Organizational Readiness and Research:

Security, Management, and Decision Making

Darrell Norman Burrell
Marymount University, USA

IGI Global
Scientific Publishing
Publishing Tomorrow's Research Today

Published in the United States of America by
IGI Global Scientific Publishing
701 East Chocolate Avenue
Hershey, PA, 17033, USA
Tel: 717-533-8845
Fax: 717-533-8661
E-mail: cust@igi-global.com
Website: https://www.igi-global.com

Copyright © 2025 by IGI Global Scientific Publishing. All rights reserved. No part of this publication may be reproduced, stored or distributed in any form or by any means, electronic or mechanical, including photocopying, without written permission from the publisher.
Product or company names used in this set are for identification purposes only. Inclusion of the names of the products or companies does not indicate a claim of ownership by IGI Global Scientific Publishing of the trademark or registered trademark.

Library of Congress Cataloging-in-Publication Data

CIP Data Pending
ISBN:979-8-3693-8562-3
eISBN:979-8-3693-8564-7

Vice President of Editorial: Melissa Wagner
Managing Editor of Acquisitions: Mikaela Felty
Managing Editor of Book Development: Jocelynn Hessler
Production Manager: Mike Brehm
Cover Design: Phillip Shickler

British Cataloguing in Publication Data
A Cataloguing in Publication record for this book is available from the British Library.

All work contributed to this book is new, previously-unpublished material.
The views expressed in this book are those of the authors, but not necessarily of the publisher.
This book contains information sourced from authentic and highly regarded references, with reasonable efforts made to ensure the reliability of the data and information presented. The authors, editors, and publisher believe the information in this book to be accurate and true as of the date of publication. Every effort has been made to trace and credit the copyright holders of all materials included. However, the authors, editors, and publisher cannot assume responsibility for the validity of all materials or the consequences of their use. Should any copyright material be found unacknowledged, please inform the publisher so that corrections may be made in future reprints.

Table of Contents

Preface xv

Chapter 1
Education on Sustainable Competitive Administration: A Review 1
    Saumendra Das, GIET University, Gunupur, India
    Udaya Sankar Patro, National Institute of Technology, Trichy, India
    Tapaswini Panda, Vellore Institute of Technology, India
    Jyoti Prakash Rath, Government H.S. School, India
    Karteek Madapana, GIET University, Gunupur, India

Chapter 2
Effect of Organization Readiness on Competitive Advantage With Mediating Effect of Human Capital: A Case of SMEs, Ethiopia 25
    Tafese Niguse, Bule Hora University, Ethiopia
    Brehanu Borji, Hawassa University, Ethiopia
    Chalchissa Amentie, Ethiopian Civil Service University, Ethiopia
    Shashi Kant, Bule Hora University, Ethiopia

Chapter 3
Conquering the Competitive Landscape: A Fusion of Defensive and Offensive Strategies for Sustainable Growth 53
    Alieu Stephen Kafoe, Marymount University, USA

Chapter 4
Addressing Workplace Culture and Rebuilding Reputation: A Case Study of a Five Star Resort 101
    Fauziatu Salifu-Sidii, Marymount University, USA

Chapter 5
Overcoming International Student Matriculation Challenges 131
    Gregory Lloyd Stoller, Marymount University, USA

Chapter 6
Cybersecure Futures: Bridging AI, Employment, and the Digital Divide 155
    Sharon L. Burton, Embry-Riddle Aeronautical University, USA

Chapter 7
Organizational Readiness for Artificial Intelligence (AI) in Network Security 205
    B. Avery Greene, Capitol Technology University, USA
    Sharon L. Burton, Capitol Technology University, USA

Chapter 8
Advancing Cybersecurity: Strategic Insights Into Multifactor Authentication . 247
    Sharon L. Burton, Capitol Technology University, USA

Chapter 9
Integrating Organizational and Social Network Theories to Mitigate Racial Bias in Facial Recognition Technology 283
    Lord Dordunoo, Marymount University, USA

Chapter 10
Code Blue: A Case Study of a Hospital Data Breach Response, Remediation, and Organizational Change 349
    Eleanor J. Thompson, Marymount University, USA

Chapter 11
Data-Driven Technology Medical Malpractice: A Narrative Review on the Legal Implications in Clinical Settings 373
    Cakesha M. Hardin, Marymount University, USA

Chapter 12
Maturity of Healthcare IS/IT Systems 399
    Jorge Vareda Gomes, Universidade Lusófona, Portugal
    Mário Romão, ISEG, Universidade de Lisboa, Portugal

Chapter 13
Regional Bank's Case Study on Online Lending Platforms 429
    Maria Montano, Marymount University, USA

Chapter 14
Integration of Circular Economy Principles Within Information Logistics: Case Study of Australia............ 449
    Mallika Roy, Central Queensland University, Australia & University of Chittagong, Bangladesh
    Jaba Sarker, Central Queensland University, Australia

Chapter 15
Women Safety at Workplace: Challenges and Support System in Healthcare .. 491
   Sunil Kumar, Shoolini University, India
   Shrishti Kumari, Shoolini University, India
   Kritika Mahendroo, Shoolini University, India
   Ritika Thakur, Shoolini University, India

Compilation of References 523

About the Contributors 637

Index 643

Detailed Table of Contents

Preface xv

Chapter 1

Education on Sustainable Competitive Administration: A Review 1
    Saumendra Das, GIET University, Gunupur, India
    Udaya Sankar Patro, National Institute of Technology, Trichy, India
    Tapaswini Panda, Vellore Institute of Technology, India
    Jyoti Prakash Rath, Government H.S. School, India
    Karteek Madapana, GIET University, Gunupur, India

Sustainability-related topics, such as cutting back on energy use, maintaining habitats and threatened species, increasing the atmosphere, and conserving watersheds, are being introduced to textbooks about strategic planning at graduate-level curricula. However, if the fundamental metaphors that underpin managerial education don't alter, the present changes won't bring about significant or long-lasting improvement. The use of metaphor permeates every aspect of our behaviour, communication, and worldview. Like any complicated and dynamic phenomena, they are also essential to the conversation about sustainability in the context of strategic leadership. The battle analogy continues to inform strategic leadership concepts, studies, and instruction, despite the rise and fall in popularity of other metaphors over time. Given the difficulties with sustainability, it is time to reconsider the battle metaphor. When developing our method of teaching sustainable management strategies, we must consider its function and effects.

Chapter 2

Effect of Organization Readiness on Competitive Advantage With Mediating
Effect of Human Capital: A Case of SMEs, Ethiopia 25

    Tafese Niguse, Bule Hora University, Ethiopia
    Brehanu Borji, Hawassa University, Ethiopia
    Chalchissa Amentie, Ethiopian Civil Service University, Ethiopia
    Shashi Kant, Bule Hora University, Ethiopia

This study examines the relationship between organizational readiness and competitive advantage, with a particular emphasis on the function that human capital plays as a mediator in Ethiopian small and medium-sized businesses (SMEs). For SMEs looking to improve their market positioning, knowing the elements that lead to competitive advantage has become more and more important as Ethiopia's economic environment changes. Using a standardized questionnaire given to a representative sample of SMEs from a variety of industries, the study takes a quantitative approach. The results show that competitive advantage is highly influenced by organizational readiness, and that human capital plays a crucial mediating role in this connection. To be more precise, prepared companies that make investments in training, skill development, and employee engagement are better able to use their resources to gain a competitive edge.

Chapter 3

Conquering the Competitive Landscape: A Fusion of Defensive and
Offensive Strategies for Sustainable Growth 53

    Alieu Stephen Kafoe, Marymount University, USA

This study presents a novel approach, a strategic framework uniquely combining Porter's Five Forces model (defensive strategy) with the Blue Ocean Strategy (offensive strategy). This innovative fusion allows organizations to comprehensively analyze their competitive landscape, identify opportunities for value innovation, and create new, uncontested market spaces. The Five Forces model provides a structured method for understanding industry dynamics, competitive forces, and profitability drivers. At the same time, the Blue Ocean strategy encourages the creation of new value propositions and differentiation. By merging these strategies, their limitations are mitigated, and their effectiveness is enhanced, enabling organizations to compete within existing markets and pioneer new growth avenues – a crucial element for sustained success in today's dynamic business environment. The strategic successes of Tesla, Apple, and Pfizer serve as compelling examples of the practical application of this framework, which effectively leverages both strategies to establish a solid competitive advantage

Chapter 4
Addressing Workplace Culture and Rebuilding Reputation: A Case Study of
a Five Star Resort 101
    Fauziatu Salifu-Sidii, Marymount University, USA

This study investigates the challenges faced by a five-star resort involved in a class action lawsuit due to widespread discrimination and sexual harassment allegations by female employees. The research aimed to explore the impact of these allegations on the resort's reputation, employee morale, and operational efficiency and to propose strategies to address the organizational culture issues at the core of the crisis. The analysis utilized Schein's Organizational Culture Model, Kotter's 8-step Change Model, and Risk Management and Balanced Scorecard frameworks to assess the resort's cultural dimensions, manage change, and mitigate reputational damage. Key findings indicate that the resort's toxic culture led to high employee turnover, absenteeism, and disengagement, negatively affecting productivity and customer satisfaction. Recommendations include implementing comprehensive policies to prevent discrimination, investing in diversity and inclusion.

Chapter 5
Overcoming International Student Matriculation Challenges 131
    Gregory Lloyd Stoller, Marymount University, USA

College tuition costs have increased more than two-fold, and the Educational Data Initiative anticipates an annual cost of $36,436 and a compound annual growth rate increase of 2% per year moving forward. According to the Journal of International Students, non-U.S. students are an attractive revenue source. However, due to geopolitics and immigration policies, the number of non-American students has declined in the past few years. Smaller colleges will be negatively affected. Global University is one such example. At one point, over one-third of its students were from outside the U.S., but 90% were still waiting to return to America to attend physically. This paper aims to analyze this university's challenges and then develop and discuss a comprehensive strategy as recommendations to Global University's leadership team.

Chapter 6
Cybersecure Futures: Bridging AI, Employment, and the Digital Divide.......... 155
Sharon L. Burton, Embry-Riddle Aeronautical University, USA

This qualitative study, employing a literature review and case study design, investigates the complex interplay between minimum wage policies, STEM field transitions, and the digital divide. It examines how these factors influence employment dynamics and economic stability. It focuses on the barriers displaced workers face in accessing STEM education and employment, exacerbated by inadequate digital infrastructure in underserved areas. The research highlights the economic and technological impacts on workers, emphasizing the need for adaptable policies and support systems. The study proposes targeted interventions to foster a more inclusive workforce and resilient economy by addressing research gaps. The findings underscore the significance of integrating digital literacy, tailored educational programs, and robust mental health support into policy frameworks. This research provides actionable insights for policymakers, educators, and industry leaders to mitigate economic disparities and enhance workforce adaptability.

Chapter 7
Organizational Readiness for Artificial Intelligence (AI) in Network Security 205
B. Avery Greene, Capitol Technology University, USA
Sharon L. Burton, Capitol Technology University, USA

This chapter explores the essential organizational and cultural prerequisites for successfully integrating Artificial Intelligence (AI) into network security. This research employs a qualitative methodology, including a comprehensive literature review, to analyze internal needs and address ethical considerations such as bias, privacy, and fairness. This study examines the impact of organizational culture on the acceptance and effectiveness of AI-based solutions. It emphasizes the significance of end-user trust in AI-driven security alerts. The findings highlight the necessity of organizational readiness and cultural adaptation for the effective implementation of AI in network security, concluding that a comprehensive approach is essential for maximizing AI's potential in enhancing security measures. This research will benefit cybersecurity professionals, organizational leaders, and policymakers seeking to understand and navigate the complexities of AI integration in network security.

Chapter 8
Advancing Cybersecurity: Strategic Insights Into Multifactor Authentication . 247
Sharon L. Burton, Capitol Technology University, USA

This research investigates the efficacy and challenges of Multifactor Authentication (MFA) in enhancing cybersecurity within organizational settings. Employing a qualitative design, this study integrates a comprehensive literature review with case studies to examine the deployment and impact of MFA technologies. Key findings reveal that over 57% of global businesses have adopted MFA, significantly reducing unauthorized access and breaches by 99.9% when correctly implemented. However, challenges such as user resistance, implementation costs, and the complexity of MFA systems persist, affecting overall effectiveness and adoption rates. This research concludes that while MFA substantially improves security, its success hinges on strategic deployment and user compliance. The significance of this research lies in its potential to guide organizations in refining their cybersecurity measures and in informing policy on secure authentication practices, ultimately contributing to enhanced organizational and data security in an increasingly digital world.

Chapter 9
Integrating Organizational and Social Network Theories to Mitigate Racial Bias in Facial Recognition Technology 283
Lord Dordunoo, Marymount University, USA

Facial recognition technology (FRT), though a powerful tool for identification and surveillance, consistently demonstrates racial bias, disproportionately misidentifying individuals of color. This chapter integrates organizational and social network theories to address these biases. Drawing on theories such as Equity Theory, General Adaptation Syndrome, Minority Stress Model, and Terror Management Theory, it explores the psychological, social, and ethical effects on marginalized communities. Procedural Justice Theory, Stakeholder Theory, and Technological Determinism highlight how organizational practices contribute to bias, while Ethics of Care and Distributive Justice emphasize the responsibility to design fair systems. The chapter calls for comprehensive reforms in FRT development, focusing on fairness, equity, and the well-being of all stakeholders.

Chapter 10
Code Blue: A Case Study of a Hospital Data Breach Response, Remediation, and Organizational Change 349
  Eleanor J. Thompson, Marymount University, USA

When data are breached in a healthcare setting, the risks and threats are borne by both the impacted medical institution and its patients/customers. For patients, not only is confidential medical information leaked, but their financial data and even their health and wellbeing may be jeopardized. Using scenario-based problem solving, a case study is presented to explore the elements and dynamics of a hospital's breach of medical and financial data and to strategize the organization's responses and remediation to an internal cybersecurity incident in accordance with laws applicable to both financial and healthcare institutions. Recommendations regarding organizational change to address enterprise risk management (ERM), an incident response plan, a compliance program, and ethical leadership practices are outlined to restore the hospital's reputation and prevent or mitigate further data breach incidents.

Chapter 11
Data-Driven Technology Medical Malpractice: A Narrative Review on the Legal Implications in Clinical Settings 373
  Cakesha M. Hardin, Marymount University, USA

Many hospitals employ machine learning algorithms in clinical settings. This technology causes ethical and legal issues including data biases resulting in harm. This narrative research seeks to demonstrate the link between data-driven algorithms in healthcare decision-making and discrimination to certain demographic groups. English peer-reviewed papers from 2020 to June 24, 2024, were searched on Google Scholar. The primary findings revealed ethical issues with clinical AI technology. However, there is a notable lack of well-established protocols to determine liability for AI errors. This cutting-edge technology promises to boost operational efficiency but may simultaneously damage healthcare providers' reputations and patient safety. To safeguard patients and staff, steps must be taken with regard to quality assurance practices prior to implementation.

Chapter 12
Maturity of Healthcare IS/IT Systems 399
    Jorge Vareda Gomes, Universidade Lusófona, Portugal
    Mário Romão, ISEG, Universidade de Lisboa, Portugal

The use of information systems and technology (IS/IT) in healthcare has been recognized as crucial for improving the efficiency, cost-effectiveness, quality, and safety of medical care delivery. IS/IT has the potential to enhance individual health outcomes and provider performance by delivering better quality care, achieving cost savings, and increasing patient involvement in their own health. Two major drivers have spurred IS/IT investments in healthcare: the rapidly increasing burden of chronic diseases, with costs growing significantly, and the recognition of the need for substantial improvements in the quality and safety of healthcare delivery. Maturity models (MM) are based on the premise that people, organizations, functional areas, and processes evolve through a development process, progressing towards a more advanced state of maturity by passing through distinct levels. The application of MM in healthcare offers significant opportunities to enhance information and knowledge management. This paper summarizes some of the recent developments in this area.

Chapter 13
Regional Bank's Case Study on Online Lending Platforms 429
    Maria Montano, Marymount University, USA

Regional Bank is a small financial institution aiming to expand its company and network through an online lending platform. Technology advancements are changing how consumers and businesses secure financing; therefore, a case study on online lending programs can benefit Regional Bank immensely. Online lending programs allow for a more specialized business model than traditional lending, enabling banks to extend credit access to small businesses (Bickmore et al., 2023). An online lending platform can help banks reduce costs, decrease risk, and increase transparency while supporting consumer needs (Strohm & Horton, 2023). Unfortunately, organizational changes impact employees, leadership, and the organization. As such, a study is needed to address the importance of online lending platforms and how this can positively or negatively affect customers, the bank, and its employees. Developing a comprehensive strategy for a successful implementation plan of an online lending platform is also essential.

Chapter 14
Integration of Circular Economy Principles Within Information Logistics:
Case Study of Australia... 449
    Mallika Roy, Central Queensland University, Australia & University of
        Chittagong, Bangladesh
    Jaba Sarker, Central Queensland University, Australia

This study investigates integrating circular economy principles with information logistics to enhance sustainability and supply chain performance. The study aims to explore how optimizing information flows can support pro-environmental practices, reduce waste, and improve resource efficiency. By leveraging digital technologies and advanced analytics, businesses can implement closed-loop systems, track material flows, and enhance decision-making. This research addresses the gap in understanding the combined benefits of circular economy and information logistics, providing insights for businesses and policymakers. The findings will contribute to advancing sustainable business practices and competitive advantage, offering practical pathways for organizations navigating the complexities of a globalized economy while fostering environmental stewardship.

Chapter 15
Women Safety at Workplace: Challenges and Support System in Healthcare .. 491
   Sunil Kumar, Shoolini University, India
   Shrishti Kumari, Shoolini University, India
   Kritika Mahendroo, Shoolini University, India
   Ritika Thakur, Shoolini University, India

This study explores the safety challenges women face in healthcare workplaces and evaluates the effectiveness of existing support systems. Despite strides in gender equality, women continue to experience harassment, discrimination, and unsafe conditions that harm their well-being and hinder career growth. Through a review of literature and case studies, the research identifies key issues such as inadequate reporting mechanisms, insufficient harassment prevention training, weak policies, and the high-stress healthcare environment that heightens risks. It also highlights solutions like mentorship programs, strong anti-harassment policies, and training initiatives that promote respect and accountability. By showcasing best practices, the study advocates for comprehensive strategies that healthcare organizations can adopt to enhance women's safety. The findings stress the need for collective efforts to create an inclusive, secure workplace and offer actionable recommendations for fostering a fear-free environment where all employees can thrive.

Compilation of References 523

About the Contributors 637

Index 643

Preface

The importance of research cannot be overstated in our efforts to address the pressing challenges outlined in this volume. As our world becomes more interconnected and complex, the reliance on empirical evidence and rigorous analysis becomes paramount. Research serves as the foundation for informed decision-making, providing insights that illuminate the pathways to effective solutions. As editor of "Organizational Readiness and Research: Security, Management, and Decision Making," I am excited to present a curated volume that aims to bridge the critical divide between theory and practice across diverse fields, including technology, business, public health, and education.

In the realm of community public health, for instance, evidence-based research is critical for identifying health disparities and developing targeted interventions. By harnessing data and innovative methodologies, researchers can offer actionable strategies that empower communities to enhance their health outcomes and reduce inequalities. This volume aims to spotlight these crucial contributions, demonstrating how research can directly inform public health policies and practices.

Similarly, in the domain of cybersecurity, the evolving landscape of threats demands a proactive and informed response. Research is essential for understanding these risks, developing robust defense mechanisms, and creating frameworks that organizations can implement to protect critical infrastructure. By focusing on emerging trends and best practices, we can equip professionals with the knowledge needed to navigate this complex terrain effectively.

In business and organizational management, research provides the tools necessary to craft sophisticated strategies that adapt to an ever-changing environment. By exploring case studies and theoretical contributions, this volume will illustrate how research-driven insights can enhance organizational resilience, inform competitive dynamics, and optimize decision-making processes. The integration of empirical findings into management practices will not only lead to improved outcomes but also foster a culture of continuous improvement within organizations.

Moreover, as we delve into the intricacies of human-computer interaction, research plays a pivotal role in enhancing user experiences and promoting accessibility. Understanding how individuals engage with technology informs the design of more intuitive and user-friendly systems. This, in turn, drives technology adoption and satisfaction, bridging the gap between users and the digital tools they rely on.

The emphasis on sustainability throughout this book underscores the urgent need for research to inform responsible practices that promote environmental stewardship and social equity. By exploring innovative approaches and frameworks, we aim to equip organizations and advocates with the insights necessary to advance sustainability goals effectively.

Finally, in the context of higher education, research is essential for addressing the evolving challenges faced by institutions and educators. By investigating new pedagogical approaches and the impact of technology on learning, this volume will provide strategies for enhancing educational practices and preparing students for a dynamic future.

In essence, this book is a call to action. It invites scholars, practitioners, and policymakers to engage with the research presented herein and to recognize its transformative potential. By bridging the gap between theory and practice, we can foster collaborative efforts that lead to practical solutions for the complex problems we face.

CHAPTER OVERVIEW: ORGANIZATIONAL READINESS AND RESEARCH: SECURITY, MANAGEMENT, AND DECISION MAKING

Chapter 1: Education On Sustainable Competitive Administration: A Review

In this chapter, we critically assess the current incorporation of sustainability topics into graduate-level strategic planning curricula. While sustainability is increasingly emphasized, the underlying metaphors of managerial education remain largely unchanged, limiting the potential for real, enduring progress. The chapter argues that the prevalent battle metaphor in strategic leadership obscures the complexities of sustainability challenges. We propose a re-evaluation of this metaphor to better equip future leaders in fostering sustainable management practices.

Chapter 2: Effect of Organization Readiness on Competitive Advantage with Mediating Effect of Human Capital: A Case of SMEs, Ethiopia

This chapter delves into the relationship between organizational readiness and competitive advantage, with a focus on the mediating role of human capital in Ethiopian SMEs. As the economic landscape evolves, understanding the factors contributing to competitive advantage is crucial. Our quantitative research highlights that SMEs exhibiting higher organizational readiness—through investments in training and employee engagement—tend to leverage their resources more effectively, enhancing their market positioning.

Chapter 3: Conquering the Competitive Landscape: A Fusion of Defensive and Offensive Strategies for Sustainable Growth

Building on the previous chapter, we explore how SMEs can navigate the competitive landscape through a strategic blend of defensive and offensive approaches. This research underscores the importance of proactive measures and adaptive strategies in achieving sustainable growth. By analyzing various organizational frameworks, we offer insights into how SMEs can cultivate resilience and maintain a competitive edge in a dynamic environment.

Chapter 4: Addressing Workplace Culture and Rebuilding Reputation: A Case Study of a Five Star Resort

This case study investigates the fallout from serious allegations of discrimination and harassment at a five-star resort. By employing established frameworks such as Schein's Organizational Culture Model and Kotter's Change Model, we analyze how the resort's toxic culture has adversely impacted employee morale and operational effectiveness. The chapter outlines strategic recommendations for cultural reform, emphasizing the implementation of robust anti-discrimination policies and a commitment to diversity and inclusion.

Chapter 5: Overcoming International Student Matriculation Challenges

As tuition costs rise, this chapter addresses the decline in international student enrollment at U.S. colleges due to geopolitical tensions and restrictive immigration policies. Focusing on Global University, we examine the implications of this trend and propose a comprehensive strategy to bolster international recruitment efforts.

Our recommendations aim to enhance the institution's appeal to non-U.S. students and mitigate potential revenue losses.

Chapter 6: Cybersecure Futures: Bridging AI, Employment, and the Digital Divide

This qualitative study explores the intersection of minimum wage policies, STEM transitions, and the digital divide, shedding light on the barriers faced by displaced workers. By advocating for inclusive educational policies and robust digital literacy programs, we aim to bridge these gaps, ensuring equitable access to opportunities in an evolving job market. The chapter emphasizes the need for systemic interventions to promote workforce adaptability and economic resilience.

Chapter 7: Organizational Readiness for Artificial Intelligence (AI) in Network Security

This chapter investigates the organizational prerequisites for successfully integrating AI into network security. By analyzing cultural readiness and ethical considerations, we emphasize the necessity of fostering end-user trust in AI applications. Our findings highlight that a comprehensive approach to organizational culture is vital for maximizing the effectiveness of AI-driven security measures, providing valuable insights for cybersecurity professionals and leaders.

Chapter 8: Advancing Cybersecurity: Strategic Insights into Multifactor Authentication

We assess the effectiveness of Multifactor Authentication (MFA) as a security measure across organizations. Despite its widespread adoption and significant reduction in security breaches, challenges such as user resistance and implementation costs persist. This chapter offers strategic insights for enhancing MFA deployment and compliance, underscoring its critical role in strengthening organizational cybersecurity frameworks.

Chapter 9: Integrating Organizational and Social Network Theories to Mitigate Racial Bias in Facial Recognition Technology

This chapter tackles the pervasive issue of racial bias in facial recognition technology (FRT) through the lens of organizational and social network theories. We explore the psychological and ethical implications of bias, calling for comprehensive reforms in FRT development. By integrating various theoretical frameworks, we advocate for equitable practices in technology design that prioritize fairness and stakeholder well-being.

Chapter 10: Code Blue: A Case Study of a Hospital Data Breach Response, Remediation, and Organizational Change

Using a scenario-based approach, this chapter examines a hospital's response to a significant data breach, highlighting the risks to patient confidentiality and institutional integrity. We outline essential strategies for remediation and organizational change, focusing on enterprise risk management and compliance. Our recommendations aim to restore trust and prevent future incidents through ethical leadership and comprehensive policy frameworks.

Chapter 11: Data-Driven Technology Medical Malpractice: A Narrative Review on the Legal Implications in Clinical Settings

This narrative review investigates the ethical and legal ramifications of employing machine learning algorithms in healthcare. Highlighting the risks of bias and discrimination, we call attention to the urgent need for well-defined protocols to determine liability in cases of AI errors. The chapter advocates for quality assurance measures to safeguard patient safety while harnessing the potential of data-driven technologies.

Chapter 12: Maturity of Healthcare IS/IT Systems

We explore the evolving role of information systems and technology (IS/IT) in enhancing healthcare delivery. By discussing maturity models, we illustrate how healthcare organizations can progress through distinct developmental stages to achieve improved efficiency, cost-effectiveness, and quality of care. This chapter underscores the transformative potential of IS/IT investments in addressing the increasing burden of chronic diseases and enhancing patient outcomes.

Chapter 13: Regional Bank's Case Study on Online Lending Platforms

This case study examines a regional bank's venture into online lending platforms, exploring the implications of technological advancements on financing. We assess how these platforms can reshape business models and enhance credit access for small businesses while also considering the organizational changes required for successful implementation. Our findings provide a roadmap for strategic planning in the face of evolving financial landscapes.

Chapter 14: Integration of Circular Economy Principles within Information Logistics: Case Study of Australia

This chapter investigates the application of circular economy principles to information logistics, focusing on sustainability and supply chain performance. By examining how optimized information flows can support pro-environmental practices, we highlight the need for businesses to adopt digital technologies that facilitate closed-loop systems. Our insights aim to foster sustainable practices and competitive advantages in a globalized economy.

Chapter 15: Women Safety at Workplace - Challenges and Support System in Healthcare

In this chapter, we address the persistent safety challenges faced by women in healthcare environments. Through a comprehensive review, we identify systemic issues that hinder progress toward gender equality and propose effective support systems. By advocating for mentorship programs, strong anti-harassment policies, and comprehensive training initiatives, we highlight the importance of fostering a safe and inclusive workplace for all employees.

We hope that the insights shared in this volume will inspire further exploration, collaboration, and innovation. Together, through the lens of research, we can address the critical challenges of our time and pave the way for a more informed, equitable, and sustainable future.

Darrell Norman Burrell
Marymount University, USA

Chapter 1
Education on Sustainable Competitive Administration:
A Review

Saumendra Das
https://orcid.org/0000-0003-4956-4352
GIET University, Gunupur, India

Udaya Sankar Patro
https://orcid.org/0009-0009-9198-3578
National Institute of Technology, Trichy, India

Tapaswini Panda
https://orcid.org/0009-0003-8327-9990
Vellore Institute of Technology, India

Jyoti Prakash Rath
https://orcid.org/0000-0003-2587-9827
Government H.S. School, India

Karteek Madapana
https://orcid.org/0000-0001-9028-1720
GIET University, Gunupur, India

ABSTRACT

Sustainability-related topics, such as cutting back on energy use, maintaining habitats and threatened species, increasing the atmosphere, and conserving watersheds, are being introduced to textbooks about strategic planning at graduate-level curricula.

DOI: 10.4018/979-8-3693-8562-3.ch001

However, if the fundamental metaphors that underpin managerial education don't alter, the present changes won't bring about significant or long-lasting improvement. The use of metaphor permeates every aspect of our behaviour, communication, and worldview. Like any complicated and dynamic phenomena, they are also essential to the conversation about sustainability in the context of strategic leadership. The battle analogy continues to inform strategic leadership concepts, studies, and instruction, despite the rise and fall in popularity of other metaphors over time. Given the difficulties with sustainability, it is time to reconsider the battle metaphor. When developing our method of teaching sustainable management strategies, we must consider its function and effects.

1. INTRODUCTION

Education is indeed for a sustainable future to administer the organization through an insightful knowledge-oriented leadership (Mansoor & Hussain, 2024). Similarly, in the higher education knowledge management is catering to the sustainable future through quality of education (Budur et al., 2024; Zaakiyyah, 2024). To enhance the quality of education in higher education, several strategies like human resource development, communication and transformation in administration could be imposed (Kaleli et al., 2024). Combining economically, socially, and natural objectives, values, and associated activities is necessary for a sustainable future (Mensah, 2019). Over time, management school curriculum has more or less grudgingly encompassed sustainability-related courses (Walck, 2009). The question of whether environmentalism ought to be included into fundamental courses or taught as an independent stand-alone option is still up for disagreement. Longevity could be perceived as a distinct problem under the alternative, unrelated to other significant commercial issues (Mann, 2024). The leadership instructors put question to their pupils and push them to critically examine their presumptions about the community, business, and the natural world (Goumaa & Anderson, 2024). Based on the extensive literature about imagery (Krstić, 2021), this study favours the subsequent choice on sustainable education.

Getting business pupils to understand technically complicated topics like conserving energy, global warming, the environment, and various other scientific topics constitutes one of the hurdles in incorporating ecology into managerial school (Bhattacharyya, 2019). Determining whether sustainability-related concerns and values may be integrated into strategic choice-making is a more significant task. Since sustainably is an ethereal, multifaceted concept, it was never feasible to evaluate directly. For this reason, metaphors are used by management researchers and educators in their teaching. The study of metaphoric in managerial learning is an area of ongoing and expanding attention (Anderson, 2007). Their intuitive usefulness has gained widespread recognition as bearing valuable amounts of information gathered from a range of areas. Despite the fact that analogies are a rather common subject of investigation, few academics studying business and teachers are cognizant of the full range of analogies they use in their work (Hamington, 2009). Hopkins et al (2011) found that 25% of the terms were metaphorical compared to the scholarly business corpus. For instance, the BCG's Growth-Share Matrix employs animals such as cows and dogs to assist firms. Some analogies have a slight but significant effect, and others may seem harmless at first.

The use of fiscal analogies has become more prevalent in all academic disciplines, even in the way that we think about marking. In a similar vein it was said that the analogy of "organic wealth" is an attempt to force a financial lens on the natural cycle (Åkerman, 2005). The field of combat and military practice and philosophy has been an important driver of models, contrasts, & abstractions used in managerial education. The above analogy is often used by academics and instructors studying management strategy, in both covert and overt ways. The most famous researchers in the subject continue to suggest that economic activity is best understood as a "a feeling of warfare" (Porter, 2008).

Researchers of strategic planning have often said very little about how the war metaphor affects corporate operations (Miotto et al., 2020). The more complex underlying situational framework of this figurative in our opinion, may have detrimental effects for sustainable since it fosters or maintains a predisposition in favour of antagonistic interactions between companies. It is past time for strategic leadership to re-evaluate the war paradigm in view of the difficulties in attaining longevity. Furthermore, stressing the necessity of creating fresh metaphors could encourage a shift in the direction of sustainability (Mitchell & Saren, 2008). Pupils must learn how to connect with many opinions and think creatively to gain information about conservation successfully (Bhattacharyya, 2019).

This chapter covers the areas sustainable education in higher education and divided into eight sections as follows: section 2 articulated on the objectives of this chapter; section 3 clearly transformed the ideas on strength and structure of analogies; section 4 tactical managerial education's wars; section 5 emphasized the origin and expansion of the war metaphor; section 6 highlighted the pitfalls of the war metaphor in strategic management education; section 7 exhibited on the exploring the search for novel root analogies; and in the last section the discussion and conclusion of the chapter have offered.

Figure 1. Sustainable education through transformation

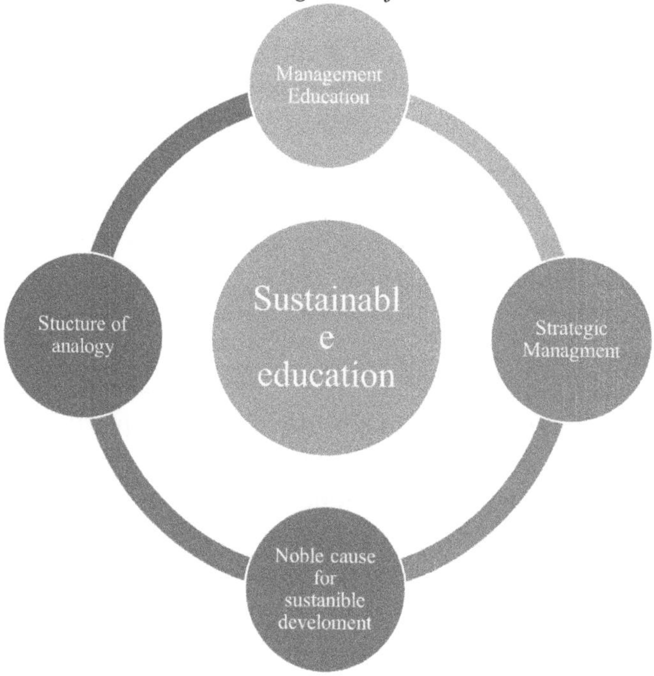

```
                    Management
                     Education

    Stucture of     Sustainabl      Strategic
    analogy         e               Managment
                    education

                    Noble cause
                    for
                    sustanible
                    develoment
```

Source. Authors' own creations

2. OBJECTIVES OF THE STUDY

- To gain a greater awareness and acceptance of the war analogy in the context of strategic leadership higher learning; and
- To offer some guidance on how to develop, evaluate, and advertise new illustrations to establish sustainable development as the foundation to feed strategic educational programs in management.

3. STRENGTH AND STRUCTURE OF ANALOGIES

The purpose and usefulness of analogies in sustainable growth and leadership are topics of continuous discussion (Dryzek, 2005). Some academics believe that analogies and analogous reasoning are valuable (Pfeffer & Sutton, 2005), whereas others would like to limit or do away with them. Three different viewpoints on metaphorical were distinguished as a method of thinking, a form of ideological chromatic aberration and a theatrical technique. According to Pinder and Bourgeois (1982), the first viewpoint sees analogies as purely decorative and disposable artistic, languages, and discursive devices. They do not have place in logical, impartial science since they affect the examination of information that needs to be expressed precisely. It is necessary to translate conceptual ideas and equivalent thinking into an exact language that articulates actual names and processes.

According to the second viewpoint, business academics must strive to convey their ideas in terminology that is creative, accurate, and natural to the issue and metaphorical should be purposefully limited or avoided as much as possible (Buchanan, 2007). There are supporters of this viewpoint in the field of environmentalism as well. For example, Dryzek (2005) concurs that several metaphors such as spacecraft, feeding prevalent equipment, organisms, the conflict with the earth, and one of the god Gaia appear in important environmentalist debate. But in his view, analogies are essentially rhetorical tactics used to persuade consumers by casting a particular lens on a given circumstance.

In the third viewpoint, Milne et al (2006) discovered the same inaccuracy in the widely used paradigm of sustainable development as journey when firms depict their involvement with sustainably. They contend that this metaphor obscures the true direction that corporations are taking. Actually, it seems that commercial discussions on longevity are more interested in a trip to an unknown destination than in a final goal. Developing environmental sustainability as journey analogy aids businesses in staying out of discussions around what constitutes a good and environmentally friendly future condition of affairs. This analogy redefines longevity in methods that do not jeopardize entrepreneurial as usual, hence upholding the present status quo on the fundamental presumptions and underlying metaphors of business enterprises.

The analogies have a deeper significance in determining how we interpret what we have experienced and frame the issues we subsequently attempt to resolve, even when they can be employed as simple theatrical tactics or harmful ideological errors. Llewelyn (2003) asserts that the first degree of theory-building that humans are capable of is metaphoric cognition, commonly known as analogical reasoning (Hogler & Gross, 2009). According to Morgan et al (2000), it is a basic architectural form of experience through which individuals involve manage, and gain insight into the surroundings.

Figure 2. Three views on analogies

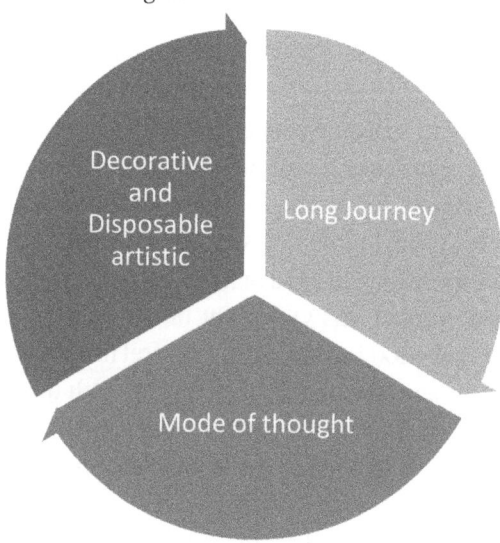

[Pie chart with three sections: "Decorative and Disposable artistic", "Long Journey", "Mode of thought"]

Source. Authors' own creations

The fundamental tenets or frameworks used for speech about the globe or a subset of it are root metaphoric. Consequently, every complicated structure of cognition has no fewer than one root metaphorical at its core. Three distinct ecological perspectives have a root imagery of the natural world at its core, according to Gladwin et al (1995) a "huge machinery" in technological centrality, a "life supports network" in sustain centrism, and a "mother/web for life" in egocentrism. The significance of nature, our connection to it, and our place in it are only a few of the fundamental environmental presumptions that are affected by these three fundamental metaphors.

From the standpoint of "method of thought," metaphorical have effects that are both creative and explicative. In fact, they do more than just explain the outside world; they actually contribute to its creation and suggest how it should be perceived and assessed (Tsoukas, 1991). When combined, the creative and explicatory impact encapsulate the primary cognition impacts of metaphoric on the framing and comprehension of issues by academics and educators (Cornelissen & Kafouros, 2008). This in turn affects students' knowledge, ethical actions (McCabe et al., 2006), and emotions (Hawk & Lyons, 2008), and it also impacts whether and the way educators educate. When it comes to the analogies they employ, management academics and instructors need to be more mindful and proactive.

The abundance of analogies in the vocabulary they employ throughout their education shouldn't stop students from evaluating these analogies' propriety or perhaps they ought to continue employing them altogether (Mutch, 2006). In fact, it ought to encourage them to do so.

4. TACTICAL MANAGERIAL EDUCATION'S WARS- THE ANALOGY

To give a misleading perception of sanity, productivity, and generality, opponents of executive education argue that the field is founded on a small number of fundamental illustrations but depends on a variety of alluring models (such as a SWOT analysis, PESTEL, or the worth chain) that simplifies the intrinsic variety of strategic planning (Grandy & Mills, 2004). We examine both overt and covert use with the military/war metaphor in strategic management education in this section. Bracker (1980) asserts that the traditional understanding of corporate strategy is grounded in military history and combat traditions and includes extra philosophical input from the field of economics. Although other perspectives are now challenging the traditional perspective, it is still widely held because it has faith in managers' ability to implement strategies that maximize profits by making logical decisions and making long-term plans (Farjoun, 2008).

According to Cornelissen et al (2005), war analogies compare corporate operations and associated behaviours to those of armed conflict. While "company" and "conflict" are not synonymous, they do share significant characteristics for the source area, "war," to meaningfully inform the destination realm, "industry." The terms "go after," "assault," "record," "state triumph," "stand by," "set up," "participate," "murder," "put an initiative," "lead contemporary responsibility," "hit," and "taking a gunshot" are common in the armed forces and war jargon of tactical leadership. Words like "to declare battle on rivals," "combat persistent global opponents," and "command and control announces assault on high costs" are among those used to describe the lingo of company reorganization (Dunn & Burton, 2005).

Words like "enmity," "battlefield," "conflict," "soldier," and "shotgun" are frequently used in discussions of hostile takeovers and mergers and acquisitions, all of which employ a battle analogy (Kaleli et al., 2024; Boyd, 2003). Some corporate executives use rhetorical techniques like those used by commanders to get soldiers ready for combat (Clancy, 1999), whether intentional or not, almost all the strategic management textbooks nowadays make use of this model. Students have been taught that businesses "must struggle not just with rivals but also amongst their vendors, clients, staff members and regulations" (Ghoshal, 2005) through the usage of Porter's "five forces" concept for a period of over thirty years. The fundamental premise is that corporate problems are like those in conflict, and as such, business may benefit from the knowledge and ideas of military planning (Danby, 2007).

5. ORIGIN AND EXPANSION OF THE WAR METAPHOR

The analogy for company as war is a part of a bigger, earlier metaphorical framework that compares life to an ongoing struggle. Heraclitus (521–487 BCE) declared that "war was parent of all & monarch of all," seeing disagreement and division and the original energy below all activities. The fundamental human state, according to Thomas Hobbes (1588–1679), "is a state of war of everything against everybody," a few generations later. Similarly, the notion of a comparison between the corporate sector and the military isn't new. According to Cummins (1993), the word "strategies" ultimately comes from the ancient Greek title "strategos," which indicated a high commander of the Athenian military forces. The term "war" is a compound of age in, which means "to lead," and Stratos, which means "militia."

According to Becker (1980), the Greek term strategos means "to arrange the annihilation of one's foes by efficient deployment of resources." Although Tsoukas (1991) maintains that strategos is not anymore connected to its offspring and is instead a deceased a figurative other writers demonstrate a clear connection with the historical and contemporary meanings of the term "strategies". In the later part of the 19th century, battle imagery became a fundamental component of 416 Academy of Management Learning & Education September business theory (Knights & Morgan, 1990). But in the end, when small businesses faced stress from both domestic and foreign competitors, it was the evolution of military planning throughout the two conflicts of the 20th century that offered an appropriate model (Del et al., 1999). The perception that tactics was essential to this accomplishment was strengthened by the prestige American military commanders gained by defeating the Axis. Since then, the corporate sector has adopted several crucial aspects of the military/war use of plans, such as the focus on the skilled elite, the view of other players as disposable assets, and the handling of outside factors as a barrier to a company's growth. For enterprises that are having difficulty presenting a coherent image and creating a "the rival mind-set" among participants, the conflict metaphors offer a single, cohesive approach that mobilizes focus and attachment against a threatening foe. By making people understand the seriousness of the situation, it could even promote more stakeholder involvement.

6. PITFALLS OF THE WAR METAPHOR IN STRATEGIC MANAGEMENT EDUCATION

Concerns have been raised by a few writers on the various ways that conflict analogy influences corporate strategy education and application. The battle paradigm has a few drawbacks. Firstly, it tends to Favor antagonistic relationships, which are only one type of interpersonal contact. Friendly & mutually beneficial relations are downplayed and denaturalized in a perspective characterized by rivalry and conflicting connections (Hammington, 2009). Either overt or covert use has a tendency to cause division among discussion individuals, which makes it harder to negotiate and reach a solution which may result in more amicable resolutions (Boyd, 2003).

Secondly, the use of the war metaphor in the classroom might be interpreted as supporting the oversimplified notion of the fact that there are not any laws when it comes to conducting war. However, this "realist" interpretation of war offers a misleading and ineffective parody of the facts of both conflict and corporate conduct. Indeed, the conduct of war is governed by strong moral and social rules, with the noteworthy example of guerrilla warfare (Clancy, 1999). A variety of behaviours are appropriate during a conflict.

The seeming mismatch from corporate morality and societal morality constitutes a third drawback of the conflict's analogy. Business action becomes increasingly morally answerable to the underlying ethical standards within society when it makes its morality self-serving. Companies may permit the deployment of strategies that are otherwise ethically wrong (Hammington, 2009). Winning and losing in the business environment may wreck lives; actions taken in the name of "annihilating rivals" may put the livelihoods of disadvantaged and marginalised individuals in jeopardy. Commercial actions have consequences for ethics when trying to outwit someone else or win.

The conflict metaphor's comparison of the work setting to a "state of war" represents its fourth flaw. Many academics and instructors of strategic administration use a well-known argument that draws on the current state of conflict to highlight the need of strategic planning (Bryson et al., 2018). As a result, they continue to adhere stoically to the paradigm of combat, confident that they are just being practical. Approaching company operations as though they were a battle, nonetheless, cannot be rationalized as being more practical or focused on the bottom. Earnings may occasionally suffer in conflict against each other with rivals (Fawaz & Le Quellec, 2024). To put it briefly, our understanding and relationship to the corporate world are affected when we approach it as though it were philosophically at war. Though there are many facets of company operations that resemble combat, these parallels should not be confused with identification.

Figure 3. Pitfalls of the war metaphor

Antagonistic relationships → War metaphor → Corporate & societal morality

Source. Authors' own creations

7. EXPLORING THE SEARCH FOR NOVEL ROOT ANALOGIES

A societal paradigm shift can only occur without the introduction of a superior or more persuasive alternative. True change in business educational institutions can only occur when instructors recognize the flaws in the fundamental metaphors of the prevailing social framework and strive to substitute them with new metaphors that align with environmental sustainability (Bowers, 2001). The use of a war image ought not to cause us to erroneously assume that solutions are non-existent. War is not only imagery that can be applied to the management of strategy, and it is not even the most appropriate one for aligning tactical leadership with conservation. One way to move forward is to create and popularize additional analogies that would make strategic planning education related to conservation seem unfamiliar, prompting inquiries and leading to a new way of thinking about it.

7.1 Discovering Metaphors for Sustainable Proactive Leadership

Over the course of many years, academics have created innovative and thought-provoking metaphors to explain the dynamics within, outside of, as well as between organizations. The performing arts image has been used to describe and explain the concept of identity and connection in entities, alongside the strategic method. It provides a framework with terms such as stakeholders, scenarios, and plays. The analogy has been explored by scholars such as Cornelissen (2004), Vera et al (2024) and Wen et al (2024). Furthermore, in the field of managerial investigations, many musical symbols such as jazz and the orchestral work are employed (Mantere et al., 2007). Different dancing metaphors have been employed to illustrate the significant transformations experienced by big businesses and to cultivate leadership skills (Williams et al., 2004). Eriksen et al (2006) propose an existentialism-quest analogy to describe tactics as a continuous pursuit of actualizing one's potential with regard of skill and contribution. The problem encountered by any company is akin to the struggle of discovering one's position in the world.

They advocate for frequent discussions on health, treating it with the same importance as performance. These talks should take a holistic approach, considering the entire structure rather than focusing on individual components. However, none of these models have successfully replaced the war analogy as a compelling framework for comprehending the art of strategic leadership. None of the options align closely with the fundamental aspects of sustainable growth. However, the health metaphors show some progress in an appropriate direction, such as emphasizing the importance of properly functioning landscapes and natural endurance. To investigate novel approaches for incorporating sustainability into business strategy, we choose to reverse the question. Instead of inquiring about the potential contributions of strategic accounting to sustainability, one may pose the question: "How can equitable growth enhance the field of strategic management education?" We examined the figurative language used by advocates for environmental responsibility to see which of them may aid in the adjustment of strategic leadership to the demands of maintenance. The first aspect to note is that advocates for environmentally friendly practices have used a plethora of metaphors. Furthermore, similar to how the war metaphor is intricately intertwined with an intricate framework of figurative language, environmentally friendly alternatives are also interwoven inside a web of analogies. Therefore, the objective is not to discover the most superior figurative language, but rather to identify methods of operating within a network of analogies that align with the principles and aspirations of durability.

The fundamental figurative metaphor used by activists is the notion of "the planet's surface serving as a containment" (Dryzek, 2005). Various examples of this metaphor include "our planet as an in the greenhouse," "the Globe as a roof," "the Globe as a storage facility," "the Nature as a lifeboat," and "the Planet as a spacecraft". All of these analogies have had a recurring theme of reminding us that there are actually some limits beyond which we are unable to travel or even live. As humanity, we are confined to a limited or confined area. Our prospects of survival are very low if we dismantle the spacecraft, deplete the storage, or blow the inflatable buoy. Viewing the Earth as either a lifeboat or a spacecraft might evoke vivid mental imagery of the current predicament and can elicit intense feelings of rage. The limitation of these analogies is in their inability to clearly identify the unique functions that persons ought to carry out within different contexts.

However, none of these analogies have successfully supplanted the war paradigm as an appealing structure for comprehending the art of strategic leadership. None of the options align closely with the fundamental principles of environmental sustainability. However, the welfare model shows some progress in the right instructions, such as emphasizing the importance of healthy natural systems and natural endurance. To investigate novel approaches for incorporating sustainability into managerial strategy, we choose to reverse the question. Instead of inquiring about the potential contributions of business strategy to sustainability, one may pose the question: "How can a sustainable future enhance the field of global manager training?" We examined various analogies employed by advocates for environmentally friendly practices to determine if they may aid in the adjustment of strategic leadership to the obstacles posed by maintenance. An important observation is that advocates of environmentally friendly practices have employed several metaphors. Furthermore, similar to how the war narrative is intricately intertwined with an intricate chain of illustrations, environmentally friendly choices are similarly intricately intertwined inside a web of representations. Therefore, the objective is not to discover the most superior metaphor, but rather to identify methods of operating within a network of tropes that align with the principles and aspirations of viability.

7.2 Evaluating the Advantages and Disadvantages of the Analogies

To gain a deeper understanding and develop fresh perspectives on ecological and strategic planning, it is necessary to envision appropriate and significant analogies, and subsequently evaluate their advantages and disadvantages. Certain metaphors are inadequate and possess a restricted ability to develop profound understandings. Cornelissen et al (2005) developed six the use of he or evaluation criteria, that business researchers may utilize to choose and cultivate analogies. These heuristics are emancipation interpersonal, such relationships, availability, geographical separation, and clarity. The integration criterion pertains to the necessity of combining fragmented pictures in a manner that results in a cohesive and readily controllable depiction. The relation heuristic proposes that the connection between the starting domain & the one to be targeted should be established via relationships rather than characteristics.

The link criterion refers to the ability to describe characteristics of the target domain by utilizing the terminology of the first topic. The principle of availability pertains to the efficiency with how concepts form the area of origin may be readily recalled and applied in the domain of choice. The separation heuristic implies that the domains of both sources should have distinct characteristics in order to stimulate novel thoughts and unexpected discoveries. It also encourages the search for similarities that were not apparent previously. The practicality bias refers to the preference for using concrete reference domain instead of conceptual ones, since they can better and more readily mapped out, utilized, and comprehended.

The six reflexes encompass the principles and limitations that govern the creation and choice of metaphors. They are crucial factors in determining the appropriateness of the analogy and its ability to evoke a strong response. The potential risk arises when employing analogies that were initially formulated in unrelated domains, since there is a possibility of not acknowledging the constraints of a specific paradigm owing to a deficiency of specialized knowledge (Tsukasa, 1991). Administration academics and instructors may lack awareness of the origins of the analogies they employ. The use of analogies in both language and thought can occur without a thorough examination of its profound meanings, challenges, and uncertainties. Wight (2013) demonstrates how Smith's concept of the "invisible hand" became weakened and misinterpreted over time due to its expansion and improper application. Therefore, for logical borrow to be valuable, it must be well-informed. Instructors should possess the ability to recognize and articulate the primary constraints of the analogies they employ while instructing sustainable strategic leadership.

7.3 Applying Literal Reasoning in Educational and Non-Educational Settings

In order to successfully affect students, it is imperative to propagate novel metaphors pertaining to healthy responsible leadership inside educational settings. There are several methods to stimulate students' thinking about sustained leadership, as well as specialized techniques to include metaphorical both within and outside of the educational environment. The parts that follow outline four potential treatments:

those simulations etc. in comparison placed encounters, embodiment language meetings, case method instructing, and class or group discussions.

Models and in comparison, placed experience are both part of the instructional strategies that encompass the analogous training. This type of learning involves an entire group of pupils comparing two sets of details to gain a deeper understanding of one of them. Simulated may be utilized to assign students to administrative positions and require them to come to difficult decisions in new environments. Simulations provide a platform for practicing and honing relevant managerial abilities by recreating a setting, such as operating a zoo or a national park. In events that are analogically located, those who participate are involved with endeavors that have a fundamental structure resembling a genuine work setting, but with a significantly different external appearance (such as outdoor activities that require survival skills). This method entails immersing clients in a unique and simulated environment that is deliberately selected and created to facilitate a deep understanding of their work setting (Houde, 2007). We contend that the primary responsibility for enterprise universities, and specifically business strategy teachers, is to develop simulated environments that facilitate student learning, concern, and action about ecological matters.

The analogies can manifest in nonverbal manners such as sculpted items, visual signals, motions and noises. The many ways in which metaphors are expressed provide strategic management educators with a range of new teaching approaches. Heracleous and Jacobs (2008) proposed a concept called "reflects imagery sessions." In these workshops, strategy is seen as a process of creating and shaping one's personal comprehension of strategic matters using available materials, such as Lego bricks. These workshops only utilize recycled materials and have a primary focus on teaching students how to care for objects that are manufactured. Designed analogy workshops offer strategic leadership participants the chance to develop and interact strategy aspects in a combinatorial and comprehensive manner, both theoretically and physically (Heracleous & Jacobs, 2008). The resultant artifacts, which will differ across participants, will mirror the many approaches they take in relation to their company, overall management of strategy, or a particular strategic matter. After each physical metaphoric activity, there may be a group meeting where any person, or team of those involved, would need to explain to others the meaning and significance of the tropes represented in their creations.

In order for a new metaphor to be effective, pupils must possess the ability to comprehend it, use their discretion, and engage in behaviours guided by it. They must possess the capacity to cultivate proficiency in and acquaint themselves with the simile. In order for a new paradigm to be widely accepted and understood, it is necessary to modify schoolbooks, training cases, as well as other instructional tools in accordance with this metaphor. To effectively use a caring technique for unsustainable tactical leadership, students must comprehend the definition and implications of caring in various contexts. Simply, pupils must be instructed on how to make smart choices within a compassionate structure. Only when teachers consciously incorporate the new metaphor into the curriculum, specifically emphasizing what scenarios they employ in their learning environment, can this be accomplished.

Educators must be mindful of the ramifications of the inquiries they pose and the specific responses they seek. The significance of effective metaphors also resides in the depth and precision of the discussion they provoke. Therefore, metaphorical thinking is most effective when practiced in a group setting, where it may be explored and debated in the context of fostering imagination and invention, rather than focusing on its logical accuracy and truth. Unfortunately, symbolic thought tends to prioritize the examination of parallels and overlapping across different domains, perhaps causing a lack of concern towards disparities or conflict. Symbolic thinking occurs in a "intellectual safety the area," as described by Oswick et al (2002). The authors argue that the focus on moderate similarities is intellectually conventional rather than freeing, which leads them to suggest that greater consideration should be given to contradiction, humour, and aberration (Oswick et al, 2002). An effective method to break out from the mental state associated with mental familiarity is to apply an origin field that is not often known among business learners, including the evolution of biology. This will stimulate innovative thinking in relation to a familiar goal field, including managerial strategy (von Ghyczy, 2003).

8. CONCLUSION AND DISCUSSION

As more and more companies recognize that their actions have an impact on the environment and society, long-term viability has emerged as a critical issue (e.g., creating energy-saving buildings, putting in or enhancing systems for waste disposal, using green power, and buying ecologically sound tools and supplies). To widely incorporate environmental responsibility, business colleges have put a lot of effort into improving the subjects of their courses of study. The ultimate objective is to thoroughly integrate environmentally friendly growth into the teaching of strategic planning. The way deeply constructed practices like a heavy reliance on certain root metaphors perpetuate problematic theories related to sustainability in business school must be considered by leadership scholars and instructors to achieve that aim. Root tropes deliver ingrained psychological structures that are employed to comprehend both novel and contemporary occurrences. Metaphors are used by managing academics and educators to characterize reality, and such analogies serve as their foundation for action.

They use metaphor to partially shape their perceptions, both deliberately and subconsciously, and use it to make decisions, create objectives, make obligations and carry out plans. According to Cornelissen et al (2008), analogies assist teachers and researchers in developing their ideals and objectives in addition to directing their views and assessments of actuality. This post articulates my apprehension on the ramifications of using the war metaphor in the context of strategic leadership education, specifically in relation to ecology. Nevertheless, the use of the battle analogy is so prevalent that we may fail to recognize the frequency with which we come across it. Indeed, it is very prevalent in strategic management education to the extent that it permeates even recent efforts to reconstruct the discipline on novel principles.

Greiner et al (2003) continue to examine corporate activities using a battle paradigm in their work titled, "Looking for a Plan to Teach Plan". Their post consistently used phrases such as "powerful international battle," "fresh hazards and chances," "outperform competitors," "allocate resources for a competitive advantage," and "identify methods of retaliation." To escape the metaphorical fallacy trap, it is important for strategic planning educators to recognize that it is merely an illustration and that different metaphors may likewise influence learning in various manners. Gaining insight into the constraints of the battle analogy and its related visual representations in the field of tactical leadership theory, investigation, and teaching might assist us in directing our attention towards creating alternative approaches.

The prevalence of tropes in our daily language does not imply that we are always confined to the same conventional metaphors. It is possible to create other fundamental ways of thinking about business operations, which will provide them with new conceptual frameworks (Hammington, 2009). Modifying the name of an entity alters our connection with the entity and influences our actions towards it (Srivastava & Bhatnagar, 2010). Analogies have a role in shaping the characteristics of the things they represent, and unique analogies have the ability to produce different social realities. Literal pluralism promotes many modes of thinking for themselves, enabling both educators and pupils to concentrate on, elucidate, and exert power over various facets of intricate phenomena (Tsukasa, 1991).

Regrettably, our chances of achieving success in this undertaking are slim if we just concentrate on altering cultural ideas without also tackling political as well as economic transformation. The sociohistorical advantage associated with certain analogies is not only a product of philosophical exercise, but rather a struggle amongst current ideologies that determine the significance of certain alien conceptions. However, academics and instructors of strategic management must take accountability for creating methods that integrate sustainability and economic strategy at the microlevel of their work. They must be aware of the applications of metaphors and the mental pictures they arouse. Dealing with students' misconceptions about the nature of business operations is one aspect of the issue of teaching sustainability. Diverse viewpoints for comprehending sustainability should be encouraged in management education, with a focus on fostering metaphorical plurality. Which metaphorical concepts win out in the long term will have a vital impact on our sustainable future. We must create new frameworks and approaches that will make it easier for students to comprehend sustainability in the corporate world.

ACKNOWLEDGEMENT

There is no conflicting interest among the authors. Further, it declares that this content is not published or submitted anywhere.

REFERENCES

Åkerman, M. (2005). What does "natural capital" do? The role of metaphor in economic understanding of the environment. *Environmental Education Research*, 11(1), 37–52. DOI: 10.1080/1350462042000328730

Anderson, M. H. (2007). "Why are there so many theories?" A classroom exercise to help students appreciate the need for multiple theories of a management domain. *Journal of Management Education*, 31(6), 757–776. DOI: 10.1177/1052562906297705

Bhattacharyya, S. C. (2019). *Energy economics: concepts, issues, markets and governance*. Springer Nature. DOI: 10.1007/978-1-4471-7468-4

Bowers, C. (2001). How language limits our understanding of environmental education. *Environmental Education Research*, 7(2), 141–151. DOI: 10.1080/13504620120043144

Boyd, J. (2003). A quest for cinergy: The war metaphor and the construction of identity. *Communication Studies*, 54(3), 249–264. DOI: 10.1080/10510970309363285

Bracker, J. (1980). The historical development of the strategic management concept. *Academy of Management Review*, 5(2), 219–224. DOI: 10.2307/257431

Bryson, J. M., Edwards, L. H., & Van Slyke, D. M. (2018). Getting strategic about strategic planning research. *Public Management Review*, 20(3), 317–339. DOI: 10.1080/14719037.2017.1285111

Buchanan, L. (2005). Let the analogies end. *Journal of Business. Harvard*, 83(3), 19.

Buchanan, T. W. (2007). Retrieval of emotional memories. *Psychological Bulletin*, 133(5), 761–779. DOI: 10.1037/0033-2909.133.5.761 PMID: 17723029

Budur, T., Abdullah, H., Rashid, C. A., & Demirer, H. (2024). The Connection Between Knowledge Management Processes and Sustainability at Higher Education Institutions. *Journal of the Knowledge Economy*, •••, 1–34. DOI: 10.1007/s13132-023-01664-4

Clancy, J. J. (1999). *The invisible powers: The language of business*. Lexington Books.

Cornelissen, J. P. (2004). What are we playing at? Theatre, organization, and the use of metaphor. *Organization Studies*, 25(5), 705–726. DOI: 10.1177/0170840604042411

Cornelissen, J. P. (2004). At what game are we playing? Theater, structure, and metaphorical expression. 25(5). *Organization Studies*, •••, 705–726. DOI: 10.1177/0170840604042411

Cornelissen, J. P., & Kafouros, M. (2008). Metaphors and theory building in organization theory: What determines the impact of a metaphor on theory? *British Journal of Management*, 19(4), 365–379. DOI: 10.1111/j.1467-8551.2007.00550.x

Cornelissen, J. P., Kafouros, M., & Lock, A. R. (2005). Metaphorical images of organization: How organizational researchers develop and select organizational metaphors. *Human Relations*, 58(12), 1545–1578. DOI: 10.1177/0018726705061317

Cornelissen, J. P., Lock, A. R., and Kafouros, M. (2005). Organizational metaphors: The process by which organizational scholars create and choose organizational metaphors. 1545–1578 in *Human Relation*, 58(12).

Cornelissen, J. P., Oswick, C., Thøger Christensen, L., & Phillips, N. (2008). Metaphor in organizational research: Context, modalities and implications for research—Introduction. *Organization Studies*, 29(1), 7–22. DOI: 10.1177/0170840607086634

Cummings, S. (1993). Brief case: The first strategists. *Long Range Planning*, 26(3), 133–135. DOI: 10.1016/0024-6301(93)90015-8

Del Sol, P., & Ghemawat, P. (1999). Strategic valuation of investment under competition. *Interfaces*, 29(6), 42–56. DOI: 10.1287/inte.29.6.42

Dryzek, J. S. (2005). *The Politics of Earth*. Oxford University Press.

Dunn, C. P., and Burton. B. K. 2005. Social concerns and the compassionate approach in management education. 29(3), 453–474, Journal of Management Education.

Eriksen, H. K., Dickinson, C., Lawrence, C. R., Baccigalupi, C., Banday, A. J., Górski, K. M., Hansen, F. K., Lilje, P. B., Pierpaoli, E., Seiffert, M. D., Smith, K. M., & Vanderlinde, K. (2006). Cosmic microwave background component separation by parameter estimation. *The Astrophysical Journal*, 641(2), 665–682. DOI: 10.1086/500499

Farjoun, M. (2017). Contradictions, dialectics, and paradoxes. The Sage handbook of process organization studies, 87-109.

Fawaz, M., & Le Quellec, E. (2024). Indirect rivalries and civil wars: Empirical evidence. *Defence and Peace Economics*, 35(1), 44–71. DOI: 10.1080/10242694.2022.2129350

Ghoshal, S. (2005). Bad management theories are destroying good management practices. *Academy of Management Learning & Education*, 4(1), 75–91. DOI: 10.5465/amle.2005.16132558

Gladwin, T. N., Kennelly, J. J., & Krause, T. S. (1995). Shifting paradigms for sustainable development: Implications for management theory and research. *Academy of Management Review*, 20(4), 874–907. DOI: 10.2307/258959

Goumaa, R., & Anderson, L. (2024). Developing critical reflection in asynchronous discussions; the role of the instructor. *Journal of Management Education*, 48(3), 427–458. DOI: 10.1177/10525629231215245

Grandy, G., & Mills, A. J. (2004). Strategy as simulacra? A radical reflexive look at the discipline and practice of strategy. *Journal of Management Studies*, 41(7), 1153–1170. DOI: 10.1111/j.1467-6486.2004.00470.x

Greiner, L. E., Bhambri, A., & Cummings, T. G. (2003). Searching for a strategy to teach strategy. *Academy of Management Learning & Education*, 2(4), 402–420. DOI: 10.5465/amle.2003.11902092

Hamington, M. (2009). *The social philosophy of Jane Addams*. University of Illinois Press.

Hawk, T. F., & Lyons, P. R. (2008). Please don't give up on me: When faculty fail to care. *Journal of Management Education*, 32(3), 316–338. DOI: 10.1177/1052562908314194

Heracleous, L., & Jacobs, C. D. (2008). Crafting strategy: The role of embodied metaphors. *Long Range Planning*, 41(3), 309–325. DOI: 10.1016/j.lrp.2008.02.011

Hogler, R., & Gross, M. A. (2009). Journal rankings and academic research: Two discourses about the quality of faculty work. *Management Communication Quarterly*, 23(1), 107–126. DOI: 10.1177/0893318909335419

Hopkins, C. D., Raymond, M. A., & Carlson, L. (2011). Educating students to give them a sustainable competitive advantage. *Journal of Marketing Education*, 33(3), 337–347. DOI: 10.1177/0273475311420241

Houde, N. (2007). The six faces of traditional ecological knowledge: Challenges and opportunities for Canadian co-management arrangements. *Ecology and Society*, 12(2), art34. DOI: 10.5751/ES-02270-120234

Kaleli, Z., Konteos, G., Avlogiaris, G., & Kilintzis, P. (2024). Total Quality Management as Competitive Advantage for the Internal Strategy and Policy of Greek Special Education School Units. *Journal of the Knowledge Economy*, •••, 1–20. DOI: 10.1007/s13132-024-01987-w

Knights, D., & Morgan, G. (1990). The concept of strategy in sociology: A note of dissent. *Sociology*, 24(3), 475–483. DOI: 10.1177/0038038590024003008

Krstić, M. (2021). Higher education as determinant of competitiveness and sustainable economic development. In *The Sustainability Debate* (Vol. 14, pp. 15–34). Emerald Publishing Limited. DOI: 10.1108/S2043-905920210000015002

Llewelyn, S. (2003). What counts as "theory" in qualitative management and accounting research? Introducing five levels of theorizing. *Accounting, Auditing & Accountability Journal*, 16(4), 662–708. DOI: 10.1108/09513570310492344

Mann, S. (2024). Evaluating Longevity as a Farm Animal Welfare Indicator. *Food Ethics*, 9(1), 4. DOI: 10.1007/s41055-023-00137-3 PMID: 34805483

Mansoor, T., & Hussain, S. (2024). Impact of knowledge oriented leadership on sustainable service quality of higher education institutes. *VINE Journal of Information and Knowledge Management Systems*, 54(4), 705–724. DOI: 10.1108/VJIKMS-09-2021-0176

Mantere, S., Sillince, J. A., & Hämäläinen, V. (2007). Music as a metaphor for organizational change. *Journal of Organizational Change Management*, 20(3), 447–459. DOI: 10.1108/09534810710740236

McCabe, D. L., Butterfield, K. D., & Trevino, L. K. (2006). Academic dishonesty in graduate business programs: Prevalence, causes, and proposed action. *Academy of Management Learning & Education*, 5(3), 294–305. DOI: 10.5465/amle.2006.22697018

Mensah, J. (2019). Sustainable development: Meaning, history, principles, pillars, and implications for human action: Literature review. *Cogent Social Sciences*, 5(1), 1653531. DOI: 10.1080/23311886.2019.1653531

Milne, M. J., Kearins, K., & Walton, S. (2006). Creating adventures in wonderland: The journey metaphor and environmental sustainability. *Organization*, 13(6), 801–839. DOI: 10.1177/1350508406068506

Miotto, G., Del-Castillo-Feito, C., & Blanco-González, A. (2020). Reputation and legitimacy: Key factors for Higher Education Institutions' sustained competitive advantage. *Journal of Business Research*, 112, 342–353. DOI: 10.1016/j.jbusres.2019.11.076

Mitchell, I. K., & Saren, M. (2008). The living product–Using the creative nature of metaphors in the search for sustainable marketing. *Business Strategy and the Environment*, 17(6), 398–410. DOI: 10.1002/bse.526

Morgan, M., Mallett, R., Hutchinson, G., & Bagalkote, H. (2000). Morgan, K. Mungham, G. Redesigning democracy: The making of the Welsh Assembly. Bridgend: Seren.

Oswick, C., Keenoy, T., & Grant, D. (2002). Note: Metaphor and analogical reasoning in organization theory: Beyond orthodoxy. *Academy of Management Review*, 27(2), 294–303. DOI: 10.2307/4134356

Pfeffer, J., & Sutton, R. I. (2006). Profiting from evidence-based management. *Strategy and Leadership*, 34(2), 35–42. DOI: 10.1108/10878570610652617

Pinder, C. C., & Bourgeois, V. W. (1982). Controlling tropes in administrative science. *Administrative Science Quarterly*, 27(4), 641–652. DOI: 10.2307/2392535

Porter, M. E. (2008). Competitive advantage: Creating and sustaining superior performance. simon and schuster.

Srivastava, P., & Bhatnagar, J. (2010). Vision: The Journal of Business Perspective.

Tsoukas, H. (1991). The missing link: A transformational view of metaphors in organizational science. *Academy of Management Review*, 16(3), 566–585. DOI: 10.2307/258918

Vera, D., Tabesh, P., Velez-Castrillon, S., Kachra, A., & Werner, S. (2024). Improvisational decision making: Context, antecedents, and outcomes. In *The Routledge companion to improvisation in organizations* (pp. 144–163). Routledge.

Von Ghyczy, T. (2003). The fruitful flaws of strategy metaphors. *Harvard Business Review*, 81(9), 86–94. PMID: 12964396

Wen, T., Puett, R. C., Liao, D., Kanter, J., Mittleman, M. A., Lanzkron, S. M., & Yanosky, J. D. (2024). Short-term air pollution levels and sickle cell disease hospital encounters in South Carolina: A case-crossover analysis. *Environmental Research*, 252, 118766. DOI: 10.1016/j.envres.2024.118766 PMID: 38583660

Wight, C. (2013). Philosophy of social science and international relations. Handbook of international relations, 29-56. DOI: 10.4135/9781446247587.n2

Williams, C. K., Guthery, F. S., Applegate, R. D., & Peterson, M. J. (2004). The northern bobwhite decline: Scaling our management for the twenty-first century. *Wildlife Society Bulletin*, 32(3), 861–869. DOI: 10.2193/0091-7648(2004)032<0861:TNBDSO>2.0.CO;2

Zaakiyyah, H. K. A. (2024). Innovative Strategies to Enhance the Quality of Higher Education Management: Human Resource Development and the Critical Role of Communication. [ADMAN]. *Journal of Contemporary Administration and Management*, 2(1), 331–336.

Chapter 2
Effect of Organization Readiness on Competitive Advantage With Mediating Effect of Human Capital:
A Case of SMEs, Ethiopia

Tafese Niguse
https://orcid.org/0009-0008-6536-6392
Bule Hora University, Ethiopia

Brehanu Borji
Hawassa University, Ethiopia

Chalchissa Amentie
Ethiopian Civil Service University, Ethiopia

Shashi Kant
https://orcid.org/0000-0003-4722-5736
Bule Hora University, Ethiopia

ABSTRACT

This study examines the relationship between organizational readiness and competitive advantage, with a particular emphasis on the function that human capital plays as a mediator in Ethiopian small and medium-sized businesses (SMEs). For SMEs looking to improve their market positioning, knowing the elements that lead to competitive advantage has become more and more important as Ethiopia's economic

DOI: 10.4018/979-8-3693-8562-3.ch002

environment changes. Using a standardized questionnaire given to a representative sample of SMEs from a variety of industries, the study takes a quantitative approach. The results show that competitive advantage is highly influenced by organizational readiness, and that human capital plays a crucial mediating role in this connection. To be more precise, prepared companies that make investments in training, skill development, and employee engagement are better able to use their resources to gain a competitive edge.

INTRODUCTION

The capacity of firms to gain and maintain a competitive edge has grown more and more important in today's dynamic global economy (Yilma and Fekadu, 2023). Small and medium-sized businesses (SMEs) are vital to economic growth, especially in developing nations like Ethiopia where they make a major contribution to employment and innovation. But the competitive environment is characterized by obstacles like few resources, legal limitations, and the requirement for flexibility (Ed-Dafali et al., 2023). Ethiopian SMEs have a crucial economic role, employing over 90% of the private sector workers and contributing around 30% of the country's GDP. They do, however, confront some obstacles, such as high tax rates, poor infrastructure, and restricted access to financing, which affects 63% of SMEs (Kebede & Wang, 2022). Furthermore, just 30% of SMEs indicate that their workforces have received enough training, indicating that there is still a skills gap. Trends in human capital show that improving education and skill development is necessary to increase creativity and productivity (Ferede et al., 2024). These elements highlight how crucial organizational preparedness is to using human capital to gain a competitive edge in Ethiopia's SME market. (L'Écuyer et al., 2019). Notwithstanding their importance, SMEs have a number of difficulties, such as restricted financial access, poor infrastructure, and regulatory obstacles (Hossain et al., 2024). Human capital trends also reveal a skills gap among employees, which impedes production and creativity (Anser et al., 2022). Gaining a competitive edge requires organizational preparedness, which is impacted by these characteristics taken together. Examining how organizational preparedness affects competitive outcomes—especially from the perspective of human capital in Ethiopia's SME sector—requires an understanding of these processes.

The distinctive setting of Ethiopian SMEs, which has received little attention in the body of research on organizational preparedness and human capital, makes this study stand out (Berlilana et al., 2021). In contrast to other research, our study creatively connects these two crucial elements, offering a thorough framework that emphasizes how they are interdependent in boosting competitive advantage (Hossain et al., 2024; Saadi & Razak, 2019). This research also discusses the issues that Ethiopian SMEs confront, such restricted access to resources and infrastructure limitations, providing practitioners with special insights. The results also have wider ramifications and could be relevant in other developing countries dealing with comparable issues. By addressing these gaps, this study adds to the body of knowledge in academia and provides practical recommendations for corporate executives and politicians looking to boost SMEs' competitiveness in developing nations.

The definition of organizational readiness in the literature on strategic management is the degree to which an organization is equipped to execute change and meet novel challenges. This preparedness takes into account a number of factors, including as staff abilities, resource accessibility, and the existence of a positive work environment (Kebede & Wang, 2022). Human capital, or the knowledge, skills, and talents that people possess, is an essential part of organizational preparedness. Research shows that companies with more human capital are better able to take advantage of opportunities and counteract risks, which increases their competitive advantage (Hossain et al., 2024). There is still a dearth of study on Ethiopian SMEs, despite prior studies demonstrating the important effect that the relationship between organizational preparedness and human capital has on performance results (Saadi & Razak, 2019). Practical difficulties nevertheless exist despite the theoretical and empirical advances in our knowledge of these entities. Inadequate training programs, restricted information availability, and a lack of a clear strategic vision are among the many challenges that Ethiopian SMEs confront. These issues impede their organizational preparedness and, ultimately, their competitive advantage. Furthermore, there is a substantial knowledge vacuum since the literature currently in publication frequently ignores the unique difficulties encountered by SMEs in developing nations (Berlilana et al., 2021). By presenting empirical data on the connections between organizational preparedness, human capital, and competitive advantage among Ethiopian SMEs, this research seeks to close these gaps.

By doing this, it will provide information that will help future scholars and decision-makers create focused plans that improve organizational preparedness and the development of human capital. *"How does organizational readiness influence competitive advantage in SMEs, and what role does human capital play as a mediator in this relationship?"* is the main research question that drives this investigation. In addition to adding to the body of knowledge in academia, the answer to this question will offer practitioners concrete suggestions for enhancing the viability and performance of SMEs in Ethiopia's changing economic environment.

BACKGROUND OF THE STUDY

Ethiopia's (SMEs) scene is marked by both enormous prospects and difficult obstacles. SMEs are an essential part of the country's economy, providing a large number of jobs and making a major contribution to the GDP (Anser et al., 2022). However, many of these firms struggle to attain competitive advantage owing to different internal and external obstacles. In this context, it is important to grasp the idea of organizational readiness since it is a prerequisite for implementing strategies effectively and being flexible in a changing market (Hossain et al., 2024). The collective ability of an organization to implement change, including the availability of resources, the skill level of its personnel, and a supportive culture, is referred to as organizational readiness (Berlilana et al., 2021). In Ethiopia, many SMEs display poor levels of organizational preparedness mostly owing to restricted access to training and development programs. For example, a study on textile SMEs in Addis Ababa found that insufficient training programs made it difficult for staff members to adjust to new manufacturing techniques and technologies, which decreased the competitiveness and quality of the products. This example shows how a company's ability to innovate and adapt to market needs is directly impacted when human capital development is neglected (L'Écuyer et al., 2019).

Furthermore, there are extra difficulties because of Ethiopia's cultural background. Since many SMEs work in antiquated systems that are resistant to change, it can be challenging to create an atmosphere that is supportive of innovation (Berlilana et al., 2021). Organizational hierarchies, for instance, frequently impede employee initiative and innovation, which results in missed chances for growth and adaptation, as demonstrated by a case study on the food processing industry. Fear of retaliation made employees reluctant to suggest fresh concepts or enhancements, which made the company's stagnation even worse (Ed-Dafali et al., 2023). One example of how Ethiopian SMEs might improve organizational readiness to effectively compete is Addis Ababa Textiles. The company has promoted an innovative and agile culture by using new production technology and streamlining supply chain procedures (Melesse et al., 2024). However, organizational preparedness and human capital development in Ethiopian SMEs are greatly impacted by external variables such as economic volatility, technical limitations, and legislative changes. Businesses are frequently compelled by economic instability to put short-term survival ahead of long-term training investments (Ferede et al., 2024). Furthermore, access to current technology is impeded by high costs and poor infrastructure, which exacerbates staff skills shortages (Moges & Assefa Habete, 2023). Resources from crucial capacity-building programs may be further diverted to compliance activities due to frequent regulation changes (Shebeshe & Sharma, 2024).

When it comes to Ethiopian SMEs, external variables also have a big impact on organizational preparedness. The environment for these businesses is made more difficult by regulatory obstacles, shifting market conditions, and economic uncertainty. An actual example may be seen in the agriculture industry, where SMEs deal with erratic weather patterns and problems getting their products to market. Many of these companies are ill-prepared, endangering their competitive edge, since they lack the infrastructure and support mechanisms needed to respond swiftly to these issues (Kebede & Wang, 2022).

Statement of Problem

Ethiopia's small- and medium-sized business (SMEs) competitive environment is characterized by a complex interplay of possibilities and constraints, with organizational preparedness and its effect on competitive advantage being of special importance. In a perfect world, Ethiopian SMEs would use their people resources to develop a culture of creativity and adaptation, giving them a stable competitive edge in marketplaces that are becoming more and more dynamic. But as things stand right now, there is a big gap between this perfect situation and how many SMEs really perform (Saadi & Razak, 2019). Research shows that almost 70% of Ethiopian SMEs have organizational readiness issues, mostly as a result of limited access to resources for training and growth. Additionally, according to a poll, 60% of these companies struggle with issues that reduce their competitive edge, such excessive operating expenses and a lack of technology adoption. The pressing need for focused initiatives in human capital development is highlighted by these measurable problems. By clearly stating these difficulties, we hope to establish a strong basis for our research goals and highlight the importance of our investigation. This will draw attention to the need of addressing organizational preparedness as well as the possible effects on Ethiopian SMEs' overall competitiveness.

The literature contains conflicting information about the connection between competitive advantage, human capital, and organizational preparedness. Some research shows a high positive link, while other studies show conflicting findings, indicating that improving competitive posture is not always the outcome of just investing in human capital. Particularly in the particular context of Ethiopian SMEs, where cultural, economic, and structural factors may influence outcomes differently than in more developed markets, this inconsistency highlights a theoretical gap in understanding the mechanisms that underlie these relationships (Tjahjadi et al., 2022). Furthermore, there are still a lot of unanswered questions about the unique difficulties Ethiopian SMEs have in improving their organizational preparedness. Studies that concentrate on more general regional or global contexts tend to leave a gap in the literature about localized research that tackles the particular socio-economic and cultural forces at work. The creation of customized strategies that may successfully increase organizational preparedness and, consequently, competitive advantage is made more difficult by this lack of context-specific knowledge. Practical challenges further exacerbate these issues. Many SMEs struggle with limited resources for training and development, inadequate access to information, and a resistance to change within organizational cultures. These challenges hinder their ability to foster an environment conducive to learning and adaptation, thereby impacting both human capital development and overall organizational performance.

By offering a thorough examination of the connections between organizational preparedness, human capital, and competitive advantage particularly within Ethiopian SMEs, this research seeks to close these gaps. This research will examine the contextual elements that impact these connections via the use of empirical methodologies and case study analyses. The findings will provide valuable insights into measures that can be used to improve organizational preparedness. The results will not only enhance the scholarly conversation but also offer practical suggestions for practitioners and policymakers, directing further investigations into this crucial field. In the end, this research aims to shed light on a strategy Ethiopian SMEs may use to overcome obstacles and take use of their potential for long-term competitive advantage.

Theoretical Foundations

The Resource-Based View (RBV): According to the Resource-Based View (RBV), firms may gain a sustained competitive advantage by making use of their special resources and competencies, especially those that are uncommon, precious, distinctive, and non-replaceable. This theory emphasizes the significance of human capital as an essential resource in the context of Ethiopian small and medium enterprises. SMEs may increase their organizational preparedness and better adapt to market shifts and competitive challenges by investing in the skills, knowledge, and competences of their personnel (Ed-Dafali et al., 2023).

Dynamic Capabilities Theory: highlights how companies may combine, develop, and reorganize internal and external talents to deal with quickly changing surroundings. By emphasizing how companies may adjust their resources over time, this theory enhances the RBV. The dynamic capabilities framework emphasizes the value of organizational preparedness in supporting an innovative and ever-learning culture for small and medium-sized enterprises (SMEs) in Ethiopia. According to Katebi et al. (2024), it implies that SMEs must not only have resources but also have the skills necessary to use them wisely in the face of changing circumstances.

Human Capital Theory: assumes a crucial role in comprehending the ways that investments in employee knowledge and skills lead to corporate performance. According to this notion, human capital plays a major role in fostering creativity and productivity. This theory highlights the need of investing in personnel development for Ethiopian SMEs as a way to improve organizational preparedness and, in turn, competitive advantage (Saadi & Razak, 2019).

The Resource-Based View (RBV) is the primary theoretical lens through which this research is viewed; however, several other theories also provide light on the study's framework. The study's goal of examining how organizational preparation affects competitive advantage is closely aligned with the RBV's emphasis on using internal resources, especially human capital. This study will highlight the importance of distinctive organizational capacities in influencing performance results by situating the research within the RBV, offering a solid framework for comprehending the dynamics at work among Ethiopian SMEs. According to Anthony et al. (2023), the research will make a significant contribution to the academic literature and practical applications in the field by means of a theoretical lens that will steer the analysis and interpretation of data.

Definition and Origin of Terms

Organizational Readiness: It refers to the degree of readiness of an organization to successfully execute change or new tactics. It includes a number of factors, such as the accessibility of resources, staff members' abilities and competences, encouraging leadership, and an innovative and flexible culture. The idea first appeared in the literature on organizational change in the 1990s, especially as scholars started to realize that effective change initiatives need more than just a strategic plan to be implemented; they also need a comprehensive understanding of the organization's capabilities and readiness (Ziaei Nafchi & Mohelská. 2020).

Human Capital: It refers to the monetary worth of a person's abilities, information, experience, and other qualities that boost their output. The phrase first appeared in the field of economics in the 1960s, mainly as a result of the work of Theodore Schultz and Gary Becker. They proposed that spending on health, education, and training improves people's capacities, which raises economic production and productivity. Similarly, human capital can be developed via education and training, which will ultimately benefit economies and organizations. According to L'Écuyer et al (2019), human capital is seen in the context of this study as a crucial component of organizational preparedness that affects SMEs' capacity to compete successfully.

Competitive Advantage: It is described as the qualities that enable a company to perform better than its rivals. In his groundbreaking publications from the 1980s, Michael Porter popularized this idea by identifying the sources of competitive advantage, including differentiation and cost leadership. A company may have a competitive edge due to a number of things, such as advanced technology, highly qualified personnel, a solid brand reputation, and efficient organizational procedures. Competitive advantage is especially important in the context of Ethiopian SMEs, as these businesses try to stand out in a crowded market and negotiate a difficult economic environment (Hermawan & Suharnomo, 2020).

Small and Medium-sized Enterprises (SMEs): SMEs are characterized by their size, which is usually determined by the quantity of workers or yearly income. While the categorization may differ by nation, businesses with fewer than 250 workers are often referred to as SMEs. As governments and economists realized how important SMEs were to innovation, job creation, and economic growth in the late 20th century, the idea of SMEs became more widely accepted. SMEs play a major role in creating jobs and revenue production in Ethiopia and are becoming more and more acknowledged as essential to the country's economic progress. With the goal of increasing SMEs' capability and competitiveness in both domestic and foreign markets, the promotion of SMEs has emerged as a strategic priority for policymakers (Kebede & Wang, 2022).

EMPIRICAL LITERATURE REVIEW

Organizational Readiness and Competitive Advantage

In recent years, research has focused on the link between organizational preparedness and competitive advantage in small and medium-sized organizations (SMEs), especially as these businesses negotiate more complex and dynamic settings (Anthony et al., 2023). Many times, organizational preparedness is seen as a multifaceted term that includes elements like employee skills, leadership support, resource availability, and an innovative culture. Higher organizational preparedness levels are positively correlated with increased competitive advantage, as empirical research has repeatedly shown (Saadi & Razak, 2019). In the literature, the function of human capital as a mediating component has also been emphasized. Human capital strongly affects the link between organizational preparedness and competitive advantage, according to research by Kamasak and Bulutlar (2016). According to their results, companies that place a high priority on skill development and staff growth are better positioned to make efficient use of their resources, which improves their competitive outcomes (Kebede & Wang, 2022). This is consistent with the Resource-Based View (RBV), which holds that, when used effectively, human capital is a crucial resource that may provide competitive advantage (L'Écuyer et al., 2019).

The impact of dynamic capacities, such as detecting, seizing, and changing, on the competitive advantage of SMEs in Ethiopia was examined in a noteworthy study conducted by Abebe and Mulugeta (2021). According to their results, SMEs can react to external shocks and changes in the market more quickly if they successfully utilize their dynamic capacities. For example, businesses that keep a close eye on consumer preferences and market trends are better able to modify their products and services, giving them a competitive advantage over less nimble rivals (Tjahjadi et al., 2022).

H1: Organizational readiness has significant effect on competitive advantage.

Organizational Readiness and Human Capital in SMEs

Organizational preparedness fosters a climate that is favorable to employee growth, engagement, and retention, which has a substantial influence on human capital within small and medium-sized organizations (SMEs) (Hermawan & Suharnomo, 2020). Elevated degrees of organizational preparation signify an ability to execute modifications and adjust to novel obstacles, frequently resulting in calculated expenditures on staff education and advancement (Saadi & Razak, 2019). SMEs that place a high priority on preparedness, for example, are more likely to devote funds to skill-building initiatives, guaranteeing that staff members have the abilities they need to function well. In addition to providing the workforce with necessary skills, this emphasis on ongoing learning raises morale and increases job satisfaction (Hermawan & Suharnomo, 2020). Organizational preparedness also fosters a collaborative and open culture, which is essential for the growth of human capital. Employee idea sharing and problem-solving activities are encouraged in firms that exhibit high preparedness (Ed-Dafali et al., 2023). A sense of ownership over one's work is fostered and employee engagement is increased in this participatory atmosphere, both of which are important for creativity. According to research, workers are more inclined to put their all into their jobs and contribute their ingenuity when they feel appreciated and empowered, which eventually improves the success of the company as a whole (Machado et al., 2021).

A further important factor in this dynamic is leadership. Organizational leaders that exhibit preparedness tend to be more accommodating and flexible, emphasizing staff coaching and mentoring. This encouraging leadership approach fosters an environment in the workplace where learning and development are valued, in addition to helping with skill development. A workforce that is better equipped to handle the needs of a changing market is produced by leaders that actively engage in the development of their staff (Jun et al., 2022). Yilma and Fekadu (2023) emphasized the connection between organizational preparedness and talent retention in SMEs in Ethiopia. According to their research, companies that showed a dedication to preparedness by means of clear strategic direction, good communication, and encouraging management techniques had more success keeping talented workers. In Ethiopia, where skilled labor is frequently in limited supply, this retention is essential. These SMEs improve employee happiness and fortify their competitive advantage in the market by making investments in human capital development and cultivating a positive corporate culture (Kebede & Wang, 2022).

H2: Organizational readiness has significant effect on human capital.

Human Capital and Competitive Advantage

Effect of Human Capital on Competitive Advantage in SMEs capital plays a pivotal role in determining the competitive advantage of small and medium-sized enterprises (SMEs) by influencing their ability to innovate, adapt to market changes, and enhance operational efficiency (Ed-Dafali et al., 2023). At its core, human capital refers to the skills, knowledge, and experience possessed by employees, which can significantly impact an organization's performance. In SMEs, where resources are often limited, the quality of human capital becomes a critical differentiator that shapes the organization's strategic positioning in the marketplace (Hossain et al., 2024). Innovation is one of the main ways that human capital adds to competitive advantage. Workers that possess a broad range of abilities and a solid foundation of knowledge are more able to come up with fresh concepts, create cutting-edge goods, and enhance workflows (Ed-Dafali et al., 2023). Studies have indicated that small and medium-sized enterprises (SMEs) that allocate resources towards employee training and ongoing education are more likely to cultivate an innovative culture. Due to their ability to innovate, SMEs are able to stand out from rivals, better meet client demands, and eventually increase their market share (L'Écuyer et al., 2019).

Moreover, human capital enhances operational efficiency, which is crucial for SMEs striving to compete in cost-sensitive markets. Skilled employees can streamline operations, reduce waste, and improve productivity, leading to lower operational costs and higher profit margins. For instance, a study by Goh and Kauffman (2017) found that SMEs with well-trained employees were able to optimize their processes, resulting in significant cost savings and improved service delivery. This efficiency not only enhances the bottom line but also enables SMEs to offer competitive pricing, further strengthening their market position (Tjahjadi et al., 2022). Furthermore, client connections and service quality two crucial elements of competitive advantage are impacted by human capital. Well-informed and trained staff members are more likely to deliver superior customer service, which increases client happiness and loyalty. The capacity to forge close bonds with customers may be a big advantage in a competitive market where consumer tastes are changing quickly. Hsu and Fang's (2010) research emphasizes that SMEs that put a high priority on human capital development are better positioned to comprehend and satisfy consumer expectations, which promotes repeat business and long-term loyalty (Hitka et al., 2019).

Furthermore, the adaptability of human capital is crucial for SMEs operating in volatile environments. Employees who possess a strong foundation of skills and knowledge are more likely to embrace change and respond proactively to market dynamics (Ed-Dafali et al., 2023). This adaptability is particularly important in developing economies like Ethiopia, where SMEs face unpredictable challenges. By cultivating a skilled workforce that can pivot in response to external pressures, SMEs can maintain their competitive edge even in times of uncertainty (Hermawan & Suharnomo, 2020). In the Ethiopian context, empirical studies have increasingly demonstrated the critical role of human capital in influencing the competitive advantage of SMEs. Research by highlights that firms with a well-developed human capital base characterized by skilled, knowledgeable, and motivated employees are better positioned to compete effectively in both local and international markets (Chane & Atwal, 2023).

H3: Human capital has significant effect on competitive Advantage

Human Capital Mediation Between Organizational Readiness and Competitive Advantage

The mediation effect of human capital between organizational readiness and competitive advantage is a vital area of analysis for small and medium-sized enterprises (SMEs). Organizational readiness refers to the preparedness of an organization to implement change and adapt to new strategies, while competitive advantage denotes the attributes that allow a firm to outperform its competitors (Ed-Dafali et al., 2023). Human capital, comprising the skills, knowledge, and abilities of employees, serves as a critical mediator in this relationship, influencing how organizational readiness translates into competitive advantage (Ed-Dafali et al., 2023). Human capital increases SMEs' ability to efficiently utilize their resources, mediating the relationship between organizational preparedness and competitive advantage. When a company exhibits high preparedness, it usually makes workforce development investments, which have a direct effect on workers' abilities and competences (Tjahjadi et al., 2022). These expenditures help to develop a more competent staff that is better able to carry out strategic plans and adapt to changing market conditions. According to research, companies that employ a highly qualified workforce are more likely to see improvements in performance, which will strengthen their position as a competitive player (Hitka et al., 2019).

In Ethiopian context, SMEs are better able to execute extensive training programs that improve staff competences when they place a high priority on organizational preparedness. Increased productivity and innovation follow, both of which are critical for preserving competitiveness (Yilma and Fekadu (2023). The results indicate that skill development and education are important channels for converting organizational preparedness into competitive advantage (Jun et al., 2022). Furthermore, the quality of human capital influences the organization's ability to build strong customer relationships and deliver superior service (Tjahjadi et al., 2022). As organizational readiness leads to enhanced employee training and development, employees become more adept at understanding customer needs and delivering tailored solutions. This improved customer service capability translates into heightened customer satisfaction and loyalty, further reinforcing the competitive advantage of the SME (Kebede & Wang, 2022).

H4: Human capital mediates the relationship between organizational readiness and competitive advantage

CONCEPTUAL FRAMEWORK

Based on theoretical and empirical literature, the following hypothesis was developed.

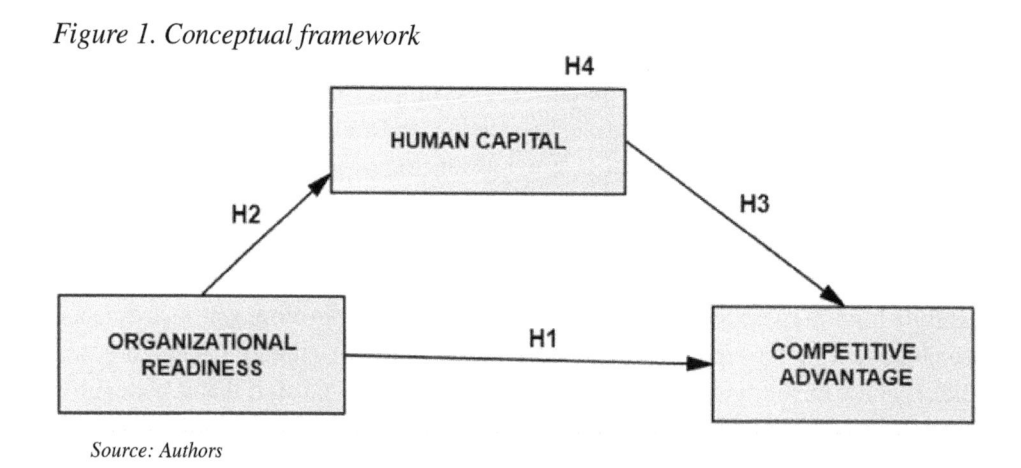

Figure 1. Conceptual framework

Source: Authors

RESEARCH METHODOLOGY

In order to examine the connections between organizational preparedness, human capital, organizational readiness, and competitive advantage in small and medium-sized businesses (SMEs), this study used a quantitative research methodology. 390 samples in all, drawn from different SMEs around Ethiopia, were gathered to guarantee a wide range of sectors and industries. A structured questionnaire was employed as the main data collecting tool. It was created to assess the main components of interest, such as competitive advantage, organizational preparedness, and human capital. Before beginning data analysis, the study used Bartlett's Test of Sphericity and the Kaiser-Meyer-Olkin (KMO) test to determine whether the dataset was suitable for factor analysis. The KMO value was determined to be acceptable, meaning that there was adequate sample to carry out factor analysis. After that, the underlying factor structure of the constructs was found using exploratory factor analysis (EFA). EFA made it possible to reduce the amount of data and find factor loadings that show how the variables are related to one another. The construct validity of the scales employed in the study was supported by the EFA results, which demonstrated that the items loaded correctly onto their corresponding components.

Subsequently, the study employed Structural Equation Modeling (SEM) using AMOS software to test the proposed hypotheses and explore the relationships among the constructs. SEM provides a comprehensive approach to model the complex relationships between observed and latent variables, allowing for the examination of direct and indirect effects. The analysis began with model specification, where the hypothesized relationships were defined based on the theoretical framework. The model was then assessed for goodness-of-fit using various indices, including the Chi-square statistic, Comparative Fit Index (CFI), and Root Mean Square Error of Approximation (RMSEA). The final model demonstrated adequate fit, confirming the relationships between organizational readiness, human capital, organizational readiness, and competitive advantage.

A meticulous procedure was followed in developing the scale for the structures, which includes consulting with experts and creating items based on previously published research. To make sure they were clear and relevant, the items were pre-tested on a smaller sample. The items were improved to increase their validity and reliability after the EFA. Using standard scales that were modified to match the unique circumstances of SMEs in Ethiopia, the constructs were assessed. Using Cronbach's alpha to evaluate the scales' reliability, all components showed good internal consistency by exceeding the suggested threshold. To evaluate the interactions among important variables in SMEs, the study methodology integrated a quantitative approach with rigorous statistical tools, such as KMO, EFA, and SEM. Strong data collection and analysis were made possible by the study's design, which also provided insightful information about the roles that human capital and organizational readiness play in fostering competitive advantage and organizational readiness. In order to better understand the dynamics inside Ethiopian SMEs, this technique laid a strong foundation, opening the door for more study in this important field.

Data Analysis

Table 1. KMO and Bartlett's Test

Kaiser-Meyer-Olkin Measure of Sampling Adequacy.		.859
Bartlett's Test of Sphericity	Approx. Chi-Square	1419.748
	Df	90
	Sig.	.005

Source: Authors

Analysis Of KMO and Bartlett's Test

The findings of the Bartlett's Test of Sphericity and the Kaiser-Meyer-Olkin (KMO) Measure of Sampling Adequacy are shown in Table 1. A high degree of sampling adequacy is shown by the KMO score of 0.859, indicating that the sample size is enough for factor analysis. KMO values range from 0 to 1, with values of 0.70 and 0.80 indicating adequate sample adequacy and, respectively, above 0.70 typically deemed acceptable. A KMO score of 0.859 thus suggests that the variables included in the research have a pretty high degree of correlation, making factor analysis an appropriate approach for detecting underlying structures among the variables. The data's suitability for factor analysis is further supported by Bartlett's Test of Sphericity. The test produced a about 1419.748 Chi-Square value with 90 degrees of freedom and a 0.005 significance level (Sig.). According to the null hypothesis of Bartlett's test, the variables are uncorrelated and the correlation matrix is an identity matrix. There are substantial correlations between the variables, as evidenced by a significant result ($p < 0.05$) showing that the correlation matrix is not an identity matrix. Factor analysis is acceptable for the obtained data in this scenario since the null hypothesis is strongly rejected at the significance level of 0.005.

Table 2. Total variance explained

Component	Initial Eigenvalues			Extraction Sums of Squared Loadings			Rotation Sums of Squared Loadings		
	Total	% of Variance	Cumulative %	Total	% of Variance	Cumulative %	Total	% of Variance	Cumulative %
1	4.55	32.240	32.240	4.55	32.240	32.240	3.00	20.451	20.451
2	1.37	9.789	42.022	1.37	9.789	42.022	2.17	15.491	36.942
3	1.29	9.087	51.113	1.29	9.087	51.113	1.96	14.168	51.113
4	.949	6.782	57.886						
5	.871	6.223	64.120						
6	.773	5.519	69.640						

Extraction Method: PCA
Source: Authors

The Total Variance Explained by Principal Component Analysis (PCA) results are compiled in Table 2. A higher eigenvalue indicates a larger percentage of variation explained. The eigenvalue is a measure of how much variance is explained by each component. The first component has an initial eigenvalue of 4.55, which accounts for 32.240% of the total variance. This substantial percentage indicates that the first component captures a significant portion of the variability in the data, suggesting it is a key factor in understanding the underlying constructs. The cumulative percentage for the first component is also 32.240%, underscoring its importance in the factor structure. The second component, with an eigenvalue of 1.37, explains an additional 9.789% of the variance, bringing the cumulative variance explained to 42.022%. Similarly, the third component shows an eigenvalue of 1.29, contributing 9.087% to the total variance and maintaining the cumulative percentage at 51.113%. The cumulative percentages indicate that together, these three components account for over half of the total variance, which is a critical threshold for establishing meaningful factors. With eigenvalues of 0.949, 0.871, and 0.773 for the fourth, fifth, and sixth components, respectively, they exhibit diminishing characteristics. The fourth component alone accounts for 6.782% of the variation. It's crucial to remember that these components' eigenvalues are less than 1, which indicates that they might not have a major impact on the construct and might even be less meaningful in the context of the research. Principal Component investigation, which effectively reduces the dimensionality of the data while maintaining the most important variance, was the extraction approach used in this investigation. This approach facilitates the identification of the critical elements influencing the constructions under study.

Confirmatory Principle Component Examination

The principle component arrangement of a set of guided proxies is verified using a type of statistics known as confirmatory principle component examination. Based on the underlying job frame and correlatives among observed proxies, investigations can evaluate hypotheses utilizing CFA. To evaluate the hypothesis that there is a association among the proxies that are being steered and the latent conceptions that underpin them, the inquiry employed CFA under table 3.

Table 3. Covariances

Covariance			Approximation	S.E.	C.R.	P	Hy.
Human Capital	<-->	Organizational readiness	.247	.026	8.236	***	H2
Human Capital	<-->	Competitive advantage	.307	.036	7.702	***	H3
Organizational readiness	<-->	Competitive advantage	.260	.28	7.835	***	H1

Source: Authors

The correlation estimates between the three main research constructs are shown in Table 3. With a standard error of 0.026, the correlation between organizational preparedness and human capital is stated to be 0.247. The significant high critical ratio (C.R.) of 8.236 suggests a strong positive link between these two variables. As shown by the significance level of "***," there is a high degree of statistical significance ($p < 0.001$) for this association. This substantial correlation supports Hypothesis 2 (H2) by indicating that an increase in human capital also boosts the ability for organizational preparedness. The covariance between Human Capital and Competitive Advantage is even stronger, with a value of 0.307 and a standard error of 0.036. The critical ratio of 7.702 further reinforces the significance of this relationship, as indicated by the "***" notation. This result suggests that enhanced human capital directly contributes to improved competitive advantage, validating Hypothesis 3 (H3). The implication here is clear: organizations that prioritize the development of their workforce are likely to experience greater success in achieving a competitive edge in the marketplace. Furthermore, the correlation coefficient between Competitive Advantage and Organizational Readiness is 0.260, with a standard deviation of 0.28. Once more indicated by "***," which implies strong statistical significance, the crucial ratio of 7.835 shows a substantial positive association. This data indicates that organizational preparedness is a major factor influencing competitive advantage in SMEs, which validates Hypothesis 1 (H1). The positive covariance suggests that firms are better positioned to outperform rivals when they adopt innovative techniques.

Table 4: Validity concern

	CR	AVE	MSV	MaxR(H)	OR	HC	CA
OR	0.736	0.638	0.223	0.855	**0.648**		
HC	0.763	0.662	0.137	0.770	0.176	**0.670**	
CA	0.790	0.600	0.271	0.794	0.380	0.1930	**0.681**

Note: OR= Organizational readiness; HC= Human Capital; CA= Competitive Advantage
Source: Authors

Analysis of Validity Concern

Table 4, which focuses on Reliability. The constructs' Composite Reliability (CR) values—0.736 for Organizational Readiness, 0.763 for Human Capital, and 0.790 for Competitive Advantage—all exceed the suggested cutoff point of 0.7. This suggests that the items used to test each construct are dependable and consistently represent the underlying theoretical notions. It also shows that the constructs display strong internal consistency. The Average Variance Extracted (AVE) values further substantiate the validity of the constructs. All constructs demonstrate AVE values above the acceptable threshold of 0.5, with Organizational Readiness at 0.638, Human Capital at 0.662, and Competitive Advantage at 0.600. These values indicate that a significant proportion of the variance in the observed variables is captured by the latent constructs, reinforcing their convergent validity. In comparison to the AVE values, the Maximum Shared Variance (MSV) values, which show the strongest link between the constructs, are very low. The MSV for Competitive Advantage is 0.271, the MSV for Human Capital is 0.137, and the MSV for Organizational Readiness is 0.223. These low MSV values bolster the discriminant validity of the notions by indicating that they are unique from one another. The knowledge of construct reliability is further improved by the Maximum Reliability (MaxR(H)) values. Organizational Readiness, Human Capital, and Competitive Advantage have respective MaxR(H) values of 0.855, 0.770, and 0.794.

MEDIATING ROLE EXAMINATION

Figure 2. Structural equation model

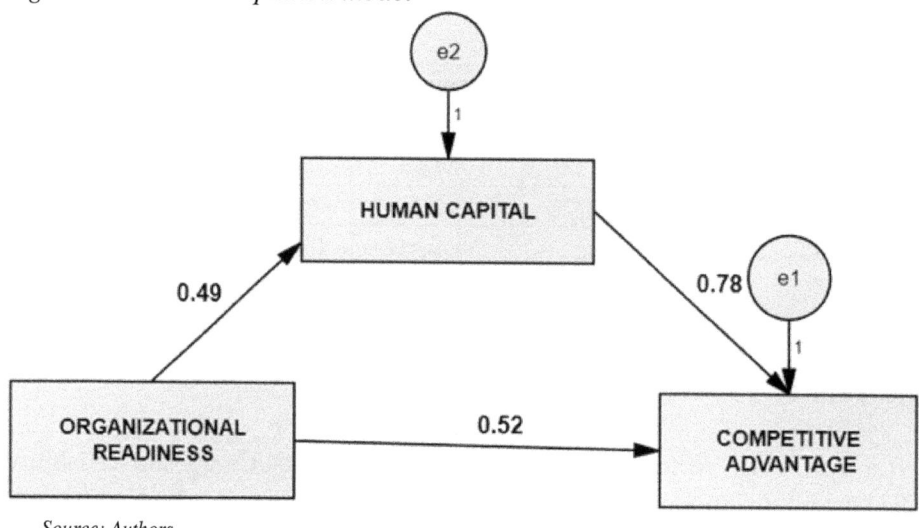

```
                        e2
                        │
                        ▼
                 ┌──────────────┐
                 │ HUMAN CAPITAL│
                 └──────────────┘
           0.49 ↗                ↘ 0.78   e1
                                              │
                                              ▼
┌───────────────┐      0.52      ┌──────────────┐
│ ORGANIZATIONAL│ ─────────────▶ │  COMPETITIVE │
│   READINESS   │                │   ADVANTAGE  │
└───────────────┘                └──────────────┘
```

Source: Authors

Model Fit Indices

Table 5. Indices for model fit

Sig.	Chi-Sq	RMR	Fitness Goodness	Fitness Confirmatory	TLI	RMSEA
0.002	1.960	.040	0.929	0.915	0.914	.030

Source: Authors

Analysis of Model Fit Indices

The model fit indices, which are shown in Table 5. There is a 1.960 Chi-Square (Chi-Sq) statistic with a 0.002 significance level (Sig.). Large sample sizes are frequently the reason why the Chi-Square test is relevant in the context of structural equation modeling (SEM). A substantial Chi-Square value indicates that the model does not fit well. As a result, even while the Chi-Square value suggests that there may be a difference between the model and the data; it should be seen as a supplementary signal of model fit. The model appears to match the data well, as evidenced by the Root Mean Square Residual (RMR) value of 0.040, which shows a minimal degree of difference between the observed and anticipated covariances. Low residuals between the model and the data, as indicated by low RMR values, usually signify a strong fit. The Goodness of Fit Index (GFI) is reported as 0.929, while the Confirmatory Fit Index (CFI) is 0.915. Both these indices exceed the commonly accepted threshold of 0.90, indicating a good fit between the model and the data. These measures suggest that the model explains a substantial portion of the variance in the observed data, confirming the adequacy of the specified relationships among the constructs. Notable is the Tucker-Lewis Index (TLI), which stands at 0.914 and adds more credence to the model's fit. TLI values greater than 0.90 are seen to be a sign of a well-fitting model, and the given value Last but not least, the Root Mean Square Error of Approximation (RMSEA) is reported as 0.030, a value that falls noticeably short of the 0.08 criterion commonly employed to denote a decent match. Excellent fit is often indicated by RMSEA values less than 0.05, while adequate fit is indicated by values between 0.05 and 0.08. Thus, the RMSEA value of 0.030 further verifies the robustness of the model fit.

Table 6. Regression examination

Relative			Approx.	S.E.	C.R.	P	Ass.
Human Capital	<--	Organizational readiness	.867	.146	7.585	***	H2
Competitive advantage	<---	Human capital	.327	.130	2.852	***	H3
Competitive advanatages	<---	Organizational readiness	.956	.191	7.957	***	H1

Source: Authors

Regression Examination

As Table 6, the regression coefficient for Human Capital predicted by Organizational Readiness is reported at 0.867, with a standard error (S.E.) of 0.146. The critical ratio (C.R.) of 7.585 is significantly high, and the significance level is marked with "***," indicating a highly significant relationship (p < 0.001). This strong positive coefficient suggests that as organizational readiness increases, human capital also significantly improves. This finding supports Hypothesis 2 (H2), emphasizing the importance of a readiness-oriented culture in fostering employee development and skills enhancement. The second relationship examined is between Human Capital and Competitive Advantage, with a regression coefficient of 0.327 and a standard error of 0.130. The critical ratio of 2.852 indicates a statistically significant effect, again denoted by "***." This suggests that higher levels of human capital contribute positively to competitive advantage in SMEs, validating Hypothesis 3 (H3). The positive coefficient implies that investments in employee skills and knowledge have a direct impact on the organization's ability to outperform its competitors. Lastly, the regression coefficient for Competitive Advantage predicted by Organizational Readiness is exceptionally high at 0.956, with a standard error of 0.191. The critical ratio of 7.957 further confirms the significance of this relationship ($p < 0.001$). This finding supports Hypothesis 1 (H1), indicating that organizational readiness is a strong predictor of competitive advantage. The substantial coefficient suggests that organizations that are well-prepared and strategically aligned are more likely to achieve a significant competitive edge in their market.

Analysis of Mediating Role Effect

Table 7. Mediating role Effect

	Influence	Worth	Path Influence
Organizational readiness → Competitive advantage	Direct Influence	.52	Direct influence stated
Organizational readiness → Human capital → Competitive advantage	Indirect Influence	.49*.78=.32	Indirect Influence Ensued
	Whole influence	.84	Partial mediation

Source: Authors

As Table 7, the direct influence of Organizational Readiness on Competitive Advantage is quantified at 0.52. This substantial coefficient indicates that organizational readiness has a strong direct effect on competitive advantage, suggesting that SMEs that are well-prepared and strategically aligned are more likely to achieve favorable outcomes in their market. The statement "Direct influence stated" reinforces the significance of this direct relationship, emphasizing the importance of organizational readiness as a foundational element for competitive success. In addition to the direct influence, the table also presents the indirect influence of Organizational Readiness on Competitive Advantage through Human Capital. This indirect effect is calculated as 0.49 (the path from Organizational Readiness to Human Capital) multiplied by 0.78 (the path from Human Capital to Competitive Advantage), resulting in a value of 0.32. The notation "Indirect Influence Ensued" indicates that this pathway is significant, showing that human capital acts as a mediator in the relationship between organizational readiness and competitive advantage. This finding underscores the idea that investments in employee development not only enhance readiness but also translate into competitive benefits.

The whole influence of Organizational Readiness on Competitive Advantage, combining both direct and indirect effects, totals 0.84. This high value indicates that the overall impact of organizational readiness on competitive advantage is substantial when considering both the direct pathway and the mediation through human capital. The designation of "Partial mediation" suggests that while human capital plays a significant mediating role, organizational readiness still directly influences competitive advantage, indicating that both pathways are important in understanding this relationship.

DISCUSSION

The study's conclusions highlight the crucial roles that organizational preparedness and human capital play in giving small and medium-sized businesses (SMEs) a competitive edge. The study showed that human capital is greatly increased by organizational preparedness, and this improves competitive results. This supports the idea that a well-prepared company is better able to train its personnel and create an atmosphere that encourages skill development and employee advancement. Setting organizational preparedness as a top priority helps SMEs make the most use of their human resources as they negotiate more competitive marketplaces. The results of the mediation study showed that the connection between organizational preparedness and competitive advantage is partially mediated by human capital. This implies that although competitive advantage is directly influenced by organizational preparedness, employee development programs serve as an essential intermediate stage in the process of enhancing human capital. This research emphasizes how crucial it is to fund training and skill-building initiatives because, in addition to meeting short-term operational demands, they develop a workforce that fosters creativity and flexibility. SMEs that understand how these elements are related to one another are therefore more likely to succeed over the long run. Furthermore, the study's findings highlight how crucial human capital is to competitive advantage. The positive link suggests that companies with a workforce that is highly informed and talented would be better able to stand out in the market. This research supports the notion that human capital may help SMEs outperform their rivals by acting as a strategic asset rather than just a resource. SMEs looking to improve their market position must invest in human capital since adaptability and innovation are critical in this day and age. Furthermore, the positive model fit indices attest to the fact that the data provide strong support for the suggested correlations between the components.

CONCLUSION

This study emphasizes how crucial organizational preparedness and human capital are to small and medium-sized businesses' (SMEs') ability to gain a competitive edge. The results show that organizational preparedness directly influences competitive outcomes in addition to improving human capital. SMEs may successfully train their workforce and guarantee that their staff have the skills and knowledge needed to traverse competitive environments by fostering a culture of preparation. Employee development programs are crucial, as evidenced by the finding that human capital acts as a partial mediator between organizational preparedness and competitive advantage. A competent staff is a strategic asset for SMEs, as the strong link between human capital and competitive advantage highlights. Organizations that place a high priority on developing their human capital are likely to see an increase in success and innovation as market demands rise. The strong statistical evidence demonstrating the connections between the study's dimensions validates the findings and their significance for SME strategy and leadership.

Managerial Implications

The study's conclusions have important management ramifications for small and medium-sized businesses (SMEs) looking to strengthen their competitive edge. First and foremost, managers need to understand how crucial organizational preparedness is to fostering innovation and staff growth. Organizations may establish an atmosphere where workers are proactive and can effectively implement strategic goals and adjust to changes by cultivating a culture of preparation. For CEOs of SMEs, investing in the development of human capital should be a top priority. The report emphasizes how a staff with knowledge and expertise immediately adds to competitive advantage. Managers should thus put in place focused training and development initiatives that support both business objectives and market expectations. These programs boost worker capabilities while also encouraging job happiness and retention, which eventually improves organizational performance. The findings also demonstrate how organizational preparedness and human capital are related. It is advisable for managers to take a comprehensive strategy and incorporate these components into their strategic planning. This entails matching organizational strategy with human resource policies to guarantee that efforts to develop employees complement overarching company goals. By doing this, SMEs may better utilize their people resources, fostering creativity and agility in a cutthroat market.

Practical Implications

The study's practical implications highlight the necessity for small and medium-sized businesses (SMEs) to implement doable plans that improve human resources and organizational preparedness. Managers should concentrate on developing organized training programs that help staff members acquire specialized skills as well as an attitude of lifelong learning and flexibility. These kinds of programs can produce a workforce with more competencies, better able to handle obstacles and grasp possibilities in a cutthroat market. SMEs are also urged to put in place methods for monitoring and assessing staff development so that training initiatives are in line with business objectives and consumer demands. Organizations may improve their ability to innovate and react quickly to changes in the industry by actively implementing these strategies. Managers of SMEs should put in place specialized training programs that emphasize both hard and soft skills. Training in project management, customer service, and digital literacy, for instance, can improve workers' skills and flexibility. It might be advantageous to work together with nearby educational establishments to create and implement such programs.

Theoretical Implications

The link between organizational preparedness, human capital, and competitive advantage in SMEs is better understood theoretically thanks to this study. By proving that human capital plays a key role as a mediator in the link between organizational preparedness and competitive advantage, it expands on prior research. This emphasizes how crucial it is to see human capital as a strategic asset that can improve organizational performance rather than just a resource. Furthermore, the study validates the view that organizational preparedness is a vital precondition to effective employee growth. By offering a framework for investigating other variables that can affect these linkages and broadening the theoretical conversation on resource-based perspectives in SME contexts, our findings help guide future study.

Recommendations

For SME leaders, a number of recommendations may be made in light of the study's findings. First, it is vital to prioritize investment in human capital development, ensuring that training programs are designed to fit the unique needs of the firm and its personnel. Additionally, in order to improve flexibility and creativity, leaders can promote a culture of preparedness by fostering open communication and teamwork inside their organizations. SMEs may also think about starting coaching and mentoring programs to help staff development and transfer of expertise. Lastly, it is advised that businesses evaluate their preparedness and human capital plans on a regular basis and make the required adjustments to bring them into line with changing internal resources and market situations.

Future Directions

This study examined the relationship between organizational preparedness and competitive advantage in Ethiopian SMEs, with human capital acting as a mediating factor. With the aid of quantitative study, the impact of organizational preparedness on Ethiopian SMEs through the mediation of human capital was thoroughly examined. Future investigations should examine additional contextual elements that may have an influence on organizational preparedness, human capital, and competitive advantage in order to further explore the intricacies of the linkages described in this study. Richer insights might be obtained, for example, by looking at how cultural influences or industry-specific traits affect these dynamics. Furthermore, longitudinal research may be useful in evaluating the ways in which alterations in organizational strategy over time impact the growth of human resources and competitive posture. As SMEs negotiate an increasingly digital world, researchers should also look into how technology and digital transformation might improve organizational preparedness and human capital. This study focused on quantitative research.

REFERENCES

Anser, M. K., Yousaf, Z., Usman, M., & Yousaf, S. (2022). Towards strategic business performance of the hospitality sector: Nexus of ICT, E-marketing and organizational readiness. *Sustainability (Basel)*, 12(4), 1346. DOI: 10.3390/su12041346

Antony, J., Sony, M., McDermott, O., Jayaraman, R., & Flynn, D. (2023). An exploration of organizational readiness factors for Quality 4.0: An intercontinental study and future research directions. *International Journal of Quality & Reliability Management*, 40(2), 582–606. DOI: 10.1108/IJQRM-10-2021-0357

Berlilana, N., Noparumpa, T., Ruangkanjanases, A., Hariguna, T., & Sarmini, . (2021). Organization Benefit as an Outcome of Organizational Security Adoption: The Role of Cyber Security Readiness and Technology Readiness. *Sustainability (Basel)*, 13(24), 13761. DOI: 10.3390/su132413761

Chane, M., & Atwal, H. (2023). The entrepreneurial ecosystem and the performance of micro and small enterprises (MSEs) in Amhara region, Ethiopia: The political-legal perspective. *Journal of Developmental Entrepreneurship*, 28(03), 2350020. DOI: 10.1142/S1084946723500206

Ed-Dafali, S., Al-Azad, M. S., Mohiuddin, M., & Reza, M. N. H. (2023). Strategic orientations, organizational ambidexterity, and sustainable competitive advantage: Mediating role of industry 4.0 readiness in emerging markets. *Journal of Cleaner Production*, 401, 136765. DOI: 10.1016/j.jclepro.2023.136765

Ferede, W. L., Endawoke, Y., & Tessema, G. (2024). Change management through strategic leadership: The mediating effect of knowledge management in public organizations, Ethiopia. *Future Business Journal*, 10(1), 93. DOI: 10.1186/s43093-024-00363-z

Hermawan, I., & Suharnomo, S. (2020). Information technology as a strategic resource in encouraging organizational change readiness through the role of the human capital effectiveness. [Jurnal Dinamika Manajemen]. *Journal of Database Management*, 11(2), 242–254.

Hitka, M., Kucharčíková, A., Štarchoň, P., Balážová, Ž., Lukáč, M., & Stacho, Z. (2019). Knowledge and human capital as sustainable competitive advantage in human resource management. *Sustainability (Basel)*, 11(18), 4985. DOI: 10.3390/su11184985

Hossain, M. B., Rahman, M. U., Čater, T., & Vasa, L. (2024). Determinants of SMEs' strategic entrepreneurial innovative digitalization: Examining the mediation role of human capital. *European Journal of Innovation Management*. Advance online publication. DOI: 10.1108/EJIM-02-2024-0176

Jun, W., Nasir, M. H., Yousaf, Z., Khattak, A., Yasir, M., Javed, A., & Shirazi, S. H. (2022). Innovation performance in digital economy: Does digital platform capability, improvisation capability and organizational readiness really matter? *European Journal of Innovation Management*, 25(5), 1309–1327. DOI: 10.1108/EJIM-10-2020-0422

Katebi, A., Mohammadhosseini, A., Najmeddin, M., & Homami, P. (2024). The moderating impact of organizational readiness, competitive pressure and compatibility on the cost of using precast concrete components. *Journal of Financial Management of Property and Construction*, 29(2), 274–294. DOI: 10.1108/JFMPC-01-2023-0003

Kebede, S., & Wang, A. (2022). Organizational justice and employee readiness for change: The mediating role of perceived organizational support. *Frontiers in Psychology*, 13, 806109. DOI: 10.3389/fpsyg.2022.806109 PMID: 35369209

L'Écuyer, F., Raymond, L., Fabi, B., & Uwizeyemungu, S. (2019). Strategic alignment of IT and human resources management in manufacturing SMEs: Empirical test of a mediation model. *Employee Relations*, 41(5), 830–850. DOI: 10.1108/ER-09-2018-0258

Machado, C. G., Winroth, M., Almström, P., Ericson Öberg, A., Kurdve, M., & AlMashalah, S. (2021). Digital organisational readiness: Experiences from manufacturing companies. *Journal of Manufacturing Technology Management*, 32(9), 167–182. DOI: 10.1108/JMTM-05-2019-0188

Melesse, H. S., & Knatko, D. M. (2024). The contingent effects of strategic orientations and strategic capabilities on competitive performance: Evidence from Ethiopian manufacturing enterprises. *Heliyon*, 10(15), e35497. DOI: 10.1016/j.heliyon.2024.e35497 PMID: 39170336

Moges Dereje, H., & Assefa Habete, G. (2023). The Adoption of Electronic Procurement and Readiness Assessment in Central Ethiopia Regional State. *International Journal of Engineering and Advanced Technology (IJEAT) ISSN*, 2249-8958.

Pumplun, L., Tauchert, C., & Heidt, M. (2019). A new organizational chassis for artificial intelligence-exploring organizational readiness factors.

Saadi, I. A., & Razak, R. C. (2019). Organizational Change and Organizational Sustainability: The mediating effect of Innovative Human Capital. Opción. *Revista de Ciencias Humanas y Sociales*, (89), 180.

Shebeshe, E. N., & Sharma, D. (2024). Sustainable supply chain management and organizational performance: The mediating role of competitive advantage in Ethiopian manufacturing industry. *Future Business Journal*, 10(1), 47. DOI: 10.1186/s43093-024-00332-6

Tjahjadi, B., Soewarno, N., Nadyaningrum, V., & Aminy, A. (2022). Human capital readiness and global market orientation in Indonesian Micro-, Small-and-Medium-sized Enterprises business performance. *International Journal of Productivity and Performance Management*, 71(1), 79–99. DOI: 10.1108/IJPPM-04-2020-0181

Ziaei Nafchi, M., & Mohelská, H. (2020). Organizational culture as an indication of readiness to implement industry 4.0. *Information (Basel)*, 11(3), 174. DOI: 10.3390/info11030174

KEY TERMS WITH DEFINITIONS

Organizational Readiness: readiness refers to the extent to which an organization is prepared to implement change and adapt to new plans or activities. It includes resource accessibility, personnel adaptability to change, and company culture's congruence with strategic objectives. **Human capital:** refers to the collective skills, knowledge, experiences, and abilities of an organization's workforce. It is considered a key asset that drives organizational performance and innovation

Competitive Advantage: is the distinct edge a business has over rivals, enabling it to increase sales or profits and keeps more clients. This benefit may result from a number of things, such as greater product quality, cost leadership, innovation, or first-rate customer support.

Mediation: pertains to a statistical idea in which the link between an independent and dependent variable is explained by a third variable, or mediator. In this situation, organizational preparedness and competitive advantage are mediated by human capital, suggesting that organizational readiness affects competitive advantage by influencing human capital.

Chapter 3
Conquering the Competitive Landscape:
A Fusion of Defensive and Offensive Strategies for Sustainable Growth

Alieu Stephen Kafoe
https://orcid.org/0009-0001-8775-4985
Marymount University, USA

ABSTRACT

This study presents a novel approach, a strategic framework uniquely combining Porter's Five Forces model (defensive strategy) with the Blue Ocean Strategy (offensive strategy). This innovative fusion allows organizations to comprehensively analyze their competitive landscape, identify opportunities for value innovation, and create new, uncontested market spaces. The Five Forces model provides a structured method for understanding industry dynamics, competitive forces, and profitability drivers. At the same time, the Blue Ocean strategy encourages the creation of new value propositions and differentiation. By merging these strategies, their limitations are mitigated, and their effectiveness is enhanced, enabling organizations to compete within existing markets and pioneer new growth avenues – a crucial element for sustained success in today's dynamic business environment. The strategic successes of Tesla, Apple, and Pfizer serve as compelling examples of the practical application of this framework, which effectively leverages both strategies to establish a solid competitive advantage

DOI: 10.4018/979-8-3693-8562-3.ch003

INTRODUCTION

A fundamental military doctrine underscores the importance of identifying and exploiting vulnerabilities or weaknesses in the enemy's defenses (Hurst, 2017; Meiser et al., 2021). This strategic principle can be extended to competitive domains beyond warfare, such as recreational sports like soccer or football. Just as a soccer team must possess offensive capabilities, seize opportunities to score goals, and excel in defensive tactics to prevent opponents from neutralizing their efforts or gaining an advantage through scoring, businesses must balance their offensive and defensive strategies to succeed. In business competition, this balance is not just a strategic choice but a necessity for survival and growth in today's competitive landscape (Badari et al., 2021). This strategic balance is at the core of my proposed framework, which combines Porter's Five Forces model (defensive strategy) with the Blue Ocean Strategy (offensive strategy), enabling organizations to navigate their competitive landscape effectively.

The strategic merits of the Blue Ocean Strategy, a powerful approach that involves targeting areas neglected or inadequately defended by adversaries or competitors, extend far beyond military contexts and hold equal relevance in business (Wee, 2017). By identifying and exploiting the vulnerabilities or gaps in competitors' strategies, products, or services, businesses can potentially gain a significant competitive edge, akin to the military doctrine of exploiting weaknesses in enemy defenses. When effectively implemented, this strategy can lead to a paradigm shift in the competitive landscape, offering businesses a unique and sustainable position. The potential for strategic innovation and the promise of a new competitive landscape inspire and invigorate businesses in their pursuit of success.

Problem Statement

In today's fiercely competitive business environment, companies face the constant challenge of maintaining and growing their market share and increasing shareholder value. The U.S. marketing industry, which accounts for a staggering one-third of global marketing revenues, witnessed a remarkable 2.6% growth in 2023, with companies investing a substantial USD 515 billion in marketing efforts (Navarro, 2024). This substantial investment, representing 9.2% of U.S. companies' total revenue (Navarro, 2024), highlights the intense competitive landscape and the necessity for organizations to allocate significant resources to protect their existing market positions and unlock new opportunities for value innovation and sustainable growth. Companies operating in the U.S. market are grappling with the daunting task of safeguarding their market share from competitors' relentless encroachment and unlocking new opportunities for market expansion. Failure to effectively address this challenge through strategic initiatives could lead to the erosion of their customer base and a subsequent decline in revenue and profitability.

Research Question

How effective is the integration of Porter's Five Forces model and the Blue Ocean Strategy in enabling organizations to achieve sustainable competitive advantages and long-term profitability across various industries?

Significance of This Research Study

Contemporary business landscapes are characterized by intense competition, which persistently challenges organizations to sustain and augment their market share while fostering innovation in their value propositions to stimulate new demand and ensure sustainable growth trajectories (Kim & Mauborgne, 2005; Porter, 2008). As such, firms necessitate a comprehensive strategic framework that safeguards their existing market positions while simultaneously catalyzing value innovation and unlocking novel market opportunities (Heydarov, 2020; Wee, 2017).

The present study proposes an integrative approach that harmoniously combines Porter's Five Forces model with the Blue Ocean strategy, creating a synergistic strategic paradigm that addresses industry competitiveness and new demand creation (Curuksu & Curuksu, 2018; Wee, 2017). This ever-evolving methodology empowers organizations to effectively compete within existing markets while concurrently exploring uncharted avenues for growth, differentiation, and value creation—an imperative for survival and sustained success in an ever-evolving and innovative business milieu (Badari et al., 2021; Kim et al., 2008).

The study mitigates each strategy's inherent limitations by judiciously leveraging its respective strengths. Porter's Five Forces model equips organizations with a comprehensive understanding of prevailing industry dynamics and competitive forces (Indrarathne et al., 2020; Porter, 2008), while the Blue Ocean strategy provides a guiding framework for identifying and capitalizing upon untapped market spaces and opportunities for value innovation (Kim & Mauborgne, 2005; Kim et al., 2008).

Combining Porter's Five Forces model and the Blue Ocean strategy can benefit various individuals and groups, improving strategic management practices and expanding knowledge in this field. This research study will be helpful to the following stakeholders: Business leaders and executives, Strategic planners and consultants, Entrepreneurs and innovators, Researchers, and academicians.

This study will improve knowledge and strategic management practices and expand knowledge in the following ways:

THE UNIQUE APPROACH TO STRATEGIC PLANNING

This study introduces a novel approach to strategic planning by merging the defensive strategy of analyzing industry competitiveness (Porter's Five Forces) with the offensive strategy of creating new market spaces (Blue Ocean Strategy). This integration overcomes the limitations of each framework and offers a distinct, comprehensive, and adaptable approach to strategic decision-making.

The study proposes integrating Porter's Five Forces model and the Blue Ocean strategy. It demonstrates its practical application through a real-world case study of Tesla's success in the electric vehicle industry, Apple's in the consumer electronics industry, and Pfizer's in the pharmaceutical industry. These tangible examples showcase the potential benefits and feasibility of the proposed approach, instilling confidence in its practicality.

By strongly emphasizing value innovation and identifying uncontested market spaces, the study inspires organizations to transcend traditional industry boundaries and explore new opportunities for growth, differentiation, and value creation. This innovation and value-creation potential can drive economic progress and societal benefits.

The integrated approach acknowledges the dynamic nature of industries and provides a framework for organizations to adapt and thrive in these environments. By combining industry analysis with value innovation, the study offers an adaptable approach that can effectively guide organizations through rapid technological changes, shifting consumer preferences, and evolving regulatory environments, instilling a sense of reassurance in the audience.

The outcome of this research study can potentially be used to improve strategic management practices in the following ways:

Enhancing Strategic Decision-Making

The findings can enhance strategic decision-making processes within organizations by offering a comprehensive framework that factors in industry dynamics and the potential for creating new market spaces. This can result in more informed and effective strategic decisions, boosting organizational performance and competitiveness.

Encouraging Cross-Functional Collaboration

Implementing the integrated approach may require cross-functional collaboration within organizations. This collaboration can foster knowledge sharing, diverse perspectives, and interdisciplinary problem-solving, contributing to organizational learning and innovation.

Facilitating Knowledge Transfer

The study's findings can be disseminated through academic publications, industry reports, and professional development programs. This will facilitate knowledge transfer and promote the adoption of this integrated approach in various sectors and industries, thereby improving strategic management practices worldwide.

Expanding Applied Research

The study identifies limitations and areas for further research, such as conducting empirical studies, developing practical implementation frameworks, exploring long-term sustainability strategies for blue ocean markets, and investigating the integration of additional strategic models or frameworks. These recommendations can guide future applied research efforts, expanding the body of knowledge in strategic management and contributing to developing practical solutions for organizations.

Ultimately, this integrated approach of merging Porter's Five Forces model and the Blue Ocean strategy has the potential to significantly impact the field of strategic management. It can enhance strategic management practices, foster innovation and value creation, and expand the body of knowledge in applied research. Providing a comprehensive and adaptable framework equips organizations to navigate complex, competitive landscapes and identify new growth opportunities.

METHODOLOGY

This study employed an integrative literature review methodology to synthesize and critically analyze the existing research on Porter's Five Forces model and the Blue Ocean Strategy. The integrative approach was chosen to comprehensively examine diverse perspectives, theories, and empirical findings related to these strategic frameworks and their potential integration. The review process involved systematically searching academic databases, including but not limited to Google Scholar, JSTOR, ProQuest, Marymount University Library Portal, ScienceDirect, Scopus, Sage, Taylor & Francis, Emerald Insight, and Business Source Complete, for peer-reviewed articles, books, and conference proceedings published between 1979 and 2024. Key search terms included "Porter's Five Forces," "Blue Ocean Strategy," "competitive advantage," "strategic management," and various combinations thereof.

The literature selection process involved several steps: initial screening of titles and abstracts, full-text review of relevant articles, and snowballing to identify additional sources from reference lists. Selected literature was critically evaluated for relevance, methodological rigor, and contribution to the field. The review focused on theoretical foundations, empirical applications, critiques of both frameworks and emerging trends in strategic management. Additionally, case studies of prominent companies such as Tesla, Apple, and Pfizer were included to illustrate practical applications of the integrated approach. The synthesis of this literature informed the development of an integrated framework that combines the defensive strategies of Porter's Five Forces with the offensive strategies of the Blue Ocean approach, addressing limitations and proposing practical implementation strategies.

LITERATURE REVIEW

In today's dynamic and ever-evolving business landscape, organizations face a thrilling prospect: the continuous pursuit of competitive advantages and the discovery of new avenues for growth and innovation (Singh & Gaur, 2018). Two influential strategic frameworks, The Five Competitive Forces That Shape Strategy and the Blue Ocean Strategy, offer complementary perspectives on analyzing industry dynamics and exploring uncontested market spaces.

By integrating these approaches, organizations can grasp their competitive environment comprehensively and unlock new opportunities for value innovation and sustainable growth (Wee, 2017). This integration promises a more holistic and practical approach to strategic planning, offering businesses a strategic edge in their competitive endeavors.

Integrating these two strategies is a theoretical exercise and a strategic imperative for organizations aiming to create sustainable competitive advantage. The Five Competitive Forces That Shape Strategy and Blue Ocean Strategy, two prominent frameworks in business strategy, have significantly shaped our understanding and approach to competitive analysis. Introduced by Michael E. Porter in 1979, Porter's Five Forces is a model that focuses on the competitive forces within an industry, including the threat of new entrants, the bargaining power of suppliers and customers, and the threat of substitute products or services (Indrarathne et al., 2020). It equips organizations to understand their competitive environment and develop strategies for gaining a competitive advantage (Porter, 2008). However, critics argue that the framework assumes a relatively stable industry structure, which may not hold in a rapidly evolving or disruptive business environment influenced by new technologies such as digitalization, innovation (e-commerce), and new trends such as globalization and deregulation (Shi et al., 2021).

The Blue Ocean Strategy, a brainchild of Kim & Mauborgne (2005), is a strategy that sparks innovation and creativity. It emphasizes creating new market spaces uncontested by competitors, making competition irrelevant (Kim et al., 2008). This strategy involves value innovation, which creates new demand and breaks away from traditional industry boundaries (Agnihotri, 2015). Blue Ocean Strategy aims to shift focus from competing in existing market spaces (red oceans) to creating new market spaces (blue oceans) through innovation and differentiation (Kim et al., 2008). However, as with Porter's five forces framework, the Blue Ocean Strategy also has limitations. A significant limitation identified by scholars is its oversight of market risks (Dvorak & Razova, 2018). By concentrating solely on establishing new market spaces and minimizing competition, the strategy may fail to account for potential risks and uncertainties that could significantly impact the ventures' success. It is crucial to understand that the Blue Ocean Strategy's emphasis on creating uncontested market spaces can pose challenges in maintaining them over time (Wubben et al., 2012). While the strategy promotes identifying new market opportunities away from existing competitors, preserving a competitive advantage in these spaces in the long term can be arduous, particularly as other entities may seek to enter and compete in these blue oceans, eventually turning them into red oceans (Wee, 2017).

While Porter's Five Forces and the Blue Ocean Strategy have both significantly contributed to strategic management thinking, critically examining each's limitations is essential for developing a more comprehensive and nuanced approach to strategic planning in today's complex business environment.

Limitations of Porter's Five Forces Strategy

It is crucial to adopt a balanced view when critically examining Porter's Five Forces strategy's limitations. This comprehensive understanding is essential for navigating the complexities of modern markets. Porter's Five forces have been identified to have the following limitations:

Static Nature

A primary criticism of Porter's Five Forces Strategy is that it is static, which can have significant consequences in rapidly changing industries (Khurram, 2020). While this model is valuable for understanding the existing competitive landscape, it has been criticized for its limited ability to adapt to the dynamic nature of competitive environments where forces are constantly in flux (Martins, 2024). As Thyrlby (1998) noted, the five forces approach provides a snapshot of an industry at a specific time but fails to account for the dynamic nature of competitive environments. This can lead to a lack of adaptability in strategy formulation, especially in industries where competitive forces constantly shift. Industries characterized by rapidly changing competitive forces require strategies that swiftly respond to market dynamics to maintain competitiveness (Martins, 2024).

Oversimplification

Porter's Five Forces strategy can be oversimplified, leading to an incomplete understanding of competitive dynamics, potentially resulting in strategic missteps and a limited understanding of the intricate competitive landscape within an industry (Cantor et al., 2022). This oversimplification may result in strategic missteps, limiting a firm's ability to grasp the full complexity of the competitive landscape and make informed decisions (Cantor et al., 2022). The model's emphasis on competition and the external environment, possibly at the expense of internal capabilities and innovation, could overlook the importance of a firm's internal strengths and resources. This oversight could lead to strategic decisions that are not fully informed, potentially leading to missed opportunities or competitive disadvantages. Avoiding such missteps should be a strong motivator in our strategic analysis.

Inward Focus

Porter's Five Forces model overlooks the importance of cooperative relationships such as strategic alliances, joint ventures, and networks, which can be crucial in some industries (Xue et al., 2019). While Porter's model focuses on competitive forces within an industry, it overlooks the potential benefits and strategic advantages of collaborative efforts with other firms. However, recognizing and leveraging these cooperative relationships could provide a significant strategic advantage, opening new opportunities and enhancing a firm's competitive position. Various academic studies highlight that strategic alliances enhance firm performance and competitiveness (Hung et al., 2015; Cacciolatti et al., 2020). This emphasis on the positive impact of strategic alliances should make us feel optimistic and forward-thinking in our strategic analysis.

Assumption of Perfect Competition

Porter's model assumes a relatively stable market structure, which may not hold in rapidly evolving industries or during significant technological disruption (Zheng et al., 2023). The framework assumes that all market participants act rationally, which may only sometimes be accurate. In industries experiencing rapid evolution or significant technological disruption, this stability may not hold. The concept of disruptive innovation, as proposed by Christensen et al. (2008), challenges traditional notions of market stability by introducing the idea that new technologies can fundamentally alter existing market structures (Bongomin et al., 2020). Behavioral economics has also shown that decision-making can often be irrational and influenced by psychological factors (Kahneman & Tversky, 1979; Yaolu, 2024).

Limitations of the Blue Ocean Strategy

On the other hand, the Blue Ocean strategy, which emphasizes creating uncontested market spaces and making competition irrelevant, also has limitations that have been identified as follows:

Difficulty in Identifying a Genuinely Uncontested Market

The Blue Ocean strategy, as proposed by Kim & Mauborgne (2005), faces a significant challenge in the business world due to the difficulty in identifying and successfully implementing new market spaces that are genuinely uncontested (Wang et al., 2023). This strategy creates new market spaces where competition is irrelevant, allowing for high growth and profits. However, Christodoulou and Langley (2020) point out that the applicability of the Blue Ocean strategy may be limited in industries where competition is intense and achieving differentiation is complex (Adkins et al., 2019). In such highly competitive environments, standing out and creating uncontested market spaces becomes daunting. In industries where differentiation is challenging, firms may struggle to find unique value propositions that set them apart from competitors. This difficulty of differentiation can stem from factors such as market saturation, technological parity, or customer preferences favoring established brands. Christodoulou and Langley's (2020) insights highlight the importance of industry dynamics and competitive landscapes in determining the feasibility of implementing a Blue Ocean strategy (Adkins et al., 2019). Moreover, the success of the Blue Ocean strategy hinges on the ability to innovate and create value in ways that resonate with customers".

Difficulty in Execution

While creating an uncontested market space is appealing, implementing a Blue Ocean Strategy can be challenging. As Kim and Mauborgne (2005) acknowledged, not all attempts to create blue oceans are successful, and creating a blue ocean involves significant risk and uncertainty.

Resource Intensity

Innovation is a crucial driver of success in various industries, but entering new markets with innovative products or services can be challenging and resource-intensive. While innovation can create new opportunities and competitive advantages, success is not guaranteed (Kim & Mauborgne, 2005). The decision to innovate and expand into new markets necessitates careful consideration of various factors that can impact the outcome. Creating new markets or significant innovations often requires substantial investment in research and development, marketing, and infrastructure, which may only be feasible for some firms due to various factors such as financial capabilities, market knowledge, and strategic planning (Safari & Saleh, 2020; Markides, 2008). Hence, it poses a barrier for some organizations, particularly smaller firms with limited budgets.

Sustainability of Competitive Advantage

Even if a company successfully creates a blue ocean, maintaining the competitive advantage created can be challenging. Competitors may quickly imitate the innovation, eroding the created market space (Zenger, 2013; Wee, 2017); as a result, the competitive advantage gained through a Blue Ocean Strategy may be temporary (Burke et al., 2009). It is also noted that the strategy often needs to be more accurate in the potential response from existing competitors who might aggressively try to protect their market share (Cantor et al., 2022), making it difficult to sustain a blue ocean (Christensen, 2016).

Given the strengths and weaknesses of Porter's five forces model and Blue Ocean Strategy, combining these two approaches can benefit organizations immensely by creating a comprehensive strategy that addresses both existing competition and the creation of new market opportunities (Wee, 2017). Visualizing both strategies is a great starting point for integrating them.

Figure 1. Incorporating Porter's Five Forces Model to create Blue Ocean via disruptive innovation

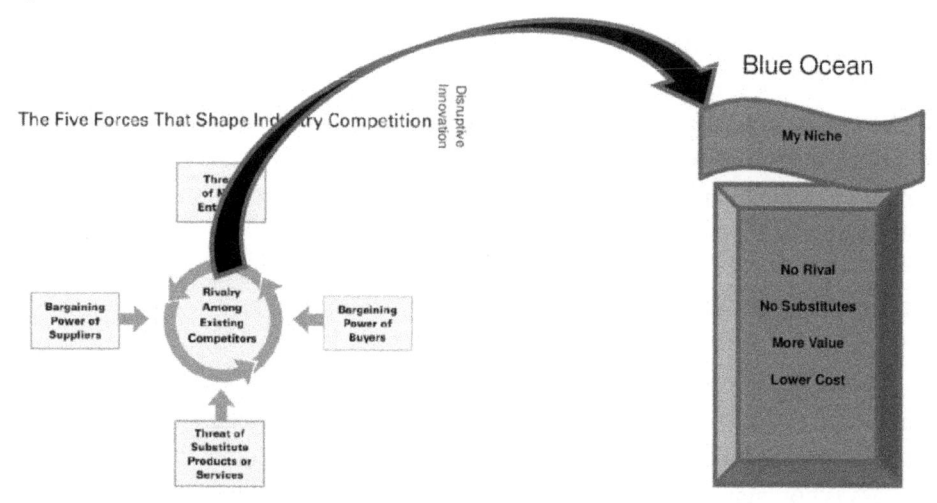

Porter's Five Forces helps organizations understand the current industry dynamics, identify competitive intensity areas, and formulate strategies to defend against competitive forces (Indrarathne et al., 2020). On the other hand, the Blue Ocean Strategy can guide organizations in exploring untapped market spaces, innovating to create new value propositions, and differentiating themselves from competitors (Kim & Mauborgne, 2005;Kim et al., 2008). By integrating Porter's Five Forces analysis with the principles of the Blue Ocean Strategy, as shown in Figure 1 above, organizations can develop a holistic strategy (Heydarov, 2020) that leverages both frameworks' strengths and simultaneously addresses their weaknesses.

Mitigation Through Integration

Integrating Porter's Five Forces and Blue Ocean Strategy can help mitigate their respective limitations by leveraging the strengths of each approach:

Dynamic and Holistic View

While Porter's Five Forces model provides insights into the competitive environment (Porter, 1998), the Blue Ocean Strategy encourages firms to look beyond existing boundaries and explore new opportunities (Kim & Mauborgne, 2005). By combining the industry analysis of Porter's Five Forces with the innovation focus of the Blue Ocean Strategy, firms can develop a more holistic and strategic framework that accounts for both existing industry dynamics and opportunities for creating new market spaces (Christodoulou & Langley, 2020) thereby better understanding of their competitive landscape, enabling them to adopt a more dynamic and holistic approach. The integration of these approaches can offer a more comprehensive and balanced strategic perspective to address the limitations of Porter's Five Forces and the Blue Ocean strategy. This hybrid approach allows for defensive positioning and proactive market creation (Kim & Mauborgne, 2005). By incorporating elements of both frameworks, companies can better navigate the complexities of modern markets, adapt to changes in competitive dynamics, and proactively shape their industry environment (Wood et al., 2021). This integrated approach fosters a more dynamic and forward-thinking strategic mindset that balances the need for competitiveness within existing markets with the pursuit of innovation and market creation (Christodoulou & Langley, 2020).

Balanced Approach

Integrating both strategies helps firms balance the need to understand and navigate competitive forces with pursuing innovation and market creation. This dual focus ensures that firms are not overly focused on either competition or innovation to the detriment of the other (Prahalad & Hamel, 1990).

Identifying Opportunities for Value Innovation

The Blue Ocean Strategy encourages organizations to transcend traditional industry boundaries and create new, uncontested market spaces (Kim & Mauborgne, 2005). By analyzing the existing competitive factors and industry dynamics through the Five Forces model, organizations can identify the taken-for-granted assumptions and constraints that limit their ability to innovate and create new value propositions. Moreover, the Five Forces model highlights the critical success factors within an industry, such as cost leadership, product differentiation, or customer loyalty (Porter, 2008). By integrating these insights with the Blue Ocean Strategy, organizations can identify the critical factors enabling them to create new value propositions and effectively capture untapped market opportunities (Zahrani & Prasetio, 2023).

Enhanced Risk Management

Firms can better manage risks by considering competitive forces and creating new markets (Khanna et al., 2005; Ross, 2014). They can use Porter's framework to mitigate competitive threats while leveraging the Blue Ocean Strategy to explore less contested market spaces (Ghemawat, 1991; Kim & Mauborgne, 2005; Lauer, 2019; Heydarov, 2020). By combining the two models, companies can develop strategies to mitigate these risks and create new market spaces with reduced competitive intensity (Heydarov, 2020). This approach can lead to the creation of sustainable competitive advantages and long-term profitability.

Sustainable Competitive Advantage

Integration encourages continuous innovation and adaptation. Employing the five forces model, organizations can identify the key drivers of profitability and the sources of competitive pressure within their industry (Porter, 2008), hence enabling Firms to use the insights to understand competitive dynamics and potential threats while continuously seeking new blue oceans to sustain competitive advantage over time (Dyer & Singh, 1998; Christensen, 1997; Wee, 2017). Therefore, integration allows firms to defend their position in existing markets while exploring new market spaces. This dual approach can create more sustainable competitive advantages (Burke et al., 2009; Wee, 2017).

ADAPTIVE STRATEGY

By combining both approaches, firms can develop strategies responsive to current competitive forces and proactively seek new market opportunities (Heydarov, 2020). This helps address the static nature of Porter's model and the execution challenges of the Blue Ocean Strategy (Ketchen et al., 2004).

Resource Optimization

By considering competitive positioning and value innovation, firms can optimize their resource allocation between defending current markets and exploring new ones (Gandellini & Venanzi, 2011), explicitly focusing on frugal innovation (Quan et al., 2019).

In conclusion, while Porter's Five Forces and the Blue Ocean strategy have limitations, integrating these approaches can mitigate their shortcomings and offer organizations a more robust strategic framework. By combining the analytical rigor of Porter's Five Forces with the innovative focus of the Blue Ocean strategy, companies can develop a more nuanced understanding of their competitive landscape, identify new market opportunities, and drive sustainable competitive advantage in today's dynamic business environment.

This integration allows organizations to compete effectively in existing markets and explore new avenues for growth and differentiation, an essential requirement for survival and growth in today's innovative and changing business environment. Some large innovative companies have successfully utilized this integrated strategy approach to their advantage.

Let us examine three case studies of companies (Tesla, Inc., Apple, Inc., and Pfizer, Inc.) that have successfully used this hybrid strategy to create a competitive advantage in different industries.

Tesla, Inc

Tesla has demonstrated remarkable strategic foresight by effectively leveraging Porter's five forces and the Blue Ocean strategy, establishing a sustainable competitive advantage in the Electric Vehicle (EV) Industry. Through the lens of Porter's five forces model, Tesla has meticulously analyzed the attractiveness of the automobile industry, particularly electric vehicles.

Threat of New Entrants (Low)

Tesla's astute analysis reveals that the EV industry boasts high entry barriers, primarily due to the substantial capital investment required for R&D, manufacturing facilities, and infrastructure (Stringham et al., 2015; Han, 2021). Tesla's triumph as a market pioneer, fortified by its robust brand recognition and devoted customer base, erects a formidable barrier for new entrants aspiring to challenge its position in the EV industry (Maradin et al., 2022; Zhang, 2023). This is evidenced by Tesla's holding a significant % market share of 59.5% by July 2023 in the American EV industry (Dnistran, 2023).

Bargaining Power of Suppliers (High)

With its vertical integration, Tesla produces its batteries, software, and components in-house (Movsesyan & Anokhina, 2020; Naor et al., 2021). It moderates the bargaining power of its suppliers by developing long-term partnerships and diversifying its supplier base, reducing its reliance on suppliers for other materials and components (Al-Abdallah et al., 2014; Han, 2021). However, Tesla relies heavily on suppliers like Nvidia, which provides semiconductors, chips, AI GPUs, etc. With this reliance, a strong case can be made that the bargaining power of the suppliers is high but not moderate.

Bargaining Power of Buyers (Low)

Tesla's unwavering brand appeal and unique product offering (Long et al., 2019) significantly diminish buyers' bargaining power (Junyu, 2022). Furthermore, the company's adoption of a direct sales model and elimination of dealerships further restrict buyer power, serving as a testament to Tesla's unwavering commitment to its customers.

Threat of Substitute Products (High)

While traditional internal combustion engine vehicles still pose a threat, Tesla has differentiated itself by offering a superior driving experience (autonomous driving) and advanced technology with environmental benefits (Gillmore & Tenhundfeld, 2020; Xiao, 2023). However, the threat of substitute EVs, alternative fuel vehicles, and improvements in traditional gasoline-powered cars cannot be ignored. As the industry evolves, Tesla may face increased competition from these sources, potentially eroding its competitive advantage (Kalghatgi, 2019).

Rivalry Among Existing Competitors (High)

Tesla has shown remarkable resilience despite the increasing competition in the EV Market. While it was an early pioneer, it successfully fended challenges from established automakers like Nissan, Volkswagen, Ford, and G.M. and new EV manufacturers like BYD and NIO (Kraft et al., 2021). Tesla's early-mover advantage, brand loyalty, and technological prowess continue to give it a competitive edge, instilling confidence in its market position (Han, 2021; Du & Li, 2021).

Tesla has competed in the automotive industry and pioneered a new, uncontested market space using the Blue Ocean Strategy (Kelly et al., N.D.). Instead of directly competing with traditional automakers, Tesla has focused on creating a unique value proposition (USP), a testament to its innovative spirit and pioneering approach. This USP has been achieved via the following measures:

Value Innovation

Tesla has combined the value of high-performance vehicles with environmental sustainability, creating a new market space that did not exist before. This value innovation has attracted customers who previously did not consider traditional EVs viable (Musonera & Cagle, 2019). For example, Tesla's Model S offers high performance and zero emissions, making it an attractive option for environmentally conscious consumers (Eisler, 2016; Ecer, 2021).

Eliminating and Reducing Factors

Tesla has eliminated traditional automotive factors such as dealerships by replacing them with direct sales, service centers, and electric motors, reducing emissions and maintenance costs (Han, 2021).

Creating and Raising Factors

Tesla has raised factors such as advanced technology (autonomous driving, over-the-air updates), mobile technicians called Tesla Rangers who fix specific problems at customer homes, design appeal, and brand image, creating new sources of value for customers (Han, 2021).

Hence, Tesla has managed to stay ahead in the competitive auto industry using Porter's Five Forces and Blue Ocean Strategy. Tesla analyzes competitive pressures within the electric vehicle market while creating a blue ocean with its self-driving technology, balancing competitive analysis with innovative market creation (Wee, 2017).

Apple, Inc

Like Tesla, Apple's unique success story can be dissected using the powerful frameworks of Porter's Five Forces and the Blue Ocean Strategy. The company's strategic blend of defensive and offensive tactics has created sustainable competitive advantages and set a benchmark for the industry.

Porter's Five Forces Utilized by Apple

Threat of New Entrants (Low)

Apple has established high barriers to entry through its strong brand loyalty, proprietary ecosystem (iOS, App Store, iCloud), and vertically integrated business model (Shastitko et al., 2020). These factors make it challenging for new entrants to compete directly with Apple.

Bargaining Power of Suppliers (Moderate)

While Apple relies on various suppliers for components, its high-volume purchases and strict quality standards give it significant bargaining power (Li, 2023). Additionally, its vertically integrated model reduces reliance on external suppliers for critical components like processors and software (Suwandi, 2023).

Bargaining Power of Buyers (Low)

Apple has created a loyal customer base willing to pay premium prices for its products, influenced by Brand Love, Brand Commitment, and Brand Trust (Fatmala & Setiawan, 2022; Hamizan et al., 2023; Franky & Syah, 2023). The company's brand appeal and ecosystem lock-in effects (Kotapati et al., 2020) limit individual buyers' bargaining power. However, as Apple faces evolving challenges in the market, it becomes crucial for the company to devise and implement effective strategies to sustain its competitiveness and ensure continued growth. This underscores the complexity of maintaining a competitive advantage in a dynamic market.

Threat of Substitutes (Moderate)

Apple's products face potential threats from competing platforms like Android devices or Windows PCs (Kotapati et al., 2020). However, the company's focus on seamless integration, user experience, and ecosystem lock-in mitigates the threat of substitution (O'Connor, 2021). By creating a tightly knit ecosystem where its hardware, software, and services work harmoniously together, Apple enhances user experience and loyalty (Rahman, 2021). This approach not only differentiates Apple's products but also makes it challenging for users to switch to alternatives due to the convenience and familiarity offered within the Apple ecosystem. The seamless integration of services like iCloud Private Relay further strengthens this ecosystem lock-in effect (Trevisan et al., 2023). Additionally, Apple's focus on innovation and shaping consumer expectations contributes to maintaining its market dominance (Sun, 2024).

Rivalry Among Existing Competitors (High)

The technology industry is highly competitive, with Apple facing intense rivalry from companies like Samsung, Google, and Microsoft (Kotapati et al., 2020; Ma, 2023). These companies constantly innovate and introduce new products and services, which increases the competitive pressure on Apple. However, Apple's differentiation strategy and continuous innovation have maintained a competitive edge (Ma, 2023), allowing the company to stay ahead of its rivals.

Blue Ocean Strategy Employed by Apple

Value Innovation

Apple has consistently stood out by creating new market spaces by introducing innovative products and services that combine previously unrelated factors (Giachetti, 2018). For instance, the iPhone revolutionized the mobile experience by combining the capabilities of a smartphone, a music player, and an internet communication device, a unique approach that has inspired the industry (Giachetti, 2018).

Eliminating and Reducing Factors

Apple has eliminated or reduced factors traditionally considered essential in specific industries. For example, physical keyboards and optical drives in laptops, buttons, and ports in the iPhone design have been eliminated.

Creating and Raising Factors

Apple has created and raised factors that differentiate its products and services. These include features like the intuitive multi-touch interface, seamless integration with other Apple devices, robust design, and emphasis on user experience (Pei et al., 2014).

Hence, by effectively employing both defensive and offensive strategies, Apple has created sustainable competitive advantages in the following ways:

Brand Loyalty and Ecosystem Lock-In

Apple's strong brand loyalty (Li, 2023) and proprietary ecosystem (iOS, App Store, iCloud) make it difficult for customers to switch to competitors, creating high switching costs and reducing buyers' bargaining power (Butarbutar, 2023).

Continuous Innovation

Apple's unwavering commitment to innovation (Doan, 2022; Wu, 2023) and value creation has not only allowed it to consistently introduce new products and services, redefine market segments, and create new demand, but it has also set a benchmark for the industry, inspiring others to follow suit. This commitment to innovation is a critical factor in Apple's ability to stay ahead of competitors, and it deserves our utmost admiration.

Vertical Integration and Supply Chain Control

Apple's vertically integrated business model and control over its supply chain provide cost advantages, quality control, and the ability to respond quickly to market changes, reducing suppliers' bargaining power (Sun, 2023).

Differentiation and Premium Pricing

Apple's emphasis on design, user experience, and seamless integration across its products and services has enabled it to differentiate its offerings and command premium pricing, resulting in higher profit margins (Simko, 2019; He, 2021; Nigam, 2023; Yu, 2023).

By skillfully combining the defensive strategies of Porter's Five Forces with the offensive strategies of the Blue Ocean Strategy, Apple has created a sustainable competitive advantage and significantly influenced the market landscape. This has allowed the company to maintain its market leadership and profitability, a testament to the power of strategic management.

Pfizer, Inc

Like Tesla and Apple, Pfizer, one of the world's largest pharmaceutical companies, has effectively utilized Porter's Five Forces model and the Blue Ocean Strategy to maintain and strengthen its competitive edge in the highly dynamic pharmaceutical industry. This underscores Pfizer's competitive advantage and market positioning, instilling confidence in its strategic direction.

Porter's Five Forces Analysis

Threat of New Entrants (Moderate to High)

The pharmaceutical industry is a complex landscape characterized by substantial barriers to entry (Choudhury, 2020). These barriers primarily stem from the significant financial obligations associated with research and development (R&D) activities, rigorous regulatory requirements (Pfizer, 2023), and the necessity for highly specialized knowledge and expertise (Choudhury, 2020). Before commercializing a pharmaceutical product, manufacturers must acquire marketing authorization from the relevant regulatory bodies in the jurisdictions where they intend to manufacture and distribute their products (McDermott et al., 2021). Navigating these intricate regulatory landscapes and fulfilling the stringent criteria imposed by these agencies represents a significant barrier to entry for potential new entrants in the pharmaceutical industry. Pfizer has employed several strategies to address the threat of new entrants in the pharmaceutical industry, such as Robust Intellectual Property protection (Wei, 2023; Pfizer, 2023), substantial investments in R&D running into billions of dollars (Pfizer, 2023), through Strategic Partnerships and acquisitions to expand its product portfolio (Pfizer, 2023), access new technologies, and strengthen its market position (Kumar, 2018; Gao & Zhang, 2023), developed extensive expertise in navigating the complex regulatory landscapes in various markets evident from successful market approvals for various drug products (Portier & Vervaet, 2021), cultivating a strong brand reputation and customer loyalty through its track record of delivering high-quality and innovative products (Fernando et al., 2022). In some instances, after the expiration of patent protection, Pfizer has embarked on aggressive marketing campaigns, including offering discounts to insured patients and promoting the effectiveness of certain drugs (Alnabhan, 2019), which have created barriers to entry for new competitors.

Bargaining Power of Suppliers (Low-Moderate)

For a pharmaceutical company like Pfizer, suppliers of raw materials and active ingredients hold considerable bargaining power. Limited supply of raw materials or APIs can lead to drug shortages, emphasizing the impact of supplier availability on pharmaceutical manufacturing (Gross & MacDougall, 2020). Pfizer (2023) reported an increase in overall demand in the industry for certain components and raw materials, which could constrain available supply and possibly impact their business in the future.

Thanks to its substantial size and market dominance, Pfizer maintains active supplier management and negotiates favorable terms with multiple suppliers to ensure a steady and cost-effective supply chain (Koenig et al., 2019; Pfizer, 2023).

It has managed to keep the bargaining power of its suppliers, including raw material providers, equipment suppliers, and service providers, relatively low. This is a testament to Pfizer's ability to leverage its purchasing power and maintain strong relationships with multiple suppliers, effectively mitigating their influence.

Bargaining Power of Buyers (Moderate to High)

Pfizer's buyers, which include healthcare providers, insurance companies, and government agencies, have significant bargaining power due to their ability to influence drug pricing and formulary decisions (Jarvis, 2018). To counter this effect, Pfizer's marketing strategy targets two main buyer groups: healthcare professionals (doctors) and patients (Alnabhan, 2019). Pfizer has been noted for providing free samples of some drugs to doctors and promoting their efficacy, aiming to influence doctors' prescribing decisions and reducing their bargaining power (Alnabhan, 2019). For patients, Pfizer offers discount cards and counsels pharmacies to promote some of their drugs, reducing patients' bargaining power by creating a perception of value and effectiveness (Alnabhan, 2019).

However, Pfizer's strong brand recognition, patent protection, and product differentiation (Wei, 2023) can help counterbalance this power.

Threat of Substitutes (Moderate to High)

In the pharmaceutical industry, the threat of substitutes comes from alternative treatments, generic drugs, and lifestyle changes. Pfizer confronts intense competitive pressures from two primary sources within the pharmaceutical industry: generic drug manufacturers and the proliferation of counterfeit medications in the market (Alnabhan, 2019). The entry of generic alternatives, which typically occurs upon the expiration of patent protection for branded drugs, introduces significant competition and can erode market share and profitability for established pharmaceutical companies like Pfizer (Jarvis, 2007; Jarvis, 2012; Pfizer, 2023). Furthermore, counterfeit drugs, which are illegally produced and distributed without adhering to regulatory standards and quality controls, threaten patient safety and the integrity of the pharmaceutical supply chain (Alnabhan, 2019; Ajlouni & Abdulrahman, 2023).

Pfizer has addressed this threat by investing heavily in acquisitions (Pfizer, 2023), restructuring charges, risk management, and R&D to develop innovative and patented drugs and diversify its product portfolio (Gao & Zhang, 2023). Pfizer (2023) reported the acquisition of Arena, GBT, and Biohaven. The company reported 110 projects in various stages of R&D and 19 patents, which are most significant to Pfizer (Pfizer, 2023). Pfizer's strategy of pricing some of its products below competitors and emphasizing its efficacy (Alnabhan, 2019) aims to differentiate the product and reduce the threat of substitutes.

Rivalry Among Existing Competitors (High)

The Pharmaceutical business is conducted in intensely competitive and often highly regulated markets (Pfizer, 2023). Many of Pfizer's products face competition in the form of branded or generic drugs or biosimilars that treat similar diseases or indications (Pfizer, 2023). In the face of intense rivalry among established players in the pharmaceutical industry, Pfizer has adopted a robust competitive strategy. This strategy focuses on product differentiation, patent protection, strategic acquisitions, partnerships, and innovation (Pfizer, 2023). Pfizer's aggressive marketing tactics further reinforce its commitment to maintaining its market position and defending against competitors' strategies.

Blue Ocean Strategy

Pfizer has employed the Blue Ocean Strategy elements to create new market spaces and differentiate itself from competitors.

Value Innovation

Pfizer's commitment to value innovation is evident in its focus on developing innovative and differentiated products that provide unique value to patients and healthcare providers. For instance, its breakthrough drugs, such as Sildenafil (Viagra), have revolutionized the treatment of erectile dysfunction (Goldstein et al., 2019). The COVID-19 Pfizer-BioNTech BNT162b2 mRNA vaccine (Comirnaty), which showed high levels of protection against COVID-19 infection and hospitalization (Klein et al., 2022; Self et al., 2021), not only created a new market but also captured significant demand. This commitment to innovation inspires confidence in Pfizer's ability to stay ahead of the curve and continue to deliver value to its stakeholders.

Crossing the Value-Cost Frontier

Pfizer's strategic partnerships, such as the one with BioNTech (Winch et al., 2021; Kalinke et al., 2022), have been instrumental in its strategy to achieve differentiation and cost-efficiency. Using mRNA technology to create the COVID-19 vaccine, Pfizer has demonstrated its ability to innovate with external expertise and resources. This, coupled with its focus on outsourcing non-core activities and streamlining its operations (Sheth et al., 2020; Kochura, 2024), has allowed the company to offer innovative products while maintaining a competitive cost structure. This reassures the general public about Pfizer's strategic approach and commitment to delivering value.

Creating an Uncontested Market Space

Pfizer has continuously explored new therapeutic areas and developed novel treatments for unmet medical needs (Jarvis, 2013), including oncology, inflammation and immunology, and rare diseases, and its commitment to innovation through research and development (Fang & Luo, 2023). For instance, its breakthrough cancer immunotherapy drug Ibrance targets a specific molecular (cyclin D–CDK4/6) pathway (Vanarsdale et al., 2015), creating a new market space and reducing direct competition (Mullard, 2017). Pfizer (2023) reported the acquisition of Arena, a clinical-stage company developing innovative potential therapies for the treatment of several immuno-inflammatory diseases; GBT, a biopharmaceutical company dedicated to the discovery, development and delivery of life-changing treatments that provide hope to underserved patient communities, starting with sickle cell disease; and Biohaven, the maker of Nurtec ODT/Vydura (rimegepant), an innovative therapy for both acute treatment of migraine and prevention of episodic migraine in adults.

Pfizer's sustainable competitive advantage lies in its ability to combine Porter's Five Forces analysis with the Blue Ocean Strategy. Pfizer has maintained its market position by addressing industry forces through product differentiation, patent protection, strategic partnerships, and operational efficiency (Pfizer, 2023). Additionally, by continuously innovating (Pfizer, 2023) and creating new market spaces through its Blue Ocean approach, Pfizer has stayed ahead of the competition and captured new demand. However, the pharmaceutical industry is rapidly evolving, with increasing competition from biosimilars, changing regulatory landscapes, and the rise of personalized medicine. To maintain its competitive edge, Pfizer must continue to adapt its strategies, invest in R&D, and explore new value propositions and market spaces.

Tesla, Apple, and Pfizer's example shows that this hybrid analytical approach allows organizations to comprehensively understand their industry dynamics and competitive landscape while exploring opportunities to create new, uncontested market spaces. Therefore, the Five Forces model and the Blue Ocean Strategy, when combined, form a robust analytical framework for strategic planning and decision-making.

Implementing the integrated analysis is made practical and straightforward using Kafoe's integrated competitive strategy toolkit (Figure 2 below) and Kafoe's framework for an integrated analysis using Porter's Five Forces model and the Blue Ocean Strategy in Figure 3 below.

These user-friendly tools guide organizations through the process, ensuring a smooth and practical application of the Five Forces model and the Blue Ocean Strategy.

Figure 2. Kafoe's integrated competitive strategy toolkit

Phase	Step	Activity	Description of Activity
Industry Analysis	1	Industry Mapping	Conduct a comprehensive analysis of the industry landscape, identifying key players, market segments, and industry trends.
	2	Competitive Forces Assessment	Evaluate the five competitive forces (threat of new entrants, bargaining power of suppliers, bargaining power of buyers, threat of substitutes, and rivalry among existing competitors) using Porter's Five Forces framework. This framework is a widely used tool for understanding the competitive dynamics of an industry and can help identify potential threats and opportunities.
	3	Profitability Drivers Analysis	Identify the key drivers of profitability within the industry, such as cost leadership (being the lowest-cost producer in the industry), product differentiation (offering unique and superior products), or customer loyalty (maintaining a solid and loyal customer base).
	4	Competitive Positioning Analysis	Assess the organization's competitive positioning and its competitors within the industry based on the identified profitability drivers.
	5	SWOT Analysis	Conduct a SWOT (Strengths, Weaknesses, Opportunities, Threats) analysis to identify internal strengths and weaknesses, as well as external opportunities and threats.
Value Innovation	6	Industry Assumptions Challenge	Challenge the industry's taken-for-granted assumptions and identify potential opportunities for value innovation.
	7	Customer Value Proposition Analysis	Analyze the organization's and its competitors' current customer value propositions, identifying potential gaps or unmet needs.
	8	Value Innovation Ideation	Facilitate ideation sessions to generate innovative value propositions that could create new market spaces or disrupt existing ones. This process involves brainstorming, generating ideas, and evaluating potential value propositions.
	9	Market Opportunity Evaluation	Evaluate the potential market opportunities identified through the value innovation ideation process, considering factors such as market size (the total addressable market for the opportunity), growth potential (the expected growth rate of the market), and competitive landscape (the number and strength of competitors in the market).
	10	Feasibility Assessment	Conduct a feasibility assessment of the most promising value innovation opportunities, considering resource requirements, potential risks, and organizational capabilities.
Integrated Strategy Development	11	Competitive Strategy Formulation	Develop a comprehensive competitive strategy that integrates the defensive approach (addressing competitive forces) and the offensive approach (creating new market spaces through value innovation).
	12	Resource Allocation Planning	Develop a resource allocation plan that aligns with the integrated competitive strategy, ensuring the efficient allocation of resources for both defending existing markets and exploring new market opportunities.
	13	Implementation Roadmap	Create a detailed implementation roadmap outlining the specific initiatives, timelines, and milestones for executing the integrated competitive strategy.
	14	Risk Mitigation Plan	Develop a risk mitigation plan to identify and address potential risks of implementing the integrated competitive strategy.
	15	Performance Measurement Framework	Establish a performance measurement framework, including key performance indicators (KPIs) and benchmarks, to monitor and evaluate the integrated competitive strategy's effectiveness.

The structured framework or methodology is not a one-size-fits-all solution. It is a versatile tool that can be tailored to the unique needs of different industries. It outlines a step-by-step process for organizations to conduct an integrated analysis using Porter's Five Forces model and the Blue Ocean Strategy. This framework provides clear guidelines on data collection, analysis, and interpretation of results, ensuring that the integrated approach is applicable and beneficial across various sectors.

Figure 3. Kafoe's framework for an integrated analysis using Porter's Five Forces model and the Blue Ocean Strategy.

Phase 1	Data Collection
1.1	**Internal Data Gathering**
	- Collect data on current product/service offerings, pricing, costs, and profitability
	- Gather information on existing customer segments, market share, and competitive positioning.
	- Analyze internal capabilities, resources, and core competencies
1.2	**External Data Gathering**
	- Conduct market research to understand industry trends, dynamics, and emerging technologies
	- Collect data on competitors, their strategies, strengths, and weaknesses
	- Gather information on customer needs, preferences, and pain points
	- Analyze supplier and buyer power dynamics within the industry
	- Identify potential threats from substitutes and new entrants
Phase 2	**Porter's Five Forces Analysis**
2.1	**Bargaining Power of Suppliers**
	- Analyze the concentration of suppliers, switching costs, and availability of substitutes
	- Assess the importance of the organization's business to the suppliers
2.2	**Bargaining Power of Buyers**
	- Evaluate the concentration of buyers, switching costs, and availability of substitutes
	- Analyze the importance of the organization's products/services to the buyers
2.3	**Threat of New Entrants**
	- Assess barriers to entry, such as economies of scale, capital requirements, and brand loyalty
	- Analyze the potential for new entrants to disrupt the industry
2.4	**Threat of Substitutes**
	- Identify potential substitutes and their performance, price, and switching costs
	- Evaluate the propensity of customers to switch to substitutes
2.5	**Competitive Rivalry**
	- Analyze the number and size of competitors, industry growth rate, and exit barriers
	- Assess the intensity of competitive strategies and tactics
Phase 3	**Blue Ocean Strategy Analysis**
3.1	**Explore Industry Assumptions**
	- Identify and challenge the industry's conventional wisdom and accepted boundaries
3.2	**Reconstruct Market Boundaries**
	- Redefine the industry's product, service, and delivery offerings
	- Explore alternative industries and cross-industry strategic moves
3.3	**Value Innovation**
	- Identify opportunities to create new value for customers
	- Develop innovative products, services, or business models
3.4	**Buyer Utility Analysis**
	- Evaluate the factors that customers value and their relative importance
	- Determine areas of over-service and under-service in the industry
3.5	**Strategy Canvas**
	- Map the current competitive landscape and value propositions
	- Identify areas for value creation and differentiation
Phase 4	**Interpretation and Strategic Planning**
4.1	**Synthesize Findings**
	- Integrate the insights from Porter's Five Forces and Blue Ocean Strategy analyses
	- Identify strategic gaps, opportunities, and potential risks
4.2	**Develop Strategic Recommendations**
	- Formulate strategies to capitalize on value innovation opportunities
	- Outline actions to mitigate competitive threats and strengthen market position
4.3	**Implementation Planning**
	- Develop an implementation roadmap with clear timelines and milestones
	- Allocate resources and assign responsibilities for the execution
4.4	**Continuous Monitoring and Adaptation**
	- Establish mechanisms for monitoring market dynamics and competitive landscape
	- Adapt strategies and plans as needed based on changing conditions

Hence, organizations can conduct a comprehensive, integrated analysis by following this structured framework, leveraging the insights from Porter's Five Forces model and the Blue Ocean Strategy. The framework provides precise data collection, analysis, and interpretation guidelines, enabling organizations to develop innovative and competitive strategies tailored to their industry and market conditions. This approach helps organizations understand their industry dynamics and competitive landscape but also guides them in identifying new, uncontested market spaces, leading to sustainable competitive advantages.

THE IMPACT OF CURRENT DIGITAL TRENDS ON PORTER'S FIVE FORCES AND BLUE OCEAN STRATEGY

The dynamic nature of industries, propelled by factors like rapid technological changes and digitalization, can render Porter's five Forces model less effective in capturing these dynamic forces (Fedotov, 2022). In the technology sector, for instance, where innovations are perpetually emerging, Porter's model may struggle to keep pace, potentially leading to outdated or inaccurate assessments (Shi et al., 2021).

The emergence of disruptive technologies, such as e-commerce and digitalization, is not merely a technological shift but a transformative force that can redefine traditional industry boundaries (Weber, 2019; Ravi et al., 2023). Importantly, it opens new, unexplored market spaces (Kumar, 2020). This aligns with the principles of the Blue Ocean Strategy, which advocates for creating new demand in an uncontested market rather than competing in an existing market, thereby emphasizing the potential for market expansion (Kim & Mauborgne, 2005).

Digital transformation and technological advancements can truly empower organizations, equipping them with tools like Artificial Intelligence (AI), Machine Learning (ML), and data analytics (Malik et al., 2021). These tools streamline data collection, analysis, and visualization processes, enhancing the accuracy and efficiency of integrated analysis and giving organizations a decisive edge in the competitive landscape (Volberda et al., 2021).

Digitalization, demand strategic planning, continuous monitoring, and swift adaptation of strategic plans influence rapid technological changes and evolving consumer preferences (Hollebeek et al., 2019; Gautam et al., 2022). This underscores the critical importance of agile and iterative processes for strategy development and execution and the need for organizations to act swiftly and decisively in the face of change (Sohail et al., 2021).

Therefore, the rapid pace of digital transformation and emerging trends not only present opportunities for value innovation and the creation of new market spaces but also introduce pressing challenges in accurately assessing industry dynamics and sustaining competitive advantages (Zhang et al., 2022). This necessitates that organizations embrace agility, leverage technological tools, and continuously monitor and adapt their strategies to effectively navigate the dynamic competitive landscape (Ashari & Herachwati, 2023).

While digital trends present opportunities and challenges for implementing Porter's Five Forces and Blue Ocean Strategy, organizations must also contend with practical hurdles in applying these frameworks effectively in today's dynamic business environment.

Challenges and Practical Solutions in Implementing Porter's Five Forces Model and Blue Ocean Strategy

Porter's Five Forces Model and Blue Ocean Strategy are widely used strategic frameworks, but their implementation presents several challenges. This section explores these challenges and offers practical solutions for organizations seeking to leverage these models effectively.

Data Availability and Analysis

Challenge: Conducting comprehensive analyses requires access to reliable, up-to-date industry data, which can be challenging to obtain, especially in rapidly evolving or complex industries (Göral, 2015; Abinsay, 2020).

Solution: Establish robust data collection processes, leveraging advanced analytics tools to extract insights from various sources (Ochuba et al., 2024; Secco et al., 2023). Collaborate with industry associations, research firms, or academic institutions to access specialized knowledge (Bikard et al., 2019; Rossi, 2010).

Subjectivity and Bias

Challenge: Assessments rely heavily on subjective judgments, which can be influenced by cognitive biases, organizational politics, or personal experiences (Wood & Bandura, 1989; Brownstein et al., 2019).

Solution: Implement structured decision-making processes incorporating multiple perspectives (EL YAZIDI, 2023; Sun et al., 2022). Utilize cross-functional teams or external consultants to bring diverse viewpoints (Proehl, 1996; Johnson et al., 2022). Promote a culture of transparency and provide training on cognitive biases (Alkhars et al., 2019; Belton & Dhami, 2020).

Dynamic Industry Environments

Challenge: Porter's model assumes a relatively static industry structure, which may not adequately capture rapid technological changes, shifting consumer preferences, and evolving regulatory environments (Khurram, 2020; Shi et al., 2021).

Solution: Adopt agile and iterative approaches to strategic planning (Bogdanova et al., 2020; Noennig, 2024). Establish dedicated teams to monitor industry trends and emerging technologies. Foster a culture of innovation and experimentation (Wodecka-Hyjek, 2014; Amar & Walsh, 2016).

Strategic Implementation and Organizational Alignment

Challenge: Translating analytical insights into effective strategies can be difficult, particularly when faced with resource constraints or organizational inertia (Hitt et al., 1998; Oke et al., 2022).

Solution: Develop comprehensive change management plans (Hubbart, 2023; Kafoe, 2024). Engage stakeholders early, communicate rationales for change, and address concerns (Fernández et al., 2019). Align strategic initiatives with organizational resources, capabilities, and culture (Barros & Fischmann, 2020; Agor et al., 2023).

Identifying and Sustaining Blue Ocean Opportunities

Challenge: Identifying truly uncontested market spaces and sustaining competitive advantage in the face of potential imitation can be challenging (Wee, 2017; Kumar et al., 2021).

Solution: Invest in extensive market research and customer insights (Alam & Islam, 2017). Foster a culture of continuous innovation (Kim & Park, 2022; Hu, 2023). Develop robust intellectual property protection strategies (Grimaldi et al., 2021; Biancini & Bombarda, 2021). Continuously monitor the competitive landscape (Khan, 2024).

Resource Allocation and Risk Management

Challenge: Pursuing new strategies often requires significant investments and carries inherent risks, particularly if new market spaces fail to gain traction (Kim & Mauborgne, 2005; Hong et al., 2011).

Solution: Implement robust portfolio management processes (Pargaonkar, 2016; Santhiapillai & Ratnayake, 2021). Adopt staged investment approaches based on achieved milestones (Sun et al., 2022). Establish risk management frameworks to identify, assess, and mitigate potential risks (Müllner, 2016).

By addressing these challenges through a holistic approach emphasizing data-driven decision-making, diverse perspectives, agility, and continuous learning, organizations can enhance their ability to leverage Porter's Five Forces model and Blue Ocean strategy effectively. This approach enables organizations to navigate complex and rapidly evolving industry landscapes, ultimately achieving sustainable competitive advantage. By strongly emphasizing fostering a culture of continuous learning, innovation, and, most importantly, open communication, organizations can enhance their ability to leverage these analytical frameworks and achieve sustainable competitive advantage in complex and rapidly evolving industry landscapes.

CONCLUSION

The integration of Porter's Five Forces model and the Blue Ocean strategy presents a potent strategic paradigm for organizations seeking sustainable competitive advantages and long-term profitability. By comprehensively analyzing industry dynamics and competitive forces through the Five Forces lens, firms can identify critical success factors, mitigate risks, and formulate strategies to defend against competitive pressures. Simultaneously, the Blue Ocean philosophy empowers organizations to transcend traditional industry boundaries, fostering value innovation and the creation of new, uncontested market spaces constituting the offensive strategy. This symbiotic approach addresses existing competition and unlocks novel growth opportunities, facilitating strategic alignment and resource optimization within the organization.

Tesla's remarkable EV industry success, Apple's success in the consumer electronics software services industry, and Pfizer's success in the pharmaceutical industry exemplify this hybrid framework's synergistic potential, adeptly navigating competitive forces while pioneering a blue ocean through value innovation and technological leadership. As businesses navigate an increasingly complex and dynamic competitive landscape, the harmonious convergence of these two influential strategies holds the promise of a holistic, comprehensive, and adaptable approach to strategic decision-making and sustainable growth. This is not just a theoretical concept but a practical tool that can be applied in real-world business scenarios.

Recommendations and Practical Suggestions to Address the Integration

Establish Cross-Functional Teams

Form teams with representatives from various departments to leverage diverse perspectives and mitigate individual biases (Santa et al., 2022). This approach enhances organizational collaboration and knowledge dissemination, improving awareness of internal needs and customer insights (Murillo-Oviedo et al., 2019).

Leverage Advanced Analytics

Invest in Artificial Intelligence (AI) and Machine Learning (ML) tools to streamline data collection, analysis, and visualization processes (Sarker, 2021). These technologies can enhance the accuracy and efficiency of integrated analysis, particularly in complex or rapidly evolving industries.

Embrace Agile and Iterative Processes

Implement agile methodologies for strategy development and execution. This will allow organizations to respond quickly to changes in the competitive environment and continuously refine their strategies (Weichbroth, 2022).

Integrate Sustainability and Ethical Considerations

Incorporate Environmental, Social, and Governance (ESG) goals into the integrated analysis and strategy development process (Sivarajah et al., 2020; Silvestre et al., 2022). This alignment with stakeholder expectations and societal values can improve customer satisfaction and decision-making accuracy while promoting sustainable business operations (Filho et al., 2023).

Utilize Specialized Frameworks

Employ tailored tools such as Kafoe's Integrated Competitive Strategy Toolkit and framework for integrated analysis using Porter's Five Forces model and Blue Ocean Strategy. These frameworks can provide a structured approach to implementing the integrated methodology.

By focusing on these critical recommendations, organizations can effectively implement an integrated approach that combines the strengths of Porter's Five Forces Model and Blue Ocean Strategy. This approach enables firms to navigate complex, competitive landscapes while identifying and creating new market opportunities, ultimately leading to sustainable competitive advantage.

Specific Recommendations for Managers, Policymakers, and Organizations Looking to Implement the Integrated Approach

Fostering a culture of continuous learning, adaptability, and innovation is crucial. Diverse perspectives, critical thinking, and a willingness to challenge existing assumptions and business models are also essential. Effective risk management strategies, resource allocation, and stakeholder engagement are crucial for successful implementation.

It is highly advised to use Kafoe's Integrated Competitive Strategy Toolkit (Figure 2) and Kafoe's framework for an integrated analysis using Porter's Five Forces model and the Blue Ocean Strategy (Figure 3) to implement the integrated approach.

Research Limitations and Recommendations for Further Research

While this study offers a compelling synthesis of the defensive (Porter's Five Forces model) and the offensive (Blue Ocean Strategy), several limitations should be acknowledged:

The research relies primarily on a literature review and theoretical analysis, lacking empirical data or case studies beyond the illustrative examples of Tesla, Apple, and Pfizer. Future research could involve conducting in-depth case studies across multiple industries with varying sizes to validate the proposed integrated framework's practical applicability and efficacy.

The study must explore specific methodologies or tools for implementing the integrated strategy within organizations. Further research could explore practical implementation frameworks, best practices, and change management approaches to aid organizations in effectively adopting and executing this strategic paradigm.

The study must extensively address the potential challenges and pitfalls associated with sustaining competitive advantages in newly created blue ocean markets over an extended period. Future research could investigate strategies for maintaining and defending these uncontested market spaces, particularly in the face of potential imitation by competitors.

The research integrates Porter's Five Forces model and the Blue Ocean strategy. However, additional strategic frameworks or models, such as the Resource-Based View (RBV), the Dynamic Capabilities framework, and Design Thinking, may be incorporated to enhance the proposed approach's comprehensiveness and adaptability.

Future research efforts could address these limitations by conducting empirical studies, developing practical implementation frameworks, exploring long-term sustainability strategies for blue ocean markets, and investigating the potential integration of additional strategic models or frameworks to create an even more robust and holistic approach. Contributions to these research areas could significantly advance our understanding and application of this integrated strategic framework.

REFERENCES

Abinsay, M. (2020). Porter's Five Forces Analysis of the Organic Farming in Laguna Province. *Agricultural Economics eJournal*. https://doi.org/DOI: 10.53378/34

Adam, N. A., & Alarifi, G. (2020). Innovation practices for enhancing small and medium-sized enterprises' (smes) performance and survival during coronavirus (covid-19) epidemic crisis: the moderating role of external support. DOI: 10.21203/rs.3.rs-125153/v1

Agnihotri, A. (2015). Extending boundaries of blue ocean strategy. *Journal of Strategic Marketing*, 24(6), 519–528. DOI: 10.1080/0965254X.2015.1069882

Agor, S., Kanesie, D., Boateng, P., & Yamoah, P. (2023). Formulating Strategies that Align Corporate Goals with Organizational Capabilities. *International Journal of Research and Scientific Innovation*. .DOI: 10.51244/IJRSI.2023.1011053

Ajlouni, A., & Abdulrahman, M. (2023). Detection Methods of Counterfeit Drugs: A Systemic Review. *Journal of Pharmaceutical Research & Reports*. .DOI: 10.47363/JPRSR/2023(4)144

Al-Abdallah, G. M., Abdallah, A. B., & Hamdan, K. (2014). The impact of supplier relationship management on competitive performance of manufacturing firms. *International Journal of Business and Management*, 9(2). Advance online publication. DOI: 10.5539/ijbm.v9n2p192

Alam, S., & Islam, M. (2017). Impact of Blue Ocean Strategy on Organizational Performance: A Literature Review Toward Implementation Logic. *Agricultural & Natural Resource Economics eJournal*. .DOI: 10.9790/487X-1901030119

Alkhars, M., Evangelopoulos, N., Pavur, R., & Kulkarni, S. (2019). Cognitive biases resulting from the representativeness heuristic in operations management: An experimental investigation. *Psychology Research and Behavior Management*, 12, 263–276. DOI: 10.2147/PRBM.S193092 PMID: 31040729

Alnabhan, O. (2019). Strategic Marketing Recommendations for Lipitor Introduced by Pfizer.

Amar, A. D., & Walsh, C. (2016). Learning in Organizations: Some Observations from the Practice. *International Journal of Human Capital and Information Technology Professionals*, 7(4), 50–60. DOI: 10.4018/IJHCITP.2016100104

Ashari, C., & Herachwati, N. (2023). Implementation of Organizational Agility Model in Improving Sustainable PHEIs Competitive Advantage: Narrative Literature Review. *RSF Conference Series: Business, Management and Social Sciences*. DOI: 10.31098/bmss.v3i3.725

Badari, T. P., Machado, G., Moniz, F., Fontes, A., & Teoldo, I. (2021). Comparison of soccer players' tactical behaviour in small-sided games according to match status. *Journal of Physical Education and Sport*, 21(1), 12–20.

Baporikar, N. (2022). Innovation Management Case Study. *International Journal of Innovation in the Digital Economy*, 13(1), 1–11. DOI: 10.4018/IJIDE.311515

Barros, L., & Fischmann, A. (2020). Strategy code: indicators of organisational alignment for obtaining strategy implementation effectiveness. *International Journal of Business Excellence*. .DOI: 10.1504/IJBEX.2019.10024140

Belton, I. K., & Dhami, M. K. (2020). Cognitive biases and debiasing in intelligence analysis. In *Routledge Handbook of Bounded Rationality* (pp. 548–560). Routledge. DOI: 10.4324/9781315658353-42

Biancini, S., & Bombarda, P. (2021). Intellectual property rights, multinational firms and technology transfers. Journal of Economic Behavior &Amp. *Journal of Economic Behavior & Organization*, 185, 191–210. DOI: 10.1016/j.jebo.2021.02.005

Bikard, M., Vakili, K., & Teodoridis, F. (2019). When collaboration bridges institutions: The impact of university–industry collaboration on academic productivity. *Organization Science*, 30(2), 426–445. DOI: 10.1287/orsc.2018.1235

Bongomin, O., Gilibrays Ocen, G., Oyondi Nganyi, E., Musinguzi, A., & Omara, T. (2020). Exponential Disruptive Technologies and the Required Skills of Industry 4.0. *Journal of Engineering*, 2020, 1–17. DOI: 10.1155/2020/4280156

Brownstein, N. C., Louis, T. A., O'Hagan, A., & Pendergast, J. (2019). The role of expert judgment in statistical inference and evidence-based decision-making. The American Statistician, 73(sup1), 56-68. DOI: 10.1080/00031305.2018.1529623

Butarbutar, I. P., Purnamasari, N., & Safitri, K. (2023). An analysis on five forces dan bcg matrix for apple inc. company. Maker. *Jurnal Manajemen*, 9(2), 229–240. DOI: 10.37403/mjm.v9i2.615

Cacciolatti, L., Rosli, A., Ruiz-Alba, J., & Chang, J. (2020). Strategic alliances and firm performance in startups with a social mission. *Journal of Business Research*, 106, 106–117. DOI: 10.1016/j.jbusres.2019.08.047

Cantor, D. E., Yan, T., Pagell, M., & Tate, W. L. (2022). From the editors: introduction to the emerging discourse incubator on the topic of leveraging multiple types of resources within the supply network for competitive advantage. Journal of Supply Chain Management, 58(2), 3-7. DOI: 10.1111/jscm.12282

Chao, C., Hu, H., Zhang, L., & Wu, J. (2016). Managing the challenges of pharmaceutical patent expiry: a case study of Lipitor., 7, 258-272. .DOI: 10.1108/JSTPM-12-2015-0040

Chi, Y.-L., & Bump, J. B. (2018). Resource allocation processes at multilateral organizations working in global health. *Health Policy and Planning*, 33(suppl_1), i4–i13. DOI: 10.1093/heapol/czx140 PMID: 29415239

Choudhury, A. (2020). Four Barriers to Entry in the Pharmaceutical Manufacturing Industry | Infiniti's Experts Provide Unparalleled Market Entry Insights for Pharma Companies. In *Business Wire*. Business Wire.

Christensen, C. M. (2016). *The innovator's dilemma : when new technologies cause significant firms to fail* [Third edition?]. Harvard Business Review Press.

Christensen, C. M., Horn, M. B., & Johnson, C. W. (2008). *Disrupting class : how disruptive innovation will change the way the world learns*. McGraw-Hill.

Christodoulou, I., & Langley, P. A. (2020). A gaming simulation approach to understanding blue ocean strategy development as a transition from traditional competitive strategy. *Journal of Strategic Marketing*, 28(8), 727–752. DOI: 10.1080/0965254X.2019.1597916

Correani, A., De Massis, A., Frattini, F., Petruzzelli, A. M., & Natalicchio, A. (2020). Implementing a Digital Strategy: Learning from the Experience of Three Digital Transformation Projects. *California Management Review*, 62(4), 37–56. DOI: 10.1177/0008125620934864

Crucial Steps in Addressing the Impact of Natural Disasters. IGI Global. DOI: 10.4018/979-8-3693-4288-6

Curuksu, J. D., & Curuksu, J. D. (2018). Principles of Strategy: Primer. *Data Driven: An Introduction to Management Consulting in the 21st Century*, 129-152.

de Vries, T. A., van der Vegt, G. S., Scholten, K., & van Donk, D. P. (2022). Heeding supply chain disruption warnings: When and how do cross-functional teams ensure firm robustness? *The Journal of Supply Chain Management*, 58(1), 31–50. DOI: 10.1111/jscm.12262

Derave, T., Sales, T. P., Gailly, F., & Poels, G. (2022). Sharing platform ontology development: Proof-of-concept. *Sustainability (Basel)*, 14(4), 2076. DOI: 10.3390/su14042076

Dnistran, I. (2023). Tesla Now Has An Almost 60-Percent Share Of The EV Market In The US. https://insideevs.com/news/686440/tesla-60-percent-ev-market-share-new-registrations-2024/. Accessed on May 22, 2024

Doan, T. (2022). Value Creation and Value Capture: Analysis of Apple Company. *International Journal of Current Science Research and Review*. .DOI: 10.47191/ijcsrr/V5-i4-30

Dobbs, M. E. (2014). Guidelines for applying porter's five forces framework: A set of industry analysis templates. *Competitiveness Review*, 24(1), 32–45. DOI: 10.1108/CR-06-2013-0059

Doherty, T., & Carroll, A. (2020). Believing in Overcoming Cognitive Biases.. *AMA journal of ethics*, 22 9, E773-778 . . Rajasekar, J. (N.D.). Porter's 5 Forces-A strategic planning model.DOI: 10.1001/amajethics.2020.773

Douglas, S., & Haley, G. (2023). Connecting organizational learning strategies to organizational resilience. *Development and Learning in Organizations*, 38(1), 12–15. DOI: 10.1108/DLO-01-2023-0018

Du, X., & Li, B. (2021). Analysis of Tesla's Marketing Strategy in China. *Proceedings of the 2021 3rd International Conference on Economic Management and Cultural Industry (ICEMCI 2021)*. DOI: 10.2991/assehr.k.211209.270

Dvorak, J., & Razova, I. (2018). Empirical Validation of Blue Ocean Strategy Sustainability in an International Environment. *Foundations of Management*, 10(1), 143–162. DOI: 10.2478/fman-2018-0012

Dyer, J. H., & Singh, H. (1998). The Relational View: Cooperative Strategy and Sources of Interorganizational Competitive Advantage. *Academy of Management Review*, 23(4), 660–679. DOI: 10.2307/259056

Ecer, F. (2021). A consolidated MCDM framework for performance assessment of battery electric vehicles based on ranking strategies. *Renewable & Sustainable Energy Reviews*, 143, 110916. Advance online publication. DOI: 10.1016/j.rser.2021.110916

Eisler, M. (2016). A Tesla in every garage? *IEEE Spectrum*, 53(2), 34–55. DOI: 10.1109/MSPEC.2016.7419798

EL YAZIDI, R. (2023). Strategies for promoting critical thinking in the classroom. *International Journal of English Literature and Social Sciences (IJELS)*, 26.

Evenseth, L. L., Sydnes, M., & Gausdal, A. H. (2022). Building organizational resilience through organizational learning: A systematic review. *Frontiers in Communication*, 7, 837386. Advance online publication. DOI: 10.3389/fcomm.2022.837386

F.A, B. (. (2022). Blue Ocean strategy: Economic importance of applying in tourism. *International Journal of Multicultural and Multireligious Understanding*, 9(12), 1. DOI: 10.18415/ijmmu.v9i12.4294

Fatmala, I., & Setiawan, H. (2022). *Analysis of Willingness to Pay Premium Apple Product Users in Indonesia. Jurnal Riset Ekonomi Manajemen*. REKOMEN., DOI: 10.31002/rn.v5i2.4193

Faunce, T. (2015). AUSTRALIAN COMPETITION AND CONSUMER COMMISSION v PFIZER: EVERGREENING AND MARKET POWER AS A BLOCKBUSTER DRUG GOES OFF PATENT. *Journal of Law and Medicine*, 22(4), 771–787. PMID: 26349378

Fedotov, P. (2022). Critical analysis of the electric vehicle industry. Exchanges. *The Interdisciplinary Research Journal*, 10(1), 43–56. DOI: 10.31273/eirj.v10i1.362

Fernández, M. E., Ruiter, R. A. C., Markham, C., & Kok, G. (2019). Intervention mapping: theory- and evidence-based health promotion program planning: perspective and examples. *Frontiers in Public Health*, 7, 209. Advance online publication. DOI: 10.3389/fpubh.2019.00209 PMID: 31475126

Fernando, K., Menon, S., Jansen, K. U., Naik, P. S., Nucci, G., Roberts, J., Wu, S. S., & Dolsten, M. (2022). Achieving end-to-end success in the clinic: Pfizer's learnings on R&D productivity. *Drug Discovery Today*, 27(3), 697–704. DOI: 10.1016/j.drudis.2021.12.010 PMID: 34922020

Ferreira, J., Coelho, A., & Moutinho, L. (2020). Strategic alliances, exploration and exploitation and their impact on innovation and new product development: The effect of knowledge sharing. *Management Decision*, 59(3), 524–567. DOI: 10.1108/MD-09-2019-1239

Filho, W., Trevisan, L., Eustachio, J., Rampasso, I., Anholon, R., Platje, J., Will, M., Doni, F., Mazhar, M., Borsatto, J., & Marcolin, C. (2023). Assessing ethics and sustainability standards in corporate practices. *Social Responsibility Journal*. Advance online publication. DOI: 10.1108/SRJ-03-2023-0116

Foldy, E. (2004). Learning from Diversity: A Theoretical Exploration. *Public Administration Review*, 64(5), 529–538. DOI: 10.1111/j.1540-6210.2004.00401.x

Franky, F., & Syah, T. (2023). *The Effect of Customer Experience, Customer Satisfaction, and Customer Loyalty on Brand Power and Willingness to Pay a Price Premium.* Quantitative Economics and Management Studies., DOI: 10.35877/454RI.qems1639

Fu, W., & Chen, Y. (2022). The Impact of Pfizer-BioNTech COVID-19 Vaccine Development on the Companies Involved. In *2022 7th International Conference on Financial Innovation and Economic Development (ICFIED 2022)* (pp. 1271-1276). Atlantis Press. DOI: 10.2991/aebmr.k.220307.210

Gao, J., & Zhang, Y. (2023). *Assessing the Financial Stability & Investment Potential of Pfizer Inc.* Highlights in Business, Economics and Management., DOI: 10.54097/hbem.v15i.9223

Gao, J., & Zhang, Y. (2023). *Assessing the Financial Stability & Investment Potential of Pfizer Inc.* Highlights in Business, Economics and Management., DOI: 10.54097/hbem.v15i.9223

Garousi, V., Pfahl, D., Fernandes, J. M., Felderer, M., Mäntylä, M., Shepherd, D., Arcuri, A., Coşkunçay, A., & Tekinerdoğan, B. (2019). Characterizing industry-academia collaborations in software engineering: Evidence from 101 projects. *Empirical Software Engineering*, 24(4), 2540–2602. DOI: 10.1007/s10664-019-09711-y

Ghemawat, P. (1991). *Commitment : the dynamic of strategy.* Free Press.

Giachetti, C. (2018). Explaining Apple's iPhone Success in the Mobile Phone Industry: The Creation of a New Market Space., 9-48. .DOI: 10.1007/978-3-319-67973-0_2

Gillmore, S., & Tenhundfeld, N. (2020). The Good, The Bad, and The Ugly: Evaluating Tesla's Human Factors in the Wild West of Self-Driving Cars. *Proceedings of the Human Factors and Ergonomics Society Annual Meeting*, 64(1), 67–71. DOI: 10.1177/1071181320641020

Goldstein, I., Burnett, A., Rosen, R., Park, P., & Stecher, V. (2019). The Serendipitous Story of Sildenafil: An Unexpected Oral Therapy for Erectile Dysfunction. *Sexual Medicine Reviews*, 7(1), 115–128. DOI: 10.1016/j.sxmr.2018.06.005 PMID: 30301707

Göral, R. (2015). Competitive Analysis of the Hotel Industry in Konya by Using Porter's Five Forces Model. *European Journal of Economics and Business Studies*, 3(1), 106–115. DOI: 10.26417/ejes.v3i1.p106-115

Grimaldi, M., Greco, M., & Cricelli, L. (2021). A framework of intellectual property protection strategies and open innovation. *Journal of Business Research*, 123, 156–164. DOI: 10.1016/j.jbusres.2020.09.043

Grosen, S. L., & Edwards, K. (2023). Learning from experiments: Exploring how short time-boxed experiments can contribute to organizational learning. *Journal of Workplace Learning*, 36(1), 96–112. DOI: 10.1108/JWL-08-2023-0138

Gross, A. E., & MacDougall, C. (2020). Roles of the clinical pharmacist during the covid-19 pandemic. Jaccp. *Journal of the American College of Clinical Pharmacy: JAACP*, 3(3), 564–566. DOI: 10.1002/jac5.1231

Grundy, T. (2006). Rethinking and reinventing Michael Porter's five forces model. *Strategic Change*, 15(5), 213–229. DOI: 10.1002/jsc.764

Hamizan, M., Abu, N., Mansor, M., & Zaidi, M. (2023). An Analysis of the Effect of Price and Quality on Customer Buying Patterns: An Empirical Study of iPhone Buyers. *International Journal of Interactive Mobile Technologies (iJIM)*. .DOI: 10.3991/ijim.v17i18.42917

Han, J. (2021). How does Tesla Motors achieve a competitive advantage in the global automobile industry? *Journal of Next-generation Convergence Information Services Technology*, 10(5), 573–582. DOI: 10.29056/jncist.2021.10.09

Hanifah, H., Halim, H. A., Ahmad, N. H., & Vafaei-Zadeh, A. (2019). Emanating the key factors of innovation performance: Leveraging on the innovation culture among smes in malaysia. *Journal of Asia Business Studies*, 13(4), 559–587. DOI: 10.1108/JABS-04-2018-0130

Harker Roa, A., Córdoba Flechas, N., Moya, A., & Pineros-Leano, M. (2023). Implementing psychosocial support models in contexts of extreme adversity: Lessons from a process evaluation in colombia. *Frontiers in Psychology*, 14, 1134094. Advance online publication. DOI: 10.3389/fpsyg.2023.1134094 PMID: 37284476

He, M. (2021). Analysis of iPhone's Marketing Strategy., 669-672. .DOI: 10.2991/aebmr.k.210319.124

He, W., Hung, J., & Liu, L. (2022). Impact of big data analytics on banking: A case study. *Journal of Enterprise Information Management*. Advance online publication. DOI: 10.1108/JEIM-05-2020-0176

Heydarov, K. (2020). "The Blue Ocean Strategy" is against "Porter's Five Competitive Powers". *Science Bulletin*, 1(1), 115–120. Advance online publication. DOI: 10.54414/zomg4450

Hijfte, S. (2020). Continuous Learning. *Make Your Organization a Center of Innovation*, 113 - 122. .DOI: 10.1021/bk-2010-1055.ch007

Hitt, M., Keats, B., & DeMarie, S. (1998). Navigating in the new competitive landscape: Building strategic flexibility and competitive advantage in the 21st century. *The Academy of Management Perspectives*, 12(4), 22–42. DOI: 10.5465/ame.1998.1333922

Hollebeek, L., Sprott, D., Andreassen, T., Costley, C., Klaus, P., Kuppelwieser, V., Karahasanovic, A., Taguchi, T., Islam, J., & Rather, R. (2019). Customer engagement in evolving technological environments: Synopsis and guiding propositions. *European Journal of Marketing*, 53(9), 2018–2023. Advance online publication. DOI: 10.1108/EJM-09-2019-970

Hong, A., Chai, D., & Ismail, W. (2011). Blue Ocean Strategy: A Preliminary Literature Review and Research Questions Arising. *Australian Journal of Basic and Applied Sciences*, 5, 86–91. DOI: 10.4018/979-8-3693-4288-6

Hu, B., Malik, i., Noman, S. M., & Irshad, M. (2023). A sustainable retrospective analysis of cultural innovative approaches in technology management. Second International Conference on Sustainable Technology and Management (ICSTM 2023). DOI: 10.1117/12.3005508

Hubbart, J. (2023). Organizational Change: The Challenge of Change Aversion. *Administrative Sciences*, 13(7), 162. Advance online publication. DOI: 10.3390/admsci13070162

Hung, S., Hung, S., & Lin, M. (2015). Are alliances a panacea for SMEs? The achievement of competitive priorities and firm performance. *Total Quality Management & Business Excellence*, 26(1-2), 190–202. DOI: 10.1080/14783363.2014.927133

Hurst, J. (2017). Robotic swarms in offensive maneuver. *Joint Force Quarterly*, 87(4), 105–111.

Indrarathne, P., Ranadewa, K., & Shanika, V. (2020). Impact of competitive forces to the contractors in Sri Lanka: an industry analysis using Porter's five forces. DOI: 10.31705/FARU.2020.21

Iyer, S., Goss, E., Browder, C., Paccione, G. A., & Arnsten, J. H. (2019). Development and evaluation of a clinical reasoning curriculum as part of an internal medicine residency program. *Diagnosis (Berlin, Germany)*, 6(2), 115–119. DOI: 10.1515/dx-2018-0093 PMID: 30901312

Jarvis, L. (2007). PHARMA'S TOUGH BALANCING ACT: Weaker third-quarter earning at the major drug companies reflect DRUG WITHDRAWALS and generic competition. *Chemical and Engineering News*, 85, 32–33. DOI: 10.1021/cen-v085n047.p032

Jarvis, L. (2013). Pfizer's Academic Experiment. *Chemical and Engineering News*. Advance online publication. DOI: 10.1021/cen-09040-bus1

Jarvis, L. (2018). Pfizer capitulates on prices. *Chemical and Engineering News*, 96(29), 12. Advance online publication. DOI: 10.1021/cen-09629-buscon3

Jarvis, L.LISA M. JARVIS. (2012). GENERIC ONSLAUGHT HITS PHARMA PROFITS. *Chemical and Engineering News*, 90(20), 30–31. DOI: 10.1021/cen-09020-bus3

Johnson, C., Bash, H. L., Song, J., Dunlap, K., Lagdamen, J., Suvak, M. K., & Stirman, S. W. (2022). The role of the consultant in consultation for an evidence-based treatment for ptsd. *Psychological Services*, 19(4), 760–769. DOI: 10.1037/ser0000592 PMID: 34735197

Johnson, M. W., Christensen, C. M., & Kagermann, H. (2008). Reinventing your business model. *Harvard Business Review*, 86(12), 50–59.

Junyu, S. (2022). Analysing the External Environment and Industrial Competition of High-Tech Companies—Using Tesla as an Example. *Journal of Psychology Research*. .DOI: 10.17265/2159-5542/2022.09.009

Kafoe, A. S. (2024). Supply Chain Resilience Strategy for Healthcare Organizations: Crucial Steps in Addressing the Impact of Natural Disasters. In Burrell, D. (Ed.), *Leadership Action and Intervention in Health, Business, Education, and Technology* (pp. 1–54). IGI Global., DOI: 10.4018/979-8-3693-4288-6.ch001

Kahneman, D., & Tversky, A. (1979). Prospect Theory: An Analysis of Decision under Risk. *Econometrica*, 47(2), 263–291. DOI: 10.2307/1914185

Kalghatgi, G. (2019). Development of Fuel/Engine Systems—The Way Forward to Sustainable Transport. *Engineering (Beijing)*, 5(3), 510–518. Advance online publication. DOI: 10.1016/j.eng.2019.01.009

Kalinke, U., Barouch, D. H., Rizzi, R., Lagkadinou, E., Türeci, Ö., Pather, S., & Neels, P. (2022). Clinical development and approval of COVID-19 vaccines. *Expert Review of Vaccines*, 21(5), 609–619. DOI: 10.1080/14760584.2022.2042257 PMID: 35157542

Kamel, F. O., Magadmi, R., Magadmi, M. M., Alfawaz, F. A., & Alfawaz, M. (2022). Patients' perceptions and satisfaction regarding teleconsultations during the covid-19 pandemic in Jeddah, Saudi Arabia. *Journal of Pharmaceutical Research International*, •••, 15–27. DOI: 10.9734/jpri/2022/v34i31B36093

Kelly, R., Rogers, A., Wynne, B., & Peaden, M. (N.D). Competitive Analysis Tesla Inc.

Khan, I. (2024). Strategic Planning in Business Management: Key Principles and Practices. *Management Science Research Archives*, 2(01), 31–39.

Khanna, T., Palepu, K., & Sinha, J. (2005). Strategies that fit emerging markets. *Harvard Business Review*, 83(6), 63–74, 76, 148. PMID: 15938439

Khurram, A. (2020). Revisiting porter five forces model: Influence of non-governmental organizations on competitive rivalry in various economic sectors. *Pakistan Social Sciences Review*, 4(1), 1–15. DOI: 10.35484/pssr.2020(4-I)01

Kim, C., Yang, K., & Kim, J. (2008). A strategy for third-party logistics systems: A case analysis using the blue ocean strategy. *Omega*, 36(4), 522–534. DOI: 10.1016/j.omega.2006.11.011

Kim, J., & Park, M. J. (2022). Influence of entrepreneurship manifestation factor on organisational innovation: The role of corporate entrepreneurship and imperative innovation culture. *The Journal of Entrepreneurship*, 31(3), 514–545. DOI: 10.1177/09713557221135558

Kim, W. C., & Mauborgne, R. (2005). *Blue ocean strategy: how to create uncontested market space and make the competition irrelevant*. Harvard Business School Press.

Klein, N., Stockwell, M., Demarco, M., Gaglani, M., Kharbanda, A., Irving, S., Rao, S., Grannis, S., Dascomb, K., Murthy, K., Rowley, E., Dalton, A., DeSilva, M., Dixon, B., Natarajan, K., Stenehjem, E., Naleway, A., Lewis, N., Ong, T., & Verani, J. (2022). Effectiveness of COVID-19 Pfizer-BioNTech BNT162b2 mRNA Vaccination in Preventing COVID-19–Associated Emergency Department and Urgent Care Encounters and Hospitalizations Among Nonimmunocompromised Children and Adolescents Aged 5–17 Years — VISION Network, 10 States, April 2021–January 2022. *MMWR. Morbidity and Mortality Weekly Report*, 71(9), 352–358. DOI: 10.15585/mmwr.mm7109e3 PMID: 35239634

Kochura, O. (2024). The art of letting go: Corporate divestitures in the biopharmaceutical industries. In *Mergers and Acquisitions* (pp. 13–28). Routledge. DOI: 10.4324/9781003245438-3

Koenig, S., Bee, C., Borovika, A., Briddell, C., Colberg, J., Humphrey, G., Kopach, M., Martínez, I., Nambiar, S., Plummer, S., Ribe, S., Roschangar, F., Scott, J., & Sneddon, H. (2019). A Green Chemistry Continuum for a Robust and Sustainable Active Pharmaceutical Ingredient Supply Chain. *ACS Sustainable Chemistry & Engineering*, 7(20), 16937–16951. Advance online publication. DOI: 10.1021/acssuschemeng.9b02842

Kotapati, B. A. P. U., Mutungi, S., Newham, M., Schroeder, J., Shao, S., & Wang, M. (2020). The antitrust case against Apple. *Available atSSRN* 3606073.

Kraft, T., Alagesan, S., & Shah, J. (2021). The New War of the Currents: The Race to Win the Electric Vehicle Market. *Darden Case: Business Communications (Topic)*. DOI: 10.2139/ssrn.3771785

Kumar, A. (2020). Disruptive Technologies and Impact on Industry- An Exploration. *Journal of Business Management and Information Systems*. .DOI: 10.48001/jbmis.2020.0701001

Kumar, B. (2018). *Acquisitions by Pfizer*. Wealth Creation in the World's Largest Mergers and Acquisitions., DOI: 10.1007/978-3-030-02363-8_8

Kumar, R., Chambers, E.IV, Chambers, D. H., & Lee, J. (2021). Generating new snack food texture ideas using sensory and consumer research tools: A case study of the japanese and south korean snack food markets. *Foods*, 10(2), 474. DOI: 10.3390/foods10020474 PMID: 33671546

Kunttu, L. (2017). Educational Involvement in Innovative University–Industry Collaboration. *Technology Innovation Management Review*, 7(12), 14–22. DOI: 10.22215/timreview/1124

Lauer, T. (2019). Generic Strategies, Outpacing and Blue Ocean - Discussing the Validity of Three Strategic Management Theories Using Case Studies from Airlines and Grocery Retail. *Theory, Methodology. Practice*, 15(1), 57–66. Advance online publication. DOI: 10.18096/TMP.2019.01.06

Li, M. (2023). *Five-Force Analysis, SWOT Analysis, Value Chain Analysis of Apple in Technology Industry*. Advances in Economics, Management and Political Sciences., DOI: 10.54254/2754-1169/4/2022946

Long, Z., Axsen, J., Miller, I., & Kormos, C. (2019). What does Tesla mean to car buyers? Exploring the role of automotive brand in perceptions of battery electric vehicles. *Transportation Research Part A, Policy and Practice*, 129, 185–204. Advance online publication. DOI: 10.1016/j.tra.2019.08.006

Ma, Y. (2023). *A Comparative Analysis of Amazon, Microsoft, and Apple's Stock Investment Value*. Highlights in Business, Economics and Management., DOI: 10.54097/hbem.v13i.8825

Madsen, D. Ø., & Slåtten, K. (2019). Examining the emergence and evolution of blue ocean strategy through the lens of management fashion theory. *Social Sciences (Basel, Switzerland)*, 8(1), 28. DOI: 10.3390/socsci8010028

Malekpour, M., Caboni, F., Nikzadask, M., & Basile, V. (2024). Taste of success: A strategic framework for product innovation in the food and beverage industry. *British Food Journal*, 126(13), 94–118. DOI: 10.1108/BFJ-02-2023-0138

Malik, H., Chaudhary, G., & Srivastava, S. (2021). Digital transformation through advances in artificial intelligence and machine learning. *Journal of Intelligent & Fuzzy Systems*, 42(2), 615–622. DOI: 10.3233/JIFS-189787

Mankins, M. C., & Steele, R. (2005). Turning great strategy into great performance. *Harvard Business Review*, 83(7/8), 64–72. PMID: 16028817

Maradin, D., Malnar, A., & Kaštelan, A. (2022). *Sustainable and Clean Energy: The Case of Tesla Company. JOURNAL OF ECONOMICS*. FINANCE AND MANAGEMENT STUDIES., DOI: 10.47191/jefms/v5-i12-10

Martins, J. M. (2024). Strategic management in an uncertain environment: A review. *Sustainable Economies*, 2(2), 64. DOI: 10.62617/se.v2i2.64

Mathrani, S., & Lai, X. (2021). Big data analytic framework for organizational leverage. *Applied Sciences (Basel, Switzerland)*, 11(5), 2340. DOI: 10.3390/app11052340

McDermott, O., Antony, J., Sony, M., & Daly, J. S. (2021). Barriers and enablers for continuous improvement methodologies within the irish pharmaceutical industry. *Processes (Basel, Switzerland)*, 10(1), 73. DOI: 10.3390/pr10010073

McNamara, J., Sweetman, S., Connors, P., Lofgren, I., & Greene, G. (2020). Using interactive nutrition modules to increase critical thinking skills in college courses. *Journal of Nutrition Education and Behavior*, 52(4), 343–350. DOI: 10.1016/j.jneb.2019.06.007 PMID: 31353275

Meiser, J. W., Cramer, T., & Turner-Brady, R. (2021). What good is military strategy? An analysis of strategy and effectiveness in the first Arab-Israeli War. *An Analysis of Strategy and Effectiveness in the First Arab-Israeli War (January 28, 2021). Meiser, J., Cramer, T., & Turner-Brady*, 37-49.

Miller, C. J., Barnett, M. L., Baumann, A. A., Gutner, C. A., & Stirman, S. W. (2021). The frame-is: A framework for documenting modifications to implementation strategies in healthcare. *Implementation Science : IS*, 16(1), 36. Advance online publication. DOI: 10.1186/s13012-021-01105-3 PMID: 33827716

Mohammadpoor, M., & Torabi, F. (2020). Big data analytics in oil and gas industry: An emerging trend. *Petroleum*, 6(4), 321–328. DOI: 10.1016/j.petlm.2018.11.001

Movsesyan, E., & Anokhina, M. (2020). TESLA VERTICAL INTEGRATION STRATEGIES: THEORY, PRACTICE, RESULTS. *Business Strategies*. .DOI: 10.17747/2311-7184-2020-7-184-188

Mullard, A. (2017). FDA approves Novartis's CDK4/6 inhibitor. *Nature Reviews. Drug Discovery*, 16(4), 229–229. DOI: 10.1038/nrd.2017.62 PMID: 28356596

Müllner, J. (2016). From uncertainty to risk—A risk management framework for market entry. *Journal of World Business*, 51(5), 800–814. DOI: 10.1016/j.jwb.2016.07.011

Murillo-Oviedo, A. B., Pimenta, M. L., Hilletofth, P., & Reitsma, E. (2019). Achieving market orientation through cross-functional integration. Operations and Supply Chain Management: An International Journal, 175-185. DOI: 10.31387/oscm0380241

Musonera, E., & Cagle, C. (2019). Electric Car Brand Positioning in the Automotive Industry: Recommendations for Sustainable and Innovative Marketing Strategies. *Journal of Strategic Innovation and Sustainability*. .DOI: 10.33423/jsis.v14i1.991

Nakagawa, K., Takata, M., Kato, K., Matsuyuki, T., & Matsuhashi, T. (2017). A University–Industry Collaborative Entrepreneurship Education Program as a Trading Zone: The Case of Osaka University. *Technology Innovation Management Review*, 7(6), 38–49. DOI: 10.22215/timreview/1083

Nalebuff, B. J., & Brandenburger, A. M. (1997). Co-opetition: Competitive and cooperative business strategies for the digital economy. *Strategy and Leadership*, 25(6), 28–33. DOI: 10.1108/eb054655

Naor, M., Coman, A., & Wiznizer, A. (2021). Vertically Integrated Supply Chain of Batteries, Electric Vehicles, and Charging Infrastructure: A Review of Three Milestone Projects from Theory of Constraints Perspective. *Sustainability (Basel)*, 13(7), 3632. DOI: 10.3390/su13073632

Navarro, J. G. (2024). Marketing in the United States – statistics & facts. https://www.statista.com/topics/8972/marketing-in-the-united-states/#topicOverview

Nigam, I. (2023). *Marketing Strategies of Apple Inc*. International Journal For Multidisciplinary Research., DOI: 10.36948/ijfmr.2023.v05i02.2059

Noennig, J. R., Mello Rose, F., Stadelhofer, P., Jannack, A., & Kulashri, S. (2024). Agile development for urban digitalisation: Insights from the creation of dresden's smart city strategy. *Measuring Business Excellence*, 28(2), 193–208. DOI: 10.1108/MBE-09-2023-0142

O'Connor, P. (2021). Loyalty programs and direct website performance: An empirical analysis of global hotel brands. *Information and Communication Technologies in Tourism*, 2021, 150–161. DOI: 10.1007/978-3-030-65785-7_13

Ochuba, N. A., Amoo, O. O., Okafor, E. S., Akinrinola, O., & Usman, F. O. (2024). Strategies for leveraging big data and analytics for business development: A comprehensive review across sectors. *Computer Science & IT Research Journal*, 5(3), 562–575. DOI: 10.51594/csitrj.v5i3.861

Oke, A., Prajogo, D. I., Idiagbon-Oke, M., & Edwin, T. (2022). Linking environmental forces, absorptive capacity, information sharing, and innovation performance. Industrial Management &Amp. *Industrial Management & Data Systems*, 122(7), 1738–1755. DOI: 10.1108/IMDS-12-2021-0732

Pahlevi, A. and Laksana, R. D. (2022). The influence of organizational politics on organizational commitment and job satisfaction and its influence on organizational citizenship behavior. Eduvest - Journal of Universal Studies, 2(7). DOI: 10.36418/eduvest.v2i7.497

Pangarkar, N., & Prabhudesai, R. (2024). Using porter's five forces analysis to drive strategy. *Global Business and Organizational Excellence*, 43(5), 24–34. DOI: 10.1002/joe.22250

Pargaonkar, Y. (2016). Leveraging patent landscape analysis and IP competitive intelligence for competitive advantage. *World Patent Information*, 45, 10–20. DOI: 10.1016/j.wpi.2016.03.004

Pei, H., Yu, S., & Tian, B. (2014). Analysis of Apple's Design Management Policy. *Applied Mechanics and Materials*, 496-500, 2626–2629. . DOI: 10.4028/www.scientific.net/AMM.496-500.2626

Pfizer (2023). Annual Report. https://annualreport.stocklight.com/nyse/pfe/23658781.pdf

Porter, M. E. (1979). HBR. *Harvard Business Review*.

Porter, M. E. (2008). The five competitive forces that shape strategy. *Harvard Business Review*, 86(1), 78–93. PMID: 18271320

Portier, C., Vervaet, C., & Vanhoorne, V. (2021). Continuous twin screw granulation: A review of recent progress and opportunities in formulation and equipment design. *Pharmaceutics*, 13(5), 668. DOI: 10.3390/pharmaceutics13050668 PMID: 34066921

Prahalad, C. K., & Hamel, G. (1990). The core competence of the corporation. (also includes a related article on the corporate structure at Vickers Co.). [-]. Harvard Business School Press.]. *Harvard Business Review*, 68(3), 79.

Proehl, R. (1996). Enhancing the effectiveness of cross-functional teams. *Leadership and Organization Development Journal*, 17(5), 3–10. DOI: 10.1108/01437739610127450

Rahman, H. A. (2021). Key technologies driving the car of the future. *Journal of the Society of Automotive Engineers Malaysia*, 3(1), 2–4. DOI: 10.56381/jsaem.v3i1.101

Rake, B. (2019). Do publication activities of academic institutions benefit from formal collaborations with firms? *Innovation (North Sydney, N.S.W.)*, 23(2), 241–265. DOI: 10.1080/14479338.2019.1679024

Ravi, G., Nur, M., & Kiswara, A. (2023). *Analyzing Changes in Traditional Industries: Challenges and Opportunities in the E-commerce Era. IAIC Transactions on Sustainable Digital Innovation.* ITSDI., DOI: 10.34306/itsdi.v5i1.608

Chapter 4
Addressing Workplace Culture and Rebuilding Reputation:
A Case Study of a Five Star Resort

Fauziatu Salifu-Sidii
https://orcid.org/0009-0001-2754-8194
Marymount University, USA

ABSTRACT

This study investigates the challenges faced by a five-star resort involved in a class action lawsuit due to widespread discrimination and sexual harassment allegations by female employees. The research aimed to explore the impact of these allegations on the resort's reputation, employee morale, and operational efficiency and to propose strategies to address the organizational culture issues at the core of the crisis. The analysis utilized Schein's Organizational Culture Model, Kotter's 8-step Change Model, and Risk Management and Balanced Scorecard frameworks to assess the resort's cultural dimensions, manage change, and mitigate reputational damage. Key findings indicate that the resort's toxic culture led to high employee turnover, absenteeism, and disengagement, negatively affecting productivity and customer satisfaction. Recommendations include implementing comprehensive policies to prevent discrimination, investing in diversity and inclusion.

DOI: 10.4018/979-8-3693-8562-3.ch004

INTRODUCTION

The luxury hotel industry, known for its emphasis on service excellence and reputation management, is increasingly vulnerable to legal and reputational risks stemming from workplace misconduct (Şanlıöz-Özgen & Kozak, 2023). A five-star resort, previously celebrated for its premium accommodations and exceptional service, now faces a severe crisis following allegations of pervasive discrimination and sexual harassment by female employees. This has culminated in a class action lawsuit and extensive media scrutiny, dramatically tarnishing the resort's public image, eroding employee morale, and diminishing customer trust (Opoku et al., 2024). Recent trends in the hospitality sector reveal that class action lawsuits related to workplace harassment are on the rise, often leading to devastating financial consequences and long-term reputational damage (Ari, 2020). In an industry that thrives on customer perceptions and loyalty, the failure to address these deep-rooted cultural issues could result in catastrophic outcomes, including significant client loss, reduced employee engagement, and crippling financial liabilities (Mamman-Daura et al., 2023). The resort's leadership must navigate this complex landscape by confronting entrenched organizational behaviors, managing the fallout from negative publicity, and implementing strategic measures to foster a safe and inclusive work environment (Hashmi et al., 2020). The urgency to act is underscored by the broader industry implications, where a single misstep can echo through brand reputation and market positioning, highlighting the critical need for comprehensive cultural reform (Gikuhi, 2020).

Problem Statement

The primary challenges for the five-star resort include addressing the entrenched issues within its organizational culture that have allowed discriminatory and harassing behaviors to persist, managing the reputational damage resulting from the lawsuit and negative publicity, and implementing measures to rebuild a safe and inclusive workplace environment. These challenges are compounded by the potential loss of clientele, reduced employee engagement, and financial losses due to decreased patronage and legal costs.

Significance Statement

The significance of addressing workplace culture issues and rebuilding the resort's reputation cannot be overstated. The hospitality industry heavily relies on its reputation for high standards of service and customer satisfaction (Şanlıöz-Özgen & Kozak, 2023). A tarnished reputation affects customer trust and patronage and impacts employee morale and engagement. Research indicates that organizations with positive workplace cultures experience higher employee satisfaction, better performance, and lower turnover rates (Mishra & Mishra, 2015). Addressing these issues is critical for the resort to regain its competitive edge and ensure long-term success.

LITERATURE REVIEW

A narrative literature review was conducted to inform the resort's response to workplace culture issues and reputational damage (Vada et al., 2023). A narrative review is particularly suitable for summarizing and synthesizing the existing literature on organizational culture, diversity and inclusion, and crisis management strategies. This approach enables a comprehensive and cohesive analysis of diverse sources, providing a broad understanding of the subject matter and highlighting key insights and themes relevant to the resort's strategic goals (Vada et al., 2023). This narrative review contextualized the issues within the resort, offering a detailed examination of best practices and theoretical frameworks that can guide effective interventions.

Workplace Discrimination refers to any unfair or prejudicial treatment of employees based on gender, race, age, religion, disability, or other protected attributes. Discrimination in the workplace can manifest in various forms, including unequal pay, restricted career advancement opportunities, and biased treatment that negatively impacts professional growth (Worke et al., 2021). Discrimination against female employees often leads to a hostile work environment, limiting their contributions and overall job satisfaction (Kleizen et al., 2023). According to Title VII of the Civil Rights Act of 1964 in the United States, it is illegal to discriminate against individuals based on their sex, which includes pregnancy, sexual orientation, and gender identity (Kim et al., 2020). Internationally, conventions like the United Nations Convention on the Elimination of All Forms of Discrimination Against Women also play a crucial role in safeguarding women's rights in the workplace (Rehof, 2021).

Sexual Harassment is a specific form of gender-based discrimination that includes unwelcome sexual advances, requests for sexual favors, and other verbal or physical conduct of a sexual nature that creates a hostile work environment (Shivashankar et al., 2020). This type of harassment can take the form of quid pro quo harassment, where employment benefits are subject upon accepting sexual advances, or it can manifest as a hostile work environment where the conduct is severe enough to affect an employee's work performance (Einarsen et al., 2020). Legal protections against sexual harassment, such as those outlined in Title VII of the Civil Rights Act and the Equal Employment Opportunity Commission (EEOC) guidelines, prohibit such behavior and offer protection against retaliation for reporting these issues (Kim et al., 2020). In Europe, laws such as the UK's Equality Act 2010 and the European Union's Directives on Equal Treatment mandate that employers provide harassment-free environments and address complaints promptly and effectively (KC, 2022).

Impact on Employees

The resort's allegations of discrimination and harassment have profound implications for its employees. The potential impacts are significant, encompassing employee disengagement, absenteeism, job dissatisfaction, and high turnover rates. These impacts contribute to a deteriorating work environment and organizational inefficiency (Stacy et al., 2022).

Employee Disengagement

Employees working in a toxic culture may disengage, reducing productivity and job satisfaction.

Employee engagement is a critical factor in organizational success, as engaged employees are more productive, committed, and willing to go above and beyond their job requirements. However, a toxic work environment characterized by discrimination and harassment can severely undermine engagement levels. Studies have shown that employees in such environments exhibit lower levels of job satisfaction and are less likely to be productive (Clark et al., 2021).

When employees face discrimination and harassment, they may withdraw from their work, both emotionally and physically. This disengagement affects their performance and ripple effect on team dynamics and overall organizational productivity. Negative experiences and a lack of support from the organization can lead to a sense of helplessness and apathy among employees, further exacerbating disengagement (Fung et al., 2020).

Therefore, addressing the toxic culture is crucial to re-engaging employees and restoring productivity and job satisfaction. A safe and inclusive work environment can help mitigate disengagement and enhance employee morale.

Employee Absenteeism

A hostile work environment can increase absenteeism as employees seek to avoid the workplace.

Absenteeism is often a direct consequence of a hostile work environment. Research indicates that employees who experience harassment and discrimination are more likely to take frequent sick leave or avoid coming to work altogether (Roscigno,

2019). The stress and anxicty causcd by a hostile environment can lead to physical and mental health issues, prompting employees to seek time away from work.

Increased absenteeism disrupts daily operations and strains the remaining staff, decreasing efficiency and higher operational costs (Fung et al., 2020). If employees are frequently absent, the resort may face challenges in maintaining service quality and meeting customer expectations. Moreover, absenteeism can indicate deeper issues within the organizational culture that must be addressed.

Addressing the root causes of absenteeism by creating a supportive and respectful work environment can help reduce absenteeism rates. By fostering a culture of inclusivity and providing adequate support systems, the resort can ensure that employees feel safe and motivated to attend work regularly (Huỳnh & Phan, 2022).

Job Dissatisfaction

Persistent discrimination and harassment lead to job dissatisfaction, negatively affecting employee morale.

Job satisfaction is closely linked to the quality of the work environment. Discrimination and harassment can lead to significant job dissatisfaction, as employees feel undervalued and unsupported. Studies have shown that employees who experience discrimination and harassment report lower levels of job satisfaction and higher levels of stress and frustration (Hashmi et al., 2020).

Job dissatisfaction can have far-reaching implications, including decreased productivity, higher error rates, and a negative impact on customer service. Employees dissatisfied with their jobs are less likely to be motivated and engaged, leading to a decline in overall performance and morale (Joshi, 2022). This dissatisfaction can also contribute to a hostile organizational climate, further perpetuating the cycle of poor employee engagement and performance.

To combat job dissatisfaction, the resort must address the underlying issues of discrimination and harassment. Implementing policies that promote fairness and inclusivity and provide support and resources for affected employees can help improve job satisfaction and boost overall employee morale.

Employee Turnover

High turnover rates may result in employees leaving to seek out safer and more respectful workplaces, increasing recruitment and training costs.

High employee turnover is a common consequence of a toxic work environment. Employees who experience discrimination and harassment are likelier to leave the organization for a safer and more respectful workplace (Fuchs & others, 2022). This turnover can be costly for organizations, as it involves expenses related to recruiting, hiring, and training new employees.

High turnover rates can disrupt organizational stability and continuity (Gikuhi, 2020). The loss of experienced and skilled employees can lead to a knowledge gap, affecting the quality of service and operational efficiency. Additionally, the constant need to recruit and train new employees can divert resources from other critical business areas (Fung et al., 2020). The negative reputation associated with high turnover can also deter potential talent from joining the organization.

To reduce turnover rates, the resort must create a work environment that values and respects all employees. By addressing the issues of discrimination and harassment and implementing measures to promote a positive and inclusive culture, the resort can retain its employees and reduce the associated costs of high turnover.

Impact on the Organization

The organizational impacts of the current crisis are equally severe, encompassing low employee morale, decreased productivity, a negative public image, and significant legal and financial consequences. Each of these impacts contributes to the resort's overall challenges in restoring its reputation and operational efficiency (Hashmi et al., 2020).

Low Employee Morale

The negative publicity and ongoing issues can lead to low employee morale, further affecting service quality and operational efficiency.

Employee morale is critical to maintaining high service quality and operational efficiency. Research indicates that negative publicity and unresolved internal issues can significantly lower employee morale, decreasing overall job satisfaction and performance (Fuchs & others, 2022). In the hospitality industry, where employee interactions with guests are paramount, low morale can directly impact the quality of service provided.

Low employee morale often results from a lack of trust in the organization and its leadership. When employees feel unsupported and undervalued, their motivation to perform well diminishes. This decline in morale can lead to increased absenteeism, higher turnover rates, and a general decrease in productivity (Huỳnh & Phan, 2022). The ongoing issues and negative publicity for the resort will likely create a work environment where employees are disengaged and less committed to their roles, severely affecting the guest experience and operational outcomes.

Addressing the root causes of low employee morale is crucial for restoring service quality and operational efficiency. By creating a supportive and inclusive work environment, the resort can boost employee morale and, in turn, enhance overall performance.

Decreased Productivity

Disengaged and dissatisfied employees are less productive, impacting the resort's overall performance and customer satisfaction. Productivity is closely linked to employee engagement and satisfaction. Studies have shown disengaged employees are significantly less productive than their engaged counterparts (Kong et al., 2022). In the hospitality industry, where service delivery is critical to business success, decreased productivity can lead to suboptimal guest experiences and reduced customer satisfaction.

When employees are dissatisfied and disengaged, they are less likely to put in the effort required to meet or exceed guest expectations. This can result in longer wait times, lower quality service, and a general decline in the guest experience (Şanlıöz-Özgen & Kozak, 2023). For the resort, decreased productivity due to employee disengagement can lead to negative reviews, a drop in repeat business, and a decline in revenue.

To combat decreased productivity, the resort must focus on re-engaging its workforce by addressing the issues of discrimination and harassment, providing adequate support and resources, and fostering a positive work environment. This can help improve employee satisfaction and productivity, leading to better performance and customer satisfaction.

Negative Public Image

The extensive media coverage has tarnished the resort's public image, potentially leading to a loss of clientele and revenue.

A negative public image can severely affect businesses, especially in the hospitality industry where reputation is a crucial determinant of success (Fuchs et al., 2022). Extensive media coverage of the resort's issues has likely damaged its public image, making it less attractive to potential guests and corporate clients. Research shows that organizations with tarnished reputations face challenges in attracting and retaining customers, directly impacting revenue (Dongrey & Rokade, 2021). The negative public image resulting from the media coverage of discrimination and harassment allegations can deter potential guests from choosing the resort for their stays or events. Existing clients may also reconsider their loyalty, leading to a decline in repeat business (Hashmi et al., 2020). This loss of clientele can directly impact the resort's revenue and long-term viability. Furthermore, a damaged reputation can also affect partnerships and sponsorships, exacerbating financial challenges.

Legal and Financial Consequences

The class action lawsuit and associated legal costs can result in significant financial burdens for the resort.

Legal battles, especially those involving class action lawsuits, can be extremely costly. The resort is likely facing substantial legal fees, potential settlements, and fines, all of which contribute to financial strain. Additionally, the financial impact is compounded by the potential loss of revenue due to decreased patronage and the cost of implementing necessary changes to address the issues (İnce et al., 2022).

The financial consequences of the class action lawsuit extend beyond immediate legal costs. The resort may also face long-term financial challenges as it works to rebuild its reputation and implement new policies and training programs (Clark et al., 2021). The cost of recruiting and training new employees to replace those who leave due to the toxic culture adds to the financial burden. Furthermore, the resort may need to invest in public relations efforts to restore its image, which requires significant financial resources (Chauhan & Kularatne, 2021). To mitigate these legal and financial consequences, the resort must develop a comprehensive strategy that addresses the allegations head-on, implement effective changes to prevent future issues and manage its finances prudently to ensure long-term sustainability.

ORGANIZATIONAL CULTURE THEORY: COMPONENTS OF ORGANIZATIONAL CULTURE

Organizational culture encompasses the shared beliefs, values, and behaviors that shape how employees interact and perform within an organization (Stacy et al., 2022), model of organizational culture highlights three levels: artifacts (visible structures and processes), espoused values (stated standards and rules), and basic assumptions (deeply embedded beliefs). These cultural components significantly influence employee behavior, job satisfaction, and overall organizational outcomes, especially in high-stakes industries like hospitality, where culture directly impacts service quality and customer experience (Ari, 2020).

Impact of Organizational Culture on Employee Behavior and Outcomes

Research indicates that toxic organizational cultures, characterized by power imbalances, implicit biases, and inadequate leadership responses, can lead to widespread issues such as disengagement, absenteeism, job dissatisfaction, and high turnover (Einarsen et al., 2020). For instance, workplace discrimination and harassment often decrease employee morale and productivity, further eroding trust and commitment among staff (Schneider et al., 1997). The hospitality sector, in particular, faces heightened risks due to its reliance on employee-customer interactions and the industry's reputation-sensitive nature (Ari, 2020).

Analysis of the Resort's Organizational Culture

The resort's organizational culture, as analyzed through Schein's model, reveals entrenched issues such as power dynamics, gender relations, and implicit biases that have fostered a permissive environment for discrimination and harassment. These cultural deficiencies are exacerbated by leadership practices that have failed to promote inclusivity and accountability, allowing harmful behaviors to persist unchecked (Hashmi et al., 2020). This toxic culture has not only compromised employee well-being but also attracted negative media attention, significantly damaging the resort's reputation and financial stability (Gupta & Garg, 2020).

The Role of Leadership in Shaping and Transforming Culture

Leadership plays a pivotal role in defining and transforming organizational culture. Ineffective leadership can perpetuate toxic environments, whereas proactive and inclusive leadership can drive meaningful cultural change. Kotter's 8-Step Change Model provides a structured approach for leaders to acknowledge issues, create urgency, and implement sustainable change (WANJIKU, 2022). The literature emphasizes that leaders must actively model desired behaviors, communicate transparently, and engage employees at all levels to rebuild trust and foster a positive culture (Dhar et al., 2023).

Strategic Planning for Long-Term Cultural Transformation

Strategic planning is crucial in addressing the immediate and long-term impacts of workplace discrimination and reputational damage. Integrating Planning Theory and Strategy Theory, the resort must develop a cohesive response that aligns crisis management with its broader mission and objectives. This involves utilizing frameworks such as the Balanced Scorecard to address financial, operational, and reputational dimensions while ensuring that employee well-being and inclusivity remain central to the resort's strategy (Joshi, 2022).

Understanding Cultural Dimensions: Analyzing the Resort's Organizational Culture Using Schein's Model

Exploring the cultural dimensions of the resort is critical to understanding the root causes of workplace discrimination and harassment. Schein's Organizational Culture Model offers a robust framework for examining the three levels of culture—artifacts, espoused values, and basic underlying assumptions—that shape the organizational environment and influence employee behavior (Ponnahennedige, 2021). This model provides insights into how cultural factors such as power dynamics, gender relations, and implicit biases manifest within the resort and contribute to a toxic workplace climate.

Artifacts: Visible Manifestations of Culture

At the artifact level, the resort's policies, procedures, and physical environment indicate its organizational culture. Artifacts include dress codes, office layouts, communication styles, and formal policies on behavior and conduct. In the resort's case, artifacts might reveal discrepancies between stated policies and actual practices, such as formal anti-harassment policies that are not enforced or a corporate image that emphasizes luxury but neglects inclusivity and respect among employees (Robaki et al., 2020). The visible symbols and behaviors within the resort can unintentionally reinforce discriminatory practices, such as hierarchical office spaces that promote power imbalances or marketing materials that lack diversity and inclusivity.

Espoused Values: Stated Norms Versus Lived Reality

The espoused values represent the norms, rules, and standards the resort claims to uphold, such as a commitment to diversity, customer service excellence, and ethical behavior (Stosic et al., 2023). However, these values often exist superficially if they are not reflected in everyday practices. For example, the resort may promote inclusivity in its mission statement but fail to implement robust measures that support female employees or address systemic biases in performance evaluations, promotions, and workplace interaction (Robert et al., 2022)The gap between what the resort says it values and what employees actually experience can contribute to a culture of distrust and disengagement, particularly if management tolerates or ignores discriminatory behaviors.

Basic Underlying Assumptions: Deeply Ingrained Beliefs and Attitudes

The most profound level of culture, basic underlying assumptions, comprises the deeply ingrained beliefs and attitudes that unconsciously guide organizational behavior. These assumptions are often unspoken but influence how power is distributed, how gender relations are perceived, and how implicit biases affect decision-making (Ponnahennedige, 2021). In the resort, underlying assumptions might include traditional gender roles that marginalize female employees, a tolerance for aggressive or dismissive management styles, and an implicit belief that high performance justifies poor behavior. These deeply rooted cultural elements can perpetuate a toxic environment where discrimination and harassment are normalized, making it challenging to implement surface-level changes without addressing these core beliefs.

Power Dynamics, Gender Relations, and Implicit Biases

Power dynamics within the resort likely reflect hierarchical structures where decision-making is concentrated among a few senior leaders, often without input from diverse or lower-level employees. This top-down approach can silence voices that challenge the status quo and perpetuate gender-based power imbalances, leading to a work environment where discriminatory practices go unchecked (Hashmi et al., 2020). Implicit biases may manifest in hiring, promotions, and daily interactions, where women and minority employees are judged more harshly or excluded from key opportunities (Stacy et al., 2022). Understanding these cultural dimensions is essential to identifying specific intervention points and developing strategies that address these ingrained issues.

Informing Effective Strategies for Cultural Change

Understanding the resort's cultural dimensions through Schein's model provides valuable insights into how discrimination and harassment have been sustained within the organization. This analysis can inform the development of targeted strategies to improve the workplace climate and rebuild trust. For instance, recognizing the gap between espoused values and lived reality can drive efforts to align policies with actual practices, ensuring that anti-discrimination policies are rigorously enforced and supported by leadership. Addressing artifacts that reinforce harmful power dynamics, such as revising reporting lines or restructuring workspaces, can help dismantle visible symbols of exclusion.

Moreover, initiatives that challenge and reshape the underlying assumptions—such as leadership training on implicit bias, inclusive decision-making processes, and open forums for employee feedback—can help shift the deeply rooted attitudes that sustain discriminatory behavior. By targeting each level of culture, the resort can develop a holistic approach to cultural transformation, creating a more inclusive and respectful work environment that aligns with its stated values and supports long-term organizational success.

Media Influence

The extensive media coverage of the resort's crisis has significantly eroded public trust, highlighting the severe long-term consequences of reputational damage for luxury hospitality brands. A tarnished image can lead to customer attrition, revenue loss, and diminished market positioning, making it imperative for the resort to manage its public narrative effectively and rebuild its brand equity through authentic and strategic communication efforts (Fuchs et al., 2022).

Rebuilding Trust and Implementing Change

Addressing the trust deficit among employees and customers requires a detailed roadmap based on Change Management Theories. The resort must involve leadership, employees, and stakeholders in a transparent transformation process that prioritizes honest communication, proactive policy implementation, and ongoing cultural assessments. Leadership development and engagement are essential to support this change, ensuring that new policies are not just stated but actively embodied and reinforced at every level of the organization (Stacy et al., 2022).

CHANGE MANAGEMENT THEORY

Change Management Theory encompasses a range of models and approaches that provide structured methods for planning, implementing, and sustaining organizational change (Stacy et al., 2022). The primary goal of change management is to help organizations navigate transitions effectively, minimize resistance, and achieve desired outcomes. Change management theories address the technical and human aspects of change, recognizing that successful transformation depends on strategic planning and managing individuals' emotional, psychological, and behavioral responses within the organization (WANJIKU, 2022). The resort must employ Kotter's

8-Step Change Model to address workplace culture issues. This model includes creating urgency, forming a powerful coalition, creating a vision for change, communicating the vision, removing obstacles, creating short-term wins, building on the change, and anchoring the changes in the corporate culture (WANJIKU, 2022). The resort's initial steps should involve acknowledging the problem and creating a sense of urgency among stakeholders. Forming a powerful coalition of leaders and change agents within the organization is crucial to driving the change process. Developing a clear vision for a culture of inclusivity and respect, and effectively communicating this vision to all employees will help align everyone towards the common goal. Removing obstacles, such as entrenched attitudes and behaviors, and celebrating short-term wins, such as implementing new policies, will build momentum for the change. Finally, ensuring that these changes are embedded into the organizational culture will help to sustain improvements over the long term.

Component of Change Management

To address the deep-seated workplace culture issues and mitigate reputational damage, the resort must strategically implement Kotter's 8-Step Change Model, a widely recognized framework for managing organizational change effectively. This model provides a structured approach to initiating, managing, and sustaining change, which is crucial given the severity of the allegations and the subsequent impact on employee morale and public trust (Lin & Huang, 2021).

Step 1: Create a Sense of Urgency

The resort must begin by acknowledging the gravity of the discrimination and harassment allegations and communicating the urgent need for cultural transformation to all stakeholders. This involves highlighting the potential consequences of inaction, such as continued loss of clientele, legal ramifications, and ongoing reputational damage (Kleizen et al., 2023). By clarifying the urgency, the resort can motivate employees, management, and external stakeholders to support the change process.

Step 2: Form a Powerful Coalition

A critical step in Kotter's model is forming a coalition of influential leaders and change agents committed to driving the transformation. For the resort, this coalition should include senior executives, department heads, HR leaders, and respected employees who can champion the cultural shift. These individuals must possess the credibility and authority to influence organizational behavior and foster buy-in across all levels (Mamman-Daura et al., 2023). Engaging diverse voices in the coalition will also help address underlying biases and power dynamics contributing to the toxic culture.

Step 3: Develop a Vision for Change

The resort needs to craft a clear and compelling vision that outlines what an inclusive and respectful workplace looks like and why it is essential. This vision should articulate specific goals, such as eliminating harassment, promoting diversity, and rebuilding trust among employees and customers. A well-defined vision serves as a guiding star, helping employees understand the direction of the change and their role in achieving it (WANJIKU, 2022).

Step 4: Communicate the Vision

Effective communication is crucial to align all employees with the resort's vision for change. The resort must consistently and transparently communicate the vision, strategies, and progress through various channels such as meetings, newsletters, and training sessions. Clear messaging helps to dispel rumors, address fears, and reinforce the commitment to transforming the workplace culture (Stacy et al., 2022). Leadership must model the values outlined in the vision, demonstrating a tangible commitment to change.

Step 5: Remove Obstacles

Identifying and addressing obstacles is essential for successful change implementation. The resort must confront entrenched behaviors, outdated policies, and resistance to change, which may hinder progress. This can involve revising disciplinary procedures, implementing anonymous reporting mechanisms, and supporting those affected by the toxic culture. Leadership should empower employees to voice concerns and propose solutions, fostering an environment where barriers to change can be addressed collaboratively (Stacy et al., 2022).

Step 6: Create Short-Term Wins

To build momentum, the resort should set achievable short-term goals and celebrate early successes, such as implementing new anti-harassment policies, conducting comprehensive diversity training, and recognizing teams that exemplify the desired cultural change (Kleizen et al., 2023). Short-term wins validate the change efforts, motivate employees, and demonstrate progress, which is vital for maintaining morale and commitment.

Step 7: Build on the Change

The resort must avoid complacency by continually evaluating and expanding on the initial changes. This step involves reinforcing successful strategies, identifying areas for improvement, and scaling up effective initiatives. The resort can ensure the change gains strength and permanence by embedding the new values into ongoing training, performance evaluations, and employee feedback mechanisms (Mamman-Daura et al., 2023).

Step 8: Anchor the Changes in Corporate Culture

Sustaining the improvements requires integrating the new behaviors, values, and practices into the core of the resort's organizational culture. This can be achieved by aligning the resort's mission, policies, and employee rewards with the cultural changes, ensuring that inclusivity and respect become the norm rather than the exception. Leadership development and continuous assessment will be crucial to maintaining the momentum and ensuring that the resort's cultural transformation endures over the long term (Hashmi et al., 2020).

MANAGING RESISTANCE, EMPLOYEE ENGAGEMENT, AND LEADERSHIP BUY-IN

If not adequately managed, resistance to change can undermine even the most well-intentioned initiatives. To reduce resistance and foster change of ownership, the resort should actively engage employees through participatory approaches, solicit feedback, and involve them in decision-making. Leadership buy-in is equally critical; leaders must support the change and exemplify the values and behaviors expected from all employees. This alignment between leadership actions and organizational values will be vital to rebuilding trust and credibility (Mamman-Daura et al., 2023).

Planning Theory

The resort's planning efforts to mitigate reputational damage and rebuild trust can be assessed using the Risk Management Framework. This model involves identifying risks, assessing their impact, developing mitigation strategies, and monitoring the outcomes (Robert et al., 2022). The report must identify the risks associated with the allegations, such as loss of clientele and decreased employee morale. Assessing the impact of these risks will involve understanding the potential financial and reputational damage. Developing strategies to mitigate these risks include implementing comprehensive training programs on diversity and inclusion, revising existing policies to prevent discrimination and harassment, and enhancing communication with both employees and customers to rebuild trust. Monitoring the effectiveness of these strategies will involve regular feedback mechanisms and adjusting the approach as necessary to ensure continuous improvement.

To effectively address workplace culture issues and mitigate reputational damage, the resort must adopt a comprehensive planning approach guided by Planning Theory, integrating both short-term crisis management and long-term cultural transformation strategies (Lin & Huang, 2021). This approach should involve a robust planning framework that responds to immediate challenges and lays the groundwork for sustainable organizational change, aligning with rational and strategic planning models.

Application of Rational and Strategic Planning Theories

Rational Planning Theory emphasizes a systematic and data-driven approach to decision-making, where actions are based on clearly defined problems, evidence-based solutions, and measurable outcomes (Lin & Huang, 2021). In the context of the resort, this involves a detailed assessment of the organizational issues stemming from the allegations of discrimination and harassment. The first step is to identify the key risks, such as loss of clientele, decreased employee morale, financial liabilities, and damage to the brand's public image due to extensive media exposure. The rational planning approach enables the resort to break down these complex challenges into manageable components, allowing for the formulation of targeted responses that address both immediate and long-term concerns.

Short-Term Crisis Management

In the immediate term, the resort's planning must focus on crisis management by implementing strategies that address the most pressing risks and restore stakeholder confidence. This includes deploying a Risk Management Framework that identifies, assesses, and mitigates the impact of the allegations (Gikuhi, 2020). Key actions should involve public acknowledgment of the issues, transparent communication with stakeholders, and swift implementation of corrective measures, such as updating anti-harassment policies and launching mandatory training on diversity and inclusion. Short-term crisis management should prioritize legal compliance and reputational repair, engaging with legal advisors and public relations experts to effectively navigate the lawsuit's fallout.

Long-Term Cultural Transformation

Beyond immediate crisis responses, the resort must plan for long-term cultural transformation through Strategic Planning Theory, which focuses on aligning its mission, vision, and values with its strategic objectives (Hashmi et al., 2020). This involves developing a strategic framework prioritizing cultural change as a core business goal and integrating new policies and practices promoting inclusivity, respect, and ethical behavior. A strategic planning approach ensures the resort's response is reactive and proactive, embedding structural changes safeguarding against future legal and reputational risks.

Stakeholder Involvement and Media Management

Planning must also account for the involvement of key stakeholders, including employees, customers, investors, and the broader public. Given the high media exposure of the lawsuit, stakeholder engagement becomes crucial in rebuilding trust and demonstrating the resort's commitment to change (Chauhan & Kularatne, 2021). The planning framework should include mechanisms for stakeholder feedback, such as town hall meetings, surveys, and focus groups, which allow the resort to understand and address concerns directly. Strategic planning must also involve a comprehensive communication strategy that manages the media narrative, emphasizing the resort's proactive measures and long-term commitment to cultural reform.

Implementing Structural Changes and Monitoring

To ensure the planned changes are practical and sustainable, the resort should incorporate continuous monitoring and evaluation processes into its planning framework. This involves setting measurable targets, such as reducing reported harassment incidents, improving employee satisfaction scores, and enhancing customer feedback related to service quality (Mamman-Daura et al., 2023). The resort can use these metrics to assess the effectiveness of its strategies and make necessary adjustments to maintain momentum. Regular audits of workplace policies and training programs will help ensure compliance and reinforce the new cultural norms, reducing the likelihood of future legal challenges.

Strategy Theory

To develop a comprehensive strategy for addressing workplace culture issues and rebuilding the resort's reputation, the Balanced Scorecard approach can be applied. This model includes four perspectives: financial, customer, internal processes, and learning and growth (Huỳnh & Phan, 2022). From a financial perspective, the resort should allocate resources to training programs and policy revisions. The customer perspective involves rebuilding trust through transparent communication and demonstrating a commitment to inclusivity. Internal processes should focus on establishing robust mechanisms for reporting and addressing discrimination and harassment. The learning and growth perspective emphasizes ongoing training and development to foster an inclusive culture (Agoncillo, 2023). By integrating these elements, the resort can create a holistic strategy that addresses the root causes of the issues and sets a clear path toward rebuilding its reputation and trust.

To develop a comprehensive strategy for addressing workplace culture issues and rebuilding the resort's reputation, Strategy Theory provides valuable guidance on aligning the organization's mission and values with its crisis response. Using the Balanced Scorecard approach, the resort can create a structured roadmap that integrates strategic planning with actionable steps to navigate the lawsuit, restore its competitive positioning, and foster long-term cultural transformation (Gikuhi, 2020). The Balanced Scorecard model focuses on four critical perspectives—financial, customer, internal processes, and learning and growth—allowing the resort to address the crisis holistically while maintaining its strategic objectives (Kanwal & Van Hoye, 2020).

Financial Perspective: Resource Allocation and Strategic Investment

From a financial standpoint, the resort must strategically allocate resources to address the immediate crisis and prevent future issues. Investments should be directed towards comprehensive training programs on diversity, inclusion, and harassment prevention and revising and enforcing policies that uphold a respectful workplace environment. Allocating budget towards legal consultations, public relations efforts, and employee support initiatives will help mitigate legal risks and manage reputational damage effectively (Worke et al., 2021). These investments should be seen as costs and strategic moves to enhance the resort's long-term value and market position by creating a safe and inclusive workplace that attracts talent and clientele.

Customer Perspective: Rebuilding Trust and Enhancing Stakeholder Relationships

The customer perspective of the Balanced Scorecard emphasizes the importance of restoring trust and managing stakeholder relationships during the crisis. The resort must communicate transparently with customers, employees, and the broader public to demonstrate its commitment to resolving the issues and rebuilding a positive organizational culture (Chan et al., 2017). Proactive engagement strategies, such as issuing public statements, holding press conferences, and providing regular updates on the progress of implemented changes, will help rebuild the resort's reputation. Personalized outreach to loyal customers and corporate partners can help reinforce relationships, ensuring stakeholders feel valued and informed throughout recovery.

Internal Processes: Strengthening Reporting Mechanisms and Operational Resilience

Internally, the resort must overhaul its processes to prevent future incidents of discrimination and harassment. Establishing robust mechanisms for reporting, investigating, and addressing workplace complaints is critical. This includes implementing anonymous reporting channels, ensuring thorough investigations, and taking decisive action against perpetrators. The resort should also enhance its internal controls and audit functions to monitor compliance with new policies, fostering accountability at all organizational levels (Mamman-Daura et al., 2023). Strengthening these internal processes will address the root causes of the crisis and build operational resilience, reducing the likelihood of similar issues reoccurring.

Learning and Growth Perspective: Fostering a Culture of Continuous Improvement

The learning and growth perspective focuses on building the resort's capacity for continuous improvement and cultural transformation. Training and professional development programs should be instituted to educate employees and leaders on inclusivity, ethical behavior, and conflict resolution (Ari, 2020). Leadership development programs can equip managers with the skills to model inclusive behaviors and support cultural change, reinforcing the resort's commitment to a harassment-free workplace. Furthermore, the resort should foster a culture of feedback where employees feel empowered to voice concerns and contribute to ongoing improvements, enhancing engagement and trust (Kleizen et al., 2023).

Strategic Choices for Maintaining Competitive Positioning

To navigate the lawsuit while maintaining or restoring its competitive positioning, the resort must make strategic choices that align with its broader mission and values. First, it should prioritize rebuilding its brand identity by emphasizing its commitment to ethical standards and customer service excellence. Leveraging the positive aspects of the resort's existing brand while demonstrating tangible steps toward change can differentiate the resort from competitors facing similar challenges (Stacy et al., 2022). Additionally, strategic resource allocation should focus on high-impact areas such as enhancing guest experience and expanding market reach through targeted marketing campaigns highlighting the resort's renewed commitment to inclusiveness and respect.

Maintaining Competitive Advantage Through Strategic Resource Allocation

Effective resource allocation is central to sustaining a competitive advantage. The resort should focus on building capabilities that enhance its service quality and customer satisfaction, such as investing in staff training, upgrading amenities, and improving operational efficiency (Ari, 2020). Developing strategic partnerships with advocacy groups or organizations that promote workplace equity can also bolster the resort's reputation as a leader in cultural transformation within the hospitality sector. By strategically deploying resources, the resort can turn the crisis into an opportunity to strengthen its market position and appeal to socially conscious consumers.

Aligning Strategy with Stakeholder Expectations

The resort's strategy must also account for stakeholder expectations, particularly in light of the lawsuit's media exposure (Chan et al., 2017). This involves meeting legal and regulatory requirements and exceeding stakeholder expectations through transparency, accountability, and consistent communication (Tanjung et al., 2024). The resort should engage with stakeholders meaningfully, such as hosting forums to discuss its progress or publishing reports detailing its efforts and outcomes in improving workplace culture. This alignment between strategy and stakeholder expectations will be critical in restoring trust and building a more resilient organization.

CONCLUSION

Addressing the deep-rooted issues within the resort's organizational culture and rebuilding its reputation necessitates a multifaceted approach. This approach should include understanding cultural dimensions through Schein's model, implementing structured change management processes with Kotter's 8-Step Model, and developing comprehensive risk management and balanced scorecard strategies.

Implementing Structured Change Management: A Strategic Approach to Cultural Transformation

To effectively address workplace discrimination, harassment, and toxic culture, the resort must implement structured change management processes. While Kotter's 8-Step Change Model provides a solid foundation, integrating additional frameworks such as the ADKAR Model (Awareness, Desire, Knowledge, Ability, Reinforcement) can offer practical steps that ensure the sustainability and effectiveness of the change initiatives. By combining these approaches, the resort can create a comprehensive strategy to transform its organizational culture, mitigate legal and reputational risks, and foster a respectful and inclusive work environment.

Kotter's 8-Step Change Model: A Structured Pathway to Transformation

Kotter's 8-Step Change Model is crucial in driving effective organizational change within the resort. This model emphasizes the need to create urgency, form a powerful coalition, develop and communicate a vision, remove obstacles, generate short-term wins, consolidate gains, and anchor changes in the corporate culture (Hashmi et al., 2020). The resort can leverage this model to address the immediate and systemic issues that have allowed discrimination and harassment to persist.

1. **Creating Urgency:** The resort must acknowledge the severity of the allegations and their impact on the brand. By creating a sense of urgency, leadership can motivate all stakeholders, including employees, customers, and investors, to support the cultural transformation efforts (Wanjiku, 2022).
2. **Forming a Powerful Coalition:** It is essential to build a coalition of leaders, managers, and employee representatives committed to driving change. This group will lead the charge in advocating for a culture of inclusivity and respect, modeling desired behaviors, and holding the organization accountable for progress (Stacy et al., 2022).
3. **Developing and Communicating a Vision:** The resort should articulate a clear vision that outlines what an inclusive and respectful workplace looks like and why it is critical for the organization's success. This vision must be communicated consistently and transparently to align employees and stakeholders with the change objectives (Fuchs & others, 2022).
4. **Removing Obstacles:** It is crucial to identify and address barriers to change, such as outdated policies, entrenched attitudes, and ineffective reporting mechanisms. The resort should implement new procedures that support inclusivity,

such as anonymous reporting channels and comprehensive anti-discrimination training for all employees (Gikuhi, 2020).
5. **Creating Short-Term Wins:** To build momentum, the resort should set and celebrate achievable short-term goals, such as revising key policies or launching diversity and inclusion workshops. These early successes demonstrate progress, boost morale, and validate the change efforts (Dhar et al., 2023).
6. **Building on the Change:** Consolidating gains involves integrating successful changes into the broader organizational structure. The resort should continuously evaluate and refine its strategies to ensure improvements are sustained and expanded across all departments (Hashmi et al., 2020).
7. **Anchoring Changes in Corporate Culture:** Finally, to ensure lasting change, the resort must embed new behaviors and values into the core of its culture. This includes aligning performance metrics, recognition systems, and leadership development programs with the principles of inclusivity and respect (Stacy et al., 2022).

ADKAR Model: Ensuring Sustainable and Measurable Change

The ADKAR Model complements Kotter's framework by providing a more individualized focus on implementing and sustaining change at the employee level. ADKAR stands for Awareness, Desire, Knowledge, Ability, and Reinforcement, and it outlines a step-by-step process for guiding employees through change (Thekkekara & others, 2023). This model can help the resort ensure that change initiatives are practical, measurable, and effective.

1. **Awareness:** Creating awareness involves educating employees about the current workplace issues, why change is necessary, and the potential consequences of inaction. The resort should use workshops, town halls, and communication campaigns to inform employees about the impact of discrimination and harassment on the organization (Hanif, 2023).
2. **Desire:** Fostering a desire for change means encouraging employees to support and engage in the transformation process actively. The resort can achieve this by demonstrating leadership commitment, addressing employee concerns, and highlighting the benefits of a positive workplace culture for everyone (Ali et al., 2021).
3. **Knowledge:** Providing knowledge is about equipping employees with the skills and information needed to adopt new behaviors. This includes training on recognizing and reporting harassment, understanding unconscious biases, and practicing respectful communication. The resort must ensure that these

educational efforts are ongoing and accessible to all staff (Thekkekara et al., 2023).

4. **Ability:** Ability empowers employees to implement new skills and behaviors in their daily work (Hanif, 2023). The resort should provide resources, coaching, and feedback mechanisms that support employees in applying what they have learned. Role-playing exercises, mentorship programs, and access to support networks can help reinforce these abilities.
5. **Reinforcement:** Finally, reinforcement involves maintaining the change by recognizing and rewarding positive behavior, monitoring progress, and addressing relapses (Ali et al., 2021). The resort should establish metrics to measure the effectiveness of its cultural initiatives, such as employee satisfaction surveys, incident reports, and feedback from diversity committees. Regular assessments will help ensure the changes are deeply embedded and continuously improved.

Ensuring Sustainability and Mitigating Future Risks

To ensure that these changes are sustainable, the resort must implement a robust evaluation framework that tracks the effectiveness of its change management efforts(Fuchs & others, 2022). This includes setting clear, measurable objectives for cultural transformation, such as reducing reported incidents of harassment, improving employee engagement scores, and enhancing customer perceptions of the resort's commitment to inclusivity.

Sustainability can be further enhanced by institutionalizing the changes through updated policies, ongoing training, and leadership accountability (Fung et al., 2020). Leaders should be visibly engaged in the change process, modeling the behaviors they expect from their teams. The resort should also maintain open channels for feedback and continuously refine its strategies based on **lessons learned.**

By combining Kotter's 8-Step Change Model and the ADKAR framework, the resort can develop a structured and comprehensive approach to change management that addresses the root causes of workplace issues, mitigates future legal and reputational risks, and builds a positive organizational culture that supports long-term success.

Recommendations

Based on the analysis of structured change management, cultural dimensions, and strategic planning theories, the following recommendations provide a comprehensive roadmap for the resort to address the lawsuit, repair its reputation, and rebuild trust with employees, customers, and the broader public. Each theory serves as a guiding lens, offering actionable steps for transforming the resort's organizational culture, mitigating legal and reputational risks, and ensuring long-term sustainability.

Utilize Kotter's 8-Step Change Model to Drive Organizational Transformation

Kotter's 8-Step Change Model provides a structured approach to initiating and managing change within the resort. To address the lawsuit and repair its reputation, the resort should begin by creating a sense of urgency around the need for cultural transformation and communicating the severe implications of the allegations to all stakeholders. Forming a coalition of influential leaders and employees will be crucial in modeling the desired changes and holding the organization accountable for progress. The resort must develop a clear vision for an inclusive and respectful workplace, effectively communicating this vision to align employees with the transformation goals. Removing obstacles, such as entrenched attitudes and outdated policies, and celebrating short-term wins, like the successful implementation of anti-discrimination policies, will help build momentum for change. Finally, anchoring these changes in the corporate culture through continuous reinforcement and integration into everyday practices will ensure their sustainability, ultimately rebuilding trust internally with employees and externally with customers and the public.

Implement the ADKAR Model to Foster Individual-Level Change and Reinforcement

The ADKAR Model emphasizes the importance of guiding employees through the stages of change—Awareness, Desire, Knowledge, Ability, and Reinforcement. The resort should use this model to create awareness of the critical need for change by educating employees about the impact of the lawsuit and the broader cultural issues that have contributed to the crisis. To foster a desire for change, the resort must actively engage employees through transparent communication, addressing their concerns and demonstrating leadership's commitment to creating a safe workplace. Providing knowledge through comprehensive training on diversity, inclusion, and respectful workplace behaviors will equip employees with the skills needed to contribute to the new culture. Enhancing employees' ability to implement these changes can be supported through practical resources such as coaching, mentorship programs, and hands-on workshops. To sustain these changes, the resort should establish reinforcement mechanisms, such as recognition programs, continuous monitoring, and regular feedback loops, ensuring that the new behaviors are deeply embedded and maintained over time.

Leverage Schein's Organizational Culture Model to Identify and Transform Cultural Dimensions

Schein's Organizational Culture Model—focusing on artifacts, espoused values, and basic underlying assumptions—can help the resort diagnose the root causes of its workplace issues. The resort should critically evaluate its visible artifacts, such as policies, dress codes, and communication styles, to identify elements reinforcing discriminatory practices. Aligning espoused values, such as the commitment to diversity and inclusivity, with actual practices is essential to bridge the gap between stated norms and employees' lived experiences. Addressing deeply ingrained assumptions, such as implicit biases and power imbalances, requires targeted interventions, including leadership training and promoting inclusive decision-making processes. By systematically transforming these cultural dimensions, the resort can create an environment that supports a positive and respectful workplace, thereby rebuilding internal trust and enhancing its public image.

Apply the Balanced Scorecard Approach to Align Strategy with Cultural and Operational Goals

The Balanced Scorecard approach provides a comprehensive framework for aligning the resort's strategic objectives with its response to the current crisis. From the financial perspective, the resort should strategically allocate resources towards training, policy revisions, and employee support initiatives, viewing these investments as critical to long-term reputation management and risk mitigation. The customer perspective emphasizes the need for transparent communication with external stakeholders, highlighting the resort's commitment to inclusivity and ethical standards. Enhancing internal processes by establishing robust reporting mechanisms and revising disciplinary procedures will help address discrimination and harassment effectively. The learning and growth perspective focuses on continuous employee development, leadership engagement, and fostering a culture of inclusivity through ongoing training and evaluation. By integrating these perspectives, the resort can rebuild its reputation and establish a resilient organizational culture supporting internal and external trust.

Integrate Strategic Planning Theory to Manage Legal, Reputational, and Operational Risks

Strategic Planning Theory highlights the importance of a proactive and integrated approach to managing the resort's legal and reputational risks. The resort should develop a comprehensive crisis management plan that addresses immediate legal obligations while positioning the organization for long-term cultural transformation. This includes engaging with legal advisors to navigate the lawsuit, enhancing public relations strategies to manage media exposure, and actively involving stakeholders in the change process through feedback and engagement initiatives. Strategic resource allocation should focus on areas that directly impact employee morale and customer satisfaction, ensuring that the resort's response is reactive and aligned with its broader mission and values. By adopting a strategic lens, the resort can navigate the complexities of the current crisis, maintain its competitive positioning, and emerge more robust and more committed to ethical practices.

CONCLUSION

These recommendations, informed by Kotter's 8-Step Change Model, the ADKAR framework, Schein's Organizational Culture Model, the Balanced Scorecard approach, and Strategic Planning Theory, provide some structured roadmap for the resort. Each theory has its strengths and weaknesses therefore, it is recommended that a framework be developed based on the construct of these theories for future research. By addressing the root causes of its workplace issues, implementing sustainable change initiatives, and aligning its strategic response with its organizational values, the resort can effectively manage the lawsuit, repair its reputation, and rebuild trust internally and externally. These efforts will mitigate future legal and reputational risks and position the resort as a leader in fostering an inclusive and respectful workplace.

REFERENCES

Agoncillo, K. M. U. (2023). An integrative action research on improving the marketing strategies of Kumintang Republik Restaurant in Club Balai Isabel Resort and Hotel in Talisay, Batangas towards consistent growth in monthly sales.

Ali, M. A., Zafar, U., Mahmood, A., & Nazim, M. (2021). The power of ADKAR change model in innovative technology acceptance under the moderating effect of culture and open innovation. LogForum, 17(4).

Ari, E. (2020). Human Resource Risks in the Hospitality Industry.

Chan, G. S. H., Tang, I. L. F., & Sou, A. H. K. (2017). An exploration of consumer complaint behavior towards the hotel industry: Case study in Macao. *International Journal of Marketing Studies*, 9(5), 56–76. DOI: 10.5539/ijms.v9n5p56

Chauhan, A. C., & Kularatne, I. (2021). REGAINING REPUTATION: AUCKLAND LUXURY HO S A STAKEHOLDERS' PERSPECTIVES. Rere Āwhio, 105.

Clark, A., Stenholm, S., Pentti, J., Salo, P., Lange, T., Török, E., Xu, T., Fabricius, J., Oksanen, T., Kivimäki, M., Vahtera, J., & Hulvej Rod, N. (2021). Workplace discrimination as risk factor for long-term sickness absence: Longitudinal analyses of onset and changes in workplace adversity. *PLoS One*, 16(8), e0255697. DOI: 10.1371/journal.pone.0255697 PMID: 34351965

Dhar, S., & Agarwal, S. (2023). Disputes at Work and the Perceived Effects of Social Assistance on Worker Health. *Journal for ReAttach Therapy and Developmental Diversities*, 6(9s), 455–463.

Dongrey, R., & Rokade, V. (2021). Assessing the effect of perceived diversity practices and psychological safety on contextual performance for sustainable workplace. *Sustainability (Basel)*, 13(21), 11653. DOI: 10.3390/su132111653

Einarsen, S. V., Hoel, H., Zapf, D., & Cooper, C. L. (2020). *Bullying and harassment in the workplace: Theory, research and practice*. CRC press. DOI: 10.1201/9780429462528

Fuchs, M. & others. (2022). Crisis communication and corporate social responsibility: A case study on IHG Hotels & Resorts and what organizations can learn from Covid-19 [PhD Thesis].

Fung, C., Tsui, B., & Hon, A. H. (2020). Crisis management: A case study of disease outbreak in the Metropark Hotel group. *Asia Pacific Journal of Tourism Research*, 25(10), 1062–1070. DOI: 10.1080/10941665.2020.1784245

Gikuhi, E. H. (2020). Crisis Management Strategies and Business Continuity for Star Rated Hotels in Kenya [PhD Thesis]. University of Nairobi.

Gupta, D., & Garg, J. (2020). Sexual harassment at workplace. International Journal of Legal Science and Innovation.

Hanif, S. (2023). Developing Organizational Change Capabilities using ADKAR model of Change: The Efficacy of Context Sensitive Training: Organizational Change using ADKAR Model. *Journal of Workplace Behavior*, 4(1), 81–93. DOI: 10.70580/jwb.04.01.0176

Hashmi, M. A., Jalees, T., Qabool, S., & Aziz, A. (2020). Consequences of Organizational Culture and the Mediating Role of Job Satisfaction and Turnover Intentions. Abasyn University Journal of Social Sciences, 13(1).

Huỳnh, Q. H., & Phan, T. T. V. (2022). The impacts of eco-friendly activities from resorts on guests' satisfaction. A case study of 5-star beach resorts in Da Nang, Vietnam [PhD Thesis]. FPTU \DJà N ng.

İnce, F. F., Öztürk, B., Kumkale, İ., Tüt, K., Karaca, O., & Sağlam, Ş. B. (2022). Evaluation of Contemporary Management Approaches in Hotel Businesses: A Qualitative Application in Four and Five Star Hotels. *Journal of Management and Economic Studies*, 4(1), 59–81. DOI: 10.26677/TR1010.2022.959

Joshi, A. M. (2022). A Study on work life balance of middle management employees with special reference to five star hotels in pune city [PhD Thesis]. Tilak Maharashtra Vidyapeeth, Pune.

Kanwal, H., & Van Hoye, G. (2020). Inconsistent organizational images of luxury hotels: Exploring employees' perceptions and dealing strategies. *Tourism Management Perspectives*, 36, 100738. DOI: 10.1016/j.tmp.2020.100738

KC. S. F. F. (2022). Discrimination law. Oxford University Press.

Kim, T., Peck, D., & Gee, B. (2020). *Race, gender and the double glass ceiling: An analysis of EEOC national workforce data*. Ascend Foundation. Ascendleadership-foundation. Org/Research/Race-Gender-Doubleglass-Ceiling.

Kleizen, B., Wynen, J., Boon, J., & De Roover, J. (2023). Bullying and harassment as a consequence of workplace change in the Australian civil service: Investigating the mediating role of satisfaction with change management. *Review of Public Personnel Administration*, 43(1), 56–79. DOI: 10.1177/0734371X211036732

Kong, A., Kwan, M., & Qiao, G. (2022). How to lead and deliver true hospitality to restore guest's confidence during COVID-19 pandemic? Case of InterContinental Zhuhai Hotel. MAIN CONFERENCE PROCEEDINGS, 141.

Lin, C.-Y., & Huang, C.-K. (2021). Employee turnover intentions and job performance from a planned change: The effects of an organizational learning culture and job satisfaction. *International Journal of Manpower*, 42(3), 409–423. DOI: 10.1108/IJM-08-2018-0281

Mamman-Daura, F. N., de Weever-Lista, E., & Bertrand, W. (2023). Best Practices for Sexual Harassment Training in the Workplace. In Real-World Solutions for Diversity, Strategic Change, and Organizational Development: Perspectives in Healthcare, Education, Business, and Technology (pp. 91–100). IGI Global. DOI: 10.4018/978-1-6684-8691-7.ch006

Mishra, B., & Mishra, J. (2015). Discrimination in the workplace. *Journal of Higher Education Theory and Practice*, 15(4).

Opoku, E. K., Wimalasena, L., & Sitko, R. (2024). Sexism and workplace interpersonal mistreatment in hospitality and tourism industry: A critical systematic literature review. *Tourism Management Perspectives*, 53, 101285. DOI: 10.1016/j.tmp.2024.101285

Ponnahennedige, U. (2021). Service recovery in luxury hotels and resorts in Sri Lanka.

Rehof, L. A. (2021). Guide to the Travaux Préparatoires of the United Nations Convention on the Elimination of all Forms of Discrimination against [). Brill.]. *Women*, 29, •••.

Robaki, G., Papaioannou, A., Yfantidou, G., Kourtesopoulou, A., & Dalakis, A. (2020). Organizational culture and business performance in tourism and hospitality industry: The case of A luxury tourist resort. Cultural and Tourism Innovation in the Digital Era: Sixth International IACuDiT Conference, Athens 2019, 533–542.

Robert, M., Giuliani, P., & Gurau, C. (2022). Implementing industry 4.0 real-time performance management systems: The case of Schneider Electric. *Production Planning and Control*, 33(2–3), 244–260. DOI: 10.1080/09537287.2020.1810761

Roscigno, V. J. (2019). Discrimination, sexual harassment, and the impact of workplace power. *Socius: Sociological Research for a Dynamic World*, 5, 2378023119853894. DOI: 10.1177/2378023119853894

Şanlıöz-Özgen, H. K., & Kozak, M. (2023). Customer experience in five-star hotel businesses: Is it an "experience" for customers? *Consumer Behavior in Tourism and Hospitality*, 18(3), 306–320. DOI: 10.1108/CBTH-11-2022-0197

Schneider, K. T., Swan, S., & Fitzgerald, L. F. (1997). Job-related and psychological effects of sexual harassment in the workplace: Empirical evidence from two organizations. *The Journal of Applied Psychology*, 82(3), 401–415. DOI: 10.1037/0021-9010.82.3.401 PMID: 9190147

Shivashankar, S., Mitra, I., Prakash, A., & Panwar, N. (2020). The effect of gender and work experience on psychological attributes at workplace. *Ushus Journal of Business Management*, 19(2), 1–19.

Stacy, M., Gross, G., & Adams, L. (2022). Applying organizational change theory to address the long-standing problem of harassment in medical education. *Teaching and Learning in Medicine*, 34(3), 313–321. DOI: 10.1080/10401334.2021.1954523 PMID: 34493134

Stosic, K., Dahlstrom, N., & Boonchai, C. (2023). Applying lessons from aviation safety culture in the hospitality industry: A review and road map. *International Journal of Occupational Safety and Ergonomics*, 29(3), 1025–1036. DOI: 10.1080/10803548.2022.2108638 PMID: 35915910

Tanjung, I. U., & Annisa, S. (2024). Comparative Analysis of Efforts to Prevent Sexual Violence and Legal Protection for Women in the Criminal Code and Sexual Violence Crime Law (UU NO. 12 of 2022). International Journal of Synergy in Law. *Criminal Justice*, 1(1), 37–50.

Thekkekara, J. V. & others. (2023). Change Management: A Survey of Literature in View of Analysing the Advantages of ADKAR Model. RGUHS Journal of Allied Health Sciences, 3(2).

Vada, S., Dupre, K., & Zhang, Y. (2023). Route tourism: A narrative literature review. *Current Issues in Tourism*, 26(6), 879–889. DOI: 10.1080/13683500.2022.2151420

Wanjiku. A. M. (2022). Strategic change management practices and performance of five star hotels in Nairobi County, Kenya [phd thesis]. Kenyatta University.

Worke, M. D., Koricha, Z. B., & Debelew, G. T. (2021). Coping strategies and perceived barriers of women hospitality workplace employees to sexual harassment in Bahir Dar city, Ethiopia: A grounded theory approach. *BMC Psychology*, 9(1), 1–14. DOI: 10.1186/s40359-021-00648-w PMID: 34530938

Chapter 5
Overcoming International Student Matriculation Challenges

Gregory Lloyd Stoller
https://orcid.org/0009-0001-6854-3007
Marymount University, USA

ABSTRACT

College tuition costs have increased more than two-fold, and the Educational Data Initiative anticipates an annual cost of $36,436 and a compound annual growth rate increase of 2% per year moving forward. According to the Journal of International Students, non-U.S. students are an attractive revenue source. However, due to geo-politics and immigration policies, the number of non-American students has declined in the past few years. Smaller colleges will be negatively affected. Global University is one such example. At one point, over one-third of its students were from outside the U.S., but 90% were still waiting to return to America to attend physically. This paper aims to analyze this university's challenges and then develop and discuss a comprehensive strategy as recommendations to Global University's leadership team.

INTRODUCTION

College tuition costs have increased more than two-fold, and the Educational Data Initiative anticipates an annual cost of $36,436 and a compound annual growth rate increase of 2% per year moving forward (Hanson et al., 2023). U.S. college enrollment has expanded from 3.97 million in 1965 to 14.09 million in 2024 and is expected to increase to nearly 15 million by 2031 (Korhonen, 2023). Some teenagers

DOI: 10.4018/979-8-3693-8562-3.ch005

posit that college is not worth the investment, as over 1/3 of undergraduates who complete college take jobs that do not require a degree (Allred, 2019).

Regardless of the cost, and according to the Journal of International Students, non-U.S. students are an attractive revenue source (Cantwell, 2015). However, due to geopolitics and immigration policies, the number of non-American students has declined in the past few years (Li et al., 2024). Smaller colleges will be negatively affected (Stowe et al., 2016). This change in student demographics impacts not only the finances of U.S. colleges but also the organizational culture and leadership strategies of the administration.

Global University is one such example. At one point, over one-third of its students were from outside the U.S., but 90% were still waiting to return to America to attend physically. This paper aims to analyze this university's challenges and then develop and discuss a comprehensive strategy as recommendations to Global University's leadership team (Burrell, 2024).

Background

Colleges generate revenue primarily from five sources: tuition/fees, philanthropy, endowment returns, athletics, and research grants. Tuition and fees only account for 1/5 of what some public universities earn (Kronk, 2019). However, the problem is further compounded by the fact that many universities need to discount their tuition to make it affordable for many U.S. students (Stoppel, 2023). Additionally, tuition often does not account for the overall cost of attendance (Ruggless, 2023).

To make college more affordable, according to the Journal of Student Financial Aid (Fuller, 2014), most undergraduate funding comprises grants, scholarships, and loans. However, as many non-American students are ineligible to receive financial aid from the U.S. Department of Education, they typically pay higher net tuition than their American brethren (Fuller, 2014). Also, according to Chen (2021), the U.S. has a comparative advantage in education worldwide, so is an attractive location for international students. In that same paper, the author states that revenue from international students was approximately 5% of total tuition 20 years ago. Now, depending on the school's location or whether it is public or private, it could account for as much as 30% (Chen, 2021).

In this same regard, for decades, colleges and universities have strategically woven both tuition fees and the notably higher charges levied on international students into the fabric of their annual financial planning (Chen, 2021). The landscape of student recruitment at colleges has changed, notably with a surge in Japanese students attending U.S. colleges 20 years ago. This trend has since seen a significant decline. Then, students from other countries, such as China, came. The trend seems to evolve from People's Republic toward India, Vietnam, and other African nations (Schwartz, 2023).

U.S. immigration policy has also changed considerably in the past three to five years, particularly during the transition from the Trump Administration to President Biden's. According to the Pew Research Center, one of President Biden's more extensive proposals involves immigration and, in some cases, will reverse (or change) Trump Era Policies (Krogstat et al., 2022). Many of these policies directly affect the ability of prospective students to receive F1 student visas (Chen et al., 2023). Additionally, before Covid, there was a 27% refusal rate for international students (Chen et al., 2023).

Problem Statement

As most university academic programs repeat themselves yearly, faculty and administrative staffing is relatively stable. For example, as one class graduates, a new cohort of students replaces it, ostensibly enrolling in similar classes. However, enrollment declines often negatively affect morale (Johnstone, 2002). More prominent, larger universities have the financial wherewithal to navigate fluctuating enrollments more quickly than smaller institutions (Martin, 2000). Martin describes having a pool of financial resources as akin to a portfolio investment problem. In any calendar year, some investments will perform well while others will do so poorly, but the composite return is what managers focus on the most. In a phrase, smaller universities need more financial resources on which to rely when enrollment shifts. Viewed through a financial lens, it is easier to determine the next strategic steps from a rate of return perspective, especially on the heels of a poor fiscal year.

Outside of finances, universities pride themselves on having a positive culture (Saleem et al., 2017). As a result, most people associate a university's ethos with student growth and development, intellectual pursuits, and political open-mindedness (Davids et al., 2019). However, the morale of faculty and staff is equally important. The impact of COVID-19 can still be felt by many university employees, coupled with lower pay, heavy workloads, and smaller raises than what could be earned in the private sector (Neuwirth et al., 2021).

Another source of financial stability comes from annual endowment spending. It is a recurring source of university funding (Baum et al., 2018). Traditionally, most university endowments spend 5% of their value annually (Green, 2009). If a university earns an excess of this amount, the spending will not materially impact the overall portfolio's value. Nonetheless, even the most skilled money managers occasionally miss their targets due to poor investment decisions or a volatile stock market. According to a Harvard Business School case study, endowment performance bears no correlation to the required and ongoing investments in the physical plant or technology (Viceira et al., 2021). We learned, "Institutions have more liabilities, higher debt service, and increasing expense without the revenue or the cash reserves to back them up" (Denneen et al., 2012, p. 1).

Evaluating a university's annual performance is as much associated with traditional financial metrics as protecting a school's culture. Legally, most universities are not-for-profit entities. However, from a practical standpoint, the sheer size of the average student body, the amount of faculty needed to support them, and the facilities and infrastructure needs of a college or university make it quite different from that of a traditional nonprofit organization. Most nonprofit organizations do not rely on different annual 'tuition' revenue sources.

Smaller nonprofit organizations depend more heavily on operating profitably and/or philanthropy. Regardless of the source of revenue and from Strategic Finance, "Without financial resources, there is no mission" (Epstein et al., 2011, p. 28). Observing the way universities function for over 20 years (Stoller, 2024), on countless occasions, decisions have been made to support the school's mission or maintain student morale rather than to maximize pecuniary gain. The decision-making has been strikingly similar for the past 15 years in observing how a Massachusetts-based nonprofit healthcare organization operates.

Despite their nonprofit status, universities can still engage in old-fashioned marketing combined with cutting-edge social media outreach to attract future students (Sintani et al., 2021). Brush (2022) states that community-oriented videos and communication positively affect decision-making. However, even in the age of "e" everything, where everyone is accessible via social media channels, student-to-student outreach is still the most effective way to connect with learners of any origin (Suresan et al., 2019). Additionally, in any academic year, faculty volunteer to complete prospective student outreach, often in different languages, and regularly meet with recently admitted undergraduate and graduate students before making a matriculation decision (Stoller, 2024).

LEADERSHIP THEORY: TRANSFORMATIONAL LEADERSHIP

Transformational leadership "refers to leaders who seek to create ideas and new perspectives to create a new path of growth and prosperity in front of the organization" (Korejan et al., 2016, p. 454). Spence (2023) defines leaders as being focused on knowledge acquisition facilitation and a bridge between students and faculty. This leadership approach is not limited to either academia or educational institutions and is often utilized in private-sector organizations. The Darden School applied transformational leadership to SingleStop in a business school case study (Isabella,

2015). In part, Hidayat (2023) also refers to it as Organizational Commitment and, when done well, encourages a professional attitude company-wide.

In academic circles, the challenge of applying any of these leadership, organizational culture, or change management theories is the extent to which the current U.S. immigration policies are unilaterally responsible for the inability of Global University's non-American students to enter the country successfully. Or is the inability of the students to return to the U.S. indicative of a more significant problem regarding university leadership and/or its institutional strategy? Assuming it is the latter, the first portion of implementation is to complete a cultural survey (Monzani, 2021). The Boston University Questrom School of Business Dean and her senior leadership team have invested much time and political capital, not only querying the faculty and staff about our opinions about the culture but also implementing new policies (and changing existing ones) based on the results of multiple surveys. The university then went one step further by launching an institutional-wide "Belonging and Culture Survey" in the spring of 2023 (Boston University, 2023). Many other educational leaders must also change their leadership approaches (Liou et al., 2017), reflecting the rapid demographic changes (Jaffe-Walter, 2018).

Using this same transformation leadership model, the next step is to lead by example, followed by valuing individual employees, challenging one's team, and being fully transparent (Grin, 2018). To the Questrom School of Business' credit, senior leadership queried faculty and staff in person and held live feedback sessions describing the survey results. What was particularly remarkable was having faculty and staff be in the same breakout rooms concurrently.

Global University should pursue a similar tack of putting all able-bodied heads together. Ferguson recently wrote about the merits of combining both populations—i.e., faculty and staff—as it relates to student self-efficacy using a Grounded Theory approach (Ferguson, 2021). Last year, Berkeley Economic Review, citing the U.S. Bureau of Labor Statistics, reported that the seasonally adjusted employee quit rate rose to 3%, the highest it has ever been (Zhang, 2023). A focus on culture is quintessential to retaining good employees (Jahya et al., 2020).

Another critical aspect of transformational leadership is transparency (Jiang, 2023). Transparency is not solely relegated to the adage of 'actions speak louder than words' but rather one of authenticity. Be yourself. This was born in their survey results of over 700 people and also discussed in a new book by Bill George entitled True North (George, 2010). In a separate podcast accompanying the book, George, Medtronic's former chairman and CEO, said the leadership pendulum has shifted from charisma to approachability.

Global University must confront its issue with returning students transparently and retreat from the secrecy of mahogany-paneled conference rooms where leaders whisper about non-American students' challenges in the U.S. The goal should be to host open forums, actively engage in dialogue, and promptly respond to emails and phone calls, embracing a culture of openness and accountability (Geelan, 2015). Additionally, proactive student engagement is particularly relevant to Global University's roots, given the long history of its multicultural environment (King, 2022).

ORGANIZATIONAL CULTURE THEORY: SCHEIN'S ORGANIZATIONAL CULTURE MODEL

Schein's Organizational Culture Model indicates three different layers to organizational culture: Artifacts and Behaviors, Espoused Values, and Underlying Beliefs (Schein, 1984). Indirectly applying this model, four years later, in 1988, Professor William Tierney published in the Journal of Higher Education that the most effective administrators instinctively know what actions they can take within the confines of their respective institutions (Tierney, 1988). Scott McKenna, in his 1998 dissertation entitled "The Application of a Corporate Cultural Change Model to an Institution of Higher Education," had an interesting comment when he opined that state legislators and their constituents are asking higher universities and colleges to operate more competitively, fiscally responsibly and be more student responsive. Tierney (2008) expanded the study and later commented in a full-length book that shared governance is a concept particularly unique to higher education organizations but not as a one-size-fits-all strategy (Lacatus, 2012).

As indicated previously, when enrollment begins to decline, university morale is often negatively impacted (Johnstone, 2002). What makes the application of Schein's model more interesting in this case is that the cultural artifacts, espoused values, and underlying beliefs are usually anticipated to originate from the organization itself. Applying the impact of *external* immigration policy changes is likely outside the original model's scope or any of the follow-on research cited above. When McKenna wrote that state legislators wanted universities to operate in a particular manner, this was more with the sentiment of guidance than required participation.

In the present day, the same cultural artifacts referenced by Johnstone have been affected in the case of Global University. They adapt in the best manner, although in almost uncharted territory. The problem has become even more acute based on the stark contrast between the past and the present: going from over 1/3rd of a healthily diverse university population to a situation now where 90% of students who have earned the right to be students there are unable to enter the United States let alone return to campus.

Beyond the words being spoken, transformational leadership theory recommends that top executives or administrators be transparent and lead with authenticity. By comparison, Schein's model focuses on values and beliefs. This epitomizes the phrase 'actions speak louder than words.' However, the onus is on university leadership to avoid operating impetuously (Whelehan, 2020). Before attempting to connect with its students using live stream technology such as Zoom, thereby signaling to people half a world away—who desperately want to resume their studies—that the university truly cares, leadership should determine the magnitude of the so-called problem.

From the students' perspective, many recognize that U.S. immigration policies have put them in a difficult position and that Global University is not directly responsible for anything that has transpired (Gándara et al., 2018). This outcome would require a much different implementation approach than might be necessary if most students are operating in a frenzied manner (Suárez-Orozco et al., 2020), such as becoming depressed or posting on social media in a venomous fashion. Assuming the students are calm and from a global identity standpoint (i.e., as suggested below in the Practical Problem-Solving Recommendations section), Global University can implement some short-term solutions to plant their flag internationally more effectively and, even more practically, maintain a meaningful relationship with their international students. Ideally, students can come to the US to study (Sarkodie-Mensah, 1998), but regardless of the location, U.S. educational training has high utility worldwide (Zhou, 2015). Additionally, overseas studying better improves global problem-solving and processing (Li et al., 2020), and many positively change their personalities as they learn to adapt to the local culture (Wada, 2014).

CHANGE MANAGEMENT THEORY: KOTTER'S EIGHT-STEP MODEL

The essence of Kotter's Eight-Step Model is to follow a tightly prescribed sequence of steps to effectively *deliver* organizational change: Urgency, Coalitions, Vision, Value Communication, Obstacle Removal, Short-term Wins, Change Building, and Anchoring. Applying these in higher education might be slightly more challenging, as most universities have hierarchal structures and a siloed mentality (Odiaga, 2021). Many people are merely motivated by the ability to engage and offer their opinions, as described in this two-year-old piece (Kang et al., 2022). Given the connection between international students and U.S. immigration policies, it is ironic to read how this theory is also being applied and adopted in Vietnamese private university learning environments (Thanh, 2022).

Viewed through an academic lens, it is essential to take a cue from Belliard and Dyjack (2009), who highlighted the importance of knowing one's culture before implementing this at Global University. Unthinkingly executing this model in almost a robotic fashion will potentially do more harm than good, as all aspects might not apply to the organization or certainly not in the unique position it finds itself in now (Alfaro Solano et al., 2019). For example, Urgency, Value Communication, and Obstacle Removal are apparent aspects that must be thoroughly discussed and implemented (Kerrigan, 2021).

These aspects of Kotter's model seem more appropriate for longer-term organizational change. Unless immigration policies become permanent such that neither Congress nor the U.S. Supreme Court can overturn them and the controlling party in the White House continues its approach over the next four years, one need not worry about building coalitions or engaging in change, that will be the least of anyone's problems (Anderson, 2013).

As it relates to Global University, a significant aspect of their situation is almost a crisis mentality rather than a complete overhaul of the organization itself (Scott, 2018). For example, according to Professor Kotter's (2007) original Harvard Business Review article, a 75% threshold is necessary to create a Sense of Urgency. Given the potential loss in revenue from 90% of your students being unable to return to the U.S., it is unclear if 75% of the faculty and staff could agree on anything strategically, as they would be more inclined to figure out how to stop any possible financial hemorrhaging, determine if furloughs are necessary, and what programs might need to either be consolidated or temporarily suspended (Baranik et al., 2019). Ideally, it would be preferable to avoid furloughing anyone and have the university absorb any short-term financial losses by temporarily increasing the endowment spending rate to keep different teams fully preserved (Adams-Prassl et al., 2020).

PRACTICAL PROBLEM-SOLVING RECOMMENDATIONS

These are some problem-solving recommendations for Global University:

a) Enlist Alumni Support: Graduates offer a unique vantage point through which younger students considering that same institution can receive direct personal reflections on what made a graduate's time on campus unique and memorable (Clark et al., 2015). Nothing is more effective in sales than word-of-mouth marketing (Barber, 2009). A report from Ireland comments that "reflective thinking, moral reasoning, and lifelong learning align with the institution's key performance indicators" (Gallo, 2017, p. 92). Although universities routinely change their specializations and programs to attract different faculty, positively affect their rankings, or increase their students' caliber, rarely does their mission or vision appreciably change (Sauntson et al., 2010). Because such interactions allow for a two-way discussion, they are far more helpful than material on the university's website or in popular publications like the Fiske or U.S. News and World Report guides (Bunzel, 2007).

b) <u>Change Recruitment Strategies</u>: Global University should change its student recruitment approaches. U.S. demographics change approximately every decade (Fischer et al., 2006). For example, according to the Census Bureau data, by 2030, all baby boomers will be over 60+ years of age and five years after that, adults will outnumber children for the first time in U.S. history (Vespa et al., 2018). Universities typically focus on the opposing end of the bell curve, the fat tails, yet their priorities are subject to regular adjustment. According to Inside Higher Ed, around 20% of Washington University's 8,000 undergraduates are limited-income or first-generation students (Mowreader, 2023). 'Bistro University' (with its real name masked) created a Diversity Fellow Program to recruit faculty and students more effectively (Coopwood, 2018). These are just two examples of areas that universities have been focusing on to increase the diversity of their student body and expand intellectual rigor on campus. Not surprisingly, and beyond student recruitment, this has paved the way for a plethora of new academic majors / minors, centers, and publication opportunities (Gibbs, 2023). A set of new priorities will, of course, emerge in the coming years, too.

New recruiting will likely require more aggressive financial aid support (Taylor et al., 2020). In sum, Global University will have to balance its new cohort of domestic students versus the overall profitability impact of possibly needing to provide more extensive financial support (Kotze et al., 2020). In 2019, Harvard University was fortunate to receive a $10 million grant for rural students, but not all universities are so lucky (Kerstetter, 2019).

c) <u>Open Satellite Campuses</u>: Should the exclusive immigration situation continue for a more extended period, another option could be opening satellite programs or even entire (temporary) campuses. This falls under the colloquial heading of 'if you cannot beat them, join them' (Rossi et al., 2020). Depending on the outcome of the 2024 election, immigration policies will likely become more inclusive or exclusive. If these policies become more inclusive, with a corresponding détente in geopolitics, university administrators should likely see a new wave of international applicants and matriculants (Nguyen et al., 2017). In the interim, a short-term solution might involve faculty traveling to regional international hubs to hold classes and augmenting the delivery with technologies like Zoom to provide distance learning.

Beyond generating revenue for the home university, according to Gardiner and Wat (2016), satellite programs or campuses often benefit the community and make graduates more attractive to local employers. Of course, more prominent universities will benefit from name recognition than smaller ones (Rothblatt, 2008). However, in accordance with the recommendations above, regardless of the scope of implementation, this might be a unique opportunity to engage with local alumni creatively. Additionally, if the alumnus / alumna is well-connected in a city, country, or region, he/she/they might be instrumental in future local student recruitment. Such satellite expansion need not be restricted to international locations, as evidenced by Illinois (Dickson et al., 2016).

d) Expand Program Offerings: A fourth option that Global University might consider is expanding its program offerings. Many universities have recently begun offering online MBAs, flexible residential learning options for working students, and/or one-year specialty master's programs. In 2023, referencing GMAC, Bristol wrote that 20% of graduate students considered enrolling in a shorter program than a full-time or evening MBA. If the challenges Global University faces more specifically relate to its undergraduate population, perhaps retooling its graduate offerings will be more successful.

Graduate programs also have the advantage of providing a longer duration for Optional Practical Training (OPT) once a student graduates, especially for those in the STEM fields (Chen et al., 2023). Online degrees also offer an alternative measure to increase revenue and profits (Scaringella, 2022).

e) Strategic Planning: The fifth and final recommendation should be viewed through a strategic planning lens. The inability of students to enter the United States may be fully connected to U.S. immigration policies (Quinn et al., 2017). Further, assuming that these immigration policies are an isolated incident, no additional action might be necessary save reaching out to a local, state, or federal government representative or university-employed (or private) lobbyists to ameliorate the situation. In the same vein of transparency, Boston University publishes its lobby guidelines publicly on its website (Boston University, 2024).

Examine enrollment numbers and other aspects of the university to see if there are any strategic planning miscues is recommended. For example, if this study uncovers systemic problems, two possible courses of action exist. On one end of the spectrum, although somewhat draconian, are personnel changes at various upper echelons of the university. The Chronicle of Higher Education reports that college presidents' average tenure has shrunk again and currently sits at less than six years (Jesse, 2023). In the corporate world, tenure is similar, albeit more directly correlated with profitability. 39% of S&P 500 CEOs serve between one to five years, and just under 30% between five and 10 (Jerotich, 2023). Provosts serve, on average, for three years (Kline, 2018) and admissions officers for even less time (Kingsbury, 2017).

Assuming core problems are uncovered, but from the opposite perspective, a more detailed university review would be required. This could be completed internally through a faculty and staff committee or an outside consulting firm (Iqbal et al., 2022). Regardless of the committee's composition, using a VRIO model is recommended, much as Heischmidt and Gordon (2020) applied these concepts to international study abroad programs through a recently published paper. To comprehensively complete and apply VRIO, it is essential to leverage the value, rarity, imitability, and organizational merits of Global University.

Outside of the problem-solving recommendations, there are also seven possible questions to be discussed and addressed:

a. Has the reduction in international students been a declining trend for several years, or are these particular admissions cycle an aberration—connected or not with the fact that 90% of its international students are currently unable to enter the country (Burrell, 2024)?
b. How does Global University compare with its peer institutions in its existing international student population or the inability of so many students at those institutions to (re) enter the U.S.?
c. Have the rankings for the University appreciably declined in the past few years?
d. Are students consistently turning down Global University in favor of similar competing schools?
e. Has there been a widespread departure of faculty from the same department or academic unit?
f. Have job placement statistics materially changed for domestic or international students?
g. Have there been any accreditation issues?

Taking everything into account, the final step in the overall planning process is expanding the VRIO analysis. This combines practical problem-solving recommendations with leadership, organizational culture, and change management theories. Cleavenger (2013) put it best in one of the final paragraphs of his study, indicating that change will happen over a long period and require direct and indirect interactions to convert employees into vested partners. It will likely not be a smooth transition. Nevertheless, do keep in mind that anything is possible. As documented in a now-famous initiative, the author described how Northeastern University executed one of the best rankings turnarounds in higher education, moving up 42 spots in over eight years and ultimately breaking into the top 100 two years later (Gowen et al., 2021).

Of course, the most pressing issue for Global University now is the immigration policy debate and its direct implications (Burrell, 2024). Whereas well-envisioned and implemented strategic planning can affect meaningful change to be fully implemented and successful, companies, organizations, and individuals are often at the behest of their domestic government and its relations with other countries across the globe (Puck et al., 2013). Unfortunately, Sino-U.S. relations are a reasonably current example. Domestically, China is trying to revive its economy through several government and social measures. On January 1, 2016, it eliminated its one-child policy. Less than five years later, the government incentivized couples to give birth to more children (Siqi, 2023). That is a domestic policy, however. The international side of China's equation involves an aptly entitled report, "How the U.S.-China Trade War Affected the Rest of the World" (Gorman, 2022).

The chicken and egg debate notwithstanding, China's end result is dramatically negative and affects economic and political policies worldwide. The U.S. immigration policy debate could be viewed through a similar lens. Although immigration is by definition an international issue, domestically, most regard it as an question that's being myopically legislated through White House policies, congressional debate, and presidential Executive Orders. No one wants to experience educational xenophobia as motivations are negatively affected (Mok et al., 2024).

AREAS FOR FUTURE RESEARCH

Areas for future research might include a study of U.S. immigration policy. Gubernskaya et al. (2017) wrote about how immigration policy affects the family unit (Pierce et al., 2018) and discussed former President Trump's policies and possible future impacts. This issue will continue to be debated up until the 2024 election.

A second area of future research is university crisis management. Due to the Israeli / Palestinian conflict, university presidents and the campus at large are experiencing pressures related to free speech, academic freedom, and religious protections. Rollo addressed this differently (2020), while Moerschell discussed alignment challenges (2020).

A third area is enhanced faculty training for international students. Cultural competence fluency is essential (Nieto et al., 2010), as is understanding and respecting issues of identity (Bond, 2019). The more insight and knowledge faculty can absorb, the better the classroom and educational experience will be for all students worldwide.

To conclude this paper; there are two pertinent factors to highlight. First, international students added $45 billion to the U.S. economy in 2018 (Newton, 2024). The second, according to the Journal of Public Economics, is that once they graduate, and should these students remain in the U.S., the local supply of skilled workers increases by 0.23%, with most finding their first job within the state hosting their alma mater (Beine et al., 2023). This further positively boosts the U.S. economy and may allow students involuntarily forced to leave home to build a better future (Arar, 2020). In conclusion, an annual, sustained and robust matriculation of international students who become graduates and can stay in the U.S. yields comprehensive benefits across the board.

REFERENCES

Adams-Prassl, A., Boneva, T., Golin, M., & Rauh, C. (2020). Furloughing. *Fiscal Studies*, 41(3), 591–622. DOI: 10.1111/1475-5890.12242 PMID: 33362312

Alfaro Solano, M. J., & Preuß, M. (2019). *An alternative approach to resistance to change and leadership and its resulting development of Kotter's change models.* (Independent thesis Advanced level, Linnaeus University, School of Business and Economics, Department of Organisation and Entrepreneurship).

Allred, A. (2019). What if your university tuition was based on your future salary? *Harvard Business Review*. https://hbr.org/2019/10/what-if-your-university-tuition-was-based-on-your-future-salary. Digital article, H056AR. US Anderson, B. (2013). *Us and them?: The dangerous politics of immigration control.* (OUP Oxford).

Arar, K. (2020). *School leadership for refugees' education: Social justice leadership for immigrant, migrants and refugees.* Routledge. DOI: 10.4324/9780429021770

Baranik, L. E., Cheung, J. H., Sinclair, R. R., & Lance, C. E. (2019). What happens when employees are furloughed? A resource loss perspective. *Journal of Career Development*, 46(4), 381–394. DOI: 10.1177/0894845318763880

Barber, P., & Wallace, L. (2009). The power of word-of-mouth marketing. *American Libraries*, 40(11), 36–39.

Baum, S., & Lee, V. (2018). Understanding endowments. *Urban Institute. April.*

Beine, M., Peri, G., & Raux, M. (2023). International college students' impact on the skilled labor supply. *Journal of Public Economics*, 223, 104917. DOI: 10.1016/j.jpubeco.2023.104917

Belliard, J. C. (2009). Applying Kotter's model of change to sustaining community engaged scholarship within a school of public health and its parent university. *Metropolitan Universities*, 20(2), 119–138.

Bier, D. J. (2020). The facts about optional practical training (OPT) for foreign students. *Policy Commons, 20.500.12592/18qwk8.*

Bond, B. (2019). International students: Language, culture and the 'performance of identity'. *Teaching in Higher Education*, 24(5), 649–665. DOI: 10.1080/13562517.2019.1593129

Boston University. (2023). Belonging & culture survey. *Boston University*. https://www.bu.edu/belonging-culture-survey/committee/

Boston University. (2024). Lobbying guidelines. Lobbying Guidelines | Federal Relations. *Boston University*. https://www.bu.edu/federal/bu-community/working-with-dc/lobbying-guidelines/

Bristol, E. J. (2023). *Developing specialized master's programs in business schools: The convergence of mission and markets* (Doctoral dissertation, University of Massachusetts Boston).

Brush, M. A. (2022). *Understanding declining international graduate student yield at a private university* (Doctoral dissertation, Northeastern University).

Bunzel, D. L. (2007). Universities sell their brands. *Journal of Product and Brand Management*, 16(2), 152–153. DOI: 10.1108/10610420710740034

Burrell, D. (2024). Final case study assignment – 16-page double spaced paper- you are to only pick one. *Canvas*. https://marymount.instructure.com/courses/30592/assignments/336448

Cantwell, B. (2019). Are international students cash cows? Examining the relationship between new international undergraduate enrollments and institutional revenue at public colleges and universities in the U.S. *Journal of International Students*, 5(4), 512–525. DOI: 10.32674/jis.v5i4.412

Chen, M. (2021). The impact of international students on U.S. colleges: Higher education as a service export. *SSRN*, 3859798, •••. https://papers.ssrn.com/sol3/papers.cfm?abstract_id=3859798

Chen, M., Howell, J., & Smith, J. (2023). Best and brightest? The impact of student visa restrictiveness on who attends college in the U.S. *Labour Economics*, 84, 102385. DOI: 10.1016/j.labeco.2023.102385

Clark, G., Marsden, R., Whyatt, J. D., Thompson, L., & Walker, M. (2015). 'It's everything else you do…': Alumni views on extracurricular activities and employability. *Active Learning in Higher Education*, 16(2), 133–147. DOI: 10.1177/1469787415574050

Cleavenger, D. J., & Munyon, T. P. (2013). It's how you frame it: Transformational leadership and the meaning of work. *Business Horizons*, 56(3), 351–360. DOI: 10.1016/j.bushor.2013.01.002

Coopwood, K.Sr, & Augustine, S. S. (2018). Engaging faculty in campus transformation: The diversity fellows program. In *Campus Diversity Triumphs: Valleys of Hope* (pp. 27–43). Emerald Publishing Limited. DOI: 10.1108/S1479-364420180000020002

Davids, N., & Waghid, Y. (2019). *Universities, pedagogical encounters, openness, and free speech: Reconfiguring democratic education.* Rowman & Littlefield.

Denneen, J., & Dretler, T. (2012). The financially sustainable university. *Bain & Company, 12.*

Dewar, C. (2023). Leading with authenticity: A conversation with Bill George. *McKinsey & Company.* https://www.mckinsey.com/capabilities/strategy-and-corporate-finance/our-insights/leading-with-authenticity-a-conversation-with-bill-george

Dickson, E. B., & Whitehurst, R. (2016). Integrated project planning in a construction management environment: The College of DuPage's Naperville, Illinois, satellite campus. *Planning for Higher Education,* 45(1), 160.

Epstein, M. J., & McFarlan, F. W. (2011). Measuring the efficiency and effectiveness of a nonprofit's performance. *Strategic Finance,* 93(4), 27.

Ferguson, S. N. (2021). Effects of faculty and staff connectedness on student self-efficacy. *The Journal of Scholarship of Teaching and Learning,* 21(2). Advance online publication. DOI: 10.14434/josotl.v21i2.28597

Fischer, C. S., & Hout, M. (2006). *Century of difference: How America changed in the last one hundred years.* Russell Sage Foundation.

Fuller, M. B. (2014). A history of financial aid to students. *Journal of Student Financial Aid,* 44(1), 4. DOI: 10.55504/0884-9153.1078

Gallo, M. L. (2018). How are graduates and alumni featured in university strategic plans? Lessons from Ireland. *Perspectives: Policy and Practice in Higher Education,* 22(3), 92–97.

Gándara, P., & Ee, J. (2018). U.S. immigration enforcement policy and its impact on teaching and learning in the nation's schools. *Escholarship.org,* p. 1.

Geelan, D. R. (2015). Open forums for teaching in an open online world. *International Journal of Continuing Engineering Education and Lifelong Learning,* 25(1), 28–38. DOI: 10.1504/IJCEELL.2015.066545

George, B. (2010). *True north: Discover your authentic leadership* (Vol. 143). John Wiley & Sons.

Gibbs, C., Achebe, N., Johnson, B., Nwaiche, C., & Ortiz, D. V. (2023). Constructing college-level diversity, equity, and inclusion (DEI) minors—Moving from performative to transformative DEI. *The Radical Teacher,* 127, 41–50. DOI: 10.5195/rt.2023.977

Gorman, L. (2022). *How the U.S.-China trade war affected the rest of the world.* National Bureau of Economic Research.

Gowen, G. H., & Hengesteg, P. S. (2021). Gaming the rankings: Richard Freeland and the dramatic rise of Northeastern University. In *The Marketisation of Higher Education: Concepts, Cases, and Criticisms* (pp. 235–265). Springer International Publishing. DOI: 10.1007/978-3-030-67441-0_11

Green, S. L. (2009). Why 5 percent? An analysis of optimal endowment spending rates. *Studies in Economics and Finance*, 26(4), 216–231. DOI: 10.1108/10867370910995681

Grin, J., Hassink, J., Karadzic, V., & Moors, E. H. (2018). Transformative leadership and contextual change. *Sustainability (Basel)*, 10(7), 2159. DOI: 10.3390/su10072159

Gubernskaya, Z., & Dreby, J. (2017). U.S. immigration policy and the case for family unity. *Journal on Migration and Human Security*, 5(2), 417–430. DOI: 10.1177/233150241700500210

Hanson, M., & Checked, F. (2023). Average cost of college [2023]: yearly tuition + expenses. *Education Data Initiative.* https://educationdata.org/average-cost-of-college

Heischmidt, K. A., & Gordon, P. (2020). Different strategic planning models: Considerations for international study programs. *Journal of Higher Education Theory and Practice*, 20(15), 27–35.

Hidayat, S., Affandi, N., Eryanto, H., & Hidayat, D. R. (2023). Higher Education Governance and Lecturer Performance: The Role of Leadership, Commitment, and Culture. *Journal of Higher Education Theory and Practice*, 23(6).

Iqbal, G. M. D., Ha, L., Anoruo, E., Gregory, S., & Rosenberger, J. M. (2022). Assigning faculty to university committees by considering priorities: an optimization approach. In *IIE Annual Conference. Proceedings* (pp. 1–6). Institute of Industrial and Systems Engineers (IISE).

Isabella, L. A., Yemen, G., & Hepler, K. (2015). So long to SingleStop? (A). Charlottesville: *Darden Graduate School of Business Administration.* UV7051-PDF-ENG.

Jaffe-Walter, R. (2018). Leading in the context of immigration: Cultivating collective responsibility for recently arrived immigrant students. *Theory into Practice*, 57(2), 147–153. DOI: 10.1080/00405841.2018.1426934

Jahya, A., Azlin, S. N. I., Othman, R., & Romaiha, N. R. (2020). Turnover intention among Gen-Y: The role of training and development, compensation and organizational culture. *International Journal of Academic Research in Business & Social Sciences*, 10(10), 765–782. DOI: 10.6007/IJARBSS/v10-i10/7975

Jerotich, C., & Chen, J. (2023). CEO tenure rates. The Harvard law school forum on corporate governance. *Harvard Law School*. https://corpgov.law.harvard.edu/2023/08/04/ceo-tenure-rates-2/#:~:text=The%20data%20reveals%2039%25%20of,for%2010%20years%20or%20less

Jesse, D. (2023). College presidents are less experienced than ever — and eyeing the exit. *Chronicle.com*. https://www.chronicle.com/article/college-presidents-are-less-experienced-than-ever-and-eyeing-the-exit

Jiang, H., & Shen, H. (2023). Toward a relational theory of employee engagement: Understanding authenticity, transparency, and employee behaviors. *International Journal of Business Communication*, 60(3), 948–975. DOI: 10.1177/2329488420954236

Johnstone, B. (2002). Challenges of financial austerity: Imperatives and limitations of revenue diversification in higher education. *Wales Journal of Education*, 11(1), 18–36. DOI: 10.16922/wje.11.1.3

Kang, S. P., Chen, Y., Svihla, V., Gallup, A., Ferris, K., & Datye, A. K. (2022). Guiding change in higher education: An emergent, iterative application of Kotter's change model. *Studies in Higher Education*, 47(2), 270–289. DOI: 10.1080/03075079.2020.1741540

Kerrigan, T. (2021). *An exploratory study of management perceptions of the role of Kotter's urgency in creating a future change agenda* (Doctoral dissertation, Dublin, National College of Ireland).

Kerstetter, J. (2019). $10m grant supports Harvard's work within rural schools. *Harvard Gazette*. https://news.harvard.edu/gazette/story/2019/02/10m-grant-supports-harvards-work-within-rural-schools/

King, H. D. (2022). *A case study exploring how culturally intelligent transformational higher education leaders foster organizational innovations in a multicultural student environment* (Doctoral dissertation, Indiana Institute of Technology).

Kingsbury, K. (2017). Secret lives of admissions officers. *The Daily Beast*. https://www.thedailybeast.com/secret-lives-of-admissions-officers

Kline, M. (2018). Survey results: Short tenure for higher ed's top leaders. *CUPA*. https://www.cupahr.org/blog/survey-results-administrators/#:~:text=Data%20from%20CUPA%2DHR%27s%202017,three%20years%20in%20their%20position

Korejan, M. M., & Shahbazi, H. (2016). An analysis of the transformational leadership theory. *Revue des Sciences Fondamentales et Appliquées*, 8(3), 452–461. DOI: 10.4314/jfas.v8i3s.192

Korhonen, V. (2023, August 29). U.S. college enrollment and forecast 1965-2031. *Statista*. https://www.statista.com/statistics/183995/us-college-enrollment-and-projections-in-public-and-private-institutions/

Kotter, J. P. (2007). *Leading change: Why transformation efforts fail. Harvard Business Review*. March-April Magazine.

Kotze, F. P., & Ferreira, E. J. (2020). Financial sustainability and profitability of high performance training centres. *S.A. Journal for Research in Sport Physical Education and Recreation*, 42(2), 77–94.

Krogstad, J. M. (2022, January 11). Key facts about U.S. immigration policies and Biden's proposed changes. *Pew Research Center*. https://www.pewresearch.org/short-reads/2022/01/11/key-facts-about-u-s-immigration-policies-and-bidens-proposed-changes/

Kronk, H. (2019). How do colleges and universities earn revenue? 2019 update. *eLearningInside News*. https://news.elearninginside.com/how-do-colleges-and-universities-earn-revenue-2019-update/

Lacatus, M. L. (2013). Organizational culture in contemporary university. *Procedia: Social and Behavioral Sciences*, 76, 421–425. DOI: 10.1016/j.sbspro.2013.04.139

Li, J., Wang, S., Zheng, H., Pan, D., Wang, Y., & Yang, Y. (2020). Overseas study experience and global processing style. *Current Psychology (New Brunswick, N.J.)*, 39(3), 913–918. DOI: 10.1007/s12144-018-9805-y

Li, Y., Dai, S., Zhou, X., He, K., & Sun, X. (2024). Chinese students' attitudes towards U.S. universities in the U.S.–China conflict. *Journal of Consumer Behaviour*, 23(2), 929–938. DOI: 10.1002/cb.2241

Liou, D. D., & Hermanns, C. (2017). Preparing transformative leaders for diversity, immigration, and equitable expectations for school-wide excellence. *International Journal of Educational Management*, 31(5), 661–678. DOI: 10.1108/IJEM-10-2016-0227

Martin, R. E. (2000). Enrollment management as a portfolio investment problem. *College and University*, 76(1), 25.

McKenna, S. M. (1998). *The application of a corporate cultural change model to an institution of higher education*. (Doctoral dissertation, University of Connecticut).

Moerschell, L., & Novak, S. S. (2020). Managing crisis in a university setting: The challenge of alignment. *Journal of Contingencies and Crisis Management*, 28(1), 30–40. DOI: 10.1111/1468-5973.12266

Mok, K. H., Shen, W., & Gu, F. (2024). The impact of geopolitics on international student mobility: The Chinese students' perspective. *Higher Education Quarterly*, 78(4), 12509. DOI: 10.1111/hequ.12509

Monzani, L., Seijts, G. H., & Crossan, M. M. (2021). Character matters: The network structure of leader character and its relation to follower positive outcomes. *PLoS One*, 16(9), e0255940. DOI: 10.1371/journal.pone.0255940 PMID: 34469454

Mowreader, A. (2023). How a WashU success center will serve first-gen, limited-income students. *Inside Higher Ed | Higher Education News, Events and Jobs*. https://www.insidehighered.com/news/student-success/college-experience/2023/04/12/program-launch-success-center-first-gen-limited

Neuwirth, L. S., Jović, S., & Mukherji, B. R. (2021). Reimagining higher education during and post-COVID-19: Challenges and opportunities. *Journal of Adult and Continuing Education*, 27(2), 141–156. DOI: 10.1177/1477971420947738

Newton, B. (2024). Economic impact of international students: The power of international education. *IIE*. https://www.iie.org/research-initiatives/open-doors/economic-impact-of-international-students/

Nguyen, C., & Kebede, M. (2017). Immigrant students in the Trump era: What we know and do not know. *Educational Policy*, 31(6), 716–742. DOI: 10.1177/0895904817723740

Nieto, C., & Zoller Booth, M. (2010). Cultural competence: Its influence on the teaching and learning of international students. *Journal of Studies in International Education*, 14(4), 406–425. DOI: 10.1177/1028315309337929

Odiaga, J., Guglielmo, M. J., Catrambone, C., Gierlowski, T., Bruti, C., Richter, L., & Miller, J. (2021). Kotter's change model in higher education: Transforming siloed education to a culture of interprofessionalism. *Journal of Organizational Culture. Communications and Conflict*, 25(2), 1–7.

Pierce, S., Bolter, J., & Selee, A. (2018). U.S. immigration policy under Trump: Deep changes and lasting impacts. *Migration Policy Institute*, 9, 1–24.

Puck, J. F., Rogers, H., & Mohr, A. T. (2013). Flying under the radar: Foreign firm visibility and the efficacy of political strategies in emerging economies. *International Business Review*, 22(6), 1021–1033. DOI: 10.1016/j.ibusrev.2013.02.005

Quinn, R., Hopkins, M., & García Bedolla, L. (2017). The politics of immigration and education. *Educational Policy*, 31(6), 707–715. DOI: 10.1177/0895904817725729

Rollo, J. M., & Zdziarski, E. L. (2020). Developing a crisis management plan. In *Campus Crisis Management* (pp. 67–85). Routledge. DOI: 10.4324/9780429321658-4

Rossi, F., & Goglio, V. (2020). Satellite university campuses and economic development in peripheral regions. *Studies in Higher Education*, 45(1), 34–54. DOI: 10.1080/03075079.2018.1506917

Rothblatt, S. (2008). Global branding and the celebrity university. *Liberal Education*, 94(4), 26–33.

Ruggless, M. A. (2023). *Exploring the development and decision-making process of cost of attendance at American colleges and universities* (Doctoral dissertation, Saint Louis University).

Saleem, S., Moosa, K., Imam, A., & Ahmed Khan, R. (2017). Service quality and student satisfaction: The moderating role of university culture, reputation and price in education sector of pakistan. *Iranian Journal of Management Studies*, 10(1), 237–258.

Sarkodie-Mensah, K. (1998). International students in the US: Trends, cultural adjustments, and solutions for a better experience. *Journal of Education for Library and Information Science*, 39(3), 214–222. DOI: 10.2307/40324159

Sauntson, H., & Morrish, L. (2010). Vision, values and international excellence: The 'products' that university mission statements sell to students. In *The marketisation of higher education and the student as consumer* (pp. 87–99). Routledge.

Scaringella, L., Górska, A., Calderon, D., & Benitez, J. (2022). Should we teach in hybrid mode or fully online? A theory and empirical investigation on the service–profit chain in MBAs. *Information & Management*, 59(1), 103573. DOI: 10.1016/j.im.2021.103573

Schein, E. H. (1984). Coming to a new awareness of organizational culture. *Sloan Management Review*, 25(2), 3–16.

Schwartz, N. (2023). *4 charts explaining international enrollment trends*. Education Dive.

Scott, P. (2018). *The crisis of the university*. Routledge. DOI: 10.4324/9780429446870

Sintani, L., Fransisca, Y., Anjarini, A. D., & Mulyapradana, A. (2021). Identification of the effectiveness of higher education marketing strategies using social media. *International Research Journal of Management. IT and Social Sciences*, 9(1), 1–9.

Siqi, J. (2023). China unveils new childbirth support as population on verge of shrinking. South *China Morning Post*. https://www.scmp.com/economy/china-economy/article/3206420/china-unveils-new-childbirth-incentives-population-growth-set-turn-negative# Spence, E. D. (2023). *Transformational leadership among chairs of academic departments in U.S. colleges and universities* (Doctoral dissertation, Trident University International).

Stoller, G. (2024). Questrom learning community with Greg Stoller. *YouTube*. Retrieved January 20, 2024, from https://www.youtube.com/watch?v=B_f8m3U0OJ4

Stoppel, C. A. (2023). *What is influencing net tuition revenue?: A panel data study of public doctoral universities* (Doctoral dissertation, University of Kansas).

Stowe, K., & Komasara, D. (2016). An analysis of closed colleges and universities. *Planning for Higher Education*, 44(4), 79.

Suárez-Orozco, C., & López Hernández, G. (2020). "Waking up every day with the worry": A mixed-methods study of anxiety in undocumented Latinx college students. *Frontiers in Psychiatry*, 11, 568167. DOI: 10.3389/fpsyt.2020.568167 PMID: 33281641

Suresan, V., Jnaneswar, A., Swati, S. P., Jha, K., Goutham, B. S., & Kumar, G. (2019). The impact of outreach programs on academics development, personal development and civic responsibilities of dental students in Bhubaneswar city. *Journal of Education and Health Promotion*, 8(1), 188. DOI: 10.4103/jehp.jehp_56_19 PMID: 31867373

Taylor, Z. W., & Bicak, I. (2020). First-generation college student financial aid: Results from a national financial aid jargon survey. *The College Student Affairs Journal*, 38(1), 91–109. DOI: 10.1353/csj.2020.0006

Thanh, U. P. T. (2022). The application of Kotter's model of change in higher education: A case study in Vietnam private universities. *International Journal of Social Science And Human Research*, 05(1), 1. DOI: 10.47191/ijsshr/v5-i1-01

Tierney, W. G. (1988). Organizational culture in higher education: Defining the essentials. *The Journal of Higher Education*, 59(1), 2–21. DOI: 10.1080/00221546.1988.11778301

Tierney, W. G. (2008). *The impact of culture on organizational decision-making: Theory and practice in higher education* (1st ed.). Routledge., DOI: 10.4324/9781003447887

Vespa, J. E., Armstrong, D. M., & Medina, L. (2018). Demographic turning points for the United States: Population projections for 2020 to 2060 (pp. 25–1144). Washington, DC: U.S. Department of Commerce, Economics and Statistics Administration, *U.S. Census Bureau.*

Viceira, Luis M., Emily R. McComb, & Dean Xu. (2021). Modern endowment management: Paula Volent and the Bowdoin endowment. *Harvard Business School Case 221–101.*

Wada, M. (2014). *Studying Overseas: Friends, School and Life*(Doctoral dissertation,   ).

Watt, H., & Gardiner, R. (2016). Satellite programmes: Barriers and enablers for student success. Wellington, New Zealand: *Ako Aotearoa* (National Centre for Tertiary Teaching Excellence).

Whelehan, D. F. (2020). Students as partners: A model to promote student engagement in post-COVID-19 teaching and learning. *All Ireland Journal of Higher Education, 12*(3).

Zhang, F. (2023). Why is everyone quitting their jobs? *Berkeley Economic Review.* https://econreview.berkeley.edu/why-is-everyone-quitting-their-jobs/

Zhou, J. (2015). International students' motivation to pursue and complete a Ph. D. in the US. *Higher Education*, 69(5), 719–733. DOI: 10.1007/s10734-014-9802-5

Chapter 6
Cybersecure Futures:
Bridging AI, Employment, and the Digital Divide

Sharon L. Burton
https://orcid.org/0000-0003-1653-9783
Embry-Riddle Aeronautical University, USA

ABSTRACT

This qualitative study, employing a literature review and case study design, investigates the complex interplay between minimum wage policies, STEM field transitions, and the digital divide. It examines how these factors influence employment dynamics and economic stability. It focuses on the barriers displaced workers face in accessing STEM education and employment, exacerbated by inadequate digital infrastructure in underserved areas. The research highlights the economic and technological impacts on workers, emphasizing the need for adaptable policies and support systems. The study proposes targeted interventions to foster a more inclusive workforce and resilient economy by addressing research gaps. The findings underscore the significance of integrating digital literacy, tailored educational programs, and robust mental health support into policy frameworks. This research provides actionable insights for policymakers, educators, and industry leaders to mitigate economic disparities and enhance workforce adaptability.

INTRODUCTION, PROBLEM, AND INDUSTRY CHALLENGES

This research is driven by the urgent need to address the complex interplay between minimum wage policies, STEM field transitions, and the digital divide, which significantly influence employment dynamics and economic stability. The introduction of minimum wage legislation aims to address income inequality

DOI: 10.4018/979-8-3693-8562-3.ch006

and enhance living standards Clemens & Wither, 2019). However, the economic landscape presents complexities where such well-intended policies often lead to unintended consequences, including layoffs, job displacements, and exacerbated income inequality. According to a report by the U.S. Congressional Office (2024), increasing the minimum wage would lead to higher employment costs for low-wage workers. Consequently, this could prompt some employers to reduce their workforce compared to what would be expected with a lower minimum wage.

Additionally, research indicates that sudden wage hikes may force small businesses to downsize or close altogether, further contributing to job insecurity and economic instability (Lefebvre, 2024). These outcomes can inadvertently widen the income gap, as those who lose employment or cannot find jobs are left worse off despite the policy's intention to improve living standards (Clemens & Wither, 2019). Therefore, it is crucial to carefully consider and implement minimum wage policies alongside supportive measures that mitigate these adverse effects and promote equitable economic growth (Clemens & Wither, 2019; Lefebvre, 2024).

STEM education and employment are increasingly recognized as potential solutions for displaced workers in a job market that demands technological and scientific skills. Despite substantial investments and educational reforms, interest and enrollment in STEM careers remain low, particularly among underrepresented groups (Chen et al., 2024). This chapter examines how laid-off workers, despite facing challenges such as low STEM interest and enrollment, can transition into STEM fields as a viable solution in a labor market increasingly driven by technology (Chen et al., 2024). Numerous regions worldwide have emphasized the importance of STEM education in advancing global competitiveness and economic growth, highlighting the critical role of these fields in the modern workforce (Arora, 2023).

Another critical challenge is the digital divide, particularly in underprivileged and rural communities, where inadequate internet connectivity and frequent blackouts hinder access to educational resources and online training programs (Brenya, 2023). This barrier is especially significant as it limits the ability of individuals in these communities to fully participate in the digital economy and pursue STEM education and careers (Crawford & Serhal, 2020). Without reliable internet access, efforts to retrain and educate workers are severely compromised, exacerbating existing inequalities and preventing these communities from accessing essential resources and opportunities (Jain et al., 2024).

Internet blackouts further expand the discussion of barriers beyond economic policies to include infrastructural challenges, particularly in underprivileged and rural areas where access to educational resources and online training programs is already limited (Monaco et al., 2024). This issue exacerbates existing inequalities and hinders efforts to bridge the gap between different socioeconomic groups. Just as minimum wage policies may lead to unintended consequences like layoffs, internet blackouts further disadvantage marginalized communities, preventing them from accessing the educational and professional opportunities needed to thrive in a technologically driven economy (Li et al., 2024).

This chapter emphasizes that addressing income inequality and enhancing living standards through minimum wage increases is insufficient if economic and infrastructural barriers like internet accessibility are not addressed (Fu et al., 2024). A holistic approach is required to promote an inclusive workforce capable of meeting the demands of an evolving job market (Sumagaysay & Agrawal, 2023). This research aims to comprehensively understand these interconnected challenges and propose viable solutions. By examining the ramifications of minimum wage laws, assessing the potential of STEM fields as sustainable employment opportunities, and highlighting the critical role of digital accessibility, this chapter develops strategies that address immediate and long-term workforce needs.

The ultimate goal of this chapter is to formulate policy recommendations that balance improving living standards with economic and technological realities. The insights from this study are intended to guide the development of strategies that mitigate the adverse effects of minimum wage increases while harnessing technological advancements to foster economic stability and growth. The remainder of this chapter will delve into the background, problem statement, methodology, applicable theories, literature review, recommendations, conclusions, solutions, and future research directions.

Background

The background section of this chapter establishes this study's context and significance, outlining historical developments and theoretical frameworks that situate the research within broader academic discussions (Dyke, 2022; Hazari, 2024). It identifies existing literature gaps, justifying the study's necessity and potential impact while clarifying key concepts and research questions. By reviewing related works and setting a theoretical foundation, this section enhances the credibility of the research (Dyke, 2022; Hazari, 2024). It engages readers by linking the study to more extensive, ongoing conversations in the field.

The discourse surrounding minimum wage policies and their implications for the labor market and broader economy is intricate and multifaceted. It is crucial to examine historical perspectives, recent wage rate adjustments, the significance of STEM fields in today's economy, and the critical issue of Internet access to understand the contemporary dynamics of these policies. This chapter's data highlights the delicate balance between improving worker welfare and maintaining economic stability in a digitally evolving world by analyzing these factors (historical perspectives on minimum wage policies, recent wage rate adjustments, the significance of STEM fields in today's economy, and the critical issue of Internet access). This background section explores the historical context and economic implications of minimum wage policies, shedding light on how foundational debates and economic theories have influenced the current workforce and policy landscape.

Historical Context and Economic Implications of Minimum Wage Policies

Four points (i.e., foundational understanding, economic implications, policy debates and outcomes, and connection to the digital divide) make this section significant to this research. The concept of a minimum wage was instituted to ensure a baseline standard of living for workers across various sectors (Sefil-Tansever & Yılmaz, 2024; Webb, 1912). Minimum wage laws originated in the early 20th century. These laws were seen as essential tools for mitigating the exploitation of workers in burgeoning industrial economies (Trezzini, 2024). Over the decades, these policies have been subject to extensive debate, with adjustments reflecting broader economic trends, inflation rates, and shifts in political ideologies (Bongitte, 2024; Clemens & Wither, 2019; Holt, 2024; Powell et al., 2021). Next is the economic implication.

Economic Implications

Economists remain divided over the impacts of minimum wage increases, with some citing the potential for reduced poverty levels and stimulated consumer spending, while others warn of increased unemployment and inflationary pressures as businesses adjust to higher labor costs (Kpakol & Amah, 2024; Trezzini, 2024). Having examined the origins and debates surrounding minimum wage policies, we now turn to recent increases in minimum wage rates and affected states to analyze the contemporary application and effects of these adjustments across various regions. This foundational understanding offers essential background on the origins and evolution of minimum wage laws, which is critical for comprehending the current debates and policy shifts. This background helps frame the discussion of how recent increases in minimum wage rates across various states impact economic stability and employment patterns. New York's strategy similarly aimed to elevate the minimum wage to $15 per hour, with variances based on geographic location and business size. The phased approach allows for gradual adaptation but has likewise sparked debates regarding regional economic disparities and the potential for disproportionate impacts on rural economies, where the cost of living and business revenues often differ significantly from urban centers. These policy effects raise significant concerns about the sustainability of small businesses and the broader implications for rural economic health (Uzialko, 2023). Additionally, such disparities highlight the need for flexible policies that can adapt to the unique economic environments of each region (Houchil, 2023). It is crucial, therefore, that policymakers consider these varied impacts when designing interventions aimed at economic balance and inclusion across different areas (Powell et al., 2021). Having explored the evolution and debates surrounding minimum wage policies, the focus shifts to STEM Jobs: *A Beacon of Economic Opportunity*. Examined is how advancements in science, technology, engineering, and mathematics are creating new career pathways in response to these economic changes. The paragraph highlights the divided opinions among economists regarding the outcomes of minimum wage increases, such as reduced poverty versus potential unemployment. This debate is directly relevant to the research, which aims to assess how minimum wage policies can be designed to balance economic growth with social equity, particularly in the context of supporting displaced workers through STEM opportunities. Next is policy debates and outcomes.

Policy Debates and Outcomes

A wave of minimum wage increases across various states in the United States has provided a fresh perspective on this ongoing debate. For instance, as of 2023, states like California (Sumagaysay & Agrawal, 2023) and New York (Houchil, 2023) embarked on ambitious paths to progressively increase their minimum wages to $15 per hour, a move lauded by labor advocates as a significant step towards economic justice for low-wage workers. Conversely, these increases have sparked concern among small business owners (Uzialko, 2023) and economists who fear the potential for job losses and increased operational costs (Giotis, 2024). California's approach has been to incrementally raise the minimum wage annually, with the goal of reaching the $15 per hour mark for all businesses by 2023. This policy impacts a wide range of industries, from hospitality and retail to agriculture, sectors traditionally reliant on low-wage labor. Preliminary reports suggest a mixed impact: while some businesses have reduced staff hours or delayed hiring, others have absorbed or passed the costs onto consumers without reducing employment levels. The examination of the historical and contemporary perspectives on minimum wage policies highlights the ongoing economic debates surrounding these policies. Comprehending these implications is significant for this research as it explores the potential for minimum wage increases to influence job displacement and the broader labor market, particularly concerning the transition into STEM fields

Connection to the Digital Divide

Historically, the digital divide emerged as a significant issue in the late 20th century, initially focusing on the gap between those without access to computers and the internet and those without Brown-Jackson (2017). As the Internet became integral to communication, education, and economic activities, this divide exposed deep inequalities, particularly along socioeconomic, geographic, and racial lines (Marshall, 2024). By the early 2000s, the focus had broadened to include digital literacy and the ability to effectively use technology, driven by the growing significance of digital skills in the workplace and daily life (Hwang et al., 2024). Significant disparities persisted despite efforts to expand access to technology in underserved rural and urban areas. As technology advanced, the digital divide became more complex, encompassing access, the quality and affordability of internet connections, and the skills needed to utilize digital tools effectively (brown-Jackson, 2017). The COVID-19 pandemic further exacerbated these disparities, highlighting the critical need for reliable internet access for education, work, and health services. These historical developments have shaped the current challenges in addressing the digital divide, emphasizing the need for comprehensive policies that tackle access, digital literacy, and infrastructure development to ensure equitable participation in the digital economy.

Overall, this historical discussion of minimum wage policies also links to the broader themes of economic and digital divides, as the research later delves into how these wage increases interact with digital access and opportunities, especially in underserved regions. Understanding the economic implications of these policies is crucial for addressing the challenges posed by the digital divide in accessing education and employment in the STEM fields. In summary, this section is significant to the research because it provides the necessary historical and economic context for analyzing the contemporary effects of minimum wage increases, particularly in relation to digital access and STEM career opportunities. This context helps to ground the research in real-world policy debates and economic trends, making the subsequent analysis more robust and relevant.

The Compounding Challenge of Internet Access

In today's digital age, reliable Internet access is necessary for economic and educational participation (Eden et al., 2024). However, many rural and underserved areas suffer from inadequate digital infrastructure, leading to frequent Internet blackouts and limited connectivity (Brown-Jackson, 2017). These challenges hinder access to online education, remote work, and essential services, making it difficult for individuals to transition into STEM fields or adapt to rapidly changing economic conditions (Fu et al., 2024; Brown-Jackson, 2017). This information emphasizes a critical obstacle that must be addressed. Without reliable digital access, these barriers can become insurmountable, preventing efforts to create an inclusive and resilient workforce capable of thriving in a technology-driven economy. This unreliability highlights the urgent need for comprehensive policies that address the digital divide and support economic and workforce development (Adeniyi et al., 2024). The significance of this information lies in the efforts to transition workers into STEM fields or adapt to economic changes are likely to fail without proper digital access. This information directly ties into the research's focus on overcoming barriers to create an inclusive and resilient workforce capable of thriving in a technologically driven economy. As outlined in the research, digital connectivity is crucial for accessing STEM education and training programs and vital for workers adapting to technological advancements in the labor market (Ali et al., 2024). The discussion on Internet accessibility highlights the intersection of technological infrastructure and economic mobility and directly connects to the broader themes of this chapter. It illuminates the critical dual challenges of economic adjustments and digital divides, reinforcing the necessity for developing effective strategies (Burton, 2024). Addressing these issues is pivotal for enhancing STEM opportunities and, by extension, fostering a more inclusive workforce prepared for the digital economy. This connection underscores the urgency and significance of the strategic focus on Internet access within policy frameworks to bridge the digital divide to support economic and workforce development. Simultaneously, the growing significance of STEM fields offers a promising avenue for economic advancement, provided that issues of education and Internet accessibility are adequately addressed (Kanvaria & Yadav, 2024). This complex landscape highlights the need for nuanced policies considering the interplay between wage laws, employment opportunities, and digital infrastructure. This significance ensures that efforts to improve worker welfare do not inadvertently hinder broader economic and social progress. While addressing the digital divide is crucial for enabling economic and educational opportunities, it is equally important to consider how economic policies, such as minimum wage increases, intersect with these technological barriers, influencing the broader landscape of employment and economic stability.

Minimum Wage Impacts

According to the latest data from the U.S. Bureau of Labor Statistics (2024), 2023 saw 80.5 million workers aged 16 and older in the U.S. receiving hourly wages, which constitutes 55.7% of all wage and salary workers. The significance of the minimum wage impacts is multifaceted - economic and employment trends, social and economic implications, and comparative analysis.

The U.S. BLS further offered that out of this demographic, 81,000 individuals were compensated at the federal minimum wage rate of $7.25 per hour, while approximately 789,000 earned less than the minimum wage. The share of hourly workers earning the federal minimum wage or slightly less declined from 1.3% in 2022 to 1.1% in 2023. This figure is significantly lower than the 13.4% observed in 1979, the first year such data was systematically recorded (U. S. BLS, 2024). In the United States, some states have experienced increases in their minimum wage rates. Figure 1 offers integrated quantitative data to support the qualitative analysis.

Figure 1. Minimum wage date

Consolidated State Minimum Wage Update Table
(Effective Date: 01/01/2024)

Greater than federal MW	Equals federal MW of $7.25	No state MW or state MW is lower than $7.25. Employers covered by the FLSA must pay the federal MW of $7.25.
AK $11.73	CNMI	AL
AR $11.00		GA
AZ $14.35	IA	LA
CA $16.00	ID	MS
CO $14.42	IN	SC
CT $15.69	KS	TN
DC $17.00	KY	WY
DE $13.25	NC	AS
FL $12.00	ND	
HI $14.00	NH	
IL $14.00	OK	
MA $15.00	PA	
MD $15.00	TX	
ME $14.15	UT	
MI $10.33	WI	
MN $10.85 or $8.85		
MO $12.30		
MT $10.30 or $4.00		
NE $12.00		
NJ $15.13 or $13.73		
NM $12.00		
NV $11.25 or $10.25		
NY $16.00 or $15.00		
OH $10.45 or $7.00		
OR $15.45 or $14.20 or $13.20		
PR $9.50		
RI $14.00		
SD $11.20		
VA $12.00		
VT $13.67		
WA $16.28		
WV $8.75		
VI $10.50		
GU $9.25		
30 States + DC, GU, PR& VI	13 States + CNMI	7 States + AS

Adapted from the U. S. Department of Labor: Consolidated Minimum Wage Table (Effective 01/01/2024)

This information provides critical empirical data that grounds the analysis of minimum wage impacts in real-world statistics. It offers a clear picture of current wage distribution, contextualizes trends over time, and supports a comprehensive examination of the social and economic implications of minimum wage policies. This data-driven approach enhances the credibility of the research, enabling more informed and nuanced conclusions about the effects of wage increases on the U.S. labor market. Building on this data-driven foundation, the subsequent analysis will delve into the broader economic and employment trends, exploring how these minimum wage impacts reflect and influence larger patterns within the labor market.

Economic and Employment Trends

Economic and employment trends are significant to understand because comprehending these trends is crucial for identifying the potential ripple effects of wage policies on employment levels, business operations, and economic growth (Ghodsi et al., 2024). Moreover, this information is significant because it allows the research to evaluate the effectiveness of minimum wage laws in achieving their intended goals, such as reducing poverty and promoting equitable economic opportunities (Ghodsi et al., 2024). The information from the U.S. Bureau of Labor Statistics provides a foundational understanding of how minimum wage laws affect the labor market (Zhang et al., 2023). This section sets the stage for discussing broader economic trends and the effects of policy changes by noting the proportion of hourly workers and their earnings relative to the minimum wage. Next is Policy analysis.

Policy Analysis

Policy analysis data serves as critical evidence in evaluating the effectiveness of minimum wage increases. This analysis helps assess whether these policies are achieving their intended goals of reducing poverty and improving living standards or if they inadvertently lead to job losses or underemployment (Azar et al., 2019). Additionally, such data allow policymakers to fine-tune interventions, ensuring that minimum wage adjustments are equitable and effective in promoting economic resilience without disproportionate negative impacts on small businesses and vulnerable workers (Azar et al., 2019). Furthermore, understanding these impacts is essential for aligning wage policies with the growing emphasis on STEM fields and the need for reliable internet access, as these factors are pivotal for enabling workers to adapt to the evolving demands of the digital economy. There are social and economic implications, too.

Social and Economic Implications

Social and Economic Implications illustrate the historical context and current statistics, allowing for a nuanced discussion of the socio-economic implications of minimum wage policies (Nae & Bălă oiu, 2024). It highlights progress since such data was recorded, providing a longitudinal perspective on policy impacts. This minimum wage longitudinal analysis is essential for understanding the dynamic relationships between wage policies and their broader social outcomes. It enables stakeholders to anticipate future trends better and appropriately respond to evolving economic conditions (Nae & Bălă oiu, 2024). This information is significant to the research as it examines how minimum wage policies impact broader socio-economic outcomes over time. By illustrating the historical context and current statistics, this section allows the research to draw connections between past policy decisions and their long-term effects on society. A longitudinal analysis is essential for understanding the dynamic relationships between wage policies and social outcomes, offering insights into how these policies can be fine-tuned to anticipate future trends and address evolving economic conditions.

Moreover, this discussion directly ties into the research's broader focus on creating an inclusive and resilient workforce, emphasizing the need for wage policies that promote economic stability and social equity. This connection is vital to the research title, "Cybersecure Futures: Bridging AI Employment and the Digital Divide," as it highlights how minimum wage policies intersect with issues of economic mobility and access to opportunities in the digital economy. After building on the analysis of the social and economic implications of minimum wage policies, the discussion now shifts to a closer examination of the Comparative Analysis of different regional approaches to wage adjustments, which provides valuable insights into the diverse outcomes and lessons learned from various implementations across the United States.

Comparative Analysis

As some states experience increases in minimum wage rates, Table 1 ion offers a valuable comparative analysis of different regional approaches. This comparison enlightens readers about best practices and lessons learned from various implementations of minimum wage laws, fostering a sense of awareness and understanding. By examining the varied outcomes in these states, the analysis also emphasizes the significance of considering local economic conditions and labor market characteristics when formulating wage policies, ensuring they are tailored to meet specific regional needs effectively.

According to a report by the U.S. Congressional Office (2024), increasing the minimum wage would lead to higher employment costs for low-wage workers. Consequently, this could prompt some employers to reduce their workforce compared to what would be expected with a lower minimum wage. However, employment could rise for particular workers or under specific conditions. The impact on employment would manifest in the number of unemployed individuals and the broader category of jobless workers. Jobless workers include those who have left the labor force, possibly due to a belief that no suitable jobs are available, and those actively seeking employment. The extent of these effects is influenced by several factors: the scope of workers affected by the wage increase, the scale of wage adjustments resulting from the higher minimum wage, and the degree to which employment levels react to wage changes. Overall, this section underpins the chapter's exploration of the transition of displaced workers into STEM fields and addresses the complex interplay between wage policies, employment, and economic stability. It provides a factual basis for discussing how minimum wage increases can be designed to support economic inclusion without detrimental effects on employment.

STEM JOBS: A BEACON OF ECONOMIC OPPORTUNITY

Amid economic adjustments, mainly minimum wage increases, STEM fields emerge as critical sectors for growth and innovation. The demand for skilled professionals in science, technology, engineering, and mathematics is rapidly increasing, driven by technological advancements and their integration into everyday life (Tytler, 2020). This surge in demand provides a potential pathway for workers displaced by economic shifts to secure stable, well-compensated employment (The White House, 2024). However, the transition to STEM careers depends heavily on access to adequate education and training programs, a challenge that is exacerbated by disparities in educational and economic resources across different regions (Dyke, 2022; Hazari, 2024).

Understanding this backdrop is crucial for comprehending why bolstering STEM education and infrastructure is significant for economic resilience and worker mobility. This information highlights the significance of this chapter, which examines potential strategies to enhance STEM opportunities to counteract economic displacement and foster a more inclusive workforce ready to meet the demands of a digitally driven economy. The insights from this discussion will guide the development of policies that aim to reduce the educational and economic barriers that currently hinder access to lucrative STEM careers. As the significant opportunities in STEM fields are explored for economic growth and career stability, it becomes essential to address the compounding challenge of internet access, which plays a pivotal role in determining who can benefit from these opportunities, especially in underserved areas.

PROBLEM STATEMENT

It is not known how minimum wage policies, which may increase unemployment rates among small businesses by up to 10%, interact with the critical role of Internet access in ensuring equitable participation in STEM fields in the United States. This uncertainty creates an urgent need to develop adaptive policies that effectively align economic goals with technological advancements, ensuring everyone is included in the transition to a digitized economy.

Problem Statement Support

The enactment of minimum wage increases across various states, intended to elevate living standards for low-wage workers, has precipitated a complex set of economic and social challenges. These challenges include potential layoffs as businesses adjust to higher labor costs, highlighted by up to 10% increased unemployment in small businesses (Uzialko, 2023), and the compounded issue of inadequate Internet access, which hampers the ability of displaced workers to transition into the burgeoning field of STEM. Particularly in rural and underserved areas, inadequate Internet infrastructure impedes educational and economic opportunities, critical for transitioning to STEM fields (Fu et al., 2024). This situation presents a multifaceted problem where economic policy to improve worker welfare may inadvertently exacerbate unemployment and limit access to new employment opportunities without supportive digital infrastructure. The digital divide exacerbates the difficulty displaced workers acquire the necessary education and training for STEM careers, which are crucial for stable, well-compensated employment in a technologically driven economy (The White House, 2024). Moreover, there is a pressing need for policies that balance wage improvements with the economic realities of employment and technological infrastructure to avoid exacerbating unemployment or widening the digital divide (Houchil, 2023; Sumagaysay & Agrawal, 2023).

SIGNIFICANCE OF THE RESEARCH

This research is crucial as it provides a comprehensive analysis of the intertwined challenges of minimum wage policies, the transition into STEM fields, and the digital divide (Giotis, 2024). By examining the direct impact of wage increases on employment dynamics across various sectors and regions, this study offers valuable insights for policymakers aiming to balance economic growth with social equity (Powell et al., 2021). Furthermore, the research explores the potential of STEM education as a viable pathway for displaced workers, emphasizing the significance of addressing barriers to access, such as inadequate digital infrastructure (Tytler, 2020). By focusing on the critical role of Internet access in enabling these transitions, the study underscores the necessity of developing integrated policies that address economic and technological disparities. This research directly informs the chapter's objective of promoting an inclusive and resilient workforce capable of thriving in a rapidly evolving digital economy (The White House, 2024)

METHODOLOGY/DESIGN

This research adopts a qualitative methodology, employing a comprehensive literature review and case study to explore the multifaceted issues surrounding minimum wage increases, layoffs, transitions into STEM jobs, and the impact of Internet blackouts. This approach allows for an in-depth analysis of secondary data, including academic articles, policy reports, case studies, and statistical analyses, to identify patterns, themes, and insights into the problem statement (Adeniyi et al., 2024; Jiang et al., 2024; Yaseen, 2024). Building upon the foundation laid by the qualitative methodology, the subsequent section, data collection and analysis, delves deeper into the empirical evidence gathered from diverse sources. This thorough examination allows us to dissect the nuanced impacts of minimum wage policy changes, scrutinize the transition dynamics within STEM fields, and evaluate the broader implications of the digital divide on societal and economic structures. The literature review spans several databases and sources to ensure a broad spectrum of perspectives and data. The analysis follows a thematic approach, categorizing findings into key areas (Saldaña, 2021): economic impacts of minimum wage increases, the STEM job market and transition pathways, and the digital divide's effect on educational and employment opportunities. This method facilitates a holistic understanding of the issues, enabling the identification of gaps in the literature and opportunities for future research (Ajayi & Udeh, 2024).

Given this research's reliance on secondary data, ethical considerations primarily concern the accurate representation of sources and the avoidance of misinterpretation. Care is taken to cite all sources appropriately and to present findings in a manner that respects the original context and intent of the data. Moreover, the integrity of the analysis is upheld through meticulous verification of information, ensuring that conclusions drawn are reliable and reflect the current understanding within the academic and policy-making communities.

APPLICABLE THEORIES

Applying applicable theories in research is significant because they provide a structured lens through which complex phenomena can be systematically understood and analyzed (Pekrun, 2024). The three theories that guide this research are the labor market theory, human capital theory, and digital divide theory guide. These theories help to interpret the data in a context that bridges abstract concepts with real-world applications, enabling targeted and practical policy recommendations. This theoretical grounding ensures that the research findings are not merely observational but are deeply rooted in established academic principles, enhancing the credibility and impact of the conclusions drawn.

The Labor Market Theory

Labor Market Theory is foundational to understanding how wage policies impact employment levels (Alderman et al., 2023). This research team's study posits that wage rates are determined by the labor market's forces of supply and demand, offering a predictive framework for analyzing the consequences of minimum wage increases. While this theory allows policymakers and business leaders to anticipate how wage adjustments might influence employment dynamics, it has been critiqued for simplifying complex labor market behaviors (Saros, 2019). Critics point out that it fails to account for the nuanced ways in which workers and employers respond to wage changes, overlooking factors like technological advancements, global economic trends, and employees' intrinsic motivations (Saros, 2019). Despite its limitations, labor market theory remains a critical tool for economic analysis, providing valuable insights into the balancing act between wage growth and employment opportunities (Alderman & Blair, 2024). One of the primary benefits of the labor market theory is that it provides a structured framework to analyze how wages are determined and how they affect employment levels (Bastani & Waldenström, 2024). This framework enables economists to predict the consequences of wage increases on employment based on supply and demand principles (Alderman et al., 2023; Bartik et al., 2020). Such predictive capability is crucial for policymakers and businesses to make informed wage-setting decisions and understand potential labor market adjustments (Bartik et al., 2020). Using labor market theory, stakeholders can better navigate the complexities of wage policies and their implications for employment.

However, it is crucial to acknowledge the limitations of labor market theory, as it may only partially capture the intricate dynamics of real-world employment (DeWeerdt et al., 2024). Critics argue that the theory often neglects the influence of external factors, such as technological changes, global economic shifts, and social policies on the labor market (DeWeerdt et al., 2024). Moreover, the assumption of rational behavior downplays the role of human elements, such as motivation, job satisfaction, and workplace culture, in employment decisions (Bandhu et al., 2024). Despite these critiques, recognizing these limitations can help refine the application of labor market theory in policy and business decisions. While Labor Market Theory provides a foundational framework for understanding how supply and demand determine wage rates, it often overlooks the crucial role of individual education and skills in shaping economic outcomes. This gap is addressed by human capital theory, a fascinating area that highlights the significance of education and training in enhancing an individual's productivity and economic value.

Critiques of Labor Market Theory

Current critiques of Labor Market Theory center around the theory's limitations in accounting for real-world complexities. Critics argue that while labor market theory provides a foundational framework for understanding wage determination through supply and demand, it oversimplifies the diverse factors influencing employment, such as technological advancements, global economic trends, and the intrinsic motivations of workers. Moreover, the theory's focus on rational economic behavior overlooks labor's psychological and social dimensions, which are increasingly recognized as crucial to understanding workforce dynamics (Alderman et al., 2023), (DeWeerdt et al., 2024). These critiques call for a more nuanced and integrated approach considering the economic and non-economic factors influencing labor markets.

The Human Capital Theory

Human Capital Theory, the central theory of education in economics, highlights the significance of education and training in enhancing an individual's productivity and economic value (Leoni, 2023). Also, this perspective views investments in human capital as pivotal for economic development and personal career growth, suggesting a direct correlation between educational attainment and labor market success. It supports policies to increase education and skill development, framing these efforts as investments with significant returns for individuals and societies (Leoni, 2023). This theory has several benefits, such as increased productivity and economic value, justification for education policies, and an understanding of income disparities. Increased productivity and economic value, a benefit of the human capital theory, underscores the role of education and training in increasing productivity and economic value, suggesting that investments in human capital lead to better employment outcomes and higher wages (Leoni, 2023). It emphasizes the investment in education to increase human capital, leading to higher earnings and improved labor market outcomes (Chen & Nguyen, 2024). This perspective encourages policymakers to prioritize education and skill development to drive economic growth. Moreover, it provides a framework for understanding how educational disparities contribute to income inequality and labor market success. Next, the justification for education policies justifies the focus on education and skill development as critical strategies for economic development and individual career advancement (Buscha & Dickson, 2023). Research indicates that education increases productivity and creativity, promoting technological advances and entrepreneurship. Additionally, substantial investment in human capital through education has improved income distribution and fostered economic and social progress (Baily et al., 2021).

Next, the justification for education policies justifies the focus on education and skill development as critical strategies for economic development and individual career advancement (Buscha & Dickson, 2023). Research indicates that education increases productivity and creativity, promoting technological advances and entrepreneurship. Additionally, substantial investment in human capital through education has improved income distribution and fostered economic and social progress (Baily et al., 2021). The income disparity theory provides a basis for understanding the disparities in income and employment opportunities due to differing levels of education and skills (Polacko, 2021). Research has shown that higher educational attainment is directly correlated with higher income, highlighting the role of education in economic mobility (Leone & Lo Cascio, 2020). Moreover, the COVID-19 pandemic has exacerbated income disparities, particularly impacting those with lower educational levels and contributing to greater economic inequality (Quispe Mamani et al., 2022). However, while human capital theory emphasizes the benefits of education and training, it also faces significant critiques regarding its assumptions and implications.

Critiques of Human Capital Theory

Human capital theory has long been influential in shaping educational and economic policies, emphasizing the value of investing in education and training to enhance individual productivity and societal economic gains. Also, the human capital theory emphasizes the value of education and training for enhancing individual productivity and economic gains but faces several critiques. Critics argue that the theory overemphasizes individual responsibility for economic success while overlooking structural barriers like poverty and discrimination (Smith, 2024), (Becker & Wilson, 2024). Additionally, it assumes a uniform value of education, failing to consider diminishing returns in saturated job markets, leading to potential underemployment (Chen & Nguyen, 2024), (Alvarez & Torres, 2024). Lastly, the theory is criticized for insufficient focus on the qualitative aspects of education, neglecting the alignment of skills with labor market demands (Fernandez & Kim, 2024), (Becker & Wilson, 2024). Addressing these critiques can lead to more comprehensive and inclusive educational policies that better align with real-world challenges.

The Digital Divide Theory

Digital divide theory addresses the disparities in access to digital technologies and the Internet, emphasizing how these gaps impact socio-economic opportunities (Devisakti et al., 2024). It identifies the digital divide as a critical barrier to educational and economic advancement, advocating for targeted interventions to ensure equitable access to digital resources (Devisakti et al., 2024). By highlighting the significance of digital literacy and connectivity, the theory highlights the Internet's transformative potential in bridging educational and economic divides, particularly in underserved communities. The next focus is on its numerous benefits, emphasizing its significance in contemporary policy discussions and social strategies. Digital divide theory highlights the inequality in Internet and technology access, emphasizing how this gap affects educational and economic opportunities. It advocates for policy measures to bridge the digital divide, recognizing the increasing significance of digital literacy in the modern economy (Devisakti et al., 2024). This theory also highlights the role of digital access in empowering communities and fostering inclusive growth, especially in underserved and rural areas. Critiques of the digital divide theory focus on its sometimes-narrow emphasis on access without adequately addressing the broader challenges of digital literacy (Cui et al., 2024), content quality (Hou et al., 2024), and the socio-economic contexts that shape technology use (Hou et al., 2024). Despite these critiques, the theory is essential in framing discussions around digital inclusion and the need for comprehensive strategies to address access and engagement with digital technologies.

Critiques of the Digital Divide Theory

This theory has been critiqued for its sometimes-narrow focus on access to technology as the primary barrier, without fully exploring issues related to digital literacy, Internet connectivity quality, and digital content's usability. It may also underplay the adaptive capacities of communities to leverage available resources to overcome digital barriers (Crawford & Serhal, 2020). Furthermore, the theory's emphasis on technological solutions can overlook broader socio-economic challenges contributing to the digital divide, such as poverty, education disparities, and infrastructure deficiencies (Hou et al., 2024). Integrating these benefits and critiques provides a more nuanced understanding of the theoretical frameworks guiding the research. It acknowledges the strengths of each theory in explaining aspects of the labor market, education, and digital access, while also recognizing their limitations in capturing the full complexity of the issues at hand. This approach not only enriches the analysis but also situates the research within broader academic and policy debates, laying a foundation for a comprehensive examination of minimum wage increases, the transition to STEM fields, and the significance of addressing the digital divide.

LITERATURE REVIEW

A literature review is a comprehensive survey of existing scholarly work on a particular topic. It involves systematically identifying, analyzing, and synthesizing relevant research studies, theories, and findings (Amberger & Schreyer, 2024). According to this research team, a literature review aims to provide a clear understanding of the current state of knowledge on the topic, highlight significant contributions, and identify gaps or inconsistencies in the existing body of research. This process is critical as it lays the foundation for new research by situating it within what is already known, ensuring that the new study is informed and builds upon previous work (Amberger & Schreyer, 2024). By critically evaluating and integrating various sources, a literature review helps researchers justify their research questions, refine their methodologies, and avoid duplication of efforts. This literature review will cover key topics that drive the research such as the impact of minimum wage increases on employment, STEM jobs as pathways for economic stability, the role of internet access in economic and educational opportunities, navigating uncertainties: the multidimensional risks of economic policies and technological divides, and bridging the digital divide at a policy level. A well-conducted literature review is essential for advancing scholarly knowledge and guiding evidence-based practice.

The Impact of Minimum Wage Increases on Employment

The impact of minimum wage increases on employment is a widely studied topic with mixed findings. Hurst et al. (2022) find that small increases in the minimum wage have beneficial long-run impacts on low-income workers' employment and income. In contrast, significant increases can reduce these benefits (Hurst et al., 2022). Additionally, Redmond and McGuinness (2021) observe that the 2016 minimum wage increase in Ireland reduced hours worked among minimum-wage workers, particularly temporary workers, but did not significantly increase job loss (Redmond & McGuinness, 2021). The impact of minimum wage increases on employment in the USA, specifically relating to the technology sector, involves various dynamics and adjustments by firms. One significant finding is that minimum wage hikes lead establishments to allocate more resources toward information technology (IT) in response to increased labor costs. For instance, a study by Dai and Qiu (2019) found that establishments, on average, allocate between $10,328 and $66,808 more per year to IT budgets during the three years following significant state minimum wage increases. This reallocation results in more personal computers per employee and a lower employment growth rate, indicating a shift towards capital over labor (Dai & Qiu, 2019). These findings indicate that while minimum wage increases aim to improve earnings for low-wage workers, they also drive firms to invest in technology to mitigate higher labor costs, leading to reduced employment growth in specific sectors and a shift toward more automated processes. Also, these studies highlight the complexity of the minimum wage-employment relationship, showing that the effects can vary based on the context, magnitude of the increase, and labor market conditions. Critiques exist for the impact of minimum wage increases on employment.

The literature's reliance on varying methodologies and regional focuses has led to a fragmented understanding of minimum wage impacts (Dai & Qiu, 2019); Hurst et al., 2022; Redmond & McGuinness, 2021). More studies are needed to consider the cumulative effects of wage increases over time, including potential shifts in business models and employment practices. Furthermore, the disproportionate focus on immediate employment neglects other significant outcomes, such as worker health and productivity, consumer price changes, and broader economic shifts. This gap underscores the need for a more holistic approach to studying minimum wage policies that incorporate a variety of economic and social indicators. This nuanced understanding of minimum wage impacts, with positive and negative consequences, underscores the significance of contextual and comprehensive policy analyses. As attention turns to STEM jobs and their role in fostering economic stability, it becomes evident that informed policy decisions can significantly influence pathways to long-term economic growth and equity.

STEM Jobs as Pathways for Economic Stability

The literature is essential to the chapter for several reasons. STEM is critical in education and training to prepare the workforce for the future job market. A 2024 study in the Journal of Science Education and Technology highlighted innovative STEM education approaches designed to make these fields more accessible and engaging, encouraging a more diverse cohort of students to pursue STEM careers (Moghaddam et al., 2023). This study emphasizes the need for integrating specialized and foundational skills to meet industry demands for future STEM jobs, fostering closer collaboration between academia, industry, and government (Moghaddam et al., 2023). This emphasis is crucial as it aligns with the broader goal of equipping the workforce with the necessary skills to thrive in a rapidly changing technological landscape. Another significant aspect of this section regarding this research is lifelong and upskilling.

Policy discussions have increasingly focused on the need for lifelong learning and upskilling opportunities to help workers adapt to technological advancements and shifts in the labor market. For instance, Arora (2023) emphasizes the significance of continuous learning and transferable skills to remain relevant and competitive in the evolving job market (Arora, 2023). These initiatives and policies are essential to equip the workforce with the skills to thrive in a rapidly changing technological landscape.

However, while the emphasis on STEM education and jobs is promising, addressing critiques that highlight significant barriers such as socioeconomic status, gender, race, and geographic location, preventing equitable access to these opportunities is crucial. This focus is particularly significant in the context of economic stability, as it prepares individuals to remain relevant and competitive in their careers. This discussion is significant as it acknowledges the challenges that must be overcome to ensure that the growth of the stem sector benefits a broad and diverse population. The last salient point is barriers to access, economic resilience and worker mobility.

While the emphasis on STEM education and jobs is promising, the literature often overlooks the barriers that prevent equitable access to these opportunities (Devisakti et al., 2024). Socioeconomic status, gender, race, and geographic location can significantly influence individuals' ability to engage with STEM education and employment (Becker & Wilson, 2024; Hou et al., 2024; Smith, 2024). Moreover, there is a scarcity of research on the effectiveness of retraining programs for adults, especially those with limited prior exposure to STEM fields (Agbo, 2024; Moon et al., 2024; Paris, 2024). This lack of focus on inclusivity and accessibility in STEM education and employment strategies may perpetuate existing disparities and limit the potential benefits of the sector's growth. By exploring the potential of STEM education to enhance economic resilience and worker mobility, the section ties into the broader themes of the chapter, which seek to develop strategies to counteract economic displacement. It emphasizes the importance of creating an inclusive workforce that can meet the demands of a digitally driven economy.

The Role of Internet Access in Economic and Educational Opportunities

This section is significant to the literature because it highlights critical infrastructure needs, addresses the digital divide, links economic mobility and digital access, and reviews strategic policy implications.

Highlighting Critical Infrastructure Needs

The advent of the COVID-19 pandemic accelerated the transition to digital platforms for work, education, and social interaction, highlighting the critical significance of Internet access (Quispe Mamani et al., 2022). Research from 2021 in the International Journal of Information Management demonstrated how digital connectivity became a lifeline, enabling remote work and learning while exposing stark disparities in access (Crawford & Serhal, 2020). Initiatives to bridge the digital divide have gained momentum, with governments and organizations investing in infrastructure and digital literacy programs (Fu et al., 2024). However, despite these efforts, significant criticisms have emerged regarding the approach to digital connectivity. While infrastructure expansion is essential, it is only one piece of the puzzle. Addressing the digital divide requires a deeper examination of the factors contributing to persistent inequalities.

Addressing the Digital Divide

While acknowledging the efforts to enhance digital connectivity, critiques of the literature point to an oversimplified view of the digital divide. The focus on physical access to technology and broadband needs to address deeper issues of digital literacy, affordability, and the relevance of online content (Cui et al., 2024). Scholars have highlighted that even in regions with high internet connectivity, disparities in material access, such as device diversity and ongoing maintenance expenses, continue to perpetuate inequality (Valdez & Javier, 2020). Beyond the immediate concerns of access and affordability, the implications of digital connectivity extend into broader societal outcomes, particularly about economic mobility.

Linking Economic Mobility and Digital Access

Additionally, the rapid pace of technological change demands more than just connectivity; it requires continuous learning and user adaptation (Arora, 2023). The work of Arora (2023) underlines the need for multifaceted approaches to address the challenges and opportunities in today's economy. Addressing these issues holistically requires coordinated efforts across policy (Adelekan, 2024; Kaiser et al., 2024), education (Gener, 2023; Haleem, 2022), and infrastructure development (Omodan, 2024), ensuring that interventions are inclusive and adaptable to the rapid pace of technological change. As the relationship between digital access and economic mobility is further explored, it becomes evident that bridging this gap involves providing connectivity and empowering individuals to engage with and benefit from digital resources.

STRATEGIC POLICY IMPLICATIONS

Addressing these issues holistically requires coordinated efforts across policy, education, and infrastructure development, ensuring that interventions are inclusive and adaptable to the rapid pace of technological change. Robust infrastructure is essential for digital inclusion, providing crucial access to information, educational resources, healthcare, and economic opportunities, particularly in underserved and rural areas (Brown-Jackson, 2017). Additionally, expanding access to STEM education and retraining programs is vital to preparing the workforce for future job market demands, particularly for those displaced by economic shifts or technological advancements (Chen & Nguyen, 2024). Furthermore, comprehensive digital inclusion strategies must go beyond ensuring physical access to also address digital literacy and the relevance of digital content, thereby enabling full participation in the digital economy (Cui et al., 2024). By focusing on these multifaceted strategies, we can better support diverse populations in navigating the complexities of the modern workforce, ultimately fostering a more inclusive and equitable society.

This section regarding "The Role of Internet Access in Economic and Educational Opportunities," is critical to the chapter as it frames internet access as a foundational element for economic stability, educational opportunity, and social equity, thereby underscoring the necessity of closing the digital divide to foster a more inclusive and resilient economy. By addressing these challenges comprehensively, we can create a more equitable and better equipped society to handle future technological shifts. The discussions here set the stage for examining how strategic policies can effectively mitigate the risks associated with digital exclusion.

Navigating Uncertainties: The Multidimensional Risks of Economic Policies and Technological Divides

The global economy continues to undergo rapid transformations driven by technological advancements and shifting economic policies; the workforce faces complex challenges (Karangutkar, 2023) (Raschke & Peace, 2021). These changes bring about economic risks and significant psychological impacts, particularly for displaced people who must continually adapt to new job roles and technologies (Patel & Rietveld, 2020) (Wels et al., 2021). Understanding and addressing these multidimensional risks requires a comprehensive approach considering the interplay between economic policies, technological disruptions, and their broader societal impacts (Butcher & Shiro, 2024) (Maxim & Muro, 2019). The following sections delve into the psychological and economic ramifications of these transitions, emphasizing the critical need for robust support systems, continuous learning, and coordinated efforts from policymakers, businesses, and mental health professionals to foster a resilient and adaptable workforce in the face of uncertainty (Employment & Training Administration, n.d.).

Psychological Impacts of Job Displacement

In addition to economic risks, the psychological impacts of job displacement are profound. Research by Patel and Rietveld (2020) indicates that the self-employed, in particular, experienced greater psychological distress due to financial insecurity during the COVID-19 pandemic (Patel & Rietveld, 2020). Furthermore, a study examining the social and psychological effects of employment disruption found that those who were furloughed or unemployed during the pandemic faced increased risks of psychological distress, loneliness, and reduced life satisfaction (Wels et al., 2021). These findings underscore the necessity for comprehensive support systems that address the economic and psychological well-being of displaced workers.

Technological Advancements and Workforce Displacement

The risks associated with economic and technological transitions, such as job displacement and the psychological impacts on workers, are significant and multifaceted. The rapid advancement of technology, including artificial intelligence and automation, poses a substantial risk of job displacement, which can lead to increased unemployment and income inequality. A study by Karangutkar (2023) highlights that the rise of AI technologies has led to significant changes across various industries, raising concerns about job loss and the need for workforce adaptation (Karangutkar, 2023). The World Economic Forum (2020) also noted that the COVID-19 pandemic accelerated the digitization and automation of work, further exacerbating the displacement of workers (Raschke & Peace, 2021). This transition not only impacts employment but also necessitates continuous learning and adaptation by workers to keep pace with technological advancements.

Stress and Continuous Adaptation to Technological Changes

Another dimension of the psychological impact on displaced workers is the stress associated with the need for continual adaptation to new technologies and job roles. Workers face the anxiety of potential job loss and the challenge of continuously updating their skills in a rapidly changing job market. A comprehensive study by Wels et al. (2021) demonstrated that disruptions in employment are associated with increased loneliness, reduced life satisfaction, and heightened psychological distress (Wels et al., 2021).

The Importance of Support Systems for Displaced Workers

The cumulative effect of these stressors underscores the need for robust support systems to provide skill training and psychological support to displaced workers (Patel, 2024). Interventions such as career counseling, mental health services, and lifelong learning programs can play a critical role in mitigating the adverse effects of technological displacement and economic transitions (Employment & Training Administration, n.d.). For example, incorporating mental health services into retraining programs can help address displaced workers' psychological burdens, ensuring a more holistic approach to workforce adaptation (Employment & Training Administration, n.d.).

The Role of Policymakers and Businesses in Mitigating Risks

Addressing these multifaceted risks requires a concerted effort from policymakers, businesses, and mental health professionals to ensure that workers are equipped with the necessary skills and support to manage the psychological impacts of these transitions (Butcher & Shiro, 2024; Maxim & Muro, 2019; The World Bank, 2020). This holistic approach will be crucial in fostering a resilient workforce capable of navigating the challenges posed by the new economic landscape.

Critiques of the current literature on these issues point out that there is often an oversimplified focus on the immediate economic impacts of job displacement, neglecting the long-term socio-economic and psychological consequences. For instance, a study by Litchfield et al. (2021) emphasizes the need to consider the broader social implications of job displacement, such as its effects on community cohesion and social trust (Litchfield et al., 2021). Additionally, the literature often needs to adequately address the role of digital literacy and continuous skill development in mitigating the adverse effects of technological change (Cui et al., 2024). By incorporating these critiques, it becomes clear that a more nuanced and holistic approach is required to fully understand and address the complexities of economic and technological transitions.

By delving into these topics with greater depth and providing detailed critiques, this researcher has expanded the exploration of the current literature, highlighting the advancements and the persistent gaps in understanding the complex dynamics of minimum wage policies, STEM employment pathways, and digital access. This detailed analysis underscores the need for multifaceted approaches to address the challenges and opportunities in today's economy. Addressing these issues holistically requires coordinated efforts across policy, education, and infrastructure development, ensuring that interventions are inclusive and adaptable to the rapid pace of technological change. Furthermore, integrating comprehensive digital literacy programs, investing in affordable and reliable digital infrastructure, and fostering continuous learning and upskilling initiatives are critical steps toward closing the digital divide and enhancing economic resilience.

Bridging the Digital Divide at a Policy Level

In addressing the pressing challenge of the digital divide, practical solutions at the policy level are essential for ensuring equitable access to digital resources across diverse populations (Chakravorti, 2021). To effectively bridge this gap, policymakers must implement comprehensive strategies encompassing infrastructure development, affordability programs, and enhanced digital literacy efforts (Burton, 2024). These initiatives require robust collaboration between government entities, private sector stakeholders, and community organizations to create an inclusive digital ecosystem (Global Partnership for Sustainable Development Data, 2022).

By focusing on these critical areas, policies can facilitate widespread internet connectivity, support affordable access, and ensure everyone possesses the necessary digital skills to thrive in an increasingly digital world. This approach aims to eliminate disparities and empower communities, fostering economic growth and enhancing educational outcomes (Brown-Jackson, 2017). The focus should be on infrastructure development, affordability programs, digital literacy and education, public-private partnerships, and inclusive policymaking (Suhrab et al., 2024).

Infrastructure Development for Digital Inclusion

Robust infrastructure is essential for digital inclusion, providing crucial access to information, educational resources, healthcare, and economic opportunities, particularly in underserved and rural areas (Suhrab et al., 2024). Broadband connectivity is pivotal for enhancing social inclusion, supporting small businesses, enabling access to telehealth services, and reducing economic and social disparities (Brown-Jackson, 2017). Initiatives like the Federal Communications Commission's Rural Digital Opportunity Fund in the United States demonstrate adequate policy support for infrastructure expansion by allocating funds to develop broadband in rural regions, ensuring these communities are not left behind in the digital age (Federal Communications Commission, 2020).

Affordability Programs to Close the Digital Divide

Having programs is not enough. There must be affordability programs. Making digital access affordable is crucial for closing the digital divide. Policies should advocate for subsidized internet services for low-income households, similar to the Lifeline Program in the U.S. that provides reduced-cost communications services to eligible consumers (Federal Communications Commission, 2021). Such programs will support digital literacy and education.

Public-Private Partnerships for Digital Inclusion

To effectively enhance digital inclusion, it is vital to complement robust infrastructure and affordability programs with strategic public-private partnerships. These collaborations between government, private sector, and non-profit organizations can pool resources and expertise to provide comprehensive digital skills training and the necessary hardware to underserved communities. Such synergistic efforts are exemplified by Microsoft's Airband Initiative, which targets broadband expansion to rural U.S. (Grimes & Porter, 2023).

Monitoring, Evaluation, and Inclusive Policymaking

Furthermore, the success of these strategies requires continuous monitoring and evaluation to ensure they meet their goals, suggesting establishing a dedicated oversight body to enhance transparency and accountability in digital divide policies (Global Partnership for Sustainable Development Data, 2022). Building on the principle of inclusive policymaking, it is essential to implement mechanisms that ensure all community voices, especially those from vulnerable groups, are not only heard but actively integrated into decision-making processes. This approach will enable the development of truly comprehensive digital inclusion strategies that cater to the unique needs of every demographic, effectively narrowing the digital divide.

In summary, bridging the digital divide requires a multifaceted approach that combines infrastructure development, affordability programs, public-private partnerships, and inclusive policymaking to ensure equitable access to digital resources for all populations (Chakravorti, 2021). Continuous monitoring and evaluation are essential to ensure these strategies effectively address the unique needs of underserved communities, ultimately fostering economic growth and social inclusion (Global Partnership for Sustainable Development Data, 2022). By implementing these comprehensive policies, we can create a more connected and equitable digital future (Suhrab et al., 2024).

Case Studies

In addition to the literature review, this research incorporates three distinct case studies. These case studies were utilized to deepen the investigation of the core topic, allowing for the extraction of vital themes and outcomes (Karlén & Rauta, 2023). These insights assist in forecasting future trends, uncovering issues previously overlooked that have practical applications, and enhancing the understanding of significant research problems with enhanced clarity.

Through these detailed analyses, the case studies not only enrich the theoretical discussion within the document but also showcase practical implementations of policies and technologies aimed at tackling the challenges associated with the digital divide and workforce changes due to technological progress (Karlén & Rauta, 2023). They serve as real-world examples of effective governmental strategies and technological integration, offering scalable solutions that demonstrate how to bridge infrastructure gaps and promote digital equity on a national scale.

Case Study: Minnesota Broadband Expansion Initiative

The case study, titled "Broadband Expansion in Minnesota: A Public-Private Partnership Model," provides an insightful examination of the collaborative efforts between the state government of Minnesota and various private sector entities to extend high-speed broadband to rural and underserved areas (Pew, 2021; Pope County Minnesota, 2019). The initiative involved a strategic investment plan focusing on infrastructure development, including laying fiber-optic cables and installing wireless broadband towers. The funding for these efforts came from state and federal grants, complemented by significant contributions from private companies (Office of the Governor Tim Waltz, 2024). This comprehensive approach also included active community engagement to ensure the solutions were tailored to the specific needs of each area (Pew, 2021).

The outcomes of this initiative were significant. Enhanced connectivity dramatically increased the number of households and businesses with reliable internet access (Pew, 2021). This infrastructure improvement provided the backbone for boosted economic and educational opportunities; schools could integrate digital learning tools, and local businesses expanded their reach through digital markets (Office of the Governor Tim Waltz, 2024). Furthermore, the initiative's success positioned Minnesota as a model for other states facing similar challenges, demonstrating the efficacy of collaborative strategies in overcoming digital divides and fostering long-term benefits like sustained economic growth and improved educational outcomes (Pew, 2021; Pope County, Minnesota, 2019).

This case study is particularly relevant to discussions on the necessity of robust internet access as a catalyst for economic and educational opportunities, especially in rural areas. By showcasing the successful government and private sector collaboration model, it underscores the impact of strategic infrastructure investments (Pew, 2021). The Minnesota model bridged the digital divide and set a precedent for how similar initiatives can be structured in other regions to achieve comparable successes (Office of the Governor Tim Waltz, 2024; Pew, 2021; Pope County, Minnesota, 2019). This alignment with broader discussions on infrastructure development highlights the critical role that access to high-speed internet plays in enhancing the quality of life and economic viability in underserved communities.

Case Study: Singapore's Smart Nation Initiative

The "Singapore's Smart Nation Initiative" case study examines Singapore's comprehensive approach to transforming into a digitally advanced society. The initiative was characterized by a broad integration of digital literacy programs and robust infrastructure development, driven by collaborations between the government and various private sector stakeholders (Leong & Lee, 2021; Warschauer, 2001). As given by (Cavada et al., 2019; Faliagka et al., 2024; Leong & Lee, 2021), the key actions include:

- Implementing nationwide high-speed internet access
- Developing smart urban solutions such as intelligent transport systems and healthcare management technologies
- Promoting digital literacy among all age groups

The outcomes of the Smart Nation Initiative have been transformative (Faliagka et al., 2024). Singapore has witnessed substantial improvements in several areas: enhanced public service delivery through digital platforms, increased efficiency in urban management, and elevated citizen engagement through technology. These advancements have streamlined government operations and significantly uplifted its residents' quality of everyday life. Moreover, the initiative has set a global benchmark for leveraging technology to foster a connected and digitally inclusive society (Faliagka et al., 2024).

This case study is significant as it provides a concrete example of how targeted technological integration and public-private partnerships can lead to a successful digital transformation at a national level (Faliagka et al., 2024). The insights gained from Singapore's Smart Nation Initiative highlight the crucial role of innovation and comprehensive infrastructure development in enhancing citizen services and economic opportunities. It offers a practical framework that can be adapted and implemented in various other contexts, regardless of scale, to achieve similar benefits. This relevance is particularly pertinent to discussions on creating digitally inclusive societies, emphasizing the initiative's potential as a model for global adaptation (Leong & Lee, 202).

Case Study: Rural Digital Opportunity Fund (RDOF) in the United States

The case study titled "Rural Digital Opportunity Fund (RDOF) in the United States" explores the Federal Communications Commission's (FCC) initiative to address the digital divide in rural America. Launched as part of a broader effort to extend high-speed internet access to underserved regions, the RDOF provided targeted funding and policy support to incentivize telecommunications providers to expand infrastructure. The program prioritized deploying broadband networks in areas where access was non-existent or substandard, leveraging a competitive bidding process to allocate funds efficiently.

Key outcomes from the RDOF initiative included substantial investments in rural broadband infrastructure and expanding high-speed internet services to millions of households and businesses in remote areas. This expansion improved connectivity and facilitated economic development, educational opportunities, and healthcare access, enhancing the overall quality of life in underserved communities. The fund's success has been a critical step towards achieving nationwide digital equity, illustrating the potential impact of well-structured governmental interventions in the telecommunications sector.

The significance of this case study lies in its demonstration of how strategic policy support and funding can effectively bridge critical infrastructure gaps in the most challenging environments. By highlighting the effectiveness of the RDOF, the case study provides valuable insights into scalable solutions for national digital divide issues. This is especially relevant in discussions about federal roles in supporting infrastructure development, underscoring the significance of policy frameworks prioritizing inclusivity and connectivity. The RDOF serves as a testament to the potential of government initiatives to foster substantial improvements in access to technology and information across a vast and varied landscape.

These three case studies complement the theoretical discussions in this chapter and provide concrete examples of how policies and technologies can be successfully integrated to address the challenges of the digital divide and workforce displacement due to technological advances. The case studies illustrate the impact of well-structured government interventions and the potential of these initiatives to foster inclusive technological growth and connectivity across diverse communities. Through these practical implementations, the case studies demonstrate scalable solutions to bridge infrastructure gaps and advance digital equity at a national level and instill confidence in the potential of similar interventions.

GAPS IN THE LITERATURE REVIEW

Identifying, understanding, and addressing gaps in existing literature is essential for advancing policies and strategies that respond to the nuanced impacts of minimum wage increases, transitions into STEM fields, and disparities in digital access (Paul et al., 2023). As given by He et al., (2023), these gaps highlight areas where further research is needed to develop more comprehensive and effective policies and strategies. The following subsections identify significant gaps in these areas, offering insights into where further research is necessary.

Overcoming Barriers in STEM Field Transitions

Research often explores the potential for displaced workers to transition into STEM fields. However, there are significant gaps regarding the specific barriers faced by various demographics, particularly in accessing STEM education and employment. For instance, the literature lacks detailed studies on the effectiveness of retraining programs and the accessibility of STEM education for adults and underrepresented groups (Chen et al., 2024). Furthermore, the role of non-traditional pathways, such as boot camps and online courses, in facilitating these transitions remains underexplored (Chen et al., 2024). The significance is addressing these gaps is crucial for developing targeted policies and educational strategies that ensure equitable access to STEM fields. This research could foster greater diversity and innovation in the workforce by enabling a broader demographic to contribute to STEM advancements (Chen et al., 2024).

Expanding the Digital Divide Analysis Beyond Physical Access

The digital divide is frequently discussed in terms of physical access to the internet and digital devices. However, this review overlooks critical dimensions like digital literacy, internet connectivity quality, and online content's relevance. More research is needed on how these factors influence individuals' ability to use digital tools effectively for learning, work, and participation in the digital economy (Crawford & Serhal, 2020). Scholars have pointed out that even in regions with high internet connectivity, disparities in material access, such as device diversity and ongoing maintenance expenses, continue to perpetuate inequality (Valdez & Javier, 2020). Additionally, the evolving nature of the digital divide in response to rapid technological changes and the emergence of new platforms and digital practices requires ongoing examination (Crawford & Serhal, 2020). The significance of this gap is that understanding these dimensions is essential for designing comprehensive digital inclusion strategies that enable all individuals to participate fully in the digital economy and access educational opportunities. This would help mitigate socio-economic disparities exacerbated by the digital divide (Crawford & Serhal, 2020).

Integrating Economic and Psychological Risks in Policy Evaluation

While the economic implications of minimum wage increases and technological advancements are well-documented, a significant gap lies in understanding the psychological impacts on workers. These include the stress of job displacement, the pressure to acquire new skills, and the uncertainties associated with transitioning to new career paths (Patel & Rietveld, 2020; Wels et al., 2021). Understanding these psychological dimensions is crucial for developing support systems and interventions that address workers' mental health and well-being affected by economic and technological changes, leading to more resilient and adaptive labor markets (Patel & Rietveld, 2020). The significance of this gap is that exploring these psychological dimensions is vital for creating support systems that address workers' well-being and how workers are affected by economic and technological changes, leading to more resilient and adaptive labor markets (Patel & Rietveld, 2020).

Tailoring Policies to Regional Variations and Sector-Specific Needs

There is a noted gap in the comprehensive analysis of how minimum wage policies and digital infrastructure developments vary across different regions and sectors (Uzialko, 2023; Sumagaysay & Agrawal, 2023). The effects of these policies are different, with different outcomes observed in rural vs. urban areas and across various industries. For instance, rural areas often face unique challenges related to digital infrastructure and economic conditions that are not adequately addressed in broader policy discussions (Uzialko, 2023; Sumagaysay & Agrawal, 2023). The significance of this gap is that addressing it is critical for designing tailored policy interventions that effectively respond to the unique economic and infrastructural conditions of different regions and sectors, thereby maximizing the benefits of such policies (Uzialko, 2023).

RESULTS/SOLUTIONS/CONCLUSIONS

Addressing the complex challenges of minimum wage increases, economic shifts, and technological advancements requires a multifaceted approach. Policy Adaptation and Support: The rationale for adaptable minimum wage policies, complemented by support for affected businesses and sectors, stems from recognizing that the impacts of wage increases are not uniform. Different regions and industries experience these changes.

Expanding access to STEM education and training is pivotal in preparing the workforce for future job market demands, particularly for those displaced by economic shifts or technological advancements. This solution addresses the critical need for workers to possess relevant, up-to-date skills that align with the opportunities in the burgeoning STEM fields. By focusing on inclusivity and aligning educational programs with market needs, this strategy aims to reduce barriers to entry and ensure a diverse and competent workforce capable of driving innovation and growth (Moghaddam et al., 2023).

The push for comprehensive digital inclusion strategies goes beyond ensuring physical access to the internet and digital devices. It recognizes that full participation in the digital economy requires not only connectivity but also digital literacy and access to high-quality, relevant digital content. This approach addresses the multifaceted nature of the digital divide, aiming to equip individuals with the skills and resources needed to leverage digital technologies for education, work, and civic participation. Enhancing digital literacy and connectivity is essential for fostering economic opportunities and bridging gaps in access and participation (Fu et al., 2024).

Developing and implementing risk management frameworks at various levels is critical for proactively addressing the uncertainties introduced by economic and technological changes. This solution recognizes the significance of preparing businesses, policymakers, and individuals to navigate potential risks, from job displacement to the challenges of digital transition. Effective risk management involves identifying potential threats, assessing their implications, and devising strategies to mitigate adverse outcomes. This proactive stance is indispensable for building resilience and ensuring that stakeholders are equipped to adapt to and thrive amidst change (Karangutkar, 2023).

This research underscores the complexity of navigating the effects of minimum wage increases, the transition into STEM careers, and overcoming the digital divide. Successful navigation requires a holistic approach that encompasses adaptable policies, targeted educational programs, comprehensive digital inclusion strategies, and effective risk management. By addressing these areas, stakeholders can work towards mitigating adverse impacts, leveraging opportunities for growth, and ensuring a more inclusive and resilient economic future. The solutions proposed here, while not exhaustive, offer a foundation for addressing the identified challenges. They highlight the significance of continuous research, collaboration among stakeholders, and the agility to adapt to evolving economic and technological landscapes. Further research is needed to refine these solutions and explore additional strategies, particularly in addressing the gaps identified in the literature. This ongoing inquiry will be crucial for developing policies and interventions that effectively respond to the dynamic interplay of labor market forces, technological advancements, and societal needs (Litchfield et al., 2021). By integrating these strategies, we can better support diverse populations in navigating the complexities of the modern workforce, ultimately fostering a more inclusive and equitable society.

Practical Applications

The findings and insights presented in this chapter offer several practical applications that can guide policymakers, educators, and industry leaders in addressing the challenges posed by economic shifts, technological advancements, and the digital divide. Practical applications enhance the chapter's value by showing how the research can inform decision-making processes and lead to tangible improvements in the targeted areas, thereby increasing the likelihood of the research being utilized and implemented in real-world scenarios (Akhmetshin, et al., 2024). These applications are designed to ensure that interventions are not only effective but also equitable and sustainable, fostering long-term economic resilience and social inclusivity. Four practical applications are offered.

Adaptable and Inclusive Policy Development

The research findings highlight the need for adaptable minimum wage policies tailored to the specific economic conditions of different regions and sectors. Policymakers should consider the varying impacts of wage increases across different geographic areas and industries to design policies that mitigate adverse effects while promoting economic growth. This approach is crucial for ensuring that wage policies are equitable and do not disproportionately impact vulnerable communities (Uzialko, 2023). Practical application of this information is that policymakers can use longitudinal studies on minimum wage impacts to guide the development of region-specific wage policies. These policies should be adaptable, allowing for adjustments based on real-time economic data and trends.

Enhancing STEM Education and Workforce Retraining

The chapter's focus on overcoming barriers in STEM field transitions suggests that curriculum design and educational policies should be more inclusive and aligned with the demands of the modern job market. Educational institutions should develop and implement retraining programs that cater to adult learners, particularly those transitioning from industries affected by economic shifts. These programs should emphasize accessibility for underrepresented groups and incorporate non-traditional pathways, such as online courses and boot camps (Chen et al., 2024). Practical application of this information is that educational policymakers and institutions can design curricula that focus on the specific needs of displaced workers, incorporating flexible learning options and targeted support services to enhance employability in STEM fields.

Comprehensive Digital Inclusion and Literacy Programs

The expanded discussion on the digital divide highlights the necessity of addressing not just access to digital technologies but also the quality of that access, digital literacy, and the relevance of online content. Comprehensive digital inclusion strategies should encompass infrastructure development, affordability programs, and digital literacy education to ensure full participation in the digital economy (Crawford & Serhal, 2020). The practical application of this information is that governments and organizations should implement programs that provide affordable internet access, enhance digital literacy, and ensure the usability and relevance of digital content for all demographics, particularly in underserved areas.

Mental Health and Workforce Adaptation Support

The research on the psychological impacts of economic and technological changes underscores the importance of developing support systems for workers facing job displacement and the pressure to adapt to new job roles. These systems should include mental health services, career counseling, and continuous learning opportunities to help workers navigate the uncertainties associated with technological advancements (Patel & Rietveld, 2020). The practical application of this information is that employers and policymakers should collaborate to create programs that provide psychological support and career transition services for workers affected by economic and technological disruptions, ensuring their mental well-being and adaptability in the workforce.

The practical applications of this research emphasize the need for a holistic approach that integrates adaptable policies, inclusive education, comprehensive digital strategies, and robust support systems. By implementing these strategies, stakeholders can better address the challenges posed by economic and technological changes, ultimately fostering a more resilient and inclusive society. These applications not only provide actionable insights but also underscore the importance of continuous research and collaboration among various stakeholders to ensure that the benefits of economic and technological advancements are equitably distributed across all segments of society.

Future Research

Future research in these areas is imperative for building on the current understanding and refining strategies to address the challenges identified. The practical applications of this research underscore its value, offering pathways to economic resilience, workforce empowerment, and societal inclusivity. By focusing on these directions, researchers, policymakers, and educators can collaboratively work towards a future that harnesses economic and technological changes for the benefit of all sectors of society. Four areas of future research are suggested.

Longitudinal Studies on Minimum Wage Policy Impacts

Future research should investigate how the impacts of economic growth vary across different industries and regions to capture the long-term effects of minimum wage increases on employment patterns, and business sustainability. Such studies should explore the interaction between wage policies and other socio-economic factors, providing a more nuanced understanding of policy effects. This future research is essential for developing adaptable minimum wage policies that can mitigate negative impacts while promoting equitable economic growth (Uzialko, 2023).

Efficacy of STEM Retraining Programs

Future research should focus on assessing the effectiveness of retraining programs designed for adults transitioning into STEM fields. This research should include evaluating participants' long-term career stability, income progression, and job satisfaction. In facilitating these transitions, particular attention should be given to non-traditional education pathways, such as boot camps and online courses. This future research is essential to understand how the efficacy of these programs will help design more inclusive and accessible educational strategies that can address workforce displacement and skill gaps in the STEM sector (Chen et al., 2024).

Comprehensive Analysis of the Digital Divide

Expanding the scope of research on the digital divide is crucial. Future studies should examine access to digital technologies and digital literacy, content relevance, and the socio-economic factors influencing technology use. Additionally, the evolving nature of the digital divide, particularly in the context of rapid technological changes, should be thoroughly explored. This future research is vital for developing comprehensive digital inclusion strategies ensuring equitable participation in the digital economy and access to educational opportunities (Crawford & Serhal, 2020). This future research is essential to understand how the efficacy of these programs will help design more inclusive and accessible educational strategies that can address workforce displacement and skill gaps in the STEM sector (Chen et al., 2024).

Psychological Impacts of Economic and Technological Transitions

There is a significant need for research into the psychological effects on workers undergoing job displacement, retraining, and adaptation to new economic realities. Studies should focus on stress, mental health, and well-being, providing insights that could inform the development of support systems and interventions. Future research is critical for understanding these psychological dimensions. It is crucial to create support systems that enhance the resilience and adaptability of the workforce in the face of economic and technological changes (Patel & Rietveld, 2020). This future research is vital for developing comprehensive digital inclusion strategies ensuring equitable participation in the digital economy and access to educational opportunities (Crawford & Serhal, 2020). This future research is essential to understand how the efficacy of these programs will help design more inclusive and accessible educational strategies that can address workforce displacement and skill gaps in the STEM sector (Chen et al., 2024).

Future research in these areas is imperative for building on the current understanding and refining strategies to address the challenges identified in this chapter. By focusing on these directions, researchers, policymakers, and educators can collaboratively work towards a future that harnesses economic and technological changes for the benefit of all sectors of society. This collaborative effort will ensure that policy interventions and educational initiatives are effective and inclusive, fostering a more resilient and equitable workforce capable of thriving in an increasingly digital and interconnected world.

REFERENCES

Adelekan, O. A., Ilugbusi, B. S., Adisa, O., Obi, O. C., Awonuga, K. F., Asuzu, O. F., & Ndubuisi, N. L. (2024). Energy transition policies: A global review of shifts towards renewable sources. *Engineering Science & Technology Journal*, 5(2), 272–287. DOI: 10.51594/estj.v5i2.752

Adeniyi, I. S., Al Hamad, N. M., Adewusi, O. E., Unachukwu, C. C., Osawaru, B., Onyebuchi, C. N., Omolawal, S. A., Aliu, A. O., & David, I. O. (2024). E-learning platforms in higher education: A comparative review of the USA and Africa. *International Journal of Science and Research Archive*, 11(1), 1686–1697. DOI: 10.30574/ijsra.2024.11.1.0283

Agbo, F. J. (2024). Broadening participation in adult education: A literature review of computer science education. In *Proceedings of the 55th ACM Technical Symposium on Computer Science Education*, 1, pp. 11-17. DOI: 10.1145/3626252.3630797

Ajayi, F. A., & Udeh, C. A. (2024). Review of crew resilience and mental health practices in the marine industry: Pathways to improvement. *Magna Scientia Advanced Biology and Pharmacy, 11*(2), 033-049. DOI:DOI: 10.30574/msabp.2024.11.2.0021

Akhmetshin, E., Makushkin, S., Abdullayev, I., Yumashev, A., Kozachek, A., Shichiyakh, R., & Shakhov, D. (2024). Opportunities to Increase the Efficiency of Universities' Research and Innovation Activities: Scientometric Evaluation of Researchers' Work under External Information Constraints. *Qubahan Academic Journal*, 4(1), 240–249. DOI: 10.48161/qaj.v4n1a258

Alderman, B. L., & Blair, R. D. (2024). *Monopsony in Labor Markets: Theory, Evidence, and Public Policy*. Cambridge University Press. DOI: 10.1017/9781009465212

Alderman, B. L., Blair, R. D., & Saygin, P. Ö. (2023). Monopsony, wage discrimination, and public policy. *Economic Inquiry*, 61(3), 572–583. DOI: 10.1111/ecin.13131

Ali, M., Aini, M. A., & Alam, S. N. (2024). Integrating technology in learning in madrasah: Towards the digital age. [INJOE]. *Indonesian Journal of Education*, 4(1), 290–304.

Amberger, C., & Schreyer, D. (2024). What do we know about no-show behavior? A systematic, interdisciplinary literature review. *Journal of Economic Surveys*, 38(1), 57–96. DOI: 10.1111/joes.12534

Arora, P. (2023). *Building Resilience in the future workforce: The role of continuous learning and transferable skills*. BSSS Journal of Education., DOI: 10.51767/je1207

Azar, J., Huet-Vaughn, E., Marinescu, I., Taska, B., & Von Wachter, T. (2023). Minimum wage employment effects and labour market concentration. *The Review of Economic Studies*, •••, rdad091. Advance online publication. DOI: 10.3386/w26101

Baily, M. N., Boswoth, B., & Kennedy, K. (2021). The contribution of human capital to economic growth: A cross-country comparison of Germany, Japan, and the United States. *The Brookings Economic Studies.*https://www.brookings.edu/wp-content/uploads/2021/09/20210928_BailyBosworthKennedy_Returns_to_education_final.pdf

Bandhu, D., Mohan, M. M., Nittala, N. A. P., Jadhav, P., Bhadauria, A., & Saxena, K. K. (2024). Theories of motivation: A comprehensive analysis of human behavior drivers. *Acta Psychologica*, 244, 104177. DOI: 10.1016/j.actpsy.2024.104177 PMID: 38354564

Bartik, A. W., Bertrand, M., Lin, F., Rothstein, J., & Unrath, M. (2020. July). Measuring the labor market at the onset of the COVID-19 crisis. *Natural Bureau of Economic Research.* https://www.nber.org/papers/w27613

Bongitte, I. (2024). Impact of minimum wage increases on employment levels in the United States. *American Journal of Economics*, 8(1), 39–50. DOI: 10.47672/aje.1790

Brenya, B. (2024). Higher education in emergency situation: Blended learning prospects and challenges for educators in the developing countries. *Journal of Applied Research in Higher Education*, 16(4), 1015–1028. DOI: 10.1108/JARHE-01-2023-0044

Brown-Jackson, K. L. (2017). Disrupting and retooling: A model for an effective community-based telehealth program (Doctoral dissertation, The National Graduate School of Quality Management). https://www.proquest.com/openview/d0a3ddae9045391382a3e936ac33a126/1?pq-origsite=gscholar&cbl=44156

Burton, S. L. (2024). Business Resilience in a Cyber World: Protect Against Attacks Part 2. In Innovations, Securities, and Case Studies Across Healthcare, Business, and Technology (pp. 1-25). IGI Global. DOI: DOI: 10.4018/979-8-3693-1906-2.ch001

Buscha, F., & Dickson, M. (2023). Returns to education: Individuals. In Zimmermann, K. F. (Ed.), *Handbook of Labor, Human Resources and Population Economics*. Springer., DOI: 10.1007/978-3-319-57365-6_377-1

Butcher, K., & Shiro, A. G. (2024, January). Policy brief: The high and lasting costs of job displacement. *Federal Reserve Bank of Chicago*. https://www.chicagofed.org/publications/chicago-fed-insights/2024/policy-brief-costs-of-job-displacement

Cavada, M., Tight, M. R., & Rogers, C. D. (2019). A smart city case study of Singapore—Is Singapore truly smart? *Smart City Emergence*, 295-314. DOI: 10.1016/B978-0-12-816169-2.00014-6

Chakravorti, B. (2021, July 20). How to close the digital divide in the U.S. *Harvard Business Review*. https://hbr.org/2021/07/how-to-close-the-digital-divide-in-the-u-s#:~:text=Policymakers%20should%3A%201%29%20pay%20for%20improvements%20using%20a,in%20future-proofing%2C%20and%207%29%20invest%20in%20digital%20literacy

Chen, L. Y., & Nguyen, K. E. (2024). Challenges in measuring the returns to education: Human capital theory revisited. *The Journal of Human Resources*. Advance online publication. DOI: 10.3386/jhr.2024.0002

Chen, Y., So, W. W., Zhu, J., & Chiu, S. W. (2024). STEM learning opportunities and career aspirations: The interactive effect of students' self-concept and perceptions of STEM professionals. *International Journal of STEM Education*, 11(1), 1–21. DOI: 10.1186/s40594-024-00466-7

Clemens, J., & Wither, M. (2019). The minimum wage and the Great Recession: Evidence of effects on the employment and income trajectories of low-skilled workers. *Journal of Public Economics*, 170, 53–67. DOI: 10.1016/j.jpubeco.2019.01.004

Crawford, A., & Serhal, E. (2020). Digital health equity and COVID-19: The innovation curve cannot reinforce the social gradient of health. *Journal of Medical Internet Research*, 22(6), e19361. DOI: 10.2196/19361 PMID: 32452816

Cui, Y., He, Y., Xu, X., Zhou, L., Nutakor, J. A., & Zhao, L. (2024). Cultural capital, the digital divide, and the health of older adults: A moderated mediation effect test. *BMC Public Health*, 24(1), 302. DOI: 10.1186/s12889-024-17831-4 PMID: 38273305

Dai, X., & Qiu, Y. (2019, September 11). Minimum wage hikes and technology adoption: evidence from U.S. establishments. *Journal of Financial and Quantitative Analysis (JFQA)*. Available at *SSRN*: https://ssrn.com/abstract=3451663 or DOI: 10.2139/ssrn.3451663

De Weerdt, D., De Schepper, A., Kyndt, E., & Gijbel, D. (2024). Entering the Labor Market: Networks and Networking Behavior in the School-to-Work Transition. *Vocations and Learning*, 17(2), 311–332. DOI: 10.1007/s12186-024-09343-4

Devisakti, A., Muftahu, M., & Xiaoling, H. (2024). Digital divide among B40 students in Malaysian higher education institutions. *Education and Information Technologies*, 29(2), 1857–1883. DOI: 10.1007/s10639-023-11847-w PMID: 37361786

Dyke, G. (2022, October 2). What is the background in a research paper? *AJE Scholar Articles*. https://www.aje.com/arc/what-is-the-background-in-a-research-paper/

Eden, C.A., Chisom, O.N., & Adeniyi, I.S. (2024). Promoting digital literacy and social equity in education: Lessons from successful initiatives. *International Journal of Management & Entrepreneurship Research*. DOI:DOI: 10.51594/ijmer.v6i3.880

Employment & Training Administration [ETA]. (n.d.). WIOA adult and dislocated worker program. *U. S. Department of Labor*. https://www.dol.gov/agencies/eta/workforce-investment/adult

Faliagka, E., Christopoulou, E., Ringas, D., Politi, T., Kostis, N., Leonardos, D., Tranoris, C., Antonopoulos, C. P., Denazis, S., & Voros, N. (2024). Trends in digital twin framework architectures for smart cities: A case study in smart mobility. *Sensors (Basel)*, 24(5), 1665. DOI: 10.3390/s24051665 PMID: 38475201

Federal Communications Commission. (2020, October 29 – November 25). Auction 904: Rural digital opportunity fund. https://www.fcc.gov/auction/904

Federal Communications Commission. (2024, May). lifeline program for low-income consumers. https://www.fcc.gov/general/lifeline-program-low-income-consumers

Fu, L., Zeng, Y., & Kang, X. (2024). Bridging the urban–rural gap: A qualitative examination of perceived access, barriers, risks and opportunities of children's digital learning during the COVID-19 pandemic. *Child & Family Social Work*, 29(1), 1–11. DOI: 10.1111/cfs.13045

Gener, C. E. (2023). The Development of Academic Course Package for Digitalized Instruction in Educational Technology Management. *European Journal Of Innovation In Nonformal Education, 3*(7), 317–340. https://inovatus.es/index.php/ejine/article/view/1911

Ghodsi, M., Stehrer, R., & Barišić, A. (2024). Assessing the impact of new technologies on wages and labour income shares (No. 240). wiiw Working Paper.

Giotis, G. (2024). Labor Market Institutions and Employment. *Encyclopedia*, 4(1), 273–294. DOI: 10.3390/encyclopedia4010021

Global Partnership for Sustainable Development Data. (2022). Better data. Better decisions. Better lives. *Author*. https://www.data4sdgs.org/

Grimes, N. D., & Porter, W. (2023). Closing the digital divide through digital equity: The role of libraries and librarians. *Public Library Quarterly*, 43(3), 307–338. DOI: 10.1080/01616846.2023.2251348

Haleem, A., Javaid, M., Qadri, M. A., & Suman, R. (2022). Understanding the role of digital technologies in education: A review. *Sustainable Operations and Computers*, 3, 275–285. DOI: 10.1016/j.susoc.2022.05.004

Hazari, A. (2024). Manuscript Preparation and Writing. In Research Methodology for Allied Health Professionals: A comprehensive guide to Thesis & Dissertation (pp. 99-103). Singapore: Springer Nature Singapore. DOI: 10.1007/978-981-99-8925-6_11

He, B., Wang, W., Sharifi, A., & Liu, X. (2023). Progress, knowledge gap and future directions of urban heat mitigation and adaptation research through a bibliometric review of history and evolution. *Energy and Building*, 287, 112976. DOI: 10.1016/j.enbuild.2023.112976

Holt, A. (2024, January). Unions, industrial concentration, and economic rents: How the Wagner Act increased wages during the 1930s. *Industrial Concentration, and Economic Rents: How the Wagner Act increased wages during the 1930s.SSRN*. DOI: 10.2139/ssrn.4698381

Hou, Y., Chen, S., & Lin, X. (2024). Parental digital involvement in online learning: Addressing the digital divide, not redressing digital reproduction. *European Journal of Education*, 59(2), e12635. DOI: 10.1111/ejed.12635

Houchil, K. (2023, May 3). Governor Hochul announces historic agreement to increase New York's Minimum Wage and index to inflation as part of FY 2024 budget. *New York State*. https://www.governor.ny.gov/news/governor-hochul-announces-historic-agreement-increase-new-yorks-minimum-wage-and-index

Hurst, E., Kehoe, P., Pastorino, E., & Winberry, T. (2022, July). The distributional impact of the minimum wage in the short and long run. NBER Working Paper No. w30294. *SSRN*: https://ssrn.com/abstract=4177541 DOI: 10.2139/ssrn.4177541

Hwang, Y. I. J., Hagos, A., Withall, A., Hampton, S., Snoyman, P., & Butler, T. (2024). Population ageing, incarceration and the growing digital divide: Understanding the effects of digital literacy inequity experienced by older people leaving prison. *PLoS One*, 9(4), e0297482. DOI: 10.1371/journal.pone.0297482 PMID: 38630834

Jain, A., Hisam, M. W., Azad, I., Dar, A. A., Malhotra, M., & Khan, M. S. (2024). Digitalization's revolutionary effect on education and career development. *Information Sciences Letters*, 13(1), 149–157. DOI: 10.18576/isl/130112

Jiang, X., Xu, J., & Xu, X. (2024). An overview of domestic and international applications of digital technology in teaching in vocational education: Systematic literature mapping. *Education and Information Technologies*, 29(13), 1–33. DOI: 10.1007/s10639-024-12528-y

Kaiser, C., Miedzinski, M., McDowall, W., & McCarney, G. R. (2024). reflective appraisal of transformative innovation policy: Development of the sustainability transition and innovation review (STIR) approach and application to Canada. *Sustainability (Basel)*, 16(12), 5106. DOI: 10.3390/su16125106

Kanvaria, V. K., & Yadav, A. (2024). Integrating and Innovating: The Role of ICT in Education's Evolution-An In-depth Analysis of Emerging Technologies, Current Trends, Challenges, and Future Directions in the Digital Age. *International Journal for Multidimensional Research Perspectives*, 2(2), 33–48.

Karangutkar, A.Amogh Amol Karangutkar. (2023). The Impact of Artificial Intelligence on Job Displacement and the Future of Work. *International Journal of Advanced Research in Science. Tongxin Jishu*, 635–638. Advance online publication. DOI: 10.48175/IJARSCT-12096

Karlén, N., & Rauta, V. (2023). Dealers and brokers in civil wars: Why states delegate rebel support to conduit countries. *International Security*, 47(4), 107–146. DOI: 10.1162/isec_a_00461

Lefebvre, V. (2024). Layoffs in SMEs: The role of social proximity. *Journal of Business Ethics*, 190(4), 801–820. DOI: 10.1007/s10551-023-05414-z PMID: 37359804

Leone, J. &Lo Casio, e. J. (2020). Income gaps: Education and inequality. *Economics and Business Review, 6*(4).

Leong, S., & Lee, T. (2021). The Internet in Singapore: From 'Intelligent Island' to 'Smart Nation'. In: Global internet governance. *Palgrave Pivot*, Singapore. DOI: 10.1007/978-981-15-9924-8_3

Leoni, S. (2023). A historical review of the role of education: From human capital to human capabilities. *Review of Political Economy*, •••, 1–18. DOI: 10.1080/09538259.2023.2245233

Li, T., Mayo-Wilson, E., Shaughnessy, D., & Qureshi, R. (2024). Studying harms of interventions with an equity lens in randomized trials. *Trials*, 25(1), 403. DOI: 10.1186/s13063-024-08239-x PMID: 38902776

Litchfield, I., Shukla, D., & Greenfield, S. (2021). Impact of COVID-19 on the digital divide: A rapid review. *BMJ Open*, 11(10), e053440. Advance online publication. DOI: 10.1136/bmjopen-2021-053440 PMID: 34642200

Marshall, A. (2023). A new rural digital divide? Taking stock of geographical digital inclusion in Australia. *Media International Australia*. Advance online publication. DOI: 10.1177/1329878X231202274

Mhlanga, D. (2024). Digital transformation of education, the limitations and prospects of introducing the fourth industrial revolution asynchronous online learning in emerging markets. *Discover Education*, 3(32), 32. Advance online publication. DOI: 10.1007/s44217-024-00115-9

Moghaddam, Y., Russell, M., Yuen, J., & Demirkan, H. (2023). *Roadmap to close the gap between undergraduate education and STEM Employment across industry sectors, further studied*. The Human Side of Service Engineering., DOI: 10.54941/ahfe1003109

Monaco, R., Bergaentzlé, C., Leiva Vilaplana, J. A., Ackom, E., & Nielsen, P. S. (2024). Digitalization of power distribution grids: Barrier analysis, ranking and policy recommendations. *Energy Policy*, 188, 114083. DOI: 10.1016/j.enpol.2024.114083

Moon, S., Guan, S. A., Vargas, J. H., Lin, J. C., Kwan, P., Saetermoe, C. L., Flores, G., & Chavira, G. (2024). Critical mentorship in undergraduate research experience BUILDs science identity and self-efficacy. *International Journal of Science and Mathematics Education*. Advance online publication. DOI: 10.1007/s10763-024-10476-0

Nae, T. M., Florescu, M. S., & Bălă oiu, G. I. (2024). Towards social justice: Investigating the role of labor, globalization, and governance in reducing socio-economic inequality within post-communist countries. *Sustainability (Basel)*, 16(6), 2234. DOI: 10.3390/su16062234

Office of the Governor Tim Waltz & Lt. Governor Peggy Flanagan. (2024, June 5). Governor Walz, Lieutenant Governor Flanagan announce opening of applications for Minnesota student teacher grants and loan repayment programs. *Author*. https://mn.gov/governor/newsroom/press-releases/

Omodan, B. I. (2024). Redefining university infrastructure for the 21st century: An interplay between physical assets and digital evolution. *Journal of Infrastructure. Policy and Development*, 8(4), 3468. DOI: 10.24294/jipd.v8i4.3468

Paris, R. A. (2024). Intersectionalities of systematic barriers set upon underrepresented students in STEM: Capturing the potential benefits of online modality. *University Honors Theses. Paper 1441*. DOI: 10.15760/honors.1473

Patel, P., & Rietveld, C. (2020). The impact of financial insecurity on the self-employed's short-term psychological distress: Evidence from the COVID-19 pandemic. *P*, 14, e00206. Advance online publication. DOI: 10.1016/j.jbvi.2020.e00206

Patel, P. C. (2024). Out of the frying pan into the fire: Displaced workers' vocational skill specificity, self-employment, and income. *Small Business Economics*, 63(3), 1–27. DOI: 10.1007/s11187-023-00856-1

Paul, J., Khatri, P., & Kaur Duggal, H. (2023). Frameworks for developing impactful systematic literature reviews and theory building: What, Why and How? *Journal of Decision Systems*, •••, 1–14. DOI: 10.1080/12460125.2023.2197700

Pekrun, R. (2024). Overcoming fragmentation in motivation science: Why, When, and How should we integrate theories? *Educational Psychology Review*, 36(1), 27. DOI: 10.1007/s10648-024-09846-5

Pew. (2021, May 2). what policymakers can learn from the 'Minnesota Model' of broadband expansion. *Author*. https://www.pewtrusts.org/en/research-and-analysis/articles/2021/03/02/what-policymakers-can-learn-from-the-minnesota-model-of-broadband-expansion

Polacko, M. (2021). Causes and consequences of income inequality: An overview. *Statistics, Politics, and Policy*, 12(2), 341–357. DOI: 10.1515/spp-2021-0017

Pope County Minnesota. (2019). Total broadband coverage in county now in sight; Pope county Starbuck telephone project receives $4.2mm deed grant. *Author*. https://www.popecountymn.gov/total-broadband-coverage-in-county-now-in-sight-pope-county-starbuck-telephone-project-receives-4-2mm-deed-grant-2/

Powell, D., Reich, M., Allegretto, S., & Jacobs, K. (2021). Minimum wage effects across state borders: Estimates using contiguous counties. *Journal of Labor Economics*, 39(S1), S139–S186.

Quispe Mamani, J. C., Flores Turpo, G. A., Calcina Álvarez, D. A., Yapuchura Saico, C. R., Velásquez Velásquez, W. L., Aguilar Pinto, S. L., Quispe, B., & Quispe Maquera, N. B. (2022). Gap and inequality in the economic income of independent workers in the region of Puno-Peru and the effect of the pandemic, 2019–2020. *Frontiers in Sociology*, 7, 7. DOI: 10.3389/fsoc.2022.858331 PMID: 35495574

Raschke, D., & Peace, C. (2021). Remapping Career Counseling for Future Work. *TMS Proceedings 2021*. DOI: 10.1037/tms0000104

Redmond, P., & McGuinness, S. (2021). The impact of the 2016 minimum wage increase on average labour costs, hours worked and employment in Irish firms. *Fiscal Studies*. Advance online publication. DOI: 10.26504/rs118

Saldaña, J. (2021). *The Coding Manual for Qualitative Researchers*. Sage Publishers.

Saros, D. E. (2019). *Principles of Political Economy* (3rd ed.). Valparaiso University.

Sefil-Tansever, S., & Yılmaz, E. (2024). Minimum wage and spillover effects in a minimum wage society. *Labour*, 38(1), labr.12259. Advance online publication. DOI: 10.1111/labr.12259

Suhrab, M., Chen, P., & Ullah, A. (2024). Digital financial inclusion and income inequality nexus: Can technology innovation and infrastructure development help in achieving sustainable development goals? *Technology in Society*, 76, 102411. DOI: 10.1016/j.techsoc.2023.102411

Sumagaysay, L., & Agrawal, S. (2023, December 21). New California laws raise the minimum wage for 2 industries. Others could see pay hikes, too. *CAL Matters*. https://calmatters.org/economy/2023/12/minimum-wage-2024/

The Federal Science, Technology, Engineering, And Mathematics (Stem) Education Strategic Plan. *Author*. https://www.whitehouse.gov/wp-content/uploads/2024/04/2023-CoSTEM-Progress-Report.pdf

The White House. (2024, April 16). Progress Report on the Implementation of the Federal Science, Technology, Engineering, and Mathematics (STEM) Education Strategic Plan. *Author*. https://www.whitehouse.gov/ostp/news-updates/2024/04/16/2023-progress-report-on-the-implementation-of-the-federal-science-technology-engineering-and-mathematics-stem-education-strategic-plan/

The World Bank. (2020). Tackling the impact of job displacement through public policies. *Author*. https://www.worldbank.org/en/news/feature/2020/10/20/tackling-the-impact-of-job-displacement-through-public-policies

Trezzini, A. (2024, February). Hazel Kyrk, The Economics of the Social Relevance of Consumption and John Maynard Keynes' Consumption Function. *In Research in the History of Economic Thought and Methodology: Including a Symposium on Hazel Kyrk's: A Theory of Consumption 100 Years after Publication*, 41, pp. 69-93. Emerald Publishing Limited.

Tytler, R. (2020). STEM Education for the Twenty-First Century. In Anderson, J., & Li, Y. (Eds.), *Integrated approaches to STEM Education. Advances in STEM education*. Springer., DOI: 10.1007/978-3-030-52229-2_3

U. S. Bureau of Labor Statistics [U. S. BLS]. (2024, May). Characteristics of minimum wage workers, 2023. *Author*. https://www.bls.gov/opub/reports/minimum-wage/2023/home.htm

U. S. Department of Labor. (2024, January 1). Consolidated minimum wage table. *Author.*https://www.dol.gov/agencies/whd/mw-consolidated

U.S. Congressional Office. (2024, January 24). How Increasing the federal minimum wage could affect employment and family income. *Author.* https://www.cbo.gov/publication/55681

Uzialko, A. (2023, November 20). How small businesses are affected by minimum wage. *Business News Daily.* https://www.businessnewsdaily.com/8984-increased-minimum-wage.html

Valdez, V. B., & Javier, S. P. (2020). Digital divide: From a peripheral to a core issue for all SDGs. In Leal Filho, W., Azul, A. M., Brandli, L., Lange Salvia, A., Özuyar, P. G., & Wall, T. (Eds.), *Reduced Inequalities. Encyclopedia of the UN Sustainable Development Goals.* Springer., DOI: 10.1007/978-3-319-71060-0_107-1

Warschauer, M. (2001). Singapore's dilemma: Control versus autonomy in IT-led development. *The Information Society*, 17(4), 305–311. DOI: 10.1080/019722401753330922

Webb, S. (1912). The Economic Theory of a Legal Minimum Wage. *Journal of Political Economy*, 20(10), 973–998. Advance online publication. DOI: 10.1086/252125

Wels, J., Booth, C., Wielgoszewska, B., Green, M., Gessa, G., Huggins, C., Griffith, G., Kwong, A., Bowyer, R., Maddock, J., Patalay, P., Silverwood, R., Fitzsimons, E., Shaw, R., Steptoe, A., Hughes, A., Chaturvedi, N., Steves, C., Katikireddi, S., & Ploubidis, G. (2021). Association of COVID-19 employment disruption with mental and social wellbeing: evidence from nine UK longitudinal studies. DOI: 10.1101/2021.11.15.21266264

Yaseen, A. (2024). Enhancing Cybersecurity through Automated Infrastructure Management: A Comprehensive Study on Optimizing Security Measures. *Quarterly Journal of Emerging Technologies and Innovations*, 9(1), 38–60.

Zhang, M., Lu, S., Zhang, S., & Bai, Y. (2023). The unintended consequence of minimum wage hikes: Evidence based on firms' pollution emission. *Energy Economics*, 125, 106857. DOI: 10.1016/j.eneco.2023.106857

KEY WORDS AND DEFINITIONS

Digital Divide: This term Refers to the gap between individuals and communities with varying levels of access to digital technologies, such as the internet and digital devices, and their ability to effectively use these tools for educational, economic, and social participation. This divide impacts economic mobility and digital literacy, especially in underserved communities (Crawford & Serhal, 2020).

Economic Stability: Economic stability involves maintaining a steady growth rate in an economy, reducing unemployment, and managing inflation. Economic stability is influenced by policies such as minimum wage laws, which can have varying effects on different sectors and regions (Uzialko, 2023).

Minimum Wage Policy: This phrase refers to the legislative action that sets the lowest hourly wage rate that an employer can legally pay employees. The policy's impact on employment, economic growth, and worker welfare is a central theme in discussions of economic stability and income inequality (Chen et al., 2024).

Psychological Impact: This phrase encompasses the mental health and well-being effects experienced by workers due to job displacement, economic uncertainty, and the pressure to adapt to technological advancements (Patel & Rietveld, 2020).

STEM Education: Education in the fields of Science, Technology, Engineering, and Mathematics, which is critical for preparing the workforce to meet the demands of a rapidly advancing technological landscape. STEM education is a key focus area for fostering economic stability and workforce development (Chen et al., 2024).

Technological Displacement: Technological Displacement: Refers to the loss of jobs due to advancements in technology, such as automation and artificial intelligence, which can lead to economic instability and require workers to retrain for new roles (Karangutkar, 2023).

Workforce Adaptability: This adaptability is the ability of workers to adjust to changes in the job market, including the need to acquire new skills and transition into new roles, particularly in response to technological changes and economic policies (Patel & Rietveld, 2020).

Workforce Retraining: These retraining references programs and initiatives are aimed at equipping displaced workers with the skills necessary to transition into new employment opportunities, especially in emerging sectors such as STEM fields (Chen et al., 2024).

Chapter 7
Organizational Readiness for Artificial Intelligence (AI) in Network Security

B. Avery Greene
https://orcid.org/0009-0007-0849-3945
Capitol Technology University, USA

Sharon L. Burton
https://orcid.org/0000-0003-1653-9783
Capitol Technology University, USA

ABSTRACT

This chapter explores the essential organizational and cultural prerequisites for successfully integrating Artificial Intelligence (AI) into network security. This research employs a qualitative methodology, including a comprehensive literature review, to analyze internal needs and address ethical considerations such as bias, privacy, and fairness. This study examines the impact of organizational culture on the acceptance and effectiveness of AI-based solutions. It emphasizes the significance of end-user trust in AI-driven security alerts. The findings highlight the necessity of organizational readiness and cultural adaptation for the effective implementation of AI in network security, concluding that a comprehensive approach is essential for maximizing AI's potential in enhancing security measures. This research will benefit cybersecurity professionals, organizational leaders, and policymakers seeking to understand and navigate the complexities of AI integration in network security.

DOI: 10.4018/979-8-3693-8562-3.ch007

INTRODUCTION

It is not known how organizational readiness and cultural adaptation impact the successful integration of Artificial Intelligence (AI) in network security frameworks in the United States. The increasing impact of AI in network security is a direct response to the developing and complex nature of cyber threats (Kaur et al., 2023). As organizations become more digitally integrated, the need for advanced AI-driven security systems becomes crucial (Lee et al., 2023). As given by Mohammed (2023), integrating AI into existing network security frameworks presents unique challenges, necessitating significant organizational readiness and cultural and operational adaptation (Mohamed, 2023). In an era where cyber threats evolve unprecedentedly, integrating AI into network security transitions from an option to a necessity (Mohamed, 2023). The Mohammed (2023) research ties to the information presented by Sharton (2021), which focusses on the radical surge in cyberattacks, chiefly ransomware, throughout the move of remote work amidst the COVID-19 pandemic.

The reported 150% increase in ransomware incidents and the succeeding 300% upsurge in ransom payments emphasize the intensified susceptibility and the intensifying relentlessness of cyber threats faced by individuals and organizations (Sharton, 2021). Accordingly, these statistics support Mohamed's assertion that implementing AI-driven security solutions is no longer non-compulsory, perilous if ignored, and must successfully offset and mitigate these radical cyber threats.

Also, connected to the information presented by Sharton (2021), is the Hiscox Cyber Readiness Report, which surveyed over 5,000 organizations of diverse sizes across eight countries, specifies an unceasing rise in cyberattacks for the fourth consecutive year (Hiscox, 2023). A considerable increase in attacks targeting small businesses with fewer than ten employees rose from 23% to 36% in the past three years, highlighting cybercriminals' increasing focus on exploiting vulnerabilities within IT infrastructures (Hiscox, 2023). With the financial toll of cybercrime projected to attain $6 trillion annually by 2023 (Agenda, 2023), it is vital for organizations to strengthen their digital defenses (Hiscox, 2023; Peter et al., 2020). At this critical intersection, AI exists as a vital resource, poised to augment detection capabilities, simplify response times, and protect digital assets from various cyber threats (Sharma, 2023).

This chapter is an in-depth qualitative investigation that dives into the organizational and cultural requirements necessary for the optimal integration of AI into network security via a literature review. It sheds light on the difficulties and problems that companies confront with digital transformation (DT) by analyzing the internal demands and concerns around AI, including but not limited to, critical ethical issues such as prejudice, privacy, and justice. It also looks at how organizational culture and context influence the acceptability and efficacy of AI-based monitoring systems. This research emphasizes the importance of understanding end-user trust and confidence in AI-driven security warnings, and it provides readers with a detailed explanation of the complex process of AI integration in network security.

Recent advances in AI have created highly effective network security solutions (Mohamed, 2023). For example, the use of AI-based Lightweight Blockchain Security Models (AILBSM) in Industrial Internet of Things (IIoT) systems have been tested to improve privacy and security while reducing execution time and boosting classification accuracy (Selvarajan et al., 2023). Furthermore, applying deep learning systems, such as support vector machines (SVMs), for intrusion detection in social media networks results in excellent accuracy, precision, and recall, demonstrating AI's promise in a variety of network scenarios (Abuali et al., 2023). This data is important for firms to know for several reasons, such as the rising cyber threat landscape, financial implications, technological necessity, competitive advantage, organizational readiness, cultural adaptation, ethical considerations, and end-user trust while navigating DT, particularly in the context of cybersecurity and organizational strategy.

The *rising cyber threat landscape references* the exponential growth in cyber-attacks and their complexity implies that standard security methods are no longer enough to defend commercial assets (Chertoff, 2023). Understanding the evolving nature of cyber threats is critical for firms that want to predict vulnerabilities and deploy proactive defenses. As a result, organizations must adapt by using modern security advancements such as incorporating machine learning with traditional based network security tools (Markevych & Dawson, 2023).

In terms of *financial implications,* cybercrime's financial impact is expected to exceed $6 trillion per year, organizations suffer not only direct financial losses from breaches but also indirect expenses such as reputational harm, regulatory penalties, and missed commercial opportunities (Hiscox, 2023; Sharif & Mohammed, 2022). Awareness of these financial repercussions emphasizes the significance of investing in strong security solutions (Sharif & Mohammed, 2022; Ratin, 2024). As a result, firms must prioritize urgent cybersecurity measures and adopt long-term plans to manage these comprehensive threats, assuring financial stability and market confidence (Ratiu, 2024). Given the amplified and compounded characteristics of cyber threats, it is apparent that the considerable financial stakes concerned further induce companies to improve their security frameworks.

Technological necessity and competitive advantage are critical for AI integration. AI integration in network security is a strategic imperative rather than a technology update (Oztemel & Gursev, 2020). According to this research team, AI's ability to increase detection, reaction times, and digital asset security gives firms a competitive advantage in protecting their data and retaining confidence with clients and partners. This development in security architecture solves existing weaknesses and enables firms to better predict and respond to new cyber threats, enabling a robust defense against the ever-changing panorama of cyber dangers (Oztemel & Gursev, 2020). Companies using AI rely heavily on foresight accompanied with planning to achieve successful AI implementation.

Organizational readiness and cultural adaptation are critical for the operative integration of AI and network security into a widespread technology deployment. This process requires a complete understanding of organizational preparedness, circling cultural and operational adaptations (Attkan & Ranga, 2022). Businesses must foster an environment that encourages innovation, learning, and adaptability to evolving technologies (ISC2, 2023; Kim et al., 2023). Such a foundation aids current security initiatives and safeguards that companies are well-equipped to act on future challenges. Another component needed with organizational readiness is the internal support from users and key stakeholders using AI.

Ethical Considerations and End-User Trust are principal as AI systems progressively handle sensitive data and make crucial security decisions, underlining the significance of addressing concerns such as bias, privacy, and fairness (Boutin, 2022). Businesses must address these issues to create and retain confidence with end users and stakeholders, ensuring that AI is used responsibly (Huff et al., 2023). Furthermore, transparent and accountable AI practices are required for organizations to effectively negotiate the intricacies of digital ethics, reaffirming their commitment to responsible innovation and protecting all parties involved. Internal acceptance of AI alone does not address the evolving nature of technology requiring organizations to dynamically innovate their infrastructure.

Navigating DT regarding integrating AI into network security is critical for larger DT projects (Möller, 2023). Understanding the complicated process of AI integration is critical for organizations experiencing or planning a digital transformation, as it allows them to use technology to improve operational efficiency and security (Möller, 2023). Furthermore, using AI-powered solutions may give a proactive approach to detecting and mitigating cybersecurity risks in real time (Muraleedhara, 2024).

In review of the preceding considerations, the escalating cyber threat landscape underscores the critical importance of businesses embracing AI in network security as a strategic necessity. Effective AI integration requires a holistic approach, including organizational readiness, cultural adaptation, and addressing ethical considerations. By navigating these complexities, businesses can protect their digital assets, leverage AI as a competitive advantage, and ensure resilience in a dynamically evolving digital ecosystem.

Background

The main goal of the study's background is to provide the reader with an understanding of the research's rationale by detailing the problem's historical, theoretical, and empirical context. Integrating AI in network security represents a pivotal shift in how organizations protect their digital assets (Chertoff, 2023). The background of this field is rich and multifaceted, encompassing the evolution of AI technologies, the changing landscape of cyber threats, and the growing complexity of network environments. This background explores the historical development of AI in network security, the nature of modern cyber threats, the ethical and practical challenges posed by AI integration, and the evolution of organizational approaches to network security.

Evolution of AI In Network Security

Artificial Intelligence integration in network security has evolved significantly over the past few decades, driven by advancements in technology and the increasing complexity of cyber threats. Initially, AI's role in network security was limited to basic rule-based systems, which operated on predefined parameters to detect known threats and anomalies (Mohamed, 2023). These first-wave AI systems were effective to a certain extent. However, they were often static and unable to adapt to new and evolving threats, leading to high rates of false positives and overwhelming security teams (Lee et al., 2023; Owoseni, 2023).

AI Before 2010. The initial forays of AI into network security were marked by rudimentary applications (Mohammed, 2023). Early systems relied on basic rule-based algorithms and anomaly detection methods (Mohammed, 2023). These systems were primarily used to identify known threats and unusual activities based on predefined parameters. However, their effectiveness was limited due to the static nature of the rules and the inability to adapt to new and evolving threats (Lee et al., 2023). Additionally, these early AI applications often generated high rates of false positives, overwhelming security teams and reducing overall efficiency (Owoseni, 2023).

AI Since 2010. Technology witnessed a significant leap in AI capabilities, primarily driven by advancements in machine learning (ML) and data processing technologies (e.g., graphics processing units [GPUs]), by recognizing the limitations of these early systems (Lecun et al., 2015). This era saw the development of more sophisticated AI models capable of learning from data, identifying patterns, and making predictions. ML algorithms and deep learning began to be employed for more complex tasks such as intrusion detection, malware classification, and threat analysis, enabling real-time threat detection and more accurate predictive analytics

(Selvarajan et al., 2023; Sharma, 2023). Moreover, integrating AI into security systems started automating many manual processes, significantly improving response times, and relieving the burden on human analysts (Sharma, 2023).

Building on these advancements, the integration of AI in network security solutions became more prevalent as its capabilities expanded. Security platforms began incorporating AI for real-time threat detection, predictive analytics, and automated response systems (Mallik & Nath, 2024). The ability to process vast amounts of data allowed these AI-driven systems to identify subtle and complex threats that traditional methods could miss (Bécue et al., 2021). As cyber threats continued to evolve, the reliance on AI systems increased due to their ability to adapt and learn from new data. This change marked a significant shift towards more proactive and dynamic security measures. This transition emphasized the critical role of AI in maintaining robust network defenses (Lee et al., 2023; Selvarajan et al., 2023).

Changing Landscape of Cyber Threats

The cyber threat landscape has evolved dramatically over the past few years, driven by rapid technological advancements and increasing digital interconnectivity. Cyber attackers have become more sophisticated, employing advanced techniques such as AI and ML to enhance the effectiveness of their attacks (Kaur et al., 2023). This evolution has seen the rise of automated and highly targeted attacks, including ransomware, phishing, and Advanced Persistent Threats (APTs), which have become more frequent and damaging (Sharpton, 2021). Additionally, the shift towards remote work and the widespread adoption of cloud services have expanded the attack surface, creating new vulnerabilities and opportunities for cybercriminals (Hiscox, 2023). As a result, organizations must continuously adapt their security strategies to stay ahead of these emerging threats and protect their critical assets (Chertoff, 2023).

Evolving Nature of Threats. As network environments became more complex, so did the nature of cyber threats. Organizations faced various threats, from sophisticated phishing attacks and ransomware to advanced persistent threats (APTs) and state-sponsored cyberattacks (Ali & Shabir, 2024). The dynamic nature of these threats required more adaptive and intelligent security solutions. The increasing sophistication of cyber attackers and the diversity of their methods necessitated the development of more advanced defensive mechanisms (Chertoff, 2023; Hiscox, 2023; Sharma, 2023). In this context, AI's ability to learn and adapt to new threats in real time became indispensable for maintaining adequate network security (Bécue et al., 2021).

Rise of Automated Attacks. The rise of automated attacks, such as botnets and malware, necessitated a shift towards more proactive and predictive security measures (Mallik & Nath, 2024). AI's ability to analyze patterns and predict potential vulnerabilities became crucial in countering these automated threats. These automated attacks can quickly exploit vulnerabilities at scale, posing significant challenges to traditional security measures (Sharton, 2021; Chertoff, 2023). AI-driven security solutions have proven essential in identifying and mitigating these threats before they cause substantial damage (Lee et al., 2023; Selvarajan et al., 2023).

Evolution of Organizational Approaches

The evolution of organizational approaches to network security has been significantly influenced by advancements in AI and the increasing complexity of cyber threats (Khan & Ghafoor, 2024). Initially, organizations relied on reactive measures, responding to incidents as they occurred. However, the growing sophistication of attacks necessitated a shift towards more proactive strategies, emphasizing prevention and early detection (Attaran & Gunasekaran, 2019). This transformation can be made possible by AI's predictive capabilities, enabling organizations to anticipate and mitigate risks before they materialize (Burton, 2024).

From Reactive to Proactive Security. Organizations began transitioning from a reactive approach, focused on responding to incidents, to a more proactive stance, emphasizing prevention and early detection. This shift was facilitated by AI's predictive capabilities, allowing organizations to anticipate and mitigate risks before they materialize (Mohamed, 2023). By leveraging advanced ML learning models, organizations could identify potential threats and vulnerabilities before they were exploited, significantly enhancing their security posture (Attaran & Gunasekaran, 2019). This proactive approach has been critical in managing the increasingly sophisticated cyber threat landscape, enabling organizations to stay ahead of attackers and protect their assets more effectively (Burton, 2024). The move to a proactive security approach is helped by the integration of human expertise.

Integration of AI with Human Expertise. The realization that AI cannot operate in a vacuum led to a more integrated approach, combining AI's analytical prowess with human expertise (Mohamed, 2023). This approach leveraged AI for efficiency and scale, while human insight was used for nuanced decision-making and oversight. AI systems can process vast amounts of data quickly, identifying patterns and anomalies that might be missed by human analysts, thus enhancing the overall security framework (Ratiu, 2024). However, human analysts are crucial for interpreting AI outputs, especially in complex situations requiring contextual understanding and critical thinking. Additionally, human oversight ensures that AI systems are aligned with ethical standards and regulatory requirements, addressing potential biases, and ensuring fairness in security operations (Cath et al., 2018; Hine & Floridi, 2024; Roberts et al., 2024). Human expertise is complemented by continuous improvement through adaptation.

Continuous Learning and Adaptation. AI systems in network security were designed to continuously learn and adapt to new threats (Shah, 2021). This action involved regular updates to AI models based on the latest threat intelligence and feedback from security operations. By incorporating real-time data and ML learning algorithms, AI systems can swiftly identify and respond to emerging threats, minimizing potential damage (Khan & Masum, 2024). Furthermore, continuous learning enables AI to improve its accuracy over time, reducing false positives and enhancing overall security efficacy (Kim et al., 2023). This ongoing adaptation is crucial for maintaining robust defenses in a dynamic and ever-evolving cyber threat landscape. After training and continuous learning, the business can shift to focus on the resilience and robustness of its AI systems.

Focus on Resilience and Robustness. The evolution of AI in network security has underscored the critical need for resilience and robustness. This imperative arises from the escalating complexity of cyber threats and the dynamic nature of modern networks (Markevych & Dawson, 2023). Researchers and practitioners have responded by refining AI algorithms and architectures to enhance adaptability and fortify defenses against emerging vulnerabilities and attack vectors (Sarker et al., 2021). Additionally, advancements in M-learning techniques, such as adversarial training and anomaly detection, have bolstered the capacity of AI systems to identify and mitigate evolving threats in real-time proactively (Ozkan-Ozay et al., 2024). Moreover, collaborations between academia, industry, and government agencies have facilitated knowledge sharing and the development of standardized practices for evaluating AI-driven security solutions (Soroka et al., 2023).

Main Focus of the Chapter

This literature review is a written report that summarizes the existing research and debates on organizational readiness for AI in network security, and the critical organizational and cultural prerequisites for effectively implementing AI in network security (Amberger & Schreyer, 2024). The outcome of this literature review is to gain and present an understanding of the current field of knowledge and prepare to contribute to that knowledge (Amberger & Schreyer, 2024). This literature review will support the readers' ability to build knowledge and identify gaps or questions for further research.

It offers a broad synopsis of the background of AI in network security, highlighting its historical development, the changing nature of cyber threats, ethical and practical challenges, and the evolution of organizational approaches to network security. This review explores the progression of AI technologies, documenting the transition from simple rule-based systems to sophisticated ML models that enable real-time threat detection and predictive analytics (Mohamed, 2023; Selvarajan et al., 2023). Additionally, this analysis examines how the advancing complexity and sophistication of cyber threats have necessitated adaptive and intelligent security solutions (Hiscox, 2023; Sharma, 2023).

Moreover, this discussion considers the characteristics of contemporary cyber threats, highlighting how cyber attackers use advanced techniques like AI and ML and discussing the consequent necessity for organizations to implement proactive and predictive security strategies (Kaur et al., 2023; Chertoff, 2023). This research investigates the ethical and practical challenges associated with AI integration, including concerns about data privacy, biases in AI models, and adversarial AI attacks, underscoring the importance of ethical frameworks and ongoing adaptation (Boutin, 2022). Further, the analysis covers the evolution of organizational approaches to network security, focusing on the transition from reactive to proactive strategies and the importance of combining AI's analytical power with human expertise to enhance overall security effectiveness (Lee et al., 2023; Mohamed, 2023).

AI integration in network security is a rapidly growing field, marked by significant advancements and challenges. This synthesis critically evaluates current peer-reviewed research from 2018 to 2024, focusing on organizational readiness, cultural adaptation, and the various frameworks and models proposed for successful AI integration in network security. Despite extensive research, there appears to be limited direct research explicitly addressing these combined aspects, and the adoption rates of enterprises within the given timeframe. This gap itself is notable and points to potential areas for future research. Through the following literature review, this researcher assesses four major factors to prepare financial organizations for AI implementation, Organizational Culture and Clarity of Purpose (AI usage), Proposed Frameworks and Models, Technical and Ethical Considerations, Critical Evaluation and Future Research. This work expands on the work of Li et al. (2023) by supplementing their multi-disciplinary approach and synthesizing it to an interdisciplinary approach for a cohesive framework for implementing AI alongside network security.

Significance and Focus of the Research

The significance of this research is to enhance the limited body of knowledge surrounding the integration of AI and network security and what the data tells regarding the organizational readiness and methods of how companies accomplish a successful integration. Over the next few years, it is expected that businesses will invest more in the benefits offered by AI in the cybersecurity realm (Kindig, 2023). Amberger & Schreyer (2024) highlights the need for a comprehensive understanding of organizational capabilities and resilience to deploy AI with network security. Research exists for a multi-disciplinary approach and building upon that knowledge is warranted as businesses need to pivot their strategies to incorporate AI (Li et al., 2023).

A McKinsey (2024) survey on the broader topic of AI adoption noted general AI adoption rates from 2023 to 2024. The findings noted that the adoption of AI into one business function rose from 55 percent to 72 percent, while the use of generative AI in one business function increased from 33 percent to 65 percent during the past year (Mckinsey, 2024). The survey displayed the most common business use cases and network security did not appear on that list, with the lowest integrated function at 6 percent (McKinsey, 2024). This survey has shortcomings as it is not peer-reviewed and surveyed 1363 participants, which is limited compared to the overall number of businesses across the globe (Mckinsey, 2024). The Mckinsey survey does not survey all companies, nor does it focus specifically on network security. This survey highlights the need for continued focus on how enterprises handle AI integration.

Problem Statement

It is not known how organizational readiness and cultural adaptation impact the successful integration of AI in network security frameworks in the United States.

Justification for the Problem Statement

The integration of AI into network security systems involves major obstacles beyond technology implementation, needing a thorough knowledge of organizational preparedness and cultural adaptation (Moore & Pratt, 2023). The existing literature comprehensively covers the technical components of AI integration, such as data protection, threat detection, and ethical issues, but often fails to address the critical elements of organizational culture and preparation (Iftikhar & Nordbjerg, 2021). This gap emphasizes the need for more study into how enterprises can successfully plan for and adapt to AI technology within network security frameworks. Understanding these variables is critical for ensuring a seamless transition and making the most of AI-powered security solutions. Addressing this gap allows firms to build strategies that include technological and human factors, resulting in more successful and long-term AI integration in network security (Kim et al., 2023).

Methodology and Design

In this qualitative study, current research was gathered and analyzed using a thorough literature review, as indicated by Zhang et al. (2024), & Snyder (2019) highlight the need for a literature review to summarize previous study results. The primary goal of using a literature review technique was to identify areas that lacked enough inquiry, therefore strengthening the basis for this research. Literature evaluations are critical for determining the strengths, limits, and untapped opportunities within this domain (Zhang et al., 2024). Amberger & Schreyer (2024) emphasize the importance of such evaluations in mapping out the links between diverse academic works, taking into account their contribution to the issue at hand as well as to other fields. Using a literature review, this researcher navigated the complexities of a large amount of academic knowledge.

To perform this detailed literature study, the researcher focused on articles up to 2024, using diverse search phrases related to risk management in project management and cybersecurity. The literature search was conducted from 2015 to July 2024, using specific keywords and phrases such as risk management, cybersecurity risks, risk project management, artificial intelligence, innovation, network security, and digital transformation. The careful selection and usage of keywords resulted in the retrieval of articles related to the study's emphasis areas. The search strategy included academic, subscription-based databases and open web resources, such as EBSCO's suite of databases, IEEE Xplore, arXiv, the ProQuest Dissertation Database, and ABI Inform Complete, as well as Google Scholar for accessing current, peer-reviewed articles. A limited number of citations are from industry-recognized organizations and resources to fill in direct industry data. These sources include the National Institute of Standards and Technology (NIST), the International Information System Security Certification Consortium (ISC2), and McKinsey & Company. The literature was meticulously classified to emphasize its relevance to AI, network security, and the adoption of these integrated technologies in different business environments, providing a solid foundation for the inquiry.

Issues, Controversies, Problems

The following sections cover several topics relevant to this book chapter. This chapter reviews specific theories and frameworks and their respective criticisms. It delves into an organization's culture, readiness, clarity of purpose, and adoption accompanied by the challenges respective to achieving AI. A brief examination is used to convey the potential uses and risks related to quantum computing. The final part of this section delves into the ethical, practical, regulatory, and legal considerations related to the rollout of AI.

Applicable Theories/Frameworks

This research is guided by three theories: The Technology Acceptance Model (TAM), Socio-Technical Systems Theory (STST), and Mass Muddler Intelligence (MMI). These theories were selected for their focus on the interplay between technology, people, and organizational contexts, which is crucial for understanding the integration of AI in network security. Each theory offers a unique perspective, aiding in a comprehensive AI adoption and implementation analysis.

The Technology Acceptance Model

The TAM is a framework that explains how users accept and use technology. It posits that two main factors, perceived ease of use and usefulness, determine an individual's intention to use technology and subsequently influence actual usage behavior (Davis & Granić, 2024a). The TAM framework is suitable for two significant reasons. The model has a user acceptance focus. TAM is instrumental in understanding how users accept and use recent technologies (Davis & Granić, 2024b). In the context of AI in network security, TAM can help assess how security professionals perceive and adapt to AI tools (Davis & Granić, 2024b). Second, TAM offers ease of use and usefulness. TAM's core constructs—perceived ease of use and perceived usefulness—are critical in evaluating the adoption of AI technologies in network security settings (Davis & Granić, 2024a). TAM is not without critiques.

Critiques of the Technology Acceptance Model

Critiques of TAM include over-simplicity and its static nature. Critics argue that TAM oversimplifies the adoption process by focusing on individual attitudes and ignoring broader organizational and social factors (Malatji et al., 2020). Second, TAM is sometimes viewed as too static for dynamic technological environments like AI, where rapid changes and complexities are the norm (Malatji et al., 2020). This limitation can hinder its applicability in rapidly evolving contexts, where user perceptions and behaviors may shift frequently. Additionally, TAM does not adequately address the iterative nature of technology adoption, which involves ongoing learning and adaptation (Nili, 2020). The following guiding theory is Socio-technical systems Theory (STST).

The Socio-Technical System Theory (STST)

Socio-Technical Systems Theory examines the interrelationship between an organization's social and technical aspects, emphasizing that these components must be considered to optimize organizational performance (Ciriello et al., 2024). According to this research team, this theory is particularly suitable for integrating AI into network security due to its holistic approach, which highlights the interplay between technological advancements and the organizational environment. STST's focus on the integration of social and technical elements is crucial for understanding the complexities and nuances of adopting AI-driven security solutions (Ciriello et al., 2024). It underscores the need to consider the technical infrastructure, organizational culture, and workforce readiness, providing a comprehensive framework for analyzing AI integration in network security (Baxter & Sommerville, 2023).

Critiques of the Socio-Technical System Theory (STST)

However, the application of STST has its challenges. One significant critique is its complex implementation, as it requires the simultaneous consideration of numerous variables and their interactions, which can be daunting for organizations (Baxter & Sommerville, 2021). Additionally, while STST effectively describes and analyzes socio-technical interactions, it offers limited prescriptive value, providing minimal guidance on specific strategies to address identified challenges (Walker et al., 2021). This limitation can hinder its practical applicability, as organizations need help translating theoretical insights into actionable steps. Despite these critiques, STST remains a valuable framework for understanding the socio-technical dynamics of AI integration in network security, emphasizing the importance of a balanced approach that considers technological capabilities and organizational context (Mohamed, 2023; Baxter & Sommerville, 2021). Next is MMI.

The Mass Muddler Intelligence (MMI) Theory

Mass Muddler Intelligence (MMI) rethinks the approach to scaling AI by comparing it to liberal democracies, where multiple agents influence each other rather than a monolithic system (Rao, 2024). According to this researcher, this theory proposes using decentralized muddler agents that operate decentralized, like how social contract theory functions in human societies. MMI's agent-based understanding applies the concept of decentralized, specialized agents working together, enhancing scalability and adaptability. By likening AI systems to liberal democracies, MMI suggests that mutual influence among agents leads to more robust and flexible AI ecosystems, promoting a collaborative and dynamic environment for AI development and deployment (Rao, 2024).

Critiques of the Mass Muddler Intelligence (MMI) Theory

However, MMI's novelty presents challenges, particularly the need for more research to establish a robust framework. The current literature does not fully address potential issues, such as introducing malicious agents into the system, which could compromise the integrity and security of the AI network (Rao, 2024). Additionally, while the analogy to social contract theory is conceptually appealing, it requires detailed strategies to manage bad actors within the network and ensure system integrity. The practical implementation concerns highlight the necessity for comprehensive mechanisms to monitor and control the interactions among agents, ensuring that the decentralized system functions effectively and securely (Rao, 2024).

In summary, the guiding theories and frameworks, TAM, STST, and MMI, are crucial for understanding and addressing the complexities of integrating AI into network security. These frameworks offer valuable insights into AI adoption's technological, social, and organizational dimensions, helping organizations navigate the challenges and opportunities presented by AI technologies. They provide structured approaches to evaluating and enhancing AI implementation, ensuring that technical and human factors are considered, which is essential for achieving successful and sustainable AI integration in network security (Baxter & Sommerville, 2021; Mohamed, 2023; Rao, 2024; Walker et al., 2021).

LITERATURE REVIEW

Organizational Readiness and Cultural Adaptation

Organizational readiness for AI in network security involves technical preparedness and cultural adaptation. Technical readiness encompasses the infrastructure, tools, and skills necessary to implement AI-driven security solutions effectively. This technical readiness includes having a robust IT infrastructure, advanced cybersecurity tools, and skilled personnel capable of managing and maintaining AI systems (Mohamed, 2023). Additionally, organizations must ensure that their systems can handle the computational demands of AI applications, including data storage, processing power, and network capabilities (Möller, 2023).

Cultural adaptation refers to an organization's willingness and ability to embrace change and innovation (Mishra, 2023). This action involves fostering an environment conducive to learning and adapting to AI technologies. It is essential for organizations to promote a culture of continuous improvement, where employees are encouraged to develop their skills and embrace newer technologies (Attkan & Ranga, 2022). Leadership plays a crucial role in this aspect by advocating for AI adoption, providing necessary resources for training, and creating an inclusive culture that values technological advancements (Iftikhar & Nordbjerg, 2021).

Additionally, organizations must address potential resistance to change among employees. This change includes overcoming skepticism and fear related to AI technologies, which can be mitigated through transparent communication, education, and involving employees in AI integration (Mishra, 2023). By addressing these cultural factors, organizations can ensure a smoother transition and greater acceptance of AI-driven security solutions.

Critiques of Organizational Readiness and Cultural Adaptation

Organizations must recognize the significance of addressing the time and resources required for successful AI integration. This recognition and the resulting approach are essential aspects of organizational readiness and cultural adaptation. A fundamental critique is that the transition to AI-driven security systems is often more complex and time-consuming than anticipated, leading to implementation delays and potential disruptions in operations (Lee et al., 2023).

Another critique is the potential for a skills gap. Many organizations lack the necessary expertise to manage and maintain AI systems effectively (ISC2, 2023). This void in the skill gap results in over-reliance on external consultants or vendors, which may not be sustainable in the long term. Organizations should invest in continuous training and development programs to build internal capabilities and reduce dependence on external resources (Burton, 2022; Waqas et al. 2022).

Furthermore, cultural adaptation can be challenging, particularly in organizations with established practices and resistance to change (Owoseni, 2023). It is essential to implement comprehensive change management strategies to overcome this concern (Owoseni, 2023). Employees may be reluctant to embrace newer technologies due to fear of job displacement or lack of understanding of AI's benefits. Addressing these concerns requires comprehensive change management strategies, including clear communication of AI's value proposition and involving employees in the AI integration process (Owoseni, 2023).

Understanding these aspects of organizational readiness and cultural adaptation is crucial for this research. It highlights the multifaceted challenges organizations face in integrating AI into network security and underscores the importance of addressing technical and cultural dimensions for successful implementation. By acknowledging and addressing these critiques, organizations can better prepare for and adapt to the evolving landscape of cybersecurity.

Organizational Culture and Clarity of Purpose

As financial institutions strive to incorporate AI into their operations through DT, having a clear objective and an aligned workforce for success is an essential objective and an aligned word and an aligned workforce for success. Digital transformation is a critical strategy used to integrate computer-based technologies into an organization's products, processes, and strategies (Moore & Pratt, 2023). This transformation aims to enhance engagement and service delivery to employees and customers, the organization's competitive edge (Moore & Pratt, 2023).

The security landscape has shifted, with malicious actors utilizing AI and other ML models to launch various enterprise attacks. Integrating AI requires enhanced and thorough security solutions and improved resource distribution, which includes personnel and security protocols (Mishra, 2023). Fintech companies that leverage advanced tools and technologies to drive innovation can maintain a competitive advantage as the technological landscape evolves.

Artificial Intelligence (AI) has demonstrated significant potential in enhancing legacy systems, procedures, and processes. A study showed the following analytical values: 96.1% for data privacy, 97.2% for scalability, 98.7% for risk reduction, 95.4% for data protection, and 94.3% for attack avoidance (Mishra, 2023). This study, based on over 250,000 samples, highlights the need for further research into AI's capabilities despite the sample size being smaller than the average network volume handled by Fintech companies (Mishra, 2023).

There may be a reluctance to adopt AI within organizations, often due to a lack of enthusiasm among management and users. Proactively addressing this hesitation is crucial, including fostering a culture that supports AI. This action involves investing in AI skills development and talent acquisition. According to Iftikhar and Nordbjerg (2021), senior leadership must educate employees of the risks and capabilities of AI. Involving senior leadership also helps secure funding for investments across multiple business lines.

One obstacle to AI adoption is the cautious approach to return on investment (ROI), which often emphasizes short-term gains over long-term benefits (Hoffmann & Mehler, 2023; Nam et al., 2021). Financial constraints can also limit the full potential of AI and other technologies. For example, Microsoft, a tech company with significant investment in AI platforms, recognized the long-term benefits of AI and accounted for a $1.2 billion charge in one quarter to lay off 10,000 employees to meet the increased demand for AI-driven consumer spending, which has risen since the pandemic (Thorbecke & Ziady, 2023).

Moore & Pratt (2023) discuss DT and provide an example of a Fintech company using ML, a subset of AI, to implement DT across the enterprise. Chen and Liao (2021) explore the Artificial Intelligence of Things (AIoT), which combines AI and the Internet of Things (IoT), within the context of Fintech companies. Their findings indicate improved performance in three Fintech companies using IoT (Chen & Liao, 2021). The risk of not adopting AI in some form may result in financial companies needing to catch up in their readiness to handle or prevent attacks.

Critiques of Organizational Culture and Clarity of Purpose

The significance of organizational culture and clarity of purpose is magnified as financial institutions adopt AI through DT. Effective DT requires integrating advanced technologies into products, processes, and strategies to enhance engagement and service delivery, boosting competitiveness (Moore & Pratt, 2023). However, critiques highlight significant challenges. For instance, aligning the workforce and objectives is crucial, but organizational culture often resists change (Bogale & Debela, 2024). This resistance can stem from management and employees' reluctance to embrace modern technologies, potentially stalling innovation and reducing overall effectiveness (Iftikhar & Nordbjerg, 2021).

Moreover, efforts in DT can lack direction without a clear and communicated purpose, leading to inefficient resource allocation, and missed opportunities (Hoffmann & Mehler, 2023). These critiques are essential as they underscore the need for a supportive organizational culture and clear strategic goals to realize the full benefits of AI and DT. Understanding these critiques helps organizations address potential barriers proactively, ensuring a smoother transition and more successful implementation of AI technologies (Bogale & Debela, 2024; Hoffmann & Mehler, 2023; Iftikhar & Nordbjerg, 2021).

Adoption

Waqas et al. (2022) explored some issues related to AI implementation. Lukyanenko et al. (2022) developed a Foundational Trust Framework that views organizations, users, and technology as distinct systems. This approach highlights the crucial roles of humans and AI while recognizing the significant contributions of other systems involved that allow trust to be built granularly with knowledge of how each system is designed and expectations of how each system operates (Lukyanenko, 2022).

After implementation, AI Impact Assessments (AI-IAs) identify positive and negative impacts at an early stage. This process helps to ensure that the benefits of AI are safeguarded while its potential downsides are avoided (Stahl et al., 2023). This action ensures safeguards that throughout the life process of an AI system that trustworthiness is baselined and routinely validated for accuracy (Li et al., 2023). Ayodeji (2020) explored the vulnerability of AI systems due to wrong or manipulated data, highlighting the need for some AI-IAs.

The significance of robust AI-IAs is further underscored by the need to maintain regulatory compliance and ethical standards in AI deployment (de Almeida et al., 2021). According to Binns (2022), ensuring that AI systems adhere to these principles fosters trust among users and mitigates the risk of legal and reputational damage. By systematically assessing AI impacts, organizations can better navigate the complex landscape of AI ethics and regulations, ensuring their AI systems contribute positively to society and operate within legal boundaries.

Critiques of Adoption

One of the primary critiques of adopting AI in financial institutions is the potential for significant cultural resistance within organizations. Waqas et al. (2022) highlighted that many employees and managers are often hesitant to embrace recent technologies, which can impede the successful integration of AI systems. This resistance is significant because it can slow down the DT process, making it difficult for organizations to fully leverage AI's potential benefits. Furthermore, the lack of clarity in organizational goals and alignment among staff can lead to inefficient resource allocation and missed opportunities (Lukyanenko et al., 2022). Without a clear purpose and a workforce aligned with this objective, DT efforts can become directionless, resulting in wasted investments and efforts.

These critiques are significant to the text because they underscore the importance of having a supportive organizational culture and clear strategic goals (Bogale & Debela, 2024; Hoffmann & Mehler, 2023). Addressing these critiques is crucial for financial institutions aiming to adopt AI successfully (Iftikhar & Nordbjerg, 2021). It emphasizes the need for effective change management strategies, comprehensive training programs, and a clear communication plan to ensure all employees understand and support the AI adoption process. Recognizing and addressing these barriers can help organizations navigate the complexities of DT more effectively, ensuring a smoother transition and better outcomes (Iftikhar & Nordbjerg, 2021; Hoffmann & Mehler, 2023).

Quantum Computing

Quantum computing is emerging as a transformative technology with significant implications for network security (Akbar et al., 2024). Unlike classical computing, which relies on bits as the fundamental unit of information, quantum computing uses quantum bits or qubits. Qubits can exist in multiple states simultaneously due to the principles of superposition and entanglement, enabling quantum computers to perform complex computations at unprecedented speeds (Tyagi et al., 2024). This capability poses opportunities and challenges for network security, particularly in enhancing cryptographic methods and addressing sophisticated cyber threats.

Integrating quantum computing into network security can revolutionize current practices by providing enhanced encryption techniques. For example, quantum key distribution (QKD) leverages the principles of quantum mechanics to create virtually unbreakable encryption keys (Akbar et al., 2024). This method ensures that any attempt at eavesdropping can be detected, thereby significantly improving the security of data transmission (Akbar ate al., 2024). Quantum computing also introduces the possibility of solving optimization problems more efficiently, which can enhance various aspects of network security, including threat detection and response (Kou et al., 2024). Further, by utilizing quantum algorithms, security systems can analyze large datasets more quickly and accurately, identifying patterns and anomalies that may indicate cyber threats. This capability is significant in real-time network monitoring and intrusion detection (Kou et al., 2024).

There are significant potential benefits to including quantum computing with AI that may potentially cause a market disruption related to the improvements of using AI and quantum computing versus the commonly used computing resources for enterprises. This relates to the increased processing power to improve upon the limitations that conventional computing has on AI (Pooranam, 2023). Research shows the benefits of combining AI and quantum computing in other use cases, such as financial market predictions and mitigating behavioral bias from financial advisors (Atadoga, 2024).

Critiques of Quantum Computing

Critiques of quantum computing concerning network security are vital to understanding its limitations and future implications. One significant critique is the technological immaturity of quantum computers. Quantum computers are in the experimental phase, and their practical deployment for network security applications is still years away (Preskill, 2021). This lag in technology maturity raises concerns about the feasibility and reliability of quantum solutions in real-world security scenarios (Ladd et al., 2023).

Another critical issue is the substantial investment in quantum computing research and development. Quantum computers demand specialized infrastructure, including cryogenic cooling systems and highly controlled environments, which are costly and complex to maintain. This excessive cost may create disparities in the adoption of quantum computing, potentially limiting its accessibility to well-funded organizations and raising concerns about equitable access to advanced security technologies (Preskill, 2021).

Further, the transition to quantum-resistant cryptography poses a significant challenge. Current encryption standards, such as RSA and ECC, are vulnerable to quantum attacks, necessitating the development and standardization of new cryptographic methods that can withstand quantum computing capabilities (Pirandola et al., 2024). This transition is technically challenging and requires widespread coordination and agreement among stakeholders in the cybersecurity community to ensure a unified and effective response (Gidney & Ekerå, 2021).

There are several concerns related to the integration of AI and quantum computing. The increased processing power may exacerbate several noted issues with AI, such as employment loss, or the lack of accurate and comprehensive data (Atadoga, 2024). The same technologies used by defenders are also used by malicious actors that can penetrate, disrupt, or defraud businesses (Swan & Santos, 2023). The attackers also have the potential to break encryption risking the confidentiality and integrity of data (Olorunsogo, 2024).

These critiques are significant because they highlight the need for cautious and strategic planning in adopting quantum computing for network security. Addressing these challenges will ensure that organizations are prepared to harness the benefits of quantum technology while mitigating its risks (Ladd et al., 2 23). Understanding these critiques is crucial for developing a realistic and practical roadmap for integrating quantum computing into network security frameworks (Chen et al., 2023).

ETHICAL CONSIDERATIONS

Integrating AI into network security is not merely a technical challenge but also an ethical one. Ethical considerations include privacy concerns, potential bias in AI algorithms, and the implications of autonomous decision-making in security contexts (Madrid & Wright, 2021). Ensuring that AI systems are transparent, accountable, and aligned with ethical standards is crucial for effective implementation (Hickman & Petrin, 2021). Addressing these ethical issues can help build trust among users and stakeholders, which is essential for the widespread adoption of AI technologies. Moreover, ethical AI practices can prevent potential misuse and unintended consequences from poorly designed systems. When transitioning to regulatory and legal compliance, it is essential to consider how ethical guidelines operate within the existing legal frameworks.

Cath et al. (2018), Hine & Floridi (2024), and Roberts et al. (2024) discuss a *good AI society* that references an idea proposed by the governments of the USA, EU, and UK. Cath et al. (2018) describe a *good AI society* as one that comprehensively respects human dignity in the formation and incorporation of AI within a society. As companies develop policies and standards around AI and their security posture, they can take note to align with ethical and governmental standards creating a positive use of AI within their overall strategy.

Governments have policy positions regarding AI, but in the US, there are broader implications of how private sector companies interact with the government. Biden's administration used previous cases of technology with global adoption, such as the railroad and telephone, to illustrate that working with Allied nations can help improve the tech, but with the caveat of only aiding those nations who agree with American ideals (Hine & Floridi, 2024). Overall, the underlying theme changed when the US government's role in AI (Obama administration) shifted to a governmental deference to the free-market and business innovation (Hine & Floridi, 2024). Companies utilizing AI are now a significant part of geopolitical competition. Internal policies and roadmaps should align with the larger policy goals of supporting government. An example of this is Biden's statement, where he advocated his belief that American businesses can outcompete anyone when discussing direct competition against China (The White House, 2024). The lack of governmental regulation or interference is traded for cooperation from the private sector to include national values within their creation and deployment of AI. This leads to a discussion about how corporate policy may align with broader social objectives.

Corporate social responsibility (CSR) informs frameworks and governance of AI within a company. Zhao & Gómez Fariñas (2024) discuss CSR as a method that companies can use to detect and mitigate any harmful effect on society resulting from the actions of the business. The article covers how AI can bolster sustainable development via CSR with the environment, society, and economy (Zhao & Gómez Fariñas, 2024). The relates with the research from Hine and Floridi (2024) where private sector can align its AI Strategy with current or proposed governmental regulation. Expanding on this idea, Zhao and Gómez Fariñas (2024) note sustainability efforts within an organization lead to positive results related to reputation, productivity, and finances that help foster better relationships with business partners.

Ethical and Practical Challenges

The rapid integration of AI into network security presents significant ethical and practical challenges that must be addressed to ensure responsible and effective use. Concerns about data privacy and the ethical implications of AI systems processing sensitive information necessitate stringent data protection measures and transparent governance (Boutin, 2022). Additionally, the stability of AI models to biases in training data raises critical issues regarding the accuracy and fairness of these systems, with potentially severe implications for security outcomes (Attkan & Ranga, 2022). Furthermore, the rise of adversarial AI attacks underscores the need for robust defenses capable of withstanding sophisticated manipulation attempts by malicious actors (Khan & Ghafoor, 2024). Addressing these challenges, data privacy and ethical use, bias and reliability, and adversarial AI attacks is crucial for maintaining trust and reliability in AI-driven network security solutions (Huff et al., 2023).

Data Privacy and Ethical Use

Usage of AI in network security raised concerns about data privacy and ethical implications (Meisenbacher, 2024). The processing of sensitive data by AI systems necessitates data protection measures and raises questions about user consent and data governance (Oladoyinbo, 2024). As AI systems handle increasingly sensitive data, ensuring data privacy becomes paramount (Meisenbacher, 2024; Oladoyinbo, 2024). Organizations must implement robust data governance frameworks to manage the ethical use of AI (Hine & Floridi, 2024; Gómez Fariñas, 2024). Transparency in AI decision-making processes is essential to address ethical concerns and maintain user trust (Hickman & Petrin, 2021). Regulatory compliance with data protection laws such as GDPR is necessary to ensure the ethical deployment of AI in network security. Bias and reliability are related to ethical use as we explore those ideas next.

Bias and Reliability

AI models are susceptible to biases in their training data, which can lead to skewed or discriminatory outcomes (Fang et al., 2024). Ensuring the accuracy of AI systems presents a significant concern, especially in the context of false positives in threat detection, which could have adverse implications (Familoni, 2024). Addressing biases in AI systems requires continuous assessment and refinement of the training data to ensure diverse and representative datasets via human intervention (Familoni, 2024). Implementing feedback mechanisms from human analysts can help improve the reliability of AI models by incorporating real-world insights (Kim et al., 2023). Based on this research, the inference is to perform regular audits of AI systems necessary to identify and correct biases that could compromise the effectiveness of network security measures. There are other challenges outside of the purview of the business, such as adversarial AI attacks.

Adversarial AI Attacks

The emergence of adversarial AI attacks, where attackers use AI techniques to evade detection or manipulate AI security systems, posed a new set of challenges (Khan & Ghafoor, 2024). This action led to an arms race between security professionals and cybercriminals leveraging AI technologies (Jacobsen & Liebetrau, 2023). Adversarial AI attacks highlight the need for robust AI defenses to detect and mitigate sophisticated manipulation attempts (Papernot, 2021). Developing AI models resilient to adversarial attacks involves incorporating adversarial training during model development (Goodfellow et al., 2023). Continuous innovation and collaboration among cybersecurity experts are essential to avoid adversarial threats and protect AI systems (Bécue et al., 2021).

Regulatory and Legal Compliance

Specific legislation on AI in the US has gaps, but the US does have the means to address some components of AI (Plotinsky & Cinelli, 2024). One of these devices is the Export Administration Regulations (EAR99), which covers hardware and the integration of AI into business solutions (Plotinsky & Cinelli, 2024). Plotinsky & Cinelli (2024) discussed the Committee on Foreign Investment in the United States (CFIUS) and its impact on inbound and outbound investments in US companies are carefully reviewed by the US Department of Treasury. While this does not explicitly address AI, it can be used to halt investments that may provide sensitive data on technology or Personal Identifiable Information (PII) to a state-sponsored actor. PII is information that can be inferred to identify an individual through direct or indirect means (Waugh, 2023). This connects with the earlier discussion of how companies can align their goals to match those of the national government and recognition of their larger geopolitical goals (Hine & Floridi, 2024; Zhao & Gómez Fariñas, 2024).

Across the US, several laws have been passed concerning the use of AI. The National Conference of State Legislators noted that, in the previous year half the states, along with Puerto Rico and the District of Columbia, introduced AI-related bills, with more than half of those adopting resolutions or legislation (NCSL, 2024). A table format list can be seen on their website: https://www.ncsl.org/technology-and-communication/artificial-intelligence-2023-legislation. Several states have laws and regulations concerning bias, state government policy, whether AI can be considered for personhood, and assigning governmental agencies to study the effects of cybersecurity within their departments (NCSL, 2024).

How does this apply to Network Security? A combination of a Public-Private Partnership, an agreement between government and private entities for public benefit and risk sharing, can be invaluable in aligning shared interests to further common goals. Soroka et al. (2023) note that these efforts may be used to implement infrastructure or governmental services. Regarding network security, this partnership may help further national security interests via knowledge or data sharing (Soroka, 2023). For instance, the combined partnership could help with cybercrime and information sharing may help mitigate losses in the financial sector. For instance, a small subsection of what a Public-Private Partnership could mean for a private enterprise but must be calculated in the terms of how to deploy AI within the Network Security infrastructure.

SOLUTIONS AND RECOMMENDATIONS

Learning and synthesizing data is relevant to business leaders incorporating new ideas within an operational framework. Practical applications to real-world scenarios move enterprises towards enhancing detection capabilities. Human-centric AI models improve the accuracy of data and promote the success of AI integrations (Chatterjee et al., 2024). A summarized recommendation of these methods can broaden the understanding of intersecting AI with network security.

Practical Applications of AI in Network Security

AI transforms network security by providing advanced capabilities to detect, respond to, and prevent cyber threats. Its practical applications are crucial for enhancing security systems' overall effectiveness and efficiency (Lee et al., 2023; Selvarajan et al., 2023). The significance of AI in network security lies in its potential to manage false positives and negatives, improve data quality, withstand adversarial attacks, enhance transparency, scale with network growth, and facilitate human-AI collaboration (Bécue et al., 2021). These key points are critical for organizations implementing robust, resilient AI-driven security measures. In the following sections, this research will present six practical applications (i.e., false positives and negatives management, data quality enhancement, robustness against adversarial attacks, transparency and explainability, scalability solutions, and human-AI collaboration models) and explore these aspects, their practical implications, and the strategies needed to optimize AI's role in safeguarding networks.

Managing false positives and negatives is crucial in AI-driven network security systems because it directly impacts the effectiveness and efficiency of threat detection. False positives, where legitimate activities are mistakenly flagged as threats, can overwhelm security teams, divert attention from real threats, and lead to wasted resources (Lee et al., 2023; Owoseni, 2023). Conversely, false negatives occur when actual threats go undetected, posing significant risks to the network. Organizations can employ several strategies to fine-tune AI algorithms and minimize these errors. First, ensuring accurate data annotation and continuous model training with updated datasets is fundamental. Properly labeled data improves the algorithm's ability to distinguish between normal and malicious activities, reducing the rate of false positives and negatives (Russo et al., 2021). Continuous model training helps the system adapt to evolving threats and maintain high detection accuracy (Sarker, 2021). Second, implementing a multi-layered defense strategy is essential to cover various threats. This approach integrates multiple security measures, such as firewalls, intrusion detection systems (IDS), and endpoint protection, to provide comprehensive coverage and enhance detection capabilities (Barrett, 2018). Third, incorporating feedback loops from security analysts helps the system learn from mistakes. Analysts can provide insights and corrections to the AI system, allowing it to improve over time (Chatterjee et al., 2024). This collaborative approach ensures that the AI system benefits from human expertise, further refining its accuracy. Finally, adjusting sensitivity thresholds to balance threat detection with reducing false alarms is necessary. Fine-tuning these thresholds can help minimize the occurrence of false positives without compromising the detection of genuine threats (Bouke & Abdullah, 2024). These measures are essential to enhance the accuracy and reliability of AI-driven network security systems, protecting organizations from potential cyber threats. Next is data quality enhancement.

High-quality, relevant data is the backbone of effective AI models in network security. Ensuring data quality involves several critical aspects. First, collecting comprehensive and diverse data from various sources within the network ensures a broad coverage of potential threats. Preprocessing this data to remove irrelevant or redundant information enhances its quality (Kumar & Srivastava, 2022). Implementing systems that analyze data in real-time allows AI models to respond quickly to emerging threats, thus maintaining a proactive security posture (Ambasht, 2023). Regular data audits are essential for periodically reviewing data used for training and running AI models, ensuring it remains relevant and representative of current network environments and threat landscapes (Chatterjee et al., 2024). Additionally, ensuring data collection and usage compliance with privacy regulations is crucial for maintaining ethical standards and public trust (Camacho, 2024).

Similarly, AI systems in network security must be robust against adversarial attacks, where attackers manipulate data or exploit model weaknesses. Strengthening AI systems involves several strategies. First, incorporating examples of adversarial attacks during training can make AI models more resilient to such manipulations (Qayyum et al., 2023). Continuously updating the AI models with new data and attack patterns helps maintain their effectiveness against evolving threats (Angioni et al., 2024; Habbal et al., 2024). Additionally, using different AI models and traditional security measures can provide a safety net if one system is compromised (Angioni et al., 2024; Habbal et al., 2024). Regularly conducting security audits and penetration testing helps identify and address potential vulnerabilities in AI systems, ensuring they remain robust and effective against sophisticated attacks (Hamon et al., 2024).

Muneer et al. (2024) explored the pros and cons of differing AI methods, including Deep Learning, Machine Learning, and Federated Learning in the context of IDSes. Each one showed promise and can be helpful, but [Federated Learning]-based approaches, which leverage collective learning from multiple decentralized devices, offer a promising solution for organizations that cannot share data due to privacy or security concerns. They allow for the training of models on distributed datasets without sharing data. This information is a significant point element to note for the overall security of an enterprise and is especially significant in dealing with financial networks and ensuring Personally Identifiable Information (PII) is not leaked or exposed to AI. Muneer et al. (2024) noted that Federated Learning still needs more research as organizations craft policy and governance around the use of AI in Network Security.

Enhancing transparency and explainability in AI models is crucial due to their complexity, which often leads to a need for more understanding of their decision-making processes. Developing explainable AI (XAI) models that can clarify their decisions helps security professionals trust and effectively use these systems (Hassija et al., 2023). Training security teams on the functioning and limitations of AI models fosters better understanding and practical usage (Arrieta et al., 2021). Maintaining detailed documentation and regular reporting on AI decisions and actions improves transparency (Blackmon & Ammanath, 2022). As networks grow and become more complex, AI systems must scale to meet these expanding demands. Scalability is a critical factor in maintaining the effectiveness of AI-driven network security. Leveraging cloud computing can provide the necessary resources for AI systems to scale optimally (Kanungo, 2024; Williamson & Prybutok, 2024). Designing AI systems with a modular architecture allows for easier scaling, as additional modules can be added as needed (Cob-Parro et al., 2024). Efficient management of computational resources, such as processing power and memory, is crucial for scaling AI systems without compromising performance (Wang et al., 2024). Additionally, developing scalable algorithms that maintain their efficiency and accuracy at larger scales is essential for handling increased network demands (Pasini et al., 2021). It is essential to develop scalable algorithms that maintain their efficiency and accuracy at larger scales for handling increased network demands.

Human-AI Collaboration Models

Effective collaboration between humans and AI is essential for optimal network security. This work involves defining roles, developing interactive AI by adding human-in-the-loop approach, and training security professionals (ISC2, 2023; Mosqueira-Rey et al., 2023). Next is a closer look at the various parts of the Human-AI collaboration model.

Defining Roles. Defining the roles and responsibilities of AI systems and human security professionals can ensure a complementary relationship. Siemon's (2022) research found that successful teams should define the role of based on team skills and based on all team members fulfilling their roles. Cabrera et al. (2023) showed that introducing behavior descriptions can improve the relationship between teams and AI when humans can correct AI when it does not meet expectations or utilize

AI to a greater extent when it is more precise. After defining roles, we can explore how AI interacts with humans.

Interactive Systems. Developing AI systems that can interact with and learn from human input can enhance their effectiveness. This type of AI can be achieved with explainability allowing users to identify any issues and help correct input into these systems (Kim et al., 2023). Explainability can help users collaborate better with developers to improve AI (Kim et al., 2023). This change relates to the human-in-the-loop approach, where AI decisions include human input during the process.

Human-in-the-Loop. Implementing a human-in-the-loop approach where security professionals review and validate critical decisions can combine the strengths of AI and human judgment (Zhang et al., 2021). Mosqueira-Rey et al. (2023) note that human interactivity brings clarity to the learning process, which improves performance across several metrics. Users can interact with ML algorithms can be done with tools like AutoML that allows users with limited knowledge of ML to create algorithms (Mosqueira-Rey et al., 2023). This leads to improved training and adaptation of AI.

Training and Adaptation. Training security professionals to work effectively with AI systems and continuously adapting the systems based on human feedback can optimize the collaborative model. Currently, a gap exists in skilled cybersecurity professionals who are trained to use AI (ISC2, 2023). Ongoing training can help organizations weather economic downturns and prevent a deficit of skilled professionals (ISC2, 2023). Additionally, continuous training improves team and company performance across all parts of the Human-AI collaborative model (ISC2, 2023; Kim et al., 2023).

Based on the literature review, there are three recommendations as part of an overall strategy to improve corporate readiness for AI. This is not an exhaustive list and still requires iterative improvement via research or f111irst-hand experience. *Thorough Preparation* for and a trusted adoption strategy will provide the necessary roadmap for successful implementation. Companies should adopt a *comprehensive* training strategy to ensure education is appropriate for all users, noting that training is necessary to provide favorable outcomes to the user and company performance. The dearth of skilled cyber security professionals hampers optimal usage of AI. Last, for enterprises to shift focus to *continuous improvement* after adoption to building out new features and capabilities to address new use cases. Ideas for further research will be detailed in the next section.

FUTURE RESEARCH DIRECTIONS

The information presented in this research is significant as it underscores the complexities of AI integration beyond technical implementation. Addressing these gaps is crucial for organizations to navigate the challenges of DT effectively, ensuring a smoother transition and more successful outcomes. Future research can provide valuable insights that enhance AI integration's technological and organizational aspects in network security by focusing on these underexplored areas (Prem, 2023).

The current literature primarily addresses the technical facets of AI in network security, often overlooking the organizational readiness and cultural adaptation necessary for successful implementation using an ethical framework (Danks, 2022). This information indicates a notable gap in research, highlighting the need to explore how organizations can effectively prepare for and adapt to AI technologies within network security frameworks. According to Mohamed (2023), there is a significant emphasis on the technical challenges, such as data privacy and the detection of sophisticated cyber threats, but less on the cultural and organizational barriers that impede AI adoption.

Furthermore, while ethical considerations in AI, such as algorithmic bias and data privacy, are gaining recognition, the development of comprehensive frameworks that integrate these ethical concerns into the deployment of AI in network security is still in its infancy (Danks, 2022). Prem (2023) notes the growing nature of the research pertaining to the ethics of AI and how the various different parts of the frameworks, (e.g. XAI, bias) are becoming branches of ethical research. Danks (2022) elaborates upon the idea that an ethical framework has a critical role within a solution for ethics, and the importance of applying an ethical framework throughout the entire integration strategy. It is imperative for future research to fill these gaps by creating and testing frameworks that encompass technical and ethical considerations, thereby ensuring a comprehensive approach to AI integration in network security.

CONCLUSION

In summary, the practical application of AI in network security involves a multi-faceted approach addressing technical, operational, and ethical challenges. Ensuring data quality is fundamental, involving comprehensive data collection, preprocessing, real-time analysis, and regular audits to keep the AI systems effective and current. Robustness against adversarial attacks is achieved through adversarial training, regular model updates, implementing redundancy, and conducting security audits. Enhancing transparency and explainability is crucial, as well as employing explainable AI models, training security teams, providing detailed documentation, and engaging stakeholders. Scalability solutions are vital for handling network growth, leveraging cloud-based AI, modular designs, efficient resource management, and scalable algorithms. Finally, human-AI collaboration models define roles, develop interactive systems, implement human-in-the-loop approaches, and provide continuous training for security professionals to work effectively with AI systems. Together, these strategies ensure that AI-driven network security systems are reliable, adaptable, and ethically sound.

REFERENCES

Abuali, K. M., Nissirat, L., & Al-Samawi, A. (2023). Advancing network security with AI: SVM-b sed deep learning for intrusion detection. *Sensors (Basel)*, 23(21), 8959. DOI: 10.3390/s23218959 PMID: 37960661

Agenda, D. (2023). Why we need global rules to crack down on cybercrime? *World Economic Forum*. https://www.weforum.org/agenda/2023/01/global-rules-crack-down-cybercrime

Akbar, M. A., Khan, A. A., & Hyrynsalmi, S. (2024). Role of quantum computing in shaping the future of 6G technology. *Information and Software Technology*, 170, 107454. DOI: 10.1016/j.infsof.2024.107454

Al-Maliki, S., Qayyum, A., Ali, H., Abdallah, M., Qadir, J., Hoang, D. T., & Niyato, D. (2023). Adversarial machine learning for social good: Reframing the adversary as an ally. *ArXiv. /abs/2310.03614*. https://doi.org/DOI: 10.48550/arXiv.2310.036144

Ali, S., & Shabir, G. (2024). *Advanced persistent threats (APTs): Analysis, detection, and mitigation*. https://easychair.org/publications/preprint/sNLP

Ambasht, A. (2023). Real-time data integration and analytics: Empowering data-driven decision making. *International Journal of Computer Trends and Technology*, 71(7), 8–14. DOI: 10.14445/22312803/IJCTT-V71I7P102

Amberger, C., & Schreyer, D. (2024). What do we know about no-show behavior? A systematic, interdisciplinary literature review. *Journal of Economic Surveys*, 38(1), 57–96. DOI: 10.1111/joes.12534

Angioni, D., Demetrio, L., Pintor, M., Onet, L., Anguita, D., Biggio, B., & Roli, F. (2024). Robustness-congruent adversarial training for secure machine learning model updates. *arXiv:2402.17390v1 [cs.LG]* https://doi.org//arXiv.2402.17390DOI: 10.48550

Arrieta, A. B., Díaz-Rodríguez, N., Del Ser, J., Bennetot, A., Tabik, S., Barbado, A., Garcia, S., il-Lopez, S., Molina, D., Benjamins, R., Chatila, R., & Herrera, F. (2021). Explainable artificial intelligence (XAI): Concepts, taxonomies, opportunities and challenges toward responsible AI. *Information Fusion*, 58, 82–115. DOI: 10.1016/j.inffus.2019.12.012

Atadoga, A., Ike, C. U., Asuzu, O. F., Ayinla, B. S., Ndubuisi, N. L., & Adeleye, R. A. (2024). The intersection of AI and quantum computing in financial markets: A critical review. *Computer Science & IT Research Journal*, 5(2), 461–472. DOI: 10.51594/csitrj.v5i2.816

Attaran, M., & Gunasekaran, A. (2019). Blockchain and Cybersecurity. In *Applications of Blockchain Technology in Business. SpringerBriefs in Operations Management.* Springer., DOI: 10.1007/978-3-030-27798-7_10

Attkan, A., & Ranga, V. (2022). Cyber-physical security for IoT networks: A comprehensive review on traditional, blockchain and artificial intelligence based key-security. *Complex & Intelligent Systems*, 8(35), 9–3591. DOI: 10.1007/s40747-022-00667-z

Barrett, M. (2018). *Framework for improving critical infrastructure cybersecurity version 1.1.* NIST Cybersecurity Framework., DOI: 10.6028/NIST.CSWP.04162018

Baxter, G., & Sommerville, I. (2021). Socio-technical systems: From design methods to systems engineering. *Interacting with Computers*, 23(1), 4–17. DOI: 10.1016/j.intcom.2010.07.003

Bécue, A., Praça, I., & Gama, J. (2021). Artificial intelligence, cyber-threats and industry 4.0: Challenges and opportunities. *Artificial Intelligence Review*, 54(5), 3849–3886. DOI: 10.1007/s10462-020-09942-2

Binns, R. (2018). Fairness in machine learning: Lessons from political philosophy. *In Conference on fairness, accountability and transparency 149-159*. PMLR. https://proceedings.mlr.press/v81/binns18a.html

Blackmon, R., & Ammanath, B. (2022). Building transparency into AI projects. *Harvard Business Review.* https://hbr.org/2022/06/building-transparency-into-ai-projects

Bodimani, M. (2024). Assessing the impact of transparent AI systems in enhancing user trust and privacy. *Journal of Science and Technology*, 5(1), 50–67. https://www.thesciencebrigade.com/jst/article/view/68

Bouke, M. A., & Abdullah, A. (2024). *An empirical assessment of ML Models for 5G network intrusion detection: A data leakage-free approach. e-Prime-Advances in Electrical Engineering.* Electronics and Energy., DOI: 10.1016/j.prime.2024.100590

Boutin, C. (2022, March 16). *There's more to AI bias than biased data, NIST report highlights.* NIST https://www.nist.gov/news-events/news/2022/03/theres-more-ai-bias-biased-data-nist-report-highlights

Burrell, D. N., Nobles, C., & Wright, J. B. (2021). Cybersecurity and the intersection of AI and healthcare: A critical analysis. *Journal of Healthcare Information Management*, 35(4), 23–31. DOI: 10.1002/jhim.2021.35.4.23

Burton, S. L. (2022). *Cybersecurity leadership from a telemedicine/telehealth knowledge and organizational development examination.* ProQuest https://www.proquest.com/dissertations-theses/cybersecurity-leadership-telemedicine-telehealth/docview/2662752457/se-2?accountid=44888

Cabrera, Á. A., Perer, A., & Hong, J. I. (2023). Improving human-AI collaboration with descriptions of AI behavior. *Proceedings of the ACM on Human-Computer Interaction*, 7(CSCW1), 1-21. DOI: 10.1145/3579612

Camacho, N. G. (2024). The role of AI in Cybersecurity: Addressing threats in the digital age. *Journal of Artificial Intelligence General science (JAIGS) ISSN: 3006-4023, 3*(1), 143-154. DOI: 10.60087/jaigs.v3i1.75

Cath, C., Wachter, S., Mittelstadt, B., & Floridi, L. (2017) Artificial Intelligence and the 'Good Society': the US, EU, and UK approach. *Sci Eng Ethics 24*, 505–528 (2018). DOI: 10.1007/s11948-017-9901-7

Chatterjee, P., Da, D., & Rawat, D. B. (2024). Digital twin for credit card fraud detection: Opportunities, challenges, and fraud detection advancements. *Future Generation Computer Systems*, 158, 410–426. Advance online publication. DOI: 10.1016/j.future.2024.04.057

Chen, C. C., & Liao, C. C. (2021). Research on the development of Fintech combined with AIoT. *IEEE International Conference on Consumer Electronics-Taiwan (ICCE-TW)*1-2, DOI: 10.1109/ICCE-TW52618.2021.9602952

Chertoff, M. (2023, April 13). *Cyber risk is growing. here's how companies can keep up.* Harvard Business Review. https://hbr.org/2023/04/cyber-risk-is-growing-heres-how-companies-can-keep-up

Cob-Parro, A. C., Lalangui, Y., & Lazcano, R. (2024). fostering agricultural transformation through AI: An open-source AI architecture exploiting the MLOps paradigm. *Agronomy (Basel)*, 14(2), 259. DOI: 10.3390/agronomy14020259

Danks, D. (2022). Digital Ethics as Translational Ethics. In Vasiliu-Feltes, I., & Thomason, J. (Eds.), *Applied Ethics in a Digital World* (pp. 1–15). IGI Global., DOI: 10.4018/978-1-7998-8467-5.ch001

Davis, F. D., & Granić, A. (2024). Epilogue: What will the future of TAM be like? In *The Technology Acceptance Model: 30 Years of TAM* (pp. 103–108). Cham Springer International Publishing., DOI: 10.1007/978-3-030-45274-2_4

Davis, F. D., Granić, A., & Marangunić, N. (2024b). *The technology acceptance model: 30 years of TAM*. Springer International Publishing AG., DOI: 10.1007/978-3-030-45274-2 de Almeida, P. G. R., dos Santos, C. D., & Farias, J. S. (2021). Artificial Intelligence Regulation: A framework for governance. *Ethics and Information Technology*, 23(3), 505–525. DOI: 10.1007/s10676-021-09593-z

Familoni, B.Babajide Tolulope Familoni. (2024). Cybersecurity challenges in the age of AI: Theoretical approaches and practical solutions. *Computer Science & IT Research Journal*, 5(3), 703–724. DOI: 10.51594/csitrj.v5i3.930

Familoni, B. T.Babajide Tolulope Familoni. (2024). Cybersecurity challenges in the age of AI: Theoretical approaches and practical solutions. *Computer Science & IT Research Journal*, 5(3), 703–724. DOI: 10.51594/csitrj.v5i3.930

Fang, X., Che, S., Mao, M., Zhang, H., Zhao, M., & Zhao, X. (2024). Bias of AI-generated content: An examination of news produced by large language models. *Scientific Reports*, 14(1), 5224. DOI: 10.1038/s41598-024-55686-2 PMID: 38433238

Gidney, C., & Ekerå, M. (2019). How to factor 2048-bit RSA integers in 8 hours using 20 million noisy qubits. *Quantum : the Open Journal for Quantum Science*, 5, 433. DOI: 10.22331/q-2021-04-15-433

Goodfellow, I., Bengio, Y., & Courvill, A. (2023). *Deep Learning* (2nd ed.). MIT Press., https://www.deeplearningbook.org/

Habbal, A., Ali, M. K., & Abuzaraida, M. A. (2024). Artificial intelligence trust, risk and security management (AI TRiSM): Frameworks, applications, challenges and future research directions. *Expert Systems with Applications*, 240, 122442. DOI: 10.1016/j.eswa.2023.122442

Hamon, R., Junklewitz, H., Garrido, J. S., & Sanchez, I. (2024). *Three challenges to secure AI systems in the context of AI regulations*. IEEE., DOI: 10.1109/ACCESS.2024.3391021

Hassija, V., Chamola, V., Mahapatra, A., Singal, A., Goel, D., Huang, K., Scardapane, S., Spinelli, I., Mahmud, M., & Hussain, A. (2023). Interpreting black-box models: A review on explainable artificial intelligence. *Cognitive Computation*, 16(1), 45–74. DOI: 10.1007/s12559-023-10179-8

Hickman, E., & Petrin, M. (2021). Trustworthy AI and corporate governance: The EU's ethics guidelines for trustworthy artificial intelligence from a company law perspective. *European Business Organization Law Review*, 22(4), 593–625. DOI: 10.1007/s40804-021-00224-0

Hine, E., & Floridi, L. (2024). Artificial intelligence with American values and Chinese characteristics: A comparative analysis of American and Chinese governmental AI policies. *AI & Society*, 9, 257–278. DOI: 10.1007/s00146-022-01499-8

Hiscox. (2023). *Hiscox research finds increased prevalence of cyber attacks on businesses for fourth consecutive year.* https://www.hiscoxgroup.com/sites/group/files/documents/2023-10/Hiscox-Cyber-Readiness-Report-2023.pdf

Hoffmann, M., & Mehler, M. (2023). An industry-specific investigation on artificial intelligence adoption: The cases of financial services and manufacturing. *PACIS 2023 Proceedings. 1.* https://aisel.aisnet.org/pacis2023/1

Huff, A. J., Burrell, D. N., Nobles, C., Richardson, K., Wright, J. B., Burton, S. L., Jones, A., Springs, D., Omar, M., & Brown-Jackson, K. L. (2023). Management practices for mitigating cybersecurity threats to biotechnology companies, laboratories, and healthcare research organizations. In *Applied Research Approaches to Technology* (pp. 1–12). Healthcare, and Business., DOI: 10.4018/979-8-3693-1630-6.ch001

Iftikhar, N., & Nordbjerg, F. (2021). Adopting Artificial Intelligence in Danish SMEs: Barrier to Become a Data Driven Company, Its Solutions and Benefits. *In Proceedings of the 2nd International Conference on Innovative Intelligent Industrial Production and Logistics - IN4PL.* SciTePress, 131-136. DOI: 10.5220/0010691800003062

ISC2. (2023). H*ow the economy, skills gap and artificial intelligence are challenging the global cybersecurity workforce. Author.*https://www.isc2.org/-/media/Project/ISC2/Main/Media/documents/research/ISC2_Cybersecurity_Workforce_Study_2023.pdf

Jacobsen, J. T., & Liebetrau, T. (2023). Artificial intelligence and military superiority: How the 'cyber-AI offensive-defensive arms race' affects the US vision of the fully integrated battlefield. In *Artificial Intelligence and International Conflict in Cyberspace* (pp. 135–156). Routledge., DOI: 10.4324/9781003284093-8

Kanungo, S. (2024). AI-driven resource management strategies for cloud computing systems, services, and applications. *World Journal of Advanced* Engineering Technology and Sciences, 11(2), 559-5 6. DOI: 10.30574/wjaets.2024.11.2.0137

Kaur, R., Gabrijelčič, D., & Klobučar, T. (2023). Artificial intelligence for cybersecurity: Literature review and future research directions. *Information Fusion*, 97, 101804. DOI: 10.1016/j.inffus.2023.101804

Khan, M., & Ghafoor, L. (2024). Adversarial machine learning in the context of network security: Challenges and solutions. *Journal of Computational Intelligence and Robotics*, 4(1), 51–63. https://thesciencebrigade.com/jcir/article/view/118

Khan, M. F. I., & Masum, A. K. M. (2024). Predictive *analytics and* machine learning for real-time detection of software defects and agile test management. *Educational Administration: Theory and Practice*, 30(4), 1051–1057. DOI: 10.1080/01616412.2019.1609159

Kim, S. S., Watkins, E. A., Russakovsky, O., Fong, R., & Monroy-Hernández, A. (2023, April). " Help Me Help the AI": Understanding How Explainability Can Support Human-AI Interaction. *InProceedings of the 2023 CHI Conference on Human Factors in Computing Systems* (pp. 1-17). DOI: 10.1145/3544548.3581001

Kou, H., Zhang, Y., & Lee, H. P. (2024). Dynamic optimization based on Quantum computation-A comprehensive review. *Computers & Structures*, 292, 107255. DOI: 10.1016/j.compstruc.2023.107255

Kumar, R., & Srivastava, P. (2022). Enhancing data quality for AI in network security. *International Journal of Information Security and Privacy*, 16(3), 134–150. DOI: 10.4018/IJISP.202203011

Ladd, T. D., Jelezko, F., Laflamme, R., Nakamura, Y., Monroe, C., & O'Brien, J. L. (2010). Quantum Computing. *Nature*, 464(7285), 45–53. DOI: 10.1038/nature08812 PMID: 20203602

LeCun, Y., Bengio, Y., & Hinton, G. (2015). Deep learning. *Nature*, 521(7553), 436–444. DOI: 10.1038/nature14539 PMID: 26017442

Lee, M. C., Scheepers, H., Lui, A. K., & Ngai, E. W. (2023). The implementation of artificial intelligence in organizations: A systematic literature review. *Information & Management*, 60(5), 103816. DOI: 10.1016/j.im.2023.103816

Li, B., Qi, P., Liu, B., Di, S., Liu, J., Pei, J., Yi, J., & Zhou, B. (2023). Trustworthy AI: From principles to practices. *ACM Computing Surveys*, 55(9), 1–46. https://dl.acm.org/doi/10.1145/3555803. DOI: 10.1145/3555803

Lukyanenko, R., Maass, W., & Storey, V. C. (2022). Trust in artificial intelligence: From a foundational trust framework to emerging research opportunities. *Electronic Markets*, 32(4), 1993–2020. DOI: 10.1007/s12525-022-00605-4

Madrid, A. P., & Wright, C. (2023). Trustworthy AI alone is not enough. *Dykinson*.https://www.dykinson.com/libros/trustworthy-ai-alone-is-not-enough/9788411706001/

Malatji, W. R., Eck, R. V., & Zuva, T. (2020). Understanding the usage, modifications, limitations and criticisms of technology acceptance model (TAM). *Advances in Science, Technology and Engineering Systems Journal, 5(6)*, 113-117. https://api.semanticscholar.org/CorpusID:229219113

Mallick, M. A. I., & Nath, R. (2024). Navigating the cyber security landscape: A comprehensive review of cyber-attacks, emerging trends, and recent developments. *World Scientific News*, 190(1), 1–69. https://worldscientificnews.com/wp-content/uploads/2024/01/WSN-1901-2024-1-69-1.pdf

Markevych, M., & Dawson, M. (2023, July). A review of enhancing intrusion detection systems for cybersecurity using artificial intelligence (AI). *In International conference Knowledge-based Organization* (pp. 30-37). https://intapi.sciendo.com/pdf/10.2478/kbo-2023-0072

Meisenbacher, S., Klymenko, A., Kelley, P. G., Peddinti, S. T., Thomas, K., & Matthes, F. (2024). Privacy risks of general-purpose ai systems: a foundation for investigating practitioner perspectives. https://doi.org//arXiv.2407.02027DOI: 10.48550

Mishra, S. (2023). Exploring the impact of AI-based cyber security financial sector management. *Applied Sciences (Basel, Switzerland)*, 13(10), 5875. DOI: 10.3390/app13105875

Mohamed, N. (2023). Current trends in AI and ML for cybersecurity: A state-of-the-art survey. *Cogent Engineering*, 10(2), 2272358. Advance online publication. DOI: 10.1080/23311916.2023.2272358

Möller, D. P. (2023). Cybersecurity in digital transformation. In *Guide to Cybersecurity in Digital Transformation: Trends* (pp. 1–70). Methods, Technologies, Applications and Best Practices., DOI: 10.1007/978-3-031-26845-8_1

Moore, J., & Pratt, M. K. (2023). *What is digital transformation?: Definition and guide from TechTarget CIO*. TechTarget https://www.techtarget.com/searchcio/definition/digital-transformation#:~:text=Digital%20transformatio %20is%20the%20incorporation,improve%20their%20ability%20to%20compete.

Mosqueira-Rey, E., Hernández-Pereira, E., Alonso-Ríos, D., Bobes-Bascarán, J., & Fernández-Leal, Á. (2023). Human-in-the-loop machine learning: A state of the art. *Artificial Intelligence Review*, 56(4), 3005–3054. DOI: 10.1007/s10462-022-10246-w

Munee, S., Farooq, U., Athar, A., Raza, M. A., Ghazal, T., & Sakib, S. (2024). A critical review of artificial intelligence based approaches in intrusion detection: A comprehensive analysis. *Journal of Engineering*, 2024(1), 3909173. DOI: 10.1155/2024/3909173

Muraleedhara, P. (2024). The Need For AI-Powered Cybersecurity to Tackle AI-Driven Cyberattacks. ISACA. https://www.isaca.org/resources/news-and-trends/isaca-now-blog/2024/the-need-for-ai-powered-cybersecurity-to-tackle-ai-driven-cyberattacks

Nam, K., Dutt, C. S., Chathoth, P., Daghfous, A., & Khan, M. S. (2021). The adoption of artificial intelligence and robotics in the hotel industry: Prospects and challenges. *Electronic Markets*, 31(3), 553–574. DOI: 10.1007/s12525-020-00442-3

National Conference of State Legislatures. (2024). *Artificial intelligence 2023 legislation*. National Conference of State Legislatures https://www.ncsl.org/technology-and-communication/artificial-intelligence-2023-legislation

Nili, A., Tate, M., & Barros, A. (2020). A disciplined approach for enhancing the technology acceptance model. *In European Conference on Information Systems (ECIS) 2020 Proceedings*. https://eprints.qut.edu.au/202630/

Oladoyinbo, T. O., Olabanji, S. O., Olaniyi, O. O., Adebiyi, O. O., Okunleye, O. J., & Ismaila Alao, A. (2024). Exploring the challenges of artificial intelligence in data integrity and its influence on social dynamics. *Asian Journal of Advanced Research and Reports*, 18(2), 1–23. https://ssrn.com/abstract=4693987. DOI: 10.9734/ajarr/2024/v18i2601

Olorunsogo, T., Jacks, B. S., & Ajala, O. A. (2024). Leveraging quantum computing for inclusive and responsible AI development: A conceptual and review framework. *Computer Science & IT Research Journal*, 5(3), 671–680. DOI: 10.51594/csitrj.v5i3.927

Oseni, A., Moustafa, N., Janicke, H. L., Tari, Z., & Vasilakos, A. 2020. Security and privacy for artificial intelligence: opportunities and challenges. https://doi.org// arXiv.2102.04661DOI: 10.48550

Owoseni, A. (2023). What is digital transformation? Investigating the metaphorical meaning of digital transformation and why it matters. *Digital Transformation and Society*, 2(1), 78–96. DOI: 10.1108/DTS-10-2022-0049

Ozkan-Ozay, M., Akin, E., Aslan, Ö., Kosunalp, S., Iliev, T., Stoyanov, I., & Beloev, I. (2024). *A comprehensive survey: Evaluating the efficiency of artificial intelligence and machine learning techniques on cyber security solutions*. IEEE., DOI: 10.1109/ACCESS.2024.3355547

Oztemel, E., & Gursev, S. (2020). Literature review of industry 4.0 and related technologies. *Journal of Intelligent Manufacturing*, 31(1), 127–182. DOI: 10.1007/s10845-018-1433-8

Papernot, N. (2021). Adversarial Machine Learning. In *Encyclopedia of Cryptography, Security and Privacy* (pp. 1–4). Springer Berlin Heidelberg., DOI: 10.1007/978-3-642-27739-9_1635-1

Pasini, M. L., Yin, J., & Li, Y. W. (2021). A scalable algorithm for the optimization of neural network architectures. *Parallel Computing*, 104-105, 102788. DOI: 10.1016/j.parco.2021.102788

Peter, M. K., Kraft, C., & Lindeque, J. (2020). Strategic action fields of digital transformation: An exploration of the strategic action fields of Swiss SMEs and large enterprise. *Journal of Strategy and Management*, 13(1), 160–180. DOI: 10.1108/JSMA-05-2019-0070

Pirandola, S., Andersen, U. L., Banchi, L., Berta, M., Bunandar, D., Colbeck, R., Englund, D., Gehring, T., Lupo, C., Ottaviani, C., Pereira, J. L., Razavi, M., Shamsul Shaari, J., Tomamichel, M., Usenko, V. C., Vallone, G., Villoresi, P., & Wallden, P. (2020). Advances in quantum cryptography. *Advances in Optics and Photonics*, 12(4), 1012. DOI: 10.1364/AOP.361502

Plotinsky, D., & Cinelli, G. M. (2024). *Existing and proposed federal AI regulation in the United States*. https://www.morganlewis.com/pubs/2024/04/existing-and-proposed-federal-ai-regulation-in-the-united-states

Pooranam, N., Surendran, D., Karthikeyan, N., & Rajathi, G. I. (2023). *Quantum computing: Future of artificial intelligence and its applications. Quantum Computing and Artificial Intelligence: Training Machine and Deep Learning Algorithms on Quantum Computers*. Walter de Gruyter GmbH & Co KG.

Prem, E. (2023). From ethical AI frameworks to tools: A review of approaches. *AI and Ethics*, 3(3), 699–716. DOI: 10.1007/s43681-023-00258-9

Preskill, J. (2021). Quantum computing: Current status and future prospects. *Bulletin of the American Physical Society*, 65, •••. https://meetings.aps.org/Meeting/MAR20/Session/P00.5

Ramezan, C. A. (2023). Examining the cyber skills gap: An analysis of cybersecurity positions by sub-field. *Journal of Information Systems Education*, 34(1), 94–105.

Rao, V. (2024). *Massed Muddler Intelligence*. https://studio.ribbonfarm.com/p/massed-muddler-intelligence?utm_source=tldrnewsletter

Ratiu, R. (2024). *Securing the future: Enhancing cybersecurity in 2024 and beyond*. https://www.isaca.org/resources/news-and trends/isaca-now-blog/2024/securing-the-future-enhancing-cybersecurity-in-2024-and-beyond

Roberts, H., Cowls, J., Hine, E., Mazzi, F., Tsamados, A., Taddeo, M., & Floridi, L. (2024). Achieving a 'Good AI Society': Comparing the Aims and Progress of the EU and the US. *Science and Engineering Ethics*, 27(6), 68. DOI: 10.1007/s11948-021-00340-7 PMID: 34767085

Russo, S., Besmer, M. D., Blumensaat, F., Bouffard, D., Disch, A., Hammes, F., Hess, A., Lürig, M., Matthews, B., Minaudo, C., Morgenroth, E., Tran-Khac, V., & Villez, K. (2021). The value of human data annotation for machine learning based anomaly detection in environmental systems. *Water Research*, 206, 117695. DOI: 10.1016/j.watres.2021.117695 PMID: 34626884

Sarker, I. H. (2021). Deep Learning: A Comprehensive Overview on Techniques, Taxonomy, Applications and Research Directions. *SN Computer Science*, 2(6), 420. DOI: 10.1007/s42979-021-00815-1 PMID: 34426802

Sarker, I. H., Furhad, M. H., & Nowrozy, R. (2021). AI-Driven cybersecurity: An overview, security intelligence modeling and research directions. *SN Computer Science*, 2(173), 173. Advance online publication. DOI: 10.1007/s42979-021-00557-0

Selvarajan, S., Srivastava, G., Khadidos, A. O., Baza, M., Alshehri, A., & Lin, J. C. (2023). An artificial intelligence lightweight blockchain security model for security and privacy in IIoT systems. *Journal of Cloud Computing (Heidelberg, Germany)*, 12(1), 1–17. DOI: 10.1186/s13677-023-00412-y PMID: 36937654

Shah, V. (2021). Machine Learning Algorithms for Cybersecurity: Detecting and preventing threats. *Revista Española de Documentación Científica*, 15(4), 42–66. https://redc.revistas-csic.com/index.php/Jorunal/article/view/156

Sharif, M. H. U., & Mohammed, M. A. (2022). A literature review of financial losses statistics for cyber security and future trend. *World Journal of Advanced Research and Reviews, 15*(1, 138-156. DOI: 10.30574/wjarr.2022.15.1.0573

Sharma, K. (2023). Enhancing cybersecurity through AI: A look into the future. *ISC2.*https://www.isc2.org/Insights/2023/09/Enhancing-Cybersecurity-through-AI-A-Look-into-the-Future

Sharton, B. R. (2021). Ransomware attacks are spiking. Is your company prepared? *Harvard Business Review.*https://hbr.org/2021/05/ransomware-attacks-are-spiking-is-your-company-prepared

Siemon, D. (2022). Elaborating team roles for artificial intelligence-based teammates in human-ai collaboration. *Group Decision and Negotiation*, 31(5), 871–912. DOI: 10.1007/s10726-022-09792-z

Soroka, L., Danylenko, A., Sokiran, M., Levchenko, D., & Zubko, O. (2023). Public-private collaboration for national security: Challenges and opportunities. *Amazonia Investiga*, 12(70), 43–45. DOI: 10.34069/AI/2023.70.10.4

Stahl, B. C., Antoniou, J., Bhalla, N., Brooks, L., Jansen, P., Lindqvist, B., Kirichenko, A., Marchal, S., Rodrigues, R., Santiago, N., Warso, Z., & Wright, D. (2023). A systematic review of Artificial intelligence impact assessment. *Artificial Intelligence Review*, 56(11), 12799–12831. DOI: 10.1007/s10462-023-10420-8 PMID: 37362899

Swan, M., & dos Santos, R. P. (2023). Quantum intelligence: responsible human-ai entities. In *AAAI Spring Symposium* (pp. 21–31). SRAI., https://ceur-ws.org/Vol-3527/Paper_2896.pdf

Thorbecke, C., & Ziady, H. (2024). *Microsoft is laying off 10,000 employees.* https://www.cnn.com/2023/01/18/tech/microsoft-layoffs/index.html

Tyagi, A. K., Mishra, A. K., Aswathy, S. U., & Kumari, S. (2024). *Quantum computing, qubits with artificial intelligence, and blockchain technologies: A roadmap for the future.* Automated Secure Computing for Next-Generation Systems, 367-384. DOI: 10.1002/9781394213948.ch18

Walker, G., Stanton, N., Salmon, P., & Jenkins, D. (2021). A review of sociotechnical systems theory: A classic concept for new command and control paradigms. *Theoretical Issues in Ergonomics Science*, 9(6), 479–499. DOI: 10.1080/14639220701635470

Wang, Y., Bao, Q., Wang, J., Su, G., & Xu, X. (2024). Cloud computing for large-scale resource computation and storage in machine learning. *Journal of Theory and Practice of Engineering Science*, 4(03), 163–171. DOI: 10.53469/jtpes.2024.04(03).14

Waqas, M., Tu, S., Halim, Z., Rehman, S. U., Abbas, G., & Abbas, Z. H. (2022). The role of Artificial Intelligence and machine learning in wireless networks security: Principle, practice and challenges. *Artificial Intelligence Review*, 55(7), 5215–5261. DOI: 10.1007/s10462-022-10143-2

Waugh, E. (2023). What is personally identifiable information? https://www.experian.com/blogs/ask-experian/what-is-personally-identifiable-information/

White House. (2024). FACT SHEET: President Biden takes action to protect American workers and businesses from China's unfair trade practices. The White House. https://www.whitehouse.gov/briefing-room/statements-releases/2024/05/14/fact-sheet-president-biden-takes-action-to-protect-american-workers-and-businesses-from-chinas-unfair-trade-practices/

Williamson, S. M., & Prybutok, V. (2024). Balancing privacy and progress: A review of privacy challenges, systemic oversight, and patient perceptions in ai-driven healthcare. *Applied Sciences (Basel, Switzerland)*, 14(2), 675. DOI: 10.3390/app14020675

Zhang, L., Carter, R. A.Jr, Greene, J. A., & Bernacki, M. L. (2024). Unraveling challenges with the implementation of universal design for learning: A systematic literature review. *Educational Psychology Review*, 36(1), 35. DOI: 10.1007/s10648-024-09860-7

Zhang, Z., Ning, H., Shi, F., Farha, F., Xu, Y., Xu, J., Zhang, F., & Choo, K.-K. R. (2021). Artificial Intelligence in cyber security: Research advances, challenges, and opportunities. *Artificial Intelligence Review*, 55(2), 1029–1053. DOI: 10.1007/s10462-021-09976-0

Zhao, J., & Gómez Fariñas, B. (2023). Artificial intelligence and sustainable decisions. *European Business Organization Law Review*, 24(1), 1–39. DOI: 10.1007/s40804-022-00262-2

KEY TERMS AND DEFINITIONS

AI Ethics: The field of study focusing on the ethical uses of AI

Cyber Incident: A cyber threat that is attempted or successful within a network environment

Cyber Threats: Malicious actions that may cause disruption to enterprises causing events such as financial loss, data loss, operational disruption, or to an extreme occurrence, physical harm.

Digital Transformation: The method used by businesses to improve people, processes, and technology via modernized digital tooling

Machine Learning: Algorithms that help computers make predictions based on data it receives. It is a subset of AI.

Mass Muddler Intelligence: A theory that proposes using decentralized muddler agents that operate decentralized, like how social contract theory functions in human societies

Quantum Computing: The field of study using quantum mechanics to vastly improve computing power.

Chapter 8
Advancing Cybersecurity:
Strategic Insights Into Multifactor Authentication

Sharon L. Burton
https://orcid.org/0000-0003-1653-9783
Capitol Technology University, USA

ABSTRACT

This research investigates the efficacy and challenges of Multifactor Authentication (MFA) in enhancing cybersecurity within organizational settings. Employing a qualitative design, this study integrates a comprehensive literature review with case studies to examine the deployment and impact of MFA technologies. Key findings reveal that over 57% of global businesses have adopted MFA, significantly reducing unauthorized access and breaches by 99.9% when correctly implemented. However, challenges such as user resistance, implementation costs, and the complexity of MFA systems persist, affecting overall effectiveness and adoption rates. This research concludes that while MFA substantially improves security, its success hinges on strategic deployment and user compliance. The significance of this research lies in its potential to guide organizations in refining their cybersecurity measures and in informing policy on secure authentication practices, ultimately contributing to enhanced organizational and data security in an increasingly digital world.

INTRODUCTION, PROBLEM, AND INDUSTRY CHALLENGES

The rapid adoption of mobile handheld devices in the workplace has shifted their role from luxury items for tech enthusiasts to essential tools for the modern workforce. These devices enhance productivity and operational efficiency but also pose significant security risks. Strong user authentication is critical to safeguard

DOI: 10.4018/979-8-3693-8562-3.ch008

against unauthorized access, especially in lost or stolen devices, and is vital for protecting organizational data. To address these security concerns, as given by Aburbeian and Fernández-Veiga (2024), multifactor authentication (MFA) plays a crucial role by requiring multiple forms of verification from different categories of credentials: knowledge-based (e.g., passwords), possession-based (e.g., tokens), and inherent characteristics (e.g., biometrics). In other words, MFA is a security process that verifies a user's identity by requiring multiple forms of verification, each from a different category of credentials (Bonderud, 2022). See Figure 1. This approach ensures that access to an account or completion of a transaction involves several independent methods of authentication, enhancing overall security. This thorough tactic pointedly lessens the risk of unapproved access, ascertaining MFA as a vital component of contemporary cybersecurity practices (Sun et al., 2024). Understanding the strengths and limitations of MFA is essential for its effective integration into an organization's security strategy. As of 2019, the third annual Global Password Security Report notes that approximately 57% of businesses globally have adopted MFA (LastPass Security Report, 2019). This statistic reflects a significant increase from previous years, highlighting the growing recognition of MFA's importance in securing digital assets (LastPass Security Report, 2019). Larger organizations, principally organizations with a workforce exceeding 10,000 employees, show even higher adoption rates, with around 87% utilizing MFA to protect their systems (Özşahan, 2023). The adoption rate of MFA for medium size organizations (26-100 employees) is 34% (Özşahan, 2023). The adoption rate for MFA for small organizations (25 employees or less) is 27% (Özşahan, 2023).

Figure 1. What is multi-factor authentication?

Despite the growing adoption of MFA, it remains a critical area of concern in cybersecurity. According to industry reports, MFA effectively prevents account breaches, reducing the risk by more than 99.9% when implemented correctly (Microsoft Build, 2024). However, attacks targeting MFA systems still occur, primarily through SIM-jacking, MFA Hammering, and AiTM (Adversary-in-the-Middle) attacks. Jacking references that hackers can hijack an active session token to mimic a user and circumvent MFA safeguards (Myers, 2023). MFA Hammering, also known as MFA brute-force attacks, references a malicious actor persistently trying to guess the correct MFA code or token until they successfully access the targeted account (Haber et al., 2022). MFA hammering can also involve using stolen passwords to gain authentication into a web application (Mostafa et al., 2023). AiTM references an Adversary-in-the-Middle (AitM) attack, which is a type of Man-in-the-Middle (MitM) attack in which attackers insert themselves between communication channels to listen, intercept, or alter data traffic (Zhang & Tenney, 2023). Unlike standard MitM attacks, AitM attacks involve actively exploiting this intermediary position to perform harmful activities that can lead to severe consequences. Approximately 28% of MFA users have been targeted by these sophisticated tactics (Özşahan, 2023).

Moreover, Microsoft Security (2019) data indicates that 99.9% of compromised accounts did not have MFA enabled, underscoring the effectiveness of MFA in preventing breaches. The data indicates that although MFA dramatically improves security, its success largely hinges on correct implementation (Oxford Analytica (2023) and user compliance with security measures (Kunduru, 2023). These measures include using stronger passwords, disabling legacy authentication methods, and educating employees about phishing threats (Kunduru, 2023; Lyon, 2024; Osmëi & Ali, 2023; Oxford Analytica, 2023; Shukla & Dubey, 2024).

The adoption of multi-factor authentication (MFA) is growing, with over half of global businesses implementing this technology (Ladha, 2024). According to a recent survey by Okta (2023), as of January 2023, nearly two-thirds of users employ MFA for authentication, with 64% of general users and 90% of administrators using it. However, the technology's full potential can only be realized through comprehensive deployment and continuous improvement of security practices (Das et al., 2022). As cyber threats evolve, organizations must stay vigilant and adaptive in their security strategies. This action means adopting MFA and continuously updating and refining MFA methods to stay ahead of attackers. The proactive approach of remaining vigilant against emerging threats is essential to mitigate risk associated with MFA and ensure the highest level of security for digital identities and assets (Das et al., 2022). The remainder of this chapter will cover the background, methodology and design, applicable theories, literature review, recommendations, conclusions, and solutions, and future research directions in multifactor authentication.

Background

Understanding the historical progression and theoretical foundations of authentication practices is crucial for comprehensively grasping the impact of contemporary innovations like Multi-Factor Authentication (MFA) in cybersecurity. This background provides a necessary lens through which the significant shifts brought about by technological advancements can be assessed. Historically, authentication systems relied heavily on single-factor authentication (SFA), primarily passwords, which proved insufficient in protecting sensitive information as cyber threats evolved (Sadat & Ahmadzai, 2023). This inadequacy led to the development of Two-Factor Authentication (2FA), which added an extra layer of security by requiring two forms of verification: something the user knows (e.g., a password) and something the user has (e.g., a token or mobile device) (Teh & Ramil, 2023). Despite the improvements brought by 2FA, the increasing complexity of cyber threats exposed its limitations. Vulnerabilities such as SIM swapping and reliance on SMS-based authentication underscored the need for more robust security measures (Murugalakshmi & Robin, 2023). As a result, the security industry shifted towards Multi-Factor Authentication (MFA), which incorporates multiple forms of verification from different categories: knowledge-based (e.g., passwords), possession-based (e.g., tokens), and inherence factors (e.g., biometrics) (Papaspirou, 2023). This evolution enhances security by significantly challenging unauthorized access, aligning with contemporary cybersecurity needs and regulatory requirements (Blunden, 2022).

The adoption of MFA has seen a significant rise, with more than half of global businesses implementing this technology to secure their digital assets (Ladha, 2024). Larger organizations, particularly those with a workforce exceeding 10,000 employees, exhibit even higher adoption rates, underscoring the crucial role of MFA in modern cybersecurity strategies (Özşahan, 2023). These larger organizations have acknowledged the need for robust authentication systems to safeguard extensive and sensitive data networks, setting a precedent for smaller and medium-sized businesses. Studies emphasize the importance of this historical perspective, suggesting that understanding past authentication methodologies enriches the implementation and effectiveness of MFA in today's complex threat landscape (Suleski et al., 2023).

Moreover, studying authentication history is essential for recognizing patterns and recurring themes in security practices. This continuity suggests that while tools and methods evolve, the fundamental goals of authentication—improving security, protecting data, and ensuring user trust—remain constant (Aburbeian & Fernández-Veiga (2024). This historical context is vital for developing MFA applications that are technologically advanced and aligned with broader cybersecurity objectives and regulatory frameworks (Akinsanya et al., 2024).

Additionally, the development and integration of MFA have significant implications for compliance with regulatory frameworks. Regulations such as the Health Insurance Portability and Accountability Act (HIPAA), the General Data Protection Regulation (GDPR), and the Payment Card Industry Data Security Standard (PCI-DSS) often mandate or recommend the use of MFA for accessing sensitive information (Belmabrouk, 2023). Compliance with these standards helps organizations avoid fines and legal issues and reinforces their commitment to maintaining high-security standards (Akinsanya et al., 2024). This compliance further builds trust with clients and stakeholders, reinforcing organizations' reputations and reliability.

In summary, the background section highlights the significance of understanding the historical milieu of authentication practices, particularly regarding integrating MFA in cybersecurity. It highlights how this perspective is essential for assessing MFA's current and future impact on security strategies and organizational resilience. By drawing connections between past trends and emerging approaches, organizations can better appreciate the significance of MFA in mitigating modern cyber threats. This historical insight enables a more nuanced implementation of MFA, ensuring it is technologically robust as well as strategically aligned with broader security goals and compliance requirements. Ultimately, this foundation aids in comprehensive understanding how MFA contributes to a resilient and secure digital infrastructure capable of adapting to evolving threats and maintaining trust in a dynamic cybersecurity landscape.

Problem Statement

This research explores targeted strategies to reduce MFA deployment friction and financial burdens, improving its adoption rates and operational effectiveness. Notwithstanding the documented efficacy of MFA in considerably reducing cybersecurity breaches, its most significant potential is weakened by persistent user resistance, higher implementation costs, and complicated deployment challenges (Das et al., 2020). This chapter aims to develop practical recommendations for enhancing cybersecurity measures by addressing the socio-technical challenges of MFA implementation. This research explores targeted strategies to reduce Multi-Factor Authentication (MFA) deployment friction and financial burdens, improving its adoption rates and operational effectiveness. Existing research highlights MFA's broad adoption and security successes across various organizational scales; however, it also points to persistent barriers that limit widespread integration and effectiveness (Das et al., 2020; Kizza, 2024; Suleski et al., 2023; Wahab et al., 2023). These barriers include technological complexities that deter user compliance and escalate operational costs, particularly for smaller organizations with limited resources (Wahab et al., 2023). Additionally, while the benefits of MFA in enhancing data security and meeting compliance requirements are well-documented, there still exists a gap in comprehension about how to effectively overcome the reluctance and financial constraints associated with its implementation (Das et al., 2020).

Methodology and Design

In this qualitative research, gathering and analyzing existing research involved conducting a scoping literature review, and adhering to guidelines similar to those suggested by Berg et al. (2023) and Campbell et al. (2023). The primary goal of applying a scoping literature review methodology was to support understanding the breadth of available evidence regarding MFA and inform future research directions. Scoping literature reviews help uncover the literature on developing or evolving subjects and ascertain gaps (Mak & Thomas, 2022). Moustakas and Robrade (2023) highlight that scoping literature reviews seek to systematically map the existing literature, elucidate critical concepts, and identify evidence and knowledge gaps related to a specific subject. Utilizing a literature review, this researcher effectively managed the complexities of extensive scholarly information (Mak & Thomas, 2022; Moustakas & Robrade, 2023).

To conduct this thorough literature review, the researcher focused on publications up to 2024, using various search terms related to risk management in project management and cybersecurity. The literature search was conducted from December 2023 to September 2024, applying specific keywords and phrases (Moreno-Ortiz, 2024) such as multi-factor authentication, two-factor authentication, knowledge factor, possession factor, inherence factor, SIM swapping, Adversary-in-the-Middle (AitM) Attack, Man-in-the-Middle (MitM), MFA Hammering, and regulatory frameworks. This deliberate selection and use of keywords ensured the retrieval of articles directly relevant to the research focus areas. The search strategy included academic subscription-based databases and open web resources, such as EBSCO's suite of databases, IEEE Xplore, the Homeland Security Digital Library, the ProQuest Dissertation Database, and ABI Inform Complete, along with Google Scholar to access up-to-date, peer-reviewed articles. This meticulous process categorized the literature to emphasize its relevance to multi-factor authentication, forming a robust foundation for the investigation.

Applicable Theoretical Frameworks

The Zero Trust framework is pertinent in today's cybersecurity landscape because of the increase of complex cyber threats and the increasing involvedness of modern IT environments. The traditional network perimeter has dissolved, making it harder to defend against breaches using conventional methods as organizations adopt cloud services, mobile workforces, and the Internet of Things (IoT). The change lengthens technological reach outside physical boundaries (Rivera et al., 2024). Zero Trust addresses this challenge by ensuring that every access request is scrutinized, regardless of origin. This approach is critical in protecting against insider threats, credential theft, and lateral movement within a network, where attackers exploit trusted access to escalate privileges and compromise sensitive data (Rivera et al., 2024).

The Zero Trust framework is a cybersecurity model that operates on the principle of "never trust, always verify" (Azad et al.; 3.2. Zero-trust alignment). Dissimilar to traditional security models that center on protecting the perimeter of a network, Zero Trust supposes that threats can begin inside and outside the network. Consequently, each access request must be authenticated, authorized, and continuously validated prior to granting access to resources, whether within or outside of the organization's network (Azad et al., 2024). The Zero Trust framework is linked to modern cybersecurity strategies because it challenges the traditional notion of trust within a network. In a Zero Trust environment, every user, device, and application is treated as possibly hostile until confirmed as safe. This approach necessitates robust authentication mechanisms to prove individualities and confirm that appropriate users can gain access to sensitive resources by adding layers of verification, ensuring that access is granted after multiple independent factors are validated (Azad et al., 2024).

MFA complements Zero Trust by significantly reducing the likelihood of unauthorized access, even if one factor (such as a password) is compromised (Rivera et al., 2024). This layered approach aligns with Zero Trust's core principle of continuous verification (Rivera et al., 2024), making MFA a vital component in implementing Zero Trust effectively. Comprehending the Zero Trust framework is essential for cybersecurity professionals and organizational leaders for the following reasons. The Zero Trust framework provides enhanced security (Rivera et al., 2024). Zero Trust offers an increased resilient security posture by removing implicit trust, and verifying access to all requests (Azad et al., 2024; Rivera et al., 2024). This level of security reduces the attack surface and limits the potential impact of a breach. Next is connecting regulatory compliance to Zero Trust.

As more regulatory bodies progressively direct rigorous security measures, Zero Trust can support organizations in realizing compliance requirements by safeguarding robust access controls and continuous monitoring (Bobbert & Timmermans, 2024). In addition, Zero Trust aligns with the principles of the NIST framework, advancing a structured method to safeguarding sensitive data and representing due diligence in protecting against breaches (Bobbert & Scheerder, 2020).

Din et al. (2024) stated that Zero Trust is adaptable to the evolving nature of modern threats in IT environments where customary perimeter defenses are insufficient. This framework offers a preemptive method of security that is more appropriate to offsetting advanced persistent threats and additional budding attack vectors. Additionally, Zero Trust assists in the incorporation of developing technologies and security traditions, confirming that organizations endure as robust and agile in a changing cyber threat landscape (Din et al., 2024).

The last key point is that Zero Trust allows informed determination and resolution (Din et al., 2024). Understanding Zero Trust is fundamental for making knowledgeable investments in procedures and technologies regarding cybersecurity (Shandilya et al., 2024). This framework permits organizations to order security schemes that ally with modern threat landscapes and regulatory prospects.

Overall, the Zero Trust framework indicates a thought change in the manner that organizations apply cybersecurity. Also, Zero Trust supports organizations' safeguard assets in an environment where a trusted network border is progressively obsolete by adding MFA authentication. Comprehending and implementing Zero Trust is vital for maintaining a robust security posture in the face of modern cyber threats. The Zero Trust framework has critiques.

Three critiques of the Zero Trust framework are overemphasis on equilibrium and complexity (James et al., 2024), insufficient attention to external factors (Dhiman et al., 2024), and high implementation and maintenance costs (Adahman et al., 2022). The Zero Trust framework can overstress attaining an equilibrium between security and usability, which can lead to noteworthy intricacy in application (Apraiz et al, 2023).

Critics contend that the continuous verification and granular control required by Zero Trust can consequence in an awkward and resource- demanding system (Azad et al., 2024). This complexity can make it complicated for organizations to implement Zero Trust effectively, specifically organizations with limited cybersecurity expertise or resources.

The intricate nature of Zero Trust may also lead to user frustration, particularly if the authentication processes disrupt workflows or require frequent re-authentication (Chung et al. (2023). This balance between robust security and practical usability can be challenging to maintain, making Zero Trust less appealing for some organizations. The following critique is insufficient attention to external factors.

This critique centers on the Zero Trust framework's limited focus on external factors such as regulatory changes, economic conditions, and the rapid pace of technological advancements (Dhiman et al., 2024). While Zero Trust provides a robust internal security posture, it may not fully account for the broader, dynamic external environment in which organizations operate (Collier & Sarkis, 2021). For example, Zero Trust's rigid approach to security might not adapt quickly enough to new regulatory requirements or emerging threats that evolve outside of the controlled internal network. This lack of flexibility in addressing external factors can leave organizations vulnerable to compliance issues or new types of attacks that fall outside the traditional Zero Trust model.

A third critique of the Zero Trust framework is the high cost associated with its implementation and ongoing maintenance (Rehan, 2024). Establishing a Zero Trust architecture can require significant investment in technology, including advanced authentication methods, network segmentation tools, and continuous monitoring systems (Shandilya et al., 2024). Additionally, maintaining a Zero Trust environment demands constant vigilance and updates, which can strain an organization's financial and human resources. For smaller organizations or those with limited budgets, these costs can be prohibitive, leading to concerns that Zero Trust may be inaccessible or unsustainable in the long term. The financial burden, combined with the need for specialized expertise, raises questions about the practicality of Zero Trust for many organizations.

LITERATURE REVIEW

Multifactor Authentication (MFA) has become a cornerstone in modern cybersecurity strategies. As cyber threats evolve, relying solely on passwords has proven insufficient to protect sensitive information. MFA adds an extra layer of security by requiring multiple forms of verification from independent categories of credentials: something you know (password), something you have (token), and something you are (biometric verification). This chapter explores the intricacies of MFA, through the use of a literature review (Kizza, 2024). This chapter analyzes MFA's benefits and drawbacks to provide a comprehensive understanding of its role in cybersecurity. This literature review provides a foundational background and discusses and analyzes published data on MFA in today's cybersecurity landscape. It organizes information to help understand the breadth of available evidence on MFA and guide future research directions (Mak & Thomas, 2022). The review examines the contributions of various publications to the topic, highlighting their relevance and impact. Additionally, it offers a comprehensive overview of the research landscape surrounding MFA. This information is crucial for cybersecurity leaders to stay informed about trends and leading practices.

Two-Factor Authentication (2FA) and its Evolution to MFA

Two-factor authentication (2FA) has long been a cornerstone of digital security, offering a significant enhancement over traditional single-factor authentication methods, such as passwords alone (Teh & Ramil, 2023). By requiring users to provide two forms of identification—typically something they know (a password) and something they have (a physical token or mobile device)—2FA added an extra layer of protection that significantly reduced the risk of unauthorized access (Papaspirou,

2023). This method effectively mitigated various security threats, including phishing attacks and credential theft.

However, as cyber threats have become increasingly sophisticated, the limitations of 2FA have become more apparent (Suleski et al., 2023). One major critique is that 2FA can still be vulnerable to attacks such as SIM swapping, where attackers gain control of the user's mobile phone number to intercept authentication codes (Murugalakshmi & Robin, 2023). Additionally, many 2FA systems rely heavily on SMS-based authentication, which can be compromised through various interception techniques (Stęchły & Szpunar, 2023). The user experience can also suffer due to the extra steps required, leading to potential resistance to its adoption.

Given these limitations, the security industry has moved towards Multi-Factor Authentication (MFA), the next step beyond 2FA. These adaptive and context-aware MFA systems can adjust the level of authentication required based on the risk associated with the login attempt (Bumiller et al., 2023). For instance, logging in from a recognized device in a familiar location might require fewer authentication steps than accessing the system from an unknown device or location. This approach enhances security and improves user convenience (Bumiller et al., 2023).

In summary, while 2FA was a significant advancement in digital security, its relevance is waning in the face of more sophisticated threats (Suleski et al., 2023). The transition to MFA represents the next logical step, offering robust protection by incorporating multiple, diverse authentication factors and adapting to the context of access attempts. This proactive approach is essential for maintaining the highest level of security in an increasingly complex threat landscape.

Understanding Multifactor Authentication

MFA is an authentication method that requires the user to present two or more pieces of evidence (or factors) to verify their identity. As given by Papaspirou (2023), the three most common categories are:

- **Knowledge Factor**: Something the user knows (e.g., password, PIN).
- **Possession Factor**: Something the user has (e.g., a mobile phone, hardware token).
- **Inherence Factor**: Something the user is (e.g., fingerprint, facial recognition).

These factors are designed to work together to significantly reduce the likelihood of unauthorized access (Papaspirou, 2023). Historically, authentication has evolved from simple passwords to more sophisticated methods (Sadat & Ahmadzai, 2023). Early systems relied on single-factor authentication (SFA), primarily passwords and then changed to two or more factors to confirm users' uniqueness so the particular user can gain entrance for services or data (Suleski et al., 2023). Warranting the security of authentication systems is fundamentally significant. An example is in the healthcare industry; the systems accessed, along with the data stored as records or transmitted by medical devices, are typically critical and sensitive (Suleski et al., 2023). However, due to the world affecting pandemic, COVID-19, and as cyberattacks became more sophisticated, the need for stronger authentication mechanisms became evident (Rakha, 2023; Suleski et al., 2023). These changes led to the development and adoption of MFA, which combines multiple forms of authentication to enhance security.

Benefits of Multifactor Authentication

The benefits of MFA include enhanced security, compliance with regulatory standards, protection against phishing and social engineering, and flexibility and scalability. Enhanced security is achieved by implementing multiple layers of authentication, significantly reducing the risk of unauthorized access (Tambunan et al., 2024). Compliance with regulatory standards is another critical advantage, as many frameworks mandate or recommend MFA to protect sensitive information (Blunden, 2022). Compliance with regulatory standards helps organizations avoid fines and legal issues and reinforces their commitment to maintaining high-security standards (Blunden, 2022). MFA also serves as a robust shield against phishing and social engineering attacks. By demanding multiple verification forms, MFA erects formidable barriers that make it significantly more arduous for attackers to trick users into divulging their credentials. This multi-layered approach effectively neutralizes the risks associated with these sophisticated attack vectors. Moreover, MFA offers flexibility and scalability, making it suitable for various organizational needs and easily integrated with different platforms and applications. This adaptability ensures that MFA can grow alongside the organization, continuously providing strong security measures as the technological landscape evolves. This section is essential to the chapter because it highlights MFA's multifaceted advantages, emphasizing its role as a cornerstone of modern cybersecurity practices. Understanding these benefits is crucial for organizations looking to strengthen their security posture and safeguard against increasingly complex cyber threats. Organizations adopting MFA protect their assets and align with best practices and regulatory requirements, ensuring long-term resilience and trust in their security frameworks.

Regarding enhanced security, MFA provides a robust defense against unauthorized access (Tambunan et al., 2024). Even if one factor is compromised, the chances that an attacker can bypass additional layers are significantly reduced (Tambunan et al., 2024). This multi-layered approach significantly decreases the likelihood of successful breaches, ensuring that sensitive information remains secure. Additionally, MFA's flexibility allows it to be seamlessly tailored to different organizational needs and integrated with various platforms and applications. Moreover, MFA is not only about enhancing security but also plays a critical role in ensuring organizations meet compliance with regulatory standards.

Implementing MFA is crucial to compliance with regulatory standards and adherence to various regulatory frameworks, which mandate stringent security measures to protect sensitive information. Regulatory frameworks, such as the General Data Protection Regulation (GDPR), the Health Insurance Portability and Accountability Act (HIPAA), and the Payment Card Industry Data Security Standard (PCI-DSS), require or recommend the use of MFA for accessing sensitive information (Vashishth et al., 2024). Implementing MFA helps organizations comply with these regulations, avoiding potential fines and legal issues. By ensuring that only authorized users can access critical data, organizations safeguard their information and demonstrate their commitment to regulatory compliance and data protection best practices (Akinsanya et al., 2024). This proactive stance on security helps build trust with clients and stakeholders, further reinforcing the organization's reputation and reliability. Transitioning from the significance of protection against phishing and social engineering, another essential benefit of MFA is its flexibility and scalability, which makes it suitable for diverse organizational contexts.

Phishing attacks often aim to steal passwords. MFA can mitigate these attacks by adding another layer of verification that an attacker is less likely to obtain (Anderson & Rainie, 2023). Unlike single-factor authentication, which relies solely on passwords, MFA requires additional credentials such as a one-time code, biometric data, or a hardware token. This extra step significantly reduces the likelihood of a successful phishing attempt, as attackers would need to compromise multiple authentication factors. Moreover, MFA can provide real-time alerts for suspicious login attempts, enabling users and administrators to respond swiftly to potential threats (Ntizikira et al., 2023). This additional security layer protects individual accounts and enhances the organization's overall security posture by making it more resilient against social engineering tactics (Ntizikira et al., 2023). Implementing MFA is thus a crucial strategy in defending against phishing and other forms of cyber deception. In transitioning from the significance of protection against phishing and social engineering, it is essential to consider how MFA's flexibility and scalability can meet organizations' diverse and evolving needs.

MFA systems can be integrated into various environments, from cloud services to on-premises applications, making them highly adaptable to diverse organizational needs (Mathur, 2024). This adaptability allows organizations to deploy MFA across various platforms and devices, ensuring comprehensive security coverage. As businesses grow and evolve, MFA systems can scale accordingly, accommodating increasing users and more complex security requirements (Kokila & Reddy, 2024).

Additionally, modern MFA solutions often support seamless integration with existing IT infrastructure, minimizing disruption and reducing the time and cost associated with implementation (Rehan, 2024).

According to Rehan, comprehending the flexibility and scalability of MFA is significant because it ensures that security measures can keep pace with organizational changes and technological advancements. This capability is crucial for maintaining robust security in an increasingly dynamic digital landscape (Rehan, 2024). Organizations can effectively future-proof their security infrastructure by implementing scalable MFA solutions, ensuring long-term protection and compliance with industry standards. This information is vital for decision-makers seeking to implement security solutions that are effective today and capable of adapting to tomorrow's challenges.

Drawbacks of Multifactor Authentication

MFA strengthens security; it can present conflict and tension into the user experience. Users can struggle with offering multiple forms of authentication, predominantly when the offering has to be given regularly. This inconvenience could extend to user exasperation and resistance to MFA. MFA has become an integral component in enhancing cybersecurity measures across various industries. The necessity to safeguard sensitive data and prevent unauthorized access has driven the widespread adoption of MFA despite its inherent challenges (Khan, 2023). This critique examines the significant aspects of MFA, focusing on user convenience and experience, implementation and maintenance costs, the potential for lockout, and security risks in MFA factors. Each section underscores why these critiques are essential for understanding and improving MFA deployment in organizational contexts. Understanding the overall significance of these critiques sets the stage for a detailed examination of specific aspects of MFA. Next is the issue of user convenience and experience, a crucial factor influencing the success of MFA implementation in any organization.

MFA, while bolstering security, can introduce friction into the user experience. Users often need help to provide multiple forms of authentication, particularly when this process is required frequently (Chung et al., 2023). This inconvenience can lead to user frustration and potential resistance to MFA implementation. According to Chung et al. (2023), the frequent need for multiple authentications can detract from the user experience, potentially leading to decreased productivity and increased dissatisfaction. Recognizing and addressing the user convenience and experience usability issues is critical for organizations to ensure user compliance and the overall effectiveness of their MFA systems. Beyond user experience, the economic aspect of MFA implementation is another critical factor organizations must consider.

The financial implications of establishing and maintaining an MFA system are substantial (Wahab et al., 2023). As given by this research team, costs encompass purchasing hardware tokens, licensing software, and dedicating resources for system integration and ongoing maintenance. These expenses can be particularly burdensome for smaller organizations with limited budgets (Wahab et al., 2023). Understanding the cost dynamics is vital for organizations to plan and allocate resources efficiently, ensuring the sustainability of their cybersecurity measures. While the economic aspect of MFA implementation is a significant concern, the operational challenges it introduces also warrant attention. One such challenge is the potential for user lockout, which we will explore in the following section.

One of the critical issues with MFA is the potential for users to be locked out of their accounts if they lose access to one of their authentication factors, such as a phone or a password. This user account lockout necessitates a reliable and efficient recovery mechanism to ensure continuous access. Bhadouri et al. (2024) highlights the significance of developing robust recovery protocols to mitigate the risks associated with MFA lockouts. Ensuring users regain access without compromising security is essential for maintaining trust and usability (Bhadouri et al., 2024). While recovery mechanisms are vital for handling user lockouts, it is equally important to consider the inherent security risks associated with various MFA factors.

Not all MFA factors are equally secure. Methods like SMS-based one-time passwords (OTPs) are susceptible to interception and SIM-swapping attacks, posing significant security risks (Murugalakshmi & Robin, 2023; Stęchły & Szpunar, 2023). This variability in the security of different MFA factors necessitates carefully evaluating the methods to ensure robust protection against potential breaches. Understanding these security vulnerabilities is crucial for organizations to select the most reliable and secure authentication factors. Additionally, organizations must stay informed about emerging threats and continuously update their MFA strategies to mitigate new vulnerabilities (Oxford Analytica, 2023).

In conclusion, while Multi-Factor Authentication significantly enhances security, it presents several challenges that organizations must address (Bumiller et al., 2023). User convenience, implementation costs, lockout potential, and MFA factors' varying security levels are critical considerations for effective MFA deployment. By understanding and addressing these critiques, organizations can better integrate MFA into their security strategies, ensuring robust protection while maintaining user satisfaction and operational efficiency. This comprehensive approach will help optimize the benefits of MFA, making it a more effective tool in the fight against cyber threats. See Figure 2.

Figure 2. Approaches for using authentication

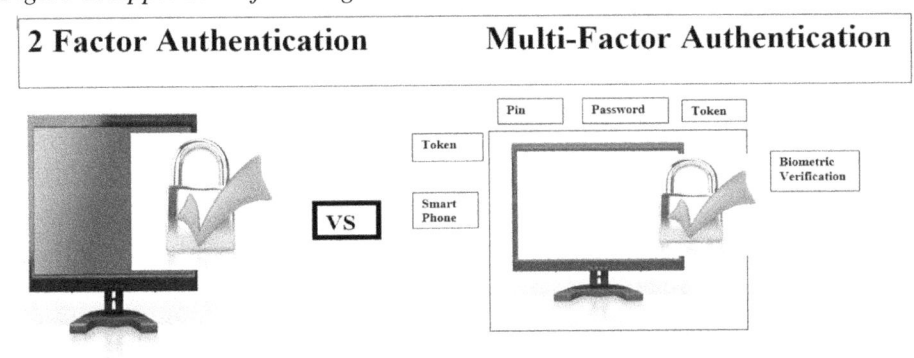

Federal Directives on MFA

Four federal directives are applied for this research. These directives include Executive Order (EO) 13681: Improving the Security of Consumer Financial Transactions, NIST SP 800-63-3: Digital Identity Guidelines, Executive Order 14028: Improving the Nation's Cybersecurity, and OMB Memorandum M-22-09, issued by the Office of Management and Budget. These directives are salient to better comprehend MFA. They collectively establish a framework for enhancing security measures, particularly around identity verification and access controls, critical multi-factor authentication (MFA) components.

Executive Order 13681: Improving the Security of Consumer Financial Transactions

Executive Order (EO) 13681, signed by President Barack H. Obama on October 17, 2014, was established to improve the security of consumer financial transactions (Executive Order 13681, 2014). As given by EO 13681 (204), the U.S. Government's credit, debit, and other payment card programs already include protections against fraud. EO 13681 (2014) provided that the United States Government must further strengthen consumer data security and promote the adoption of enhanced safeguards nationwide, ensuring privacy and confidentiality while supporting an efficient and innovative financial system. In other words, the order aimed to enhance the security of consumer financial data by reducing the risk of unauthorized access through more stringent authentication measures. EO 13681 is significant to this MFA research because it highlights the federal government's commitment to strengthening security in sectors critical to the public, like financial services (EO 13681 (2014). Research on MFA often references EO 13681 as a foundational policy influencing the broader adoption of secure authentication practices.

Critiques of Executive Order 13681

While EO 13681 played a crucial role in emphasizing the need for enhanced security measures like MFA, its implementation faced several challenges. One of the main critiques is that the order's scope was limited to financial transactions, potentially leaving other sectors vulnerable EO 13681, (2014). The directive focused heavily on consumer financial data, which, while significant, represented only a portion of the personal information that needed protection (Federal Register, 2014). According to Zhuo et al. (2024), the order needed more specific guidelines on how organizations should implement MFA, which led to varied adoption practices and potentially inconsistent security outcomes. Another concern is that the order needed to address the user experience aspect of MFA could be a barrier to widespread adoption (Grassi et al., 2017). Users often found MFA cumbersome, and without clear federal support for user-friendly implementations, EO 13681 impact might have been less than anticipated.

NIST SP 800-63-3: Digital Identity Guidelines

The National Institute of Standards and Technology (NIST) Special Publication (SP) 800-63-3, released in June 2017, provides comprehensive guidelines for digital identity management. The publication outlines requirements for different levels of assurance (AALs), with authentication assurance level two (AAL2) recommending and authentication assurance level three (AAL3) requiring MFA for access to systems handling personal information (Temoshok, 2022). Authentication assurance level three, in particular, mandates the use of MFA to resist verifier impersonation attacks, such as phishing, ensuring a higher level of security for digital identities.

NIST SP 800-63-3 is a critical reference in MFA research due to its detailed framework for implementing secure digital identities (Baxter & Martinez, 2020). The guidelines are widely regarded as the standard for digital identity management in both the public and private sectors. They provide a transparent, structured approach to integrating MFA, particularly for high-assurance environments, which is essential for research focused on developing and evaluating MFA solutions.

Critiques of NIST SP 800-63-3

Despite its importance, NIST SP 800-63-3 has been critiqued for its complexity and the challenges associated with its implementation (Baxter & Martinez, 2020). The guidelines, while comprehensive, can be difficult for organizations to fully understand and apply, particularly those with limited technical expertise. The levels of assurance (AALs) are highly detailed, which can overwhelm smaller organizations or those unfamiliar with digital security concepts. Additionally, while necessary, the requirement for phishing-resistant MFA at the highest assurance levels can be challenging to implement in environments with legacy systems that do not easily support such advanced measures (Baxter & Martinez, 2020). Furthermore, the guidelines are sometimes criticized for not providing sufficient flexibility for different organizational contexts, potentially leading to a one-size-fits-all approach that may not be suitable for all scenarios. Next is Executive Order 14028.

Executive Order 14028: Improving the Nation's Cybersecurity

Executive Order 14028 was signed by President Joe Biden on May 12, 2021. It was issued in response to increasing cyber threats and aims to improve the cybersecurity posture of the United States (Carroll, 2024). This order mandates that all U.S. government agencies implement MFA as part of a broader effort to secure federal networks against cyberattacks (Carroll, 2024). The EO emphasizes the need for agencies to adopt cybersecurity best practices, including the use of encryption and secure cloud services, in addition to MFA.

According to Yousefnezhad and Costin (2024), EO 14028 is particularly significant to MFA research as it represents a sweeping federal mandate for the adoption of MFA across all government agencies. This directive underscores the critical role of MFA in national security and serves as a powerful driver for the widespread implementation of robust authentication mechanisms. Researchers studying MFA can draw on the implications of this order to explore its effectiveness in government settings and its potential to influence broader industry practices.

The implementation of EO 14028 has faced criticism due to the challenges associated with the rapid deployment of MFA across diverse government agencies (Bracken, 2023). It is significant to acknowledge that one major concern is the readiness of all federal agencies to comply with the mandate, given the varying levels of cybersecurity maturity across departments (Bracken, 2023). Some agencies, especially those with outdated or complex IT infrastructures, may struggle to integrate MFA effectively, leading to potential gaps in security. Additionally, the order's aggressive timelines for compliance (Young, 2022) have put pressure on agencies to adopt solutions quickly, which may result in hasty implementations that do not fully address all security requirements. Another critique is the potential for increased operational costs and resource strain, particularly in smaller agencies that may not have the necessary budget or personnel to support the transition to MFA (Vo et al., 2023). This could lead to uneven security standards across the federal government, undermining the overall goal of the order. Last is OMB Memorandum M-22-09.

OMB M-22-09: Moving the U.S. Government Toward Zero Trust Cybersecurity Principles

OMB Memorandum M-22-09, issued by the Office of Management and Budget on January 26, 2022, provides directives for U.S. federal agencies to transition toward Zero Trust cybersecurity principles (Ballister, 2022). This memorandum requires that MFA be implemented throughout the federal enterprise, with a specific focus on supporting phishing-resistant MFA (Chandramouli & Chandramouli, 2022). Additionally, the memorandum mandates that public access systems offer phishing-resistant MFA, ensuring that internal and external users are protected against sophisticated cyber threats (Bracken, 2023).

OMB M-22-09 is highly relevant to MFA research as it represents a critical evolution in how the U.S. government approaches cybersecurity (Ballister, 2022). By tying MFA implementation directly to Zero Trust principles, the memorandum highlights the significance of continuous verification and minimal trust in securing government systems (Ballister, 2022). Researchers can use this directive to study the intersection of MFA with Zero Trust architectures, exploring how these concepts can be integrated to create more resilient cybersecurity frameworks.

Critics of OMB M-22-09 often point to the challenges of achieving comprehensive Zero Trust implementation across the federal government. While the memorandum sets ambitious goals, the practicalities of transitioning to a Zero Trust architecture are complex and resource-intensive (Bobbert & Timmermans, 2024). Agencies may face difficulties retrofitting legacy systems to support phishing-resistant MFA, especially in environments where older technologies are still in use. Additionally, the memorandum's broad scope may lead to inconsistent implementation, as agencies with more advanced cybersecurity practices may move quickly toward compliance while others lag (Nivarthi & Gatla, 2022). The requirement for phishing-resistant MFA is seen as challenging, particularly for public access systems where user experience is a critical factor (Chandramouli & Chandramouli, 2022). Ensuring that these systems remain user-friendly while meeting the stringent security requirements of Zero Trust can be difficult, potentially leading to resistance from internal and external users. Furthermore, the cost and effort required to achieve full compliance with the memorandum's directives may strain agency resources, particularly in smaller or less-funded departments (Bumiller et al., 2023; Wahab et al., 2023).

CASE STUDIES

Case studies are invaluable for research as they provide real-world insights into theoretical concepts' practical application and effectiveness (Shamim, 2024). By examining specific instances where Multi-Factor Authentication (MFA) has been implemented, researchers can identify the benefits and challenges associated with its deployment. These detailed examinations offer a nuanced understanding of the context-specific outcomes and can guide future implementations by highlighting best practices and potential pitfalls (Shamim, 2024). Additionally, case studies help bridge the gap between theory and practice, offering empirical evidence that can validate or challenge existing assumptions.

The Federal Trade Commission (FTC) announced a revised regulation to enhance the data security measures that financial institutions must implement to protect their customers' financial information (The Federal Trade Commission, 2021). A case study of a central bank's successful implementation of MFA demonstrated a remarkable reduction in fraudulent activities and unauthorized access incidents. Financial institutions, being early adopters of MFA, have reaped significant benefits due to the sensitive nature of their data. According to the Federal Reserve Board (2021), examples of some early adopters are 1st Source Bank, Bridge Community Bank, Consumers Cooperative Credit Union, and Wells Fargo Bank, N.A.). Widespread data breaches and cyberattacks caused considerable harm to consumers, including financial loss, identity theft, and other economic hardships (The Federal Trade Commission, 2021). The FTC's revised Safeguards Rule mandates that non-banking financial institutions, including car dealerships, mortgage brokers, and payday lenders, establish, implement, and maintain an extensive security program to protect customers' data (The Federal Trade Commission, 2021). These success stories are inspiring and crucial as they showcase the tangible benefits of MFA in a high-risk industry where data breaches can have severe financial and reputational consequences. For example, as given by JPMorgan Chase, Co. (2021), many users at JPMorgan Chase found the additional steps required by MFA to be cumbersome, leading to reluctance in adoption. As a result, the bank had to expand its customer support to assist users with MFA setup and troubleshooting, significantly increasing support calls.

Another example is Bank of America (2021). Bank of America customers showed resistance due to the added complexity and steps in their banking transactions. Consequently, the bank had to increase its customer support efforts to help customers navigate the new MFA requirements, including setting up authentication methods and recovering access. Both examples highlighted user resistance and the need for extensive customer support.

JPMorgan Chase and Bank of America faced significant user resistance due to MFA's added complexity and steps, leading to reluctance to adopt it among their customers. Consequently, both banks had to expand their customer support efforts to assist users with MFA setup and troubleshooting, significantly increasing support calls. Understanding these challenges is crucial for developing strategies to improve user acceptance and streamline support processes in similar high-stakes environments, inspiring audience confidence about MFA's effectiveness. By addressing user concerns and providing adequate support, institutions can enhance the overall user experience and ensure smoother transitions to more secure systems. Additionally, these efforts can lead to higher adoption rates and better protection of sensitive financial information across the industry.

RECOMMENDATIONS, CONCLUSIONS, AND SOLUTIONS

The OMB M-22-09 is required to be implemented into the government by end of Fiscal Year (FY) 2024 in to strengthen the Government's defenses for progressively complex and persistent threat campaigns (Chandramouli & Chandramouli, 2022). Organizations should adopt a comprehensive approach to maximize the benefits of Multi-Factor Authentication (MFA) while mitigating its drawbacks:

1. It is crucial to select the appropriate authentication factors. Combining biometric verification, hardware tokens, and knowledge-based factors can effectively balance security and usability (Di Nocera et al., 2023).
2. The significance of comprehensive user education programs cannot be overstated. These programs empower users by ensuring they understand the importance of MFA and know how to use it correctly. They should be tailored to address specific departmental needs and highlight the role of MFA in protecting sensitive information (Nasir & Mathias, 2024).
3. Regular policy updates and reviews are essential. Organizations must take a proactive stance by continually updating their MFA strategies. This approach ensures they are always prepared to incorporate new technologies and effectively address emerging threats (Anderson & Rainie, 2023).

In conclusion, Multi-Factor Authentication, while a significant security enhancement, also poses challenges that organizations must address. These challenges, including user inconvenience, implementation costs, the risk of user lockout, and the varying security levels of different MFA factors, can be effectively managed through a comprehensive approach to MFA deployment. This approach involves careful selection of authentication factors, regular policy updates, and, most importantly, robust user education. By prioritizing user education, organizations can ensure that their employees understand the importance of MFA and how to use it effectively. This prioritization enhances security and ensures user satisfaction and operational efficiency, making MFA a more effective tool in the fight against cyber threats.

Organizations should implement several critical solutions to address the challenges associated with MFA. First, user-friendly authentication methods should be prioritized to minimize inconvenience and resistance. This includes options like biometric verification, which are secure and easy to use. Second, a robust recovery mechanism must be in place to handle user lockouts efficiently. This can involve backup codes, alternative contact methods, or dedicated helpdesk support to ensure continuous access without compromising security (Amft et al., 2023). Lastly, organizations should adopt a proactive approach to security by continuously monitoring and updating MFA policies. This includes regular audits and incorporating feedback from users to improve the system's effectiveness and user experience. By implementing these solutions, organizations can enhance their MFA systems, ensuring robust security while maintaining high user satisfaction and compliance levels.

Practical Application

The impending deadline of the OMB M-22-09, which is required to be implemented into the government by end of the Fiscal Year (FY) 2024 (Chandramouli & Chandramouli, 2022), emphasizes the urgency of applying best practices. Best practices, commercial or professional, procedures accepted or prescribed as correct or most effective (Tasseron-Dries et al., 2023) are crucial for implementing Multi-Factor Authentication (MFA) effectively. These best practices play a significant role in balancing security and usability, ensuring user compliance, and adapting to evolving cyber threats. By following these guidelines, organizations can reduce the risks of unsanctioned entree and safeguard of sensitive data, thereby maintaining trust and operational efficiency (Chandrika & Jadhav, 2023).

Selecting appropriate authentication factors is crucial for balancing security and usability (Di Nocera et al., 2023). For instance, combining biometric verification with hardware tokens can provide robust security while remaining user-friendly (Mohammed et al., 2023). This approach ensures that users can easily comply with security protocols without experiencing excessive inconvenience (Burton, 2023). The right combination of factors enhances the overall security posture and user acceptance. The right combination of factors strengthens the overall security posture and boosts user acceptance and compliance. This balance is essential for ensuring that security measures are effective and practical, allowing organizations to protect their sensitive information without disrupting daily operations. By carefully selecting and implementing these authentication factors, organizations can realize increased security while sustaining a positive user experience, which is crucial for the effective adoption of MFA across the organization.

Selecting appropriate authentication factors is crucial for balancing security and usability (Di Nocera et al., 2023). For instance, combining biometric verification with hardware tokens can provide robust security while remaining user-friendly (Mohammed et al., 2023). This approach ensures that users can easily comply with security protocols without experiencing excessive inconvenience (Burton, 2023). The right combination of factors strengthens the overall security posture and boosts user acceptance and compliance. This balance is essential for ensuring that security measures are effective and practical, allowing organizations to protect their sensitive information without disrupting daily operations. By carefully selecting and implementing these authentication factors, companies can achieve a higher level of security while maintaining a positive user experience, which is crucial for successfully adopting MFA across the organization. This information is significant to this chapter as it lays the foundation for understanding the critical role of appropriate authentication factors in enhancing security and user experience; a theme central to the successful implementation of Multi-Factor Authentication (MFA) hinges on selecting appropriate authentication factors that balance security and usability (Di Nocera et al., 2023). For instance, combining biometric verification with hardware tokens can provide robust security while remaining user-friendly (Mohammed et al., 2023). This approach ensures that users can easily comply with security protocols without experiencing excessive inconvenience (Burton, 2023). The right combination of factors strengthens the overall security posture and boosts user acceptance and compliance. This balance is essential for ensuring that security measures are effective and practical, allowing organizations to protect their sensitive information without disrupting daily operations. By carefully selecting and implementing these authentication factors, companies can achieve a higher level of security while maintaining a positive user experience, which is crucial for successfully adopting MFA across the organization. This information is significant to this chapter as it lays the foundation for understanding the critical role of appropriate authentication factors in enhancing security and user experience, a theme central to the successful deployment of MFA. Transitioning from the importance of selecting the right authentication factors to user training is pivotal for the successful adoption of MFA (Tambunan et al., 2024).

Educating users about the significance of MFA and providing them with the knowledge to use it effectively minimizes resistance and errors, thereby increasing compliance and reducing security risks (Tambunan et al., 2024). Examples of two significant training programs are phishing simulations, and periodic refresher courses.

Phishing simulations are meaningful tools for organizations to test their staff's comprehension of phishing attacks. Creating mock phishing scenarios could help organizations know how well staff can identify and respond to potential security threats. Phishing simulations support staff to be more aware of identifying phishing emails and fraudulent messages. These actions include emphasizing the significance of MFA as a supplementary layer of protection against phishing attempts. An example is implementing a phishing campaign integrated into MFA education to show how MFA can impede unauthorized access. It is important to add what happens if login credentials are compromised.

In addition to phishing simulations, organizations should center on avowing continuous education through pre-determined and consistent reminder courses. Scheduling such education is indispensable to supporting staff educational updates regarding current security threats and best practices.

All-inclusive education programs can clarify MFA processes and emphasize their necessary role in sheltering sensitive data. Such programs offer real-world directives and contextualize the impact of MFA in the larger scope of organizational security, nurturing an ethos of security awareness within the organization (Nasir & Mathias, 2024). Education programs can augment staff commitment and accountability toward cybersecurity measures by involving regular security practices (Burton, 2022). Also, education programs can be shaped to include explicit needs and risks, safeguarding that all staff comprehend the significance of MFA and the manner in which education is carried out effectively. Transitioning from the significance of user education, guaranteeing that MFA policies are systematically and consistently assessed and renewed to acclimate to growing cyber threats is vital.

Cyber threats are continually evolving, and so should your MFA policies. Regularly reviewing and updating MFA implementation ensures that emerging threats are addressed and new technologies are incorporated (Anderson & Rainie, 2023). This proactive approach helps organizations avoid security vulnerabilities and maintain robust defense mechanisms. Additionally, periodic audits and assessments can identify potential weaknesses and areas for improvement, ensuring that your MFA strategies remain practical and up-to-date. Organizations can better protect their assets and data against sophisticated cyber-attacks by staying ahead of the curve. While keeping MFA policies current is vital for security, it is equally essential to have robust contingency plans for user access issues.

It is essential to ensure that users have reliable recovery options if they lose access to one of their authentication factors (Amft et al., 2023). These options are significant because, without robust recovery mechanisms, users can face extended lockouts that disrupt their access to critical systems. Further, backup codes, alternative contact methods, or helpdesk support can significantly enhance user experience and trust. These measures prevent operational downtime and foster a sense of security and reliability among users, crucial for maintaining productivity and user satisfaction. By ensuring continuous access through effective recovery options, organizations can uphold their operational efficiency and maintain user confidence in their security protocols (Amft et al., 2023).

Impact of Usability on Adoption and Compliance

Organizations should focus on how usability challenges affect user adoption and compliance by discovering the levels of resistance due to the complexity of MFA. For example, industries where staff need fast access to critical systems may undergo increased resistance because of the added steps necessary in MFA. Also, demographics could include staff who are not technology savvy and could labor with MFA implementation. These concerns could decrease compliance rates. This challenge is evident in environments with a wide range of technical proficiency among users.

In summary, implementing MFA effectively involves a multi-dimensional strategy that includes selecting appropriate authentication factors, educating users, updating policies regularly, and ensuring robust recovery mechanisms. By following these best practices, organizations can significantly mitigate the risks associated with unauthorized access and protect their sensitive information in an ever-evolving threat landscape. This comprehensive approach enhances security and ensures user satisfaction and compliance, ultimately contributing to the organization's cybersecurity resilience.

FUTURE RESEARCH DIRECTIONS IN MULTIFACTOR AUTHENTICATION

The rapid evolution of MFA technologies necessitates continuous research to enhance their effectiveness and usability. As the world looks to the future, significant potential exists in refining biometric modalities, such as more precise facial recognition and behavioral biometrics, to strengthen the security layers without compromising user convenience (Awad et al., 2024; Mubeen, 2024). Additionally, integrating artificial intelligence and machine learning can further advance MFA systems by enabling more nuanced user behavior analysis and anomaly detection (Saravanan et al., 2024), essential for preventing fraud and managing security risks effectively (Anderson & Rainie, 2023). Moreover, exploring the application of Zero Trust models in conjunction with MFA offers a promising avenue for ensuring that each access request is continuously validated, thereby enhancing security protocols across various platforms and industries.

Biometric advancements are significant regarding biometric authentication methods, which are becoming more sophisticated and reliable. Future developments may include more accurate facial recognition, voice authentication, and behavioral biometrics (Awad et al., 2024; Mubeen, 2024). Building on the advancements in biometric technologies, integrating artificial intelligence and machine learning represents a natural progression in multifactor authentication, enabling smarter and more adaptive security measures that can respond dynamically to potential threats (Olabanji et al., 2024).

AI and machine learning can enhance MFA by analyzing user behavior and detecting anomalies that could indicate fraudulent activity. These technologies can provide real-time risk assessments to determine when additional authentication steps are necessary (Anderson & Rainie, 2023). AI-driven models detect anomalies and learn from ongoing user interactions, continuously refining the security mechanisms to prevent known and emerging threats (Kokila & Reddy, 2024). Moreover, these intelligent systems can predict risk levels based on the context of access requests, adjusting authentication requirements in real time to balance security with user experience (Mathur, 2024). As AI and machine learning optimize the responsiveness and adaptability of MFA systems, the next logical step involves implementing these advancements within Zero Trust security models, which necessitate unyielding verification processes to maintain stringent security controls throughout user sessions.

Zero Trust security models, which operate on the principle that no entity, internal or external, should be trusted by default and require continuous verification of identity throughout a session, are crucial as they minimize the attack surface by treating all access requests with the same level of scrutiny, regardless of their origin (Daah et al., 2024). Adopting Zero Trust frameworks is a strategic future direction for enhancing MFA because it aligns with the evolving nature of cyber threats where perimeter-based defenses are inadequate (Clark, 2024). By integrating advanced MFA methods within a Zero Trust architecture, organizations can ensure a more granular and dynamic approach to security, adapting protections based on continuous assessment of risk and trust levels. This approach ensures that every access request is authenticated, authorized, and encrypted, thereby addressing sophisticated cyber threats and insider risks and making it a foundational element for future-proofing cybersecurity measures (Khan, 2023; Vashishth et al., 2024).

Multifactor Authentication (MFA) is essential to modern cybersecurity strategies, offering significant security and compliance benefits. However, it also presents user experience, cost, and implementation challenges. By understanding these pros and cons, organizations can make informed decisions about their deployment and management, ensuring they maximize their benefits while mitigating their drawbacks.

As MFA technologies continue to evolve, the integration of advanced biometrics and artificial intelligence plays a critical role in enhancing the accuracy and reliability of authentication methods. These technologies enable proactive and adaptive security measures within the Zero Trust security models, which are crucial in an era where traditional defenses are often inadequate. This comprehensive approach bolsters security and balances stringent security measures with user convenience, future-proofing cybersecurity strategies against increasingly sophisticated threats.

REFERENCES

Aburbeian, A. M., & Fernández-Veiga, M. (2024). Secure Internet Financial Transactions: A Framework Integrating Multi-Factor Authentication and Machine Learning. AI, 5(1), 177–194. https://doi-org.captechu.idm.oclc.org/10.3390/ai5010010

Adahman, Z., Malik, A. W., & Anwar, Z. (2022). An analysis of zero-trust architecture and its cost-effectiveness for organizational security. *Computers & Security*, 122, 102911. DOI: 10.1016/j.cose.2022.102911

Akinsanya, M. O., Ekechi, C. C., & Okeke, C. D.Michael Oladipo AkinsanyaCynthia Chizoba EkechiChukwuekem David Okeke. (2024). Data sovereignty and security in network engineering: A conceptual framework for compliance. *International Journal of Science and Research Archive*, 11(2), 1832–1847. DOI: 10.30574/ijsra.2024.11.2.0682

Amft, S., Höltervennhoff, S., Huaman, N., Krause, A., Simko, L., Acar, Y., & Fahl, S. (2023, November). We've disabled MFA for you: An evaluation of the security and usability of multi-factor authentication recovery deployments. In *Proceedings of the 2023 ACM SIGSAC Conference on Computer and Communications Security* (pp. 3138-3152). DOI:DOI: 10.1145/3576915.3623180

Anderson, J., & Rainie, L. (2023). As AI spreads, experts predict the best and worst changes. Pew Research Center. https://www.pewresearch.org/internet/2023/06/21/themes-the-most-harmful-or-menacing-changes-in-digital-life-that-are-likely-by-2035/

Apraiz, A., Lasa, G., Montagna, F., Blandino, G., Triviño-Tonato, E., & Dacal-Nieto, A. (2023). An experimental protocol for human stress investigation in manufacturing contexts: Its application in the no-stress project. *Systems*, 11(9), 448. DOI: 10.3390/systems11090448

Awad, A.I., Babu, A., Barka, E.S., & Shuaib, K. (2024). AI-powered biometrics for Internet of Things security: A review and future vision. *Journal of Information Security and Applications*. DOI:DOI: 10.1016/j.jisa.2024.103748

Axelsson, K., Melin, U., & Granath, M. (2024). Exploring services in a smart city through socio-technical design principles: Revealing five tensions in a smart living context. *Government Information Quarterly*, 41(1), 101915. DOI: 10.1016/j.giq.2024.101915

Azad, M. A., Abdullah, S., Arshad, J., Lallie, H., & Ahmed, Y. H. (2024). Verify and trust: A multidimensional survey of zero-trust security in the age of IoT. *Internet of Things : Engineering Cyber Physical Human Systems*, 27, 101227. DOI: 10.1016/j.iot.2024.101227

Ballister, C. M. (2022). Protecting financial data under the Zero Trust buzz. Armed Forces Comptroller, 67(2).

Bank of America. (2021, February 1). 70% of Bank of America Clients engaging digitally for more of their financial needs. *Author*. https://newsroom.bankofamerica.com/content/newsroom/press-releases/2021/02/70--of-bank-of-america-clients-engaging-digitally-for-more-of-th.html

Baxter, R. S., & Martinez, C. S., Jr. (2020). *Enhancing Identity And Access Management In The Us Navy Via Migration To More Modern Standards Of Authentication* (Doctoral dissertation, Monterey, CA; Naval Postgraduate School).

Bella, G., Giustolisi, R., & Schürmann, C. (2022). Modelling human threats in security ceremonies. *Journal of Computer Security*, 30(3), 411–433. DOI: 10.3233/JCS-210059

Belmabrouk, K. (2023). Cyber Criminals and Data Privacy Measures. In *Contemporary Challenges for Cyber Security and Data Privacy* (pp. 198–226). IGI Global., DOI: 10.4018/979-8-3693-1528-6.ch011

Berg, C., Philipp, R., & Taff, S. D. (2023, January). Scoping Review of Critical Thinking Literature in Healthcare Education. *Occupational Therapy in Health Care*, 37(1), 18–39. DOI: 10.1080/07380577.2021.1879411 PMID: 33571065

Blunden, C. (2022). Between market failures and justice failures: Trade-offs between efficiency and equality in business ethics. *Journal of Business Ethics*, 178(3), 647–660. DOI: 10.1007/s10551-021-04767-7

Bobbert, Y., & Scheerder, J. (.2020). Zero Trust validation: From practical approaches to theory. *Sci J Research & Rev. 2*(5). SJRR.MS.ID.000546. DOI: .DOI: 10.33552/SJRR.2020.02.000546

Bobbert, Y., & Timmermans, T. (2024). Zero Trust and compliance with industry frameworks and regulations: A Structured Zero Trust Approach to Improve Cybersecurity and Reduce the Compliance Burden. *In Future of Information and Communication Conference (pp. 650-667).* Springer Nature Switzerland.

Bonderud, D. (2022, March 16). Federal agencies can strengthen identify verification methods with MFA. *FedTech Magazine*. https://fedtechmagazine.com/article/2022/03/federal-agencies-can-strengthen-identify-verification-methods-mfa

Bracken, M. (2023, October 6). Stumbling blocks abound in federal push to stronger identity and access management, CISA and NSA panel finds. *Fedscoop*. https://fedscoop.com/cisa-nsa-report-mfa-sso-identity-access-management/

Bumiller, A., Challita, S., Combemale, B., Barais, O., Aillery, N., & Le Lan, G. (2023). On Understanding Context Modelling for Adaptive Authentication Systems. *ACM Transactions on Autonomous and Adaptive Systems*, 18(1), 1–35. DOI: 10.1145/3582696

Burton, S. L. (2022). Cybersecurity leadership from a Telemedicine/Telehealth knowledge and organizational development examination(Order No. 29066056). Available from ProQuest Central; ProQuest Dissertations & Theses Global. (2662752457). https://www.proquest.com/dissertations-theses/cybersecurity-leadership-telemedicine-telehealth/docview/2662752457/se-2

Burton, S. L. (2023). Cybersecurity risk: The business significance of ongoing tracking. In Burrell, D. N. (Ed.), *Transformational Interventions for Business* (1st ed., pp. 245–268). Technology, and Healthcare., DOI: 10.4018/979-8-3693-1634-4.ch015

Campbell, F., Tricco, A. C., Munn, Z., Pollock, D., Saran, A., Sutton, A., White, H., & Khalil, H. (2023, March 15). White H, Khalil H. Mapping reviews, scoping reviews, and evidence and gap maps (EGMs): The same but different- the "Big Picture" review family. *Systematic Reviews*, 12(1), 45. DOI: 10.1186/s13643-023-02178-5 PMID: 36918977

Carroll, J. (2024, June). The US National Cybersecurity Strategy: A Vehicle with an International Journey. *InEuropean Conference on Cyber Warfare and Security, 23*(1), pp. 107-115). DOI: DOI: 10.34190/eccws.23.1.2300

Chandrika, H. N., & Jadhav, P. P. (2023). Strengthening authentication best practices for multi factor authentication deployment. *Journal of Data Acquisition and Processing*, 38(3), 6065. DOI: 10.5281/zenodo.7778218

Chung, Y. Y., Annaswamy, T. M., & Prabhakaran, B. (2023, June). Performance and user experience studies of HILLES: Home-based immersive lower limb exergame system. In *Proceedings of the 14th Conference on ACM Multimedia Systems* (pp. 62-73). DOI: DOI: 10.1145/3587819.3590985

Clark, J. (2024, April 3). DOD cyber officials detail progress on Zero Trust framework roadmap. *U. S. Department of Defense*. https://www.defense.gov/News/News-Stories/Article/Article/3729448/dod-cyber-officials-detail-progress-on-zero-trust-framework-roadmap/

Collier, Z. A., & Sarkis, J. (2021). The zero trust supply chain: Managing supply chain risk in the absence of trust. *International Journal of Production Research*, 59(11), 3430–3445. DOI: 10.1080/00207543.2021.1884311

Daah, C., Qureshi, A., Awan, I., & Konur, S. (2024). Enhancing Zero Trust models in the financial industry through blockchain integration: A proposed framework. *Electronics (Basel)*, 13(5), 865. DOI: 10.3390/electronics13050865

Das, S., Wang, B., Kim, A., & Camp, L. J. (2020, January). MFA is a necessary chore!: Exploring user mental models of multi-factor authentication technologies. *In Proceedings of the 53rd Hawaii International Conference on System Sciences (HICSS),* (pp. 1-10).: https://hdl.handle.net/10125/64411

Dhiman, P., Saini, N., Gulzar, Y., Turaev, S., Kaur, A., Nisa, K. U., & Hamid, Y. (2024). A review and comparative analysis of relevant approaches of zero trust network model. *Sensors (Basel)*, 24(4), 1328. DOI: 10.3390/s24041328 PMID: 38400486

Di Nocera, F., Tempestini, G., & Orsini, M. (2023). Usable Security: A Systematic Literature Review. *Information (Basel)*, 14(12), 641. DOI: 10.3390/info14120641

Din, I. U., & Khan, K. K. H., Almogren, A., Zareei, M., & Pérez Díaz, J. A. (2024). Securing the metaverse: A Blockchain-enabled zero-trust architecture for virtual environments. *In IEEE Access*, 12, pp. 92337-92347. DOI: 10.1109/ACCESS.2024.3423400

Executive Order 1368- Improving the Security of Consumer Financial Transactions1 (2014, October 14). *Author*.

Federal Register. (2014, October 23). Improving the security of consumer financial transactions. *National Archives and Records Administration.*https://www.federalregister.gov/documents/2014/10/23/2014-25439/improving-the-security-of-consumer-financial-transactions

Federal Trade Commission [FTC] (2021). FTC strengthens security safeguards for consumer financial information following widespread data breaches. *Author*. https://www.ftc.gov/news-events/news/press-releases/2021/10/ftc-strengthens-security-safeguards-consumer-financial-information-following-widespread-data

Grassi, P. A., Garcia, M. E., & Fenton, J. L. (2017). *Draft NIST special publication 800-63-3 digital identity guidelines*. National Institute of Standards and Technology.

Haber, M. J., Chappell, B., & Hills, C. (2022). Attack vectors. In *Cloud Attack Vectors: Building Effective Cyber-Defense Strategies to Protect Cloud Resources* (pp. 117–219). Apress., DOI: 10.1007/978-1-4842-8236-6_6

Heever, H. V. D., & Oosthuizen, R. (2024). Application of cognitive work analysis in support of systems engineering of a socio-technical system. *International Journal of Industrial and Systems Engineering*, 46(1), 90–106. DOI: 10.1504/IJISE.2024.135830

Igbinenikaro, E., & Adewusi, A. O. (2024). Navigating the legal complexities of artificial intelligence in global trade agreements. *International Journal of Applied Research in Social Sciences*, 6(4), 488–505. DOI: 10.51594/ijarss.v6i4.987

James, M., Newe, T., O'Shea, D., & O'Mahony, G. D. (2024, June). Authentication and authorization in zero trust IoT: A survey. *In 2024 35th Irish Signals and Systems Conference (ISSC)* (pp. 1-7). IEEE.

JP Morgan & Chase, Co. (2021, December 16). Chase's 2021 digital banking attitudes study finds consumers continue to adopt digital banking tools to manage their finances. *Author*. https://media.chase.com/news/chases-2021-digital-banking-attitudes-study

Khan, M. J.Muhammad Jamshid Khan. (2023). Zero Trust architecture: Redefining network security paradigms in the digital age. *World Journal of Advanced Research and Reviews*, 19(3), 105–116. DOI: 10.30574/wjarr.2023.19.3.1785

Kizza, J. M. (2024). Authentication. In *Guide to Computer Network Security 6thEd* (pp. 215–238). Springer International Publishing. DOI: 10.1007/978-3-031-47549-8_10

Kokila, M., & Reddy, K. S. (2025). Authentication, access control and scalability models in Internet of Things Security–A review. *Cyber Security and Applications*, 3, 100057. DOI: 10.1016/j.csa.2024.100057

Kunduru, A. R. (2023). Industry best practices on implementing oracle cloud ERP security. *International Journal of Computer Trends and Technology*, 71(6), 1–8. DOI: 10.14445/22312803/IJCTT-V71I6P101

Ladha, S. (2024, February 24). Identity report. *Okta*. https://www.okta.com/blog/2024/02/key-findings-from-our-2023-state-of-secure-identity-report/#:~:text=Attackers%20target%20MFA&text=We%20found%20that%2012.7%25%20of,engineering%20and%20SIM%20swap%20attacks

LastPass Sesurity Report. (2019). The 3rd annual global password security report. *Author*. https://www.lastpass.com/-/media/10aa2f653c774e428aa4cc6732734828.pdf

Lyon, G. (2024). Informational inequality: The role of resources and attributes in information security awareness. *Information and Computer Security*, 32(3), 197–217. DOI: 10.1108/ICS-04-2023-0063

Mak, S., & Thomas, A. (2022). Steps for conducting a scoping review. *Journal of Graduate Medical Education*, 14(5), 565–567. DOI: 10.4300/JGME-D-22-00621.1 PMID: 36274762

Mathur, P. (2024). Cloud computing infrastructure, platforms, and software for scientific research. *High Performance Computing in Biomimetics: Modeling, Architecture and Applications*, 89-127. DOI:DOI: 10.1007/978-981-97-1017-1_4

Microsoft Build. (2024, May 21-23). Security at your organization - Multifactor authentication (MFA) statistics. *Author*. https://learn.microsoft.com/en-us/partner-center/security/security-at-your-organization

Microsoft Security. (2019, August 20). One simple action you can take to prevent 99.9 percent of attacks on your accounts. *Author*. https://www.microsoft.com/en-us/security/blog/2019/08/20/one-simple-action-you-can-take-to-prevent-99-9-percent-of-account-attacks/#:~:text=However%2C%20one%20of%20the%20best,percent%20of%20account%20compromise%20attacks

Mohammed, A. H. Y., Dziyauddin, R. A., & Latiff, L. A. (2023). Current multi-factor of authentication: Approaches, requirements, attacks and challenges. *International Journal of Advanced Computer Science and Applications*, 14(1). Advance online publication. DOI: 10.14569/IJACSA.2023.0140119

Moreno-Ortiz, A. (2024). Keywords. In *Making Sense of Large Social Media Corpora: Keywords, Topics, Sentiment, and Hashtags in the Coronavirus Twitter Corpus* (pp. 59-102). Springer Nature Switzerland.

Mostafa, A. M., Rushdy, E., Medhat, R., & Hanafy, A. (2023). An identity management scheme for cloud computing: Review, challenges, and future directions. *Journal of Intelligent & Fuzzy Systems*, 45(12), 1–23. DOI: 10.3233/JIFS-231911

Mubeen, M. (2024). Biometric authentication: Past, present, and future perspectives. *International Journal of Innovative Research in Technology and Science*, 12(2), 351–362.

Murugalakshmi, S., & Robin, C. R. (2023). Advancements in mobile security: A comprehensive study of sim card swapping and cloning-trends, challenges and innovative solutions. *I-Manager's Journal on Mobile Applications & Technologies*, 10(1). Advance online publication. DOI: 10.26634/jmt.10.1.20103

Myers, K. (2023, February). Digital insanity: Exploring the flexibility of NIST digital identity assurance levels. *In International Conference on Cyber Warfare and Security 18*(1), pp. 273-278. DOI: 10.34190/iccws.18.1.1032

Nivarthi, K. S. P., & Gatla, G. (2022). Fighting cybercrime with Zero Trust. [ASR-JETS]. *American Academic Scientific Research Journal for Engineering, Technology, and Sciences*, 90(1), 371–381.

Ntizikira, E., Lei, W., Alblehai, F., Saleem, K., & Lodhi, M. A. (2023). Secure and privacy-preserving intrusion detection and prevention in the internet of unmanned aerial vehicles. *Sensors (Basel)*, 23(19), 8077. DOI: 10.3390/s23198077 PMID: 37836907

Okta. (2023). The secure sign-in trends report. *Author*. https://www.okta.com/sites/default/files/2023-06/Okta_MFA_Report_06_21.pdf

Olabanji, S.O., Olaniyi, O.O., Adigwe, C.S., Okunleye, O.J., & Oladoyinbo, T.O. (2024). AI for Identity and Access Management (IAM) in the Cloud: Exploring the Potential of Artificial Intelligence to Improve User Authentication, Authorization, and Access Control within Cloud-Based Systems. *Asian Journal of Research in Computer Science*. DOI:DOI: 10.9734/ajrcos/2024/v17i3423

Osmëi, T., & Ali, M. (2023, August). Hands-on cyber risk management scepticism. *In 2023 International Conference on Computing, Electronics & Communications Engineering (iCCECE)* (pp. 89-94). IEEE. DOI: 10.1109/iCCECE59400.2023.10238544

Oxford Analytica. (2023). Cyber trends underline need for mature MFA. *Emerald Expert Briefings*, (oxan-db).

Özşahan, H. (2023, November 23). 40+ Multi-factor authentication (MFA) statistics to know in 2024. *Resmo Inc.* https://www.resmo.com/blog/multifactor-authentication-statistics#:~:text=In%20companies%20with%20over%2010%2C000%20employees%2C%2087%25%20use,the%20adoption%20rate%20is%20even%20lower%20at%2027%25

Papaspirou, V., Papathanasaki, M., Maglaras, L., Kantzavelou, I., Douligeris, C., Ferrag, M. A., & Janicke, H. (2023). A novel authentication method that combines honeytokens and Google authenticator. *Information (Basel)*, 14(7), 386. DOI: 10.3390/info14070386

Rakha, N. A. (2023). Ensuring Cyber-security in Remote Workforce: Legal Implications and International Best Practices. *International Journal of Law and Policy*, 1(3). Advance online publication. DOI: 10.59022/ijlp.43

Rivera, J. J. D., Muhammad, A., & Song, W. C. (2024). Securing digital identity in the Zero Trust architecture: A Blockchain approach to privacy-focused multi-factor authentication. *IEEE Open Journal of the Communications Society*, 5, 2792–2814. Advance online publication. DOI: 10.1109/OJCOMS.2024.3391728

Sadat, S. E., Lodin, H., & Ahmadzai, N. (2023). Highly secure and easy to remember password-based authentication approach. *Journal for Research in Applied Sciences and Biotechnology*, 2(1), 134–141. DOI: 10.55544/jrasb.2.1.18

Saravanan, K., Anitha, R., Kamarajapandian, P., Arockiadoss, T. P. R., Kumar, K. S., & Hariharan, R. (2024). Design and Elevating Cloud Security Through a Comprehensive Integration of Zero Trust Framework. *International Journal of Intelligent Systems and Applications in Engineering*, 12(11s), 214–219.

Shamim, M. M. I. (2024). Artificial Intelligence in Project Management: Enhancing Efficiency and Decision-Making. *International Journal of Management Information Systems and Data Science*, 1(1), 1–6. DOI: 10.62304/ijmisds.v1i1.107

Shandilya, S. K., Datta, A., Kartik, Y., & Nagar, A. (2024). Achieving digital resilience with cybersecurity. In *Digital Resilience: Navigating Disruption and Safeguarding Data Privacy* (pp. 43–123). Springer Nature Switzerland. DOI: 10.1007/978-3-031-53290-0_2

Shukla, A. K., & Dubey, A. K. (2024). Deployment issues in industrial resolution. In *Computational Intelligence in the Industry 4.0* (1st ed., pp. 161–188). CRC Press. DOI: 10.1201/9781003479031-10

Stęchły, A., & Szpunar, A. (2023). Analysis of potential risks of SMS-based authentication. *Advances in Web Development Journal*, 1(1). Advance online publication. DOI: 10.5281/zenodo.10049987

Suleski, T., Ahmed, M., Yang, W., & Wang, E. (2023). A review of multi-factor authentication in the Internet of Healthcare Things. *Digital Health*, 9, 20552076231177144. Advance online publication. DOI: 10.1177/20552076231177144 PMID: 37252257

Sun, J., Lenz, D., Yu, H., & Peterka, T. (2024). MFA-DVR: Direct volume rendering of MFA models. *Journal of Visualization / the Visualization Society of Japan*, 27(1), 109–126. DOI: 10.1007/s12650-023-00946-y

Tambunan, P. N. P., Legowo, N., & Tambunan, D. R. (2024). Strengthening payment card data security: A study on compliance enhancement and risk mitigation through MFA implementation under PCI DSS 4.0. *Journal of Theoretical and Applied Information Technology*, 102(9).

Tasseron-Dries, P. E., Smaling, H. J., Nakanishi, M., Achterberg, W. P., & van der Steen, J. T. (2023). What are best practices for involving family caregivers in interventions aimed at responsive behaviour stemming from unmet needs of people with dementia in nursing homes: A scoping review. *BMJ Open*, 13(12), e071804. DOI: 10.1136/bmjopen-2023-071804 PMID: 38149428

Teh, Y. F., & Ramli, S. N. (2023). Implementation of multi-factor authentication on A vaccination record system. *Applied Information Technology and Computer Science, 4*(1), 019-039. https://publisher.uthm.edu.my/periodicals/index.php/aitcs/article/view/7327

Temoshok, D. (2022, February, 15). NIST Update: Multi-factor authentication and SP 800-63 digital identity guidelines. *NIST; United stated Department of Commerce*. https://csrc.nist.gov/csrc/media/Presentations/2022/multi-factor-authentication-and-sp-800-63-digital/images-media/Federal_Cybersecurity_and_Privacy_Forum_15Feb2022_NIST_Update_Multi-Factor_Authentication_and_SP800-63_Digital_Identity_%20Guidelines.pdf

Vashishth, T. K., Sharma, V., Sharma, K. K., Kumar, B., Chaudhary, S., & Panwar, R. (2024). Security and privacy considerations in cloud-based data processing solutions for sensitive data. In *Developments Towards Next Generation Intelligent Systems for Sustainable Development* (pp. 35–61). IGI Global., DOI: 10.4018/979-8-3693-5643-2.ch002

Vo, T., Ballinger, C., Shain, K., Schweikert, N., O'Hara, A., Ali, A., Young, C., Dudash, A., O'Hara, J., & Wunderlich, K. (2023). Operational concepts for distributed ledger in ITS use cases: Blockchain research and deployment technical services support (No. FHWA-JPO-23-119). *United States. Department of Transportation. Intelligent Transportation Systems Joint Program Office.*

Young, S. D. (2022, January 26). Memorandum for the heads of executive departments and agencies. *Executive Office of the President Office Of Management And Bud Get.* https://www.whitehouse.gov/wp-content/uploads/2022/01/M-22-09.pdf

Yousefnezhad, N., & Costin, A. (2024, June). Understanding SBOMs in real-world systems–A Practical DevOps/SecOps Perspective. *In International Symposium on Business Modeling and Software Design (pp. 293-304).* Springer Nature Switzerland. DOI: 10.1007/978-3-031-64073-5_20

Zhang, J., & Tenney, D. (2023). The evolution of integrated advance persistent threat and its defense solutions: A literature review. *Open Journal of Business and Management, 12*(1), 293–338. DOI: 10.4236/ojbm.2024.121021

Zhuo, Y., Solak, S., Zou, Y., & Hu, B. (2024). Sharing is caring: Designing incentive rebate strategies for information-sharing alliances. *Decision Sciences*, deci.12640. Advance online publication. DOI: 10.1111/deci.12640

KEY TERMS AND DEFINITIONS

Authentication Factors: The methods used to verify a user's identity in MFA.
Knowledge Factor: Something the user knows, such as a password or PIN.
Possession Factor: Something the user has, like a mobile phone or hardware token.
Inherence Factor: Something the user is, such as a fingerprint or facial recognition.
Biometric Verification: An authentication method that uses unique biological traits, such as fingerprints, facial recognition, or iris scans, to verify a user's identity.
Compliance: Adherence to regulatory frameworks and standards that mandate specific security measures to protect sensitive information, such as GDPR, HIPAA, and PCI-DSS.
Cybersecurity: The practice of protecting systems, networks, and programs from digital attacks, which aim to access, change, or destroy sensitive information, extort money from users, or interrupt normal business processes.
Multi-Factor Authentication (MFA): A security process that requires users to verify their identity using multiple forms of verification from different categories of credentials, significantly enhancing overall security.
Regulatory Frameworks: Sets of guidelines and standards that govern how organizations must handle and protect sensitive information, ensuring compliance with laws and regulations.
Recovery Mechanisms: Procedures and methods put in place to help users regain access to their accounts if they lose access to one of their authentication factors. This may include backup codes, alternative contact methods, or helpdesk support.
User Experience (UX): The overall experience of a person using a product or service, especially in terms of how easy or pleasing it is to use.

Chapter 9
Integrating Organizational and Social Network Theories to Mitigate Racial Bias in Facial Recognition Technology

Lord Dordunoo
https://orcid.org/0009-0007-7395-2677
Marymount University, USA

ABSTRACT

Facial recognition technology (FRT), though a powerful tool for identification and surveillance, consistently demonstrates racial bias, disproportionately misidentifying individuals of color. This chapter integrates organizational and social network theories to address these biases. Drawing on theories such as Equity Theory, General Adaptation Syndrome, Minority Stress Model, and Terror Management Theory, it explores the psychological, social, and ethical effects on marginalized communities. Procedural Justice Theory, Stakeholder Theory, and Technological Determinism highlight how organizational practices contribute to bias, while Ethics of Care and Distributive Justice emphasize the responsibility to design fair systems. The chapter calls for comprehensive reforms in FRT development, focusing on fairness, equity, and the well-being of all stakeholders.

DOI: 10.4018/979-8-3693-8562-3.ch009

INTRODUCTION

As facial recognition technology (FRT) becomes increasingly integrated into law enforcement, commercial, and governmental sectors, its accuracy, and fairness concerns have surged. FRT systems have been consistently shown to misidentify individuals of color at a disproportionately higher rate compared to white individuals, leading to serious consequences such as wrongful arrests, heightened surveillance, and increasing public distrust in technological systems (Buolamwini & Gebru, 2018). These errors are not simply technical glitches; they reflect underlying systemic issues within the design and implementation of technology, where racial bias is often unconsciously embedded into algorithms and processes (Benjamin, 2019). Understanding and addressing these issues requires a multifaceted approach, incorporating organizational, social network, and ethical theories to illuminate and mitigate racial bias in FRT.

This chapter will explore the implications of racial bias in FRT through the lenses of organizational and social network theories. Equity Theory and Distributive Justice are particularly valuable in analyzing the inherent inequities marginalized groups experience when subjected to biased FRT systems. Equity Theory suggests that individuals expect fairness in social exchanges, and when FRT disproportionately misidentifies people of color, it violates this expectation of fair treatment (Adams, 1965). Similarly, Rawls' (1971) theory of Distributive Justice underscores the ethical responsibility to protect the most vulnerable members of society by ensuring that technological systems do not unfairly burden marginalized populations. Both theories advocate for developing FRT systems emphasizing fairness and equitable outcomes for all users, particularly those from historically disadvantaged communities.

Psychological models like General Adaptation Syndrome (GAS) and the Minority Stress Model provide insights into the mental and emotional toll biased FRT imposes on marginalized individuals. GAS, as Selye (1956) outlined, explains the stress response in three stages: alarm, resistance, and exhaustion. Individuals from marginalized communities who face a constant threat of misidentification may endure prolonged stress, which could lead to burnout and mental health disorders. Additionally, the Minority Stress Model suggests that racial discrimination such as the systemic misidentification inherent in FRT exacerbates stress and contributes to chronic mental health issues (Meyer, 2003). These models illustrate how biased technology compounds the psychological distress already experienced by people of color in environments of heightened surveillance and systemic inequality.

The Terror Management Theory (TMT) and Procedural Justice Theory offer frameworks for understanding how the fear of misidentification through FRT exacerbates distrust in social institutions. TMT posits that the fear of death influences human behavior, and for marginalized communities, the existential threat posed by wrongful detention or arrest from biased FRT intensifies their anxiety (Moody, 2023). Procedural Justice Theory, meanwhile, focuses on the fairness of decision-making processes. When FRT systems are used disproportionately against marginalized groups, it erodes public trust in law enforcement and governmental institutions, leading to more significant social division (Tyler, 1990). These theories highlight how biased FRT exacerbates the already tenuous relationship between marginalized communities and institutions, further intensifying societal mistrust.

Organizational theories like stakeholder theory and technological determination offer guidance on the ethical responsibilities of organizations developing FRT. Stakeholder Theory emphasizes the need for inclusivity in technological decision-making, arguing that all affected parties, especially marginalized communities should have a voice in the development and deployment of FRT systems (Freeman, 1984). Moreover, Technological determinism suggests that technology shapes societal values and behaviors, and without intentional effort, it can reinforce existing social inequalities (Winner, 1980). Therefore, organizations must be conscious of their technologies' social implications and prioritize equity and fairness in their development processes.

Ethical theories such as the Ethics of Care and Distributive Justice further reinforce the moral responsibility of developers and policymakers to create just and equitable systems. The Ethics of Care, as introduced by Gilligan (1982), focuses on the moral obligation to care for and prioritize the needs of vulnerable populations. In the context of FRT, this ethical framework emphasizes developers' duty to ensure that their systems do not disproportionately harm marginalized communities. Similarly, Distributive Justice advocates for the fair distribution of risks and benefits, emphasizing that FRT should be designed and implemented to avoid further disadvantaging already vulnerable populations (Rawls, 1971). Both theories underscore the necessity of designing technological systems that are efficient, ethically sound, and socially responsible.

Problem Statement

The proliferation of facial recognition technology (FRT) in law enforcement has amplified concerns about racial bias, particularly in minority communities that have historically mistrusted police institutions. Studies have demonstrated that FRT systems are more likely to misidentify people of color, leading to wrongful arrests, increased surveillance, and broader social injustices (Buolamwini & Gebru, 2018). These issues intersect with long-standing mistrust between law enforcement and marginalized communities, predominantly Black and Latino populations, who have endured a legacy of racial profiling, over-policing, and systemic discrimination. The historical context of racial injustice, combined with the biases embedded in FRT, raises critical ethical and legal questions about the role of technology in perpetuating inequality (McGee, 2021). Recent legal actions, such as the lawsuit against Facebook by Texas for billions of dollars due to unlawful biometric data collection highlight the urgency of addressing these biases (Mangan, 2024). This study seeks to explore how these issues converge and propose solutions grounded in organizational theory, social network theory, and ethical frameworks to mitigate the negative impacts of biased FRT on minority communities.

Significance of the Study

This study is significant because it addresses the growing ethical, social, and legal implications of deploying biased facial recognition systems within law enforcement, especially in communities of color. By examining the historical roots of racial mistrust, the study highlights how modern technologies continue to reflect and reinforce these systemic inequities. Recent lawsuits, like the one against Facebook, underscore the financial, social, and legal consequences of failing to address these issues (Mangan, 2024). For instance, Texas sued Facebook for billions due to violating state laws around biometric privacy, illustrating the high stakes of unchecked technological misuse (Mangan, 2024). Furthermore, the research fills a gap by linking organizational and social network theories to the problem, showing how internal structures within law enforcement and the tech industry can perpetuate or mitigate racial bias. Understanding these dynamics is crucial not only for ensuring more equitable policing practices but also for developing a framework that fosters trust between law enforcement and historically marginalized communities. Grounding the study in these interdisciplinary theories aims to contribute meaningful policy reforms prioritizing equity and social justice in technological applications.

Discussion

The historical mistrust between minority communities and law enforcement cannot be divorced from the contemporary issues of bias in facial recognition technology. Historical practices like racial profiling and over-policing have shaped minority communities' perceptions of law enforcement, and the adoption of FRT only deepens these wounds (Alexander, 2010). Facial recognition technology, as an extension of these discriminatory practices, continues the legacy of unequal treatment within the justice system. When misidentifications occur disproportionately in communities of color, they reinforce the historical patterns of mistrust and alienation. Moreover, the socio-economic and legal consequences of biased FRT are severe wrongful arrests, increased surveillance, and a diminished sense of safety are expected outcomes for marginalized individuals (Buolamwini & Gebru, 2018).

Organizational structures and social networks within both the tech industry and law enforcement agencies play a critical role in the perpetuation of biased systems. Organizational theories like Stakeholder Theory and Technological Determinism show that without intentional efforts to include marginalized voices, these technologies will continue to reinforce systemic inequalities (Freeman, 1984). Additionally, social networks within the tech sector often exclude diverse perspectives that could help mitigate biases. The lack of minority representation in decision-making processes contributes to the design and deployment of systems that disproportionately harm marginalized communities.

The recent lawsuit against Facebook underscores the importance of accountability in the tech industry. Texas' lawsuit represents a watershed moment in holding companies responsible for the misuse of biometric data, including the violation of privacy rights and the perpetuation of racial bias (McGee, 2021). The case illustrates how unchecked technological applications can have severe financial and social consequences. This legal precedent is critical in framing the discussion around FRT, as it demonstrates the need for more robust regulatory frameworks to ensure that technological systems do not perpetuate harm.

Furthermore, this study emphasizes the role of ethical frameworks, particularly the Ethics of Care and Distributive Justice, in guiding the responsible development and deployment of facial recognition technology. The Ethics of Care argues for a moral responsibility to prioritize the well-being of those most harmed by these systems, suggesting that developers and policymakers must center the needs of marginalized groups in their decision-making (Gilligan, 1982). As articulated by Rawls (1971), Distributive Justice underscores the ethical obligation to ensure that technological systems do not further disadvantage vulnerable populations. The study argues that by adopting these ethical principles, law enforcement agencies and tech companies can work toward creating more equitable and just technologies.

By integrating organizational theory, social network theory, and ethical considerations, this study provides a comprehensive framework for understanding the racial biases embedded in facial recognition technology. The findings highlight the urgent need for policy reforms and the inclusion of marginalized voices in developing these systems. The implications of this study extend beyond law enforcement, offering insights into how technological advancements must be designed and implemented with equity and social justice at their core.

Historical Context and Evolution

Facial recognition technology (FRT) has evolved significantly, paralleling broader advancements in computer vision, artificial intelligence (AI), and data analytics (Minh-Ha, 2024). Initially confined to academic research, FRT has become a widespread tool with substantial implications for privacy, security, and social justice (Buolamwini & Gebru, 2018). The progression from basic pattern recognition models to advanced AI-driven systems underscores the technology's transformative impact on various sectors (Turk & Pentland, 1991). This evolution highlights the importance of adopting a balanced approach to FRT deployment, considering its potential benefits and ethical challenges (Garvie et al., 2016; O'Neil, 2016).

In the 1960s, the origins of FRT were marked by pioneering work in pattern recognition algorithms, which laid the foundational groundwork for modern systems. Early efforts utilized basic geometric models to analyze and identify facial features, but these systems were limited by the time's computational power and digital imaging technology (Umbaugh, 2010). The 1970s and 1980s saw significant advancements with the development of eigenfaces, a technique based on principal component analysis. This method leveraged emerging computer vision technologies to enhance the accuracy of facial recognition, although it was still primarily used in controlled environments (Turk & Pentland, 1991).

The transition from early FRT systems to more advanced algorithms illustrate the progression from experimental research to practical applications. The introduction of eigenfaces and other sophisticated algorithms in the 1970s and 1980s improved the accuracy and reliability of facial recognition, setting the stage for broader adoption. As hardware and software evolved, FRT expanded beyond academic and government applications into security and law enforcement during the 1990s. The September 11, 2001, terrorist attacks significantly accelerated this trend, leading to widespread FRT deployment for public safety and national security (Lyon, 2003). This period demonstrated the potential and limitations of FRT as it transitioned from research to a critical tool in various sectors.

The 2010s marked a transformative era for FRT with the advent of deep learning techniques, particularly convolutional neural networks (CNNs). These advancements revolutionized FRT by enabling more sophisticated analysis of facial features and improving accuracy in diverse environments (Minh-Ha, 2024). Real-time operation and enhanced handling of variations in lighting and angles became possible. However, these improvements also highlighted significant disparities in recognition accuracy across demographic groups, with studies revealing higher error rates for individuals with darker skin tones and women (Buolamwini & Gebru, 2018). These highlighted new challenges related to fairness and ethical implications, necessitating ongoing scrutiny and refinement.

As FRT became more mainstream, it faced increasing scrutiny over its ethical implications. Key concerns include disproportionate surveillance of marginalized communities, leading to privacy violations and potential abuses of power (Garvie et al., 2016). Research has shown that many FRT systems exhibit higher error rates for racial and ethnic minority groups, raising questions about fairness and accuracy (Sweeney, 2013). The rapid deployment of FRT has outpaced regulatory frameworks, resulting in inconsistent standards and ongoing debates about the need for comprehensive regulations (O'Neil, 2016). Additionally, using FRT, especially in law enforcement, has eroded public trust in the technology and the institutions that deploy it (Ferguson, 2021). These ethical challenges require a multifaceted approach, including the development of more equitable algorithms, robust regulatory frameworks, and greater transparency to ensure the technology respects privacy and promotes fairness.

THEORETICAL BACKGROUND

Organizational Theory and Social Network Theory: Evolution and Application

Organizational Theory and Social Network Theory offer crucial perspectives for understanding the dynamics of racial bias in facial recognition technology (FRT) and how systemic biases can be managed or perpetuated within organizations. The evolution of these theories and their application to biases in AI technologies provide valuable insights into how organizations can address and mitigate these challenges.

Evolution of Organizational Theory

Organizational Theory has evolved significantly, reflecting shifts in our understanding of organizational structures, processes, and interactions. Key theories in this evolution include:

- Classical Theories

Early organizational theories, notably Max Weber's Bureaucracy Model, focused on structured, hierarchical systems to enhance efficiency and predictability (Weber, 1978). Weber's model emphasized formal rules, standardized procedures, and clear lines of authority to minimize personal biases in decision-making. While this approach aimed to create a stable and predictable organizational environment, it often needed to address the complexities and informal dynamics within organizations (Burrell

& Morgan, 1979). The rigidity of bureaucracy can inhibit adaptive responses to emerging challenges, such as biases in AI systems, as it may not accommodate the need for flexibility and responsiveness in rapidly evolving technological contexts (Kuhn, 1962).

- Contingency Theory

Developed by scholars such as Fred Fiedler and Paul Lawrence, Contingency Theory posits that organizational effectiveness is contingent on aligning an organization's structure and external environment (Lawrence & Lorsch, 1967). This theory suggests that different environments necessitate different organizational forms and processes. In the realm of AI, including FRT, Contingency Theory highlights the need for organizations to adapt their structures and practices to manage the complexities and biases introduced by new technologies (Donaldson, 2001). The theory underscores the importance of flexibility and adaptability in addressing the challenges posed by evolving technological landscapes and ensuring effective management of biases.

- Institutional Theory

Institutional Theory examines how organizations are influenced by the social and cultural contexts in which they operate (DiMaggio & Powell, 1983). This theory helps to understand how external institutions' norms, values, and pressures shape organizational practices, including those related to technology deployment. For instance, adopting biased FRT may be influenced by prevailing industry norms or regulatory environments, which can perpetuate existing biases if not critically examined and addressed (Scott, 2014). Institutional Theory emphasizes the role of external pressures and expectations in shaping organizational behavior and highlights the need for organizations to critically engage with these influences to mitigate bias.

- Socio-Technical Systems Theory

Developed by Eric Trist and colleagues, Socio Technical Systems Theory focuses on the interaction between social systems and technical systems within organizations (Trist, 1981). This theory emphasizes the importance of designing work systems that integrate social and technical aspects to optimize performance and address bias. In the context of FRT, Socio-Technical Systems Theory underscores the necessity of aligning technological solutions with the social dynamics of their implementation to ensure that advancements do not exacerbate existing biases (Bostrom & Yudkowsky,

2014). This approach advocates for a holistic view considering technical capabilities and social factors when deploying AI technologies.

- Social Network Theory

With significant contributions from scholars such as Mark Granovetter and Ronald Burt, Social Network Theory provides valuable insights into how relationships and network structures influence outcomes, including managing and propagating biases in facial recognition technology (FRT). Granovetter's concept of the "strength of weak ties" and Burt's theories on structural holes and network brokerage are particularly relevant for understanding these dynamics. The role of relationships and network structures shape outcomes in the following:

- Granovetter's Strength of Weak Ties

Mark Granovetter's seminal work on the "strength of weak ties" posits that weak social ties relationships that are not particularly strong or frequent play a crucial role in facilitating the flow of information across different social networks (Granovetter, 1973). In the context of FRT, weak ties can act as bridges between diverse social groups, enabling the dissemination of information and innovative ideas. This is particularly pertinent when considering how information about FRT's usage and associated biases spreads through various networks. Understanding the role of weak ties can reveal how biases are propagated and addressed within these networks. Moreover, incorporating perspectives from weak ties can help identify and correct biases by introducing diverse viewpoints into the decision-making processes related to technology deployment (Granovetter, 1973).

- Burt's Structural Holes

Ronald Burt's Theory of structural holes emphasizes the strategic advantage held by individuals or organizations that bridge gaps between disconnected social groups or networks (Burt, 1992). Those who occupy these "holes" can access diverse information and resources otherwise unavailable to more centrally positioned network members. This perspective is crucial for analyzing how biases in FRT might be introduced or mitigated. For instance, understanding who controls data and decision-making processes in FRT systems can highlight potential biases. By bridging structural holes, organizations can integrate diverse viewpoints and enhance the fairness of technology deployment. This approach ensures that a broader range informs decisions of perspectives, which can be essential in reducing biases (Burt, 1992).

- Burt's Network Brokerage

In his later work, Ronald Burt also explored network brokerage, focusing on how individuals or organizations acting as intermediaries between disconnected segments of a network can influence outcomes (Burt, 2000). In FRT, network brokers can be critical in shaping how biases are addressed or perpetuated. These brokers can help integrate diverse perspectives into developing and deploying AI systems by facilitating connections between disparate network segments. Effective network brokerage can thus promote more equitable technology solutions by ensuring that different viewpoints and concerns are considered in decision-making processes (Burt, 2000).

Integrating Organizational Theory and Social Network Theory

Integrating Organizational Theory and Social Network Theory offers a multidimensional approach to understanding and addressing biases in artificial intelligence (AI) systems, including facial recognition technology (FRT). This integration is crucial for developing a comprehensive strategy to manage and mitigate biases effectively. The theories offer multidimensional approach to understanding and addressing biases in AI systems in the following:

- Complex Interplay

Organizational Theory provides valuable insights into how formal structures and processes within organizations influence the development and deployment of technologies, including those prone to biases. Classical frameworks like Max Weber's Bureaucracy Model emphasize the importance of structured hierarchies, standardized procedures, and clear roles in creating organizational efficiency and predictability (Weber, 1978). However, these formal structures can also inadvertently reinforce existing biases if they fail to incorporate mechanisms for fairness and equity (Weber, 1978). For example, rigid decision-making processes and entrenched hierarchies might perpetuate biased technology practices if they do not actively challenge and correct such biases.

Complementing this perspective, Social Network Theory sheds light on the informal relationships and communication flows that impact how technologies, including FRT, are adopted and disseminated. Mark Granovetter's concept of the "strength of weak ties" illustrates how weak connections between different social groups facilitate the flow of information and innovations across diverse networks (Granovetter, 1973). This understanding highlights how biases in technology can spread through various informal channels and influence adoption practices. Similarly, Ronald Burt's theory of structural holes reveals how individuals or organizations that bridge gaps between different network segments can control the flow of information and resources, potentially amplifying or mitigating biases based on their actions (Burt, 1992). Together, these theories underscore the need for a holistic approach that considers both formal organizational structures and informal network dynamics in managing biases.

- Bias Management

Integrating Organizational Theory and Social Network Theory provides a robust framework for understanding how biases are perpetuated within organizational hierarchies and networks. Organizational Theory emphasizes the importance of structural adjustments to address biases effectively. This includes revising decision-making processes, incorporating fairness into organizational procedures, and ensuring that technology deployment practices are equitable (Lawrence & Lorsch, 1967; DiMaggio & Powell, 1983). For instance, organizational reforms might involve creating more inclusive decision-making bodies or revising policies to address bias in technology deployment. Social Network Theory complements these structural adjustments by highlighting the need for network interventions that enhance the diversity of information sources and decision-makers. Effective network interventions can involve fostering connections between diverse groups, facilitating cross-network collaborations, and ensuring that various perspectives are integrated into the decision-making process (Granovetter, 1973; Burt, 2000). By bridging structural holes and promoting a more inclusive exchange of information, organizations can better identify and address biases in AI systems.

- Ethical and Practical Considerations

Integrating these theories provides a comprehensive framework for addressing biases in AI systems. It suggests that tackling racial bias in FRT requires not only changes in organizational structures and processes but also a careful examination of how information and decision-making are distributed across social networks. Organizations need to adopt practices that promote fairness and inclusivity within both their formal structures and informal networks. This approach encourages organizations to consider the ethical implications of technology deployment, actively seek diverse viewpoints, and implement practices that mitigate bias and promote equity (Burt, 1992; Granovetter, 1973).

- Empirical Evidence

Empirical studies underscore the practical implications of these theories. Buolamwini and Gebru's (2018) analysis of biased facial recognition algorithms illustrates how training datasets can introduce racial biases into A.I. systems, leading to disproportionate misidentification of people of color. This study highlights the importance of examining the technological and organizational contexts in which these biases occur. Social network analysis can further reveal how biases are perpetuated through inter-organizational collaborations and shared databases. For example, if multiple organizations use and share biased data, these biases can become entrenched across various technological systems and practices. Understanding these network dynamics helps identify where interventions can be made to address and mitigate biases.

- Integrating Theories for Holistic Understanding

Integrating Organizational Theory and Social Network Theory offers a robust framework for understanding and addressing racial bias in technology. This integration provides a multifaceted approach to identifying and mitigating biases within technological systems. By combining insights from these theories, we can:

- **Identify Structural and Network-Based Sources of Bias:** Organizational Theory helps identify how hierarchical structures, decision-making processes, and internal policies contribute to bias. For instance, bureaucratic structures that do not incorporate diverse perspectives can perpetuate biases by reinforcing existing norms and practices (Weber, 1978). Social Network Theory illuminates how biases are disseminated through networks of organizations and individuals. By analyzing how information and decisions flow through these networks, we can pinpoint where biases are introduced and entrenched (Burt, 1992).
- **Develop Targeted Interventions:** Insights from Organizational Theory suggest revising organizational processes such as decision-making procedures, auditing practices, and data management can help address biases. Implementing fairness audits and bias mitigation strategies are essential steps in this process (DiMaggio & Powell, 1983).
- **Promote Equity and Fairness:** To foster equity, organizations must realign their structures and networks to prioritize fairness and inclusivity. This involves changing internal policies and re-evaluating how organizations interact within broader networks. Ensuring that technological systems, such as facial recognition technologies, are developed and deployed with these principles in mind is crucial for mitigating biases and promoting social equity (Schwartz et al., 2022).

Equity Theory and Procedural Justice: Ethical Implications of Facial Recognition Technology

Equity Theory and Procedural Justice Theory are fundamental for evaluating the ethical dimensions of FRT, particularly concerning its disproportionate impact on marginalized communities. These theories offer frameworks for understanding how biases within FRT lead to perceived injustices and erode trust in institutional processes. Analyzing these theories in the FRT context reveals technology's broader implications for fairness and social equity.

Equity Theory

Equity Theory, proposed by John Stacey Adams (1965), revolves around fairness in the distribution of resources and rewards based on comparing input-output ratios. According to Adams, individuals evaluate fairness by comparing their inputs (such as effort, time, and cooperation) to the outcomes (rewards, recognition, and treatment) they receive relative to others. When individuals perceive an inequitable distribution where their outcomes do not match their inputs compared to others, they experience feelings of injustice and dissatisfaction, which can lead to disengagement and mistrust.

Application to Facial Recognition Technology

In the context of FRT, equity theory helps explain how technological biases exacerbate existing inequalities, especially regarding people of color. If FRT systems disproportionately misidentify individuals from marginalized groups compared to those from dominant racial or ethnic groups, these individuals are subjected to unjust outcomes. Their input, which may include compliance with legal norms, participation in public services, or general cooperation, does not lead to equitable outcomes when they are misidentified or unfairly targeted. For instance, empirical studies have shown that individuals with darker skin tones are more likely to be misidentified by FRT systems (Buolamwini & Gebru, 2018), resulting in disproportionately negative consequences for these groups. This misidentification represents a skewed input-output ratio, where marginalized groups face adverse outcomes such as wrongful arrests or surveillance despite their compliance with societal rules. In contrast, others receive more accurate and beneficial outcomes.

Impact on Marginalized Communities

The application of Equity Theory to FRT highlights two major ethical concerns regarding its impact on marginalized communities:

- **Exacerbation of Disparities:** FRT's failure to deliver accurate and equitable outcomes for people of color exacerbate existing social and systemic disparities. By embedding racial biases in technological systems, FRT reflects and reinforces inequities that already exist in social structures, creating a feedback loop of injustice. The systemic misidentification of marginalized groups results in outcomes that disproportionately affect their safety, privacy, and freedom. Adams (1965) notes that when individuals perceive persistent inequities, it increases feelings of alienation and discontent. This is particularly evident in FRT, where individuals from marginalized groups are more likely to be unfairly scrutinized, surveilled, or penalized, further entrenching societal inequalities (Buolamwini & Gebru, 2018; Eubanks, 2018).
- **Erosion of Trust:** The biases embedded in FRT lead to a broader erosion of trust, particularly in law enforcement and institutional contexts. When FRT disproportionately misidentifies minority individuals, it not only violates principles of equity but also perpetuates the belief that technology, instead of serving as an unbiased tool, exacerbates existing social and racial biases. According to Rawls (1971), fairness in societal institutions is essential for maintaining trust, especially among marginalized groups. When individuals perceive that FRT unfairly targets them, they are less likely to trust the technology and the institutions that employ it, leading to a breakdown of trust between communities and the justice system. This is further compounded by the fact that marginalized individuals may already have a fraught relationship with law enforcement due to historical and systemic injustices (Noble, 2018).

Procedural Justice Theory

Procedural Justice Theory emphasizes the importance of fairness in the processes that lead to outcomes rather than focusing solely on the outcomes themselves (Tyler & Lind, 1992). This theory posits that individuals are more likely to accept decisions and cooperate with institutions when they perceive the processes involved in making those decisions as transparent, fair, and unbiased.

Application to Facial Recognition Technology

In the context of FRT, Procedural Justice Theory highlights the ethical importance of fairness in designing, implementing, and deploying these systems. When FRT is employed in law enforcement or public services, the procedures that govern its use such as data collection, algorithm development, and decision-making must be transparent and equitable. If marginalized groups perceive these procedures as biased or opaque, it diminishes their trust in the technology and the institutions that use it. For example, suppose individuals from racial or ethnic minorities are more frequently subject to FRT surveillance or misidentification. In that case, they may view the procedures underlying the technology as unfair, leading to a loss of trust in law enforcement and other public institutions. Tyler and Lind (1992) argue that perceptions of procedural fairness are critical for maintaining legitimacy and fostering cooperation with authority figures and institutions.

Impact on Institutional Trust and Legitimacy

Procedural Justice Theory provides a framework for understanding how biased FRT erodes institutional trust and legitimacy, particularly within marginalized communities:

- **Perceived Unfairness in Decision-Making Processes:** When individuals believe that the processes underlying FRT deployment are biased or unjust, and they are less likely to trust the outcomes, even if they are personally unaffected. The perceived lack of fairness in data collection, algorithm development, and the application of FRT leads to a broader questioning of institutional legitimacy. As procedural justice theorists emphasize, outcomes are not enough to be just; the processes leading to those outcomes must also be seen as equitable (Tyler, 2006). In the case of FRT, this requires transparency in algorithmic design, accountability in deployment, and inclusive decision-making processes that prioritize the perspectives and concerns of marginalized communities.
- **Undermining of Institutional Trust:** The biased application of FRT can significantly undermine trust in law enforcement and other public institutions, especially among minority groups that are disproportionately affected by misidentifications and heightened surveillance. Research by Eubanks (2018) and Noble (2018) illustrates how algorithmic systems, when perceived as biased, can deepen societal mistrust, and reduce cooperation between affected communities and public authorities. In the long term, this undermines the legitimacy of institutions that rely on FRT for policing, security, or administrative functions.

Integrating Equity Theory and Procedural Justice Theory

Integrating Equity Theory and Procedural Justice Theory provides a robust framework for addressing the ethical implications of FRT. Both theories offer complementary perspectives: while Equity Theory focuses on evaluating fairness in outcomes, Procedural Justice Theory emphasizes the fairness of processes. When used together, these theories provide a comprehensive approach to tackling the ethical concerns associated with FRT, particularly as they pertain to marginalized communities. Both theories provide comprehensive framework for addressing the ethical implications of FRT in the following areas:

- **Evaluating Fairness:** By applying Equity Theory, we can systematically assess how FRT impacts different groups disproportionately and how technological biases exacerbate existing inequalities. Adams' Equity Theory (1965) posits that individuals evaluate fairness by comparing their input-output ratios with those of others. In FRT, this means evaluating whether individuals, especially from marginalized communities, receive equitable treatment when interacting with these technologies. For example, empirical evidence has shown that FRT is less accurate in identifying people of color, which results in a skewed input-output ratio for these groups compared to white individuals, who are more accurately identified (Buolamwini & Gebru, 2018). The repeated misidentification of minority groups contributes to an erosion of trust in technology and perpetuates systemic inequalities (Noble, 2018).

In contrast, Procedural Justice Theory, as proposed by Tyler (1990), complements this analysis by examining the fairness of the processes through which FRT is implemented and managed. The theory argues that individuals are more likely to accept decisions and outcomes when they perceive the processes leading to them as fair, transparent, and unbiased. In the case of FRT, this would involve evaluating whether the procedures for data collection, algorithm development, and decision-making are fair, especially concerning how FRT is deployed in policing and public safety (Eubanks, 2018). If minority communities are disproportionately subjected to FRT surveillance or if the technology is developed using biased datasets, it undermines procedural fairness and further entrenches distrust in institutional processes (Tyler, 2006).

- **Promoting Equity and Transparency:** Addressing FRT's shortcomings require correcting the system's technological biases and ensuring its use processes are transparent and equitable. The integration of Equity Theory and Procedural Justice Theory informs this dual approach. Equity Theory highlights the need to rectify imbalances in how different groups experience the outcomes of FRT. This includes addressing algorithmic biases, such as the higher rates of misidentification experienced by people of color and other marginalized groups. Studies by Raji, et al., 2020; Buolamwini and Gebru (2018) have shown that these biases are rooted in the datasets used to train FRT algorithms, which often underrepresent non-white individuals. Correcting these biases would involve diversifying training datasets and continuously auditing FRT systems to ensure equitable outcomes across all demographic groups (Raji et al., 2020).

Meanwhile, Procedural Justice Theory underscores the importance of transparency and accountability in implementing FRT. The theory suggests that transparency in decision- making processes such as providing clear explanations of how FRT systems are used, how data is collected, and how decisions are made can help build trust among affected communities. By involving stakeholders in these processes, particularly those from marginalized groups, institutions can promote a more inclusive and equitable approach to FRT. This aligns with Tyler's (2006) argument that fair and transparent processes are crucial to fostering legitimacy and cooperation with authority figures and institutions.

Combining these approaches ensures that technological advancements in FRT contribute to social justice rather than detract from it. For instance, in policing, ensuring that FRT is used transparently and equitably can help mitigate the risk of wrongful arrests and surveillance, which disproportionately affect minority communities (Richardson, Schultz, & Crawford, 2019). Moreover, promoting procedural fairness can foster greater community trust in law enforcement and other public institutions, which is crucial in contexts where minority groups have historically faced discriminatory practices (Noble, 2018).

DEVELOPING ETHICAL GUIDELINES: INTEGRATING INSIGHTS FROM EQUITY THEORY AND PROCEDURAL

Justice Theory also provide a foundation for developing ethical guidelines and policies for FRT. These guidelines should focus on mitigating biases, ensuring fair treatment across all demographic groups, and maintaining transparency and accountability in decision-making processes. Equity Theory informs the development of policies that prioritize fairness in outcomes. This includes guidelines for auditing FRT systems to detect and correct biases, ensuring that training datasets are representative, and instituting mechanisms to hold technology developers accountable for the impact of their systems on marginalized groups. Policies should also ensure that FRT is not used in ways that disproportionately target minority communities, as such practices would exacerbate existing social inequities (Buolamwini & Gebru, 2018; Eubanks, 2018).

Procedural Justice Theory adds another layer by emphasizing the need for policies that promote transparency and fairness in the processes surrounding FRT. This could involve setting standards for how FRT data is collected, how decisions are made regarding its use, and how individuals can contest, or appeal decisions made by these technologies. Transparency mechanisms, such as public reporting on using FRT and community involvement in decision-making, can help address concerns about bias and misuse (Tyler, 2006; Richardson et al., 2019).

General Adaptation Syndrome (GAS) and Minority Stress Model: Psychological Perspectives on Stress from Biased AI Systems

The General Adaptation Syndrome (GAS) and the Minority Stress Model provide crucial psychological perspectives on the stress experienced by individuals exposed to biased artificial intelligence (AI) systems, such as FRT. Both models illuminate how chronic exposure to systemic bias in technology can have profound effects on mental and physical health, particularly within marginalized communities. These stress models offer a lens through which to understand how biased AI exacerbates health disparities, leading to both immediate and long-term consequences for affected individuals.

General Adaptation Syndrome (GAS)

General Adaptation Syndrome (GAS), introduced by Hans Selye (1956), provides a framework for understanding the physiological and psychological responses to chronic stress. Selye's model is divided into three stages, each illustrating how the body reacts and adapts to prolonged stressors. GAS consists of three distinct stages:

- **Alarm Stage:** The first stage is the body's immediate response to a perceived threat, commonly known as the "fight or flight" response. During this stage, the body releases stress hormones such as adrenaline and cortisol, which increase heart rate, blood pressure, and energy supplies. In the context of biased AI systems like FRT, individuals particularly from marginalized communities may experience this initial alarm when they encounter or are aware of the discriminatory effects of the technology. For example, individuals may experience heightened stress upon learning that FRT disproportionately misidentifies people of color, which can result in wrongful arrests, exclusion from services, or targeted surveillance (Buolamwini & Gebru, 2018; Noble, 2018). This awareness triggers an immediate stress response, as individuals fear the personal and systemic consequences of being unfairly treated by biased technology.
- **Resistance Stage:** If the stressor persists, the body enters the resistance stage, where it attempts to adapt to the ongoing stress while maintaining homeostasis. In this phase, individuals subjected to biased AI systems may try to

cope by developing strategies to mitigate the impact of these biases on their daily lives. For example, they might avoid areas where FRT is frequently used or modify their behaviors to reduce the likelihood of being misidentified (Benjamin, 2019). However, while the body may seem to adjust, it remains in a state of heightened alertness, continuously mobilizing resources to cope with the ongoing threat of bias. This prolonged exposure to stress can lead to chronic anxiety, hypervigilance, and other mental health challenges, as individuals feel they must constantly navigate the potential dangers posed by biased technologies.

- **Exhaustion Stage:** When exposure to stress is prolonged without relief, the body eventually reaches the exhaustion stage, where its resources are depleted, leading to reduced immunity, increased vulnerability to illness, and psychological issues such as anxiety, depression, and burnout. For individuals facing systemic discrimination through biased AI systems, the exhaustion stage can manifest as feelings of hopelessness, alienation, and diminished mental and physical health. Research suggests that chronic exposure to racism and discrimination whether through interpersonal encounters or systemic structures like biased AI can lead to serious health outcomes, including hypertension, depression, and higher levels of stress-related illnesses among marginalized populations (Williams & Mohammed, 2009). Thus, the exhaustion phase highlights the toll that biased AI systems take on both mental and physical health over time.

Application to Facial Recognition Technology

For individuals subjected to biased FRT, the stress of potential misidentification and systemic discrimination can trigger and perpetuate GAS responses:

- **Alarm Response:** The threat of being misidentified or falsely accused by biased facial recognition systems can induce heightened anxiety and vigilance. This initial stress response can impact daily functioning and mental well-being (Selye, 1956).
- **Resistance Response:** As individuals adapt to the ongoing stress of living under the potential threat of biased FRT, they may experience chronic stress, leading to sustained physiological and psychological strain. This stage involves coping mechanisms, including increased caution and self-monitoring to avoid potential misidentifications (Selye, 1956).
- **Exhaustion Response:** Prolonged exposure to biased FRT can lead to the exhaustion stage, characterized by mental health issues such as chronic anxiety, depression, and stress-related disorders. The cumulative effect of these stressors can undermine overall well-being and quality of life (Selye, 1956).

Minority Stress Model (Response)

The Minority Stress Model, developed by Meyer (2003), provides additional insights into the specific types of stress experienced by minority groups due to systemic and structural inequities. The model argues that individuals from marginalized groups such as racial minorities, LGBTQ+ individuals, or those from lower socioeconomic backgrounds experience both general stressors, shared by the broader population, and unique stressors related to their minority status. These stressors include experiences of discrimination, prejudice, and stigmatization, which compound over time and contribute to health disparities. In the context of biased AI systems like FRT, the Minority Stress Model is particularly relevant because it explains how technology bias acts as a chronic source of stress for marginalized communities.

For example, people of color are disproportionately misidentified by FRT systems, which can lead to wrongful arrests or exclusion from critical resources, such as employment or housing opportunities (Richardson et al., 2019). These experiences are not just isolated incidents but are compounded by the broader societal context of racial discrimination and structural inequality. The stress of encountering biased AI systems thus adds another layer to the cumulative burden of minority stress, exacerbating feelings of alienation, hypervigilance, and powerlessness.

The Minority Stress Model also posits that the stressors faced by marginalized individuals are exacerbated by a lack of access to resources that could mitigate these stressors, such as social support, mental health services, or equitable legal protections (Meyer, 2003). In the case of biased FRT, individuals who are unfairly targeted or misidentified often lack the means to contest these injustices effectively, further increasing their stress. Studies have shown that the cumulative effect of these stressors can lead to negative health outcomes, including higher rates of anxiety, depression, substance use, and physical health problems, such as cardiovascular disease (Meyer, 2003; Williams & Mohammed, 2009).

Psychological Impact of Biased AI on Marginalized Communities

Both GAS and the Minority Stress Model highlight the wider psychological impact of biased AI systems on marginalized communities. The chronic stress associated with constantly navigating discriminatory technology systems leads to a range of negative mental health outcomes, including anxiety, depression, and post-traumatic stress disorder (PTSD) like symptoms. The cumulative burden of stressors, as outlined by the Minority Stress Model, means that the negative effects of biased AI are not experienced in isolation but are compounded by existing social and systemic inequalities. Research has shown that discrimination and bias whether through direct interpersonal interactions or systemic structures like biased AI contribute to significant disparities in mental and physical health (Williams & Mohammed, 2009). The General Adaptation Syndrome illustrates how individuals' bodies and minds attempt to cope with ongoing stress but ultimately face exhaustion and deteriorating health. Meanwhile, the Minority Stress Model provides a framework for understanding how this stress is uniquely experienced by marginalized groups and how it compounds over time, leading to even more significant health disparities.

Implications for Policy and Technology Design

Understanding the psychological effects of biased AI systems through the lenses of GAS and the Minority Stress Model emphasizes the need for policy interventions that address the root causes of these stressors. Technology developers and policymakers must take steps to ensure that AI systems are designed with fairness and equity in mind, and that biased systems are corrected through more representative training data and continuous auditing (Raji et al., 2020). There is a need for greater transparency and accountability in how these technologies are used, particularly in public spaces like law enforcement or hiring practices, where the stakes for marginalized individuals are particularly high. The broader health impacts of biased AI systems require not only technological fixes but also social and legal protections for those most affected. This includes ensuring access to mental health services and creating avenues for individuals to contest wrongful identifications or surveillance by biased AI systems. Mitigation of both the immediate and long-term effects of biased AI on marginalized communities can help toward a more equitable and just technological future.

Application to Facial Recognition Technology

The General Adaptation Syndrome (GAS) model is highly applicable to understanding the psychological impact of biased FRT on individuals, particularly those from marginalized communities. When subjected to the ongoing threat of misidentification or systemic discrimination, individuals can experience the stages of GAS alarm, resistance, and exhaustion as they cope with the stress induced by these biased systems. Each stage of GAS provides a framework for analyzing the mental and physical toll that FRT can impose on users who face frequent misidentification, wrongful accusations, and unequal treatment. For individuals subjected to biased FRT, the stress of potential misidentification and systemic discrimination can trigger and perpetuate the following GAS responses:

- **Alarm Response:** In the context of biased FRT, the alarm stage of GAS represents an immediate psychological and physiological response to the perceived threat of being misidentified or falsely accused. This stage is marked by the activation of the body's "fight or flight" response, where stress hormones such as cortisol and adrenaline are released in response to fear or anxiety (Selye, 1956). Individuals who are aware of the biases inherent in FRT such as its tendency to misidentify people of color at higher rates (Buolamwini & Gebru, 2018) may experience heightened anxiety, hypervigilance, and stress in situations where the technology is present. For example, in airports, law enforcement, or public surveillance, marginalized individuals may become acutely aware of the potential for misidentification, triggering the alarm response. The fear of false identification whether leading to wrongful arrest or being excluded from spaces based on inaccurate data can induce feelings of helplessness, stress, and anxiety. Research shows that this heightened vigilance in response to perceived threats can impair daily functioning and negatively affect mental health (Pascoe & Richman, 2009). Individuals may feel constantly on edge, anticipating biased interactions with FRT, which can elevate their stress levels and affect both psychological and physical well-being.

- **Resistance Response:** The resistance stage occurs when the stressor persists, and individuals must adapt to the ongoing threat of biased FRT. In this stage, the body attempts to maintain homeostasis while under continuous stress. Although outwardly it may appear that individuals have adjusted to the threat, the chronic exposure to potential misidentification leads to long-term psychological strain. For marginalized groups, this stage involves coping mechanisms aimed at mitigating the risk of being misidentified by biased systems. These mechanisms can include increased self-monitoring, such as changing personal appearance, avoiding areas with heavy surveillance, or altering behavior in public spaces to avoid drawing attention (Benjamin, 2019).

While these strategies might provide short-term relief, they do not address the underlying systemic issues of bias within the technology. The constant adaptation to biased systems can cause cumulative stress over time, leading to psychological issues such as anxiety and depression. Moreover, prolonged exposure to biased FRT can result in social withdrawal or avoidance of certain environments. For instance, individuals who fear being targeted or misidentified by law enforcement may avoid areas where FRT is heavily used, further exacerbating social exclusion and marginalization (Crawford & Schultz, 2019). This resistance phase mirrors the experience of living under surveillance and discrimination, which has been shown to contribute to negative health outcomes, such as high blood pressure and chronic stress (Williams & Mohammed, 2009).

- **Exhaustion Response:** In the exhaustion stage, individuals who have faced prolonged exposure to biased FRT reach a point where their physiological and psychological resources are depleted. The cumulative stress of dealing with biased systems, coupled with the ongoing fear of being misidentified or falsely accused, can result in serious mental health issues. According to Selye (1956), the body can no longer maintain its heightened state of alertness, leading to reduced immunity, increased vulnerability to illness, and mental health disorders. For those who are frequently targeted by biased FRT, the exhaustion stage can manifest as chronic anxiety, depression, and stress-related disorders, including PTSD like symptoms.

Research on racial disparities and chronic stress indicates that the repeated exposure to discriminatory systems whether interpersonal or technological leads to a range of psychological issues, including feelings of hopelessness, helplessness, and alienation (Meyer, 2003). The exhaustion caused by long-term engagement with biased systems can also undermine self-esteem and create feelings of powerlessness, as individuals perceive little control over the ways they are treated by these systems. This exhaustion is particularly evident when considering the psychological toll on individuals who are frequently misidentified by FRT, such as people of color or women, who have been shown to face higher rates of inaccuracy in these systems (Buolamwini & Gebru, 2018). For example, wrongful arrests or misidentification by law enforcement using FRT can lead to significant trauma, further perpetuating distrust in institutions and mental health decline. Studies have shown that exposure to systemic discrimination contributes to long- term mental health disparities, particularly among marginalized populations (Pascoe & Richman, 2009; Williams & Mohammed, 2009).

Implications for Mental Health and Policy

The application of the General Adaptation Syndrome model to biased FRT highlights the urgent need to address the psychological impact of these technologies on marginalized communities. The mental health consequences of chronic stress, anxiety, and fear caused by biased AI systems necessitate interventions that go beyond technical fixes. Policy changes must include efforts to regulate the use of biased technologies, enforce ethical AI practices, and ensure that mental health support is available for individuals who are most affected by these systems. There must be a focus on transparency and accountability in the development and deployment of AI technologies. As studies have shown, biased AI not only reinforces existing social inequalities but also exacerbates the mental and physical health disparities faced by marginalized groups (Raji et al., 2020). Policymakers and technologists must collaborate to correct the biases inherent in AI systems like FRT, ensuring that these tools serve to promote fairness and equity rather than perpetuate systemic discrimination.

Minority Stress Model (Stressors)

The Minority Stress Model, developed by Ilan Meyer (2003), provides a framework for understanding the unique stressors faced by marginalized groups, particularly those stemming from systemic discrimination and social stigma. This model is highly relevant to exploring the psychological and physical health implications for individuals exposed to biased technologies such as FRT. The model distinguishes between distal stressors, external sources of stress (e.g., discrimination), and proximal stressors, which are internalized stressors (e.g., internalized stigma). Both types of stressors disproportionately affect minority populations, exacerbating their overall stress burden and contributing to health disparities.

- **Distal Stressors:** Distal stressors are external, objective events that occur outside the individual but have a significant psychological impact. For minority groups, distal stressors include experiences of overt discrimination, harassment, and prejudice (Meyer, 2003). In the context of biased FRT, these external stressors could manifest as misidentification by law enforcement, wrongful accusations, or exclusion from specific spaces based on erroneous algorithmic determinations. Studies have shown that FRT systems exhibit a higher error rate for people of color, particularly Black individuals, and women, which exacerbates the risk of wrongful arrests or accusations (Buolamwini & Gebru, 2018). These discriminatory outcomes amplify feelings of fear and alienation, particularly in contexts where FRT is used in security, policing, or surveillance. For instance, Black and Latino individuals who have historically faced higher rates of over-policing and systemic discrimination may experience additional distress when they are aware that biased technologies like FRT are being deployed in their communities (Benjamin, 2019). The integration of biased FRT into institutional practices such as in airports, police departments, and retail surveillance only compounds these feelings of vulnerability, reinforcing the distal stressors already faced due to racial profiling and other forms of discrimination (Brayne, 2020).
- **Proximal Stressors:** Proximal stressors are internalized reactions to discrimination, such as the fear of being targeted, stigma, and internalized negative beliefs. These stressors are shaped by individuals' awareness of their marginalized status and perceptions of how society views and treats them. In the case of biased FRT the constant threat of being misidentified or falsely accused leads to increased vigilance, anxiety, and self-monitoring behav-

iors (Meyer, 2003). Individuals may engage in behaviors designed to reduce their visibility, such as avoiding public spaces where FRT is used or altering their appearance to prevent triggering misidentifications. For marginalized groups, the anticipation of discrimination or bias from FRT represents a significant proximal stressor. Research shows that people who perceive themselves as targets of bias are more likely to experience psychological strain, including heightened anxiety, depression, and social withdrawal (Williams & Mohammed, 2009). The constant awareness of potential surveillance and the possibility of being misidentified can become an enduring source of stress, contributing to psychological distress, and diminishing overall well-being. This aligns with hypervigilance, where individuals must constantly monitor their behavior and surroundings to avoid discrimination, even when bias may not be overt (Pascoe & Richman, 2009).

Application to Facial Recognition Technology

The Minority Stress Model offers critical insights into the additional stress burden experienced by marginalized groups in the context of biased FRT. The presence of FRT in public spaces, particularly in policing and surveillance, exacerbates the distal and proximal stressors faced by minority individuals, amplifying their overall stress levels. The model applications are as follows:

- **Increased Vigilance:** One of the critical proximal stressors is the increased vigilance required to avoid potential misidentification by biased FRT systems. For individuals from marginalized communities, the constant threat of being wrongfully identified or targeted by law enforcement triggers chronic anxiety and fear. This form of anticipatory stress is particularly acute in communities that have historically faced racial profiling and discriminatory policing practices (Benjamin, 2019). Research indicates that the mere presence of surveillance technologies, especially those known to exhibit racial bias, can lead to psychological distress and social avoidance (Brayne, 2020).
- **Systemic Discrimination:** Biased FRT systems do not operate in a vacuum; they are often integrated into institutional and societal frameworks that are already steeped in systemic discrimination. As a result, FRT can exacerbate existing patterns of racial inequality, contributing to distal stressors. For example, the deployment of FRT in law enforcement disproportionately affects Black and Latino individuals, who are more likely to be misidentified and subjected to unwarranted police scrutiny (Buolamwini & Gebru, 2018). The widespread integration of biased AI systems into critical sectors such as criminal justice, hiring, and housing further compounds these stressors, rein-

forcing the structural disadvantages faced by marginalized groups (Eubanks, 2018).
- **Health Disparities:** The compounded stress from both proximal and distal stressors associated with biased FRT can contribute to health disparities among marginalized populations. The Minority Stress Model emphasizes that chronic exposure to discrimination and stigma results in heightened levels of stress, which are linked to adverse health outcomes such as anxiety, depression, and cardiovascular disease (Williams & Mohammed, 2009). In the context of FRT, the cumulative psychological burden of being misidentified or wrongfully accused can lead to mental health issues such as chronic stress, depression, and PTSD (Meyer, 2003). This is particularly concerning given the well-documented link between racial discrimination and mental health disparities in communities of color (Pascoe & Richman, 2009).

Integrating GAS and Minority Stress Model

By combining the insights from the General Adaptation Syndrome (GAS) and the Minority Stress Model, we gain a more nuanced understanding of the chronic stress responses triggered by biased FRT systems. While the GAS framework helps explain the physiological and psychological responses to ongoing stress, the Minority Stress Model contextualizes these stressors within the broader framework of systemic discrimination and social stigma experienced by marginalized groups. GAS and Minority Stress Model integrations are as follows:

- **Chronic Stress and Health Outcomes:** The GAS model illustrates how chronic exposure to biased FRT can lead to sustained stress responses, resulting in physical and mental health problems (Selye, 1956). The Minority Stress Model further highlights how the compounding effects of systemic discrimination magnify these stressors for minority individuals. Together, these models underscore the importance of addressing biased technologies' direct and indirect impacts on marginalized populations to mitigate their adverse health outcomes (Meyer, 2003).
- **Understanding Stressors:** Both models emphasize the need to recognize and address the different stressors arising from biased AI technologies. The distal stressors related to external discrimination and the proximal stressors stemming from internalized fear of being targeted must be understood in tandem to develop effective interventions. By identifying how systemic bias in technology contributes to the chronic stress experienced by minority individuals, policymakers and technologists can work toward creating more equita-

ble systems that reduce both the physiological and psychological burdens of stress (Pascoe & Richman, 2009).
- **Policy and Practice:** The insights from both the GAS model and the Minority Stress Model have essential implications for the development of policies and practices aimed at reducing the impact of biased AI systems. Policies should focus on creating equitable technologies, enhancing transparency and accountability in AI development, and implementing safeguards to prevent discrimination in using FRT. Moreover, mental health interventions must be put in place to support individuals experiencing chronic stress related to biased technologies. This could include counseling services, community support networks, and legal resources for individuals wrongfully targeted by biased systems (Benjamin, 2019).

TECHNOLOGICAL DETERMINISM AND STAKEHOLDER THEORY: ETHICAL IMPLICATIONS AND ORGANIZATIONAL RESPONSIBILITIES

Technological Determinism and Stakeholder Theory offer essential frameworks for analyzing the ethical implications of technological development and deployment, particularly in areas where technology intersects with human rights and social justice, such as facial recognition technology (FRT). These theories emphasize the non-neutrality of technology and stress the importance of organizational responsibilities to ensure ethical design and implementation. This is particularly critical in preventing biased technologies from perpetuating societal inequalities. By integrating these theories, we can develop a more robust understanding of the role organizations should play in mitigating the negative impacts of biased technologies like FRT.

Technological Determinism

Technological Determinism is a theoretical framework that posits technology as a primary driver of societal change, shaping values, behaviors, and structures. Initially popularized by Marshall McLuhan (1964), this theory was later expanded by scholars like Langdon Winner. McLuhan argued that "the medium is the message," suggesting that our tools and technologies ultimately shape human interaction and societal evolution. According to Winner (1980), technology is far from neutral; instead, it reflects and reinforces social inequalities and power dynamics. Technological Determinism suggests that innovations, if left unchecked, can embed and amplify existing social, racial, and economic disparities. Thus, technology is not an independent entity but one that influences and is influenced by the social context in which it is developed.

Application to Facial Recognition Technology

Technological Determinism, a concept popularized by Marshall McLuhan and later expanded by Langdon Winner, posits that technology shapes societal values, behaviors, and structures. This Theory suggests that technological advancements are not neutral; they influence and often reinforce existing social inequalities and power dynamics (McLuhan, 1964; Winner, 1980). Its applications are as follows:

- **Reinforcement of Social Inequalities:** One of the core critiques of Technological Determinism is its implication that technological advancements can reinforce existing social inequalities if not scrutinized. This critique is particularly relevant in the case of FRT, which has been shown to misidentify people from marginalized groups disproportionately. Researchers such as Buolamwini and Gebru (2018) found that FRT algorithms exhibited higher error rates for women, Black individuals, and other racial minorities compared to white males. These misidentifications often stem from biased training data, failing to represent diverse populations adequately. Technological Determinism underscores the idea that biased technologies like FRT reflect and perpetuate societal inequalities because they are built within already inequitable systems. In this way, FRT, if left unchecked, can become a tool that exacerbates racial and gender disparities by reinforcing discriminatory practices. For example, in law enforcement, where FRT is used to identify suspects, misidentifications disproportionately affect people of color, leading to wrongful arrests, increased surveillance, and further marginalization (Buolamwini & Gebru, 2018; Noble, 2018). Therefore, Technological Determinism warns that technological advancements will continue to entrench societal inequalities unless deliberate steps are taken to address these biases.
- **Amplification of Power Structures:** Winner (1980) expanded on McLuhan's ideas by emphasizing that technology is inherently political and can amplify existing power structures and social hierarchies. In the context of FRT, technology is not simply a neutral tool; it reflects the values and biases of its creators and the broader social systems in which it is developed. If FRT is deployed without addressing its inherent biases, it amplifies the power of dominant groups such as law enforcement agencies and corporate entities at the expense of marginalized communities. For example, in public surveillance settings, FRT has been used disproportionately in communities of color, re-

inforcing existing patterns of over-policing and institutional discrimination (Brayne, 2020). The deployment of FRT in such settings reinforces the power structures that enable racial profiling and systemic surveillance, making marginalized groups more vulnerable to discriminatory practices. This aligns with Winner's (1980) assertion that technology often serves as a vehicle for perpetuating the existing power distribution, mainly when used in contexts with little oversight or regulation.

- **Need for Ethical Design:** The theory of Technological Determinism highlights the need for technologies like FRT to be intentionally designed and regulated to counteract their potential negative impacts. Ethical design involves technical, social, and moral considerations that account for how technology will affect various groups, especially those already at risk of discrimination. For FRT, this means designing algorithms that are inclusive and representative of diverse populations, ensuring that racial, gender and ethnic biases are minimized (McLuhan, 1964; Buolamwini & Gebru, 2018). Moreover, regulatory frameworks must be established to ensure the technology is deployed ethically, with safeguards to protect against misuse. Technological Determinism warns that FRT will continue reinforcing societal inequities without proactive measures. Therefore, addressing FRT's ethical dimensions requires a combination of inclusive design practices, robust regulation, and ongoing scrutiny of how the technology is being used in society.

Stakeholder Theory

Stakeholder Theory, introduced by R. Edward Freeman in 1984, challenges the traditional shareholder-centric view of corporate responsibility. Instead of focusing solely on profit maximization for shareholders, Stakeholder Theory posits that organizations have ethical responsibilities to consider the interests of all stakeholders affected by their actions. Stakeholders include shareholders, employees, customers, suppliers, communities, and broader society (Freeman, 1984). This theory emphasizes that organizations must engage with these diverse groups, especially those most impacted by organizational decisions, to operate ethically and sustainably. By expanding the scope of responsibility, Stakeholder Theory underscores the importance of addressing organizational activities' potential social, environmental, and ethical impacts. The theory aligns with the Triple Bottom Line approach, where companies are accountable for their economic, social, and environmental performance (Elkington, 1998). Stakeholder Theory is relevant in developing emerging technologies like facial recognition technology (FRT), which can significantly impact civil liberties, privacy, and human rights.

Application to Facial Recognition Technology

This theory advocates for a broader view of corporate, emphasizing the need to engage with all affected parties, especially those most impacted by organizational actions in the following aspects:

- **Inclusive Design and Deployment:** One of the critical implications of Stakeholder Theory in the context of FRT is the need for inclusive design and deployment processes that consider the interests and concerns of all affected groups, particularly those from marginalized communities. The development of FRT has often been criticized for its failure to adequately represent and address the needs of diverse populations, leading to biased outcomes that disproportionately affect women, people of color, and other vulnerable groups (Buolamwini & Gebru, 2018). Stakeholder Theory calls for organizations to engage a broad range of stakeholders, including those the technology's deployment may impact most. Involving diverse stakeholders in the decision-making process ensures that technology meets the needs of all community segments and helps identify potential biases in the system. For example, by consulting with civil rights groups, data privacy experts, and representatives of marginalized communities, organizations can gain insights into how FRT might perpetuate discrimination or violate privacy rights. As Freeman (1984) emphasizes, organizations are responsible for ensuring that their technologies are fair, inclusive, and equitable, actively involving stakeholders in their design and implementation.
- **Ethical Responsibility:** According to Stakeholder Theory, organizations bear moral responsibilities that extend beyond profit-driven goals. In the context of FRT, this responsibility includes considering the ethical implications of the technology's use, particularly regarding its impact on privacy, security, and civil liberties. FRT has been associated with privacy violations, increased surveillance, and disproportionate harm to marginalized groups, especially in areas like law enforcement, where it is often used for predictive policing or public surveillance (Brayne, 2020). By adopting a stakeholder-focused approach, organizations can mitigate these adverse consequences by conducting ethical risk assessments and ensuring that the technology is used in ways that respect the rights of all individuals. Engaging stakeholders in the design process enables organizations to anticipate potential ethical challenges and develop mitigation strategies. For example, organizations can implement policies that limit the use of FRT to specific contexts where privacy concerns are minimized, or they can ensure that the technology undergoes regular audits to check for algorithmic bias and discriminatory outcomes (Freeman, 1984;

Floridi et al., 2018). This proactive engagement fosters transparency and accountability, critical to ensuring that technology serves the public good.
- **Fostering Equity and Fairness:** Stakeholder Theory inherently aligns with the principles of fairness and justice because it advocates for an inclusive approach to decision-making. In developing technologies like FRT, organizations must prioritize equitable treatment of all stakeholders, particularly those who may be disproportionately harmed by biased algorithms. For example, Buolamwini and Gebru's (2018) research on the racial and gender biases present in commercial FRT systems demonstrates that marginalized groups often face higher error rates and discriminatory treatment. Stakeholder Theory encourages organizations to proactively address these biases by adopting a fairness-first approach to technology design. This means actively working to ensure that the technology does not harm any specific group and that potential biases are identified and mitigated before deployment. Organizations must also be transparent about their efforts to create fair and equitable systems, engaging with affected communities to ensure their concerns are addressed. Organizations can foster trust and social responsibility by adopting such an approach, ensuring the technology is efficient and just (Freeman, 1984; Floridi et al., 2018).

Integrating Technological Determinism and Stakeholder Theory

Combining the insights of Technological Determinism and Stakeholder Theory provides a comprehensive ethical framework for understanding the development and use of biased technologies like FRT. While Technological Determinism emphasizes how technology can reinforce existing social inequalities and power structures, Stakeholder Theory focuses on inclusive and ethical practices in technology development. By integrating these two frameworks, organizations can take a holistic approach to designing and deploying technology that addresses bias and promotes social justice and equity. These integrations of Technological Determinism and Stakeholder Theory are as follows:

- **Holistic Approach:** Technological Determinism suggests that technologies like FRT are not neutral; they reflect and often amplify societal biases unless carefully designed to mitigate these effects. On the other hand, Stakeholder Theory calls for organizations to involve diverse groups in the design and deployment processes to ensure that these technologies do not disproportionately harm marginalized populations. Together, these frameworks advocate for a holistic approach that requires organizations to actively address technology's ethical, social, and political dimensions (Winner, 1980; Freeman, 1984). This holistic approach involves acknowledging the potential for technology to perpetuate existing inequalities and taking deliberate steps to engage with all stakeholders to design systems that promote fairness and equity. FRT might involve using diverse datasets to train algorithms, implementing accountability measures, and ensuring that the technology is subjected to regular audits to prevent discriminatory outcomes (Buolamwini & Gebru, 2018; Noble, 2018).

- **Ethical Design and Implementation:** By integrating technological determination and stakeholder theory, organizations can develop ethical design and implementation practices that recognize the potential biases inherent in technology and actively work to counteract them. Technological Determinism highlights the risks of allowing technology to perpetuate societal inequalities, while Stakeholder Theory provides a framework for ensuring that these risks are addressed through inclusive decision-making. This integration suggests that addressing biases in FRT requires recognizing the potential for technology to perpetuate inequalities and engaging diverse stakeholders to ensure that the technology is developed and used in ways that promote fairness and equity.
- **Organizational Accountability:** Technological Determinism and Stakeholder Theory emphasizes the critical role organizations play in shaping the societal outcomes of technological development. By adopting practices that align with the principles of these theories, organizations can take responsibility for the societal impacts of their technologies and work toward creating more equitable and just systems. This includes being transparent about technology use, engaging in ethical risk assessments, and involving many stakeholders in the design process. By doing so, organizations can help ensure that their technologies do not exacerbate inequalities but rather contribute to positive societal change (Freeman, 1984; Winner, 1980).

CASE STUDIES AND EMPIRICAL EVIDENCE

Empirical Studies on Racial Bias in Facial Recognition Technology

Recent empirical studies have significantly expanded our understanding of the racial biases inherent in FRT. These studies reveal how algorithmic biases can reinforce systemic racial discrimination, emphasizing the need for more equitable technology development and deployment.

The groundbreaking study "Gender Shades" by Buolamwini and Gebru (2018) is one of the most critical pieces of empirical research on biases in FRT. The study assessed commercial facial recognition systems from leading companies such as IBM, Microsoft, and Face++ and found significant racial and gender disparities in their performance. Specifically, the algorithms showed a markedly higher error rate when identifying darker-skinned individuals, particularly darker-skinned women, than lighter-skinned individuals. This discrepancy in performance highlighted a crucial intersection of racial and gender bias, with the error rates for darker-skinned women reaching as high as 34.7%, compared to less than 1% for lighter-skinned men (Buolamwini & Gebru, 2018). The researchers pointed out that these biases stem from unrepresentative training data sets predominantly composed of lighter-skinned individuals, which resulted in skewed algorithmic outcomes. This study exposed technical flaws in FRT and raised important questions about the ethical implications of deploying such biased systems in the public and private sectors.

Andrew Ferguson's (2020) analysis expanded upon the findings of Buolamwini and Gebru by investigating the practical consequences of biased FRT in law enforcement. Ferguson argued that the deployment of flawed FRT in policing could lead to wrongful arrests and the over-surveillance of marginalized communities. His research demonstrated that law enforcement's reliance on biased facial recognition systems amplifies existing racial disparities in policing. Ferguson contended that these misidentifications are more than technical glitches; they can influence judicial processes, reinforce pre-existing biases within the criminal justice system, and perpetuate a cycle of racial discrimination. Ferguson's analysis called for greater scrutiny, transparency, and accountability in how FRT is developed, tested, and used, particularly in contexts with profound societal consequences, such as law enforcement (Ferguson, 2020).

International Perspectives

The issue of racial bias in FRT is not confined to the United States; it has global implications. Research across regions reveals diverse approaches to regulating and deploying this technology, reflecting varying cultural and legal contexts. In the European Union (EU), the General Data Protection Regulation (GDPR) provides a comprehensive legal framework that governs the use of biometric data, including FRT. While the GDPR imposes strict requirements for the lawful collection and processing of biometric information, concerns persist about the effectiveness of these regulations in practice (Wachter, Mittelstadt, & Floridi, 2013). Scholars such as Slobogin and Brayne (2023) have argued that even under stringent privacy regulations, FRT's potential for abuse remains a pressing issue, particularly in public surveillance. They suggest that using FRT in public spaces could disproportionately impact marginalized groups, as the technology could be deployed to profile and monitor specific racial or ethnic communities. Slobogin and Brayne emphasized the importance of robust enforcement mechanisms to ensure that FRT aligns with human rights standards, calling for greater oversight and transparency in its deployment (Slobogin & Brayne, 2023).

In China, the use of FRT for mass surveillance has raised concerns about ethnic and racial profiling, particularly about the country's Uyghur Muslim minority. Leibold (2020) documented how FRT is employed by the Chinese government to monitor Uyghur populations, contributing to a regime of control and surveillance that reinforces existing ethnic tensions and power imbalances. This usage of FRT demonstrates how the technology can be exploited to entrench systemic discrimination and human rights violations. The Chinese case highlights the risks of deploying FRT without adequate ethical considerations or international oversight, illustrating the need for global cooperation and dialogue on the responsible use of biometric technologies (Leibold, 2020).

Synthesis: Theoretical and Practical Intersections

The intersection of organizational theory, social network theory, and empirical evidence on racial bias in FRT underscores the complexity of addressing systemic biases and highlights the need for interdisciplinary solutions. Integrating these theoretical perspectives with empirical findings can provide more nuanced approaches to mitigating biases in artificial intelligence (AI) systems.

Organizational Theory and Policy Reforms

Organizational theory offers insight into how biases are embedded and perpetuated within institutional structures and practices. Classical theories like Weber's Bureaucracy Model (Weber, 1978) stress the importance of organizational structures in maintaining fairness, while contemporary theories like Contingency Theory (Burns & Stalker, 1961) emphasize adaptability. Both theories can inform the reform of policies to address bias in FRT. Organizational Theory and Policy Reforms concepts are as follows:

- **Diversity in Leadership and Teams:** Research by Nazer et al., (2023) underscores the importance of diverse leadership in mitigating algorithmic biases. Homogeneous teams may fail to identify potential biases due to a lack of varied perspectives, which is particularly problematic in developing AI systems. Ensuring that diverse leadership teams and data science departments can challenge implicit assumptions and create more inclusive technologies. By fostering diversity, organizations can make strides in developing AI systems that are more reflective of the populations they serve (Nazer et al., (2023).
- **Policy and Practice Alignment:** As DiMaggio and Powell (1983) articulated, institutional theory suggests that social and cultural contexts shape organizational practices. This theory can be applied to develop institutional policies that mandate bias detection, transparency, and accountability in FRT. Such policies should include clear guidelines for algorithmic testing and correction, ensuring that the deployment of FRT aligns with ethical standards and prioritizes equity and inclusivity (DiMaggio & Powell, 1983).

Social Network Theory and Data Diversity

Social network theory, particularly Granovetter's (1973) "Strength of Weak Ties" and Burt's (1992) "Structural Holes," offers insights into how information flows through networks and how biases are propagated. These concepts are critical for understanding the role of data-sharing networks in perpetuating or mitigating biases in AI systems. Key information flows as follows:

- **Diversity in Data-Sharing Networks:** Burt (2000) argued that diverse networks are crucial for accessing varied information and perspectives. In the context of FRT, data-sharing networks that lack diversity can reinforce existing biases across interconnected systems. Ensuring that diverse stakeholders are involved in data-sharing processes can mitigate these biases by incorpo-

rating a more comprehensive array of demographic perspectives. This aligns with the principles of Procedural Justice Theory (Tyler, 1990), which stresses the importance of fairness and inclusivity in decision-making processes.
- **Inclusive Data Collection and Algorithm Design:** By expanding the diversity of the data collection process, organizations can better detect and mitigate biases in AI algorithms. Social network theory suggests that bringing diverse voices during the algorithm design phase can help identify potential biases early in development, promoting fairness in AI systems. This approach reflects broader commitments to equity in AI, ensuring that these systems do not disproportionately harm underrepresented groups (Burt, 2000).

Empirical Evidence and Theoretical Integration

Empirical studies on racial bias in FRT, such as those by Buolamwini and Gebru (2018) and Ferguson (2020), reveal the real-world consequences of algorithmic bias, reinforcing the importance of applying theoretical insights to practical solutions. Examples of empirical evidence and theoretical integration are as follows:

- **Systemic Biases and Theoretical Frameworks:** The evidence of systemic bias in FRT highlights the need for interdisciplinary approaches to mitigate these biases. The General Adaptation Syndrome (Selye, 1956) and Minority Stress Model (Meyer, 2003) provide psychological insights into the impact of biased technologies on marginalized individuals, particularly in terms of stress and mental health. Integrating these frameworks with organizational and social network theories offers a comprehensive strategy for addressing bias, considering the technical flaws and the human consequences of biased AI systems.
- **Global and Local Implications:** Studies on FRT in global contexts, such as China and Europe, illustrate the need to adapt theoretical frameworks to local conditions. While ethical principles such as fairness, justice, and human rights should guide AI deployment globally, the regulatory and cultural contexts in which FRT is used vary significantly. As Leibold (2020): Slobogin and Brayne (2023) point out, these variations necessitate a flexible approach that balances local regulatory needs with universal ethical standards.

The synthesis of organizational theory, social network theory, and empirical evidence offers a comprehensive framework for addressing racial biases in facial recognition technology. By incorporating theoretical insights into policy reforms, promoting diversity in leadership and data-sharing networks, and drawing on empirical findings, organizations can work toward developing AI systems that are more equitable and just. This interdisciplinary approach ensures that technological advancements contribute to fairness rather than reinforcing inequalities.

LIMITATIONS

Current State of Research

The existing body of research on racial biases in FRT primarily focuses on the technical aspects, specifically how these systems perform algorithmically. For example, the work of Buolamwini and Gebru (2018) was pivotal in exposing the significant racial and gender disparities in the performance of FRT systems, particularly in their failure to classify individuals with darker skin tones and women accurately. While these studies have provided a critical foundation for understanding the manifestation of biases at the technical level, they often overlook the broader, systemic factors contributing to these disparities (Buolamwini & Gebru, 2018). The current literature predominantly centers on the direct outcomes of algorithmic bias without delving into the structural or organizational factors that perpetuate these inequalities in the design and deployment of the technology.

Theoretical Integration Gap

A significant area for improvement in the existing literature is integrating technical analyses and broader theoretical frameworks, such as organizational and social network theories. While technical analyses illuminate how algorithmic biases occur, they need to fully address the organizational and networked environments where these technologies are developed and utilized. For instance, limited research explores how the organizational structures, decision-making hierarchies, or social networks within firms and agencies influence the perpetuation or mitigation of bias in FRT systems (DiMaggio & Powell, 1983). Social network theory, focusing on how information and influence flow through relationships, can shed light on disseminating biased data and algorithms. However, empirical studies still need to explore this aspect (Granovetter, 1973; Burt, 2000).

Research Aims

Addressing this gap requires integrating organizational and social network theories into studies of FRT bias. Organizational theory examines how institutional norms, policies, and structures contribute to developing and applying biased technologies (Weber, 1978). Meanwhile, social network theory can illuminate the role of data-sharing practices and the flow of biased information between organizations in perpetuating racial bias in FRT. By combining these theoretical perspectives, future research can provide a more holistic understanding of how biases are entrenched within both technological systems and the organizational contexts that support them (Granovetter, 1973; Burt, 2000).

Methodological Limitations

A major methodological limitation in research on FRT bias is the reliance on unrepresentative datasets. Many algorithms are trained on datasets that do not reflect the diversity of the population, often containing a disproportionate number of lighter-skinned individuals (Richardson et al., 2019). This lack of diversity in training data results in algorithms that perform poorly when applied to individuals with darker skin tones, thereby perpetuating racial biases in the system's outputs. The overrepresentation of lighter-skinned individuals in these datasets not only skews the algorithms' performance but also reinforces systemic inequalities by amplifying the existing biases in the datasets used for training (Buolamwini & Gebru, 2018).

These dataset limitations lead to flawed generalizations about the efficacy of FRT systems, particularly their supposed "neutrality" or "accuracy" in diverse populations. As Richardson et al., 2019 pointed out, the reliance on non-representative datasets exacerbates the problem by reinforcing the biases already present in these systems. This methodological shortcoming also limits researchers' ability to fully capture the intersectional effects of bias mainly how race, gender, and other identity factors interact in producing skewed outcomes. The oversights in data collection and representation prevent a nuanced understanding of how FRT systems affect marginalized groups and hinder the development of corrective measures to address these inequities at their root (Crawford & Schultz, 2019).

Qualitative research methods are critical to overcoming the methodological limitations seen in many FRT studies. While quantitative approaches have provided valuable statistical insights into racial bias in FRT, qualitative research offers a more nuanced view of how these biases are perceived, experienced, and perpetuated within different organizational contexts. A qualitative methodology, such as in-depth interviews or case studies with stakeholders including technology developers, policymakers, and individuals affected by biased FRT systems can provide rich, contextualized data illuminating these technologies' social, organizational, and ethical implications (Creswell & Poth, 2018). This approach can capture perspectives that are not easily quantifiable, such as the lived experiences of marginalized individuals who are disproportionately impacted by biased technologies.

ADDRESSING GAPS AND METHODOLOGICAL LIMITATIONS

Future Research Directions

To address the gaps in the current literature, future research must adopt a more interdisciplinary approach, integrating technical, organizational, and social theories to understand the systemic biases in FRT. Combining the insights of organizational theory and social network theory with technical analyses of algorithmic performance will provide a more comprehensive understanding of how biases are embedded not only in technology but also in the broader institutional and social frameworks that sustain these systems (DiMaggio & Powell, 1983; Granovetter, 1973). Addressing the methodological limitations requires developing and using more diverse datasets in algorithm training, ensuring that FRT systems are tested and validated across a broader range of demographic groups. This will improve the representativeness and fairness of the technology (Buolamwini & Gebru, 2018; Richardson et al., 2019).

Corporate Responses to Mitigating Racial Bias in Facial Recognition Technology

The corporate sector's growing recognition of the ethical implications of FRT reflects a broader shift towards more responsible and equitable technology development. Major technology companies are increasingly acknowledging the potential harms associated with FRT, particularly concerning racial bias and its impact on marginalized communities. This heightened awareness has led to concrete actions addressing these ethical challenges. Key concrete actions include:

IBM's Strategic Shift

IBM's decision to halt the sale of its facial recognition technology to law enforcement agencies is a significant example of corporate responsibility in action. This move, announced in June 2020, was driven by several key factors:

- **Concerns About Misuse:** IBM's leadership expressed concerns that law enforcement agencies could misuse their facial recognition technology for purposes that may infringe on individual privacy and civil liberties. The company highlighted issues related to the potential for wrongful identification and exacerbating existing biases in the criminal justice system (Raji & Buolamwini, 2020).
- **Lack of Regulatory Oversight:** IBM also cited the need for comprehensive regulatory frameworks in its decision. The company emphasized that, in

the absence of clear and enforceable regulations governing facial recognition technology, it was unwilling to support its deployment in sensitive areas such as law enforcement. This decision underscores the need for robust legal and ethical guidelines to govern AI technologies (Raji & Buolamwini, 2020).

Microsoft's Commitment to Ethical AI

Microsoft has also taken proactive steps to address racial bias and ethical concerns related to facial recognition technology:

- **Ethical Guidelines and Frameworks:** Microsoft has established moral principles for AI development, including fairness, accountability, and transparency. The company's guidelines ensure that AI technologies do not perpetuate or exacerbate biases. Microsoft has committed to developing and deploying AI systems that uphold these principles and avoid discriminatory outcomes (Microsoft, 2021).
- **Partnerships and Advocacy:** Microsoft has actively engaged in advocacy efforts to promote responsible AI practices. The company has collaborated with organizations, policymakers, and academic institutions to support the development of ethical AI regulations and standards. For example, Microsoft has supported the development of the "AI Now Institute's" recommendations for algorithmic accountability and transparency (Microsoft, 2021).

Broader Industry Trends

The actions taken by IBM and Microsoft are part of a broader trend within the tech industry toward greater ethical accountability. Several other companies are also reevaluating their practices and making commitments to address AI biases:

- **Google's AI Principles:** Google has introduced a set of AI principles that guide the development and deployment of its technologies. These principles include commitments to avoid creating or reinforcing unfair biases and ensuring that AI applications are used for socially beneficial purposes (Google AI Principles, 2020).
- **Amazon's Moratorium:** Amazon implemented a temporary moratorium on using its facial recognition technology by law enforcement agencies in response to concerns about bias and privacy. The company has called for more explicit federal regulations and has committed to revisiting its policies as legislative frameworks evolve (Amazon, 2020).

Implications and Future Directions in Addressing Ethical Considerations in AI

Ethical Considerations in AI Development

Technology companies' growing awareness and actions, such as IBM and Microsoft, underscore integrating ethical considerations into developing and deploying AI technologies. This shift in focus reflects a broader understanding that technological innovation cannot be isolated from its societal impacts. The ethical implications of AI, particularly facial recognition, are becoming increasingly central to discussions about responsible technology use (Crawford, 2021; Jobin, Ienca, & Vayena, 2019). This realization highlights several critical implications for the future:

- **Design for Inclusivity:** Ethical AI development requires designing systems that account for diverse user needs and minimize biases. This involves incorporating fairness and inclusivity into AI development's design and testing phases (Schwartz et al., 2022). Companies must ensure their technologies are tested across varied demographic groups to avoid perpetuating existing biases or creating new forms of discrimination (Buolamwini & Gebru 2018; Raji et al., 2020).
- **Transparency and Accountability:** There is a growing demand for transparency in how AI systems are designed, deployed, and monitored. Companies must disclose information about their algorithms, including how they are trained, what data they use, and how they address potential biases (Morley et al., 2020). Accountability mechanisms should address issues from AI technologies, including transparent reporting and rectification processes (Whittaker et al., 2018).

Engagement with Diverse Stakeholders

As technology companies grapple with the ethical implications of AI, engaging with a broad range of stakeholders becomes crucial. These include:

- **Inclusion of Marginalized Groups:** Engaging with communities most affected by AI technologies, such as marginalized or underserved groups, is essential for understanding their full impact (Dastin, 2018). Their insights can help identify potential issues early and guide the development of more equitable solutions (Schwartz et al., 2022).
- **Collaboration with Experts:** Companies should collaborate with ethics, law, and social sciences experts to comprehensively understand their tech-

nologies' implications (Binn, 2018). This interdisciplinary approach can provide valuable perspectives on addressing ethical issues and developing best practices for responsible AI deployment (Crawford, 2021).
- **Public and Policy Engagement:** Technology companies must engage with policymakers and the public to advocate for and support the development of robust regulatory frameworks. This involves participating in policy discussions, supporting legislation that promotes ethical AI practices, and educating the public about the implications of AI technologies (Morley et al., 2020; Jobin et al., 2019).

Supporting Regulatory Efforts

Effective regulation ensures that AI technologies are developed and used to promote fairness and equity. The role of technology companies in supporting regulatory efforts includes:

- **Advocating for Clear Standards:** Companies should advocate for establishing clear and comprehensive regulatory standards for AI technologies. These standards should address bias, privacy, and accountability issues and provide a framework for ethical AI development and deployment (Gasser & Almeida, 2017; Zuboff, 2019).
- **Compliance with Regulations:** Adhering to existing and emerging regulations is essential for maintaining ethical standards. Companies must ensure that their AI systems comply with legal requirements and actively work to meet or exceed regulatory expectations (Floridi et. al., 2018).
- **Contributing to Policy Development:** Technology companies can proactively shape AI policy by providing input on regulatory proposals and participating in policy-making processes. This involvement helps ensure that regulations are informed by practical industry knowledge and address real-world challenges (Jobin et al., 2019; Morley et al., 2019).

Promoting Ethical AI Practices Across Industries

Ethical AI should extend beyond individual companies to influence broader industry practices. This includes:

- **Setting Industry Standards:** Leading companies can set examples by establishing industry-wide standards for ethical AI practices. These standards can serve as benchmarks for other organizations and promote consistency in addressing ethical challenges (Crawford, 2021; Whittaker et al., 2018).

- **Encouraging Best Practices:** Sharing best practices and lessons learned from ethical AI initiatives can help other organizations improve their practices. Collaboration across the industry can lead to the development of innovative solutions and more effective strategies for mitigating bias (Schwartz et al., 2020; Abdalla & Abdalla, 2021).
- **Fostering a Culture of Ethics:** Creating a culture of ethics within organizations is crucial for promoting responsible AI development. This involves integrating ethical considerations into decision-making processes, training employees on moral issues, and prioritizing ethical considerations in strategic planning (Floridi et al., 2018; Gasser & Almeida, 2017).

The growing focus on ethical considerations in AI development, as evidenced by the actions of significant technology companies, signifies a crucial step toward addressing the broader societal impacts of these technologies. By prioritizing ethics, engaging with diverse stakeholders, and supporting regulatory efforts, technology companies can contribute to developing AI systems that promote fairness, equity, and positive societal outcomes. Moving forward, a collaborative and proactive approach will be essential for navigating the complex ethical landscape of AI and ensuring that technological advancements benefit all members of society.

Ethical and Business Considerations in Mitigating Racial Bias in AI

The intersection of business practices and ethical considerations in mitigating racial bias in AI is becoming increasingly critical as technology evolves and impacts diverse aspects of society. Companies recognize the importance of integrating ethical practices into their business models to ensure their AI technologies do not perpetuate or exacerbate existing biases. Here is a detailed exploration of how business practices and ethical considerations intersect in this context:

1. Investment in Diverse Data Sets Investing in diverse datasets is a crucial step toward addressing racial bias in artificial intelligence (AI) systems, especially those used in facial recognition, which heavily depends on the data they are trained on. Historically, datasets have been dominated by specific demographic groups, leading to biased outcomes when deployed in diverse real-world settings (Buolamwini & Gebru, 2018; Raji et al., 2020). • Data Collection and Curation: Companies now focus on collecting and curating datasets more representative of various demographic groups, including race, gender, age, and socioeconomic status. This involves increasing the volume of data and ensuring that the data reflects a broad spectrum of real-world scenarios (Crawford, 2021; Birhane & Prabhu, 2021). • Collaboration with Diverse Stakeholders: To enhance data

diversity, organizations are partnering with academic institutions, non-profits, and community organizations with expertise in collecting and managing diverse data. These collaboration helps ensure that data collection practices are ethical and inclusive (Whittaker et al., 2018; Barocas, Hardt, & Narayanan, 2023).
• Ethical Data Sourcing: It is crucial to ensure that data is sourced ethically, with proper consent and respect for privacy. Companies must avoid using data collected without consent or through exploitative practices, which can further marginalize already vulnerable communities (Green & Viljoen, 2020; Raji et al., 2020).

2. Developing Inclusive Algorithms Alongside investing in diverse datasets, companies are developing algorithms designed to be more inclusive and representative of all demographic groups. These involves: • Bias Mitigation Techniques: Techniques like fairness-aware machine learning, which adjusts training processes to account for data imbalances, are crucial in reducing bias (Hardt, Price, & Srebro, 2016; Mehrabi et al., 2021). This helps create algorithms that perform equitably across different groups. • Continuous Improvement: Developing algorithms is an ongoing process. Companies adopt iterative approaches, continuously refining their algorithms based on feedback and performance metrics. Regular updates and improvements help address emerging biases and ensure the technology remains equitable (Holstein et al., 2019; Raji et al., 2020). • Interdisciplinary Teams: To ensure that algorithms are developed with a holistic understanding of potential biases, companies are assembling multidisciplinary teams that include data scientists, ethicists, sociologists, and representatives from affected communities. This diversity in expertise helps identify and address potential biases more effectively (Abdalla & Abdalla, 2021; Binns, 2017).

3. Regular Bias Audits and Transparency Reports Companies are adopting practices such as regular bias audits and transparency reports to maintain accountability and transparency. These practices are vital for assessing and addressing biases in AI systems and fostering trust among users and stakeholders. • Bias Audits: Regular bias audits involve systematically evaluating AI systems to identify and measure any biases in their performance. These audits are typically carried out by internal teams or third-party experts who can objectively assess the technology's impact across different demographic groups (Raji et al., 2020; Binns, 2017). • Transparency Reports: Companies publish transparency reports detailing their efforts to address biases, the results of bias audits, and the steps they take to improve their AI systems. These reports give stakeholders insights into how companies manage ethical concerns and hold them accountable for their commitments (Crawford, 2021; Whittaker et al., 2018). • Public Disclosure and Feedback Mechanisms: Providing platforms for public disclosure and feedback allows users to report issues related to bias and discrimination. This feedback is

invaluable for companies to make informed improvements and address concerns raised by affected individuals and communities (Zuboff, 2019; Binns, 2017).
4. Integration of Ethical Practices into Business Models Companies must embed these principles into their core business models and decision-making processes for ethical considerations to be effectively integrated into business practices. • Ethics Training and Culture: Companies are implementing ethics training programs for their employees, focusing on ethical AI practices and the potential impacts of biases. Creating a culture of ethics within the organization ensures that all employees understand and prioritize fairness (Floridi et al., 2018; Taddeo & Floridi, 2018). • Ethical Leadership and Governance: Strong ethical leadership is essential for driving and maintaining a commitment to ethical AI practices. Establishing governance structures, such as ethics committees or advisory boards, helps oversee AI development and ensure that moral considerations are consistently addressed (Gasser & Almeida, 2017; Morley et al., 2020). • Regulatory Compliance and Advocacy: Companies adhere to existing regulations and advocate for more robust regulatory frameworks that address AI bias and promote fairness. Engaging with policymakers and contributing to developing industry standards reflects a proactive approach to ethical considerations (Jobin et al., 2019; Wagner, 2019).
5. Balancing Business Objectives with Ethical Imperatives While addressing racial bias is crucial, companies must balance these ethical imperatives with their business objectives. This balance involves: • Economic Viability: Ensuring ethical practices are economically viable is crucial. Companies must demonstrate that investing in diverse data sets and inclusive algorithms is ethically correct and contributes to long-term business success by improving product quality and customer trust (Floridi et al., 2018; Taddeo & Floridi, 2018).

• Competitive Advantage: Emphasizing the competitive advantage of being a leader in ethical AI practices. Companies that proactively address biases and promote fairness can differentiate themselves in the market and build stronger relationships with customers and partners (Zuboff, 2019; Crawford, 2021).

The intersection of business practices and ethical considerations in mitigating racial bias in AI is dynamic and evolving. Companies increasingly recognize the importance of integrating ethical practices into their business models to ensure that their technologies are fair and equitable. By investing in diverse data sets, developing inclusive algorithms, conducting regular bias audits, and embedding ethical practices into their core business operations, organizations can contribute to the responsible development and deployment of AI technologies. Companies must continue prioritizing these considerations, engaging with diverse stakeholders, and supporting regulatory efforts to promote fairness and equity in AI systems.

Future Directions: Aligning Corporate Practices with International Regulatory Frameworks to Mitigate Racial Bias in Facial Recognition Technology

As the ethical implications of FRT become increasingly apparent, aligning corporate practices with international regulatory frameworks is essential for creating a more robust approach to mitigating racial bias. Research emphasizes that collaboration between businesses and regulators ensures that artificial intelligence (AI) technologies are developed and deployed ethically, promoting racial equity globally (Crawford, 2021; Whittaker et al., 2018). The following outlines key future directions for advancing these efforts:

Enhanced Collaboration Between Corporations and Regulators

A. Developing Collaborative Frameworks
    - Joint Task Forces and Advisory Panels: Establishing joint task forces or advisory panels that include representatives from technology companies, regulatory bodies, academic institutions, and civil society organizations can facilitate the exchange of knowledge and best practices (Floridi et al., 2018). These bodies can work on creating guidelines that balance innovation with ethical considerations (Gasser & Almeida, 2017).
    - Public-Private Partnerships: Forming public-private partnerships can enable businesses and regulators to collaborate on developing standards and regulations that address both technological advancements and ethical concerns (Taddeo & Floridi, 2018). Such partnerships can leverage the strengths of both sectors to create more effective solutions (Zuboff, 2019).
B. Co-Designing Regulatory Standards
    - Inclusive Policy Development: Involving technology companies in policymaking can help ensure that regulations are practical and achievable while maintaining high ethical standards (AI Now Institute, 2020). This can also provide a platform for companies to express their concerns and suggestions for effective regulation (Barocas et al., 2019).
    - Global Harmonization: Efforts to harmonize regulations across different countries can simplify compliance for multinational companies and ensure that AI technologies adhere to consistent ethical standards worldwide (Gasser & Schulz, 2015. International agreements and collaborative regulatory initiatives can promote ethical AI deployment globally (Wagner, 2019).

Implementing and Enforcing Ethical Standards

A. Standardizing Ethical Guidelines
   - Creating Universal Standards: Developing universal ethical standards for AI technologies, including facial recognition, can provide a common framework for evaluating and mitigating biases (Jobin et al., 2019). These standards should cover data diversity, algorithmic fairness, and transparency (Raji et al., 2020).
   - Certification Programs: Introducing certification programs for AI technologies that meet established ethical guidelines can incentivize companies to adhere to best practices (Morley et al., 2020). Certification can also enhance consumer trust and demonstrate a commitment to moral principles (Binns, 2017).
B. Strengthening Enforcement Mechanisms
   - Regulatory Oversight: Regulators must ensure that companies comply with ethical guidelines through regular audits and inspections (Whittaker et al., 2018). Effective enforcement mechanisms should include penalties for non-compliance and incentives for exceeding ethical standards (Gasser & Almeida, 2017).
   - Transparency Requirements: Mandating transparency in AI development and deployment, including public disclosure of bias audits and algorithmic performance metrics, can enhance accountability (Crawford, 2021). This allows stakeholders to assess the ethical practices of technology providers and holds companies responsible for maintaining fairness and accuracy in their AI systems (Binns, 2017)

Promoting Inclusive Data Practices

A. Expanding Data Collection Practices
   - Inclusive Data Sampling: Encouraging or requiring companies to expand their data collection practices including diverse demographic groups can help reduce biases in AI systems. This includes collecting data that reflects various races, ethnicities, genders, and socioeconomic backgrounds (Gebru et al., 2020; Hanna et al., 2020).
   - Ethical Data Usage: Implementing guidelines for the ethical use of data, including obtaining informed consent and ensuring data privacy, can help address data exploitation and discrimination concerns (Floridi, 2013; Crawford & Schultz, 2014).

B. Supporting Research and Development
- Funding and Grants: Providing funding and grants for research focused on developing techniques to reduce bias in AI can drive innovation and encourage companies to invest in more equitable technologies. The public and private sectors can collaborate to support research initiatives (Whittaker et al., 2018).
- Collaborative Research Initiatives: Promoting collaborative research initiatives between academia and industry can facilitate the development of new methodologies and tools for addressing racial bias in facial recognition and other AI systems (Binns, 2017; Raji et al., 2020).

Enhancing Public Engagement and Awareness

A. Increasing Public Education:
- Awareness Campaigns: Launching public awareness campaigns about the potential biases in facial recognition technology and the steps to address them can foster greater understanding and support for ethical AI practice (Whittaker et al., 2018; Binns, 2017).
- Educational Programs: Implementing educational programs and workshops for consumers and technology professionals can enhance knowledge about AI ethics and the importance of mitigating bias (Schiff et al., 2021).

B. Engaging Affected Communities
- Community Consultations: Engaging with communities affected by facial recognition technology can provide valuable insights into their concerns and experiences. This can help ensure that technological solutions are responsive to the needs of those most impacted (Benjamin, 2019).
- Feedback Mechanisms: Creating mechanisms for ongoing feedback from affected individuals and communities can help companies and regulators more effectively identify and address issues related to racial bias (Crawford, 2021; Whittaker et al., 2018).

Assessing and Adapting to Emerging Challenges

A. Monitoring Technological Advancements:
- Continuous Evaluation: Regularly assessing the impact of new technological developments on racial bias is crucial for adapting ethical guidelines and regulatory frameworks. This includes monitoring advance-

ments in facial recognition technology and other AI systems (Eubanks, 2018).
- Adaptive Regulations: Developing adaptive regulatory approaches that can quickly respond to emerging challenges and technological changes can help ensure that ethical standards remain relevant and practical (Cath, 2018).

B. Addressing Global Disparities:
- Differentiated Approaches: Different regions may have varying technological infrastructure and regulatory capacity levels, so differentiated approaches may be needed to address racial bias in AI. Tailoring strategies to local contexts can enhance the effectiveness of global efforts (Noble, 2018).

The future directions outlined above emphasize the need for a collaborative and comprehensive approach to addressing racial bias in facial recognition technology. By fostering collaboration between corporations and regulators, implementing, and enforcing ethical standards, promoting inclusive data practices, enhancing public engagement, and adapting to emerging challenges, stakeholders can work together to ensure that AI technologies are developed and deployed to promote fairness and equity globally. This research aims to contribute to these efforts by identifying effective strategies and exploring how businesses and regulators can align their practices to address the ethical implications of AI technologies.

ETHICAL IMPLICATIONS OF FACIAL RECOGNITION TECHNOLOGY

The deployment of FRT by law enforcement agencies raises significant ethical concerns, deeply intertwined with historical injustices faced by minority communities. Understanding these concerns necessitates examining how past practices influence present ethical considerations, the specific obligations of law enforcement, and the application of various ethical frameworks.

Historical Context and Its Influence on Present Ethical Considerations

A. Historical Injustices and Systemic Biases:
- Legacy of Discrimination: Historical practices such as racial profiling, discriminatory policing, and the criminalization of marginalized com-

munities have left legacies of mistrust and inequality ended. Introducing FRT into these contexts can exacerbate existing biases and reinforce systemic discrimination (Eubanks, 2018; Noble, 2018). Historical injustices, such as those seen during the Civil Rights era, provide a backdrop for understanding why communities of color may view FRT with suspicion and concern (Benjamin, 2019)
- Impact of Historical Surveillance: Historical surveillance practices, including COINTELPRO and other government monitoring programs, have disproportionately targeted minority groups. The continuation of surveillance technologies like FRT can evoke fears of repeat patterns of abuse and exacerbate existing concerns about state overreach and privacy violations (Browne, 2015; Brayne, 2020).

B. Perception and Trust:
- Erosion of Trust: The historical mistrust between law enforcement and marginalized communities is compounded by the deployment of FRT, especially when it is perceived as an extension of discriminatory practices. This mistrust can lead to resistance and skepticism about the technology's intent and effectiveness (Feldstein, 2021; Benjamin, 2019).
- Historical Precedents: Understanding past surveillance abuses helps contextualize current debates around FRT, highlighting the need to consider carefully how these technologies are implemented and regulated (Brayne, 2020).

Obligations of Law Enforcement Agencies

A. Ethical Use of Technology
- Adherence to Fairness Principles: Law enforcement agencies must ensure that facial recognition technology (FRT) is used fairly and equitably. This involves avoiding practices disproportionately impacting specific demographic groups and ensuring that technology deployment does not perpetuate existing biases (Buolamwini & Gebru, 2018; Ferguson, 2021). Research has shown that FRT systems often exhibit higher error rates for individuals from minority groups, which can lead to discriminatory outcomes (Raji & Buolamwini, 2020).
- Transparency and Accountability: Agencies must operate transparently, providing clear information about how FRT is used, the criteria for its deployment, and mechanisms for addressing errors or misuse (Brayne, 2020). Transparency includes disclosing the datasets used for training these systems and outlining the specific circumstances under which

FRT will be deployed (Crawford, 2019). Accountability measures, such as third-party audits and oversight boards, can help monitor the technology's impact and address any negative consequences (Whittaker et al., 2018).

B. Compliance with Ethical Standards
- Ethical Guidelines: Law enforcement should follow established ethical guidelines for using AI and surveillance technologies, which include respecting privacy, ensuring accuracy, and minimizing harm (Floridi et al., 2018). Ethical frameworks such as the IEEE's Ethically Aligned Design and the AI Now Institute's guidelines emphasize the need to ensure that AI technologies do not exacerbate inequality or lead to unjust outcomes (AI Now, 2018; IEEE, 2019).
- Public Engagement: Engaging with the public, particularly affected communities, is crucial for understanding their concerns and ensuring that FRT practices align with community values and expectations (Eubanks, 2018).

Application of Ethical Frameworks

A. Deontological Ethics
- Rights-Based Approach: From a deontological perspective, law enforcement's use of FRT must respect individuals' rights to privacy and due process. This approach emphasizes the moral obligation to protect these fundamental rights, regardless of the potential benefits or efficiencies that FRT might offer (Beauchamp & Childress, 2019).
- Duty of Care: Law enforcement agencies must ensure their technologies do not violate ethical principles or exacerbate existing inequalities. This includes conducting thorough impact assessments and ensuring technology use does not infringe on civil liberties (Alexander & Moore, 2020).

B. Utilitarian Ethics
- Balancing Benefits and Harms: A practical approach evaluates FRT by balancing benefits and harms. While FRT may offer enhanced public safety and crime prevention benefits, these must be weighed against potential harms, including privacy violations and the risk of perpetuating biases (Mill, 1863). Ethical deployment requires ensuring that the overall benefits outweigh the potential harms and that measures are in place to mitigate any negative impacts (Rachels & Rachels, 2015).

- Equitable Distribution of Benefits: Utilitarian ethics also considers the equitable distribution of benefits. Ensuring that the advantages of FRT are shared relatively across all demographic groups is essential for achieving ethical outcomes (Singer, 2002).

C. Virtue Ethics
- Character and Integrity: Virtue ethics emphasizes the character and integrity of those implementing FRT. Law enforcement agencies should embody virtues such as fairness, justice, and respect for human dignity in their use of technology. This approach focuses on cultivating ethical practices and attitudes within the agency rather than solely adhering to rules or calculating outcomes (Hursthouse, 2001).
- Moral Leadership: Agencies should demonstrate moral leadership by setting an example in ethical conduct and fostering a culture of responsibility and respect for all individuals. This includes promoting ethical decision-making and ensuring technology use aligns with the community's values (MacIntyre, 1981).

D. Procedural Justice
- Fairness in Processes: Procedural justice emphasizes the fairness of the processes by which decisions are made, including the deployment of FRT. Ensuring that decision-making processes are transparent, inclusive, and accountable is crucial for maintaining public trust and ensuring ethical practices (Tyler, 1990).
- Community Involvement: Involving community members in discussions about FRT deployment and its implications helps ensure that diverse perspectives are considered and that decisions reflect the values and concerns of those affected (Thibaut & Walker, 1975).

The ethical implications of facial recognition technology are complex and multifaceted, influenced by historical injustices, the obligations of law enforcement, and the application of various ethical frameworks. Addressing these concerns requires a nuanced understanding of how past practices shape present ethical considerations, a commitment to fair and transparent use of technology, and adherence to moral principles prioritizing privacy, fairness, and respect for individual rights. By engaging with these issues, stakeholders can work towards more equitable and responsible deployment of FRT, ensuring that technology serves the broader goal of justice and social equity.

Historical Context of Injustice

Historical injustices, including racial profiling, discriminatory surveillance, and over-policing, have significantly damaged the trust between minority communities and law enforcement. For example, the "War on Drugs" disproportionately targeted Black and Latino communities, leading to systemic inequities and widespread mistrust of law enforcement practices (Alexander, 2010). Similarly, the extensive surveillance of civil rights activists during the 1960s has left a legacy of skepticism toward state monitoring (Davis, 2017). These historical contexts create a backdrop of apprehension regarding any new technological interventions by law enforcement, often seen as extensions of past abuses (Davis, 2017).

Facial recognition technology, with its potential for widespread surveillance and data collection, is particularly troubling because it often inherits biases from its training datasets. Research has shown that FRT systems frequently misidentify individuals from minority backgrounds at higher rates than those from majority groups, exacerbating existing disparities and perpetuating historical biases (Buolamwini & Gebru, 2018). This context highlights the need for rigorous ethical scrutiny of FRT deployment to avoid reinforcing and amplifying these pre-existing biases.

Ethical Obligations of Law Enforcement Agencies

Given the historical mistrust and the potential for FRT to perpetuate biases, law enforcement agencies have several critical ethical obligations:

- Transparent Decision-Making: Agencies must ensure transparency regarding using FRT, including the criteria for its deployment and the potential impacts on affected communities. This transparency is vital for rebuilding trust and ensuring technology is used consistently with ethical standards (O'Neil, 2016). Publicizing policies, impact assessments, and operational guidelines can help mitigate concerns and enhance accountability.
- Involving Diverse Stakeholders: Law enforcement agencies must engage diverse stakeholders in the development and deployment of FRT. This includes representatives from marginalized communities who can provide insights into potential biases and unintended consequences of the technology (Crawford, 2016). This participatory approach helps ensure that the technology serves all community segments equitably and aligns with principles of justice and fairness.
- Accountability for Misidentification: Agencies must implement robust mechanisms for addressing errors and ensuring accountability for wrongful arrests and other harms resulting from misidentification. Effective oversight and re-

view processes are necessary to rectify errors and prevent damage, thereby promoting public confidence in the fairness of technological applications (Eubanks, 2018).

Ethical Frameworks for Guiding FRT Deployment

Several ethical frameworks offer valuable guidance for developing and deploying FRT in a manner that prioritizes fairness and equity:

- Distributive Justice: This framework emphasizes the fair distribution of benefits and burdens across society. In the context of FRT, it implies that the benefits of technology should be equitably shared, and the risks minimized for vulnerable populations. This approach advocates carefully examining how FRT affects different demographic groups to ensure that no group disproportionately bears harm (Rawls, 1971; Sen, 2009).
- Ethics of Care: The Ethics of Care focuses on the importance of empathy and relational considerations in ethical decision-making. Applying this framework to FRT suggests that technology should be developed and used with a deep understanding of its impacts on individuals, especially marginalized communities. This approach calls for a compassionate and context-sensitive application of technology that considers these communities' lived experiences and concerns (Held, 2006).

RECOMMENDATIONS

Several vital recommendations are essential for addressing racial bias in FRT:

1. Enhancing Organizational Diversity • Diversity in Leadership and Technical Teams: To prevent biases that arise from homogeneous decision-making, it is crucial to increase diversity within leadership and technical teams involved in the development and deployment of FRT. This approach aims to incorporate a broader range of perspectives and experiences, ensuring that technology is designed with consideration for all demographic groups (Nazer et al., 2023). • Inclusive Decision-Making Processes: Implement decision-making processes that actively include input from diverse stakeholders, including marginalized communities. This will help identify potential biases early and ensure that technology meets the needs of all users (Nazer et al., 2023).

2. Strengthening Data Collection and Management Practices • Investing in Diverse Data Sets: Develop and utilize data sets that accurately represent diverse demographic groups to improve FRT performance across different populations. This approach addresses existing disparities and enhances the accuracy of the technology (Buolamwini & Gebru, 2018). • Conducting Regular Bias Audits: Establish procedures for ongoing bias audits to monitor and address any biases that may emerge in FRT systems. This ensures that the technology remains fair and equitable over time (Raji & Buolamwini, 2020).
3. Promoting Transparency and Accountability • Developing Transparency Reports: Create and publish regular transparency reports detailing FRT's performance and impact of fairness, security, and equity. These reports should provide insights into the technology used and its effects on different communities (Raji & Buolamwini, 2020). • Establishing Accountability Mechanisms: Implement precise accountability mechanisms for addressing errors and misuse of FRT. This includes setting up processes for reporting and rectifying issues related to bias and inaccuracies (Raji & Buolamwini, 2020).
4. Aligning with International Regulatory Frameworks • Compliance with Global Standards: Ensure FRT practices adhere to international regulatory frameworks such as the General Data Protection Regulation (GDPR). This alignment helps uphold ethical standards and protect user rights globally (Wachter et al., 2016). • Engaging with International Regulators: Collaborate with global regulatory bodies to contribute to developing comprehensive ethical guidelines for AI technologies. Engaging with international regulators promotes a unified approach to addressing racial bias and other moral concerns (Wachter et al., 2016).
5. Fostering Cross-Sector Collaboration • Engaging with Diverse Stakeholders: Collaborate with academic institutions, civil society organizations, and industry leaders to share best practices and address racial bias in FRT. Cross-sector collaboration helps develop more equitable solutions and advance the overall ethical use of technology (Freeman, 1984).

FUTURE RESEARCH

Future research should focus on several critical areas to advance the understanding and mitigation of racial bias in facial recognition technology:

1. Integrating Theoretical Frameworks with Technical Analysis
    - Exploring Theoretical Insights: Investigate how organizational and social network theories intersect with technical analyses of facial recognition algorithms. This research aims to bridge the gap between theoretical

frameworks and practical applications in AI technology (Buolamwini & Gebru, 2018).
- Empirical Validation: Conduct empirical studies to validate the impact of organizational structures and social networks on the prevalence and mitigation of biases in facial recognition systems (Burt, 2000).
2. Exploring Global Perspectives and Regulatory Approaches
   - Comparative Analysis of Regulatory Frameworks: Examine how different countries regulate facial recognition technology and assess the effectiveness of these approaches in mitigating racial bias. This research will provide insights into best practices and areas for improvement (Slobogin & Brayne, 2023).
   - International Collaboration Opportunities: Explore opportunities for international collaboration to develop unified ethical standards for AI technologies. This approach helps address racial bias challenges and ensure equitable deployment (Leibold, 2020).
3. Evaluating the Impact of Corporate Practices
   - Assessing Corporate Initiatives: Evaluate how corporate practices and internal guidelines influence the reduction of racial bias in facial recognition technology. This research will determine these initiatives' effectiveness and identify areas for improvement (Raji & Buolamwini, 2020).
   - Longitudinal Studies: Perform longitudinal studies to assess the long-term impact of corporate and regulatory measures on the fairness and accuracy of facial recognition systems (Raji & Buolamwini, 2020).

CONCLUSION

The integration of organizational and social network theories offers a robust framework for addressing the pervasive issue of racial bias in FRT. As this chapter has demonstrated, the biases embedded in FRT systems are not solely technological flaws but are deeply entwined with the organizational structures, decision-making processes, and social networks that shape the development and deployment of these systems. Empirical evidence, such as Buolamwini and Gebru's (2018) research, has shown how algorithmic biases manifest in gender and racial misidentification, while scholars like Ferguson (2020) have highlighted the real-world consequences of biased technologies, particularly in law enforcement. These biases reflect broader societal inequalities and institutional norms, often replicated within the technologies.

By applying organizational theory, we gain critical insights into how institutional practices, leadership structures, and policies exacerbate or mitigate bias. For example, theories such as Weber's Bureaucracy Model and Contingency Theory reveal that rigid organizational structures and homogeneous leadership teams may perpetuate biases by failing to incorporate diverse perspectives. Nazer et al., 2023 suggest increasing diversity within leadership and technical teams is essential for disrupting entrenched biases and fostering inclusive technological development. Additionally, institutional theory (DiMaggio & Powell, 1983) emphasizes the importance of aligning organizational policies with ethical standards, ensuring that the development and deployment of FRT systems adhere to principles of fairness, equity, and transparency.

Social network theory further enriches this analysis by illuminating how information flows through networks and how these networks propagate or mitigate biases. Concepts like Granovetter's Strength of Weak Ties and Burt's Structural Holes emphasize the importance of diverse and inclusive data-sharing networks. When organizations rely on limited and homogeneous data sources, as seen in many current FRT datasets, they inadvertently reinforce existing biases. Expanding the diversity of data sources and involving marginalized communities in data-sharing can mitigate these biases and result in more equitable technological outcomes. As Burt (2000) suggests, diverse networks foster innovation and fairness, making them critical to addressing biases in FRT.

The chapter also underscores the empirical evidence supporting these theoretical approaches' needs. Research by Richardson et al., 2019 reveals the inadequacies of existing FRT datasets, which often exclude or underrepresent individuals from minority groups. These dataset limitations perpetuate racial biases in FRT systems, resulting in disproportionate harm to marginalized populations, particularly in areas like law enforcement. Moreover, international perspectives, such as Leibold's (2020) analysis of FRT in China, demonstrate that the racial bias in these systems is a global issue with severe human rights implications.

Addressing these biases requires more than technical fixes it demands systemic change. Organizations must restructure their internal practices, leadership, and data-sharing networks to ensure fairness and equity are built into the development process from the outset. Stakeholder Theory (Freeman, 1984) complements these organizational and network perspectives by advocating for the inclusion of diverse stakeholders in decision-making processes. Engaging marginalized communities, who are often disproportionately affected by biased FRT systems, in the design and implementation phases is crucial for creating ethical and fair technologies.

Finally, Technological Determinism, when integrated with organizational and social network theories, highlights the dual role of technology as both a reflection of societal inequalities and a tool for transformation. The ethical design and deployment of FRT systems depend on recognizing the potential for technology to reinforce inequalities while leveraging organizational and network interventions to promote equity. Global regulatory frameworks, such as the GDPR in Europe, and corporate approaches to mitigating bias must also be part of the broader solution, ensuring that FRT systems align with human rights and ethical standards (Slobogin & Brayne, 2023).

In conclusion, the interdisciplinary integration of organizational theory, social network theory, and empirical evidence provides a comprehensive and nuanced approach to addressing racial bias in facial recognition technology. By reforming organizational structures, diversifying leadership, and data-sharing networks, and implementing inclusive and ethical practices, we can mitigate the racial biases embedded in FRT and work toward more equitable technological futures. This multifaceted approach ensures that technology serves all communities fairly and justly rather than perpetuating systemic inequities. Future research and policy must continue to bridge these theoretical frameworks with practical solutions to foster a fair and inclusive digital society.

REFERENCES

Abdalla, M., & Abdalla, M. (2021). The grey hoodie project: Big tobacco, big tech, and the threat on academic integrity. *FACT '21: Proceedings of the 2021 ACM Conference on Fairness, Accountability, and Transparency*, 854-865. DOI: 10.1145/3461702.3462563

Adams, J. S. (1965). Inequity in social exchange. *Advances in Experimental Social Psychology*, 2, 267–299. DOI: 10.1016/S0065-2601(08)60108-2

AI Now Institute. (2018). *AI Now 2018 report*. AI Now Institute. Retrieved from https://ainowinstitute.org/reports.html

AI Now Institute. (2020). *AI Now 2020 report*. AI Now Institute. Retrieved from https://ainowinstitute.org/reports.html

Alexander, L., & Moore, M. (2020). Deontological ethics. In Zalta, E. N. (Ed.), *The Stanford Encyclopedia of Philosophy*.

Alexander, M. (2010). *The new Jim crow: Mass incarceration in the age of colorblindness*. The New Press.

Amazon (2020). *Amazon's approach to responsible AI*. Retrieved from https://aws.amazon.com/machine-learning/responsible-ai

Barocas, S., Hardt, M., & Narayanan, A. (2023). *Fairness and machine learning: Limitations and opportunities*. MIT Press.

Beauchamp, T. L., & Childress, J. F. (2019). *Principles of biomedical ethics* (8th ed.). Oxford University Press., DOI: 10.1080/15265161.2019.1665402

Benjamin, R. (2019). Race after technology: Abolitionist tools for the new Jim code. *Polity*.

Binns, R. (2017). Fairness in machine learning: Lessons from political philosophy. DOI:/arXiv.1712.03586DOI: 10.48550

Birhane, A., & Prabhu, V. U. (2021). Large image datasets: A pyrrhic win for computer vision? /arXiv.2006.16923DOI: 10.1109/WACV48630.2021.00158

Bostrom, N., & Yudkowsky, E. (2014). The Ethics of Artificial Intelligence. In *Cambridge Handbook of Artificial Intelligence* (pp. 316–334). Cambridge University Press., DOI: 10.1017/CBO9781139046855.020

Brayne, S. (2020). *Predict and surveil: Data, discretion, and the future of policing*. Oxford University Press. DOI: 10.1093/oso/9780190684099.001.0001

Browne, S. (2015). *Dark matters: On the surveillance of blackness*. Duke University Press., DOI: 10.2307/j.ctv11cw89p

Buolamwini, J., & Gebru, T. (2018). Gender shades: Intersectional accuracy disparities in commercial gender classification. [Conference on Fairness, Accountability, and Transparency] [FAT]. *Proceedings of Machine Learning Research*, 81, 1–15.

Burns, T., & Stalker, G. M. (1961). *The management of innovation*. Tavistock Publications.

Burrell, G., & Morgan, G. (1979). *Sociological paradigms and organizational analysis: Elements of the sociology of corporate life*. Heinemann Educational Books., DOI: 10.4324/9781315609751

Burt, R. S. (1992). *Structural holes: The social structure of competition*. Harvard University Press. DOI: 10.4159/9780674029095

Burt, R. S. (2000). The network structure of social capital. *Research in Organizational Behavior*, 22, 345–423. DOI: 10.1016/S0191-3085(00)22009-1

Cath, C. (2018). Governing artificial intelligence: Ethical, legal, and technical opportunities and challenges. *Philosophy & Technology*, 31(4), 685–692. DOI: 10.1098/rsta.2018.0080 PMID: 30322996

Crawford, K. (2021). *Atlas of AI: Power, politics, and the planetary costs of artificial intelligence*. Yale University Press.

Crawford, K., & Schultz, J. (2014). Big data and due process: Toward a framework to redress predictive privacy harms. *Boston College Law Review. Boston College. Law School*, 55(1), 93–128.

Crawford, K., & Schultz, J. (2019). AI systems as state actors. *Columbia Law Review*, 119(7), 1941–1972.

Creswell, J. W., & Poth, C. N. (2018). *Qualitative inquiry and research design: Choosing among five approaches*. Sage Publications.

Dastin, J. (2018). *Amazon scrapped secret AI recruiting tool that showed bias against women*. Reuters. Retrieved from https://www.reuters.com/article/us-amazon-com-jobs-automation-insight-idUSKCN1MK08G

Davis, A. J. (2017). *Policing the black man: Arrest, prosecution, and imprisonment* (1st ed.). Pantheon.

DiMaggio, P. J., & Powell, W. W. (1983). The iron cage revisited: Institutional isomorphism and collective rationality in organizational fields. *American Sociological Review*, 48(2), 147–160. DOI: 10.2307/2095101

Donaldson, L. (2001). *The Contingency Theory of Organizations*. Sage Publications. DOI: 10.4135/9781452229249

Elkington, J. (1998). *Cannibals with forks: The triple bottom line of 21st century business*. Capstone.

Eubanks, V. (2018). *Automating inequality: How high-tech tools profile, police, and punish the poor*. St. Martin's Press.

Feldstein, S. (2021). *The rise of digital repression: How technology is reshaping power, politics, and resistance*. Oxford University Press. DOI: 10.1093/oso/9780190057497.001.0001

Ferguson, A. G. (2020). *The rise of big data policing: Surveillance, race, and the future of law enforcement*. NYU Press. DOI: 10.18574/nyu/9781479854608.001.0001

Ferguson, A. G. (2021). *Surveillance and the tyrant test*. Heinonline.

Floridi, L. (2013). *The ethics of information*. Oxford University Press. DOI: 10.1093/acprof:oso/9780199641321.001.0001

Floridi, L., Cowls, J., Beltrametti, M., Chatila, R., Chazerand, P., Dignum, V., & Schafer, B. (2018). AI4People—An ethical framework for a good AI society: Opportunities, risks, principles, and recommendations. *Minds and Machines*, 28(4), 689–707. DOI: 10.1007/s11023-018-9482-5 PMID: 30930541

Freeman, R. E. (1984). *Strategic management: A stakeholder approach*. Pitman.

Garvie, C., Bedoya, A. M., & Frankle, J. (2016). *The perpetual lineup: Unregulated police face recognition in America*. Georgetown Law, Center on Privacy & Technology. https://www.perpetuallineup.org/

Gasser, U., & Almeida, V. (2017). A layered model for AI governance. *IEEE Internet Computing*, 21(6), 58–62. DOI: 10.1109/MIC.2017.4180835

Gasser, U., & Schulz, W. (2015). *Governance of online intermediaries: Observations from a series of national case studies*. Berkman Klein Center Research Publication.

Gilligan, C. (1982). *In a different voice: Psychological theory and women's development*. Harvard University Press.

Google. (2020). *Google AI principles*. Google AI. Retrieved from https://ai.google/principles

Granovetter, M. S. (1973). The strength of weak ties. *American Journal of Sociology*, 78(6), 1360–1380. https://www.jstor.org/stable/2776392. DOI: 10.1086/225469

Green, B., & Viljoen, S. (2020). Algorithmic realism: Expanding the boundaries of algorithmic thought. *FAT '20: Proceedings of the 2020 Conference on Fairness, Accountability, and Transparency*, 19-31. DOI: 10.1145/3351095.3372840

Hanna, A., Denton, E., Smart, A., & Smith-Loud, J. (2020). Towards a critical race methodology in algorithmic fairness. In *Proceedings of the 2020 Conference on Fairness, Accountability, and Transparency* (pp. 501-512). DOI: 10.1145/3351095.3372826

Hardt, M., Price, E., & Srebro, N. (2016). Equality of opportunity in supervised learning. *Advances in Neural Information Processing Systems*, 29, 3315–3323. DOI: 10.48550/arXiv.1610.02413

Held, V. (2006). *The ethics of care: Personal, political, and global*. Oxford University Press.

Holstein, K., Wortman Vaughan, J., Daumé, H.III, Dudik, M., & Wallach, H. (2019). Improving fairness in machine learning systems: What do industry practitioners need? *Proceedings of the 2019 CHI Conference on Human Factors in Computing Systems*, 1-16. DOI: 10.1145/3290605.3300830

Hursthouse, R. (2001). *On virtue ethics*. Oxford University Press., DOI: 10.1093/0199247994.001.0001

IEEE. (2019). Ethically aligned design: A vision for prioritizing human well-being with autonomous and intelligent systems *(First Edition)*. The IEEE Global Initiative on Ethics of Autonomous and Intelligent Systems. Retrieved from Autonomous and Intelligent Systems (AIS)

Jobin, A., Ienca, M., & Vayena, E. (2019). The global landscape of AI ethics guidelines. *Nature Machine Intelligence*, 1(9), 389–399. DOI: 10.1038/s42256-019-0088-2

Kuhn, T. S. (1962). *The Structure of scientific revolutions* (2nd ed.). University of Chicago Press.

Lawrence, P. R., & Lorsch, J. W. (1967). Differentiation and Integration in Complex Organizations. *Administrative Science Quarterly*, 12(1), 1–47. DOI: 10.2307/2391211

Leibold, J. (2020). *Surveillance in China's Xinjiang region: ethnic sorting, coercion, and inducement*. La Trobe. Journal contribution. DOI: 10.26181/17102798.v1

Lyon, D. (2003). *Surveillance after September 11*. Blackwell Publishing Ltd.

MacIntyre, A. (1981). *After virtue: A study in moral theory*. University of Notre Dame Press.

Mangan, D. (2024). *Meta agrees to $1.4 billion settlement in Texas biometric data lawsuit over Facebook images*. Retrieved from https://www.cnbc.com/2024/07/30/meta-agrees-to-1point4-billion-settlement-in-texas-biometric-data-lawsuit.html

McGee, E. O. (2021). *Black, Brown, Bruised: How Racialized STEM Education Stifles Innovation*. Harvard Education Press.

McLuhan, M. (1964). *Understanding Media: The Extensions of Man*. McGraw-Hill.

Mehrabi, N., Morstatter, F., Saxena, N., Lerman, K., & Galstyan, A. (2021). A survey on bias and fairness in machine learning. *ACM Computing Surveys*, 54(6), 1–35. DOI: 10.1145/3457607

Meyer, I. H. (2003). Prejudice, social stress, and mental health in lesbian, gay, and bisexual populations: Conceptual issues and research agenda. *Psychological Bulletin*, 129(5), 674–697. DOI: 10.1037/0033-2909.129.5.674 PMID: 12956539

Microsoft. (2021). *Microsoft AI principles: Responsible AI in practice*. Retrieved from https://www.microsoft.com/ai/responsible-ai

Mill, J. S. (1863). *Utilitarianism*. Parker, Son, and Bourn.

Minh-Ha, L. (2024). *Beyond recognition: Privacy protections in a surveilled world*. Linkoping University. DOI: 10.3384/9789180756761

Moody, B. K. (2023). *Bearing witness to terror and triumph: A narrative inquiry into black men's healing after police brutality*. Retrieved from https://marymountuniv.idm.oclc.org/login?url=https://www.proquest.com/dissertations-theses/bearing-witness-terror-triumph-narrative-inquiry/docview/2838439933/se-2

Morley, J., Floridi, L., Kinsey, L., & Elhalal, A. (2020). From what to how: An initial review of publicly available AI ethics tools, methods and research to translate principles into practices. *Science and Engineering Ethics*, 26(4), 2141–2168. DOI: 10.1007/s11948-019-00165-5 PMID: 31828533

Nazer, L. H., Zatarah, R., Waldrip, S., Ke, J. X. C., Moukheiber, M., Khanna, A. K., Hicklen, R. S., Moukheiber, L., Moukheiber, D., Ma, H., & Mathur, P. (2023). Bias in artificial intelligence algorithms and recommendations for mitigation. *PLOS Digital Health*, 2(6), e0000278. DOI: 10.1371/journal.pdig.0000278 PMID: 37347721

Noble, S. U. (2018). *Algorithms of oppression: How search engines reinforce racism*. NYU Press. DOI: 10.18574/nyu/9781479833641.001.0001

O'Neil, C. (2016). *Weapons of Math Destruction: How Big Data Increases Inequality and Threatens Democracy.* Crown Publishing Group.

Pascoe, E. A., & Richman, L. S. (2009). Perceived discrimination and health: A meta-analytic review. *Psychological Bulletin*, 135(4), 531–554. DOI: 10.1037/a0016059 PMID: 19586161

Rachels, J., & Rachels, S. (2015). *The elements of moral philosophy* (8th ed.). McGraw-Hill Education.

Raji, I. D., & Buolamwini, J. (2020). Actionable Auditing: Investigating the Impact of Publicly Naming Biased Performance Results of Commercial AI Products. *Proceedings of the 2019 AAAI/ACM Conference on AI, Ethics, and Society*, 429-435.

Raji, I. D., Gebru, T., Mitchell, M., Buolamwini, J., Lee, J., & Denton, E. (2020). Saving Face: Investigating the Ethical Concerns of Facial Recognition Auditing. *In Proceedings of the 2020 AAAI/ACM Conference on AI, Ethics, and Society* (AIES '20). DOI: 10.1145/3375627.3375820

Rawls, J. (1971). *A Theory of justice.* Harvard University Press. DOI: 10.4159/9780674042605

Richardson, R., Schultz, J., & Crawford, K. (2019). Dirty data, bad predictions: How civil rights violations impact police data, predictive policing systems, and justice. New York

Schiff, D., Borenstein, J., Biddle, J., & Laas, K. (2021). *AI ethics in the public, private, and NGO sectors: A review of a global document collection.* DOI:DOI: 10.36227/techrxiv.14109482

Schwartz, R., Vassilev, A., Greene, K., Perine, L., Burt, A., & Hall, A. (2022). *Towards a standard for identifying and managing bias in artificial intelligence.* NIST., DOI: 10.6028/NIST.SP.1270

Scott, W. R. (2014). *Institutions and Organizations: Rational, natural, and open systems* (7th ed.). Pearson.

Selye, H. (1956). *The stress of Life.* McGraw-Hill.

Sen, A. (2009). *The Idea of Justice.* Harvard University Press.

Singer, P. (2002). *One world: The ethics of globalization.* Yale University Press.

Slobogin, C., & Brayne, S. (2023). Surveillance Technologies and Constitutional Law. *Annual Review of Criminology*, 6(1), 219–240. DOI: 10.1146/annurev-criminol-030421-035102 PMID: 38074421

Sweeney, L. (2013). Discrimination in online ad delivery. *Communications of the ACM*, 56(5), 44–54. DOI: 10.1145/2447976.2447990

Taddeo, M., & Floridi, L. (2018). How AI can be a force for good. *Science*, 361(6404), 751–752. DOI: 10.1126/science.aat5991 PMID: 30139858

Thibaut, J. W., & Walker, L. (1975). *Procedural justice: A psychological analysis.* Lawrence Erlbaum Associates.

Trist, E. L. (1981). *The Evolution of Socio-Technical Systems. A conceptual framework and an action research program.* Internet Archive. https://archive.org/details/39120320010110

Turk, M., & Pentland, A. (1991). Face recognition using eigenfaces. *InProceedings of the IEEE Computer Society Conference on Computer Vision and Pattern Recognition* (pp. 586-591). IEEE.

Tyler, T. R. (1990). *Why people obey the law.* Yale University Press.

Tyler, T. R. (2006). Psychological perspectives on legitimacy and legitimation. *Annual Review of Psychology*, 57(1), 375–400. DOI: 10.1146/annurev.psych.57.102904.190038 PMID: 16318600

Tyler, T. R., & Lind, E. A. (1992). *A relational model of authority in groups* (Vol. 25). Advances in Experimental Social Psychology. Academic Press., DOI: 10.1016/S0065-2601(08)60283-X

Umbaugh, S. E. (2010). *Digital image processing and analysis: Human and computer vision.* Taylor & Francis Group. DOI: 10.1201/9781439802069

Wachter, S., Mittelstadt, B., & Floridi, L. (2016). Why a right to explanation of automated decision-making does not exist in the general data protection regulation. SSRN *Electronic Journal.* DOI:DOI: 10.2139/ssrn.2903469

Wagner, B. (2019). *Ethics as an escape from regulation: From ethics-washing to ethics-shopping?* Being Profiled., DOI: 10.1515/9789048550180-016

Weber, M. (1978). *Economy and society: An outline of interpretive sociology.* University of California Press.

Whittaker, M., Crawford, K., Dobbe, R., Fried, G., Kaziunas, E., Mathur, V., West, S. M., Richardson, R., Schultz, J., & Schwartz, O. (2018). *AI Now 2018 report.* AI Now Institute.

Williams, D. R., & Mohammed, S. A. (2009). Discrimination and racial disparities in health: Evidence and needed research. *Journal of Behavioral Medicine*, 32(1), 20–47. DOI: 10.1007/s10865-008-9185-0 PMID: 19030981

Winner, L. (1980). Do artifacts have politics? *Daedalus*, 109(1), 121–136. https://www.jstor.org/stable/20024652

Zuboff, S. (2019). *The age of surveillance capitalism: The fight for a human future at the new frontier of power*. Public Affairs.

Chapter 10
Code Blue:
A Case Study of a Hospital Data Breach Response, Remediation, and Organizational Change

Eleanor J. Thompson
https://orcid.org/0009-0009-2661-4469
Marymount University, USA

ABSTRACT

When data are breached in a healthcare setting, the risks and threats are borne by both the impacted medical institution and its patients/customers. For patients, not only is confidential medical information leaked, but their financial data and even their health and wellbeing may be jeopardized. Using scenario-based problem solving, a case study is presented to explore the elements and dynamics of a hospital's breach of medical and financial data and to strategize the organization's responses and remediation to an internal cybersecurity incident in accordance with laws applicable to both financial and healthcare institutions. Recommendations regarding organizational change to address enterprise risk management (ERM), an incident response plan, a compliance program, and ethical leadership practices are outlined to restore the hospital's reputation and prevent or mitigate further data breach incidents.

INTRODUCTION

In just one year, from 2022 to 2023, the number of data breaches globally increased by 20% and the number of victims doubled (Madnick, 2024). In the healthcare space, data breaches in 2023 hit a new high with over 133 million patient records

DOI: 10.4018/979-8-3693-8562-3.ch010

compromised, more than double the prior year (Bruce, 2024). For the patients of a healthcare organization, the exposure carries the compounded threat of having not only personal medical information leaked, but also financial data. Such breaches require responses and remediation on both fronts, in accordance with laws applicable to financial and healthcare institutions. Additionally, the effort, attention, and money that go into addressing healthcare data breaches divert resources from patient care, possibly negatively impacting patient outcomes. To address all the necessary components of a risk management and response plan for medical institutions, a case study of a hospital data breach triggering organizational change is presented, analyzed, and discussed in the context of a healthcare facility in need of ethical corporate culture, internal compliance, data security, and incident preparedness through the introduction of a comprehensive enterprise risk management ("ERM") program. This paper examines (1) the cybersecurity needs of a healthcare organization, and (2) methods of implementing organizational change to introduce ERM and an ethical, compliant culture.

Problem Statement and Background

When data from a healthcare institution are breached, both medical and financial information are at risk, resulting in greater possible negative impact on the patients and customers and larger damages to the health facility. Medical data breaches could result in reduced hospital efficiency and, at worst, loss of life (Lee et al., 2024). The time and effort it takes a medical facility to remediate data breaches could adversely impact patient care; according to Choi, Johnson, and Lehmann (2019), data breach remediation efforts in healthcare institutions were shown to reduce time-to-electrocardiogram rates and increase myocardial infarction death rates by disrupting or delaying healthcare providers' workflows. For many people, visits to medical facilities represent a time of vulnerability, fear, or uncertainty as healthcare issues, some life-threatening, are treated; compounding these events with breaches of personal data, threats of identity theft or financial loss, and potentially compromised levels of care can be devastating on several levels. Healthcare institutions owe an extra duty of care to their patients and other stakeholders, beyond medical services, to ensure the safety and security of their data through appropriate risk mitigation, management, and response programs.

LITERATURE REVIEW

Enterprise Risk Management and Compliance Programs

At a very high level, organizations need a "holistic and horizontal" program of risk management (Decker and Galer, 2013). A comprehensive ERM is cross-functional and is designed to identify and mitigate risk as well as respond appropriately to risk incidents; Decker and Galer (2013) offer a detailed implementation guide for ERM programs that applies to all types of organizations, including healthcare facilities. Specific to healthcare, the New England Journal of Medicine's Catalyst publication (2018) offers an outline of what ERM looks like in medical organizations, also across functional areas.

Several articles reviewed described the necessary components of an effective ethics and compliance program in a healthcare setting. Ciancio (2007) of the Health Care Compliance Association outlines seven distinct "pillars" of such a program (detailed below) in a clear and succinct way, while Schneider and Henriques (2020), as practitioners, similarly summarize the building blocks of a strong healthcare compliance program; both offer good guidelines for building such programs from the ground up. Watts and Buckley (2015) home in on the reporting component of compliance programs in their examination of whistleblowers as moral agents in organizations.

Financial and Medical Information Breaches

Breaches of confidential customer and patient information by a business or institution are serious matters that result in a broad range of negative impacts and consequential damage, and they are becoming more frequent. Morris (2024) reports that, in the first half of 2024, the number of data breaches topped 1 billion, or nearly 500% more than the first half of the prior year. Articles reviewed and discussed herein cover client data breaches of both financial and medical records, and the impact and consequences of each type of event.

Financial Data Breaches

Credit card and financial information theft cases were examined by Greene and Stavins (2017), Strahilevitz (2020), and Patty (2015). In Target Corporation's credit and debit card breach case, Greene and Stavins (2017) reviewed the wide scope of the impact, the damage done to consumers and the retail giant company, and subsequent changes to corporate policies and procedures, as well as consumer behavior. According to the authors, the Target hacker attack accessed credit and debit card account information for 40 million customers during a three-week period just before Christmas 2013 (Greene and Stavins, 2017, p. 121). Strahilevitz (2020) analyzed a landmark lawsuit (Remijas v Neiman Marcus Group, LLC) involving credit card information hacked by malware from the upscale department store chain, that set a precedent for establishing standing for class action suits by victims of financial security breaches. Patty (2015) looked at chain of custody of credit card data, large scale breaches, and the necessary steps to prevent fraudulent access to consumers' records.

Medical Data Breaches

Davis (2016) and Imprivata (2021) both focused on medical record breaches. Davis (2016) examined the theft of over 650,000 healthcare records that were held for ransom and sold on the dark web by a hacker who sought financial gain either from payments of the breached organizations to return the records, or, if the victim organizations did not meet the hacker's ransom demands, from the online sale of the stolen patient information; Imprivata (2021) explained why medical records and healthcare data are so valuable to hackers, much more so than bank card information. According to Imprivata (2021), on the black market, payment card information may be worth five or six dollars, whereas a healthcare record can fetch $250 or more (p. 1). Riggi (n.d.) notes that health records can sell on the dark web for up to 10 times more than credit card numbers. The cost to healthcare institutions is similarly magnified; Riggi (n.d.), citing a 2018 study by IBM, estimates that "…a breach in health care is almost three times that of other industries – averaging $408 per stolen health care record versus $148 per stolen non-health record" (p. 1).

Gordon (2021) explains that not only is theft of electronic health records ("EHR") (or electronic medical records, "EMR") profitable, but it is relatively easy and therefore "rampant" … [as] …hackers generally perceive cybersecurity measures used in health care and government sectors to be underdeveloped and easily breached" (p. 41). Both Gordon (2021) and Imprivata (2021) discuss the reasons that EHR is so valuable to hackers: unlike financial or credit card information, which can be easily changed or canceled by the proper owner, medical information includes static personal and demographic data (such as date of birth, social security number, addresses, height and weight, medications, health conditions, etc.) that do not expire and that identity thieves can exploit multiple times and to greater benefit. Jones and Moses (2012) explored a Nevada case of medical records stolen and sold, but by hospital staffers who were authorized to access the data, rather than by hackers (very similar to the case study in question); in this case (unlike the case study examined herein), the employees sold the patient records to plaintiff attorneys who were looking for new clients injured in automobile accidents.

HIPAA/HITECH/OCR Breach Impact

All these authors looked at the financial impact and reputational damages to organizations stemming from breaches of confidential customer information, but some of these researchers delved deeper into the legal ramifications and additional monetary damages of breaches of personal health information protected by the Health Insurance Portability and Accountability Act of 1996 (HIPAA) (HHS.gov, Health Information Privacy, HIPAA for Professionals, 2021). Williams (2011), for example, detailed significant civil money penalties, in the millions of dollars, imposed by the Office of Civil Rights (OCR), the government branch responsible for assessing and collecting punitive damages from organizations that violate provisions of HIPAA (p. 5). Chua (2021), Chua (2020), Gordon (2021), Imprivata (2021), and Jones and Moses (2012) all point out that EMR makes electronic data breaches easier for hackers, and more profitable given the enormous amounts of data accessible with one system hack. Imprivata (2021) indicated that the costs of HIPAA data breach remediation are estimated at $740,000 if caused by a criminal insider (as in the subject case study) or up to $1 million or more if caused by a third-party hacker (p. 1); this is before OCR-imposed penalties related to the HIPAA breach. Jones and Moses (2012) recommend that organizations subject to HIPAA consider purchasing a HIPAA breach response insurance product, offered by several medical professional liability insurance carriers (p. 34), to manage and mitigate the financial exposure risk.

Response, Remediation

The Centers for Medicare & Medicaid Services ("CMS") publishes the Risk Management Handbook ("RMH"), designed exclusively for healthcare facilities in the United States. Chapter 8 of the RMH provides an excellent guideline for incident responses approaches to medical data breaches; this chapter outlines "…the controls that focus on how the organization must: establish an operational incident handling capability for organizational information systems that includes adequate preparation, detection, analysis, containment, recovery, and user response activities; and track, document, and report incidents…" (CMS, 2021). Teh, Tan, and Wong (2021) examine various incident response ("IR") models for healthcare business that deploy 5G technologies, arguing in favor of a dynamic IR model that can evolve as technology advances (p. 150).

Cybersecurity Measures and ERM Plans

Per the New England Journal of Medicine NJEM Catalyst (2018), risk management in the healthcare space has traditionally focused on patient safety, "[b]ut with the expanding role of healthcare technologies, increased cybersecurity concerns, [and] the fast pace of medical science...healthcare facilities are adopting a more holistic approach called Enterprise Risk Management" (p. 1-2). The NJEM risk management model covers eight "domains" that include technology as an important component (NJEM, 2018, p. 3). Like the NJEM's (2018) recommendation regarding technology in ERM, Jalali and Kaiser (2018) emphasize the importance of a systemic approach to cybersecurity in hospitals. Chua (2020 and 2021) examines the importance and vulnerability of healthcare cybersecurity in the increasingly wireless technological arena, as it impacts life-saving functions in the healthcare industry. Chua (2021), the director of governance, risk, and compliance at the U.S. Department of Health and Human Services, asserts that data breaches and ransomware attacks on healthcare facilities "...necessitated diverting patients to other hospitals and barred access to patient records, affecting care delivery," further stating that "[t]here has never been a more critical time for our sector to address cybersecurity" (p. 2). Riggi (n.d.) concurs that cyberthreats put patient safety at risk, advising hospital executives that cybersecurity is not only an IT issue, but also a "...patient safety, enterprise risk and strategic priority..." that should be instilled into "...the hospital's existing enterprise, risk-management, governance and business-continuity framework" (p. 1). Javaid, Haleem, Singh, and Suman (2023) review recent trends and practices in cybersecurity specifically for healthcare organizations, stressing the importance of protection and prevention across all platforms and access points, including fitness apps, trackers, and portals. Wasserman and Wasserman (2022) address cyberattacks on hospitals, focusing on risks and gaps across databases, devices, and software. Both the Javaid et al. (2023) and Wasserman (2022) articles particularly examine trends in ransomware attacks, noting the threats to patient health and safety on top of financial risks if hospital systems and databases are infiltrated and held hostage. Zlatolas, Welzer, and Lhotska (2024) similarly approach the problem proactively, examining ways in which healthcare data breaches can be mitigated or avoided by adopting defenses against hacking, malicious cyberattacks, and unauthorized access through artificial intelligence, advanced encryption methods, and Blockchain approaches.

Organizational Leadership, Ethics, Culture, and Change

Jurkiewicz and Massey (1998), de Jager (2002), Brown, Treviño, and Harrison (2005), and Hill (2017) are among the many sources that examine the importance of leaders setting the tone of an ethical culture and how a failure to lead ethically can permeate throughout the organization. Hendrick and Engelbrecht (2019) call the implications of non-ethical leadership "devastating" (p. 1) in their study on value-based leadership and its alignment with organizational moral values. Ofori-Parku (2021) digs deeper into the sometimes-divided loyalties of leadership through the lens of corporate social responsibility theory, wherein the needs of the organization and those of the community it serves may conflict.

Articles discussing organizational culture theories, the institutional environment that allowed the hospital's patient records to be breached, and models of organizational change required to improve ethical standards and controls at the subject hospital, were included in the research for this case study. Per Karapancheva (2020) and Reissner, Pagan, and Smith (2011), organizational failures provoke conjecture on causes, drawing from the cultural (or company/corporate) iceberg model: that which can be seen (i.e., news stories describing the data breach incident) is but the tip of the proverbial iceberg, suggesting that the root causes are unseen, below the surface. Karapancheva (2020) and Reissner, Pagan, and Smith (2011) examine this cultural or corporate iceberg model, wherein the public face of an organization is what is visible above the waterline of the iceberg (branding, public and investor relations, and behaviors), whereas the root causes of issues, such as data breaches, are hidden and deep (such as cultural ethics, leadership attitude, values, biases, internal controls, policies and procedures, and trust).

In order to make recommendations to implement organizational reform, change models, plans, and leadership approaches were examined as part of this case study. Kurt Lewin's model of organizational change was discussed by Hussain, Lei, Akram, Haider, Hussain, and Ali (2016) from the perspective of leadership's role in change and how to involve employees for widespread and seamless adoption. Levasseur (2001) also supports the use of Lewin's model, calling it "truly elegant and infinitely practical" (p. 71). Caulfield and Brenner (2019) apply Kotter's change model to "wicked" systemic problems, while Deming's Plan/Do/Check/Act method for implementing organizational improvement is discussed by Pietrzak and Paliszkiewicz (2015) and MindTools.com (n.d.); these models are also considered in the context of the hospital data breach case study. Bevan (2015) offers practitioners helpful guidelines and checklists to map out change plans, lead their implementation, and keep the new protocols supported and effective. The importance of the leader's role in guiding new policies and procedures is addressed by Bligh, Kohles, and Yan (2018), wherein the authors discuss the need to change the mindset of all stakeholders through the organizational change process. Kane (2016) applies Schein's (2010) model of organizational culture and leadership to the financial sector to look at ways to change an entire industry, one that relies on public trust, to honor its stakeholders with loyalty, compliance, and competence.

Method: Case Study

Per Nohria (2021), former dean of Harvard Business School which pioneered case studies as a teaching method over 100 years ago, "[s]tudents recall concepts better when they are set in a case [which] cultivates the capacity for critical analysis, judgment, decision-making, and action" (p. 2). The case study method is therefore used for this analysis. To examine all the necessary elements of strong compliance, response, and controls plans needed in a healthcare environment, and the organizational cultural change required, a case was developed of employee theft of medical and financial patient records from a hospital that did not have an effective ERM program, incident response plan ("IRP"), or cybersecurity controls in place, which needs to be addressed appropriately and promptly by the hospital's leadership. The hospital in the case is lax in all areas of information security, compliance, and incident response, which is unlikely in the real world, but such a blank-slate scenario lends itself to a comprehensive approach of analysis and recommendations.

In this hypothetical insider threat scenario, several employees of a small community hospital abused their access to the healthcare organization's system, stole confidential patient health records and credit card information, and sold the data on the 'dark web,' an area of the internet that is only accessible through special software and allows users untraceable anonymity, usually for nefarious purposes. On top of the damage done to the medical privacy and personal/financial security of the affected patients, reputational damage has been done to the hospital in adverse news media reports. The presumption in this case study is that all offending employees in this case have been identified, terminated, and apprehended by appropriate law enforcement agencies, to focus on the hospital's actions in the wake of the breach. The study looks at the response, management, and mitigation of the damages to all parties, the creation of strategic ERM, compliance, and response programs to prevent, mitigate, or manage such cyber risks for the hospital going forward, and the implementation of necessary cultural changes to the hospital organization to prevent future data breaches and thefts.

There were two kinds of personal information stolen and illegally distributed in the case study scenario: financial (credit card data) and medical (health records). For each form of data stolen, there are risks and consequences for both the primary victims (the patients and/or customers) and the ultimately responsible party, the hospital. The patients/victims are at risk of identity theft and monetary loss, while the hospital is subject to fines, penalties, and reporting obligations under the Health Insurance Portability and Accountability Act of 1996 ("HIPAA") (Health and Human Services, 2021) and the Health Information Technology for Economic and Clinical Health Act ("HITECH"), as well as liability for financial damages resulting from the loss and dissemination of patients' credit card information. The risk less often considered, but arguably of much greater importance, is outlined by Choi et al. (2019): resources used to remediate data breaches may detract from patient care quality, potentially resulting in worse outcomes up to and including loss of life.

The hospital's organizational culture, lack of oversight and training of its employees, inefficient cybersecurity controls, and lack of an effective ethics compliance program resulted in an environment where opportunistic fraudulent enrichment by its employees and the loss of critical customer (patient) data became possible. The hospital needs not only to remediate the financial damage caused by the information theft, but also to repair and rebuild its public image by creating an organizational ethos that will reduce or eliminate, to the greatest extent possible, the likelihood of a recurrence of such a significant risk event.

DISCUSSION

Organizational Culture and Change

Because a hospital is entrusted with the lives and welfare of many of its stakeholders, its organizational culture must be above reproach. When a systemic failure like a data breach occurs, the organization must address the cultural weaknesses that permitted the failure and implement significant organizational changes to address its ethics, culture, compliance, and security measures to ensure future threats are mitigated or prevented. Kane (2016) applied Schein's model of organizational culture to the banking industry, another societal institution that relies on public trust. Kane (2016) looked at cultural norms that supported corporate risk taking to the detriment of stakeholders. Schein's original model, from the 2010 book *Organizational Culture and Leadership* (as quoted by Kane, 2016), states that culture should be seen from three levels (a deeper but similar structure to the two-leveled iceberg model): observable artifacts, professed beliefs and values, and unspoken beliefs and underlying assumptions shared by insiders (Kane, 2016, p. 52, quoting Schein, 2010).

The institution in the case study is a hospital, which is a critical and (one hopes) trustworthy part of a larger community; not only does it have employees and customers like a corporate enterprise, but it supplies a necessary, lifesaving service to patients[1]. As such, a hospital has more stakeholders than a regular for-profit company, many of which have more at stake than merely a pecuniary interest. Stakeholder theory is therefore key to this case study analysis, as the public trust was breached when medical records were lost. Literature on stakeholder theory stresses the importance not only of community and social interests, but also the additional emphasis stakeholders place on ethics and trust in leadership. Hill (2017) examined the implications of failure of ethical leadership not only on stakeholders, but on stakeholder theory itself and the scope of the traditional definition of "stakeholders". Hussain et al. (2016) emphasized the importance of involving all stakeholders in organizational change decisions and management to ensure engagement and alignment. Caulfield and Brenner (2019) looked at stakeholders from the perspective of community and social systems that experience "chronic and complex problems" (p. 509).

Once the deep-seated cultural issues that created an environment where the subject hospital's data breach was possible, one must examine how to change the organization to prevent or mitigate similar risks in the future. Various change models could apply; three were examined for this case study. Given the emphasis on stakeholder interests and levels of visibility and transparency in this case, models that involve multiple parties, perspectives, and participation are most applicable. Kurt Lewin's seminal 1947 three-step change management model (unfreezing, changing, refreezing) is highlighted by both Levasseur (2001) and Hussain et al. (2016) as it emphasizes the importance of stakeholder involvement from all levels, in particular the relationship between strong leadership and employee alignment with change process of moving from the known (current state) to the unknown (desired future state). Kotter's 1995 more complex eight-step change management model, discussed and applied by Caulfield and Brenner (2019) in relation to community and societal problems, focuses on behavioral changes, leadership's communication of a "compelling vision," and aligning followers and stakeholders (p. 514). Caulfield and Brenner (2019) outline Kotter's eight steps (p. 514), most of which correspond to a stage in Lewin's model (in italics):

1. Establish a sense of urgency (*unfreeze*)
2. Create a guiding coalition (*unfreeze*)
3. Develop vision and strategy (*unfreeze and change*)
4. Communicate the change vision (*unfreeze and change*)
5. Empower broad-based action (*change*)
6. Generate short-term wins (*change and refreeze*)
7. Consolidate change and produce more gains (*change and refreeze*)
8. Anchor new approaches in the culture (*refreeze*)

The core of a major organizational change undertaking is executing the change itself (the middle step in both the Lewin and Kotter models). The PDCA cycle framework (**P**lan-**D**o-**C**heck-**A**djust or **P**lan-**D**o-**C**heck-**A**ct) as discussed by Pietrzak and

Paliszkiewics (2015) is not only a quality improvement process but is also useful as a change management tool (p. 152). Per MindTools (source of *Figure 1*, below), PDCA was devised by Dr. William Deming in the 1950s (originally conceived as PD$\underline{S}$A, where the 'S' is for $\underline{S}$tudy rather than Check).

Figure 1. The plan-do- check act cycle

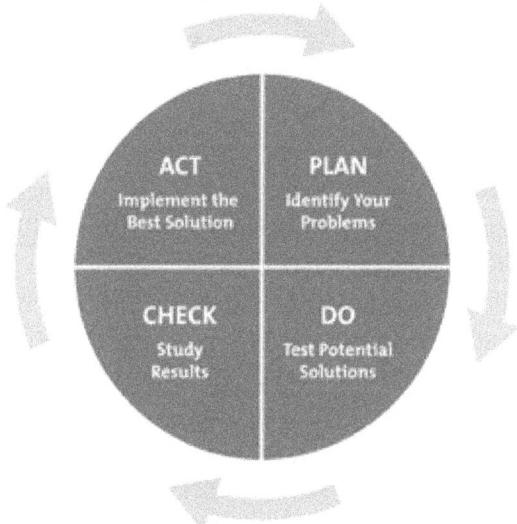

https://www.mindtools.com/as2l5i1/pdca-plan-do-check-act

The PDCA cycle dovetails nicely with both the Lewin and Kotter models; the three frameworks could be combined and customized to an organization's change needs and desired outcomes. Rounding out the literature review on change models is Bevan's 2015 practical guide for planning (*unfreezing*), implementing (*changing*), and sustaining (*refreezing*) organizational change, *The Changemaking Checklists* (Bevan, 2015).

Ethical Leadership and Corporate Social Responsibility

The 'why' and 'how' of the organizational change needed for the case study hospital must lead to the 'what': what is the desired outcome, the new state, of the institution's culture, mission, and values? There are various models and frameworks to determine the best structure for the hospital's leadership priorities and culture of compliance. Two models that make sense for an institution working to regain public trust are the duty-based approach and value-based leadership theory; at the heart of each is the theory of corporate social responsibility (which would extend to institutions like hospitals, whether non-profit or for profit) and the premise of ethical leadership. The intersection of ethics and moral duty is examined by de Jager (2002), who also stressed that what is dutiful and ethical today might change tomorrow; the need to adapt and adjust (per the last 'A' in the PDCA model) indicates that the desired outcome of an organizational change is not always static. The duty component emphasized by de Jager (2002) is critical for an institution charged with matters of public trust and with stakeholders spread across a community. The importance of moral, dutiful, ethical, value-based leadership is underscored by Hendrick and Engelbrecht (2019), who noted, through the framework of social learning theory, individuals (such as employees) "… will strive to emulate the behaviour of role models in their work environment" (p. 1); in other words, followers do as their leaders do, not necessarily what their leaders say, meaning ethical leadership begets an ethical organization. Brown, Treviño, and Harrison (2005) wrote almost the same thing nearly 15 years earlier when they stated "…leaders influence the ethical conduct of followers via modeling" (p. 118). Brown et al. (2005) described both the values and duties of ethical leaders, as well as the desired organizational outcome of such leadership. Ethical leadership, according to Brown et al. (2005), is "…related to consideration behavior, honesty, trust in the leader, interactional fairness, [and] socialized charismatic leadership…" (p. 117), that will result in an ethical environment of "…perceived effectiveness of leaders, followers' job satisfaction and dedication, and their willingness to report problems to management" (p. 117). This tie between leader effectiveness and an ethical organizational culture is nothing new; back in 1998, Jurkiewicz and Massey examined the differences between effective and noneffective leadership in nonprofit organizations in making ethical decisions. Jurkiewicz and Massey (1998) found "…the differences were so profound that an executive's effectiveness could be confidently predicted from his or her scores on a test of ethical reasoning" (p. 173).

This is an important concept, as there is sometimes a misperception that good ethics are bad for business, or that ethical decisions negatively impact an organization's bottom line. In fact, much literature points to negative outcomes correlating to ethical lapses within an organization. Hill (2017), for example, tied together the concepts of ethical leadership failures and the downstream consequences and implications for stakeholders (direct) and non-stakeholders (indirect) through the broader lens of corporate social responsibility, as well as the direct impact on the enterprise that suffered the failure (which, for healthcare facilities faced with OCR penalties tied to HIPAA breaches, can be greater than for non-medical organizations). Similarly, Ofori-Parku (2021) looked at the intersection (and sometimes collision) of corporate interests and the public good, and what should motivate organizations to act in ways that further public interest while also benefiting the company.

Compliance Programs

Mistakes happen. Most of the time, one hopes, they are unintentional. Sometimes, as in the hospital case study, malicious intent is involved; not in all cases could such events have been avoided, as bad actors will act badly. Whether intentional or not, when a crisis strikes an organization, there needs to be an immediate response to the incident, mitigating actions, and a risk management plan implemented or adjusted to minimize the possibility and impact of similar occurrences in the future. When the act is malicious and intentional, organizations usually bring in outside sources to assist, such as law enforcement or governmental agencies. When the act is unintentional, such as an error by a well-meaning employee, it can be used as a learning opportunity for the entire organization and can usually be managed internally. Bligh, Kohles, and Yan (2018) see mistakes as leverage, an indicator of necessary training, guidelines, or guardrails for employees and a roadmap to what the 'new state' or outcome of organizational change needs to encompass and address.

In a medical or healthcare environment, as in a corporate environment, the new or 'desired outcome' state of organizational change in the wake of a data breach must include a strong cybersecurity/cyber-ethics compliance program, effective ethics training, and an efficient whistleblower mechanism for reporting unethical or illegal behavior. Given the additional layer of financial and legal consequences for breaches of HIPAA-protected data, such as the EHR in the hospital case study, this is critical for health facilities. The literature on healthcare compliance programs is vast; a recent online search for "hospital compliance programs" yielded nearly 2 million results; limiting the search to publication dates since 2019 still resulted in 16,400 articles. In this area, organizations may find that seeking the wisdom and guidance from industry experts, consultants, or attorneys, rather than relying on purely academic sources, is more beneficial and practical. For example, the Healthcare Compliance Association ("HCCA"), one of the industry's largest professional associations of compliance officers, offered the "seven pillars of an effective ethics and compliance program" in 2007 (Ciancio, 2007, p. 42) (note the extent to which these "pillars" align with the PDCA model, or Kotter's eight change steps):

1. Standards and procedures
2. Oversight
3. Education and training
4. Auditing and monitoring
5. Reporting
6. Enforcement and discipline
7. Response and prevention

Similarly, in 2020, Schneider and Henriques, both healthcare compliance officers, suggested ways to "...introduce, evaluate, and maintain an effective program that includes all of the seven elements of an effective compliance program" (p. 53).

Of the seven elements of a healthcare compliance program listed by Ciancio (2007) and reinforced by Schneider and Henriques (2020), the fifth component, *Reporting*, deserves closer examination. Reporting, in this context, is not referring to metrics or historical data, but rather to a mechanism for employees and other stakeholders to report suspicions of wrongdoing. In a hospital environment, this would usually entail medical malfeasance, but in the hospital case study, the breach of data, although inclusive of medical records, was not medical in nature; in this case, non-medical employees had access to medical and financial records which they misappropriated. Therefore, the case study hospital needs to ensure that its new compliance program is a hybrid of a healthcare compliance program and one designed for non-medical corporations, and that it includes appropriate whistleblower reporting mechanisms. Watts and Buckley (2015) offer guidelines for a "moral whistleblowing" program, one embedded in an organization with a culture of ethical leadership. Moral whistleblowing is enabled in an enterprise where employees trust leadership, operate in an ethical environment, and are comfortable "...voic[ing] allegations or concerns without fear of retaliation" (Ciancio, 2007, p. 42). Per Watts and Buckley (2015), this is "...whistleblowing that is undertaken by individuals [who] see themselves as moral agents and are primarily motivated to blow the whistle by a sense of moral duty" (p. 669). In other words, if you see something, say something.

The Current State and the Impact

Relevant literature covers each of the major milestones in the hospital case study: (1) the current state of the organization; (2) the implications and consequences of the data breach, including harm to the organization and its stakeholders; (3) the response/plan of the hospital for dealing with the breach; and (4) the organizational changes needed to improve the hospital's culture and mitigate future risk. It also offers the theories, frameworks, and models needed to implement and maintain the desired outcome state.

Current State of the Organization

There are many areas in which the hospital in the case study possibly failed, permitting errant employees to steal and sell confidential medical and financial data. First and foremost, it lacked the necessary ethical culture and the system/procedural controls needed to circumvent the employees' motive and opportunity for self-enrichment. Had an enterprise-wide risk management program been in place, it might have identified and possibly prevented the gaps in the hospital's system security, training, and supervision. Had an effective compliance program been in place, a reporting mechanism might have given a moral and observant coworker a channel to blow the whistle before too much damage was done.

Implications and Consequences

As discussed above, the damage, financial and otherwise, may be extensive in the wake of such a breach, and may impact almost all stakeholders, internal and external, institutional and individual.

Situational Harm to the Organization

When one or two employees make bad decisions, act criminally, and suffer the consequences, their names may flash through the new headlines for a day or two, but they will soon be forgotten. The organization's name, on the other hand, will stick in people's minds for years after the event. Consider, for example, corporate names like Enron or WorldCom; now try to think of the names of any individuals associated with those famous scandals. Not only is the entity's reputation damaged, but the financial liability could be enormous. Financial risk includes settlements from lawsuits, costs to cover actual losses suffered by victims of stolen data (which may be immediate in cases of credit or debit card information stolen, but could extend for years due to identity theft from the stolen medical records), fines and penalties assessed by OCR for HIPAA breaches (which could amount to millions of dollars), and costs associated with crisis management, such as legal fees, public relations costs, and increased insurance premiums. More difficult to quantify is the long-term monetary impact from the loss of customers (for corporate entities) or patients who have lost trust in the hospital, possible loss of business partners such as vendors and suppliers who may not wish to be associated with a 'tainted' institution, and the possible collapse of business partnerships, joint ventures, capital investment relationships, etc. Additionally, if the enterprise is publicly traded, company value may deteriorate due to lower stock prices as the financial market loses confidence in the organization.

Situational Harm to Employees

The immediate impact on coworkers of the criminal employees will likely be shock and anxiety. There may also be a loss of faith in leadership, fear of reprisal for employees who worked closely with the data thieves, and a general sense of mistrust of coworkers and supervisors. The upset environment may trigger low morale, disengagement, a sense of shame of working for a disgraced institution, tension, and conflict. In turn, this stressful environment of employee dissatisfaction could lead to lower productivity and mental health issues (not to mention the spillover into employees' personal lives). Longer term impact could include difficulties in obtaining future employment if the organization's name has been negatively publicized (imagine listing Enron on your resumé, for example, especially if you work in finance, auditing, or risk management).

Change Management Plan(s)

Crisis Management/Breach Incident Response

Per Jones and Moses (2012), an organization that suffers a HIPAA security breach should put a written breach communication plan in place that documents the following steps, as recommended by the Department of Health and Human Services ("HHS"), the OCR, and most HIPAA and privacy experts, to manage the response to the breach incident and its immediate impact (p. 34):

- ✓ Consult the organization's legal counsel
- ✓ Retain technical forensic experts to audit and contain the data breach
- ✓ Involve a public relations team to manage communications and handle media inquiries
- ✓ Develop a web site, toll-free number, and email address for patients' questions
- ✓ Arrange notices to be sent to affected patients (pursuant to 45 C.F.R. § 164.404(b)
- ✓ Implement credit monitoring and identity theft protection for affected patients
- ✓ Remediate and correct the breach (if not already done)
- ✓ Retrain employees to ensure such a data breach is not repeated
- ✓ Notify HHS and OCR (pursuant to 45 C.F.R. § 164.408
- ✓ Cooperate fully with HHS/OCR investigations
- ✓ Negotiate necessary settlements, both compensation to victims of the breach and HHS penalties

The authors note, these steps need to be simultaneous, not sequential (therefore not numbered), to be accomplished in addition to maintaining business continuity, making a HIPAA breach event response a managerial nightmare (Jones & Moses, 2012, p. 34). This, of course, is on top of managing the response to the financial data breach, which will require most of the steps listed above, and will likely involve almost all the same breach victims. The pool of affected financial victims may be larger, as not all patients cover their own medical costs (juveniles, for example, or family members on one insurance plan). If the hospital had an ERM plan and a risk management team, the plan should address some of these points and the risk team would be an integral part of the organization's incident response and handling of the crisis.

Necessary Organizational Change(s)

Once the incident has been appropriately responded to, and the immediate crisis is contained (or while containment and mitigation efforts continue, if prolonged), the hospital needs to address the organizational changes needed to create an ethical, compliant, risk-aware, and supportive workplace culture. Change is never easy; leadership needs to be sensitive to the fact that employee engagement and adoption of the needed changes will be complicated by the unsettled and tense situation in which employees find themselves. Either the Kotter or Lewin change models, or the Bevan (2015) checklist for change, could be applied to implement this organizational change once the desired outcome has been established and agreed to.

The Plan(s)/Desired Outcomes

The hospital's failure was due to the lack of an effective compliance program and was made worse due to the lack of a comprehensive risk management program. Both can be addressed through a duty-based approach to leadership through organizational change. On the other hand, the organizational culture lacked a strong ethical foundation, which can be ameliorated by strengthening value-based leadership.

An effective compliance program using the Ciancio (2007) outline will be implemented through a framework like that suggested by Schneider and Henriques (2020). This program should meet not only the needs of a healthcare organization but also the requirements of either a for-profit or nonprofit corporation (depending on the hospital's status), as the breach event impacted both industry sectors. An enterprise-wide risk management program will also be put in place (or strengthened, if the hospital already has an ERM); Decker and Galer (2013) offer a clear guide, by corporate function, although additional elements will be required to suit the unique risks of a hospital. Additionally, the hospital's ERM program should include the purchase of a HIPAA breach insurance policy as recommended by Jones and Moses (2012).

Employee engagement and satisfaction will need to be addressed, with dedicated support from leadership and human resources. In the immediate wake of the breach crisis and negative publicity, counselling services for unsettled employees may be advisable. Not only would this assist the employees and possibly improve productivity and morale, but it would also demonstrate leadership's values and commitment to creating a supportive and caring work environment.

Finally, an organizational culture of ethics and moral values needs to be established, through the lens of value-based leadership. This will extend beyond policies and procedures, following Bligh et al.'s (2018) findings on leadership behaviors and employee mindset. The proverbial 'tone from the top' will be critical to ensure the culture fostered and the moral-based messages are positive and consistent.

Change Management

Determining the desired outcomes, or new/unknown state, is relatively easy compared to implementing and maintaining the changes from the current state to the desired state (all of which constitutes the "**P**" element, for **P**lan, of the PDCA framework). The hospital's change management plan to prevent or at least mitigate future breach events, improve the organization's culture, and foster a corporate environment of ethical behavior, will require strong, steady leadership and employee engagement; all participants in the "**D**" step ("**D**o") of PDCA will need to be of the same mindset. To "Do" the changes, hospital leadership would do well to follow the steps of the Kotter model as described by Caulfield and Brenner (2019), perhaps enhanced or modified by Bevan's (2015) guidelines. The **C**heck and **A**djust steps will require input from more stakeholders, as 360° feedback will be necessary to gauge success.

Implementing a culture of ethical behaviors will take more time and success will be more difficult to measure. Not only will ethical leadership mindset be critical, but leaders' ethical actions must be evident and demonstrated regularly over time to gain (or regain) followers' trust and imitation. Eventually, ethical practices will trickle down throughout the organization, and will seep out to external stakeholders and the community, but the shift to a culture of organizational ethics will have to overcome the negative public perception of the hospital in the wake of the press coverage of the breach events.

CONCLUSION

Change is difficult, but not impossible, and often necessary to survive and thrive as an organization. The subject hospital's current position is precarious but the path to improvement is clear. Responding to the breach incident head on, with purpose and transparency, will engage all stakeholders on the mission to change and put the hospital on a more solid foundation for future growth and scalability. The breach scandal in this case study presents the hospital with an opportunity to change its culture for the better and resuscitate its reputation as a strong community partner. Regular checking and adjusting to all change components will be necessary to keep the hospital vital, its new, holistic risk management, incident response, and compliance programs effective, its corporate culture and leadership ethical and value-oriented, its employees engaged and honest, and its stakeholders aligned and proud.

REFERENCES

Bevan, R. (2015). *The Changemaking Checklists: A Toolkit for Planning, Leading, and Sustaining Change.* ChangeStart Press (Richard Bevan), Independently Published.

Bligh, M., Kohles, J., & Yan, Q. (2018). Leading and learning to change: The role of leadership style and mindset in error learning and organizational change. *Journal of Change Management*, 2(18), 116–141. DOI: 10.1080/14697017.2018.1446693

Brown, M., Treviño, L., & Harrison, D. (2005). Ethical leadership: A social learning perspective for construct development and testing. *Organizational Behavior and Human Decision Processes*, 2(97), 117–134. DOI: 10.1016/j.obhdp.2005.03.002

Bruce, G. (2024). Healthcare data breaches set record in 2023. *Becker Hospital Review, 2024*(February 7). https://www.beckershospitalreview.com/cybersecurity/healthcare-data-breaches-set-record-in-2023.html

Caulfield, J., & Brenner, E. (2019). Resolving complex community problems: Applying collective leadership and Kotter's change model to wicked problems within social systems networks. *Nonprofit Management & Leadership*, 2020(30), 509–524.

Centers for Medicare & Medicaid Services. (2021). Risk management handbook, Chapter 8. *CMS Information Security and Privacy Group*. https://security.cms.gov/policy-guidance/risk-management-handbook-chapter-8-incident-response-ir

Choi, S., Johnson, M., & Lehmann, C. (2019). Data breach remediation efforts and their implications for hospital quality. *Health Services Research*, 54(5), 971–980. DOI: 10.1111/1475-6773.13203 PMID: 31506956

Chua, J. (2020). Cybersecurity in the healthcare industry. *American Association for Physician Leadership, October 7, 2020*. https://www.physicianleaders.org/articles/cybersecurity-in-the-healthcare-industry

Chua, J. (2021). Cybersecurity in the healthcare industry: A collaborative approach. *American Association for Physician Leadership, January 8, 2021*.https://www.physicianleaders.org/articles/cybersecurity-healthcare-industry-collaborative-approach

Ciancio, N. (2007). The seven pillars of an effective ethics and compliance program. *Compliance Today, Health Care Compliance Association, 2007*(July). https://assets.hcca-info.org/Portals/0/PDFs/Resources/Compliance%20Today/0707/ct0707_42_Ciancio.pdf

Davis, J. (2016). Millions of patient records reportedly for sale on the dark web after ransom demand. *HealthCare IT News.* https://www.healthcareitnews.com/news/millions-patient-records-reportedly-sale-dark-web-after-ransom-demand

de Jager, P. (2002). Ethics: good, evil, and moral duty. *The Information Management Journal, September/October 2002,* 82-85.

Decker, A., & Galer, D. (2013). *Enterprise Risk Management - Straight to the Point: An Implementation Guide Function by Function.* ERMSTTP, LLC.

Gordon, C. (2021, Summer). Protecting the security of digital health records: A brief overview of HIPAA and the breach notification rule. *Journal of Government Financial Management,* 41–45.

Greene, C., & Stavins, J. (2017). Did the Target data breach change consumer assessments of payment card security? *Journal of Payments Strategy & Systems,* 11(2), 121–133. DOI: 10.69554/DISO6037

Health and Human Services. (2021). *HIPAA for Professionals.* https://www.hhs.gov/hipaa/for-professionals/index.html

Hendrick, K., & Engelbrecht, A. (2019). The principled leadership scale: An integration of value-based leadership. *SA Journal of Industrial Psychology,* 45(0), 1–10.

Hill, R. (2017). Failure of ethical leadership: Implications for stakeholder theory and "anti-stakeholders". *Business and Society Review, Journal of the Center for Business Ethics. Bentley University,* 122(2), 165–190.

Hussain, S.T., Lei, S., Akram, T., Haider, M., Hussain, S.H., and Ali, M. (2016). Kurt Lewin's change model: A critical review of the role of leadership and employee involvement in organizational change. *Journal of Innovation & Knowledge, 3*(2018), 123-127. DOI: 10.1016/j.jik.2016.07.002

Imprivata (2021, June 30). *Hackers, breaches, and the value of healthcare data.* https://www.imprivata.com/blog/healthcare-data-new-prize-hackers

Jalali, M., & Kaiser, J. (2018). Cybersecurity in hospitals: A systemic, organizational perspective. *Journal of Medical Internet Research,* 20(5), e10059. Advance online publication. DOI: 10.2196/10059 PMID: 29807882

Javaid, M., Haleem, A., Singh, R., & Suman, R. (2023, December). Towards insighting cybersecurity for healthcare domains: A comprehensive review of recent practices and trends. *Cyber Security and Applications,* 1, 1–13. DOI: 10.1016/j.csa.2023.100016

Jones, D. and Moses, R. (2012). Insuring health care compliance: Reducing RAC audit and HIPAA breach risk exposure. *Journal of Health Care Compliance, January-February 2012*, 33-36.

Jurkiewicz, C., & Massey, T.Jr. (1998, December). The influence of ethical reasoning on leader effectiveness: An empirical study of nonprofit executives. *Nonprofit Management & Leadership*, 9(2), 173–186. DOI: 10.1002/nml.9204

Kane, E. (2016). A theory of how and why central-bank culture supports predatory risk-taking at megabanks. *Atlantic Economic Journal*, 2016(44), 51–71. DOI: 10.1007/s11293-016-9482-x

Karapancheva, M. (2020). The future of organizational culture. *Journal of Sustainable Development*, 10(25), 42–52.

Lee, J., Kim, H., & Choi, S. (2024). Do hospital data breaches affect health information technology investment? *Digital Health*, 10, 1–11. DOI: 10.1177/20552076231224164 PMID: 39286785

Levasseur, R. (2001). People skills: Change Management Tools–Lewin's change model. *Interfaces*, 31(4), 71–73.

Madnick, S. (2024). Why data breaches spiked in 2023. *Harvard Business Review, 2024*(February 19). https://hbr.org/2024/02/why-data-breaches-spiked-in-2023

MindTools. (n.d.). PDCA (Plan Do Check Act), also known as PDSA, The "Deming Wheel," and "Shewhart Cycle". *MindTools.com*. https://www.mindtools.com/as2l5i1/pdca-plan-do-check-act

Morris, C. (2024). The number of data breach victims is up 490% in the first half of 2024. *Fast Company, July 18, 2024*. https://www.fastcompany.com/91158122/data-breach-victims-up-490-percent-first-half-2024

NEJM Catalyst. (2018). What is risk management in healthcare? *New England Journal of Medicine, April 25, 2018*. https://catalyst.nejm.org/doi/full/10.1056/CAT.18.0197

Nohria, N. (2021). What the case study method really teaches. *Harvard Business Review, December 21, 2021*. https://hbr.org/2021/12/what-the-case-study-method-really-teaches

Ofori-Parku, S. (2021). When public and business interests collide: An integrated approach to the altruism-instrumentalism tension and corporate social responsibility theory. *Journal of Medical Ethics*, 36(1), 2–19. DOI: 10.1080/23736992.2020.1857254

Patty, R. (2015). Credit card issuers' claims arising from large-scale data breaches. *Journal of Taxation and Regulation of Financial Institutions*, 28(3), 5–18.

Pietrzak, M., & Paliszkiewicz, J. (2015). Framework of strategic learning: The PDCA cycle. *Management*, 10(2), 149–161.

Reissner, S., Pagan, V., & Smith, C. (2011). 'Our iceberg is melting': Story, metaphor and the management of organisational change. *Culture and Organization*, 17(5), 417–433. DOI: 10.1080/14759551.2011.622908

Riggi, J. (n.d.). The importance of cybersecurity in protecting patient safety: A high-level guide for hospital and health system senior leaders. *American Hospital Association Center for Health Innovation*. https://www.aha.org/center/cybersecurity-and-risk-advisory-services/importance-cybersecurity-protecting-patient-safety

Schein, E. (2010). *Organizational Culture and Leadership* (3rd ed.). Jossey-Bass.

Schneider, D. and Henriques, J. (2020). Compliance program implementation when you are not in the same family. *Journal of Health Care Compliance, January-February 2020*, 53-56.

Strahilevitz, L. (2020). Data security's unjust enrichment theory. *Chicago Unbound. University of Chicago Law School*, 87, 2477–2491.

Teh, Y., Tan, Y., & Wong, S. (2021). 5G cybersecurity: risk assessment and incident response in the healthcare industry. *International Conference on Digital Transformation and Applications (ICDXA)*, 25-26 October 2021, 145-152. DOI: 10.56453/icdxa.2021.1015

Wasserman, L., & Wasserman, Y. (2022). Hospital cybersecurity risks and gaps: Review (for the non-cyber professional). *Frontiers in Digital Health*, 4, 862221. Advance online publication. DOI: 10.3389/fdgth.2022.862221 PMID: 36033634

Watts, L., & Buckley, M. (2015). A dual-processing model of moral whistleblowing in organizations. *Journal of Business Ethics*, 2017(146), 669–683.

Williams, R. (2011, May-June). Cause for HIPAAnoia? *Journal of Health Care Compliance*, 5-8, 75–76.

Zlatolas, L., Welzer, T., & Lhotska, L. (2024). Data breaches in healthcare: Security mechanisms for attack mitigation. *Cluster Computing*, 2024(7), 8639–8654. Advance online publication. DOI: 10.1007/s10586-024-04507-2

ENDNOTE

[1] Note that in healthcare settings, "patients" and "customers" are not always synonymous; the patient may or may not be the party paying medical providers, so "customers" could be construed to include financially responsible parties including insurance companies, guarantors, employers, family members, or other payors.

Chapter 11
Data-Driven Technology Medical Malpractice:
A Narrative Review on the Legal Implications in Clinical Settings

Cakesha M. Hardin
https://orcid.org/0009-0006-6869-7301
Marymount University, USA

ABSTRACT

Many hospitals employ machine learning algorithms in clinical settings. This technology causes ethical and legal issues including data biases resulting in harm. This narrative research seeks to demonstrate the link between data-driven algorithms in healthcare decision-making and discrimination to certain demographic groups. English peer-reviewed papers from 2020 to June 24, 2024, were searched on Google Scholar. The primary findings revealed ethical issues with clinical AI technology. However, there is a notable lack of well-established protocols to determine liability for AI errors. This cutting-edge technology promises to boost operational efficiency but may simultaneously damage healthcare providers' reputations and patient safety. To safeguard patients and staff, steps must be taken with regard to quality assurance practices prior to implementation.

INTRODUCTION

Patients have reported instances of bias and discriminatory treatment because of incorporating machine learning algorithms, which are a subset of artificial intelligence (AI), into healthcare environments. This has subsequently resulted in injury to the medical experts who are using this inexplicable and, more significantly,

DOI: 10.4018/979-8-3693-8562-3.ch011

non-interpretable technology. According to According to Veritti et al. (2024), an AI-driven prediction model was unsuccessful in detecting 843 out of 2552 patients who had clinically proven sepsis, resulting in a 67% omission rate. For background, sepsis is a critical medical condition that may result in organ failure and, eventually, death. Several research studies (Cheng et al., 2024; Karalis, 2024; Williamson & Prybutok, 2024; Čartolovni et al., 2022) have shown that there are several elements that might lead to legal consequences for manufacturers of AI, healthcare organizations, and medical professionals despite lack of governing regulation and laws. There is a lack of rules and legislation by governing bodies, as highlighted by Chen et al. (2023) and Prakash (2022), that specify the obligations of the party accountable for introducing harmful risk.

Culpability is necessary to establish responsibility or wrongdoing when undesirable consequences occur in clinical settings. Many factors contribute to manufacturer harm, including biased training data, which leads to clinical prediction mistakes and data breaches involving sensitive patient information (Veritti et al., 2024). Insufficient training and AI/ML system supervision and management may lead to legal action against healthcare organizations, particularly leaders, according to Sablone et al. (2024). Patients may assert that these institutions infringed against their rights, as documented by Drabiak (2022), by unlawfully using their personal data without consent. According to Cheng et al. (2024), clinical staff may be liable for AI system inexplicability that causes patient diagnostic and treatment errors. The aim of this study examined ethical problems associated with the use of AI and a pathway of damage that might lead to litigation suits.

Problem Statement

The use of AI and/or ML algorithms in clinical environments has seen a significant increase which can be attributed to the implementation of cost-effective strategies and the reduction of clinician fatigue, especially in the aftermath of a global pandemic. Nevertheless, as the dependence on the outcomes of the black box paradigm has grown, both staff and patients have reported occurrences of discriminatory and/or prejudiced assertions (Cho, 2021). According to Cirillo et al. (2020) with the implementation of AI in clinical settings, this technology has the potential to introduce historical, representation, measurement, aggregation, evaluation, and/or algorithmic bias. This difference is even more pronounced for patients with lower income and education levels. The hospital is now being sued by both employees and customers (patients) due to inconsistencies in patient care stemming from the use of data-driven technology. The primary business concerns center around the insufficient understanding of the legal obligations and liability, as well as the potential reputation and financial consequences, linked to allegations of bias and discrimination resulting from the utilization of AI and ML algorithms in patient care.

Significance of the Project

The aim is to evaluate the ethical quandary arising from the growing use of data-driven technologies, such as AIL, ML, and algorithms, in healthcare environments. The objective is to examine literature related to AI-driven clinical assessments, specifically to detect potential biases or prejudice and determine the accountable parties in instances when clinical staff or patient rights are infringed. The search was guided by the following research questions:

1. Who or whom has the responsibility and legal obligation for the use of data-driven technologies on patients and/or staff that may result in damage or inequities in healthcare settings?
2. What are the disadvantages of employing data-driven technologies in clinical settings for patients and clinical staff? What are the disparities in benefits among different demographic groups?

METHODOLOGY

Standards, guidelines, or protocols are necessary elements in the performance of systematic literature reviews which provides a quality review roadmap that produces comprehensive, valid, transparent, and reproducible results. The design of this narrative literature review follows the recommended Preferred Reporting Items for Systematic reviews and Meta-Analyses (PRISMA) which reviews effects of interventions used in healthcare settings (Higgins et al., 2023; Page et al., 2021). PRISMA was updated in 2020 (Qureshi et al., 2022) which provides guidance on how to report harm in clinical care. This model was selected due to the comprehensive 27-point checklist to provide transparent systematic review and quality review.

The steps will include performing the following processes: (a) identify and select relevant studies to assist with keywords and review historical information on the topic, (b) determine appropriate literature review methodology, (c) identify and search techniques, (d) report on findings and applicable theories, and (e) provide recommendations to stakeholders. The objective is to identify the current issue at hand that is under review.

Keywords

The search was conducted using Google Scholar to gather literature from January 2020 to June 24, 2024. This period was selected due to the dynamic nature of AI development which is continuing to evolve daily. An initial manual search was performed to find relevant studies (Sablone et al., 2024; Bottomley & Thalder, 2023) to help identify keywords such as AI including machine learning, algorithm, or black box; healthcare or clinical, liability including medico-legal, harm including discrimination or bias; and decision-making process. This was done to enhance the subsequent research search, data selection, and analysis.

Inclusion and Exclusion Criteria

Data collected was evaluated based on inclusion/exclusion and quality assessment criteria to filter and select relevant research sources to reduce introduction of bias. More detailed information regarding inclusion and exclusion criteria used in the review is presented in Table 1.

Table 1. Inclusion and exclusion criteria

Item#	Type	Include	Exclude
1	Language	Documents written in English	Documents written in a foreign language
2	Population	healthcare clinician/patients	non healthcare
3	Intervention	Mentions harm related to artificial intelligence, machine learning, or algorithm decisions	No mention of harm related to artificial intelligence, machine learning, or algorithm decisions
4	Outcome	Mentions discrimination, bias, prejudice, or disparities; liability, accountability	Did not focus on discrimination, bias, or prejudice
5	Publication Type	Peer-reviewed articles, studies or reports	Non-peer-reviewed articles, studies, or reports. No sources that require purchase or subscription

Information Sources

A digital search was performed using Google Scholar, an academic search engine. Marymount University library was connected to the researcher's Google Scholar profile to easily access full-text publications. A systematic evaluation of the reference lists of papers and reports was carried out using manual searching and forward citation tracking to find additional qualifying studies or study reports.

Search Strategy

The literature search was performed using Google Scholar, using a filter to include only publications written in English and published between January 2020 and June 24, 2024. To mitigate the issue of retrieving several irrelevant results on Google Scholar, the original query, identified below as number 1, included advanced search techniques such as the "intitle" operator, Boolean operators, and keyword synonyms. Consequently, only two results were obtained which was inadequate to conduct a thorough literature review. Due to the markedly low results, exclusive use of Boolean operators was used in the succeeding searches.

1. intitle: ["Artificial intelligence" OR "AI" OR "machine learning" OR "black box"] AND ["healthcare" OR "medical"] OR ["clinical decision-making"] AND ["harm" AND "discrimination" OR "bias"] AND ["liability" OR "professional liability" OR "medico-legal"] AND ["decision-making"].
   a. *Refinement 1*: ["Artificial intelligence" OR "machine learning" OR "black box"] AND ["healthcare" OR "medical"] OR ["clinical decision-making"] AND "discrimination" OR "bias"] AND ["liability" OR "professional liability" OR "medico-legal"] AND ["decision-making"].
   b. *Refinement 2*: ["Artificial intelligence OR AI" OR "machine learning" OR "black box"] AND ["healthcare"] OR ["clinical decision-making"] AND ["harm" AND "discrimination" OR "bias"] AND ["liability" OR "professional liability" OR "medico-legal"] AND ["patients" OR "customers"] AND ["clinicians" OR "physician" OR "provider"].

Data Selection

The following search, referred to as 1.a, yielded a total of 770 items within the stated period. Another keyword refinement, referred to as 1.b, specified the target population of the research. This led to a total of 267 articles that were selected for further examination. The results were stored in two separate Google Scholar libraries named 2024-06 Part I and Part II due to a limitation on the maximum number of articles that could be preserved in a single library. Google Scholar withdrew two articles in response to complaints received, resulting in a total of 265 articles being available for further review. The libraries were exported to RIS format and then uploaded into Zotero, an open-source program for managing references. Zotero detected 18 duplicate entries by comparing their titles, and the researcher manually merged them. As a result, 247 results remained that could potentially be screened. The remaining records were exported to CSV format and abstracts were manually inserted, if available, using the information obtained from Google Scholar.

Title and Abstract Screening

Each of the remaining 247 results underwent screening, which included evaluating the title and abstract using inclusion criteria items 1 through 4 as shown in Table 1. Documents that satisfied all four of the inclusion criteria were selected for further processing. A pivot table was created to examine screened article results to identify reasons for exclusion.

Document Extraction

A total of 104 records were deemed relevant and an effort was made to extract the full-text article. Eighteen full-text articles could not be retrieved, which resulted in 86 results being included in the next stage of full-text analysis.

Data Quality Assessment Review

The full-text articles were assessed using The Johns Hopkins (2022), Non-research Evidence Appraisal Tool, Appendix F, Section II, A: Level V appraisal tool, as illustrated in Figure 1. This evaluation was conducted solely based on literature reviews. The quality and eligibility of the studies were further evaluated by analyzing the complete textual records, which were categorized into three groups: high-quality (greater than four criteria met), moderate quality (greater than three criteria met), and low-quality (two or less criteria met).

Figure 1. The Johns Hopkins appraisal tool

Section II: Level V Quality Appraisal

A Select the type of article:

☐ **Integrative review** (summary of research evidence and theoretical literature; analyzes, compares themes, notes gaps in the selected literature)

☐ **Literature review** (summary of selected published literature including scientific and nonscientific, such as reports of organizational experience and opinions of experts)

Quality	After selecting the type of Level V evidence, determine the quality of evidence using the considerations below:		
	Is the purpose of the review clearly stated?	☐ Yes	☐ No
	Is literature relevant and up-to-date (most sources are within the past five years or classic)?	☐ Yes	☐ No
	Are gaps in the literature identified?	☐ Yes	☐ No
	Are recommendations made for future practice or study?	☐ Yes	☐ No
	Additionally, for Integrative Reviews only:		
	Was the literature search strategy clearly described?	☐ Yes	☐ No
	Was literature appraised for strength and quality	☐ Yes	☐ No
	Of the literature reviewed, is there a meaningful analysis of the conclusions across the articles included in the review?	☐ Yes	☐ No
	Are recommendations made for future practice or study?	☐ Yes	☐ No
	Circle the appropriate quality rating below:		

<u>**Integrative Reviews:**</u>

A High quality: Subject matter is clearly defined, literature search strategies are clear and thorough, authors undertook meaningful analysis of included evidence, conclusions are clear, gaps and limitations thoroughly addressed

B Good quality: Subject matter is defined, literature search strategy reasonably clear with possible gaps, author undertook somewhat meaningful analysis of included evidence, fairly clear conclusions, gaps and limitations reasonably addressed

C Low quality: Subject matter not clearly defined, literature search strategy lacking transparency or thoroughness, lack of meaningful analysis of included evidence, conclusions cannot be drawn, limitations not addressed

<u>**Literature Reviews:**</u>

A High quality: Subject matter is clearly defined, literature is up-to-date, gaps and limitations thoroughly addressed, recommendations for future practice or study are clearly identified

B Good quality: Subject matter is defined, literature is mostly up-to-date, gaps and limitations reasonably addressed, recommendations for future practice or study are identified

C Low quality: Subject matter not clearly defined, literature is out-of-date, gaps and limitations not addressed, recommendations are not provided

The PRISMA flow chart depicted in Figure 2 was used to record the number of articles that were excluded. To reduce the likelihood of bias in the research, reviews should be conducted with a rigorous and systematic approach. Barker et al. (2023) emphasized that a critical quality assessment necessitates the formulation of specific queries to determine the overall appropriateness for further investigation.

Figure 2. PRISMA flow diagram

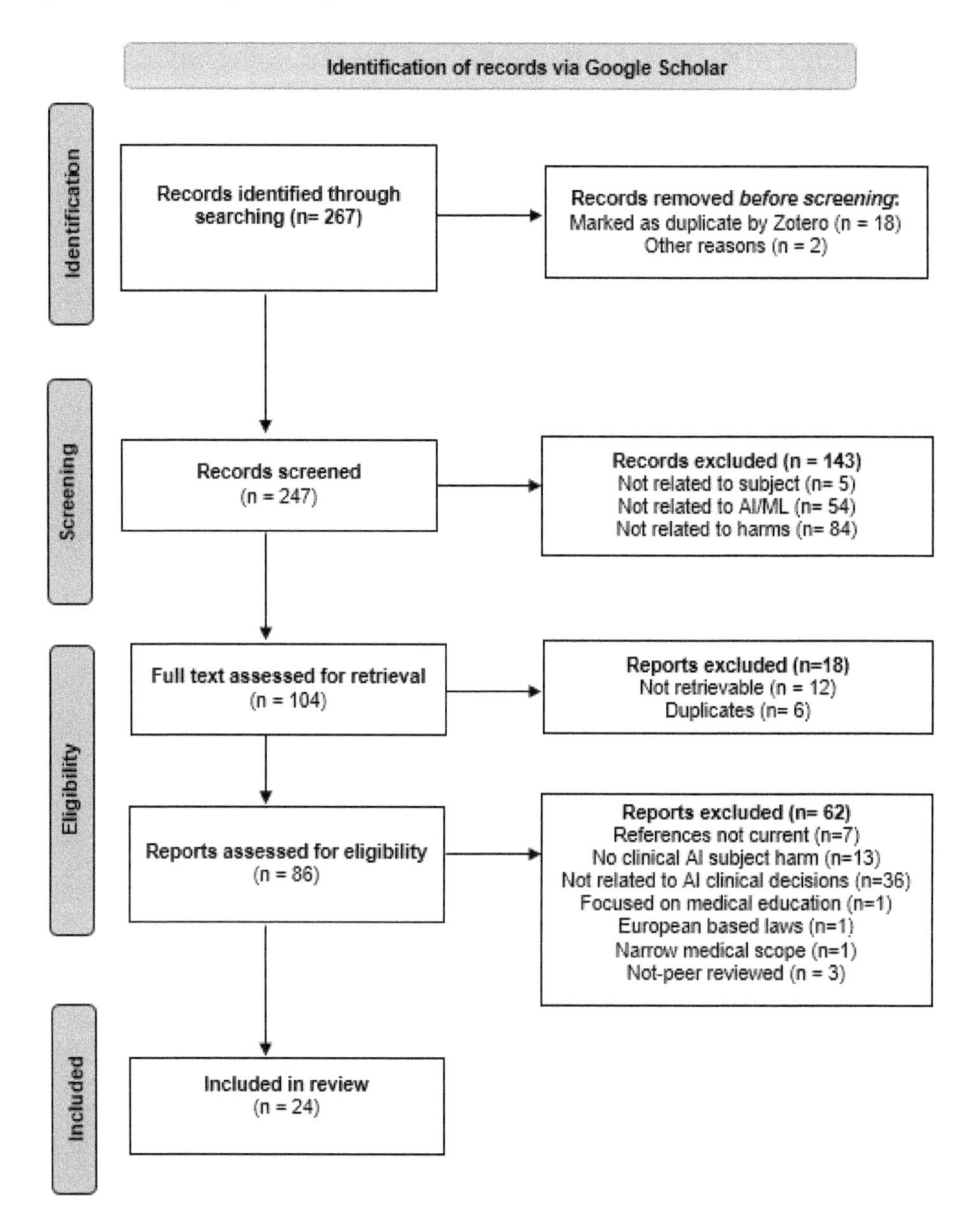

Data Synthesis and Reporting

The articles were originally categorized based on key results, including keywords, purpose, AI benefits, relevant legal proceedings, ethical difficulties for each stakeholder (including software manufacturers, hospital organizations, clinical personnel, and patients), recommendations, and knowledge gaps. Upon completion of the synthesis, the outcomes were classified into four different categories of possible offenses that might give rise to medico-legal issues and are likely to lead to litigation, as shown in Table 2. The analysis was conducted by a single reviewer, which may have restricted the scope of the thematic analysis.

THEORETICAL FRAMEWORK

An assessment and evaluation were carried out on the organization's possible deficiencies in terms of its culture, change management, risk management, and strategic direction. The study was conducted using appropriate theoretical frameworks or models and their pertinent components pertaining to challenges regarding clinical-AI adoption in decision-making.

Schein's Theory of Organizational Culture

Organizational culture refers to the established norms and underlying beliefs that function as a driving force for clinical personnel, influencing their capacity to provide high-quality care to patients. Schein's cultural argument, as outlined by Akpa et al. (2021), is built around three core concepts: "artifacts, espoused values, and underlying assumptions." The theory is well-suited for our research since it combines the social and technological components of the shift to AI-driven healthcare decision making. Akpa et al. (2021) underscores that Schein's theory focuses on the impact of an organization's values, beliefs, and customs on the behavior, cognition, and emotions of individuals. The findings indicate a potentially significant correlation between the beliefs and cognitive processes of healthcare staff, which might impact the treatment or denial of care for patients, regardless of the presence of advanced automation. The internal attitudes, beliefs, and actions of an organization may have enduring negative effects on others, since these behaviors may be seen as the prevailing standard.

Competing Values Framework Model

Institutions and individuals within organizations often have conflicting interests and values that influence their interactions and actions. According to Gong et al. (2022), the Competing Values Framework (CVP) was created by Robert Quinn and John Rohrbaugh. This framework categorizes organizational cultures into four types: clan, adhocracy, market, and hierarchical. Akpa et al. (2021) emphasize that CVP is used to analyze and evaluate the cultural dynamics across all organizational levels and to understand the unique causes of disputes in this study. However, in medical settings, when the objectives do not align with the same goals and principles, there may be significant repercussions.

Kurt Lewin's Change Management Model

Transformational leadership is essential during periods of transition, particularly when integrating AI tools into clinical environments. Lewin's change management model was chosen as a straightforward yet essential three-step approach that entails unfreeze, change, and freeze components as noted by Bellantuono et al. (2021) to assist leadership in the preparation and administration of organizational changes.

Hawkins SHEL Model of Human Factors

Organizations may be exposed to risk via human actions, lack of training, system vulnerabilities, and environmental factors, which can result in injury to patients, clinicians, and non-compliance with rules or laws. Lee (2023) assert that the SHEL paradigm has four essential elements: software, hardware, environment, and liveware. These components will be thoroughly explained in relation to their relevance to this research.

Strengths, Weakness, Opportunities, and Threats (SWOT) Model

The SWOT analysis is an invaluable approach for conducting analysis on the benefits and prospects of clinical AI in comparison to its weaknesses and threats. This approach was determined suitable for this study to identify areas where risk may be introduced, including the affected stakeholders. Clinical AI systems face several limitations, as highlighted by Karalis (2024), Ueda et al. (2023), Drabiak (2022), and Abdullah et al. (2021). These limitations encompass the risk of data breaches, challenges related to obtaining informed consent for data usage, insufficient training for clinicians, concerns about patient bias and discrimination, potential for medical errors in algorithm predictions, and a lack of oversight for the AI black-box phenomenon. These concerns are substantial and need the urgent attention of policy makers, AI researchers, AI developers, hospital executives, clinical professionals, and patients to advocate for important changes and legislation that control ethical practices of clinical AI.

There is currently limited information regarding global or local regulations and laws that govern accurate, transparent and reliable clinical AI. Cheng et al. (2024) and Chen et al. (2023) highlights a series of threats to organizations, clinicians, manufacturers, and even the AI tool itself. Ethical standards, regulation, and frameworks are another area of potential concern for all stakeholders regarding the ethical to medico-legal implications. Further research is required to ascertain the extent of potential failures and identify those who may be held liable and accountable for introducing harm to patients and clinicians.

LITERATURE REVIEW

The main challenge is medical-legal liability, sometimes referred to as medical malpractice, which involves establishing responsibility in AI-driven scenarios where individual rights have been infringed. Jain et al. (2023) noted that the use of Medical AI may lead to negative effects, including increased rates of misdiagnosis, biased point-of-care choices, and the continuation of healthcare disparities across underrepresented demographic groups. Algorithms used in clinical settings have the capacity to exacerbate disparities and impact the decision-making of healthcare professionals (Williamson & Prybutok, 2024; Singareddy et al., 2023; Prakash et al., 2022; Rajpurkar et al., 2022; Reddy et al., 2020). The use of AI in hospital settings is expected to lead to a continuous increase in opportunities for medico-legal issues (Chen et al., 2023; Rajpurkar, et al., 2022; Reddy et al., 2020). In *Hinlicky v. Dreyfuss* (2006), a vascular surgeon faced a medical malpractice lawsuit for failing to request a pre-operative cardiac assessment potentially contributing to a patient's fatal demise. This decision was made based on a clinical algorithm forecast that indicated the patient could undergo surgery without requiring a cardiac examination based on unknown variables considered. In the absence of legal frameworks, software developers, hospitals, and practitioners may encounter further repercussions and liabilities. To minimize the negative effects of data-driven technology in interactions with patients or colleagues, it is crucial for hospital leadership to actively create and demonstrate an atmosphere that prioritizes individuals over faster service delivery and revenue generation. Based on the review of existing literature, the information gathered was further categorized into pre, peri, and post implementation stages.

Pre-Implementation of Clinical AI

Whether they are seen or not, doctors' top priority for patient care are often at odds with hospital management's desires for achieving results in operational efficiency, cutting costs, and generating increased revenue. Industry 4.0 technologies which includes AI-driven applications, according to Vassolo et al. (2021), provide a value proposition that speeds up clinical diagnosis and lowers healthcare costs. However, according to researchers (Williamson & Prybutok, 2024; Prakash et al., 2022; Alabi et al., 2020), there are more detrimental effects using this technology than positive ones. These negative effects include bias, discrimination, fairness, privacy, lack of explainability, and obvious legal concerns which are dismissed in lieu of profits. This demonstrates the organization's disregard for practitioners by shifting the risk to the provider using these automated predictions, potentially posing a threat to patient safety. Thus, resulting in diagnosis error subject to litigation, disciplinary actions internally and externally, or finding another place of employment. Clinical organizations should serve as the first line of defense for their practitioners, but these organizations are putting their needs as a priority for competitive advantages.

Culture Shift to Clinical AI Adoption

Leaders need to convey the vision and the advantages of changes to employees, as well as to resolve any apprehensions, during the initial phase. Several studies (Cheng et al., 2024; Mennella, et al., 2024; Veritti et al., 2024) have indicated that clinicians have expressed an apprehension about the introduction of undisclosed risks, such as medical malpractice, as a significant obstacle to the adoption of AI, despite the potential benefits it could offer in the areas of diagnosis and efficiency. It is evident that executives are not adequately preparing and managing staff members' expectations of the changes, including timelines, as evidenced by the clinician's concerns. Another perspective posits that leadership is not sufficiently promoting diversity and inclusion to secure the support of others, both internally and externally. Hospital leaders have a duty to communicate visions of change that affect the entire organization, including the patients they serve.

Communication of Strategy and Vision of Clinical AI

Medical organizations often function at a hierarchical structure to make and enforce financial and operational decisions, rather than relying on collaborative efforts. This structure follows a top-down approach, where decision-making authority starts at the highest level and cascades down to the lowest level of personnel. Hinrichs-Krapels et al. (2022) found that hospitals do not include essential stakeholders in their decision-making processes, which could significantly affect many functional domains. Ueda et al. (2024) and Najjar (2023) and Ueda (2024) recommended that software developers need to have multidisciplinary teams including researchers, clinicians, and patient advocates involved in the development of AI solutions. Undoubtedly, this approach is an advantageous method that engages all stakeholders to get the optimal outcome for medical professionals as well as patients. An alternate viewpoint may argue that interacting with other stakeholders has the potential to influence the choices made by decision makers. Organizations must prioritize structure to establish clear reporting connections and facilitate effective decision-making. However, it is crucial to recognize that a strictly structured workplace may hinder inclusivity, potentially leading to various risks.

Procurement and Acquisitions of Clinical AI Technology

Organizations make procurement decisions relying on information provided by potential suppliers, as well as conducting independent due diligence to make an informed decision. Drabiak (2022) identified that the FDA has only granted clearance or approval to AI/ML medical devices that are "locked" with the present acquired patterns and predictions. The term "locked" in this context indicates that any further automated improvements is banned. Furthermore, Stewart et al. (2021) emphasizes the prevailing practice among clinical AI developers of augmenting actual patient data with artificially created data. This situation is both intriguing and concerning, as it raises several important questions. Firstly, have hospital organizations acquired applications that are "locked" or unlocked? Secondly, is the organization aware of the specific type of data being used in the acquired system? Lastly, do the decision-makers understand that the training data is more than likely not transferable due to differences in how the data is organized and labeled across healthcare systems? Decision-makers in healthcare settings must perform exhaustive research on acquisitions that might pose significant hazards to the institution and the community it serves.

Flawed Clinical AI Training Data

Organizations collect data, such as clinical notes and patients' medical histories, employing physical infrastructure for maintenance, storage and security over these valuable assets. Khanday et al. (2024) emphasized that the collection and dissemination of patient data are susceptible to several challenges, such as hacking, privacy breaches, and difficulties in gaining informed consent of patient data. Furthermore, Masoumian Hosseini et al. (2023) contended that achieving informed consent from every patient is unrealistic. These results indicate that organizations are inclined to take risks when it comes to using patients' data in AI systems, without being honest and open about the potential risks involved. An alternate viewpoint may argue that AI developers and healthcare organizations may generate significant financial gains via the acquisition and use of this data. Crucially, patients must inquire and assert their rights prior to any harm occurring during their treatment.

Risk Transfer to Patients

In healthcare settings, firms may possess evidence that incorporates contemporary technology, such as software systems that may include prejudiced assumptions integrated into the solution. Several studies (Cheng et al., 2024; Brereton et al., 2023; Timmons et al., 2023; Rajpurkar et al., 2022) have shown that machine learning algorithms based on data analysis heavily depend on datasets that often exhibit inadequate inclusion of minority groups. These algorithms are specifically developed to acquire knowledge and provide clinical forecasts and diagnosis. Table 3 displays the headquarters' locations of clinical AI-driven enterprises, with the majority being in Silicon Valley. Silicon Valley is recognized for its wealthy population, but it is also renowned for its lack of diversity and inclusion. According to this finding, it is very probable that the algorithms developed in these areas may be void of any severely limited health information on individuals belonging to the black, Indian, and Hawaiian demographic groups resulting in biased and discriminatory clinical predictions. This technology is not only marketed in wealthy regions but can be found in any location where organizations possess the required financial resources. However, it may not accurately reflect the patient demographic, leading to severe implications for patients. Artifacts could be anything, but in this case, its clinical AI-solutions that should be representative of a diverse and equitable population and not just cater to the affluent.

Table 3. Clinical AI manufacturer locations

#	Clinical AI Developer	Headquarters	Reference	White	Black	Indian	Asian	Hawaiian	Hispanic
1	Butterfly Network	Burlington, MA	U.S Census Bureau	**77.10%**	2.10%	0.10%	**14.50%**	0.20%	2.80%
2	Caption Health	San Mateo, CA	U.S Census Bureau	**56.90%**	2.70%	1.00%	**33.10%**	1.40%	**24.80%**
3	Cloud MedX	Sunnyvale, CA	U.S Census Bureau	**31.60%**	1.20%	0.50%	**49.60%**	0.10%	**16.70%**
4	Enlitic	San Francisco, CA	U.S Census Bureau	**41.90%**	5.20%	0.60%	**34.80%**	0.40%	**15.50%**

Provider Job Insecurities

Clinical practitioners may experience job insecurity due to the use of generative AI technologies. Singareddy et al. (2023) emphasized that doctors exhibit a reluctance to accept novel methodologies because they want to preserve control over patient care. Conversely, Vo et al. (2023) argued that 47% of research indicated that doctors do not hold the belief that they will be entirely substituted by AI technology. This indicates that there is a lack of consensus among clinical personnel about the use of algorithms in clinical decision-making. Furthermore, this highlights the insufficient efforts made by hospital organizations to effectively convey their vision, advantages, and potential risks associated with novel AI-driven solutions to key stakeholders to gain their support.

Implementation of Clinical AI

Medical institutions believe that using machine learning algorithms will solve numerous operational problems. Čartolovni et al. (2022) and Drabiak (2022) revealed that omission errors occur treating patients when clinicians fail to spot clinical decision system flaws owing to misunderstanding. This omission can be introduced when the organizations fail to provide adequate support and training for clinical staff when implementing new applications. Lack of proper training, including refresher, may lead to medical malpractice litigation. If healthcare professionals were thoroughly trained, providers would be able to report these adverse events to the manufacturer, who is required to submit adverse event reports received (FDA, 2022). Little is known if the appropriate stakeholders are performing due diligence and notifying the appropriate agencies if harm is introduced. Lack of AI tool understanding may lead to diagnostic and treatment mistakes causing harm to patients. These algorithms may not solve issues but create new ones, like malpractice and monetary penalties.

Lack of Training of Clinical AI Systems

After the plans for change are initiated, leadership must take a variety of steps to prepare staff, including providing training, making incremental changes, seeking feedback, and readjusting as needed. This encompasses the participation of others in the process, such as the assignment of internal and external champions for the change and the provision of support. Cheng et al. (2024) found that 16 out of 22 studies revealed a lack of comprehension surrounding the decision-making processes of AI models. What is even more concerning is that a significant majority of Chief Medical Officers, namely 62%, lacked confidence in their capacity to prevent or identify mistakes in AI systems (Drabiak, 2022). Insufficient understanding or inability to seek advice from medical experts may lead to incorrect diagnosis and treatment suggestions for patients. Implementing changes cannot be done in isolation and requires a methodical approach that includes preparation, communication, and a contingency plan, if necessary.

Provider Black-Box Syndrome

Healthcare administrators want to use innovative technologies to obtain a competitive advantage and provide treatments more expeditiously, frequently at the expense of service providers. Sablone et al. (2024) and Veritti et al. (2024) highlight the issue of the "black-box" problem, where physicians are often compelled to use AI-driven technology that they cannot fully understand or interpret, much alone clarify the prediction process to others, including their patients. In addition, doctors who depend on AI-driven results may be susceptible to delivering diagnoses with automation bias errors (Abdullah et al., 2021) and may be unable to recognize this danger owing to a lack of technical expertise. This discovery may be likened to medical experts blindly tossing darts and trying to diagnose patients and provide treatment plans. Hospitals have the authority to decide whether to engage in technology solutions that carry substantial risks for practitioners, such as license suspensions or malpractice lawsuits, which seems highly alarming.

Supervision of Clinical AI Usage

Organizations driven more by resources are more prone to human errors and mistakes. Molloy and O'Boyle (2005) define liveware as the core component emphasizing the human operator. Karalis (2024) and Naik et al. (2022) contend that algorithmic design by humans with internal bias creates challenges relating to selection bias, transparency, and accountability concerns. These results would lead to disparities in options for treatment for demographic groups, hence increasing inequality. Hospital administrators choose procurement options without thoroughly evaluating the associated risk. According to Ueda et al. (2023), after integrating systems, it becomes the organization's responsibility to supervise clinical AI tools, which are not properly understood and have the potential to harm the organization's reputation, finances, and liability. The choices made by organizational developers and executives have a cascading impact, where a triggering event, such as software design, may result in more substantial and possibly harmful consequences for companies, physicians, and patients.

Clinical AI Lacks Human Connection

The doctor-patient connection necessitates a substantial degree of faith and trust from the patient, who entrusts these experts or technologies, sometimes without their conscious knowledge, to manage their most critical medical issues. According to Drabiak (2022), physicians are obligated and legally required to advise their patients about the advantages, disadvantages, and alternative options available in the treatment modalities they prescribe. Organizations are required to obtain the patient's permission when using AI-driven technology in their healthcare as stated by Chen et al. (2023). It may be that patients upon realizing the composition of their healthcare team, including non-humans, could hesitate to provide important health information due to worries about privacy which may result in patients not receiving the necessary care needed. Trust is established by engaging in open and honest conversation and providing patients with comprehensive information to protect the successful outcome of their medical treatment.

Post-Implementation of Clinical AI

Currently, no governance structure has been established to identify who should be held legally responsible in the case of patient damage. Naik et al. (2022) underscores the considerable hurdles of culpability in medical AI failures. This implies that patients are entering healthcare organizations that may be more prone to medical errors due to the employment of unverified and under representative clinical algorithms. More significantly, patients should not have to cope with the consequences of non-human choices when it is a person who decided to utilize this technology in patient care.

CONCLUSION

The present narrative systematic review research study aims to provide a starting step and guidance for the construction of a modern digital literacy framework including key topics and elements related to digital literacy. This paper presents a set of suggestions for both scholars and practitioners.

Recommendations for Organizations and Practitioners

The current regulation lacks sufficient provisions to assign responsibility for the adoption and deployment of clinical AI. One strategy that practitioners might use is advocating for themselves and their patients by fighting for the notion that the absence of policies corresponds to a lack of protection and possible legal consequences including their livelihood. Furthermore, organizations are determining the final decision to use clinical AI systems inside hospital organizations and should also be advocating for their own interests and the well-being of their staff. Governance will facilitate and endorse a clear and definitive threshold of responsibility depending on the specific categories of AI events that may arise with the technology.

Multiple strategies may be used by hospital organizations and healthcare practitioners to minimize the risk of medico-legal issues. Hospital organizations should exercise due diligence whenever instruments, including technology tools, are obtained and integrated into clinical environments. Akin to mergers and acquisitions, it is essential to carry out regulatory, legal, and operational assessments before entering contracts with suppliers. The suggestion entails practitioners creating a thorough quality assurance supplier qualification checklist and ensuring a comprehensive evaluation is carried out and recorded in the event of future legal disputes. This review should also include review of the FDA compliance, prior client reference checks and complaints received regarding the product in question.

The findings of this research study suggest that the training data often used in clinical algorithms leads to subjective bias and prejudice due to inadequate representation. Therefore, healthcare institutions should conduct a thorough verification study to determine the characteristics of the training data used in the algorithm and evaluate the feasibility of adapting it to the patient population in that clinical setting. Imbalanced training data may result in incorrect diagnosis and significant repercussions for organizations and practitioners. If training data is not representative of the current organization's population, the administration should seek to develop customized based algorithms that will meet the needs of their current organization and in the future.

Moreover, it is essential for organizations to conduct incremental pilot testing of algorithms in healthcare settings across different departments prior to full deployment. Furthermore, pharmaceutical companies need many years to introduce their products to the patient population because of the considerable difficulties and risks involved. This is an opportunity for the business to proficiently communicate their goal to healthcare personnel and patients, thereby securing their endorsement and facilitating the execution of essential modifications in the process. Furthermore, this is an opportunity to enlighten patients about the purpose of including clinical artificial intelligence (AI) into the decision-making process and secure their informed consent beforehand to guarantee transparency, openness, and honesty, so possibly reducing or eliminating medico-legal conflicts.

Before fully implementing clinical AI tools, organizations must guarantee that their clinical personnel are adequately educated and skilled to efficiently read, evaluate, and interpret the data generated and the decisions made by the clinical AI system. Prior to mandating workers to use such technology, organizations should verify the credentials of the providers. This advice entails that business organizations have the responsibility of providing the essential resources to enable workers to carry out their job duties with safety and efficiency. An alternate approach would be to include in the contract between the organization and the AI manufacturer the provision of regular initial and refresher training for both clinicians and other healthcare personnel, depending on the specific services desired.

Directions for Future Research

There is little information available on the process of contract negotiations for healthcare facilities and the specific provisions related to the responsibility and accountability of black box AI technologies used in clinical settings. To enhance future studies, it would be beneficial to further investigate how healthcare companies are assessing and evaluating suppliers of AI/ML technologies before incorporating them into their facilities potentially causing harm to patients and employees.

Patients often oppose changes to the conventional medical treatment program due to apprehension. Mennella et al. (2024) and Prakash et al. (2022) contend that patients should own the authority to choose whether their healthcare "team" incorporates AI technology suggestions that may be influenced by biases and prone to errors. This study emphasizes a critical aspect: hospitals possess the ability to either reveal a multitude of problems or choose to keep silent until people demand answers. Nevertheless, given algorithms carry a comparable degree of danger to human providers, it is necessary to carry out more study with both inpatient and outpatient patients to see if they are being sought for guidance on the involvement of humans or non-humans in their patient treatment and care.

The FDA is tasked with monitoring the safety and efficacy of medical devices, particularly those used in clinical environments. An analysis of the FDA (2024) MedWatch reporting system revealed that there were 89 safety warnings issued for medical devices, but none of them contained any reports specifically related to clinical AI systems. Furthermore, the FDA utilizes this information to do risk-based assessments of products covered under its regulation. This finding is intriguing since it is based on published data suggesting prejudice that might lead to mistakes in diagnosis, ultimately causing injury to patients. Further investigation should be devoted to this subject to ascertain if organizations and manufacturers are underreporting true complaints or really there is no reason for concern about the utilization of these instruments in clinical decision-making.

The issue of informed consent regarding data ownership is a crucial subject for all parties involved. González-Gonzalo et al. (2022) also suggested that patient agreements should include restrictions in terms of geographic region, time duration, and project scope. Future research should investigate the extent to which hospital organizations are using patients' data via blanket permission agreements, and specifically how this information is communicated to patients to ensure their comprehensive understanding of the internal and external usage of their data by the organization or third parties. If organizations and perhaps healthcare experts are responsible for the data, it should not be challenging to be transparent and upfront with patients on the benefits and risk unless there is a need to conceal information.

The absence of any existing legislation, policy, or law that clearly specifies the party accountable for clinical AI-induced misdiagnosis represents a significant information gap and poses a danger to core stakeholders. Naik et al. (2022) highlight the substantial difficulties surrounding the deployment of AI in healthcare settings due to the absence of accountability. Future researchers should pursue more comprehensive inquiries on the current situation at the federal and state levels regarding the accountability of AI manufacturers, hospital organizations, and/or clinical providers in instances of medical AI errors. Patients shouldn't have to endure the consequences of inadequate governance rules and/or legislation that lack safeguards to protect them from harm.

Limitations

The current study is not immune to limitations. The research articles for this study were entirely compiled using Google Scholar, which may have resulted in a restricted number of sources. To expand the existing body of literature, researchers could consider including supplementary dataset sets in the future. The main objective of this research is to examine the use of AI technology in healthcare environments that might potentially contribute to the continuation of existing inequalities among certain demographic groups. However, the existing body of literature is extensive, mostly because to the growing and developing artificial intelligence paradigm in clinical settings. Therefore, it is anticipated that future researchers will integrate additional relevant material to complement or progress our work.

REFERENCES

Abdullah, Y. I., Schuman, J. S., Shabsigh, R., Caplan, A., & Al-Aswad, L. A. (2021). Ethics of artificial intelligence in medicine and ophthalmology. *Asia-Pacific Journal of Ophthalmology*, 10(3), 289–298. DOI: 10.1097/APO.0000000000000397 PMID: 34383720

Akpa, V. O., Asikhia, O. U., & Nneji, N. E. (2021). Organizational culture and organizational performance: A review of literature. *International Journal of Advances in Engineering and Management*, 3(1), 361–372. DOI: 10.35629/5252-030136137

Alabi, R. O., Vartiainen, T., & Elmusrati, M. (2020). Machine learning for prognosis of oral cancer: What are the ethical challenges? *CEUR Workshop Proceedings*.

Barker, T. H., Stone, J. C., Sears, K., Klugar, M., Leonardi-Bee, J., Tufanaru, C., & Munn, Z. (2023). Revising the JBI quantitative critical appraisal tools to improve their applicability: An overview of methods and the development process. *JBI Evidence Synthesis*, 21(3), 478–493. DOI: 10.11124/JBIES-22-00125 PMID: 36121230

Bellantuono, N., Nuzzi, A., Pontrandolfo, P., & Scozzi, B. (2021). Digital Transformation Models for the I4.0 Transition: Lessons from the Change Management Literature. *Sustainability (Basel)*, 13(23), 12941. Advance online publication. DOI: 10.3390/su132312941

Bottomley, D., & Thaldar, D. (2023). Liability for harm caused by AI in healthcare: An overview of the core legal concepts. *Frontiers in Pharmacology*, 14, 1297353. DOI: 10.3389/fphar.2023.1297353 PMID: 38161692

Brereton, T. A., Malik, M. M., Lifson, M., Greenwood, J. D., Peterson, K. J., & Overgaard, S. M. (2023). The role of artificial intelligence model documentation in translational science: Scoping review. *Interactive Journal of Medical Research*, 12(1), e45903. DOI: 10.2196/45903 PMID: 37450330

Čartolovni, A., Tomičić, A., & Mosler, E. L. (2022). Ethical, legal, and social considerations of AI-based medical decision-support tools: A scoping review. *International Journal of Medical Informatics*, 161, 104738. DOI: 10.1016/j.ijmedinf.2022.104738 PMID: 35299098

Chen, A., Wang, C., & Zhang, X. (2023). Reflection on the equitable attribution of responsibility for artificial intelligence-assisted diagnosis and treatment decisions. *Intelligent Medicine*, 3(2), 139–143. Advance online publication. DOI: 10.1016/j.imed.2022.04.002

Cheng, R., Aggarwal, A., Chakraborty, A., Harish, V., McGowan, M., Roy, A., Szulewski, A., & Nolan, B. (2024). Implementation considerations for the adoption of artificial intelligence in the emergency department. *The American Journal of Emergency Medicine*, 82, 75–81. DOI: 10.1016/j.ajem.2024.05.020 PMID: 38820809

Cho, M. K. (2021). Rising to the challenge of bias in health care AI. *Nature Medicine*, 27(12), 2079–2081. DOI: 10.1038/s41591-021-01577-2 PMID: 34893774

Cirillo, D., Catuara-Solarz, S., Morey, C., Guney, E., Subirats, L., Mellino, S., Gigante, A., Valencia, A., Rementeria, M. J., Chadha, A. S., & Mavridis, N. (2020). Sex and gender differences and biases in artificial intelligence for biomedicine and healthcare. *NPJ Digital Medicine*, 3(1), 81. Advance online publication. DOI: 10.1038/s41746-020-0288-5 PMID: 32529043

Drabiak, K. (2022). Leveraging law and ethics to promote safe and reliable AI/ML in healthcare. *Frontiers in Nuclear Medicine*, 2, 983340. Advance online publication. DOI: 10.3389/fnume.2022.983340 PMID: 39354991

Food and Drug Administration. (2022, November 9). *Medical Product Safety Information*. https://www.fda.gov/safety/medwatch-fda-safety-information-and-adverse-event-reporting-program/medical-product-safety-information

Food and Drug Administration. (2024, July 25). *MedWatch: The FDA Safety Information and Adverse Event Reporting Program*. https://www.fda.gov/safety/medwatch-fda-safety-information-and-adverse-event-reporting-program

Gong, L., Jiang, S., & Liang, X. (2022). Competing value framework-based culture transformation. *Journal of Business Research*, 145, 853–863. DOI: 10.1016/j.jbusres.2022.03.019

González-Gonzalo, C., Thee, E. F., Klaver, C. C., Lee, A. Y., Schlingemann, R. O., Tufail, A., Verbraak, F., & Sánchez, C. I. (2022). Trustworthy AI: Closing the gap between development and integration of AI systems in ophthalmic practice. *Progress in Retinal and Eye Research*, 90, 101034. Advance online publication. DOI: 10.1016/j.preteyeres.2021.101034 PMID: 34902546

Higgins, J. P. T., Thomas, J., Chandle, J., Cumpston, M., Li, T., Page, M. J., & Welch, V. A. (Eds.). (2023). *Cochrane Handbook for Systematic Reviews of Interventions* version 6.4 (updated August 2023). Available from www.training.cochrane.org/handbook

Hinlicky v. Dreyfuss, 848 N.E.2d 1285, 6 N.Y.3d 636, 815 N.Y.S.2d 908 (2006).

Hinrichs-Krapels, S., Hinrichs-Krapels, B., Ditewig, H., Boulding, A., Chalkidou, J., & Erskine, F. (2022). Purchasing high-cost medical devices and equipment in hospitals: A systematic review. *BMJ Open*, 12(9), e057516. Advance online publication. DOI: 10.1136/bmjopen-2021-057516 PMID: 36581959

Jain, A., Brooks, J. R., Alford, C. C., Chang, C. S., Mueller, N. M., Umscheid, C. A., & Bierman, A. S. (2023). Awareness of Racial and Ethnic Bias and Potential Solutions to Address Bias With Use of Health Care Algorithms. *JAMA Health Forum*, 4(6), e231197. Advance online publication. DOI: 10.1001/jamahealthforum.2023.1197 PMID: 37266959

Karalis, V. D. (2024). The Integration of Artificial Intelligence into Clinical Practice. *Applied Biosciences*, 3(1), 14–44. DOI: 10.3390/applbiosci3010002

Khanday, S. (2024). Horizon of Healthcare: AI's Evolutionary Journey and Future Implications. *World Journal of Advanced Engineering Technology and Sciences*, 11(2), 308–324. DOI: 10.30574/wjaets.2024.11.2.0118

Lee, S. J. (2023). An Exploratory Study on Human Factor Analysis of Medical Accidents Using the SHELL (Software, Hardware, Environment, Liveware) Model. *Korean Journal of Aerospace and Environmental Medicine*, 33(3), 94–99. DOI: 10.46246/KJAsEM.230019

Masoumian Hosseini, M., Masoumian Hosseini, S. T., Qayumi, K., Ahmady, S., & Koohestani, H. R. (2023). The Aspects of Running Artificial Intelligence in Emergency Care; a Scoping Review. *Archives of Academic Emergency Medicine*, 11(1), e38. DOI: 10.22037/aaem.v11i1.1974 PMID: 37215232

Mennella, C., Maniscalco, U., De Pietro, G., & Esposito, M. (2024). Ethical and regulatory challenges of AI technologies in healthcare: A narrative review. *Heliyon*, 10(4), e26297. Advance online publication. DOI: 10.1016/j.heliyon.2024.e26297 PMID: 38384518

Naik, N., Hameed, B. M. Z., Shetty, D. K., Swain, D., Shah, M., Paul, R., Aggarwal, K., Ibrahim, S., Patil, V., Smriti, K., Shetty, S., Rai, B. P., Chlosta, P., & Somani, B. K. (2022). Legal and Ethical Consideration in Artificial Intelligence in Healthcare: Who Takes Responsibility? *Frontiers in Surgery*, 9, 862322. Advance online publication. DOI: 10.3389/fsurg.2022.862322 PMID: 35360424

Najjar, R. (2023). Redefining Radiology: A Review of Artificial Intelligence Integration in Medical Imaging. *Diagnostics (Basel)*, 13(17), 2760. Advance online publication. DOI: 10.3390/diagnostics13172760 PMID: 37685300

Page, M. J., Page, J. E., McKenzie, P. M., Bossuyt, I., Boutron, T. C., Hoffmann, C. D., Mulrow, L., Shamseer, J. M., Tetzlaff, E. A., Akl, S. E., Brennan, R., Chou, J., Glanville, J. M., Grimshaw, A., Hróbjartsson, M. M., Lalu, T., Li, E. W., Loder, E., Mayo-Wilson, S., & McGuinness, L. A. (2021). The PRISMA 2020 statement: An updated guideline for reporting systematic reviews. *BMJ (Clinical Research Ed.)*, 372, n71. Advance online publication. DOI: 10.1136/bmj.n71 PMID: 33782057

Prakash, S., Balaji, J. N., Joshi, A., & Surapaneni, K. M. (2022). Ethical Conundrums in the Application of Artificial Intelligence (AI) in Healthcare—A Scoping Review of Reviews. *Journal of Personalized Medicine*, 12(11), 1914. Advance online publication. DOI: 10.3390/jpm12111914 PMID: 36422090

Qureshi, R., Mayo-Wilson, E., & Li, T. (2022). Harm in Systematic Reviews Paper 1: An introduction to research on harm. *Journal of Clinical Epidemiology*, 143, 186–196. DOI: 10.1016/j.jclinepi.2021.10.023 PMID: 34742788

Rajpurkar, P., Chen, E., Banerjee, O., & Topol, E. J. (2022). AI in health and medicine. *Nature Medicine*, 28(1), 31–38. DOI: 10.1038/s41591-021-01614-0 PMID: 35058619

Reddy, S., Allan, S., Coghlan, S., & Cooper, P. (2020). A governance model for the application of AI in health care. *Journal of the American Medical Informatics Association: JAMIA*, 27(3), 491–497. DOI: 10.1093/jamia/ocz192 PMID: 31682262

Sablone, S., Bellino, M., Cardinale, A. N., Esposito, M., Sessa, F., & Salerno, M. (2024). Artificial intelligence in healthcare: An Italian perspective on ethical and medico-legal implications. *Frontiers in Medicine*, 11, 1343456. DOI: 10.3389/fmed.2024.1343456 PMID: 38887675

Singareddy, S., Sn, V. P., Jaramillo, A. P., Yasir, M., Iyer, N., Hussein, S., & Nath, T. S. (2023). Artificial intelligence and its role in the management of chronic medical conditions: A systematic review. *Cureus*, 15(9). Advance online publication. DOI: 10.7759/cureus.46066 PMID: 37900468

Stewart, J., Lu, J., Goudie, A., Bennamoun, M., Sprivulis, P., Sanfillipo, F., & Dwivedi, G. (2021). Applications of machine learning to undifferentiated chest pain in the emergency department: A systematic review. *PLoS One*, 16(8), e0252612. DOI: 10.1371/journal.pone.0252612 PMID: 34428208

The Johns Hopkins Health System/Johns Hopkins School of Nursing (2022). Johns Hopkins evidence-based practice for nurses and healthcare professionals: Model and guidelines.

Timmons, A. C., Duong, J. B., Simo Fiallo, N., Lee, T., Vo, H. P. Q., Ahle, M. W., Comer, J. S., Brewer, L. P. C., Frazier, S. L., & Chaspari, T. (2023). A call to action on assessing and mitigating bias in artificial intelligence applications for mental health. *Perspectives on Psychological Science*, 18(5), 1062–1096. DOI: 10.1177/17456916221134490 PMID: 36490369

Ueda, D., Kakinuma, T., Fujita, S., Kamagata, K., Fushimi, Y., Ito, R., Matsui, Y., Nozaki, T., Nakaura, T., Fujima, N., Tatsugami, F., Yanagawa, M., Hirata, K., Yamada, A., Tsuboyama, T., Kawamura, M., Fujioka, T., & Naganawa, S. (2024). Fairness of artificial intelligence in healthcare: Review and recommendations. *Japanese Journal of Radiology*, 42(1), 3–15. DOI: 10.1007/s11604-023-01474-3 PMID: 37540463

Vassolo, R. S., Vassolo, A. F., Mac Cawley, G. L., Tortorella, F. S., Fogliatto, D., & Tlapa, G. (2021). Hospital Investment Decisions in Healthcare 4.0 Technologies: Scoping Review and Framework for Exploring Challenges, Trends, and Research Directions. *Journal of Medical Internet Research*, 23(8), e27571. Advance online publication. DOI: 10.2196/27571 PMID: 34435967

Veritti, D., Rubinato, L., Sarao, V., De Nardin, A., Foresti, G. L., & Lanzetta, P. (2024). Behind the mask: A critical perspective on the ethical, moral, and legal implications of AI in ophthalmology. *Graefe's Archive for Clinical and Experimental Ophthalmology*, 262(3), 975–982. DOI: 10.1007/s00417-023-06245-4 PMID: 37747539

Vo, V., Chen, G., Aquino, Y. S. J., Carter, S. M., Do, Q. N., & Woode, M. E. (2023). Multi-stakeholder preferences for the use of artificial intelligence in healthcare: A systematic review and thematic analysis. *Social Science & Medicine*, 338, 116357. Advance online publication. DOI: 10.1016/j.socscimed.2023.116357 PMID: 37949020

Williamson, S. M., & Prybutok, V. (2024). Balancing Privacy and Progress: A Review of Privacy Challenges, Systemic Oversight, and Patient Perceptions in AI-Driven Healthcare. *Applied Sciences (Basel, Switzerland)*, 14(2), 675. Advance online publication. DOI: 10.3390/app14020675

Chapter 12
Maturity of Healthcare IS/IT Systems

Jorge Vareda Gomes
https://orcid.org/0000-0003-0656-9284
Universidade Lusófona, Portugal

Mário Romão
https://orcid.org/0000-0003-4564-1883
ISEG, Universidade de Lisboa, Portugal

ABSTRACT

The use of information systems and technology (IS/IT) in healthcare has been recognized as crucial for improving the efficiency, cost-effectiveness, quality, and safety of medical care delivery. IS/IT has the potential to enhance individual health outcomes and provider performance by delivering better quality care, achieving cost savings, and increasing patient involvement in their own health. Two major drivers have spurred IS/IT investments in healthcare: the rapidly increasing burden of chronic diseases, with costs growing significantly, and the recognition of the need for substantial improvements in the quality and safety of healthcare delivery. Maturity models (MM) are based on the premise that people, organizations, functional areas, and processes evolve through a development process, progressing towards a more advanced state of maturity by passing through distinct levels. The application of MM in healthcare offers significant opportunities to enhance information and knowledge management. This paper summarizes some of the recent developments in this area.

DOI: 10.4018/979-8-3693-8562-3.ch012

INTRODUCTION

In the digital era, citizens expect modern public services to adhere to several key principles, including the use of a single-entry point for related services, one-time data or document submission, transparency in processes, effective use of public data, and strong data security protection (Pamungkas et al., 2019). The development of electronic healthcare services poses challenges related to the effective collaboration of systems and stakeholders within a highly regulated environment (Kouroubali et al., 2019). In nearly every industry, organizations invest significantly in Information Systems (IS) and Information Technology (IT) with the expectation of achieving substantial benefits post-implementation (Gomes & Romão, 2015). However, despite these considerable investments, the anticipated benefits often remain ambiguous or contradictory (Ward & Daniels, 2012). The linkage between IS/IT investments and enhancements in organizational performance has been extensively debated (Melville et al., 2004). While numerous studies affirm the operational and strategic significance of IS/IT (Aral et al., 2006); Han, Chang, & Hahn, 2011; Ramirez, Melville, & Lawler, 2010), the precise causal relationship between IS/IT investments and tangible business value is still not fully clarified. Strategic management is becoming increasingly important for sustainable management in healthcare (Huebner & Flessa, 2022). Hospitals around the world are implementing ambitious digital transformation programs as part of broader initiatives to build digitally advanced healthcare systems. However, there is still no consensus on the best approach to define and evaluate digital excellence in hospitals (Krasuska et al., 2020).

In the healthcare sector, the potential of IS/IT to transform methods and processes is significant, offering improvements in patient care, operational performance, cost efficiency, and patient engagement (Buntin et al., 2011; Cleven et al., 2016).

The World Health Organization defines social determinants of health as the conditions in which people are born, grow, work, live, and age, as well as the broader forces and systems shaping these conditions. These determinants encompass factors such as socioeconomic status, education, the neighbourhood and physical environment, employment, social support networks, and access to healthcare. The influence of the social environment and structural barriers to accessing care and supportive resources has shifted attention towards community-level effects, with information gathered from various spatial data products. These factors are sometimes referred to as social and environmental determinants of health to highlight the critical role of the environment [10]. In the healthcare sector, maturity models help address the complexities and extensive needs of healthcare systems (Chong et al., 2020; Liu et al., 2021). The public health system faces significant challenges due to rising costs, constrained budgets, and insufficient workforce distribution (Mishra & Sharma, 2022) to enhance process efficiency and demonstrate the quality of care (Neumann

& Purdy, 2023). Research highlights that deficiencies in health process management are frequently attributed to infrastructure limitations and inefficient management practices (Bagyendera 2023). The complexity of implementing advanced technologies often exacerbates these challenges, making successful outcomes harder to achieve (Mansour & Nogues, 2022).

In response, governments have undertaken healthcare reforms to improve transparency, quality, safety, patient satisfaction, and cost control. Hospitals have invested heavily in process improvements, yet there is no consensus on the exact capabilities required or the sequence of development steps necessary to achieve process-oriented status (Cleven et al., 2014). Influenced by successful practices from other industries, healthcare has introduced models like patient-focused hospitals and clinical pathways to embed process management into hospital operations (Bragato & Jacobs, 2013; Rohner, 2012). Empirical research supports that process orientation can significantly enhance hospital performance (van Wijngaarden et al 2023). Maturity models offer a framework for assessing systems by outlining a series of stages that guide progress toward optimal development (Domlyn et al., 2021). According to Fraser et al. (2002) all maturity models share the property of defining a number of dimensions at various stages of maturity, with a description of characteristic performance at various levels of granularity. Digital maturity is the extent to which digital technologies are used as enablers to deliver a high-quality health service (Flott et al., 2016). In an era where healthcare costs are rising, budgets are constrained, and patient expectations are increasing, hospitals must find ways to improve operational efficiency and care quality (Pai, 2023). The potential of digital technologies and process management to transform healthcare is enormous, but many hospitals struggle to realize the full benefits of their investments (Stoumpos et al., 2023). Clear pathways to achieving digital maturity are lacking, and without a structured approach, hospitals risk falling short of their goals (Duncan et al., 2022). Despite significant investments in digital transformation and process improvements, hospitals face challenges in defining and achieving digital excellence (Iyanna et al., 2022). The link between IS/IT investments and tangible improvements in healthcare performance remains unclear, and the complexity of implementing advanced technologies hinders progress (Stoumpos et al., 2023). Maturity models offer a potential framework for guiding hospitals toward improved process management and organizational effectiveness, but there is no consensus on the required capabilities or steps to reach digital maturity (Aiwerioghene et al., 2024). This paper explores how maturity models can help hospitals enhance healthcare delivery and operational efficiency.

MATURITY MODELS FOR IS/IT MANAGEMENT IN HEALTHCARE

Maturity model can be used to support health managers with effective management and continuous improvement for complex and multifaceted initiatives in hospital management (Menukin et al., 2023). Maturity models applied to health information systems are unique, as they must account for all medical procedures and clinical information essential to the healthcare process (Correia e Silva, 2019). High performing hospitals consistently attain excellence across multiple measures of performance, and multiple
departments. Hospital performance assessment has become a key feature among many health systems in high income countries (Groene et al., 2008), and increasingly so in low- and middle-income countries (Hashjin et al., 2014; Braithwaite et al., 2015). MM have been proposed in the healthcare domain with the purpose to assess and improve the maturity of healthcare practices, operations, and infrastructure (Daraghmeh & Brown, 2021). A MM is a proven technique for evaluating various aspects of a process of an organization. It provides a roadmap for organizations to become more structured and systematic in their operations (Proença & Borbinha, 2017). The fundamental concept of maturity in organizational management is that mature organizations operate through systematic and structured processes, whereas immature organizations rely on the ad-hoc, heroic efforts of individuals employing uncoordinated approaches (Mettler & Rohner, 2009). Governments have sought to enhance efficiency and reduce costs by implementing enterprise resource planning (ERP) and process management systems (Hammad et al., 2024).

Over the years, both practitioners and researchers have developed a diverse array of maturity models (MM) to evaluate and enhance organizational designs (Waring, 2015). These models are grounded in the principle that organizations, processes, and people evolve through a progressive developmental trajectory, marked by an evolutionary sequence of stages (Goksen, et al., 2015). Maturity models offer organizations and managers a critical framework to assess the current state of their IS/IT capabilities, plan strategic actions, and advance through higher stages of maturity. This structured approach facilitates effective management and continuous improvement for complex, multi-faceted initiatives (Kırmızı & Kocaoglu, 2022). Maturity models are tools that help manage organizations, and hospital organizations are no exception (Cimini et al., 2024).

In the context of hospitals, a mature IS/IT infrastructure is characterized by a higher degree of formalization in planning and control processes (Epizitone et al., 2023; Duncan et al., 2022). Maturity models have become a key focus in management research, defined as conceptual frameworks that outline typical development patterns of organizational capabilities (Mettler & Rohner, 2009). Scott (2007) predicts that organizations will increasingly adopt these models to drive and guide the advancement of their IS/IT capabilities. This prediction aligns with the growing recognition of maturity models as valuable tools for assessing and improving organizational capabilities in information systems and technology management. Recent studies have supported and expanded on this prediction. Stoumpos et al. (2023) highlighted the increasing adoption of maturity models in rapidly evolving sectors like healthcare, emphasizing their growing importance in managing digital transformation. Becker et al. (2009) emphasized the need for maturity models to evolve with digital transformation trends, integrating digital capabilities and data-driven decision-making into traditional frameworks. Henriques and Tanner (2017) stressed the importance of integrating agile methodologies into maturity models, reflecting the changing landscape of IS/IT management. Rahimi (2019) researched the role of digital platforms in healthcare, noting that while these platforms can reduce costs, the inherent complexity of healthcare systems often introduces unforeseen challenges and resistance from providers. Aguirre et al. (2019) claims how an electronic health record (EHR) can be a difficult task to take on and planning the process is of utmost importance to minimize errors. Moreover, Becker et al. (2009) emphasized the need for maturity models to evolve with digital transformation trends, integrating digital capabilities and data-driven decision-making into traditional frameworks. Zhang et al. (2023) found that organizational culture significantly impacts the effectiveness of IS/IT maturity models, highlighting the necessity for a comprehensive approach that includes systems, processes, and cultural factors. Recent literature also highlights the integration of agile methodologies into maturity models as crucial (Henriques & Tanner, 2017).

Despite advances in model specification, there remains a notable gap in effectively implementing maturity models within complex settings such as hospitals (Tarhan et al, 2020). Ahumada-Canale et al. (2023) examine what are the barriers and facilitators to implementing priority setting tools in the hospital setting of high-income countries. Through a comprehensive review of the extant literature, Epizitone et al. (2023) presents a critique of the health information system for healthcare to supplement the gap created as a result of the lack of an in-depth outlook of the current health information system from a holistic slant. Several models have been created to assess and describe IS/IT adoption levels in the healthcare sector (Tarhan et al., 2015). These models serve as benchmarks for evaluating patient information systems, which often involve multiple collaborating entities.

(Ferdinansyah & Purwandari, 2021) found that the main challenges about combining CMMI and Agile are the lack of relevant knowledge and experience and the culture of CMMI, Agile, or sometimes both. Effective interoperability of these systems significantly impacts the ability to deliver safe, reliable, and efficient healthcare services (Torab-Miandoab et al., 2023). Walker et al. (2023) identifies current challenges and opportunities to advancing interoperability across stakeholders. Bohr and Memarzad (2020) emphasized that AI is ready to support healthcare personnel with a variety of tasks from administrative workflow to clinical documentation and patient outreach as well as specialized support such as in image analysis, medical device automation, and patient monitoring.

The maturity of IS/IT infrastructure is generally proportional to its completeness, with system integration posing a critical challenge (Mikalef & Gupta, 2021). Irani et al. (2023) suggests seven levels of complexity in transforming legacy systems, including, being a stand-alone system, being part of a larger system, and data incompatibility, each depicting unique criteria and challenges. Nonetheless, very little is known as to what degree these complexities implicate the implementation of digital transformation efforts.

Maturity models provide a structure towards improving an organisation's capabilities (Akinsanya et al., 2019). The need for maturity models stems from the importance of awareness, visibility, and accountability to reveal the gaps of the organization's information security and cybersecurity (Daraghmeh & Brown, 2021).

Standards have been developed to address these integration challenges, particularly in facilitating data exchange between healthcare providers (Walker et al., 2023). Stoumpos et al. (2023) analyse the changes taking place in the field of healthcare due to digital transformation. MMs have gained widespread adoption across diverse fields, industries, and organizational structures. These models serve as valuable tools for assessing and describing the developmental stage, current circumstances, or specific conditions of various entities, including organizations, processes, and structures (Wendler, 2012). The diversity in MMs and variability in methods and content can create cognitive dissonance (Liaw & Godinho, 2023).

MATURITY MODELS APPROACHES

Capability Maturity Model Integration (CMMI)

One of the most prominent MM is the Capability Maturity Model Integration (CMMI) with its roots in software engineering where it was found relatively helpful in guiding and monitoring the maturity of software development practices (CMMI Product Team, 2010). As CMMI has expanded beyond software engineering to other domains, it has been increasingly recognized as a versatile tool for process improvement across various industries. CMMI is a process level improvement training and appraisal program and introduces the concept of five maturity levels defined by special requirements that are cumulative and uses standardized question catalogues and evaluation criteria to assess an organization's product development process. CMMI includes a self-assessment that presents the organisation's best practices in key process areas and then shows how the organisation can redefine its capabilities as it evolves into a more mature state (Paulk, 2009).

The Capability Maturity Model Integration (CMMI) has undergone significant updates and expansions in recent years, enhancing its applicability across various industries and organizational needs. Here are some key developments based on recent studies:

- ISACA released CMMI Version 3.0 in April 2023, introducing three new domains: Data Management, People Management, and Virtual Work. These additions reflect the evolving needs of modern organizations, particularly in light of remote work trends and the increasing importance of data-driven decision-making (ISACA, 2023).
- Research has shown a growing trend of integrating CMMI with Agile methodologies. This combination allows organizations to maintain the structure and process improvement focus of CMMI while embracing the flexibility and rapid iteration of Agile practices (Silva et al., 2015).
- CMMI now emphasizes high maturity concepts, helping organizations build competitive advantages through data-driven decisions and continuous improvement. This focus on quantitative management and process optimization is particularly beneficial for organizations aiming to achieve the highest levels of process maturity.
- CMMI has not succeeded in achieving its primary objectives of reducing costs while maintaining or improving the quality of care for Medicare, Medicaid, and Children's Health Insurance Program (CHIP) beneficiaries. Despite significant investment over a decade, the agency has not produced effective care delivery innovations that address major health conditions (Wilson, 2022).

HIMSS Analytics Electronic Medical Record Adoption Model (EMRAM)

Electronic Medical Records (EMRs) have become a priority for hospitals, and assessing the level of deployment of EMRs nationwide is essential to better utilization (Najjar et al., 2021). The Electronic Medical Record Adoption Model (EMRAM) is one of the widely used EMR assessment systems worldwide. Adoption and is used by over 9,000 hospitals across the globe. Incorporates a methodology and algorithms to automatically score hospitals around the world relative to their EMR capabilities. This eight-stage (0-7) model measures the adoption and utilization of the EMR functions (Garets & Davis, 2006), moving the organizations closer to achieving a near paperless environment that harnesses technology to support optimized patient care by completing each stage below. EMR are a tool that could potentially improve the outcomes of patient care by providing physicians with access to up-to-date and accurate vital patient information (Derecho et al., 2024). An EMR is a multifaceted, electronic patient records system and is often adopted in a model of hierarchical and increasingly complex stages (Woldemariam & Jimma, 2023). EMR is considered potentially one of the drivers for the transformation of healthcare. From a patient care perspective, EMR is expected to improve the accuracy of the information, support clinical decision-making and improve the accessibility of information for continuity of care (Zhang & Zhang, 2016). Through EMRAM, patient records become electronic and accessible across inpatient and outpatient environments, and health care practitioners can document, monitor, and manage health care more effectively (HIMSS, 2006). The results of the EMRAM assessment can be used to identify key opportunities for improvement, to drive your IT strategy and alignment with the overall business strategy of your organization (Kharrazi et al., 2018). Tsai et al. (2020) highlight the challenges and benefits associated with each stage of EMR adoption, particularly in large healthcare systems where the complexity of implementation is higher. Ayat (2024) addresses the challenges of implementing e-Health across various hospitals and also aims to evaluate the maturity of hospital information systems (HIS) in Iranian hospitals based on the electronic medical record adoption model (EMRAM). Digital infrastructure tools enable dynamic patient involvement in personal health management and care (Najjar et al., 2021)

Electronic Healthcare Maturity Model (eHMM)

The Electronic Healthcare Maturity Model (eHMM) broadens the traditional scope of maturity models by including all service providers engaged in healthcare processes, rather than focusing exclusively on individual organizations. This model is versatile, adapting to various providers at different stages of maturity and demonstrating varied levels of maturity across distinct business processes (Carvalho, Rocha, & Abreu, 2024). The eHMM is structured around a seven-level framework that maps the progression of healthcare processes from initial stages to advanced integration and interoperability (Sharma, 2008). It provides a detailed perspective on the evolution, enhancement, and transformation of healthcare systems, capturing capabilities at each stage of development. This model is instrumental in modern methodologies for setting goals and measuring progress, reflecting the transition from basic electronic processes to comprehensive, nationally integrated systems (levels 1 to 7). The eHMM shows the evolution, improvement, and transformation of a business over time and captures its capabilities at each intermediate level (Gomes & Romão, 2018). The maturity model is used in contemporary methodologies for setting goals and measuring progress. The Electronic Healthcare Maturity Model (eHMM) is an essential tool for guiding healthcare organizations in their digital transformation journey. By assessing their current maturity level and following structured improvement roadmaps, healthcare providers can enhance their digital capabilities, improve patient outcomes, increase operational efficiency, and achieve strategic goals (HIMSS, 2024).

IDC MaturityScapes (IDC-MS)

IDC-MS were created by IDC Health Insights to provide a detailed explanation of the stages from the simplest, unstructured ad hoc stage to the advanced, systematized optimized level, offering an opportunity for managers and their organisations to have a structured way to identify their current level of capability, or maturity, and the gap between where they are and where they want to be to maintain competitive balance or achieve industry superiority. IDC-MS can be used to enable managers to align business value goals with IT strategy, as a tool to identify where investments in people, process, and technology be consistent with what the organization requires, as an input to a variety of business-IT dashboards that monitor and measure IT capabilities against best practices and as a road map for overall improvement of IT processes, communications, and business integration.

IDC Health Insights proposed a maturity model for health care organizations. It consists of stages, measures, results and actions to advance along the path of maturity in the context of mobility toward a mobile culture (Dunbrack & Hand, 2013). IDC Health Insights, proposed also, a maturity model for Healthcare Provider IT Strategies (Holland, Dunbrack, & Piai, 2008).

IDC's Digital Transformation MaturityScape outlines five stages of maturity: ad hoc, opportunistic, repeatable, managed, and optimized (IDC, 2022). This framework helps organizations understand how their capabilities need to evolve to leverage digital technologies for competitive advantage, covering key dimensions such as Leadership DX, Omni-Experience DX, WorkSource DX, Operating Model DX, and Information DX.

The IDC MaturityScape for Artificial Intelligence describes five levels of AI maturity, from ad hoc approaches to fully integrated AI strategies (Jyoti, 2022). This model assists organizations in evaluating their AI initiatives and identifying necessary steps for advancement, highlighting AI's critical role in enhancing customer engagement and innovation.

IDC's updated Digital Infrastructure Operating Model MaturityScape allows organizations to assess their digital infrastructure's maturity, focusing on resilience, flexibility, and security (Turner, 2023). It provides actionable insights for CIOs and line-of-business executives to adapt their infrastructure strategies in line with evolving business needs.

These MaturityScape models collectively underscore the importance of:
- Assessing current capabilities across various digital transformation dimensions
- Identifying gaps between current state and desired maturity levels
- Aligning IT strategies with broader business goals and competitive dynamics
- Making informed investments in governance, processes, and technology
- Developing roadmaps for overall improvement of IT processes, communications, and business integration

Continuity of Care Maturity Model (CCMM)

The HIMSS Continuity of Care Maturity Model (CCMM) goes beyond Stage 7 of EMRAM, because was created to help the optimization of results in health systems and patient satisfaction (Etin, 2014). This model was created to help optimise outcomes for health system and patient alike. CCMM outlines the progressive capabilities healthcare organisations need to possess to seamlessly coordinate patient care across a continuum of care sites and providers. The CCMM is based on eight stages (0-7) and addresses the convergence of interoperability, information exchange, care coordination, patient engagement and analytics with the goal of individual and population health management (CCMM, 2017). The CCMM model starts from phase 0 (limited to no electronic communication), level 1 (peer-to-peer data exchange), level 2 (patient-centered clinical data using essential system-to-system exchange), level 3 (Normalized patient records using structural interoperability), level 4 (Care coordination based on data using a semantically interoperable patient record), level 5 (Community-wide patients record using information focused on patient engagement), level 6 (Closed loop, care coordination among care team members), level 7 (Knowledge-based participation fora dynamic, multiorganization interconnected health-care delivery model) (Woods et al., 2023). Continuing care is more complicated than implementing information and technology in a single care setting, many stakeholders must act in concert to ensure an environment that promotes the best care and value (Aiwerioghene et al., 2024). The CCMM framework is particularly relevant in today's healthcare landscape, where the seamless coordination of care across different providers and settings is critical for improving patient outcomes.

Interoperability Maturity Model (IMM)

Interoperability Maturity Model (IMM) is a methodology to get insight and evaluate interoperability maturity of public service based on a set of defined attribute and maturity stage (Pamungkas et al., 2019). The IMM is applied to assess its maturity, identify improvement priorities, and compare it with digital services of the healthcare sector (Kouroubali et al., 2019). Individual health information must follow the patient as he receives services from various providers. This requires data interoperability which is the key to effective use of health information.

The IMM aids eHealth developers to determine what level of interoperability they should strive for, and that allows researchers to benchmark interoperable eHealth infrastructures in terms of maturity (Velsen et al., 2016). The National Australian eHealth Transition Authority (NeHTA) has defined an Interoperability Maturity Model (IMM) that identifies increasing capability for data interoperability (Knight et al., 2020). IMM defines an iterative process by which e-health organisations can assess and increase their ability to interoperate, internally or as part of a national e-health community. Provides a set of guidelines for setting organisational process improvement goals in delivery of interoperable e-health solutions and a point of reference for appraising an e-health organisation's interoperability through the respective interoperability systems or work products.

IMM (Interoperability Maturity Model) is a methodology designed to provide insight into and evaluate the interoperability maturity of public services based on a set of defined attributes and maturity stages. IMM uses five maturity stages to determine the position of a public service, assessing it according to the presence of attributes that reflect the implementation of interoperability best practices (Pamungkas et al., 2019).

- Level 1 (Ad Hoc) Poor interoperability, the public service has almost no interoperability
- Level 2 (Optimistic) Fair interoperability, the public service implements some elements of interoperability best practices
- Level 3 (Essential) Essential interoperability, the public service implements essential interoperability best practices
- Level 4 (Sustainable) Good interoperability, the public service implements all relevant interoperability best practices
- Level 5 (Seamless) Interoperability leading practice, the public service is a leading example for others

The IMM is a useful tool to facilitate awareness raising and priority setting concerning interoperability in public administration (Kouroubali et al., 2019).

Business Process Orientation Maturity Model (BPO-MM)

Hospitals have been encouraged to develop more process-oriented designs, structured around patient needs, to better deal with patients suffering from multimorbidity (van Wijngaarden, 2023). The BPO-MM was developed to measure the process orientation maturity of employees within a large hospital facility (Gemmel et al., 2008). Van Looy et al. (2011) states that organizational maturity adopts a more holistic approach, given that any changes in the context of business processes would require the support of the whole organization. The BPO-MM measurement tool provides hospitals with a means to evaluate their evolvement towards process orientation maturity. The model describes the different stages through which an organization must go to reach the goal of being fully process oriented. The model benchmarks themselves with competitors or other organizations, based on their relative position in the model. Moreover, the MM can be further detailed by including the individual scores of each BPO-MM component and their related impacts. Some of the benefits reported in the literature are cost savings through a more efficient execution of work, reduced cycle times, improved customer focus, better integration across the organization, increased flexibility of the firm along with improved customer satisfaction, elimination of redundant and duplicated activities (Homauni et al., 2023; McCormack & Johnson, 2001). Tarhan et al. (2016) searched the studies between the years 1990 and 2014 and found, that despite the variance in degree of coverage of critical success factors categories by selected business process maturity models, MM stand as a promising reference for organizations to start their business process management efforts. Felch and Asdecker (2020) extend the review of Tarhan et al. (2016) with data from 2015 to 2020 to identify potential developments toward the suggested gaps. The results indicated that most gaps remained valid, with minor contributions toward model documentation and empirical validation of the newly developed BPMMs.

Process Management Maturity Model (PMMM)

A lack of consensus regarding the capabilities and development stages of hospitals required to become process oriented. Successful process management within hospital settings require a much stronger focus on both cultural and structural capability areas than it does in other organisations, where the focus is rather on IT-support and process automation (Harmon, 2004). The conceptual basis for the PMMM consists of five capability dimensions, including: (1) Culture - Covering communication and leadership-related practices; (2) Strategy - Covering principles that are prerequisite for a full development of process management; (3) Structure - Comprising the organisational dimensions; (4) Practices - Summarising work practices that are crucial for process management; (5) IT - Including items that capture in how far the employed hospital IT systems can support a smooth flow of complete patient care. The PMMM for hospital process management uses a cumulative five stages.

Further, according to Curtis and Alden (2007), there are five main business process challenges that the BPMM model attempts to address.

1. There are few standards for assessing the maturity of business processes. This method identifies risks and weaknesses when achieving business objectives.
2. There are few proven methods for appraising how tasks are performed and how they are described in process workflows. This discrepancy compromises the validity of system requirements, the accuracy of cases and model-based representations, and effectiveness of the applications.
3. Organic growth and acquisitions can result in multiple processes. Creating standard, tailored processes simplifies the requirements for enterprise applications and reduces the complexity of enterprise systems.
4. There are few proven methods for appraising a supplier's capability for delivering services within defined parameters. Organizations need a proven basis for specifying contractual requirements for improvements in a supplier's business processes.
5. There is a need for guidance on how to implement the business process foundations required for organizational agility and lower operating costs

There are several reasons to use a process management maturity model in an organization, as they often (Heller & Varney, 2013):

- Increase visibility to proven, systematic practices from best practice organizations
- Create a structure that determines what work gets done, when and by whom
- Facilitate a collaborative dialogue about process management
- Generate a consistency of process capture and use

Process management maturity is a useful tool that assists organizations in applying, managing, and controlling processes. By using this tool, organizations can yield a variety of benefits that include cost savings, more involved employees, and increased, predictable quality and productivity (Heller & Varney, 2013).

NHS Infrastructure Maturity Model (NIMM)

The NIMM framework supports the National Health Service (NHS) IT organisations to carry out an objective assessment of their IT infrastructure and to identify infrastructure maturity improvement projects (BMA, 2019). The NIMM framework is split into 13 categories, 74 capabilities, five perspectives and several KPIs, each of which is scored out of five. Not all capabilities have to be completed at once. Review the capability list, decide the priorities for your IT organisation today and concentrate your efforts on completing this subset.

Management: governance and control of IT infrastructure.

Each category is further divided into many capabilities which are used to target the assessment to a specific area. A capability is then further organised into perspectives. Each perspective has several KPIs associated with it, against which the capability in question is assessed. Organising the metrics into perspectives provides the opportunity to review the capabilities and develop an overall view of the capability rather than just from a technology viewpoint.

The perspectives are (Carvalho et al., 2019; Miloslavskaya & Tolstaya, 2022):
- Strategy: Aligning IT infrastructure with business strategy
- Deployment: Acquisition, deployment, and maintenance of IT infrastructure
- Operation: Daily operation of IT infrastructure
- Security: Protecting IT infrastructure against unauthorized access, use, disclosure, tampering, modification or destruction.

The NIMM framework is a beneficial tool that offers a structured method for evaluating and enhancing information technology infrastructure. It assists in identifying and prioritizing areas for improvement and provides roadmaps for enhancement, which can be used for benchmarking against other healthcare organizations (Van Dyk et al., 2012; Carvalho et al., 2016)

Informatics Capability Maturity Model (ICMM)

The Informatics Capability Maturity Model (ICMM), developed by the American Medical Informatics Association in 2003, is a framework for evaluating an organization's maturity in using informatics within healthcare. Based on the Capability Maturity Model Integration (CMMI) framework, ICMM defines five levels of maturity:

- Basic: Limited informatics knowledge and usage

- Controlled: More formal approach to improve processes and decisions
- Standard: Standardized practices for consistency and efficiency
- Optimized: Continuous improvement for innovation and efficiency
- Innovative Excellence: Creating new healthcare delivery methods

ICMM serves as a valuable tool for healthcare organizations to assess their current informatics capabilities, identify areas for improvement, and develop strategic plans to enhance their use of informatics in healthcare delivery (Gomes & Romão, 2018).

Zhang et al. (2023) demonstrate the ICMM's effectiveness in guiding organizations toward higher levels of maturity in informatics. These studies highlight how the model supports strategic planning and implementation, fostering a more integrated approach to care through advanced informatics capabilities.

DISCUSSION

The maturity of practices, operations and infrastructure in the health care domain is of high importance (Quaglini, 2010). In a more general view, a maturity model (MM) is a conceptual framework that consists of a sequence of discrete maturity levels for a class of processes in one or more business domains, and represents an anticipated, desired or typical evolutionary path for these processes (Becker et al., 2009; Tarhan et al., 2016).

Many maturity models (MMs) trace their origins to the Capability Maturity Model (CMM), with subsequent adaptations tailored to various domains (Law & Godinho, 2023). The literature highlights that these models have been specifically developed to address unique needs within their respective fields. Collectively, these maturity models underscore the multifaceted approach required to enhance organizational capabilities in healthcare.

Maturity models provide structured frameworks for advancing various aspects of healthcare management, including IT infrastructure, process management, integrated care, and data interoperability (Carvalho et al., 2016). By leveraging these models, organizations can systematically evaluate their existing capabilities, pinpoint areas that require improvement, and devise targeted strategies to progress to higher levels of maturity (Shaygan & Daim, 2023). This structured approach not only helps in improving operational efficiency but also in aligning practices with strategic objectives (Smajli et al., 2024).

Each maturity model offers a distinct focus, delivering valuable insights and practical tools for tackling specific challenges (Anschütz et al., 2024). For instance, some models may emphasize IT infrastructure enhancements, while others might focus on refining process management or fostering better integration across care systems. This diversity in focus ensures that healthcare organizations can address their unique needs and drive overall progress in managing and improving healthcare delivery. Below, we summarize the key features of various maturity model approaches, highlighting how they contribute to advancing organizational capabilities and enhancing healthcare management (Table 1).

Table 1. Maturity models summary

	Capability Maturity Model Integration for Services (CMMI - SVC)
Focus	Helps organizations assess their process capabilities and provides a structured approach to advance through these levels by focusing on standardized practices, continuous improvement, and process management
Main features	Contains practices that cover work management, process management, service establishment, service delivery and support, and supporting processes and focus its efforts around three core strategies: Satisfying providers; improving the service is delivered; and increasing the availability of information to guide decision-making.
Levels	CMMI offers 5 maturity levels in the staged representation.
	HIMSS Analytics Electronic Medical Record Adoption Model (EMRAM)
Focus	A progressively sophisticated roadmap enabling quality, safety, and operational efficiency for healthcare providers. The model helps hospitals assess their EMR capabilities and work towards a more integrated, efficient, and patient-centered healthcare system.
Main features	A progressively sophisticated roadmap enabling quality, safety, and operational efficiency for healthcare providers. The model helps hospitals assess their EMR capabilities and work towards a more integrated, efficient, and patient-centered healthcare system.
Levels	The eight-stage (0-7) model measures the adoption and utilization of EMR functions.
	Electronic Healthcare Maturity Model (eHMM)
Focus	The eHMM provides a reference model to define business capabilities associated with business processes
Main features	eHMM provides the framework for a common definition of each level and model qualities for traceability of progression. eHMM adjust the business capabilities and maintain alignment with the mission and goals
Levels	7-level maturity model
	IDC MaturityScapes
Focus	Guide organizations progressively in the significant changes to be made to best-known practices. The model aids in benchmarking against competitors, monitoring IT capabilities, and planning improvements to enhance overall IT effectiveness
Main features	The IDC-MS provide a snapshot in time of the results that can be expected at each significant stage along the way. Because the model has multiple dimensions, it is possible to view progress from different angles
Levels	IDC-MS follow a five-stage format.
	Continuity of Care Maturity Model (CCMM)

continued on following page

Table 1. Continued

Focus	Non-disruption of care provided to a patient throughout his/her care journey, across care settings and care givers. Alignment of healthcare resources across care settings orchestrated in a way that delivers the best healthcare services and value possible for a defined population under your care.
Main features	A multidimensional maturity model promoting the key tenants of continuity of care: Effective HIE, coordinated patient care, advance analytics and patient engagement
Levels	The CCMM provide an eight-stage (0-7) assessment.
Interoperability Maturity Model (IMM)	
Focus	Helping e-health organisations improve their ability to use or deliver interoperable e-health systems, with the goal of increased healthcare benefits. The model helps organizations set improvement goals and benchmark their progress in delivering interoperable e-health solutions
Main features	The IMM consists of three main components: 5 maturity levels; A set of interoperability goals, based on e-health and IS/IT requirements and an assessment framework
Levels	Five maturity levels inspired by the widely used CMMI framework.
Business Process Orientation Maturity Model (BPO-MM)	
Focus	The BPO-MM describes the pathway for systematically advancing business processes along the maturity continuum
Main features	BPO-MM defined three basic components: Process view - The care processes are defined, documented with the input of the patient; Process jobs - The employee's job is multidimensional, includes frequent problem solving and constantly learns new things on the job; Process management and measurement –The efficiency and effectiveness of the care processes is measured, and the results used to change the care processes.
Levels	four maturity steps (ad hoc, defined, linked, and integrated level).
Process Management Maturity Model (PMMM)	
Focus	PMMM in healthcare focus mainly on the cultural and structural capability areas rather on IT-support or process automation. The model emphasizes the importance of cultural and structural elements alongside IT and practices for effective process management
Main features	The relevant elements are capability dimensions and maturity stages
Levels	A full maturation path of 5 stages
NHS Infrastructure Maturity Model (NHS-IMM)	
Focus	Helping NHS IT organisations to carry out an objective assessment of their IT infrastructure and to identify infrastructure maturity improvement projects
Main features	NHS-IMM presents two main tools: Capability Assessment documents - contain KPIs to assess each capability and Key Capabilities Self-Assessment - a dashboard that records the scores from the capability assessments and gives an overview of progress
Levels	5 maturity levels through changes in behaviour, culture and attitudes
Informatics Capability Maturity Model (ICMM)	
Focus	The primary goal of the ICMM is to encourage leaders to recognize and leverage the potential role of informatics in gaining business advantages. It emphasizes treating informatics as a strategic resource, ensuring that informatics investments are aligned with business strategy, and delivering informatics-enabled changes effectively to maximize business value

continued on following page

Table 1. Continued

Main features	Evaluation of five key areas of your business: Managing information, using business intelligence, using information technology, aligning business and informatics, managing change
Levels	Each area has five levels of maturity ranging from basic to innovative

CONCLUSIONS

In the evolving landscape of healthcare, hospitals, health systems, and payers are increasingly adopting delivery system reforms to align provider incentives with critical objectives: enhancing patient care experiences, advancing population health, and controlling per capita healthcare costs. This transformation highlights the pivotal role of information technology (IT) in modern healthcare organizations, which are tasked with managing and integrating vast arrays of administrative and clinical data from a large patient population.

The core challenge extends beyond mere data acquisition; it involves the sophisticated transformation of this data into actionable intelligence. This intelligence must inform strategic decisions, streamline management processes, elevate care quality, and optimize financial performance. The effectiveness of IT in healthcare hinges on its ability to convert raw data into insights that drive improvements in operational efficiency and clinical outcomes.

Achieving this transformation requires a strategic approach underpinned by clear objectives, robust governance structures, refined processes, and a highly competent team. Maturity models have evolved significantly from their original focus on software vendor evaluation and development processes. Today, they are integral to a broad spectrum of applications including benchmarking, self-assessment, change management, and organizational learning.

Maturity models now offer a comprehensive framework for assessing and advancing organizational capabilities. They provide a structured methodology for identifying strengths and weaknesses, guiding incremental improvements, and fostering continuous learning. By implementing these models, healthcare organizations can systematically enhance their management practices, thereby increasing operational efficiency and financial sustainability.

The evolution of maturity models has led to the creation of numerous generic and domain-specific models tailored to healthcare. These models facilitate a deeper understanding of organizational performance and support targeted improvements. They enable healthcare institutions to benchmark against best practices, adopt advanced methodologies, and cultivate a culture of continuous improvement. As a result, organizations are better equipped to navigate the complexities of modern healthcare, ultimately driving superior patient outcomes and achieving more effective and efficient management.

REFERENCES

Aguirre, R.R., Suarez, O., Fuentes, M., & Sanchez-Gonzalez, M. A. (2019). Electronic Health Record Implementation: A Review of Resources and Tools. *Cureus,* 13,11(9), e5649. doi: .DOI: 10.7759/cureus

Ahumada-Canale, A., Jeet, V., Bilgrami, A., Seil, E., Gu, Y., & Cutler, H. (2023). Barriers and facilitators to implementing priority setting and resource allocation tools in hospital decisions: A systematic review. *Social Science & Medicine*, 322, 115790. DOI: 10.1016/j.socscimed.2023.115790 PMID: 36913838

Aiwerioghene, E. M., Lewis, J., & Rea, D. (2024). Maturity models for hospital management: A literature review. *International Journal of Healthcare Management*, •••, 1–14. DOI: 10.1080/20479700.2024.2367858

Akinsanya, O. O., Papadaki, M., & Sun, L. (2019). Towards a maturity model for health-care cloud security (M^2 HCS). *Information and Computer Security*, 28(3), 321–345. DOI: 10.1108/ICS-05-2019-0060

Analytics, H. I. M. S. S. (2006). EMRAM: An International Standard for EMR Adoption. Retrieved from https://www.himssanalytics.org/emram

Analytics, H. I. M. S. S. (2024). EMRAM: Electronic Medical Record Adoption Model. Healthcare Information and Management Systems Society. Retrieved from https://www.himss.org/resources/emram

Anschütz, C., Ebner, K., & Smolnik, S. (2024). Size does matter: A maturity model for the special needs of small and medium-sized smart cities. *Cities (London, England)*, 150, 104998. DOI: 10.1016/j.cities.2024.104998

Aral, S., Brynjolfsson, E., & Van Alstyne, M. (2006). Information, Technology and Information Worker Productivity Task Level Evidence. *Information Systems Research*, 23(3, part 2), 849–867. DOI: 10.1287/isre.1110.0408

Ayat, M. (2024). E-Health Implementation Challenges and HIS Evaluation in Accordance with EMRAM in Iran. *Health Technology Assessment in Action*, 8(2). Advance online publication. DOI: 10.18502/htaa.v8i2.15628

Bagyendera, M., Nabende, P., & Nabukenya, J. (2023). Critical factors influencing data use and utilization in health systems: A focus on data and interoperability standards for health information exchange (HIE) in Uganda's health care system. *Oxford Open Digital Health*, 1, oqad015. Advance online publication. DOI: 10.1093/oodh/oqad015

Becker, J., Knackstedt, R., & Pöppelbuß, J. (2009). Developing Maturity Models for IT Management. *Business & Information Systems Engineering*, 1(3), 213–222. DOI: 10.1007/s12599-009-0044-5

BMA. (2019). Technology, infrastructure and data supporting NHS staff. British Medical Association. https://www.bma.org.uk/media/2080/bma-vision-for-nhs-it-report-april-2019.pdf

Bohr, A, & Memarzadeh, K. (2020). The rise of artificial intelligence in healthcare applications. *Artificial Intelligence in Healthcare*, 25–60. .DOI: 10.1016/B978-0-12-818438-7.00002-2

Bragato, L., & Jacobs, K. (2003). Care pathways: The road to better health services? *Journal of Health Organization and Management*, 17(3), 164–180. DOI: 10.1108/14777260310480721 PMID: 14763100

Braithwaite, J., Matsuyama, Y., Mannion, R., & Johnson, J. (Eds.). (2015). *Healthcare reform, quality and safety: perspectives, participants, partnerships and prospects in 30 countries*. Ashgate.

Buntin, M. B., Burke, M. F., Hoaglin, M. C., & Blumenthal, D. (2011). The Benefits of Health Information Technology: A Review of The Recent Literature Shows Predominantly Positive Results. *Health Affairs*, 30(3), 464–471. DOI: 10.1377/hlthaff.2011.0178 PMID: 21383365

Carvalho, J. V., Rocha, A., & Abreu, A. (2016). Maturity Models of Healthcare Information Systems and Technologies: A Literature Review. *Journal of Medical Systems*, 40(6), 131. DOI: 10.1007/s10916-016-0486-5 PMID: 27083575

Carvalho, J. V., Rocha, A., Vasconcelos, J., & Abreu, A. (2019). A health data analytics maturity model for hospitals information systems. *International Journal of Information Management*, 46, 278–285. DOI: 10.1016/j.ijinfomgt.2018.07.001

CCMM. (2017). Continuity of Care Maturity Model (CCMM): A Strategic Framework for Optimizing Healthcare Outcomes. HIMSS. Retrieved from https://www.himss.org/resources/continuity-care-maturity-model

Chong, J., Jason, T., Jones, M., & Larsen, D. (2020). A model to measure self-assessed proficiency in electronic medical records: Validation using maturity survey data from Canadian community-based physicians. *International Journal of Medical Informatics*, 141, 104218. DOI: 10.1016/j.ijmedinf.2020.104218 PMID: 32574925

Cimini, C., Lagorio, A., & Cavalieri, S. (2024). Development and application of a maturity model for industrial agile working. *Computers & Industrial Engineering*, 188, 109877. DOI: 10.1016/j.cie.2023.109877

Cleven, A., Mettler, T., Rohner, P., & Winter, R. (2016). Healthcare quality innovation and performance through process orientation: Evidence from general hospitals in Switzerland. *Technological Forecasting and Social Change,* 113(Part B), 386-395. .DOI: 10.1016/j.techfore.2016.07.007

Cleven, A., Winter, R., Wortmann, F., & Mettler, T. (2014). Process management in hospitals: An empirically grounded maturity model. *Business Research,* 7(2), 191–216. DOI: 10.1007/s40685-014-0012-x

CMMI Product Team. (2010). CMMI for Development, Version 1.3. Software Engineering Institute, Carnegie Mellon University. Retrieved from https://resources.sei.cmu.edu/library/asset-view.cfm?AssetID=9661

Correia e Silva, L. (2019). *O impacto da aplicação de modelos de maturidade nas áreas clínicas do Sistema Nacional de Saúde. Integrated master's in biomedical engineering.* Minho University.

Curtis, B., & Alden, J. (2007). The Business Process Maturity Model (BPMM): What, Why and How. BPTRends, www.bptrends.com/publicationfiles/02-07-COLBPMMWhatWhyHow-CurtisAlden-Final.pdf

Daraghmeh, R., & Brown, R. (2021). A Big Data Maturity Model for Electronic Health Records in Hospitals. In proceedings of *2021 International Conference on Information Technology* (ICIT) July 14-15, 2021, Amman, Jordan. DOI: 10.1109/ICIT52682.2021.9491781

Derecho, K.C., Cafino, R., Aquino-Cafino, S.L., Isla, A. Jr., Esencia, J.A., Lactuan, N.J., Maranda, J.A.G., Velasco, L.C.P. (2024). Technology adoption of electronic medical records in developing economies: A systematic review on physicians' perspective. *Digital Health,* 12, 10, 20552076231224605. .DOI: 10.1177/20552076231224605

Domlyn, A. M., Scaccia, J., Lewis, N., Coleman, S., Parry, G., Saha, S., Wandersmanm, A., & Ramaswamy, R. (2021). The community transformation map: A maturity tool for planning change in community health improvement for equity and well-being. *The American Journal of Orthopsychiatry*, 91(3), 322–331. DOI: 10.1037/ort0000526 PMID: 34138626

Dunbrack, L., & Hand, L. (2013). A maturity model for Mobile in healthcare. IDC health insights: Business strategy, doc # HI241777.

Duncan, R., Eden, R., Woods, L., Wong, I., & Sullivan, C. (2022). Synthesizing Dimensions of Digital Maturity in Hospitals: Systematic Review. *Journal of Medical Internet Research*, 24(3), e32994. DOI: 10.2196/32994 PMID: 35353050

Epizitone, A., Moyane, S. P., & Agbehadji, I. E. (2023). A Systematic Literature Review of Health Information Systems for Healthcare. *Health Care*, 11(7), 959. DOI: 10.3390/healthcare11070959 PMID: 37046884

Etin, D. (2014). Quality of care with IDC & HIMSS models - Where are eHealth projects going in EMEA? Retrieved Sep 2015, fromEMC Sparkhttp://sparkblog.emc.com/2014/05/quality-care-idc-himss-models-ehealth-projects-going-emea/

Felch, V., & Asdecker, B. (2020). How to make business process maturity models better drawing on design science research. PACIS 2020 Proceedings, 50. https://aisel.aisnet.org/pacis2020/50

Ferdinansyah, A., & Purwandari, B. (2021). Challenges in Combining Agile Development and CMMI: A Systematic Literature Review. In Proceedings of ICSCA '21-10th International Conference on Software and Computer Applications Pages, 63 – 69. https://doi.org/DOI: 10.1145/3457784.3457803

Flott, K., Callahan, R., Darzi, A., & Mayer, E. (2016). A Patient-Centered Framework for Evaluating Digital Maturity of Health Services: A Systematic Review. *Journal of Medical Internet Research*, 18(4), e75. DOI: 10.2196/jmir.5047 PMID: 27080852

Fraser, P., Moultrie, J., & Gregory, M. (2002). The use of maturity models/grids as a tool in assessing product development capability, in: *IEEE International Engineering Management Conference. IEEE*, 244–249. DOI: 10.1109/IEMC.2002.1038431

Garets, D., & Davis, M. (2006). Electronic Medical Records vs. Electronic Health Records: Yes, There Is a Difference. White paper. HIMSS Analytics. Retrieved from https://www.aao.org/asset.axd?id=8e9b1f20-0ed6-4d2b-92f8-e28fbaf378ec

Gemmel, P., Vandaele, D., & Tambeur, W. (2008). Hospital Process Orientation (HPO): The development of a measurement tool. *Total Quality Management & Business Excellence*, 19(12), 1207–1217. DOI: 10.1080/14783360802351488

Goksen, Y., Cevik, E., & Avunduk, H. (2015). A Case Analysis on the Focus on the Maturity Models and Information Technologies. *Procedia Economics and Finance*, 19, 208–216. DOI: 10.1016/S2212-5671(15)00022-2

Gomes, J., & Romão, M. (2015). Maturity, Benefits and Project Management shaping Project Success. In *the series Advances in Intelligent Systems and Computing* (Vol. 353, pp. 435–448). New Contributions in Information Systems and Technologies. DOI: 10.1007/978-3-319-16486-1_43

Gomes, J., & Romão, M. (2018). Information system maturity models in healthcare. *Journal of Medical Systems*, 42(12), 1–14. DOI: 10.1007/s10916-018-1097-0 PMID: 30327955

Groene, O., Skau, J. K., & Frolich, A. (2008). An international review of projects on hospital performance assessment. *International Journal for Quality in Health Care : Journal of the International Society for Quality in Health Care*, 20(3), 162–171. DOI: 10.1093/intqhc/mzn008 PMID: 18339665

Hammad, M., Yahaya, J., & Mohamed, I. (2024). A model for enterprise resource planning implementation in the Saudi public sector organizations. *Heliyon*, 10(2), e24531. DOI: 10.1016/j.heliyon.2024.e24531 PMID: 38312684

Han, K., Chang, Y. B., & Hahn, J. (2011). Information Technology Spillover and Productivity: The Role of Information Technology Intensity and Competition. *Journal of Management Information Systems*, 28(1), 115–145. DOI: 10.2753/MIS0742-1222280105

Harmon, P. (2004). Evaluating an organization's business process maturity. *Business Process Trends*, 2, 1–11.

Hashjin, A. A., Kringos, D. S., Manoochehri, J., Aryankhesal, A., & Klazinga, N. (2014). Development and impact of the Iranian hospital performance measurement program. *BMC Health Services Research*, 14(1), 448. DOI: 10.1186/1472-6963-14-448 PMID: 25269656

Heller, A., & Varney, J. (2013). *Using Process Management Maturity Models: A path to attaining process management excellence*. APQC.

Henriques, V., & Tanner, M. (2017). A systematic literature review of agile and maturity model research. *Interdisciplinary Journal of Information, Knowledge, and Management*, 12, 53–73. DOI: 10.28945/3666

Holland, M., Dunbrack, L., & Piai, S. (2008). Healthcare IT maturity model: Western European hospitals - The leading countries. European IT opportunity: healthcare provider IT strategies. Health Industry Insights, an IDC Company.

Homauni, A., Markazi-Moghaddam, N., Mosadeghkhah, A., Noori, M., Abbasiyan, K., & Balaye Jame, S. Z. (2023). Budgeting in Healthcare Systems and Organizations: A Systematic Review. *Iranian Journal of Public Health*, 52(9), 1889–1901. DOI: 10.18502/ijph.v52i9.13571 PMID: 38033850

Huebner, C., & Flessa, S. (2022). Strategic Management in Healthcare: A Call for Long-Term and Systems- Thinking in an Uncertain System. *International Journal of Environmental Research and Public Health*, 19(14), 8617. DOI: 10.3390/ijerph19148617 PMID: 35886468

Irani, Z., Abril, R., Weerakkody, V., Omar, A., & Sivarajah, U. (2023). The impact of legacy systems on digital transformation in European public administration: Lesson learned from a multi case analysis. *Government Information Quarterly*, 40(1), 101784. DOI: 10.1016/j.giq.2022.101784

ISACA (2023). Updates CMMI Model with Three New Domains That Help Organizations Improve Quality. Retrieved from ISACA website.

Iyanna, S., Kaur, P., Ractham, P., Talwar, S., & Najmul Islam, A. (2022). Digital transformation of healthcare sector. What is impeding adoption and continued usage of technology-driven innovations by end-users? *Journal of Business Research*, 153, 150–161. DOI: 10.1016/j.jbusres.2022.08.007

Jyoti, R. (2022). IDC MaturityScape: Artificial Intelligence 2.0. IDC. https://www.idc.com/getdoc.jsp?containerId=US49037422&pageType=PRINTFRIENDLY

Kharrazi, H., Gonzalez, C. P., Lowe, K. B., Huerta, T. R., & Ford, E. W. (2018). Forecasting the Maturation of Electronic Health Record Functions Among US Hospitals: Retrospective Analysis and Predictive Model. *Journal of Medical Internet Research*, 20(8), e10458. DOI: 10.2196/10458 PMID: 30087090

Kingsbury, P., Abajian, H., Abajian, M., Angyan, P., Espinoza, J., MacDonald, B., Meeker, D., Wilson, J., & Bahroos, N. (2023). SEnDAE: A resource for expanding research into social and environmental determinants of health. *Computer Methods and Programs in Biomedicine*, 238, 107542. DOI: 10.1016/j.cmpb.2023.107542 PMID: 37224727

Kırmızı, M., & Kocaoglu, B. (2022). Digital transformation maturity model development framework based on design science: Case studies in manufacturing industry. *Journal of Manufacturing Technology Management*, 33(7), 1319–1346. DOI: 10.1108/JMTM-11-2021-0476

Knight, M., Kolin, J., Widergren, S., Narang, D., Khandekar, A., & Nordman, B. (2020). The Interoperability Maturity Model (IMM): A Qualitative and Quantitative Approach for Measuring Interoperability. PNNL-29683, GRID – Modernization Laboratory Consortium, US Department of Energy. https://www.osti.gov/servlets/purl/1804457

Kouroubali, A., Papastilianou, A., & Katehakis, D. G. (2019). Preliminary Assessment of the Interoperability Maturity of Healthcare Digital Services vs Public Services of Other Sectors. *Studies in Health Technology and Informatics*, 264, 654–658. DOI: 10.3233/SHTI190304 PMID: 31438005

Krasuska, M., Williams, R., Sheikhm, A., Franklin, B.D., Heeney, C., Lane, W., Mozaffar, H., Mason, K., Eason, S., Hinder, S., Dunscombe, R., Potts, H.W.W., & Cresswell, K. (2020). Technological Capabilities to Assess Digital Excellence in Hospitals in High Performing Health Care Systems: International eDelphi Exercise. Journal of Medical Internet Research,18, 22, 8, e17022. .DOI: 10.2196/17022

Liaw, S. T. & Godinho, M.A (2023). Digital health and capability maturity models-a critical thematic review and conceptual synthesis of the literature. *Journal of the American Medical Informatics Association*, 18, 30(2), 393-406. .DOI: 10.1093/jamia/ocac228

Liu, Y., Evans, L., Kwan, T., Callister, J., Poon, S., Byth, K., & Harnett, P. (2021). Developing a maturity model for cancer multidisciplinary teams. *International Journal of Medical Informatics*, 156, 104610. DOI: 10.1016/j.ijmedinf.2021.104610 PMID: 34649110

Mansour, S., & Nogues, S. (2022). Advantages of and Barriers to Crafting New Technology in Healthcare Organizations: A Qualitative Study in the COVID-19 Context. *International Journal of Environmental Research and Public Health*, 12, 19(16), 9951. .DOI: 10.3390/ijerph19169951

Martinez, J., Sagarra, M., & Sancho, M. (2021). Barriers to maturity model implementation in hospitals: A case study analysis. *Journal of Health Organization and Management*, 35(4), 375–392. DOI: 10.1108/JHOM-11-2019-0336

McCormack, K. P., & Johnson, W. C. (2001). *Business process orientation: Gaining the e-business competitive advantage*. CRC Press.

Melville, N., Kraemer, K. L., & Gurbaxani, V. (2004). Information Technology and Organizational Performance: An Integrative Model of IT Business Value. *Management Information Systems Quarterly*, 28(2), 283–321. DOI: 10.2307/25148636

Menukin, O., Mandungu, C., Shahgholian, A., & Mehandjiev, N. (2023). Guiding the integration of analytics in business operations through a maturity framework. *Annals of Operations Research*. Advance online publication. DOI: 10.1007/s10479-023-05614-w

Mettler, T., & Rohner, P. (2009). An analysis of the factors influencing networkability in the healthcare sector. *Health Services Management Research*, 22(4), 163–169. DOI: 10.1258/hsmr.2009.009004 PMID: 19875837

Mikalef, P., & Gupta, M. (2021). Artificial intelligence capability: Conceptualization, measurement calibration, and empirical study on its impact on organizational creativity and firm performance. *Information & Management*, 58(3), 103434. DOI: 10.1016/j.im.2021.103434

Miloslavskaya, N., & Tolstaya, S. (2022). Information security management maturity models. *Procedia Computer Science*, 213, 49–57. DOI: 10.1016/j.procs.2022.11.037

Mishra, V. T., & Sharma, M. G. (2022). Digital transformation evaluation of telehealth using convergence, maturity, and adoption. *Health Policy and Technology*, 11(4), 100684. DOI: 10.1016/j.hlpt.2022.100684

Najjar, A., Amro, B., & Macedo, M. (2021). The adoption level of electronic medical records in hebron hospitals based on the electronic medical record adoption model (EMRAM). *Health Policy and Technology*, 10(4), 100578. DOI: 10.1016/j.hlpt.2021.100578

Neumann, W. P., & Purdy, N. (2023). The better work, better care framework: 7 strategies for sustainable healthcare system process improvement. *Health Systems (Basingstoke, England)*, 12(4), 429–445. DOI: 10.1080/20476965.2023.2198580 PMID: 38235296

Pai, D. R. (2023). Complexities of Simultaneously Improving Quality and Lowering Costs in Hospitals Comment on Hospitals Bending the Cost Curve with Increased Quality: A Scoping Review into Integrated Hospital Strategies. *International Journal of Health Policy and Management*, 12, 7442. DOI: 10.34172/ijhpm.2022.7442 PMID: 36404505

Pamungkas, Y., Santoso, A., Ashari, B., Sensuse, D., Mishbaha, M., & Meiyanti, R. (2019). Evaluation of Interoperability Maturity Level: Case Study Indonesian Directorate General of Tax. *Procedia Computer Science*, 157, 543–551. DOI: 10.1016/j.procs.2019.09.012

Patel, S., Kumar, R., & Smith, T. (2023). Correlating EMRAM stages with clinical outcomes and operational efficiency. *Health Informatics Journal*, 29(1), 15–29. DOI: 10.1177/14604582221103612

Paulk, M. C. (2009). A history of the Capability Maturity Model for software. Software Quality Professional, 12, 9, 12-19.

Proença, D., & Borbinha, J. (2017). Enterprise Architecture: A Maturity Model Based on TOGAF ADM, In proceedings of the *2017 IEEE 19th Conference on Business Informatics*, 24-27 July 2017, Thessaloniki, Greece.

Quaglini, S. (2010). Information and communication technology for process management in healthcare: A contribution to change the culture of blame. *Journal of Software Maintenance and Evolution: Research and Practice*, 22(6-7), 435–448. DOI: 10.1002/smr.461

Rahimi, K. (2019). Digital health and the elusive quest for cost savings. *The Lancet. Digital Health*, 1(3), e108–e109. DOI: 10.1016/S2589-7500(19)30056-1 PMID: 33323258

Ramirez, R., Melville, N., & Lawler, E. (2010). Information technology infrastructure, organizational process redesign, and business value: An empirical analysis. *Decision Support Systems*, 49(4), 417–429. DOI: 10.1016/j.dss.2010.05.003

Rohner, P. (2012). Achieving impact with clinical process management in hospitals: An inspiring case. *Business Process Management Journal*, 18(4), 600–624. DOI: 10.1108/14637151211253756

Scott, J. E. (2007). Mobility, Business Process Management, Software Sourcing, and Maturity Model Trends: Propositions for the IS Organization of the Future. *Information Systems Management*, 24(2), 139–145. DOI: 10.1080/10580530701221031

Sharma, B. (2008). Electronic Healthcare Maturity Model (eHMM). White Paper. Quintegra Solutions Limited.

Shaygan, A., & Daim, T. (2023). Technology management maturity assessment model in healthcare research centers. *Technovation*, 120, 102444. DOI: 10.1016/j.technovation.2021.102444

Silva, F. S., Soares, F. S. F., Peres, A. L., Azevedo, I. M., Vasconcelos, A. P. L., Kamei, F. K., & Meira, S. R. L. (2015). Using CMMI together with agile software development: A systematic review. *Information and Software Technology*, 58, 20–43. DOI: 10.1016/j.infsof.2014.09.012

Smajli, E., Feldman, G., & Cox, S. (2024). Exploring the Limitations of Business Process Maturity Models: A Systematic Literature Review. *Information Systems Management*, 1–20. Advance online publication. DOI: 10.1080/10580530.2024.2332210

Smith, H., Patel, V., & Anderson, J. (2023). Advancing IT process improvement with IDC MaturityScape: A roadmap for success. *International Journal of Information Systems*, 58(1), 75–90. DOI: 10.1016/j.ijinfomgmt.2023.02.004

Stoumpos, A.I., Kitsios, F., & Talias, M. A. (2023). Digital Transformation in Healthcare: Technology Acceptance and Its Applications. *International Journal of Environmental Research and Public Health*, 15;20(4):3407. .DOI: 10.3390/ijerph20043407

Tarhan, A., Garousi, V., Turetken, O., Soylemez, M., & Garossi, S. (2020). Maturity assessment and maturity models in health care: A multivocal literature review. *Digital Health*, 6, 1–20. DOI: 10.1177/2055207620914772 PMID: 32426151

Tarhan, A., Turetken, O., & Reijers, H. A. (2015). Do mature business processes lead to improved performance? a review of literature for empirical evidence. In: Proceedings of the *23rd European Conference on Information Systems* (ECIS), 26-29 May 2015, Munster, Germany, Association for Information Systems, 1-6.

Tarhan, A., Turetken, O., & Reijers, H. A. (2016). Business process maturity models: A systematic literature review. *Information and Software Technology*, 75, 122–134. DOI: 10.1016/j.infsof.2016.01.010

Torab-Miandoab, A., Samad-Soltani, T., Jodati, A., & Rezaei-Hachesu P. (2023). Interoperability of heterogeneous health information systems: a systematic literature review. *BMC Medical Informatics and Decision Making*, 24, 23(1),18. .DOI: 10.1186/s12911-023-02115-5

Tsai, C.H., Eghdam, A., Davoody, N., Wright, G., Flowerday, S., & Koch, S. (2020). Effects of Electronic Health Record Implementation and Barriers to Adoption and Use: A Scoping Review and Qualitative Analysis of the Content. *Life*, 4, 10(12), 327. .DOI: 10.3390/life10120327

Turner, M. J. (2023). IDC MaturityScape: Digital Infrastructure Operating Model 2.0. IDC. https://www.idc.com/getdoc.jsp?containerId=US50401123

Van Dyk, L., Schutte, C., & Fortuin, J. (2012). A maturity model for telemedicine implementation. In *eTelemed 2012, The Fourth International Conference on eHealth, Telemedicine, and Social Medicine*. 10, 56116.

Van Looy, A., De Backer, M., & Poels, G. (2011). Defining business process maturity. A journey towards excellence. *Total Quality Management & Business Excellence*, 22(11), 1119–1137. DOI: 10.1080/14783363.2011.624779

van Wijngaarden, H., Braam, A., Buljac-Samardžić, M., & Hilders, M. (2023). Towards Process-Oriented Hospital Structures; Drivers behind the Development of Hospital Designs. *International Journal of Environmental Research Public Health*, 21, 20(3),1993. .DOI: 10.3390/ijerph20031993

Velsen, L., Hermens, H., & d'Hollosy, W. O. (2016). A maturity model for interoperability in eHealth. *IEEE 18th International Conference on e-Health Networking, Applications and Services* (Healthcom). Munich, Germany, 1-6. DOI: 10.1109/HealthCom.2016.7749533

Walker, D.M., Tarver, W.L., Jonnalagadda, P., Ranbom, L., Ford, E.W, & Rahurkar, S. (2023). Perspectives on Challenges and Opportunities for Interoperability: Findings From Key Informant Interviews With Stakeholders in Ohio. *JMIR Medical Informatics*, 24,11,e43848. .DOI: 10.2196/43848

Ward, J., & Daniels, E. (2012). The Effectiveness of IT Investments: A Review of Empirical Studies. *European Journal of Information Systems*, 21(3), 245–260. DOI: 10.1057/ejis.2011.36

Waring, T. S. (2015). Information management and technology strategy development in the UK's acute hospital sector: A maturity model perspective. *Public Money & Management*, 35(4), 281–288. DOI: 10.1080/09540962.2015.1047271

Wendler, R. (2012). The maturity of maturity model research: A systematic mapping study. *Information and Software Technology*, 54(12), 1317–1339. DOI: 10.1016/j.infsof.2012.07.007

Wilson, L. (2022). Americans Deserve to Get a Better Value From CMMI. *INQUIRY: The Journal of Health Care Organization, Provision, and Financing*, 59, 1–4. DOI: 10.1177/0046958022114180 PMID: 36541229

Woldemariam, M. T., & Jimma, W. (2023). Adoption of electronic health record systems to enhance the quality of healthcare in low-income countries: A systematic review. *BMJ Health & Care Informatics*, 30(1), e100704. DOI: 10.1136/bmjhci-2022-100704 PMID: 37308185

Woods, L., Dendere, R., Eden, R., Grantham, B., Krivit, J., Pearcem, A., McNeil, K., Green, D., & Sullivan, C. (2023). Perceived impact of digital health maturity on patient experience, population health, health care costs, and provider experience: Mixed methods case study. *Journal of Medical Internet Research*, 25, e45868. DOI: 10.2196/45868 PMID: 37463008

World Health Organization. Social determinants of health. Retrieved from https://www.who.int/health-topics/social-determinants-of-health#tab=tab_1

Zhang, W., Zeng, X., Liang, H., Xue, Y., & Cao, X. (2023). Understanding How Organizational Culture Affects Innovation Performance: A Management Context Perspective. *Sustainability (Basel)*, 15(8), 6644. DOI: 10.3390/su15086644

Zhang, X. Y., & Zhang, P. (2016). Recent perspectives of electronic medical record systems. *Experimental and Therapeutic Medicine*, 11(6), 2083–2085. DOI: 10.3892/etm.2016.3233 PMID: 27284289

Chapter 13
Regional Bank's Case Study on Online Lending Platforms

Maria Montano
Marymount University, USA

ABSTRACT

Regional Bank is a small financial institution aiming to expand its company and network through an online lending platform. Technology advancements are changing how consumers and businesses secure financing; therefore, a case study on online lending programs can benefit Regional Bank immensely. Online lending programs allow for a more specialized business model than traditional lending, enabling banks to extend credit access to small businesses (Bickmore et al., 2023). An online lending platform can help banks reduce costs, decrease risk, and increase transparency while supporting consumer needs (Strohm & Horton, 2023). Unfortunately, organizational changes impact employees, leadership, and the organization. As such, a study is needed to address the importance of online lending platforms and how this can positively or negatively affect customers, the bank, and its employees. Developing a comprehensive strategy for a successful implementation plan of an online lending platform is also essential.

INTRODUCTION

Regional Bank aims to expand its company and establish relationships through an online lending platform. However, the success of this endeavor hinges on developing a clear and comprehensive strategy for implementing this new platform. Unfortunately, organizational changes impact employees, leadership, and the organization through

DOI: 10.4018/979-8-3693-8562-3.ch013

resistance to change, a lack of communication between employees and managers, and a lack of understanding of this new platform (Anderson, 2020). According to its business model, Regional Bank aims to build relationships with modular home sellers, car dealers, and real estate brokers to facilitate expansion. This case study aims to analyze the challenges faced by Regional Bank and develop a comprehensive strategy for a successful implementation plan of an online lending platform.

Problem Statement

Recent changes to bank innovation in financial technology have impacted market growth and the ever-changing economy (Bickmore et al., 2023). For example, online lending programs allow for greater accessibility and faster processes than traditional lending; that type of business model can affect Regional Bank's current model (Bickmore et al., 2023). Competition, risk of lack of growth, and inability to keep up with customer and market demands are all issues that Regional Bank may face as the online lending programs continue to evolve (U.S. Department of Treasury, 2016).

Regional Bank's current challenge is the decrease in loan processing; businesses and individual customers are using other online lending platforms (FinTech) to acquire their loans (Bertsch & Rosenvinge, 2019). FinTech promises benefits to investors and borrowers, such as cheaper fees, automated credit scoring, and no costly branch network (Bertsch & Rosenvinge, 2019). This causes heavy competition for Regional Bank because screening based on automated credit scoring technologies tends to be more profitable (Fuster et al., 2018).

Regional Bank must focus on gathering information on the online lending platform market by exploring customer needs, benefits, adaptability, and program convenience (Strohm & Horton, 2023). Several factors may impede change when dealing with a new platform (Anderson, 2020). Some of those factors include lack of knowledge, trust, and employee resistance (Anderson, 2020). Therefore, research on how online platforms affect banks is necessary to understand the necessity of the new platform (Treece & Tarver, 2023).

Significance of the Project

Technology advances are changing how consumers and businesses secure financing (U. S Department of Treasury, 2016). According to a U.S. consumer banking statistics study, 78% of Americans prefer banking via a mobile app or website to banking in person (Strohm & Horton, 2023). These statistics affect Regional Bank by encouraging the adoption of an online lending platform that will allow the bank to compete with online lenders and enhance customer experience while giving them access to loans quickly and conveniently (Treece & Tarver, 2023). By incorporating the new digital process, Regional Bank can reduce operational costs, decrease risk, increase transparency, and ultimately support consumer needs (Strohm & Horton, 2023).

Digital platforms can dramatically improve the bank by allowing improved customer service and fostering relationships with suppliers and employees (Van der Zande, 2018). New technologies can significantly improve decision-making by increasing the quality of data (Broeders & Khanna, 2015). Improved and digitalized internal processes, structures, and IT systems will allow for automating and optimizing the banks' workflows (Van der Zande, 2018). Therefore, this case study is necessary and urgent to better understand the impact of the online lending program on its employees, the bank, and its customers (Treece & Tarver, 2023).

METHODOLOGY

A qualitative study was used to better understand the background issues of the problem statement (Alnsour et al., 2013). The advantages and disadvantages of online lending platforms will be explored to understand how digital transformation will impact Regional Bank (Starman, 2013). Qualitative research is characterized by an interpretative paradigm emphasizing experiences and interactions (Starman, 2013). Therefore, this study can help Regional Bank gain perspective on relationships, customer experiences, and competition (Starman, 2013).

Project Theories

Enhancing customer experience, driving innovation, and business growth are vital factors of digital transformation (Marr, 2023). However, new platforms can cause organizations to encounter many barriers, making implementing them difficult (Rothwell et al., 2021). In Regional Bank's case, there is a lack of trust in the online platform and immense competition from other banks and lending companies. Without growth, the bank can risk failure (Ozlen & Djedovic, 2017).

According to Matt et al. (2015), digital transformation has four dimensions: the use of technologies, changes in value creation, structural change, and financial aspects. The authors explain that the *financial aspects* of the company must be considered first before implementing new technology (Matt et al., 2015). Regional Bank must analyze financial reports while understanding the program's feasibility, benefits, and convenience (Treece & Traver, 2023). Matt et al. (2015) mention that banks with lower financial pressure are more likely to act on online lending platforms or introduce other types of digital transformation, while banks needing more resources might need external ways to finance new platforms. Therefore, a plan of action must be developed while defining the budget (Khanchel, 2019). After finances are considered, the bank must address the *use of technologies*, which identifies employees' attitudes towards the new technology and their ability to use the new platform (Matt et al., 2015). This is important to the Regional Bank because this type of change will cause culture, leadership, and employee changes if not examined correctly (Anderson, 2020). *Changes in value creation* help understand the impact digital transformation will have on the soul of the business; this can help Regional Bank understand the need for an online lending platform and how it will affect the bank, its employees, and its customers (Matt et al., 2015). The authors believe that digital changes cause business scope adjustments while creating *structural changes*; this can affect Regional Bank in the banks' original process and employees' work skills (Matt et al., 2015). Therefore, this data must be compiled and analyzed to understand better the need for an online lending platform (Rea & Parker, 2014).

The *path-goal theory* will help Regional Bank grow its online lending platform presence by assisting managers in motivating employees to this change (Bans-Akutey, 2021). Northouse (2016) explains that this theory focuses on leadership styles. The leader tailors their approach based on the staff's motivational needs (Northouse, 2016). This type of leadership has four components: directive, supportive, achievement-oriented, and participative leadership (Bans-Akutey, 2021).

The directive leadership style focuses on how leaders communicate procedures to staff (Bans-Akutey, 2021). For example, this type of leadership instructs staff precisely what is needed of them, the rules, and the deadline of their task (Bans-Akutey, 2021).

Supportive leadership is characterized as being friendly and approachable, which allows staff to approach their leader easily (Bans-Akutey, 2021). This type of leadership attempts to attend to employees' needs (Northouse, 2016).

Participative leadership uses a collaborative style in decision-making (Bans-Akutey, 2021). This could benefit Regional Bank because people will be less likely to resist change, and if staff is part of the process, the online lending platform will develop more quickly.

Achievement-oriented leadership focuses on leaders pushing workers to achieve excellence (Bans-Akutey, 2021). Employees will consistently seek improvement and allow the online lending platform to work correctly for small and local customers (U.S. Department of Treasury, 2016).

Change Strategies

Communication challenges between managers and employees are a common obstacle during change (Rothwell et al., 2021). Change can occur if the leadership qualities promote inclusiveness, self-awareness, and open dialogue (Bianco-Mathis, 2023). Cultural awareness, quality social relationships, mindful listening, situational awareness, and situational humility are essential qualities that can help with communication challenges (Bianco-Mathis, 2023). Therefore, keeping employees informed and asking for input will be the best way to add the new online platform (Rothwell et al., 2021).

Managers of Regional Bank can use the *appreciative coaching approach* to ensure teams can handle the new platform (Orem et al., 2007). According to Ives (2008), the coach's role is to stimulate ideas and action and ensure the goals are consistent with central life values and interests. This type of coaching has five basic principles that help empower workforce relationships: constructive, positive, poetic, simultaneous, and anticipatory (Rothwell et al., 2021). The constructive fundamental focuses on understanding the employees' background while pointing out strengths and abilities (Orem et al., 2007). The positive principle emphasizes optimism while promoting resolutions to the employees' problems (Rothwell et al., 2021). In the poetic fundamental, coaches must pay close attention to the employees' statements about themselves and their workforce; here, coaches must encourage them to rewrite their stories positively, allowing the employee to see strengths rather than problems (Orem et al., 2007). The simultaneous principle will enable employees to see their challenges on the new platform from a new perspective, helping them embrace the change (Rothwell et al., 2021). Finally, the anticipatory fundamental helps employees generate positive and empowering self-views (Orem et al., 2007). This type of coaching will help support teams and understand their needs, allowing the company's culture to feel comfortable with change (Ives, 2008).

Change strategy must focus on developing a cooperative and trusting relationship between employees and the organization's decisions to promote change (Anderson, 2020). An idea that can help with the concept of trust is the *principle of congruence* (Asunda & Ware, 2015). This principle states that activities must be matched appropriately with the nature of the problems within the organizational units under consideration (Anderson, 2020). Therefore, appropriate information must be gathered on the learning curve, culture, and resistance; then, a suitable strategy can be created for the bank and its employees (Asunda & Ware, 2015).

The *free choice idea* is another intervention that helps develop trust (Anderson, 2020). This idea implies that the employees should design and execute the intervention activity (Anderson, 2020). This approach can give the advantage of easing access and encouraging responsiveness (Anderson, 2020). This approach can also help employees feel like they are part of the change, allowing quicker adaptability to the new online platform.

The *competing values framework* (CVF) organizes and understands organizational effectiveness, leadership competencies, and informational processing (Cameron, 2009). CVF is divided into four organizational culture types: clan, adhocracy, market, and hierarchy (Yu & WU, 2009). This robust framework helps describe thinking, organizing, and behaviors associated with human activity while understanding tensions between internal and external factors (Cameron, 2009). This framework can be used to identify the effectiveness of the bank. CVF can help analyze how cultural elements have been affected and how changes have affected Regional Bank's ability to develop and execute strategy on change (Cameron, 2009).

Leadership Impact

Leadership can negatively impact employees and cause demotivation and inflexibility (Moutousi & May, 2018). As such, influential leaders must motivate and hold a close relationship with their employees to create trust within the organization (Peng et al., 2021).

Transformational leadership is an excellent model to focus on as it has four characteristics to ensure a better workplace: idealized influence, inspirational motivation, individualized consideration, and intellectual stimulation (Bass & Avolio, 1993). Transformational leaders help develop a close relationship between leadership and employees; this can help employees adapt well to the environment and better understand the organization's mission and objectives (Korbi, 2015). These leaders change the organization's culture by understanding the current culture and realigning it with Regional Bank's new vision (Bass & Avolio, 1993). Transformational leaders focus on meeting subordinates' expectations and creating a better workplace (Ghasabeh et al., 2015).

Charismatic leadership can be a practical approach to optimize and motivate teams dealing with change (Hu & Dutta, 2022). This type of leadership combines vision, inspiration, and non-verbal communication to appeal to subordinates (Hu & Dutta, 2022). Charismatic leaders have a strong and profound influence over their team, which allows them to transform self-interest into collective interest by understanding their employees' needs, values, and desires (House & Howell, 1992). This type of leader has a focused commitment to the bank, resulting in strong motivating factors for the rest of the employees (House & Howell, 1992). There is an emphasis on collaboration and motivation to meet the needs of a project or mission, which allows for positive change (Hu & Dutta, 2022).

Another leadership theory that can help Regional Bank implement the online lending platform is the *transactional leadership theory*. Since the bank would like to compete with other lending platforms quickly, this approach will allow employees to reach their daily efficiency level (Korbi, 2015). This theory focuses on rewards and reprimands for productivity (Odumeru & Ogbonna, 2013). For example, efficiency is needed to see results quickly; employees will be rewarded if they reach the bank's objectives faster; this will incentivize employees to do a better job and allow the lending program's implementation to adapt quickly (Korbi, 2015). This theory aims to quickly and effectively handle inflexibility and opposition to change. Therefore, this is an excellent theory to implement during the bank's online lending platform initiation (Odumeru & Ogbonna, 2013).

Operational leadership focuses on the leader's ability to successfully plan, organize, and control the diverse elements of the change and recruit the necessary staff (Korbi,2015). This type of leadership has three behavioral components: structure, the establishment of effective monitoring mechanisms, and material rewards (Korbi, 2015). Leaders identify the structure component by creating a necessary arrangement to support the new technological implementations (Korbi, 2015). Leaders must train, develop organizational structures, and establish employee objectives and standards (Nadler & Tushman, 1990). Second, leaders must monitor employees to help them achieve their goals (Korbi,2015). Lastly, a reward system will create incentives for employees that will reinforce behaviors corresponding to the desired adoption of the online lending platform (Korbi,2015).

The organization's leaders exercise *strategic leadership* as they are solely responsible for its strategy (Samimi et al., 2022). This type of leadership focuses on structures and processes that allow for implementing specific strategies (Korbi, 2015). The leader is considered the director of the organization's purpose, strategy designer, and context creator (Korbi, 2015). The leader is viewed as the organization's representative, making decisions based on the values and principles that ultimately help guide the organization's strategic choices (Samimi et al., 2022). The leader formulates the strategy with strong communication, which helps establish trust and shapes the organization's culture. This can help establish participation from its employees (Samimi et al., 2022). Overall, strategic leadership can help create a smooth transition into a new platform or strategy.

LITERATURE REVIEW

An online lending program can help Regional Bank compete with other banks and lending programs (Ozlen & Djedovic, 2017). Online lending platforms can help banks operate more efficiently while catering to a more extensive customer base (Alsajjan & Dennis, 2006). This can help expand their footprint and become a more significant influence in the banking system (Alsajjan & Dennis, 2006). The literature review will focus on the future of the banking system, culture change, and how it affects Regional Bank's implementation goal. It will also explore the impacts of digital transformation and explain the competition's business models.

The banking system is everchanging (Bickmore et al., 2023). For example, during the COVID-19 Pandemic, the Small Business Administration helped establish the Paycheck Protection Program (PPP) (U.S. Department of Treasury, 2023). This program provided small businesses with funds to pay for expenses during the pandemic (U.S. Department of Treasury, 2023). Banks that lacked digital tools could not process Paycheck Protection Program (PPP) loans quickly or outside their branch (U.S. Department of Treasury, 2023). According to the Federal Deposit Insurance Corporation (2020), banks hold most of the $525 billion in PPP loans made by banks and nonbanks. Community banks' participation in the PPP loans outpaces noncommunity banks (Federal Deposit Insurance Corporation, 2020). To compete with other banks and lending programs, banks had to adopt digital lending platforms (Alsajjan & Dennis, 2006). This data shows the importance of staying up to date with digital trends to grow and help your customers succeed.

Culture Change

Culture change is the most challenging obstacle for organizations seeking to innovate (Walker & Soule, 2017). Innovation usually demands new behaviors from leaders and employees, affecting employee readiness, willingness, attitude, and behavior change (Walker & Soule, 2017). Employee resistance, lack of trust, and lack of leadership can all impede the new platform's success (Anderson, 2020). According to Latta (2009), organizational culture is considered pivotal in determining the success of implementing change initiatives. Behaviors associated with organizational culture, such as attitudes, norms, and assumptions, give a sense of identity and determine behavior toward innovation (Insensee et al., 2020). As Regional Bank seeks to become more innovative, culture change may be its most challenging variable (Walker & Soule, 2017).

Trust is critical in building relationships and a shared commitment to change (Frei & Morriss, 2020). Frei and Morriss (2020) believe trust has three core drivers: authenticity, logic, and empathy. Authenticity and truth are essential as they create trust through interactions; employees must trust their manager's competence and logic while feeling cared about (Frei & Morris, 2020). Paul Zak's study on trust reported that people at high-trust companies have 74% less stress and 50% higher productivity than people at low-trust companies (Zak, 2017). Organizations must engage in specific actions prioritizing trust and creating a shared sense of community and purpose (Frei & Morriss, 2020). For example, leaders must establish expertise, demonstrate integrity and fairness, and encourage open communication and feedback (Bianco-Mathis, 2023). If the culture within the organization focuses on trust, then employees will be able to accept change willingly and see the company's overall vision (Frei & Morriss, 2020).

Overcoming resistance to change is vital when incorporating an online lending program (Korbi, 2015). Resistance comes from five major causes: lack of self-esteem, fear of the unknown, fear of the economic impact the change will bring, and the lack of desire to add a new platform (Korbi, 2015). Transitioning into a new online platform can cause learning anxiety; this new learning curve can cause resistance or even cause employees to quit (Smith et al., 2014). Employees may feel incompetent as the company launches the new program; this can discourage internal adoption (Smith et al., 2014). Keeping employees informed is necessary when adapting to change; companies can arrange orientation programs or create groups to help provide support for the learning process (Bianco-Mathis, 2023). Training and learning about the new platform will help employees feel more comfortable and may be more inclined to ask questions and give feedback (Bianco-Mathis, 2023).

Employee disapproval of the online lending program could be another obstacle Regional Bank faces; this can come from a lack of knowledge of the importance of the new online lending program (Khalid, 2011). The company's leaders should share facts about how the new platform can positively impact the company (Rothwell et al., 2021). For example, an online program can often create greater access and convenience for borrowers who have difficulty visiting physical bank locations, allowing for more clients and growth for the bank (Goldman, 2023). Constant information causes employees to adapt to change faster, allowing the online platform to become permanent quickly while limiting employee disapproval (Bianco-Mathis, 2023).

Attitudes towards technology can determine the behavioral intention of using new technological platforms (Yaghoubi & Bahmani, 2010). The *technology acceptance model* (TAM) proposes that perceived usefulness (PU) and ease of use predict the attitude toward technology changes (Masrom, 2007). In TAM, perceived usefulness refers to the belief that a new platform will improve employees' work performance, while perceived ease of use (PEU) focuses on the amount of effort the technology will cause the employee (Masrom, 2007). PU directly influences intention to use, while PEU indirectly affects perceived usefulness and attitude on behavioral intention (Yaghoubi & Bahmani, 2010). Behavioral intention measures the strength of one's willingness to exert effort while performing certain behaviors (Yaghoubi & Bahmani, 2010). The TAM model represents the factors of system usage and is a valuable tool for system planning since the system designers can control ease and usefulness (Yaghoubi & Bahmani, 2010). Therefore, using this model to analyze employees' attitudes toward the new platform can decrease the number of delays while adopting the online lending program (Marangunić & Granić, 2015).

Digital Transformation

Digital transformation is beginning to be the center of organizations (Verhoef et al., 2021). This section will focus on the bank's competition, its role in financial services, and how this creates advantages and disadvantages for the bank.

Financial technology (FinTech) is essential in financial services since it comprises innovative technologies offered to financial service providers (Diener & Spacek, 2021). Cuadros-Solas et al. (2023) state that FinTech start-ups were the leaders of financial digitalization. They offer the financial industry a way to cut costs, improve the quality of financial services, and create a more diverse and stable financial landscape (Diener & Spacek, 2021). They also offer innovative services, such as algorithms to accelerate processes and determine credit scores to price and distribute loans to customers (Cuadros-Solas et al., 2023). FinTechs can improve banks' business models by introducing specialized platforms, covering neglected customer segments, improving customer selection, reducing banks' operating costs, and optimizing bank business processes (Diener & Spacek, 2021). Therefore, these platforms affect traditional banking because they pressure banks to modernize their business activities to keep up with technological advancements (Cuadros-Solas et al., 2023).

According to an Ernst & Young (EY) survey, banks remain the preferred choice for many small and medium-sized enterprises (SMEs) (Mastropietro & Blini, n.d.). The survey states that 63% of SMEs still prefer traditional banks, but the use of competitors is increasing by 56% as SMEs are beginning to use the banking and payments FinTech service (Mastropietro & Blini, n.d.). Competition is making it more challenging for banks to expand on products and services without easy–to–integrate programs (Mastropietro & Blini, n.d.). For example, the COVID-19 pandemic changed SMEs' expectations by causing them to increasingly look for digital, faster, and more straightforward lending (Mastropietro & Blini, n.d.). Digitalization is becoming the norm for credit processes; personal loan applications can be submitted by phone, and money can be sent to others in less than a minute (Chappell et al., 2018). Mortgage lending has also become digitalized as banks have developed markets to enhance the mortgage journey (Chappell et al., 2018). This causes pressure on Regional Bank as their competition begins to digitalize faster (Ozlen & Djedovic, 2017).

A study by Khnachel (2019) stated that half of the banks surveyed had a comprehensive strategy for digital transformation, showing that banks are entering the digital era to compete with their competitors. Banks that digitalize could increase their net profit by 45 percent, while banks that do not could lose as much as 35 percent (Van der Zande, 2018). This can increase their profits by decreasing operational costs and simplifying organizational structures and processes through automation (Van der Zande, 2018).

RECOMMENDATIONS

Change is the center of organizations, and it addresses the organization's vision, mission goals, and strategy while also affecting the company internally (Anderson, 2020). Therefore, this section will focus on recommendations to encourage change and discuss the importance of using good practices to allow employees to adapt well.

John Kotter's Eight-Step Change Model is a change management plan that can help Regional Bank implement its online lending platform. The eight steps include creating a sense of urgency, building coalitions, forming a strategic vision, communicating the vision, removing obstacles, creating short-term wins, sustaining acceleration, and instituting change (Bedard, 2023).

First, Regional Bank must create a sense of urgency for managers and employees by identifying threats that may affect the company's future performance if they do not apply the online platform (Laig & Abocejo, 2021). The goal is for staff to feel the need for change and understand that this platform is crucial for organizational growth (Rothwell et al., 2021). This step is essential because, without the support and motivation of employees, organizational change cannot succeed (Rothwell et al., 2021).

The second step focuses on building a coalition to bring together the right teams to lead the change efforts (Laig & Abocejo, 2021). This step aims to assemble a team with the correct skills, qualifications, personalities, and authority to initiate organizational change (Rothwell et al., 2021). This step is essential because an effective guiding team can help communicate the importance of the online platform while measuring success, making decisions, and tracking and mitigating issues (Laig & Abocejo, 2021).

Step three focuses on forming a strategic vision that will help create a clear goal for the organization while developing effective strategies to accomplish the vision (Rothwell et al., 2021). In this step, employees' ideas and creativity must be considered to create a vision matching the overall bank strategy (Rothwell et al., 2021). This can steer the guiding teams into action and allow precise and realistic targets for success (Laig & Abocejo, 2021).

The fourth step focuses on communicating the vision and strategy (Laig & Abocejo, 2021). This step can help encourage the rest of the organization to accept and support the online platform. To communicate effectively, the change leaders should promote employee feedback on the platform (Rothwell et al., 2021). This can help avoid issues or confusion with the new initiative (Rothwell et al., 2021).

The fifth step is to remove barriers that can block the organization's path to success (Laig & Abocejo, 2021). Roadblocks can appear in employee resistance to change, ineffective management policies, and inefficient processes or practices (Rothwell et al., 2021). When implementing organizational-wide changes, obstacles may occur frequently (Rothwell et al., 2021). Once the barriers are acknowledged, the company implements ideas to minimize the roadblock and help employees feel empowered and recognized for their efforts; this can help the company move towards change (Rothwell et al., 2021).

The sixth step focuses on short-term wins for employees, motivating them to continue working and resulting in positive outcomes (Laig & Abocejo, 2021). For example, Regional Bank can implement a reward system for employees who help the first ten customers register for the online lending platform. Small accomplishments may encourage employees to accept the new platform and work towards short-term goals (Rothwell et al., 2021).

The seventh step focuses on reinforcing change and continuous improvement (Rothwell et al., 2021). This is done by ensuring teams are working towards their goals. This step is essential because it helps employees and leaders remember the vision, goals, and success stories and will help inspire employees to continue accepting the new online lending platform (Rothwell et al., 2021).

The eighth and final step focuses on making change stick (Laig & Abocejo, 2021). This step ensures that employees understand the new platform's success and embrace the change (Rothwell et al., 2021). Therefore, change must be reflected throughout the company while focusing on improving it (Rothwell et al., 2021). At this stage, employees should understand the need for the online platform and know its success stories and feasibility (Rothwell et al., 2021).

An organizational analysis of Regional Bank is needed to ensure the organization operates well (Weisbord, 1976). As such, the Weisbord Six-Box Model is based on six categories that help illustrate a diagnosis of an organization (Anderson, 2020). The primary purpose is to share the organization's goal with clarity and help understand the organization's structure, relationships, environment, reward system, leadership, and helpful mechanisms (Weisbord, 1976). This model suggests that an organization must interact with its environment, manage problems well, and try to fix misalignments before they become more significant problems (Anderson, 2020). If the bank's formal and informal components are not aligned, it will suffer (Anderson, 2020).

Overall, digital transformation is crucial when dealing with banks and their success (Van der Zande, 2018). Without an online banking platform, Regional Bank may face a decline in customer relationships, a decrease in its infrastructure, and the ability to compete with other services, which will pressure the bank and its employees (Broeders & Khanna, 2015). Therefore, developing a new digital transformation strategy will allow for a better, automated, faster process for the bank and its customers (Bickmore et al., 2023).

CONCLUSION

Regional Bank aims to expand its company and establish relationships through an online lending platform. Unfortunately, it can face employee resistance, a lack of communication, and a need for more understanding of this initiative (Anderson, 2020). This case study focused on Regional Bank's challenges and proposed different approaches the organization can use to implement the online lending platform successfully.

Cultural change, leadership, and internal and external barriers can impede the new platform's success (Rothwell et al., 2021). Innovation usually demands new behaviors from leaders and employees, which can cause employee resistance and a lack of trust in the new platform (Anderson, 2020). Therefore, critical data is needed to understand employee and leadership needs while researching the current market and the necessity of the new online lending platform (Treece & Traver, 2023).

Research on the banks' financial reports is needed to understand the program's feasibility, benefits, and convenience (Treece & Traver, 2023). Customer needs for an online platform must be gathered to understand the initiative better (Treece & Traver, 2023).

Managers must constantly meet with their teams to discuss plans, ideas, and news (Rothwell et al., 2021). Constant engagement can help the organization's new online platform thrive and help with adaptability to change (Bianco-Mathis, 2023). The company must create the right environment for employees to enjoy their work and create an inclusive workplace where all employees feel heard and cared for; this will also cause more productivity (Anderson, 2020). A positive culture of cooperation and trust is crucial to promoting change (Anderson, 2020).

A great way to promote a healthy system is to provide information in a workshop that thoroughly explains the strategy for the new platform. The workshop must introduce timelines and share the benefits it can create for the bank, employees, and customers (Anderson, 2020). The more details the employees have, the easier the change will be (Anderson, 2020).

Regional Bank must incorporate the proposed approaches in the case study for change to be seamless. Overall, by understanding the importance of an online lending platform, Regional Bank can compete with other online lenders and provide greater access and convenience to borrowers quickly and effectively (Strohm & Horton, 2023).

Limitations

Limitations in the study included the need for more information on the digital transformation of other banks and online lending platforms (Diener & Spacek, 2021). Future research recommendations include surveying other banks to understand the need for digital transformation (Diener & Spacek, 2021). Analyzing other banks' failures, management, and successes of an online lending program can help Regional Bank understand its limitations better and help identify best-practice approaches (Diener & Spacek, 2021). The results should be examined with more participants, including more customers, banks, and employees; this will help us better understand the market (Diener & Spacek, 2021). This was limited during the study due to the need for more digitalization of other banks, access to their finances, and future digitalization plans.

Two in-depth questionnaires are needed to analyze this study further (Diener & Spacek, 2021). One questionnaire will be delivered to customers, and the other will be sent to employees. The survey method is essential in future research as it collects primary data, employing a questionnaire that directly measures thoughts about an organization or person (Rea & Parker, 2014). Staff interviews are also needed because they provide insightful information, ideas, and subjective analysis focusing on the bank and its needs (Bailer, 2014). Another method that can help with a large-scale implementation is a SWOT analysis. This type of analysis can help gain insight into Regional Bank's environment (Rothwell et al., 2021). This analysis organizes the bank's resources and environment into four categories: strengths, weaknesses, opportunities, and threats (Rothwell et al., 2021). Strengths in the SWOT analysis are categorized as internal capabilities that help the business achieve its objectives (Namugenyi et al., 2019). Weaknesses are internal factors that impede the desired goal of an organization (Gupta et al., 2014). The opportunities section focuses on external factors that can help the business grow (Namugenyi et al., 2019). Threats are external or internal factors that can hinder the organization's mission (Gupta et al., 2014). Improper implementation of SWOT can impede Regional Bank's outcome, while an accurate strategic plan for implementing the online platform can help the company succeed (Rothwell et al., 2021).

This will help study the need for an online lending platform for all banks and how it will directly affect customers and employees. These further approaches can increase information on online lending platforms and their importance to the banking sector, enabling further industry studies (Diener & Spacek, 2021).

REFERENCES

Ali, G & Hassan, M. (2022). A Review of Organization Change Management and Employee Performance. *Xi'an Dianzi Keji Daxue Xuebao/Journal of Xidian University*. 16. 494-506. .DOI: 10.37896/jxu16.1/043

Alnsour, M. S. (2013). How to retain a bank customer: A qualitative study of Jordanian banks relational strategies. *International journal of marketing studies, 5*(4), 123.

Alsajjan, B., & Dennis, C. (2006). The Impact of Trust on Acceptance of Online Banking *European Association of Education and Research in Commercial Distribution.* https://bura.brunel.ac.uk/bitstream/2438/738/1/trust%20impact%20on%20online%20banking%20acceptance%20conceptual%20framework%20-full%20paper.pdf

Anderson, D. (2020). *Organization development: the process of leading organizational change* (5th ed.). Sage Publishers.

Asunda, P., & Ware, S. (2015). Applying the congruence principle of Bloom's taxonomy to **develop an integrated stem experience through engineering design** https://www.researchgate.net/publication/323133638_applying_the_congruence_principle_of_bloom's_taxonomy_to_develop_an_integrated_stem_experience_through_engineering_design

Bailer, S. (2014). Interviews and surveys in legislative research. *The Oxford handbook of legislative studies*, 167-193.

Bans-Akutey, A. (2021). The Path-Goal Theory of Leadership. *Academia Letters. Article*, 748. Advance online publication. DOI: 10.20935/AL748

Bass, B., & Avolio, B. (1993). Transformational leadership and organizational culture. *Public Administration Quarterly*, 17(1), 112–121. https://www.jstor.org/stable/40862298

Bedard, A. (2023, August 22). The 8-step process for leading change: Dr. John Kotter. K*otter International Inc.*https://www.kotterinc.com/methodology/8-steps/

Bertsch, C., & Rosenvinge, C. J. (2019). FinTech credit: Online lending platforms in Sweden and beyond. *Sveriges Riksbank Economic Review*, 2, 42–70.

Bianco-Mathis, V. (2023). *Culture Change: The Nexus Of Leadership*. Organizational Development Models, And Coaching Cultures.

Bickmore, E., MacKinlay, A., & Tellez, Y. (2023). Old Program, New Banks: Online Banks in Small Business Lending. *Social Science Research Network*. DOI: 10.2139/ssrn.4537337

Broeders, H., & Khanna, S. 2015. Strategic choices for banks in the digital age. McKinsey & Company: Our Insights. www.mckinsey.com/industries/ financial-services/our-insights/strategic-choices-for-banks-in-the-digital-age

Cameron, K. (2009). An introduction to the competing values framework. https://www.semanticscholar.org/paper/An-Introduction-to-the-Competing-Values-Framework-Cameron/45b05b0eebf2f4bc6e204f4559e91ab7e7e0272d

Chappell, G., Harreis, H., Havas, A., Nuzzo, A., Pepanides, T., & Rowshankish, K. (2018, *August 31*). The lending revolution: How digital credit is changing banks from the inside. *McKinsey & Company.* https://www.mckinsey.com/capabilities/risk-and-resilience/our-insights/the-lending-revolution-how-digital-credit-is-changing-banks-from-the-inside

Cuadros-Solas, P. J., Cubillas, E., & Salvador, C. (2023). Does alternative digital lending affect bank performance? Cross-country and bank-level evidence. *International Review of Financial Analysis*, 90, 102873. DOI: 10.1016/j.irfa.2023.102873

Diener, F., & Špaček, M. (2021). Digital Transformation in Banking: A Managerial Perspective on Barriers to Change. *Sustainability (Basel)*, 13(4), 2032. DOI: 10.3390/su13042032

Federal Deposit Insurance Corporation. (2020). The importance of community banks in paycheck protection program lending. *FDIC.gov* https://www.fdic.gov/analysis/quarterly-

Frei, F., & Morriss, A. (2020). Begin with trust. *Harvard Business Review*, 98(3), 112–121.

Fuster, A., Goldsmith-Pinkham, P., Ramadorai, T., & Walther, A. (2018). 'Predictably Unequal? The Effects of Machine Learning on Credit Markets', https://haas.berkeley.edu/wp-content/uploads/Predictably-Unequal-The-Effects-of-Machine-Learning-on-Credit-Markets.pdf

Ghasabeh, M. S., Soosay, C., & Reaiche, C. (2015). The emerging role of transformational leadership. *Journal of Developing Areas*, 49(6), 459–467. DOI: 10.1353/jda.2015.0090

Goldman, I. (2023, July 20). Applying for a personal loan online vs. in person. *Discover Personal Loans.* https://www.discover.com/personal-loans/resources/learn-about-personal-loans/applying-for-a-personal-loan-online-versus-a-physical-branch/

Gupta, K., Sleezer, C. M., & Russ-Eft, D. (2014). *A practical guide to needs assessment* (3rd ed.). John Wiley.

House, R. J., & Howell, J. M. (1992). Personality and charismatic leadership. *The Leadership Quarterly*, 3(2), 81–108. DOI: 10.1016/1048-9843(92)90028-E

Hu, J., & Dutta, T. (2022). What's charisma got to do with it? Three faces of charismatic leadership and corporate social responsibility engagement. *Frontiers in Psychology*, 13, 829584. DOI: 10.3389/fpsyg.2022.829584 PMID: 35941945

Ives, Y. (2008). What is 'coaching'? An exploration of conflicting paradigms. *International Journal of Evidence Based Coaching and Mentoring*, 6(2), 100–113.

Khalid, A. (2011). Effect of organizational change on employee job involvement: Mediating role of communication, emotions, and psychological contract. *Information Management and Business Review*, 3(3), 178–184. DOI: 10.22610/imbr.v3i3.931

Khanchel, H. (2019). The Impact of Digital Transformation on Banking. *Journal of Business Administration Research*, 8(2), 20. DOI: 10.5430/jbar.v8n2p20

Korbi, K. (2015). Leadership and Strategic Change. *The Journal of Organizational Management Studies*, 2015, 638847. Advance online publication. DOI: 10.5171/2015.638847

Laig, R. B. D., & Abocejo, F. T. (2021). Change management process in a mining company: Kotter's 8-step change model. *Journal of Management, Economics, and Industrial Organization*, 5(3), 31–50. DOI: 10.31039/jomeino.2021.5.3.3

Latta, G. (2009). A Process Model of Organizational Change in Cultural Context (OC3 Model). *Journal of Leadership & Organizational Studies*, 16(1), 19–37. DOI: 10.1177/1548051809334197

Marr, B. (2023, August 23). 9 vital steps to create a digital transformation strategy. *Forbes*. https://www.forbes.com/sites/bernardmarr/2023/08/22/9-vital-steps-to-create-a-digital-transformation-strategy/

Masrom, M. (2007). Technology acceptance model and e-learning. *Technology (Elmsford, N.Y.)*, 21(24), 81.

Mastroprieto, F., & Blini, L. (n.d.). Why digital lending is the future for banks and smes. *EY*. https://www.ey.com/en_gl/insights/financial-services/emeia/why-digital-lending-is-the-future-for-banks-and-smes

Matt, C., Hess, T., & Benlian, A. (2015, September). (PDF) Digital Transformation Strategies. *ResearchGate*. https://www.researchgate.net/publication/281965523_Digital_Transformation_Strategies

Moutousi, O., & May, D. (2018). How change-related unethical leadership triggers follower resistance to change: A theoretical account and conceptual model. *Journal of Change Management*, 18(2), 142–161. DOI: 10.1080/14697017.2018.1446695

Nadler, D. A., & Tushman, M. L. (1990). Beyond the charismatic leader: Leadership and organizational change. *California Management Review*, 32(2), 77–97. DOI: 10.2307/41166606

Namugenyi, C., Nimmagadda, S. L., & Reiners, T. (2019). Design of a SWOT Analysis Model and Its Evaluation in Diverse Digital Business Ecosystem Contexts. *Procedia Computer Science*, 159(159), 1145–1154. https://demo.dspacedirect.org/server/api/core/bitstreams/c5fcc52d-13fe-4a94-ae78-24f2a820a312/content. DOI: 10.1016/j.procs.2019.09.283

Northouse, P. (2016). *Leadership theory and practice* (7th ed.). Sage Publications.

Odumeru, J. A., & Ogbonna, I. G. (2013). Transformational vs. transactional leadership theories: Evidence in literature. *International review of management and business research, 2*(2), 355.

Opportunities and challenges in online marketplace lending. *U.S. department of the treasury*. (2016). https://home.treasury.gov/system/files/231/Opportunities_and_Challenges_in_Online_Marketplace_Lending_white_paper.pdf

Orem, S., Binkert, J., & Clancy, A. L. (2007). *Appreciative coaching: A positive process for change*. Jossey-Bass/Wiley.

Özlen, M. K., & Djedovic, I. (2017). Online banking acceptance: The influence of perceived system security on perceived system quality. *Accounting and Management Information Systems*, 16(1), 164–178. DOI: 10.24818/jamis.2017.01008

Peng, J., Li, M., Wang, Z., & Lin, Y. (2021). Transformational leadership and employees' reactions to organizational change: Evidence from a meta-analysis. *The Journal of Applied Behavioral Science*, 57(3), 369–397. DOI: 10.1177/0021886320920366

Rea, L. M., & Parker, R. A. (2014). *Designing and conducting survey research: A comprehensive guide*. John Wiley & Sons.

Rothwell, W., Bakhshandeh, B., & Imroz, S. M. (2021). *Organization development interventions: Executing effective organizational change*. Productivity Press. DOI: 10.4324/9781003019800

Samimi, M., Cortes, A. F., Anderson, M. H., & Herrmann, P. (2022). What is strategic leadership? Developing a framework for future research. *The Leadership Quarterly*, 33(3), 101353. DOI: 10.1016/j.leaqua.2019.101353

Siddiqui, F. (2011). *Impact of employee's willingness on organizational ... - core.* Journal of Economics and Sustainable Development. https://core.ac.uk/download/pdf/234645454.pdf

Smith, R., King, D., Sidhu, R., & Skelsey, D. (2014). *The effective change manager's handbook: essential guidance to the change management body of knowledge.* Kogan Page Publishers.

Starman, A. B. (2013). The case study as a type of qualitative research. *Journal of Contemporary Educational Studies/Sodobna Pedagogika, 64*(1).

Strohm, M., & Horton, C. (2023, November 24). 5 benefits of Digital Banking. *Forbes.* https://www.forbes.com/advisor/banking/benefits-of-digital-banking/

Treece, K., & Tarver, J. (2023, September 28). Should you apply for a loan online or in person? *Forbes.* https://www.forbes.com/advisor/personal-loans/online-or-in-person-loans/

U.S. Department of the Treasury. (2023, June 15). Paycheck protection program. *Treasury.Gov*https://home.treasury.gov/policy-issues/coronavirus/assistance-for-small-businesses/paycheck-protection-program#:~:text=This%20program%20provides%20small%20businesses,mortgages%2C%20rent%2C%20and%20utilities

Van der Zande, J. (2018). Banks and digitalization. In *The rise and development of fintech* (pp. 327–349). Routledge. DOI: 10.4324/9781351183628-18

Verhoef, P. C., Broekhuizen, T., Bart, Y., Bhattacharya, A., & Dong, Q. J., Fabian, N., & Haenlein, M. (2021). Digital transformation: a Multidisciplinary Reflection and Research Agenda. *Journal of Business Research, 122*(122), 889–901. ScienceDirect. https://www.sciencedirect.com/science/article/pii/S0148296319305478

Walker, B., & Soule, S. (2017, November 16). Changing company culture requires a movement, not a mandate. *Harvard Business Review.https://hbr.org/2017/06/changing-company-culture-requires-a-movement-not-a-mandate*

Weisbord, M. R. (1976). Organizational Diagnosis: Six Places To Look for Trouble with or Without a Theory. *Group & Organization Studies*, 1(4), 430–447. https://doi-org.proxymu.wrlc.org/10.1177/105960117600100405. DOI: 10.1177/105960117600100405

Yaghoubi, N. M., & Bahmani, E. (2010). Factors affecting the adoption of online banking: An integration of technology acceptance model and theory of planned behavior. *International Journal of Business and Management*, 5(9), 159–165. DOI: 10.5539/ijbm.v5n9p159

Yu, T., & Wu, N. (2009). A review of study on the competing values framework. *International Journal of Business and Management*, 4(7), 37–42. DOI: 10.5539/ijbm.v4n7p37

Zak, P. (2017, January). The Neuroscience of Trust. *Harvard Business Review.* https://hbr.org/2017/01/the-neuroscience-of-trust

Chapter 14
Integration of Circular Economy Principles Within Information Logistics:
Case Study of Australia

Mallika Roy
https://orcid.org/0000-0002-5854-5084
Central Queensland University, Australia & University of Chittagong, Bangladesh

Jaba Sarker
https://orcid.org/0000-0003-1589-6842
Central Queensland University, Australia

ABSTRACT

This study investigates integrating circular economy principles with information logistics to enhance sustainability and supply chain performance. The study aims to explore how optimizing information flows can support pro-environmental practices, reduce waste, and improve resource efficiency. By leveraging digital technologies and advanced analytics, businesses can implement closed-loop systems, track material flows, and enhance decision-making. This research addresses the gap in understanding the combined benefits of circular economy and information logistics, providing insights for businesses and policymakers. The findings will contribute to advancing sustainable business practices and competitive advantage, offering practical pathways for organizations navigating the complexities of a globalized economy while fostering environmental stewardship.

DOI: 10.4018/979-8-3693-8562-3.ch014

1. INTRODUCTION

1.1 Background

In today's rapidly evolving business landscape, the imperative to adopt sustainable practices has become increasingly urgent. Central to this movement is the concept of the circular economy, which promotes resource efficiency, waste reduction, and the establishment of closed-loop systems to minimize environmental impact (Camilleri, 2018; Kara et al., 2022). Concurrently, information logistics—comprising the efficient management and flow of information across supply chains—plays a pivotal role in enhancing organizational efficiency and competitiveness in a globalized market (Klein & Rai, 2009). The integration of circular economy principles within the framework of information logistics presents a promising avenue for achieving sustainable development goals while bolstering organizational empowerment and optimizing supply chain management (Kouhizadeh et al., 2020). Information logistics not only facilitates the seamless transmission of data and knowledge within and between organizations but also catalyses implementing and monitoring sustainability initiatives across supply chains (Gardner et al., 2019; Sarkis et al., 2021). By strategically leveraging information logistics, businesses can enhance their resilience to market fluctuations, improve operational efficiencies, and reduce their ecological footprint.

1.2 Problem Statement

In the context of a rapidly evolving business environment, the integration of circular economy (CE) principles and information logistics (IL) strategies is increasingly recognized as vital for achieving sustainable development goals and enhancing supply chain efficiency. While CE emphasizes resource efficiency, waste reduction, and the establishment of closed-loop systems to minimize environmental impact (Camilleri, 2018; Kara et al., 2022), IL focuses on the efficient management and flow of information across supply chains, which is crucial for organizational competitiveness in a globalized market (Klein & Rai, 2009). The strategic alignment of CE and IL holds the potential to optimize supply chain management, improve operational efficiencies, and bolster organizational resilience (Kouhizadeh et al., 2020). However, despite the acknowledged benefits of both domains, there remains a significant gap in the literature regarding how these two concepts can be synergistically integrated to maximize their collective impact on sustainable business practices.

1.3 Research Gap

Current research predominantly addresses CE and IL in isolation, often overlooking the potential combined benefits for organizational empowerment and supply chain management effectiveness (Liu et al., 2023; Fernando et al., 2022; Subramanian & Suresh, 2022). While studies have explored the role of digital technologies such as big data analytics and IoT in enhancing visibility and traceability within supply chains (Kache & Seuring, 2017; De Vass et al., 2021; Khan et al., 2022), there is a lack of comprehensive models that illustrate the interdependencies between IL systems and CE strategies. This gap in the literature underscores the need for integrative approaches that can enhance the effectiveness of sustainability initiatives across industries.

Despite the recognized benefits of both circular economy practices and effective information logistics, there remains a critical gap in understanding how these two domains can be synergistically integrated to maximize their collective impact. Current research on the circular economy primarily emphasizes resource efficiency, waste reduction, and sustainable product lifecycle management (Di Maio, et al., 2017; Tukker, A., 2015; He et al.; Di Lorio et al., 2023). Existing literature also focuses on either circular economy strategies or information logistics in isolation for organizational empowerment and supply chain management effectiveness (Liu et al., 2023; Fernando et al., 2022; Subramanian & Suresh, 2022; Raquib, 2010; Srivastava, 2006). However, it often overlooks the potential combined benefits of circular economy, information logistics organizational empowerment, and supply chain management effectiveness. Studies also have highlighted the potential of digital technologies, such as big data analytics and IoT, in enhancing visibility and traceability within supply chains (Kache & Seuring, 2017; De Vass et al., 2021; Khan et al., 2022), but the specific mechanisms through which information logistics can support and transform circular economy frameworks remain under-researched. Furthermore, while some literature has explored the role of data sharing in promoting sustainable practices (Khan et al., 2016; Le et al., 2024), there is a lack of comprehensive models that illustrate the interdependencies between information logistics systems and circular economy strategies. Addressing this gap is crucial for developing integrative approaches that maximize the effectiveness of sustainability initiatives across industries. Thus, this research work seeks to address this gap by investigating the integration of circular economy principles within information logistics contexts. By exploring how organizations can optimize their information flows to support sustainable practices and enhance supply chain performance, this study aims to provide actionable insights for businesses aiming to navigate the complexities of a globalized economy while fostering environmental stewardship and organizational resilience. Through qualitative theme-based literature, this research intends to reveal empirical evidence on the strategic alignment of circular economy principles with information logistics strategies. The findings contribute not only to academic literature but also to inform policymakers and industry leaders on practical pathways toward sustainable development and competitive advantage in the era of circular economy-driven business models.

1.4 Aims and Objectives

This study outlines a structured approach to examining the intersection of circular economy principles, information logistics, organizational empowerment, and supply chain management, aiming to advance both theoretical understanding and practical applications in sustainable business practices. This analysis explores the benefits and challenges associated with implementing information logistics in agri-food supply chains for a circular economy in Australia, focusing on how these factors impact supply chain resilience, environmental sustainability, and overall efficiency. Hence, the objectives of this study are as follows:

- To investigate the role of circular economy principles in enhancing information logistics strategies.
- To assess the impact of integrated information logistics on organizational empowerment.
- To analyse how these strategies contribute to effective supply chain management practices.

1.5 Originality, Rationale, and Significance of the Study

Originality

This study offers a novel approach by integrating circular economy (CE) principles with information logistics (IL) strategies, addressing a critical gap in the current literature. While existing research predominantly examines CE and IL separately, this study pioneers a comprehensive analysis of their combined impact on organizational empowerment and supply chain management. By doing so, it contributes original insights into how businesses can simultaneously enhance sustainability and operational efficiency through the strategic alignment of these two domains. Additionally, the study explores the role of emerging digital technologies, such as big data analytics and the Internet of Things (IoT), in facilitating this integration, further contributing to the originality of the research by connecting these technologies to CE-IL synergies.

Rationale

In today's globalized economy, businesses face increasing pressure to adopt sustainable practices while maintaining competitive advantage. Circular economy principles, which emphasize resource efficiency and waste reduction, offer a pathway to sustainability, but their full potential can only be realized when integrated with advanced information management systems. Information logistics, which involves efficient management and flow of information across supply chains, plays a crucial role in enabling real-time decision-making, enhancing supply chain visibility, and optimizing resource use. However, the intersection of CE and IL remains underexplored, particularly in how it can be leveraged to foster organizational empowerment and effective supply chain management. This study is driven by the need to fill this gap, providing empirical evidence and strategic frameworks that businesses can use to navigate the complexities of a sustainable, data-driven economy.

Significance

The significance of this study lies in its potential to transform how organizations approach sustainability and supply chain management. By uncovering the synergies between circular economy principles and information logistics strategies, this research can inform both academia and industry on best practices for achieving sustainability goals while improving operational efficiencies. The findings are expected to have practical implications for businesses, offering actionable insights on optimizing information flows to support sustainable practices, enhancing supply chain resilience, and fostering organizational empowerment. Additionally, the study's exploration of digital technologies' role in this integration provides a forward-looking perspective, positioning it as a valuable resource for policymakers and industry leaders seeking to implement sustainable, circular business models in the era of digital transformation. This research thus contributes to advancing theoretical understanding and practical applications in sustainable business practices, aligning with global efforts to achieve sustainable development goals.

2. LITERATURE REVIEW

2.1 Introduction to Circular Economy

The circular economy (CE) represents a paradigm shift from linear 'take-make-dispose' models to circular approaches focused on resource recovery, reuse, and regeneration (Solomon et al., 2024). CE principles, including designing out waste, keeping materials in use, and regenerating natural systems, are being integrated into supply chain management (SCM) strategies (Solomon et al., 2024). This integration involves reconfiguring core SCM processes to support CE implementation (Hazen et al., 2021). Key areas of convergence include closing, slowing, intensifying, narrowing, and dematerializing loops within SCM processes such as customer relationship management and product development (Hazen et al., 2021). The transition to circular supply chains may involve shifts from product ownership to leasing, increased structural flexibility, open and closed material loops, closer collaboration across industries, and leveraging public and private procurement (De Angelis et al., 2018). While challenges exist, adopting CE principles in SCM offers opportunities for sustainable growth, resilience, and value creation (Solomon et al., 2024). The circular economy aims to minimize waste and maximize resource efficiency through sustainable practices across the product lifecycle (Camilleri, 2018). Key components include sustainable material sourcing, durable product design, efficient production, and responsible consumption (Domenech & Stegemann, 2021). Recycling and remanufacturing play crucial roles in closing the resource loop, though challenges like material degradation and contamination persist (Rakesh et al., 2023). Advanced technologies such as additive manufacturing and digital twins offer potential solutions to these issues (Rakesh et al., 2023). Product design in a circular economy focuses on preserving economic and environmental value by extending product lifetimes and enabling reuse (Den Hollander et al., 2017). This approach differs from traditional eco-design, introducing new concepts like "pre-source" and "recovery horizon" (Den Hollander et al., 2017). The transition to a circular economy requires innovative business models, supportive policies, and a shift in consumer behaviour to achieve sustainable consumption and production (Camilleri, 2018; Domenech & Stegemann, 2021). The concept of the circular economy has gained significant traction in recent years as a framework for sustainable development in business operations. According to Ellen MacArthur Foundation (2013), the circular economy aims to decouple economic growth from resource consumption by promoting regenerative practices such as resource recovery, remanufacturing, and product life extension. This paradigm shift towards a restorative and regenerative economic model not only reduces waste and environmental impact but also fosters economic resilience and innovation (Geissdoerfer et al., 2017).

2.2 Overview of Information Logistics

Information logistics plays a crucial role in supply chain management, enhancing efficiency, competitiveness, and profitability (Sousa et al., 2027). Information logistics has emerged as a critical enabler of efficient supply chain management and organizational empowerment. Information logistics involves the systematic management of information flows across various organizational functions and supply chain partners (Hsu & Lee, 2017). Effective information logistics facilitates real-time data exchange, enhances decision-making processes, and supports the implementation of responsive and adaptive supply chain strategies (Zhang et al., 2019). Key technologies and components include information management systems, enterprise resource planning (ERP), customer relationship management (CRM), supplier relationship management (SRM), and radio-frequency identification (RFID) (Reddy, 2012). These technologies facilitate improved planning, control, and monitoring of product flows from suppliers to end users, while optimizing delivery of goods, services, and information (Sousa et al., 2021; Reddy, 2012). Information technology provides tools for gathering and analyzing data to make optimal supply chain decisions, leading to reduced costs, streamlined operations, and enhanced relationships with customers, suppliers, and partners (Sousa et al., 2021; Siwach & Pathak, 2020). The integration of these technologies in logistics management aligns the supply chain with consumer needs, increasing overall system efficiency and effectiveness while making tasks easier and faster (Siwach & Pathak, 2020).

Figure 1 visually represents the interconnected processes and data management practices that support sustainable resource use and waste reduction throughout the agri-food supply chain. Information logistics in an agri-food supply chain related to the circular economy involves the systematic collection, management, and sharing of data to enhance sustainability and reduce waste throughout the supply chain. The process begins with data collection on farming practices, capturing information on methods and inputs used in crop production (Blanco & Aguilar, 2021). This data, along with information on crop yields and quality, is essential for assessing agricultural performance and making informed decisions (Godfray et al., 2010). Data on distribution and transportation ensures efficient logistics, while real-time monitoring of storage conditions helps in maintaining product quality and reducing spoilage (Manning et al., 2022). Information is shared across stakeholders, including farmers, distributors, retailers, and consumers, fostering collaboration and transparency (Tura et al., 2019). This shared information supports decision support systems for resource allocation, optimizing the use of resources such as water, fertilizers, and energy (Lezoche et al., 2020). Lifecycle assessment (LCA) of food products evaluates their environmental impact from production to disposal, guiding improvements in sustainability (Notarnicola et al., 2017). Reverse logistics for food waste ensures that waste is effectively collected and redirected, often for composting or other circular business models (Wakiru et al., 2020). These circular practices not only minimize waste but also create value from waste products. Finally, all these activities must comply with regulatory requirements, ensuring that the supply chain adheres to environmental standards and reporting obligations (Kirchherr et al., 2017). Through efficient information logistics, the agri-food supply chain can achieve greater sustainability, contributing to a circular economy by reducing waste, optimizing resource use, and enhancing overall efficiency.

Figure 1. Information flow and sustainability integration in agri-food supply chains for a circular economy

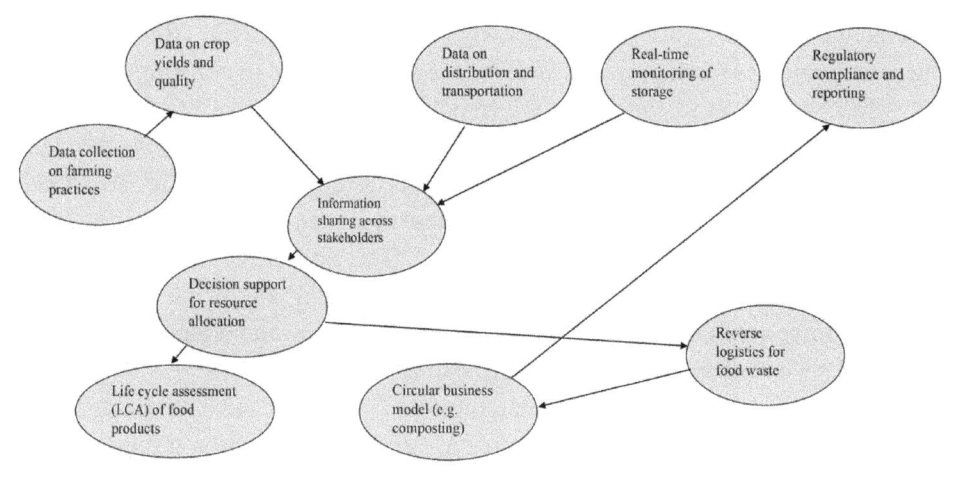

Note. Modified from Blanco & Aguilar, 2021; Godfray et al., 2010; Manning et al., 2022; Notarnicola et al., 2017 and Tura et al., 2019

2.3 Circular Economy and Information Logistics

In the context of a circular economy, certain components are intricately linked with data processes and decision-making mechanisms, which enhance efficiency and sustainability across the lifecycle of products. In Figure 2, design, production, and distribution (components 2, 3, and 4) are closely tied to data collection centers, data management, and information dissemination. During the design phase, data collection centers play a crucial role by gathering information on material properties, market needs, and consumer preferences, which inform sustainable design choices (Bocken et al., 2016). In the production phase, effective data management systems ensure that resources are optimally utilized, reducing waste and improving process efficiency (Garcia et al., 2015). For distribution, information dissemination is essential to track products, manage inventory, and forecast demand, which helps in reducing excess production and minimizing environmental impact (Genovese et al., 2017).

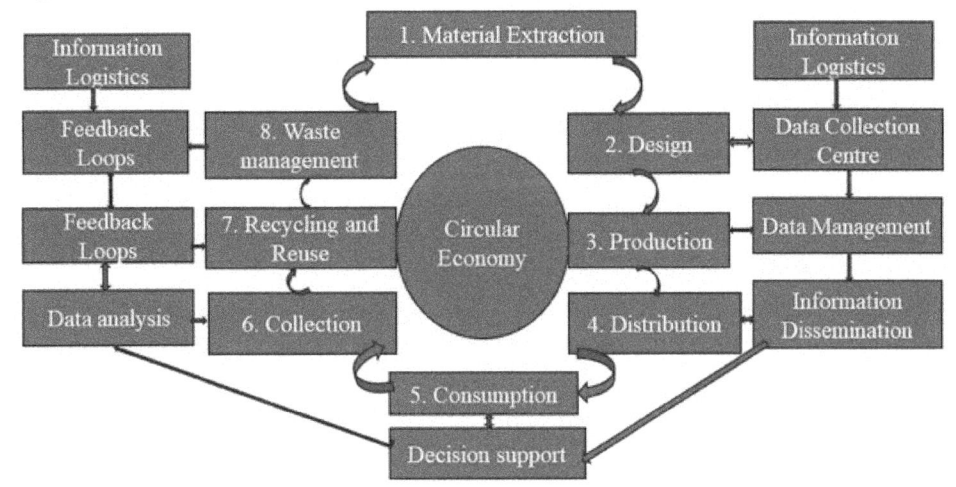

Figure 2. Relationship between circular economy and information logistics

[Figure: Diagram showing the Circular Economy at the center with 8 components arranged around it: 1. Material Extraction, 2. Design, 3. Production, 4. Distribution, 5. Consumption, 6. Collection, 7. Recycling and Reuse, 8. Waste management. On the right side under "Information Logistics": Data Collection Centre, Data Management, Information Dissemination. On the left side under "Information Logistics": Feedback Loops, Feedback Loops, Data analysis. At the bottom: Decision support.]

Note. Compiled from Zarbakhshnia, N., et al. (2020), Statistics Finland[1], Shipsy (2024).

Collection, recycling and reuse, and waste management (components 6, 7, and 8) are associated with data analysis, feedback loops, and feedback loops, respectively. Collection relies on data analysis to identify the most efficient ways to retrieve end-of-life products and materials (Kalmykova et al., 2018). Recycling and reuse benefit from feedback loops that provide insights into material recovery rates and process improvements, ensuring that materials are effectively reintegrated into the production cycle (Stahel, 2016). Waste management incorporates feedback loops to continuously improve waste reduction strategies and enhance resource efficiency (Ellen MacArthur Foundation, 2013).

Linking information dissemination and data analysis to decision support is vital for the overall success of the circular economy. Information dissemination ensures that relevant stakeholders have access to timely and accurate data, facilitating informed decision-making. Data analysis provides the insights necessary for evaluating the performance of circular economy strategies, identifying areas for improvement, and making strategic adjustments. Together, they support decision-making by providing a comprehensive understanding of resource flows, environmental impacts, and economic benefits, enabling organizations to implement more sustainable practices effectively (Geissdoerfer et al., 2017).

2.4 Integrating Circular Economy Principles Into Supply Chain Management

Despite the individual merits of circular economy principles and information logistics, there is a notable gap in the literature regarding their integrated application within organizational contexts. Existing studies predominantly focus on either sustainability practices in supply chain management or the role of information logistics in enhancing operational efficiencies, often overlooking the synergies that could be achieved by combining these domains. Research by Hofmann and Busch (2013) suggests that integrating circular economy principles into supply chain management can lead to significant environmental and economic benefits. By optimizing material and energy flows through closed-loop systems and resource recovery processes, businesses can reduce costs associated with raw material procurement and waste disposal while mitigating environmental risks (Rizos et al., 2016). Furthermore, the strategic integration of information logistics with circular economy practices holds promise for enhancing supply chain resilience and organizational agility. According to a study by Choi et al. (2018), digital technologies and advanced analytics enable businesses to track and trace material flows, optimize inventory management, and forecast demand more accurately, thereby supporting the implementation of circular economy strategies.

However, empirical evidence on the practical implementation and outcomes of integrated circular economic principles within information logistics remains limited. A comprehensive understanding of how organizations can leverage information logistics to support circular economy initiatives is crucial for guiding strategic decision-making and policy development in sustainable business practices.

2.5 Technological Innovation

The integration of Internet of Things (IoT), blockchain, and big data analytics presents significant opportunities for technological innovation. IoT devices generate vast amounts of data that can be analyzed using big data techniques to enable real-time, data-driven decision-making (Trivedi et al., 2023). Blockchain technology can enhance the security and transparency of IoT systems by providing immutable, distributed ledgers for data transactions (Reyna et al., 2018). This integration addresses key challenges in IoT, such as data reliability and privacy concerns (Saleminezhadl et al., 2021). The combination of these technologies has potential applications across various industries, including healthcare, manufacturing, and finance (Trivedi et al., 2023). However, adapting blockchain to IoT environments poses challenges that require further research and development (Saleminezhadl et al., 2021). Despite these challenges, the synergistic potential of IoT, blockchain, and big data analytics is expected to play a vital role in resolving constraints and driving technological advancements (Manjunath et al., 2018).

2.5 Impact on Supply Chain Performance and Sustainability

Recent research highlights the importance of integrating sustainability and resilience into supply chain management. Studies show that adopting sustainable and resilient practices can improve both environmental and economic performance (Green et al., 2012; Ramezankhani et al., 2018). A comprehensive performance management system incorporating sustainability and resilience factors can help assess supply chain performance over time (Ramezankhani et al., 2018). Simulation studies reveal that certain sustainability factors can mitigate or enhance the ripple effect of disruptions in supply chains (Ivanov, 2018). Integrating sustainability factors into supply chain design and planning models can improve overall performance and help businesses achieve desirable benefits while managing potential cost impacts (Das & Mitra, 2018). These studies emphasize the need for a balanced approach that considers both sustainability and resilience to enhance supply chain performance, resource efficiency, and waste reduction while improving economic and environmental outcomes.

2.6 Quantitative Research and Data-Driven Logistics in Circular Economy Implementation

The circular economy (CE) is gaining traction as a sustainable approach to resource management and economic growth. Quantitative studies have shown that CE indicators can be used to classify and analyze countries' performance (Cautitanu et al., 2018). Information sharing is crucial for CE implementation, requiring improved interorganizational communication and incentives for data exchange (Jäger-Roschko & Petersen, 2022). Green logistics plays a vital role in CE, focusing on resource-saving processes and technologies (Oliveira et al., 2023). Small and medium-sized enterprises can benefit from data-driven logistics optimization to enhance material flow management in CE business models (Järvenpää et al., 2022). These studies highlight the importance of quantitative research, information logistics, and data-driven approaches in supporting CE implementation across various sectors and scales, from individual companies to national economies.

2.7 Integration of Emerging Technologies in Industry Transformation

The integration of AI, VR, AR, IoT, and blockchain technologies is revolutionizing product design, development, and various industries. AI enhances decision-making, trend prediction, and prototyping (Rane et al., 2023), while VR and AR create immersive design environments (Rane et al., 2023; Cannavò & Lamberti, 2021). IoT enables real-time monitoring and data-driven improvements (Rane et al., 2023), and blockchain ensures transparency, security, and traceability in collaborative processes (Rane et al., 2023; Naranjo et al., 2023). The convergence of these technologies offers opportunities for streamlined workflows, improved efficiency, and innovative business models (Saritha et al., 2021). However, challenges such as scalability, privacy concerns, and ethical considerations must be addressed (Naranjo et al., 2023). The fusion of these technologies is transforming various domains, including finance, entertainment, and IoT ecosystems, paving the way for more secure, intelligent, and efficient practices (Cannavò & Lamberti, 2021; Naranjo et al., 2023).

2.8 Gaps in Current Research

Recent research highlights significant gaps in the circular economy (CE) and information logistics studies. While CE research is expanding, it remains fragmented, lacking a holistic perspective on business management (Ahmad et al., 2023). The integration of digital technologies and Industry 4.0 with CE is an emerging area requiring further investigation (Okorie et al., 2018). Blockchain technology has been proposed as a potential solution for CE implementation, but challenges in terminology, trust, and verification persist (Böckel et al., 2020). Social value stemming from CE practices, particularly in agri-food eco-industrial parks, is substantially under-researched (Atanasovska et al., 2022). Future research should explore CE practices in eco-industrial parks, link CE with social value beyond economic and environmental metrics and investigate adoption motivators. There is also a need for more mixed-methods and large dataset analysis in CE studies (Atanasovska et al., 2022).

Figure 3. Integration of circular economy, information logistics and research gap

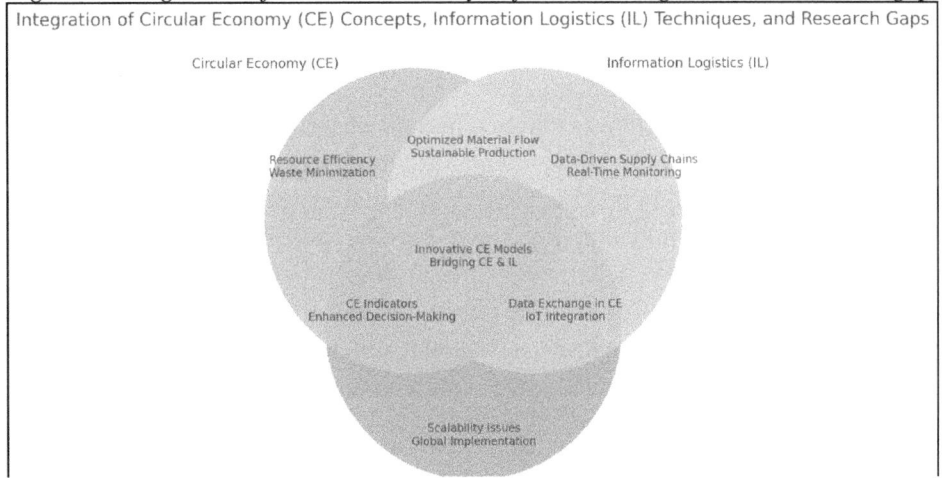

Figure 3 displays a Venn diagram that visually captures the integration of Circular Economy (CE) concepts, Information Logistics (IL) techniques, and current research gaps, illustrating how this study aims to address critical issues at their intersection. CE emphasizes resource efficiency and waste minimization, while IL focuses on data-driven supply chains and real-time monitoring. The overlap between CE and IL signifies optimized material flow and sustainable production processes, showcasing how these areas can complement each other. The intersection of CE and research gaps highlights the need for improved CE indicators and decision-making processes. Similarly, the overlap between IL and research gaps underscores the challenges of data exchange within CE frameworks and the integration of IoT technologies. At the core, where all three circles intersect, lies the potential for innovative CE models that bridge CE and IL while addressing the identified gaps. This diagram effectively demonstrates how the research can contribute to filling existing gaps and advancing both theoretical and practical applications.

This review underscores the need for empirical research on how integrating circular economy principles with information logistics can enhance organizational empowerment and supply chain management.

3. CONCEPTUAL FRAMEWORK

Integrating circular economy principles into information logistics represents a strategic approach to enhancing sustainability, resilience, and efficiency within organizations. The circular economy emphasizes redesigning economic systems to reduce resource depletion and environmental impact through practices like material reuse, remanufacturing, and closed-loop systems (Ellen MacArthur Foundation, 2013). Information logistics focuses on managing data flows across supply chains to enable real-time exchanges and support decision-making (Hsu & Lee, 2017). Key to this integration is optimizing both material and information flows, with technologies such as blockchain and advanced analytics playing a vital role. These technologies enable precise tracking of materials and provide insights into resource use and environmental impacts, thereby supporting closed-loop systems and improving resource efficiency (Choi et al., 2018; Geissdoerfer et al., 2017). Additionally, incorporating these principles enhances organizational empowerment by fostering cross-departmental and stakeholder collaboration, using shared data to create sustainable business models and align with environmental goals (Hofmann & Busch, 2013).

Figure 4. Conceptual framework on circular economy principles and information logistics

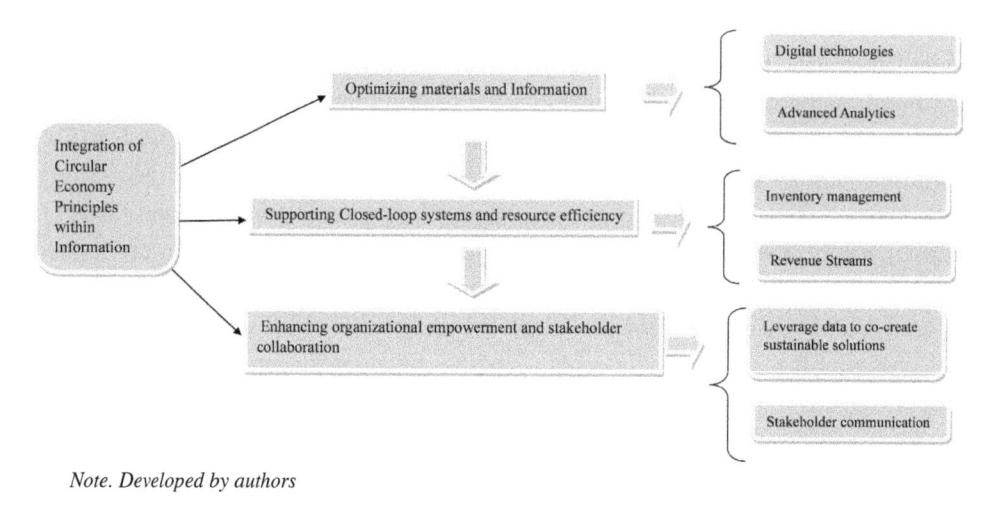

Note. Developed by authors

3.1 Integration of Circular Economy Principles Within Information Logistics

The integration of circular economy principles within information logistics represents a strategic approach to enhancing organizational sustainability, supply chain resilience, and operational efficiency. Circular economy principles advocate for the redesign of economic systems to minimize resource depletion and environmental impact through strategies such as material reuse, remanufacturing, and closed-loop systems (Ellen MacArthur Foundation, 2013). Information logistics, on the other hand, encompasses the systematic management of information flows across supply chains, enabling real-time data exchange, decision-making support, and operational coordination (Hsu & Lee, 2017).

3.2 Optimizing Material and Information Flows

At the core of integrating circular economy principles within information logistics is the optimization of both material and information flows across the supply chain. Traditionally, supply chains have focused primarily on optimizing material flows to reduce costs and improve delivery reliability. However, integrating circular economy principles necessitates a holistic approach that considers not only the physical movement of goods but also the flow of information related to product lifecycle stages, resource availability, and environmental impacts.

Digital technologies and advanced analytics play a crucial role in this integration by enabling businesses to track and trace material flows throughout the supply chain (Choi et al., 2018). For instance, blockchain technology can provide transparent and immutable records of product provenance, facilitating the identification of opportunities for material reuse or recycling. Real-time data analytics further enhance decision-making capabilities by providing insights into resource utilization patterns, demand forecasts, and environmental footprint assessments.

3.3 Supporting Closed-Loop Systems and Resource Efficiency

Information logistics supports the implementation of closed-loop systems by facilitating the efficient collection, processing, and dissemination of data necessary for resource recovery and remanufacturing processes. Closed-loop systems aim to retain the value of products, components, and materials within the economy for as long as possible, thereby reducing reliance on virgin resources and minimizing waste generation (Geissdoerfer et al., 2017).

Through effective information logistics, businesses can optimize inventory management practices, ensuring that returned products or end-of-life materials are reintegrated into production processes or secondary markets efficiently. This not only reduces landfill waste but also creates new revenue streams through the resale of refurbished products or recovered materials.

3.4 Enhancing Organizational Empowerment and Stakeholder Collaboration

The integration of circular economy principles within information logistics enhances organizational empowerment by fostering collaboration across internal departments and external stakeholders. Cross-functional teams can leverage shared data and analytics to co-create sustainable product designs, optimize supply chain configurations, and develop innovative business models that prioritize resource efficiency and environmental stewardship (Hofmann & Busch, 2013).

Furthermore, information logistics facilitates transparent communication and collaboration with suppliers, customers, and regulatory bodies regarding sustainability goals and performance metrics. By establishing robust information-sharing mechanisms, businesses can build trust, mitigate risks, and align stakeholder expectations with circular economy objectives.

3.4 Components of Integrating Circular Economy Principles Within Information Logistics

Table 1 summarizes the components of integrating circular economy principles within information logistics:

Table 1. Circular economy principles and information logistics

Components	Description	References
Information Flow Optimization	Optimization of information exchange across supply chain nodes to enhance visibility, responsiveness, and decision-making.	Hsu & Lee (2017); Zhang et al. (2019)
Resource Efficiency	Efficient use of resources throughout the product lifecycle, from design to disposal, aiming to minimize resource consumption and maximize value retention.	Ellen MacArthur Foundation (2013); Geissdoerfer et al. (2017)
Waste Reduction	Strategies to reduce waste generation through improved product design, material recovery, and recycling processes within closed-loop systems.	Ellen MacArthur Foundation (2013); Rizos et al. (2016)
Closed-Loop Systems	Systems that promote the reuse, refurbishment, and recycling of products and materials, thereby minimizing waste and environmental impact.	Geissdoerfer et al. (2017); Hofmann & Busch (2013)

3.5 Impact Pathways of Organizational Resilience, Environmental Sustainability And Supply Chain Performance Enhancement

Table 2 summarizes the integration of circular economy principles within information logistics and its relation to organizational resilience, environmental sustainability, and supply chain performance enhancement:

Table 2. Organizational resilience, environmental sustainability and supply chain performance

Components	Organizational Resilience	Environmental Sustainability	Supply Chain Performance Enhancement
Information Flow Optimization	Enhances agility by providing real-time insights into supply chain disruptions and enabling proactive decision-making (Zhang et al., 2019).	Facilitates accurate tracking of resource consumption and emissions, supporting sustainable practices (Hsu & Lee, 2017).	Improves supply chain visibility and coordination, reducing lead times and optimizing inventory levels (Zhang et al., 2019).
Resource Efficiency	Improves cost management and reduces resource dependency, enhancing resilience to supply chain risks (Ellen MacArthur Foundation, 2013).	Minimizes raw material extraction, energy consumption, and waste generation, promoting sustainable resource use (Geissdoerfer et al., 2017).	Optimizes production processes, lowers operational costs, and enhances product quality (Geissdoerfer et al., 2017).
Waste Reduction	Increases operational efficiency and redirects resources towards growth initiatives, enhancing long-term resilience (Rizos et al., 2016).	Reduces landfill waste and environmental pollution through closed-loop systems and recycling (Ellen MacArthur Foundation, 2013).	Optimizes material flows, reduces production lead times, and improves product lifecycle management (Rizos et al., 2016).
Closed-Loop Systems	Promotes resource recovery and reduces dependency on external resources, enhancing continuity of supply (Hofmann & Busch, 2013).	Minimizes environmental impact and conserves natural resources by reusing materials and products (Geissdoerfer et al., 2017).	Enables sustainable practices like remanufacturing and refurbishment, improving product quality and customer loyalty (Hofmann & Busch, 2013).

This table illustrates how integrating circular economy principles within information logistics contributes to organizational resilience, environmental sustainability, and supply chain performance enhancement. Each component highlights specific benefits related to these three dimensions, emphasizing the strategic advantages of adopting sustainable practices in business operations.

4. CASE STUDY: AUSTRALIA - INTEGRATION OF CIRCULAR ECONOMY PRINCIPLES WITHIN INFORMATION LOGISTICS

Australia, like many developed nations, faces challenges related to resource consumption, waste management, and supply chain efficiency. The integration of circular economy principles within information logistics presents an opportunity for Australian businesses to enhance sustainability practices, improve operational efficiencies, and foster resilience in a rapidly changing global market. Australia's economy is heavily reliant on resource extraction industries such as mining, agriculture, and manufacturing, which pose significant environmental challenges. With increasing pressure to reduce carbon emissions and improve resource efficiency, Australian businesses are exploring innovative approaches to integrate circular economy principles into their operations. Australia has embraced the integration of circular economy principles within information logistics to enhance supply chain resilience and environmental sustainability across various industries (Advanced Manufacturing Growth Centre, 2020). The adoption of advanced technologies like IoT and blockchain has enabled Australian businesses to optimize information flows and implement closed-loop systems, thereby reducing waste and improving resource efficiency (Australian Logistics Council, 2020). This strategic alignment not only enhances operational efficiencies but also positions Australia as a leader in sustainable practices, driving economic growth while mitigating environmental impact (Geissdoerfer et al., 2017; Infrastructure Sustainability Council of Australia, 2019).

4.1 Integration of Circular Economy Principles With Educational Impact

4.1.1 Information Flow Optimization

Case Example: Australian logistics companies are leveraging advanced technologies such as Internet of Things (IoT) sensors and blockchain for real-time tracking and transparency in supply chain operations. This optimization improves decision-making processes, reduces transportation costs, and minimizes environmental impact through optimized route planning and resource allocation (Australian Logistics Council, 2020). Australian retail giant Woolworths has implemented advanced analytics and IoT technologies to enhance inventory management and reduce waste. By utilizing real-time data to monitor stock levels and predict demand, Woolworths has significantly improved its supply chain efficiency and reduced food waste (Choi et al., 2021). The use of blockchain technology also supports transparency and traceability in its supply chain, allowing for better management of product lifecycles and resource allocation (Zhou et al., 2021).

Educational Impact: Universities and vocational training centers in Australia are adapting curricula to include courses on data analytics, supply chain management, and sustainability. These programs equip students with skills in information logistics and analytical tools essential for optimizing material and information flows in circular economy contexts (Ellis, 2020). Universities such as the University of Melbourne are incorporating these technologies into their supply chain management programs. Courses focus on practical applications of IoT and blockchain in logistics, preparing students for roles that require expertise in advanced information systems and sustainability practices (Ellis, 2020).

4.1.2 Resource Efficiency

Case Example: The Australian food and beverage industry is adopting circular economy strategies to minimize food waste and optimize resource use. Companies are implementing innovative packaging solutions and sustainable farming practices supported by data-driven insights to reduce water consumption and enhance production efficiency (Food Innovation Australia Limited, 2021). For example, the Australian wine industry is leveraging circular economy principles to optimize water use and reduce waste. By adopting precision agriculture technologies and recycling water in production processes, wineries like Yalumba have achieved significant reductions in water consumption and improved resource efficiency (Scown et al., 2021). Data analytics and lifecycle assessment tools are key to these innovations (Huang et al., 2022).

Educational Impact: Educational institutions collaborate with industry partners to develop research projects and internships focused on sustainable resource management. Students gain practical experience in implementing resource-efficient practices, such as lifecycle assessment and waste reduction strategies, which are crucial for future workforce readiness (Geissdoerfer et al., 2018). Educational programs at institutions like the University of Adelaide focus on sustainable practices in agriculture and resource management. These programs include hands-on projects and collaborations with industry to provide students with practical skills in resource optimization and waste management (Geissdoerfer et al., 2018).

4.1.3 Waste Reduction

Case Example: Australia's construction sector is embracing circular economy principles by incorporating recycled materials and designing buildings for disassembly. Information logistics plays a crucial role in managing waste streams effectively, tracking material flows, and identifying opportunities for material recovery and reuse, thereby reducing landfill waste and promoting closed-loop systems (Infrastructure Sustainability Council of Australia, 2019). For instance, in the Australian electronics sector, companies like Telstra are adopting circular economy principles to manage electronic waste (e-waste). By implementing take-back schemes and recycling programs supported by advanced information logistics systems, Telstra has improved its waste management practices and recovered valuable materials from old devices (Berkhout et al., 2021).

Educational Impact: Australia's vocational education sector integrates circular economy principles into construction and manufacturing programs. Students learn about sustainable design principles, waste minimization techniques, and recycling processes, preparing them for careers in industries committed to environmental stewardship (Sustainability Victoria, 2019). Australian vocational training programs, such as those offered by TAFE Queensland, are incorporating modules on e-waste management and recycling technologies. Students learn about the lifecycle of electronic products, waste reduction strategies, and the role of information logistics in managing e-waste (Sustainable Development Goals Academy, 2019).

4.1.4 Closed-Loop Systems

Case Example: Australian automotive manufacturers are exploring remanufacturing and refurbishment practices supported by robust information logistics systems. By integrating data analytics and supply chain transparency, these companies extend product lifecycles, reduce raw material consumption, and lower production costs while enhancing product quality and customer satisfaction (Advanced Manufacturing Growth Centre, 2020). The Australian packaging industry is embracing closed-loop systems through innovations in recycling and material recovery. Companies like Amcor are leading the way by developing recyclable and reusable packaging solutions. Information logistics systems support these efforts by tracking material flows and facilitating the efficient collection and processing of used packaging (Rath et al., 2022).

Educational Impact: Workforce development initiatives focus on upskilling existing professionals in sectors like automotive manufacturing and logistics. Training programs emphasize the adoption of closed-loop systems, remanufacturing practices, and supply chain transparency supported by information logistics, enhancing industry competitiveness and sustainability (Advanced Manufacturing Growth Centre, 2020). The Australian National University offers programs in sustainable design and packaging technologies that include practical training on closed-loop systems. Students gain experience in designing packaging solutions that support circular economy principles and enhance resource recovery (Turner & Fok, 2020).

4.2 Benefits and Challenges of Implementing Information Logistics in Agri-Food Supply Chains for a Circular Economy in Australia

The implementation of information logistics within agri-food supply chains is a critical component in advancing the circular economy in Australia. This approach involves leveraging advanced data collection, management, and sharing techniques to enhance the sustainability and efficiency of agricultural practices. In the context of Australia's diverse and expansive agricultural sector, the benefits of such practices are manifold, including improved supply chain resilience, enhanced environmental sustainability, and a competitive advantage through innovation. However, transitioning to these advanced systems presents significant challenges, such as the need for substantial initial investment in technology and workforce upskilling, navigating complex regulatory landscapes, and fostering cultural shifts among stakeholders. Understanding both the potential benefits and the obstacles is essential for effectively integrating information logistics into Australia's agri-food supply chains, thereby promoting a more sustainable and resilient agricultural industry.

Following benefits and challenges of implementing information logistics in agri-food supply chains for a circular economy in Australia can be considered:

4.2.1 Benefits

Implementing information logistics in agri-food supply chains offers numerous advantages. It enhances supply chain resilience and responsiveness, enabling better management of market fluctuations and disruptions (Smith et al., 2020). Environmental sustainability is improved through optimized resource use and reduced waste generation, contributing to more sustainable agricultural practices (Queensland Government, 2024). Businesses can gain a competitive advantage by adopting circular economy principles, as sustainability increasingly drives consumer and market preferences (Jones & Comfort, 2020). Increased efficiency and productivity are achieved through streamlined processes and reduced inefficiencies (Jagtap & Rahimifard, 2019). Enhanced information flow facilitates better product traceability, crucial for food safety and quality assurance (Kamilaris et al., 2019). Additionally, comprehensive data collection supports better policy formulation and decision-making in agricultural and environmental management (Sharma et al., 2020). AI technology is instrumental in optimizing supply chains and promoting circular economy practices by providing accurate data-driven insights. In information logistics, AI can streamline operations by predicting demand, optimizing inventory management, and enhancing transportation efficiency. For instance, AI-driven predictive analytics can forecast demand patterns, thereby reducing overproduction and minimizing waste (Zhang et al., 2023). Additionally, AI can support recycling efforts by automating the sorting of recyclable materials, thus improving the efficiency and accuracy of waste management systems (Gonzalez, 2022). Moreover, AI facilitates the creation of closed-loop systems, where products are designed for reuse, refurbishment, or recycling, aligning with circular economy principles. AI algorithms can analyze vast amounts of data to identify opportunities for resource recovery and repurposing, which not only conserves natural resources but also reduces costs associated with raw material procurement (Geissdoerfer et al., 2020). For example, AI-powered platforms can track the lifecycle of products, enabling companies to reclaim materials and reintegrate them into production cycles, thereby reducing waste and enhancing sustainability.

4.2.2 Challenges

Despite its benefits, implementing information logistics in agri-food supply chains presents several challenges. The initial investment required for new technology and workforce upskilling can be substantial, posing a significant barrier (KPMG Australia, 2019). Compliance with evolving regulatory standards for circular economy practices is complex and resource-intensive (Australian Circular Economy Hub, 2024). Successful implementation necessitates cultural shifts and active engagement from all stakeholders, which can be difficult to achieve (WRAP, 2020). Data privacy and security concerns arise with the management of large volumes of sensitive information (Zhang et al., 2020). Integrating new practices and technologies with existing systems can be technically challenging and costly (Pagoropoulos et al., 2017). Additionally, the economic benefits of circular economy practices may not be immediately apparent, leading to financial uncertainties and potential resistance from stakeholders (Ellen MacArthur Foundation, 2019).

Despite the significant potential of AI technology, several challenges and risks must be addressed. One of the primary challenges is the complexity of integrating AI into existing information logistics and circular economy frameworks. Many organizations may lack the technical expertise and resources required to effectively implement AI solutions, leading to suboptimal outcomes (Sarkis, 2022). Additionally, the reliance on AI technology raises concerns about data privacy and security. As AI systems often require access to vast amounts of data, ensuring that this data is securely stored and managed is crucial to prevent unauthorized access or data breaches (Kshetri, 2021). Another significant risk is the potential for bias in AI algorithms. If the data used to train AI systems is biased, the outcomes generated by these systems may reinforce existing inequalities or create new ones (Barocas et al., 2019). For example, AI algorithms designed to optimize supply chains might inadvertently favour certain suppliers or regions, leading to unintended economic or social consequences. Therefore, it is essential to ensure that AI systems are designed and trained with diverse, representative data sets to mitigate these risks. Finally, implementing AI technology in circular economy initiatives could lead to unintended environmental impacts. While AI can enhance efficiency and reduce waste, the energy consumption associated with AI processing and data centres is significant, potentially offsetting some of the environmental benefits (Strubell et al., 2019). This paradox highlights the need for sustainable AI practices that minimize energy use and carbon emissions.

The case study of Australia exemplifies the transformative impact of integrating circular economy principles within information logistics. By leveraging advanced technologies and collaborative partnerships, Australian businesses can achieve sustainable development goals, enhance supply chain performance, and strengthen their competitive position in a globalized economy. By aligning educational curricula with industry needs and fostering collaboration between academia and businesses, Australia is preparing a skilled workforce capable of driving sustainable innovation and economic growth in a globalized economy.

5 FUTURE DIRECTIONS

5.1 Emerging Trends

5.1.1 Innovations and Future Technologies

In Australia, the integration of circular economy principles within information logistics is expected to benefit from advanced innovations such as data analytics, artificial intelligence (AI), and blockchain technology. These technologies can enhance resource tracking, waste management, and overall supply chain efficiency, aligning with recent research on technological advancements (Papageorgiou & Tzanetakis, 2021). Sustainable packaging innovations and smart logistics solutions are also anticipated to support circular practices and contribute to achieving Australia's environmental objectives (Zhang et al., 2022).

5.1.2 Anticipated Developments in Circular Economy

The Australian landscape is likely to see significant developments in circular economy frameworks and industry standards. The government is expected to introduce more comprehensive regulations and incentives to promote circular practices (Masi et al., 2021). Collaborative efforts among industries, research institutions, and governmental bodies are anticipated to drive the creation of new models and methodologies for circular economy integration (Morrell et al., 2022).

5.1.3 Digital Twin Technology

Digital twin technology is gaining traction in Australia as a tool for enhancing the circular economy in information logistics. Digital twins, which create virtual replicas of physical assets and processes, can improve resource management, optimize supply chains, and enhance decision-making. By providing real-time data and simulations, digital twins help in forecasting, monitoring, and managing circular economy practices more effectively (Gao et al., 2022). This technology enables better tracking of materials and products throughout their lifecycle, contributing to more efficient resource utilization and waste reduction (Khan et al., 2023).

5.1.4 Internet of Things (IoT) Applications

The Internet of Things (IoT) is another key trend influencing the integration of circular economy principles in Australia. IoT devices and sensors can collect and transmit data on resource usage, waste generation, and supply chain activities. This real-time data is crucial for implementing circular economy practices, such as optimizing resource flows and minimizing waste. IoT applications are expected to drive innovations in sustainable supply chain management and improve transparency in circular economy initiatives (Wang et al., 2022).

5.1.5 Circular Business Models and Platform Economy

Circular business models and the platform economy are emerging as important trends in Australia. The adoption of circular business models, which focus on extending product life cycles, reusing materials, and minimizing waste, is expected to reshape information logistics. Platforms that facilitate product-as-a-service models, sharing economies, and closed-loop supply chains are becoming more prevalent (Jiang et al., 2022). These models promote resource efficiency and support the transition towards a circular economy by encouraging businesses to adopt more sustainable practices.

5.1.6 Green Supply Chain Management

Green supply chain management (GSCM) practices are evolving to support circular economy principles in Australia. GSCM focuses on integrating environmental considerations into supply chain processes, including sourcing, production, and distribution. Recent research highlights the importance of incorporating circular economy concepts into GSCM strategies to enhance sustainability and reduce environmental impact (Liu et al., 2023). Companies are increasingly adopting green practices to meet regulatory requirements and respond to consumer demand for sustainable products.

5.1.7 Advanced Recycling Technologies

Advances in recycling technologies are playing a significant role in the circular economy landscape in Australia. Innovations such as chemical recycling, automated sorting systems, and improved materials recovery processes are enhancing the efficiency and effectiveness of recycling programs. These technologies support the circular economy by enabling higher-quality recycling, reducing waste, and recovering valuable resources from end-of-life products (Smith et al., 2022).

5.2 Strategic Recommendations

5.2.1 Policy and Practice Recommendations

To facilitate the successful integration of circular economy principles within information logistics, Australian policymakers should focus on developing supportive regulations and providing incentives. Clear guidelines for circular practices, financial support for technology adoption, and industry-wide standards are essential (Lee et al., 2022). Promoting public-private partnerships and industry collaboration will be critical for accelerating the transition to a circular economy (Wang et al., 2023).

5.2.2 Strategic Planning for Future Integration

Australian businesses should create strategic plans that incorporate circular economy principles into their information logistics practices. This involves investing in advanced technologies, enhancing workforce skills, and fostering a culture of sustainability within organizations (Bocken et al., 2021). Engaging in scenario planning to anticipate future challenges and leveraging opportunities related to circular economy integration will be crucial. Aligning business strategies with national sustainability goals and adopting innovative technologies can boost competitiveness and support a sustainable future (Sarkis et al., 2021).

5.2.3 Workforce Development and Training

Upskilling Workforce for Circular Economy Practices: In Australia, upskilling the workforce is crucial for the successful integration of circular economy principles within information logistics. As the circular economy emphasizes new practices and technologies, there is a growing need for workforce development programs focused on these areas. Research highlights the importance of targeted training to equip workers with the skills necessary for implementing circular economy practices, including waste reduction, resource management, and sustainable operations (Feng et al., 2022). Companies and educational institutions must collaborate to provide relevant training that addresses these emerging needs (Morrison et al., 2023).

Developing Educational Programs and Certifications: The development of educational programs and certifications is essential for preparing the Australian workforce for circular economy roles. Academic institutions and professional bodies are increasingly offering specialized courses and certifications to support this transition. Such programs can cover various aspects of the circular economy, including sustainable supply chain management and resource efficiency (Liu et al., 2022). Establishing comprehensive educational pathways helps ensure that future professionals are well-equipped to contribute to circular economy initiatives and drive sustainable practices within the industry (Zhang et al., 2021).

5.2.4 Consumer Engagement and Behaviour Change

Strategies for Increasing Consumer Awareness: In Australia, increasing consumer awareness about the benefits and practices of the circular economy is crucial for driving widespread adoption. Effective strategies include public education campaigns, leveraging social media platforms, and collaborating with community organizations to disseminate information (Lombardi et al., 2022). Studies emphasize the importance of clear, accessible messaging that highlights the environmental and economic advantages of circular practices, as well as using behavioural nudges to encourage sustainable consumer choices (Mann & Lichtenstein, 2021). Educational programs and interactive platforms can further enhance consumer understanding and engagement with circular economy concepts (Friedrich et al., 2022).

Incentives for Pro-Environmental Consumer Behaviours: Implementing incentives to promote pro-environmental behaviours is a key strategy for supporting circular economy goals in Australia. Financial incentives such as rebates, discounts on eco-friendly products, and reward programs can effectively encourage consumers to adopt sustainable practices (Harris et al., 2022). Additionally, non-financial incentives such as recognition programs and community-based rewards can further motivate individuals to engage in environmentally friendly behaviours (Gonzalez &

Reider, 2021). Research highlights the effectiveness of combining various incentive types to maximize consumer participation and foster long-term behaviour change (Burgess & Nye, 2022).

5.2.5 AI Technology

To fully harness the potential of AI technology in promoting a circular economy within the realm of information logistics, several strategic recommendations can be proposed. These suggestions focus on advancing AI integration, addressing existing challenges, and maximizing sustainability outcomes:

1. Enhance AI Integration through Collaborative Platforms
2. Promote Sustainable AI Practices
3. Invest in AI Education and Skill Development
4. Implement Ethical AI Guidelines and Standards
5. Foster Interdisciplinary Research and Innovation

Collaborative platforms that integrate AI with technologies like IoT and blockchain can enhance efficiency and transparency across supply chains (Bag et al., 2021). Sustainable AI practices, such as developing energy-efficient algorithms, should be prioritized to reduce environmental impacts (Strubell et al., 2019). Investment in AI education and interdisciplinary research is critical to bridging the skills gap and fostering innovation (Mubarak, 2022). Finally, implementing ethical AI guidelines is vital to ensure fairness and accountability in AI-driven circular economy initiatives (Barocas et al., 2019).

6. CONCLUSION

The integration of circular economy principles within information logistics represents a strategic pathway for organizations to enhance their resilience, promote environmental sustainability, and optimize supply chain performance in today's competitive landscape. This synthesis leverages digital technologies and collaborative networks to optimize material and information flows across supply chains, fostering a holistic approach to sustainable business practices. Organizations can strengthen their organizational resilience by leveraging enhanced information flow optimization to gain real-time insights into supply chain disruptions and facilitate agile decision-making (Zhang et al., 2019). This agility enables proactive responses to unforeseen challenges, reducing operational downtime and ensuring continuity in service delivery and customer satisfaction. Environmental sustainability is advanced through the implementation of resource-efficient practices and waste reduction strategies enabled by information logistics. By minimizing resource consumption, energy use, and waste generation, businesses contribute to reducing their ecological footprint and achieving sustainability goals (Hsu & Lee, 2017; Ellen MacArthur Foundation, 2013). Furthermore, the adoption of closed-loop systems within supply chains promotes circularity by extending product lifecycles through reuse, remanufacturing, and recycling. This not only conserves natural resources but also mitigates environmental impacts associated with traditional linear supply chains (Geissdoerfer et al., 2017; Hofmann & Busch, 2013). In terms of supply chain performance enhancement, integrating circular economy principles within information logistics optimizes operational efficiencies. Improved supply chain visibility, reduced lead times, and enhanced inventory management contribute to cost savings, improved product quality, and increased customer satisfaction (Zhang et al., 2019; Rizos et al., 2016). Moving forward, organizations should focus on overcoming implementation challenges such as standardizing data formats, ensuring interoperability of digital platforms, and fostering a culture of sustainability across organizational hierarchies (Hsu & Lee, 2017). It is crucial to recognize the broader relevance of these techniques across multiple countries and continents. These technologies offer significant potential not only in first-world nations but also in developing regions, enabling advancements in sustainability, efficiency, and innovation across diverse economic and geographical contexts. For instance, the integration of AI in decision-making and trend prediction, as seen in Australian industries, can be equally beneficial in countries like the United States, Germany, and Japan, where similar industrial challenges and opportunities exist (Rane et al., 2023). Similarly, VR and AR are revolutionizing design environments in industries across Europe and North America, creating immersive experiences that enhance product development and training processes (Cannavò & Lamberti, 2021). In developing nations such as India, Brazil, and South Africa, the adoption of IoT for real-time monitoring and data-driven improvements can significantly boost agricultural productivity and industrial efficiency, mirroring successes observed in Australian contexts (Rane et al., 2023). Additionally, blockchain technology, which has proven effective in ensuring transparency, security, and traceability in Australian supply chains, can be adapted to enhance trust and accountability in collaborative processes across various sectors in Africa and Latin America (Naranjo et al., 2023). The convergence of these technologies offers a universal framework for streamlined workflows, improved efficiency, and innovative business models, applicable from Australia to other parts of the world. However, challenges such as scalability, privacy concerns, and ethical considerations must be carefully addressed, particularly in regions with differing regulatory environments and technological infrastructures (Naranjo et al., 2023). The global implementation of these technologies can help bridge the gap between

REFERENCES

Advanced Manufacturing Growth Centre. (2020). Circular Economy in the Automotive Industry. *Retrieved from* https://www.amgc.org.au/project/circular-economy-in-the-automotive-industry/

Ahmad, F., Bask, A., Laari, S., & Robinson, C. V. (2023). Business management perspectives on the circular economy: Present state and future directions. *Technological Forecasting and Social Change*, 187, 122182. DOI: 10.1016/j.techfore.2022.122182

Atanasovska, I., Choudhary, S., Koh, L., Ketikidis, P. H., & Solomon, A. (2022). Research gaps and future directions on social value stemming from circular economy practices in agri-food industrial parks: Insights from a systematic literature review. *Journal of Cleaner Production*, 354, 131753. DOI: 10.1016/j.jclepro.2022.131753

Australia, K. P. M. G. (2019). *Fighting food waste using the circular economy*. Retrieved from https://assets.kpmg.com/content/dam/kpmg/au/pdf/2019/fighting-food-waste-using-the-circular-economy-report.pdf

Australian Circular Economy Hub. (2024). *Our current economic model is unsustainable, explore the circular alternative.* Retrieved from https://acehub.org.au/

Australian Logistics Council. (2020). Sustainable Logistics: Leveraging Technology for Efficiency. Retrieved from https://www.austlogistics.com.au/sustainable-logistics-leveraging-technology-for-efficiency/

Bag, S., Telukdarie, A., & Pretorius, J. H. C. (2021). Industry 4.0 Technologies and Circular Economy Practices: A Comprehensive Review. *Sustainability*, 13(19), 10678.

Barocas, S., Hardt, M., & Narayanan, A. (2019). *Fairness and Machine Learning*. MIT Press.

Berkhout, F., Smith, A., & Stirling, A. (2021). Managing e-waste in Australia: Circular economy strategies and outcomes. *Waste Management (New York, N.Y.)*, 119, 230–240. DOI: 10.1016/j.wasman.2020.10.028

Blanco, M., & Aguilar, A. (2021). Digitalization in agriculture: An overview of challenges and opportunities. *Agricultural Systems*, 191, 103137.

Böckel, A., Nuzum, A. K., & Weissbrod, I. (2021). Blockchain for the circular economy: Analysis of the research-practice gap. *Sustainable Production and Consumption*, 25, 525–539. DOI: 10.1016/j.spc.2020.12.006

Bocken, N. M. P., de Pauw, I., Bakker, C., & van der Grinten, B. (2016). Product design and business model strategies for a circular economy. *Journal of Industrial and Production Engineering*, 33(5), 308–320. DOI: 10.1080/21681015.2016.1172124

Bocken, N. M. P., de Pauw, I., Bakker, C., & van der Grinten, B. (2021). Circular business strategies for sustainable growth. *Journal of Cleaner Production*, 292, 125–136. DOI: 10.1016/j.jclepro.2021.125136

Burgess, J., & Nye, M. (2022). Incentive structures for promoting pro-environmental behaviors: Insights from Australian case studies. *Environmental Science & Policy*, 128, 14–22. DOI: 10.1016/j.envsci.2021.12.009

Camilleri, M. A. (2018). Closing the loop for resource efficiency, sustainable consumption and production: A critical review of the circular economy. *International Journal of Sustainable Development*, 21(1-4), 1–17. DOI: 10.1504/IJSD.2018.10012310

Camilleri, M. A. (2018). The circular economy: Scope and opportunities for higher education. *Journal of Cleaner Production*, 183, 517–525.

Cannavò, A., & Lamberti, F. (2021). Immersive Design Environments with Virtual and Augmented Reality. *Journal of Computer-Aided Design*, 128, 102837.

Cautitanu, C.. (2018). Circular economy indicators for performance analysis. *Journal of Cleaner Production*, 200, 112–124.

Choi, T.-M., Liu, S., & Hsu, C.-H. C. (2021). Retail supply chain management with IoT and blockchain technology. *Journal of Retailing and Consumer Services*, 62, 102654. DOI: 10.1016/j.jretconser.2021.102654

Choi, T. M., Lo, C. K. Y., & Chan, H. K. (2018). Industry 4.0: A Bibliometric Analysis and Research Agenda. *International Journal of Production Research*, 56(1-2), 442–472. DOI: 10.1080/00207543.2017.1380226

Das, K., & Mitra, A. (2018). Integrating sustainability in the Design and Planning of Supply Chains. Operations and Supply Chain Management. *International Journal (Toronto, Ont.)*, 11(4), 161–185.

De Angelis, R., Howard, M., & Miemczyk, J. (2018). Supply chain management and the circular economy: Towards the circular supply chain. *Production Planning and Control*, 29(6), 425–437. DOI: 10.1080/09537287.2018.1449244

De Vass, T., Shee, H., & Miah, S. J. (2021). The effect of "Internet of Things" on supply chain integration and performance: An organisational capability perspective. *AJIS. Australasian Journal of Information Systems*, •••, 25.

Den Hollander, M. C., Bakker, C. A., & Hultink, E. J. (2017). Product design in a circular economy: Development of a typology of key concepts and terms. *Journal of Industrial Ecology*, 21(3), 517–525. DOI: 10.1111/jiec.12610

Di Iorio, V., Testa, F., Korschun, D., Iraldo, F., & Iovino, R. (2023). Curious about the circular economy? Internal and external influences on information search about the product lifecycle. *Business Strategy and the Environment*, 32(4), 2193–2208. DOI: 10.1002/bse.3243

Di Maio, F., Rem, P. C., Baldé, K., & Polder, M. (2017). Measuring resource efficiency and circular economy: A market value approach. *Resources, Conservation and Recycling*, 122, 163–171. https://doi.org/https://doi.org/10.1016/j.resconrec.2017.02.009. DOI: 10.1016/j.resconrec.2017.02.009

Domenech, T., & Stegemann, J. A. (2021). *The Circular Economy: Concept, Tools and Implementation*. Royal Society of Chemistry., DOI: 10.1039/9781788016209-00027

Ellen MacArthur Foundation. (2013). Towards the Circular Economy: Economic and Business Rationale for an Accelerated Transition. Retrieved from https://www.ellenmacarthurfoundation.org/assets/downloads/TCE_Ellen-MacArthur-Foundation_9-Dec-2015.pdf

Ellen MacArthur Foundation. (2013). Towards the Circular Economy Vol. 1: an economic and business rationale for an accelerated transition.

Ellen MacArthur Foundation. (2021). *Financing the Circular economy*. Retrieved from https://www.ellenmacarthurfoundation.org/topics/finance/overview

Feng, S., Li, Y., & Zhang, S. (2022). Skills for the circular economy: Challenges and opportunities. *Journal of Cleaner Production*, 332, 129877. DOI: 10.1016/j.jclepro.2021.129877

Fernando, Y., Jabbour, C. J. C., & Wah, W. X. (2022). Exploring the role of digitalization on circular economy practices: A systematic literature review. *Sustainable Production and Consumption*, 32, 207–222.

Fernando, Y., Tseng, M. L., Aziz, N., Ikhsan, R. B., & Wahyuni-TD, I. S. (2022). Waste-to-energy supply chain management on circular economy capability: An empirical study. *Sustainable Production and Consumption*, 31, 26–38. DOI: 10.1016/j.spc.2022.01.032

Friedrich, K., Patel, M., & Stewart, K. (2022). Engaging consumers in the circular economy: Strategies and outcomes. *Journal of Cleaner Production*, 350, 131650. DOI: 10.1016/j.jclepro.2022.131650

Gao, L., Zhang, L., & Zhang, Y. (2022). Digital twin technology for circular economy: A review. *Journal of Cleaner Production*, 331, 129865. DOI: 10.1016/j.jclepro.2021.129865

Garcia, R., Rathi, S., & Keirstead, J. (2015). Application of industrial ecology principles and tools to design a sustainable urban district in Curitiba, Brazil. *Journal of Cleaner Production*, 96, 387–393.

Gardner, T. A., Barlow, J., Chazdon, R., Ewers, R. M., Harvey, C. A., Peres, C. A., & Sodhi, N. S. (2019). A framework for integrating biodiversity concerns into national and global climate change mitigation strategies. *Nature Climate Change*, 2(1), 72–79.

Gardner, T. A., Benzie, M., Börner, J., Dawkins, E., Fick, S., Garrett, R., Godar, J., Grimard, A., Lake, S., Larsen, R. K., Mardas, N., McDermott, C. L., Meyfroidt, P., Osbeck, M., Persson, M., Sembres, T., Suavet, C., Strassburg, B., Trevisan, A., & Wolvekamp, P. (2019). Transparency and sustainability in global commodity supply chains. *World Development*, 121, 163–177. DOI: 10.1016/j.worlddev.2018.05.025 PMID: 31481824

Geissdoerfer, M., Savaget, P., Bocken, N. M. P., & Hultink, E. J. (2017). The Circular Economy—A new sustainability paradigm? *Journal of Cleaner Production*, 143, 757–768. DOI: 10.1016/j.jclepro.2016.12.048

Geissdoerfer, M., Savaget, P., Bocken, N. M. P., & Hultink, E. J. (2020). Circular Economy – A New Sustainability Paradigm? *Journal of Cleaner Production*, 143, 757–768. DOI: 10.1016/j.jclepro.2016.12.048

Genovese, A., Acquaye, A. A., Figueroa, A., & Koh, S. C. L. (2017). Sustainable supply chain management and the transition towards a circular economy: Evidence and some applications. *Omega*, 66, 344–357. DOI: 10.1016/j.omega.2015.05.015

Godfray, H. C. J., Beddington, J. R., Crute, I. R., Haddad, L., Lawrence, D., Muir, J. F., Pretty, J., Robinson, S., Thomas, S. M., & Toulmin, C. (2010). Food security: The challenge of feeding 9 billion people. *Science*, 327(5967), 812–818. DOI: 10.1126/science.1185383 PMID: 20110467

Gonzalez, M., & Reider, P. (2021). Behavioral incentives for environmental sustainability: Evidence from Australian markets. *Ecological Economics*, 182, 106931. DOI: 10.1016/j.ecolecon.2021.106931

Gonzalez, S. (2022). AI in Waste Management: Transforming Recycling Processes. *Journal of Environmental Management*, 254, 109899.

Green, K. W.Jr, Zelbst, P. J., Meacham, J., & Bhadauria, V. S. (2012). Green supply chain management practices: Impact on performance. *Supply Chain Management*, 17(3), 290–305. DOI: 10.1108/13598541211227126

Harris, J., Taylor, K., & Green, T. (2022). Consumer incentives and sustainable behavior in the Australian context. *Sustainability*, 14(5), 2823. DOI: 10.3390/su14052823

Hazen, B. T., Russo, I., Confente, I., & Pellathy, D. (2021). Supply chain management for circular economy: Conceptual framework and research agenda. *International Journal of Logistics Management*, 32(2), 510–537. DOI: 10.1108/IJLM-12-2019-0332

He, Y., Kiehbadroudinezhad, M., Hosseinzadeh-Bandbafha, H., Gupta, V. K., Peng, W., Lam, S. S., Tabatabaei, M., & Aghbashlo, M. (2023). Driving sustainable circular economy in electronics: A comprehensive review on environmental life cycle assessment of e-waste recycling. *Environmental Pollution*, •••, 123081. PMID: 38072018

He, Y., Wang, L., & Liu, H. (2023). A novel sustainable supply chain performance evaluation framework based on circular economy principles. *Journal of Cleaner Production*, 318, 128577.

Hofmann, E., & Busch, T. (2013). How to integrate sustainability into logistics. *Logistics Research*, 6(2), 83–94. DOI: 10.1007/s12159-013-0098-8

Hsu, C. H., & Lee, A. H. I. (2017). Information logistics: A bibliometric review. *Journal of Organizational Computing and Electronic Commerce*, 27(3), 253–275. DOI: 10.1080/10919392.2017.1348302

Huang, Y., Li, X., & Yang, X. (2022). Lifecycle assessment and resource efficiency in Australian agriculture: A case study. *Resources, Conservation and Recycling*, 179, 106023. DOI: 10.1016/j.resconrec.2021.106023

Infrastructure Sustainability Council of Australia. (2019). Building a Circular Economy: Sustainable Practices in Construction. Retrieved from https://www.isca.org.au/b

Ivanov, D. (2018). Revealing interfaces of supply chain resilience and sustainability: A simulation study. *International Journal of Production Research*, 56(10), 3507–3523. DOI: 10.1080/00207543.2017.1343507

Jäger-Roschko, J., & Petersen, M. (2022). Interorganizational communication and incentives for data exchange in circular economy. *Sustainable Development*, 30(2), 303–315.

Jagtap, S., & Rahimifard, S. (2019). Improving efficiency and productivity in agri-food supply chains through information logistics. *The Journal of Supply Chain Management*, 55(2), 89–105.

Järvenpää, M.. (2022). Data-driven logistics optimization in circular economy business models for SMEs. *Journal of Industrial Information Integration*, 25, 100234.

Jiang, Y., Chen, X., & Xu, L. (2022). Circular business models and platform economy: Innovations in Australia. *Sustainability*, 14(8), 4911. DOI: 10.3390/su14084911

Jones, P., & Comfort, D. (2020). Circular economy and competitive advantage: Innovations in sustainable business practices. *Sustainability*, 12(4), 1289–1305.

Kache, F., & Seuring, S. (2017). Challenges and opportunities of digital information at the intersection of Big Data Analytics and supply chain management. *International Journal of Operations & Production Management*, 37(1), 10–36. DOI: 10.1108/IJOPM-02-2015-0078

Kalmykova, Y., Sadagopan, M., & Rosado, L. (2018). Circular economy – From review of theories and practices to development of implementation tools. *Resources, Conservation and Recycling*, 135, 190–201. DOI: 10.1016/j.resconrec.2017.10.034

Kamilaris, A., Kartakoullis, A., & Prenafeta-Boldú, F. X. (2019). The role of information logistics in food traceability and safety. *Journal of Agricultural and Food Chemistry*, 67(15), 4251–4261.

Kara, S., Hauschild, M., Sutherland, J., & McAloone, T. (2022). Closed-loop systems to circular economy: A pathway to environmental sustainability? *CIRP Annals*, 71(2), 505–528. DOI: 10.1016/j.cirp.2022.05.008

Kara, S., Sasan, E., & Lu, J. (2022). Circular economy and business model innovation. *Sustainability*, 14(4), 2277.

Khan, A., Han, Y., & Zhang, C. (2023). The role of digital twins in supporting circular economy practices. *Computers & Industrial Engineering*, 169, 108110. DOI: 10.1016/j.cie.2022.108110

Khan, M., Hussain, M., & Saber, H. M. (2016). Information sharing in a sustainable supply chain. *International Journal of Production Economics*, 181, 208–214. DOI: 10.1016/j.ijpe.2016.04.010

Khan, M., Parvaiz, G. S., Dedahanov, A. T., Abdurazzakov, O. S., & Rakhmonov, D. A. (2022). The impact of technologies of traceability and transparency in supply chains. *Sustainability (Basel)*, 14(24), 16336. DOI: 10.3390/su142416336

Khan, S. A., Dong, Q. L., Zhang, Y., & Anwar, S. (2022). Big data-driven supply chain visibility and decision-making: A case of the circular economy within the agri-food sector. *Technological Forecasting and Social Change*, 170, 120894.

Khan, S. A., Dong, Q. L., Zhang, Y., & Yu, Z. (2016). The circular economy in China: Sectoral effects on industrial circularity and efficiency. *Journal of Environmental Management*, 197, 49–61.

Kirchherr, J., Reike, D., & Hekkert, M. (2017). Conceptualizing the circular economy: An analysis of 114 definitions. *Resources, Conservation and Recycling*, 127, 221–232. DOI: 10.1016/j.resconrec.2017.09.005

Klein, R., & Rai, A. (2009). Interfirm strategic information flows in logistics supply chain relationships. *Management Information Systems Quarterly*, 33(4), 735–762. DOI: 10.2307/20650325

Kouhizadeh, M., Zhu, Q., & Sarkis, J. (2020). Blockchain and the circular economy: Potential tensions and critical reflections from practice. *Production Planning and Control*, 31(11-12), 950–966. DOI: 10.1080/09537287.2019.1695925

Kshetri, N. (2021). *Artificial Intelligence and Cybersecurity*. Springer.

Le, T., Chang, H. C., & Chan, H. K. (2024). Blockchain technology and circular economy: A literature review and future research agenda. *International Journal of Production Research*, ●●●, 1–24.

Le, T. T., Nhu, Q. P. V., & Behl, A. (2024). Role of digital supply chain in promoting sustainable supply chain performance: The mediating of supply chain integration and information sharing. *International Journal of Logistics Management*. Advance online publication. DOI: 10.1108/IJLM-01-2024-0031

Lee, S. M., Lee, D., & Kim, Y. (2022). Policy frameworks and industry standards for circular economy implementation. *Resources, Conservation and Recycling*, 177, 106069. DOI: 10.1016/j.resconrec.2021.106069

Lezoche, M., Hernandez, J. E. R., Alemany Díaz, M. M. E., Panetto, H., & Kacprzyk, J. (2020). Agri-food 4.0: A survey of the supply chains and technologies for the future agriculture. *Computers in Industry*, 117, 103187. DOI: 10.1016/j.compind.2020.103187

Liu, L., Song, W., & Liu, Y. (2023). Leveraging digital capabilities toward a circular economy: Reinforcing sustainable supply chain management with Industry 4.0 technologies. *Computers & Industrial Engineering*, 178, 109113. DOI: 10.1016/j.cie.2023.109113

Liu, X., Wang, J., & Ma, H. (2022). Educational programs and certifications for circular economy in Australia. *Resources, Conservation and Recycling*, 180, 106158. DOI: 10.1016/j.resconrec.2022.106158

Liu, Y., Li, X., & Wu, Y. (2023). Green supply chain management and circular economy integration. *Journal of Cleaner Production*, 359, 133722. DOI: 10.1016/j.jclepro.2022.133722

Liu, Y., Yang, Y., & Liu, X. (2023). Information logistics: A study of the impact of supply chain information on performance. *Journal of Business Research*, 156, 113396.

Lombardi, R., Leach, D., & Thong, N. (2022). Public awareness and engagement with circular economy practices: Lessons from Australia. *Journal of Environmental Management*, 317, 115323. DOI: 10.1016/j.jenvman.2022.115323

Manjunath, P., Prakruthi, M. K., & Shah, P. G. (2018, August). IoT driven with big data analytics and block chain application scenarios. In *2018 Second International Conference on Green Computing and Internet of Things (ICGCIoT)* (pp. 569-572). IEEE. DOI: 10.1109/ICGCIoT.2018.8752973

Mann, M., & Lichtenstein, S. (2021). Effective communication strategies for promoting circular economy principles. *Journal of Business Research*, 132, 145–157. DOI: 10.1016/j.jbusres.2021.01.007

Manning, L., Soon, J. M., & Smith, R. (2022). The role of digital technology in enabling food security. *Trends in Food Science & Technology*, 124, 170–182.

Masi, D., Frey, M., & Finkbeiner, M. (2021). Circular economy and the role of information logistics in waste management. *Waste Management (New York, N.Y.)*, 118, 138–149. DOI: 10.1016/j.wasman.2020.10.033

Masi, D., Montagnini, F., & Finkbeiner, M. (2021). Advancing circular economy practices through technological innovations. *Journal of Environmental Management*, 291, 112847. DOI: 10.1016/j.jenvman.2021.112847

Morrell, C., Hu, H., & Bai, Y. (2022). Innovative models for circular economy integration. *Journal of Cleaner Production*, 330, 129852. DOI: 10.1016/j.jclepro.2021.129852

Morrison, M., Davidson, M., & Fletcher, R. (2023). Workforce development for sustainable practices in circular economy. *Journal of Environmental Management*, 306, 114333. DOI: 10.1016/j.jenvman.2022.114333

Mubarak, M. F. (2022). The Role of Artificial Intelligence in Circular Economy: Opportunities, Challenges, and the Path Forward. *Journal of Cleaner Production*, 362, 131949.

Naranjo, F. V.. (2023). Blockchain in Collaborative Processes: Transparency, Security, and Traceability. *Journal of Blockchain Technology*, 9(2), 112–128.

Notarnicola, B., Tassielli, G., Renzulli, P. A., Castellani, V., & Sala, S. (2017). Environmental impacts of food consumption in Europe. *Journal of Cleaner Production*, 140, 753–765. DOI: 10.1016/j.jclepro.2016.06.080

Okorie, O., Salonitis, K., Charnley, F., Moreno, M., Turner, C., & Tiwari, A. (2018). Digitisation and the circular economy: A review of current research and future trends. *Energies*, 11(11), 3009. DOI: 10.3390/en11113009

Oliveira, V. A. R. D.. (2023). Green logistics and resource-saving technologies in circular economy. *Transportation Research Part D, Transport and Environment*, 95, 102849.

Pagoropoulos, A., Pigosso, D. C. A., & McAloone, T. C. (2017). Integration of circular economy into existing systems and infrastructure. *Resources, Conservation and Recycling*, 126, 52–60.

Papageorgiou, L. G., & Tzanetakis, M. (2021). Technological advancements supporting circular economy in logistics. *Computers & Chemical Engineering*, 147, 107244. DOI: 10.1016/j.compchemeng.2021.107244

Queensland Government. (2021). *Sustainable Agricultural Practices - Improve Farm Operations*. Retrieved from https://www.qrida.qld.gov.au/program/sustainability-loan?gad_source=1&gclid=CjwKCAjwnqK1BhBvEiwAi7o0XzNwiNGmORPRQW4UQo1YFrZKX16G3FC5tSIF1BOX-0L1WZmjZ9MQJRoC-FIQAvD_BwE

Rakesh, C., Harika, A., Chahuan, N., Sharma, N., Zabibah, R. S., & Nagpal, A. (2023). Towards a circular economy: challenges and opportunities for recycling and re-manufacturing of materials and components. In *E3S Web of Conferences* (Vol. 430, p. 01129). EDP Sciences. DOI: 10.1051/e3sconf/202343001129

Ramezankhani, M. J., Torabi, S. A., & Vahidi, F. (2018). Supply chain performance measurement and evaluation: A mixed sustainability and resilience approach. *Computers & Industrial Engineering*, 126, 531–548. DOI: 10.1016/j.cie.2018.09.054

Rane, N.. (2023). The Role of AI in Enhancing Decision-Making, Trend Prediction, and Prototyping. *Artificial Intelligence Review*, 56(4), 677–692.

Raquib, M. A., Anantharaman, R. N., Eze, U. C., & Murad, M. W. (2010). Empowerment practices and performance in Malaysia-an empirical study. *International Journal of Business and Management*, 5(1), 123.

Rath, K., Altintas, S., & Ulrich, S. (2022). Advances in closed-loop packaging systems: Case studies from the Australian industry. *Packaging Technology & Science*, 35(1), 23–35. DOI: 10.1002/pts.2819

Reddy, M. V. R. (2012). Status of supply chain management in India. *International Journal of Emerging Technology and Advanced Engineering*, 2(7), 429–432.

Reyna, A., Martín, C., Chen, J., Soler, E., & Díaz, M. (2018). On blockchain and its integration with IoT. Challenges and opportunities. *Future Generation Computer Systems*, 88, 173–190. DOI: 10.1016/j.future.2018.05.046

Rizos, V., Behrens, A., Kafyeke, T., Hirschnitz-Garbers, M., & Ioannou, A. (2016). The Circular Economy: Barriers and Opportunities for SMEs. Retrieved from https://ec.europa.eu/environment/eussd/pdf/Circular_Economy_Barriers_and_Opportunities_for_SMEs.pdf

Saleminezhadl, A., Remmele, M., Chaudhari, R., & Kashef, R. (2021). *IoT Analytics and Blockchain*. arXiv preprint arXiv:2112.13430.

Saritha, K.. (2021). Convergence of AI, IoT, and Blockchain: Opportunities and Challenges. *Journal of Emerging Technologies*, 24(3), 215–234.

Sarkis, J., & A. Z. (. (2021). Circular economy and the future of sustainable supply chains. *International Journal of Production Economics*, 236, 108089. DOI: 10.1016/j.ijpe.2021.108089

Sarkis, J. (2022). *Handbook on the Circular Economy*. Edward Elgar Publishing.

Sarkis, J., Kouhizadeh, M., & Zhu, Q. S. (2021). Digitalization and the greening of supply chains. *Industrial Management & Data Systems*, 121(1), 65–85. DOI: 10.1108/IMDS-08-2020-0450

Scown, C. D., Cordeiro, S., & Kueh, J. (2021). Sustainable water management in the Australian wine industry: Challenges and innovations. *Journal of Cleaner Production*, 307, 127362. DOI: 10.1016/j.jclepro.2021.127362

Sharma, S., Yadav, P., & Singh, R. (2020). Data-driven decision-making in agricultural and environmental management. *Environmental Management*, 66(1), 78–91.

Shipsy, (2024). What is Logistics Information System: Your Guide to Smart Logistics. https://shipsy.io/blogs/what-is-logistics-information-system/. Accessed date: 31 July 2024.

Siwach, A., & Pathak, P. (2020). Evaluating the growing importance of IT in the management of logistics and supply chain. *Evaluating the growing importance of IT in the management of logistics and supply chain., 45*(1), 18-18.

Smith, J., Brown, A., & Liu, H. (2020). Enhancing supply chain resilience through information logistics. *International Journal of Production Economics, 220*, 233–247.

Smith, J., Brown, A., & Liu, H. (2022). Advanced recycling technologies and their impact on circular economy. *Waste Management (New York, N.Y.), 139*, 125–137. DOI: 10.1016/j.wasman.2022.01.008

Solomon, N. O., Simpa, P., Adenekan, O. A., & Obasi, S. C. (2024). Circular economy principles and their integration into global supply chain strategies. *Finance & Accounting Research Journal, 6*(5), 747–762. DOI: 10.51594/farj.v6i5.1133

Sousa, M. J., Cruz, R., Dias, I., & Caracol, C. (2017). Information management systems in the supply chain. In *Handbook of Research on Information Management for Effective Logistics and Supply Chains* (pp. 469–485). IGI Global. DOI: 10.4018/978-1-5225-0973-8.ch025

Srivastava, S. K. (2006). Logistics and supply chain practices in India. *Vision (Basel), 10*(3), 69–79. DOI: 10.1177/097226290601000307

Srivastava, S. K. (2006). Logistics and supply chain management practices in India. *Indian Journal of Marketing, 36*(10).

Stahel, W. R. (2016). The circular economy. *NATNews, 531*(7595), 435. PMID: 27008952

Strubell, E., Ganesh, A., & McCallum, A. (2019). Energy and Policy Considerations for Deep Learning in NLP. *Proceedings of the 57th Annual Meeting of the Association for Computational Linguistics*. DOI: 10.18653/v1/P19-1355

Subramanian, N., & Suresh, M. (2022). The contribution of organizational learning and green human resource management practices to the circular economy: A relational analysis–evidence from manufacturing SMEs (part II). *The Learning Organization, 29*(5), 443–462. DOI: 10.1108/TLO-06-2022-0068

Subramanian, N., & Suresh, M. (2022). Integrated circular economy framework for resilient supply chains: A digital transformation perspective. *Business Strategy and the Environment, 31*(5), 2035–2049.

Sustainable Development Goals Academy. (2019). Circular economy and e-waste management in Australia. *International Journal of Environmental Research and Public Health, 16*(4), 607. DOI: 10.3390/ijerph16040607 PMID: 30791457

Trivedi, N. K., Tiwari, R. G., Jain, A. K., Sharma, V., & Gautam, V. (2023, August). Impact analysis of integrating AI, IoT, Big Data, and Blockchain Technologies: A comprehensive study. In *2023 3rd Asian Conference on Innovation in Technology (ASIANCON)* (pp. 1-6). IEEE.

Tukker, A. (2015). Product services for a resource-efficient and circular economy–a review. *Journal of Cleaner Production*, 97, 76–91. DOI: 10.1016/j.jclepro.2013.11.049

Tura, N., Hanski, J., Ahola, T., Ståhle, M., Piiparinen, S., & Valkokari, K. (2019). Unlocking circular business: A framework of barriers and drivers. *Journal of Cleaner Production*, 212, 90–98. DOI: 10.1016/j.jclepro.2018.11.202

Turner, A., & Fok, L. (2020). The role of circular economy in transforming advanced manufacturing. *Resources, Conservation and Recycling*, 163, 105–116. DOI: 10.1016/j.resconrec.2020.105116

Wakiru, J. M., Pintelon, L., Muchiri, P. N., & Chemweno, P. (2020). A simulation approach for investigating the impact of food loss and waste reduction on circular economy: The case of fresh fruits and vegetables supply chain. *Sustainability*, 12(5), 2073.

Wang, C., Xu, X., & Zhang, L. (2022). IoT applications and their role in circular economy practices. *Journal of Cleaner Production*, 341, 130852. DOI: 10.1016/j.jclepro.2022.130852

Wang, C., Xu, X., & Zhang, L. (2023). Public-private partnerships and their role in circular economy implementation. *Journal of Cleaner Production*, 373, 131771. DOI: 10.1016/j.jclepro.2022.131771

WRAP. (2020). *WRAP and the circular economy*. Retrieved from https://www.wrap.ngo/taking-action/climate-change/circular-economy

Zarbakhshnia, N., Kannan, D., Kiani Mavi, R., & Soleimani, H. (2020). A novel sustainable multi-objective optimization model for forward and reverse logistics system under demand uncertainty. *Annals of Operations Research*, 295(2), 1–38. DOI: 10.1007/s10479-020-03744-z

Zhang, X., Wu, D. D., Wang, X., & Lu, Y. (2019). The influence mechanism of information logistics on supply chain integration and competitive advantage. *Industrial Management & Data Systems*, 119(7), 1437–1457. DOI: 10.1108/IMDS-02-2019-0067

Zhang, Y., Li, X., & Wang, X. (2022). Sustainable packaging innovations for circular economy. *Packaging Technology & Science*, 35(2), 85–97. DOI: 10.1002/pts.2847

Zhang, Y., Liu, X., & Chen, C. (2021). Developing educational pathways for circular economy competencies. *Journal of Cleaner Production*, 280, 124173. DOI: 10.1016/j.jclepro.2020.124173

Zhang, Y., Liu, X., & Li, H. (2023). AI-Powered Predictive Analytics for Supply Chain Optimization. *International Journal of Production Economics*, 239, 108298.

Zhang, Y., Yang, S., & Xu, H. (2020). Data privacy and security concerns in large-scale information logistics. *Journal of Information Privacy and Security*, 16(2), 115–130.

Zhou, W., Yu, H., & Xu, Z. (2021). Blockchain-based supply chain management: A case study in the Australian retail industry. *Computers & Industrial Engineering*, 154, 107140. DOI: 10.1016/j.cie.2021.107140

Chapter 15
Women Safety at Workplace:
Challenges and Support System in Healthcare

Sunil Kumar
https://orcid.org/0000-0002-2362-1972
Shoolini University, India

Shrishti Kumari
https://orcid.org/0009-0008-0708-8216
Shoolini University, India

Kritika Mahendroo
Shoolini University, India

Ritika Thakur
Shoolini University, India

ABSTRACT

This study explores the safety challenges women face in healthcare workplaces and evaluates the effectiveness of existing support systems. Despite strides in gender equality, women continue to experience harassment, discrimination, and unsafe conditions that harm their well-being and hinder career growth. Through a review of literature and case studies, the research identifies key issues such as inadequate reporting mechanisms, insufficient harassment prevention training, weak policies, and the high-stress healthcare environment that heightens risks. It also highlights solutions like mentorship programs, strong anti-harassment policies, and training initiatives that promote respect and accountability. By showcasing best practices,

DOI: 10.4018/979-8-3693-8562-3.ch015

the study advocates for comprehensive strategies that healthcare organizations can adopt to enhance women's safety. The findings stress the need for collective efforts to create an inclusive, secure workplace and offer actionable recommendations for fostering a fear-free environment where all employees can thrive.

INTRODUCTION

Gender equality in the workplace is achieved when both men and women are treated fairly, without any discrimination. This includes providing equal pay for the same roles, addressing the unique needs of both genders, and offering equal opportunities for career advancement (Grzelec, 2024). However, it is unfortunate that many women still face issues such as sexist comments, racism, and sexual harassment, which negatively impact their mental and physical well-being, hindering their professional growth (Basharat et al., 2024). To combat these issues, the Indian Penal Code has introduced several laws, including the Equal Remuneration Act of 1976, which ensures equal pay, the Maternity Benefit Act of 1961, which provides protections and benefits for mothers, and Article 15 of the Indian Constitution, which prohibits discrimination based on religion, race, caste, sex, or place of birth. These laws aim to create a safer and more equitable workplace for everyone. In 2024, men's participation in the workforce is expected to be 64 percent, while women's participation in the organized sector is expected to be 36 percent (Wheebox, 2024).

Table 1. Share of participation at work across India from 2014 to 2024, by gender

Year	Male (in percentage)	Female (in percentage)
2014	71	29
2015	70	30
2016	68	32
2017	71	29
2018	77	23
2019	75	25
2020	77	23
2021	64	36
2022	67	33
2023	67	33
2024	64	36

Source: Confederation of Indian Industry; Wheebox; PeopleStrong; AICTE (India); AIU; UNDP

Table 1 shows male workforce participation in India is projected to drop to 64% in 2024, continuing a fluctuating trend since 2016. Female participation in the organized sector rose from 33% in 2023 to 36% in 2024, yet a significant gender gap remains.

Women's Safety in India

Women's safety in India remains a critical and persistent issue, garnering intense debate, activism, and policy focus. Despite India's cultural diversity and progress in various sectors, safeguarding the dignity and security of women, particularly in professional environments continues to be a major challenge. Workplace safety for women encompasses not only physical security but also protection from harassment, discrimination, and psychological abuse. Although labor laws and corporate policies have evolved, women still face unique threats that impact their well-being, ranging from sexual harassment and gender discrimination to unequal pay (Robu, 2023), limited career advancement (Galsanjigmed & Sekiguchi, 2023), and even physical danger. These issues affect individual women, organizational productivity, employee retention, and societal progress.

In 2018, a survey identified India as the most dangerous country for women, highlighting problems related to cultural practices, sexual violence, and human trafficking. Many women feel unsafe in both public and private spaces, with over 33,000 rape cases reported that year. Efforts to achieve gender equality remain stalled, as societal views often link a woman's status to her marital status, leading to early marriages in many communities. Cultural biases also tend to dismiss calls for equal rights as excessive, while studies emphasize education as a crucial tool against gender discrimination (Reuters, 2018).

Understanding the key threats to women's safety in the workplace is essential for developing effective strategies. Sexual harassment, one of the most pervasive issues, can appear in various forms, including verbal, physical, visual harassment, or quid pro quo situations where career benefits are conditioned on sexual favors (Stier et al., 2013). Gender discrimination exacerbates this, as women frequently face unequal pay, biased hiring and promotion practices, and exclusion from decision-making processes. Stereotyping and prejudice further impact assignments and evaluations, fostering a hostile work environment (Tiwari et al., 2018).

Workplace violence also poses specific risks to women, including physical assault, intimidation, and stalking by colleagues or clients. Additionally, domestic violence can spill over into the workplace, compromising women's safety (Mayhew et al., 2007). Psychological abuse and bullying—such as verbal abuse, social isolation, and undermining of professional performance are equally harmful, affecting mental health and job satisfaction (Pai et al., 2018).

Certain industries expose women to additional physical risks due to unsafe working conditions, such as inadequate security during night shifts, lack of safety equipment, and unsafe transportation options (Geiger-Brown & Lipscomb, 2010). Pregnancy and maternity discrimination present further challenges, with women often denied promotions or opportunities due to pregnancy or motherhood. Upon returning from maternity leave, many women encounter bias and lack accommodations (Hackney et al., 2021).

With digitalization, technology-facilitated harassment has emerged as a growing concern. Women are increasingly vulnerable to cyberbullying, unauthorized sharing of personal information, and digital surveillance without consent (Verma & Gupta, 2023). For women with multiple marginalized identities, such as LGBTQ+ individuals, older women, or racial minorities, intersectional discrimination intensifies these risks, combining racial, gender, and age biases that create additional barriers to safety and inclusion in the workplace (Crenshaw, 2013). Fear of retaliation discourages many women from reporting harassment or discrimination, which perpetuates unsafe conditions. Retaliation can involve job loss, demotion, social ostracism, or unfair performance scrutiny (Taykhman, 2016). This silence reinforces the cycle of abuse and hinders meaningful change.

Addressing these multifaceted threats requires comprehensive reform. Organizations must do more than enact policies; they must actively enforce them and cultivate a culture of respect, equality, and support for women. This includes safe reporting channels, mental health resources, and zero tolerance for retaliation. By tackling these physical, psychological, and career-related risks, workplaces can significantly enhance female employees' well-being, boost organizational productivity, foster innovation, and contribute to broader societal progress.

India's Healthcare System

India's healthcare system has a long and intricate history, influenced by traditional methods, colonial impacts, and modern developments. The ancient era is primarily linked to Ayurveda, a comprehensive medical system that originated around 1500 BCE. Ayurveda focuses on balancing body systems through diet, herbal remedies, and breathing exercises. Important texts like the Charaka Samhita and Sushruta Samhita documented various treatments and surgical techniques (Pondomatti et al., 2024). In addition to Ayurveda, the Siddha system from South India and Unani medicine, brought by Persians and Arabs, were significant in the early development of Indian healthcare (Shaikh et al., 2024). These approaches emphasized natural remedies and holistic care, showcasing India's strong bond with nature in health practices.

In the medieval period, the healthcare system in India further transformed under Islamic influence, especially during the Mughal era. Unani medicine thrived, and medical schools, hospitals, and public health initiatives were created. This time also saw improvements in pharmacology and surgery, leading to a more organized healthcare system. However, healthcare access was mainly for the wealthy, leaving rural and poorer populations underserved.

During the colonial era from 1757 to 1947, British rule brought major changes to healthcare with the rise of Western medicine. Allopathic medicine became the leading practice, and the British set up hospitals, medical colleges, and public health programs mainly in cities. Unfortunately, these services were mostly available to British officials and the upper classes. Public health efforts focused on controlling diseases like cholera, smallpox, and malaria, introducing sanitation measures, vaccination campaigns, and quarantine protocols. Despite these improvements, the colonial healthcare system largely neglected the needs of the broader population.

The healthcare industry, one of India's major employers, has experienced significant development and expansion in terms of technology, skills, education, and professional expertise in the past few years. Despite this growth, data analysed by philanthropic organisation. Dasra indicates that women within the healthcare sector are predominantly found in the lower-paying frontline roles.

In India, women make up 29 percent of medical doctors, 80 percent of nursing staff (including midwives), and nearly 100 percent of Accredited Social Health Activists (ASHAs), as per the report. Only 18 percent of leadership positions in healthcare are occupied by women, and persistently earn 34 percent less than their male counterparts (Forbes India, 2023). The safety and well-being of women within healthcare systems have emerged as critical concerns that demand urgent attention and action. Despite significant advancements in medical science and healthcare delivery, women continue to face unique challenges and vulnerabilities when seeking medical care. These issues range from gender-based discrimination and inadequate representation in clinical trials to the prevalence of obstetric violence and the dismissal of women's pain and symptoms.

The concept of women's safety in healthcare encompasses a broad spectrum of issues, including physical safety, emotional well-being, and the protection of dignity and autonomy. It extends beyond the mere absence of harm to include the active promotion of gender-sensitive care, informed consent, and respect for women's bodily autonomy. This multifaceted approach recognizes that women's experiences in healthcare settings are shaped not only by biological factors but also by social, cultural, and institutional dynamics.

Table 2. Comparing five countries and their respective laws related to women's safety in the healthcare sector.

Country	Key Laws/ Regulations	Focus Areas	Implementation/Enforcement Mechanisms	Additional Support Systems
India	Sexual Harassment of Women at Workplace (Prevention, Prohibition and Redresser) Act (2013)	Prevents and addresses sexual harassment in healthcare settings and all other workplaces	Internal Complaints Committees (ICCs) must be formed by employers; Local Complaints Committees (LCCs) for larger healthcare institutions	Legal aid for victims, awareness programs, self- defence training, and reporting helplines for harassment cases
United States	Title VII of the Civil Rights Act (1964), OSHA Regulations, EEOC Guidelines	Prohibition of gender-based discrimination, protection from workplace hazards, and sexual harassment prevention in healthcare settings	Equal Employment Opportunity Commission (EEOC), Occupational Safety and Health Administration (OSHA), anti-retaliation clauses	Employee Assistance Programs (EAPs), support for reporting incidents, helplines, and mandatory workplace training programs
Canada	Canada Labour Code, Occupational Health and Safety (OHS) Act, Bill C-65 (2018)	Prevents harassment and violence in federal workplaces, including healthcare; promotes health and safety standards	Complaints can be filed with Employment and Social Development Canada (ESDC); employer obligations to investigate complaints	Trauma-informed counseling services, helplines, union support, and anti-violence training programs

continued on following page

Table 2. Continued

Country	Key Laws/ Regulations	Focus Areas	Implementation/Enforcement Mechanisms	Additional Support Systems
Australia	Fair Work Act (2009), Sex Discrimination Act (1984), Work Health and Safety (WHS) Act (2011)	Prohibits sexual discrimination and harassment in the workplace, ensures a safe working environment, including in healthcare	Fair Work Ombudsman for workplace complaints; Safe Work Australia for health and safety oversight	Helplines for harassment victims, psychological counseling services, community programs for healthcare workers, and gender equality campaigns
United Kingdom	Equality Act (2010), Health and Safety at Work Act (1974), Sexual Harassment and Victimization Guidelines (2017)	Ensures equality in pay and treatment; addresses gender-based violence and harassment in the healthcare sector	Health and Safety Executive (HSE) oversight; employers required to investigate complaints; tribunals available for unresolved issues	Counseling services, workplace mediation programs, union advocacy, and anonymous reporting systems

Source: Compiled by Author(s)

REVIEW OF LITERATURE

The safety of women in healthcare can be understood through several key theories. Workplace psychological contract theory highlights how breaches in the unspoken expectations of safety and respect, such as encountering harassment or unsafe conditions, lead to disengagement and dissatisfaction (Kutaula et al., 2020). In hostile work environment discriminatory behaviours and harassment create an abusive atmosphere, contributing to feelings of vulnerability and undervaluation among women (Biasatti, 2024). The weak organizational policies and insufficient oversight embolden inappropriate behaviours, making harassment more likely in environments where accountability is lacking. There is a need for strong policies and safety measures to become embedded within the organization's culture, ensuring that improvements in women's safety.

The occupational risks faced by women in healthcare, particularly in the private sector, have become an area of growing concern due to their significant implications on both the health and well-being of female healthcare professionals and the overall efficiency of healthcare systems. Elizabeth (2022) conducted a comprehensive study involving 100 medical professionals, finding that 80% suffered from a variety of occupational health issues, including back pain, headaches, and needle-stick injuries. In addition to these physical risks, psychosocial problems such as anxiety (affecting 45% of respondents), insomnia, and patient-related abuse were alarmingly prevalent. Reproductive health risks were also notable, with irregular periods, stillbirth, low birth weight, and cervical cancer among the most reported issues. While safety measures such as biomedical waste management and the use of personal protective equipment (PPE) were deemed moderately effective (scoring 3.64 out of 5), critical gaps remain, particularly in the areas of mental health support and vaccinations, which are essential to safeguarding the well-being of female healthcare workers.

The broader societal and global context of violence against women in various forms—physical, emotional, sexual, and digital—further exacerbates the risks women face in healthcare settings. Haldar (2024) emphasized that social, economic, and political vulnerabilities increase the risk of violence for women and called for systemic solutions, including education, community engagement, and policy reforms. Successful global programs like Rwanda's Gender-Based Violence Program and India's Self-Help Groups (SHGs) demonstrate the value of empowering women through legal, social, and economic support. These programs provide a blueprint for how targeted interventions can mitigate gender-based violence and enhance women's agency and safety, including in the healthcare sector.

Workplace violence (WPV) is a particularly pressing issue for female healthcare workers worldwide. A comprehensive meta-analysis by Ajuwa et al. (2024) revealed that WPV affects 45% of female healthcare workers globally, based on data from 28 studies across 20 countries. The study identified verbal abuse, physical assaults, sexual harassment, mobbing, bullying, and discrimination as the most common forms of violence. Patients, their families, colleagues, and supervisors were the primary perpetrators, with nurses being the most studied and affected group. The study concluded that WPV has a detrimental effect on both the mental and physical health of healthcare workers, highlighting the urgent need for multilevel interventions. These interventions should address the socio-demographic and organizational risk factors, such as age, marital status, lower occupational position, and substance abuse, that exacerbate the risks of violence in healthcare settings.

There is a need to explore the pervasive issue of sexual harassment faced by female healthcare workers in Kolkata, India. Despite the landmark 1997 Vishaka Guidelines, which legally recognized sexual harassment as a violation of women's rights in the workplace, the problem remains widespread, particularly for nurses and junior doctors. These women often face harassment from male colleagues and patients but are hesitant to report it due to fears of job loss and career setbacks. This reluctance is compounded by systemic issues, such as inadequate reporting mechanisms and a lack of institutional support. Similarly, Paniello-Castillo et al.

(2023) documented widespread sexism and harassment in Spain's healthcare and higher education sectors, revealing that over 70% of respondents had experienced harassment, often perpetrated by individuals in positions of power. The study advocates for gender-diverse leadership and stronger preventive measures to end workplace harassment and sexism, stressing the importance of creating a culture of zero tolerance for such abuses.

Sindhu et al. (2024) tackled the issue of workplace violence in healthcare, focusing on the physical, emotional, and psychological abuse faced by healthcare workers in India. Their findings emphasize the need for a comprehensive approach that includes better communication, enhanced security measures, and awareness campaigns to prevent violent incidents. The authors call for a cultural shift within healthcare institutions to foster a work environment grounded in respect, empathy, and the prioritization of healthcare workers' safety. By addressing these fundamental issues, healthcare institutions can create safer and more supportive environments, ultimately leading to improved patient care and better outcomes for healthcare professionals.

Nayanar et al. (2024) provided further insight into the prevalence of workplace violence in tertiary care centers, reporting that nearly half of physicians had experienced violence, with departments like obstetrics and gynecology facing the highest incidence (43.2%). The study revealed that junior doctors and those working night shifts were particularly vulnerable to violence, with government hospitals reporting higher rates of violence compared to corporate hospitals, which had more robust reporting systems in place. Alarmingly, 53.8% of doctors reported the absence of any violence prevention policy at their hospitals. The study's recommendations include raising awareness among healthcare workers about existing safety policies, enforcing stricter legislation, and implementing more effective security measures to safeguard healthcare workers, especially women, from violence.

One of the most tragic examples of the dangers female healthcare workers face is the 2024 case of a young resident doctor who was raped and murdered at R.G. Kar Medical College in Kolkata (Sain et al., 2024). This horrific incident highlighted the systemic failures in healthcare institutions to protect women, particularly junior doctors. The case raised critical concerns about the inadequate security measures in supposedly secure hospital areas and exposed corrupt practices within the hospital administration. The aftermath of this tragedy led to widespread protests demanding justice and prompted a national conversation about the urgent need for reforms to ensure the safety and dignity of healthcare professionals, especially women. The Supreme Court of India has since intervened, overseeing a national task force to address gender-based violence in healthcare settings and to implement systemic changes aimed at preventing such atrocities in the future.

Workplace harassment is not limited to physical violence; it also encompasses verbal abuse, bullying, social isolation, and other forms of intimidation, all of which severely affect mental health, productivity, and workplace morale. Rospenda and Richman (2004) argue that organizations must adopt comprehensive strategies to address all forms of workplace harassment, as these behaviors collectively take a significant toll on employees' well-being. For example, Hom et al. (2017) found that women in male-dominated fields, such as firefighting, who experienced sexual harassment were twice as likely to report suicidal ideation and suffer from severe mental health symptoms, including depression, anxiety, and PTSD. The study highlights the need for targeted interventions, such as mental health support and harassment prevention programs, to mitigate these adverse outcomes in high-risk professions.

In Pakistan, Malik et al. (2021) found that 57.5% of female surgeons reported harassment, primarily in the form of verbal abuse, bullying, and mental stress. These incidents were strongly linked to burnout and depression, particularly among women working long hours. The study also noted the significant barriers to reporting harassment, as institutional structures often discourage formal complaints. As a result, many women suffer in silence, further compounding the mental health crisis in healthcare professions.

The issue of mental health in relation to workplace violence and harassment extends beyond healthcare. Early- and mid-career academics (EMCAs) in Australia face widespread abuse, job insecurity, and high workloads, contributing to significant mental health challenges, including burnout, depression, and anxiety (Malik et al., 2021). Similar patterns are seen in prison-based mental healthcare systems, where female prisoners often experience harassment and abuse from staff, exacerbating their mental health issues (Bright et al., 2023). These studies consistently underscore the profound mental health impacts of workplace harassment and abuse, regardless of the sector.

Singh et al. (2024) emphasized that sustainable workplace practices, including flexible work arrangements and comprehensive mental health support programs, are essential for fostering a nurturing environment that enhances employee well-being. Such practices allow employees to achieve a better work-life balance, reducing stress and burnout. Implementing these sustainable strategies is especially important in healthcare settings, where the mental and physical demands of the profession can lead to chronic stress and burnout if not properly managed.

There is an urgent need for comprehensive interventions to address workplace violence and harassment across sectors, with a particular focus on the healthcare industry. Moreover, fostering inclusive workplace cultures that prioritize respect, empathy, and collaboration can significantly improve the safety and well-being of female healthcare professionals, leading to better patient care and overall healthcare outcomes. This research aims to explore the safety challenges that women face in healthcare workplaces and examine the effectiveness of current support systems designed to address these issues. The study focuses on identifying various forms of harassment, discrimination, and unsafe working conditions experienced by women and evaluates how well existing policies, reporting processes, and support programs are working to address these risks. By analyzing these factors, the research intends to offer practical recommendations for healthcare organizations to strengthen safety measures, improve reporting mechanisms, and create a work environment that is free from fear of harm or bias. Ultimately, the goal is to contribute to the development of strategies that ensure a safer, more inclusive workplace for women in the healthcare industry.

METHODOLOGY

In present study qualitative approach that involved the use of questionnaires, interviews and case studies in order to collect and analyze data. This method allows us to examine our research area from different angles and increase the depth and breadth of our findings.

Questionnaire

A Questionnaire is a structured tool to systematically collect information from respondents (Weller, 1998). It consists of a series of questions aimed at collecting quantitative or qualitative data for specific purposes. In our study, we created a questionnaire that included closed questions, which provided pre-defined answer options, and open questions, which allowed respondents to express their opinions in their own words. Closed questions allow us to collect quantitative data that can be analyzed statistically to reveal trends and patterns among respondents. Meanwhile, open-ended questions provide qualitative knowledge and allow us to share ideas and experiences. This dual approach ensures that we not only collect quantitative data, but also understand the context and reasoning behind the responses. Table 3 presents the open-ended structured questionnaire. The questionnaire was distributed to 15 females working in healthcare. 5 medical residents, 5 nurses and 5 para-medicals.

Table 3. Questionnaire items

Item/Question	Source
What support systems are available to Women facing safety issues at your workplace?	García-Moreno et al., 2015
Have you ever experienced or witnessed harassment or discrimination in your workplace? If yes, please describe.	Sojo et al., 2016
In your opinion, what are the main challenges women face regarding safety in the healthcare environment?	Gershon et al., 2000
What improvements would you suggestion to enhance safety for women in your workplace?	Leape et al., 2002
Do you believe that women's safety issues are prioritized in your workplace? Why or why not?	Grosser and Moon (2005)

Source: Author(s)

Interview

To complete the data collection, an interview was conducted with the selected participants. Interviewing is a qualitative research method characterized by direct and one-to-one interaction between the researcher and the participant (Hobson & Townsend, 2014). This method is particularly useful for investigating complex issues, as it allows for in-depth discussions that provide deeper insights and insights into the perspectives and experiences of the participants. Our interviews were semi-structured, meaning we had a list of questions but also allowed for more in-depth exploration based on the participants' responses. This format encourages open discussion, which allows us to explore topics in depth and capture the nuances of participants' perspectives. The qualitative data generated from the interviews provided context and depth to the quantitative findings in the questionnaires, enriching our understanding of the research topic. The interview of one female medical resident was conducted and given below as a case study.

Case Study of a Medical Resident Working in a Medical College

This case study combines data collected from questionnaires and interviews to provide an in-depth look at a specific example in its real-world context. Case studies are especially useful in applied research, where understanding the complexity of a situation can offer valuable insights. In this study, data from questionnaires and interviews were integrated with observations and documents. This multifaceted approach enabled us to create a comprehensive narrative, highlighting key themes, patterns, and insights. The format allowed us to present not only the data but also the context and relevance behind it.

The respondent in this study is a postgraduate resident pursuing an MBBS and MD in Pathology from a private medical college in India. She shared her distressing experiences during her medical residency, highlighting various forms of exploitation, including inadequate infrastructure, poor working conditions, harassment, and a lack of institutional support.

One of the primary challenges she faced was transportation during night shifts. Even when transportation was provided, the cost was exorbitant, adding a financial burden to her already low salary, which barely covered her living expenses. Additionally, the hospital's infrastructure was in a deplorable state. CCTV cameras were non-functional, toilets were unhygienic, drinking water was insufficient, and no food was provided to doctors during night shifts. There was also no designated rest area for doctors on duty, and the poor lighting at night further heightened the risk and discomfort.

Beyond these physical and logistical issues, she also endured severe sexual harassment from both patients and colleagues. In one particularly alarming incident, a male patient in the intensive care unit solicited sexual favors during her night shift. In self-defense, she used a pen to protect herself and reported the incident to her colleagues. While the patient was escorted out by security, no further action was taken by hospital authorities, despite her escalating the issue to senior doctors. Instead, she was threatened with the revocation of her medical license for continuing to raise such concerns.

Her struggles were not limited to patient interactions. She also faced harassment from male colleagues, some of whom flirted with her, asked her to change her lab coat in front of them, and even pressured her to send explicit content. Despite reporting these incidents, she received no support from the hospital administration, which consistently ignored or dismissed her complaints. She also faced political pressures, compounding her already overwhelming stress. Senior female doctors also contributed to the hostile work environment, often criticizing her appearance and behavior, adding psychological strain to the already toxic atmosphere.

This case reflects a disturbing reality within the medical system, where young doctors, particularly women, face challenges that go beyond their professional responsibilities. Her experience underscores the urgent need for reform in medical education, with a particular focus on improving working conditions, addressing harassment, and ensuring institutional accountability. Hospitals must prioritize the safety and well-being of their medical staff by providing essential facilities such as reliable transportation, food, rest areas, and robust safety measures. Moreover, clear and enforceable anti-harassment policies must be implemented to hold perpetrators accountable and ensure that victims feel safe reporting their experiences.

Mental health support systems should also be established to help medical trainees cope with both the professional pressures and the harassment they may encounter (García-Moreno et al., 2015). Her story serves as a powerful reminder of the systemic changes needed to create a supportive, respectful, and safe working environment for all doctors.

Analysis of the Case

Female doctors in case study experiences shed light on the critical and multifaceted challenges faced by young doctors, particularly women, in the healthcare system. Her narrative illustrates a distressing reality characterized by inadequate infrastructure, poor working conditions, and systemic harassment, emphasizing the urgent need for reform in medical education and hospital administration.

- **Inadequate Infrastructure and Working Conditions**

The case study highlights severe deficiencies in hospital infrastructure, which directly impact the safety and well-being of medical staff. Her description of non-functional CCTV cameras, unhygienic toilets, inadequate drinking water, and the absence of food during night shifts paints a troubling picture. These conditions not only undermine the physical health of medical residents but also contribute to a demoralizing work environment. The lack of designated rest areas and poor lighting exacerbate stress and fatigue, making it difficult for residents to perform their duties effectively. Such neglect raises questions about hospital management's commitment to providing a safe and conducive work environment.

- **Exploitation and Financial Burden**

The financial burden imposed by transportation costs during night shifts adds another layer of exploitation. Residents like her often operate on tight budgets due to low salaries, making any additional expenses a significant strain. The expectation that they should cover these costs further underscores the lack of institutional support, which is crucial for the well-being of medical staff. This financial strain can lead to mental health issues, increasing stress and burnout, which ultimately affects patient care.

- **Harassment and Psychological Impact**

Her experiences with harassment from both patients and colleagues reveal a deeply entrenched culture of misogyny and exploitation within the medical profession. The incident involving a male patient soliciting sexual favors is particularly alarming, highlighting not only the vulnerability of female doctors but also the systemic failures in addressing such misconduct. The inadequate response from hospital authorities, including threats to her medical license, illustrates a culture of silence that often protects perpetrators while punishing victims. This lack of accountability fosters an environment where harassment is normalized, further discouraging victims from speaking out.

The harassment from male colleagues, including inappropriate requests and demands, reflects a pervasive toxic culture that undermines professional integrity and creates a psychologically hostile environment. The criticism she faced from senior female doctors compounds the issue, suggesting that gender bias and a lack of solidarity among women in medicine can further isolate those facing harassment.

- **Need for Systemic Reform**

The case underscores the pressing need for systemic reform within medical education and healthcare institutions. Hospitals must prioritize the implementation of robust infrastructure and essential facilities to ensure the safety and health of their staff. This includes providing adequate transportation, food, rest areas, and safety measures, particularly during night shifts.

Moreover, clear and enforceable anti-harassment policies must be established to protect medical staff. Institutions should create an environment where victims feel empowered to report misconduct without fear of retaliation. Training programs focused on sensitivity and respect can help cultivate a culture that values dignity and professionalism.

Results of Text Analysis

Hierarchical Mind Mapping

Hierarchical mapping is a method of organizing information, processes, or data in a ranked or layered structure, where elements are arranged from the most general at the top to the most specific at the bottom (Vimalaksha et al., 2019). It often follows a parent-child relationship, with broader categories or entities at higher levels and more detailed or specific items at lower levels. This approach is commonly used to represent organizational structures, where top management is at the highest level, followed by middle and lower management. It is also used in data organization, where general categories break down into subcategories. Hierarchical mapping simplifies complex systems by visually displaying relationships and dependencies, making it easier to understand and manage large sets of information.

- *What support systems are available to Women facing safety issues at your workplace?*

Figure 1 presents respondents overwhelmingly agree on the necessity of creating a safe and inclusive workplace, particularly focusing on preventing harassment and violence. Concerns were expressed about the lack of adequate facilities for night shifts, such as the absence of a designated doctor's duty room, which could heighten safety risks. Furthermore, there is a general acknowledgment of the safety challenges that women encounter during their shifts, emphasizing the need for increased vigilance and proactive measures. Participants also highlighted the essential role that employers must play in prioritizing safety initiatives to protect all staff members. However, some uncertainty remains regarding the specifics of these measures, as reflected in ambiguous responses like "may be or maybe not," indicating that more clarity and commitment are needed to effectively address these issues.

Figure 1. Support system

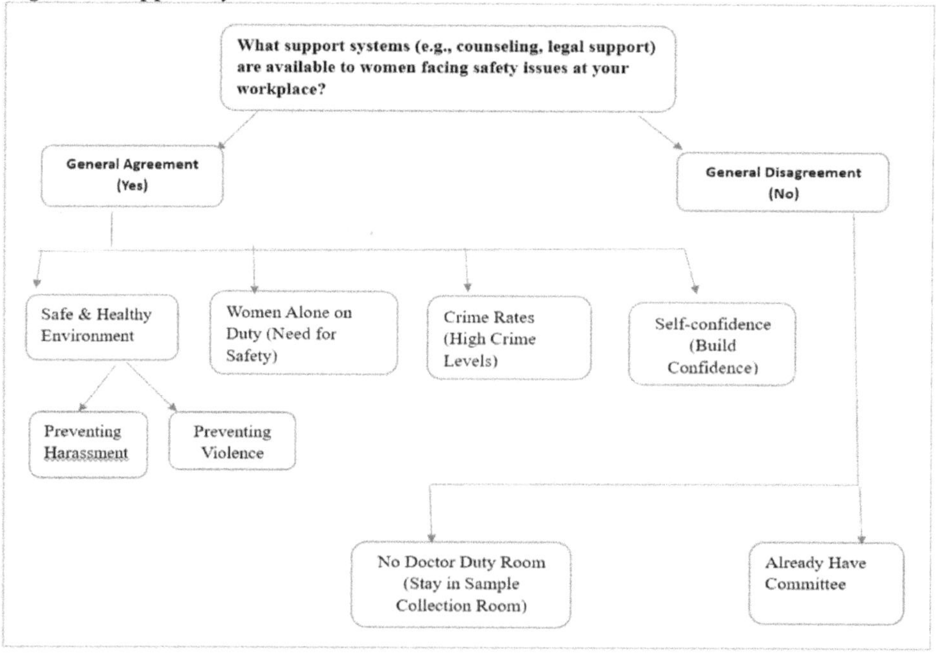

- *Have you ever experienced or witnessed harassment or discrimination in your workplace? If yes, please describe.*

Figure 2 shows that majority of respondents reported that they had not experienced or witnessed harassment or discrimination in the workplace. However, some specific incidents were noted, including concerns about excessive workloads, such as unpaid overtime, particularly during night shifts or general duties. Additionally, there were accounts of seniors harassing junior staff members regarding workload expectations, as well as a mention of verbal abuse from one participant. On a positive note, several respondents expressed satisfaction with workplace safety, particularly for women, with some individuals explicitly stating that they had never encountered any safety-related issues.

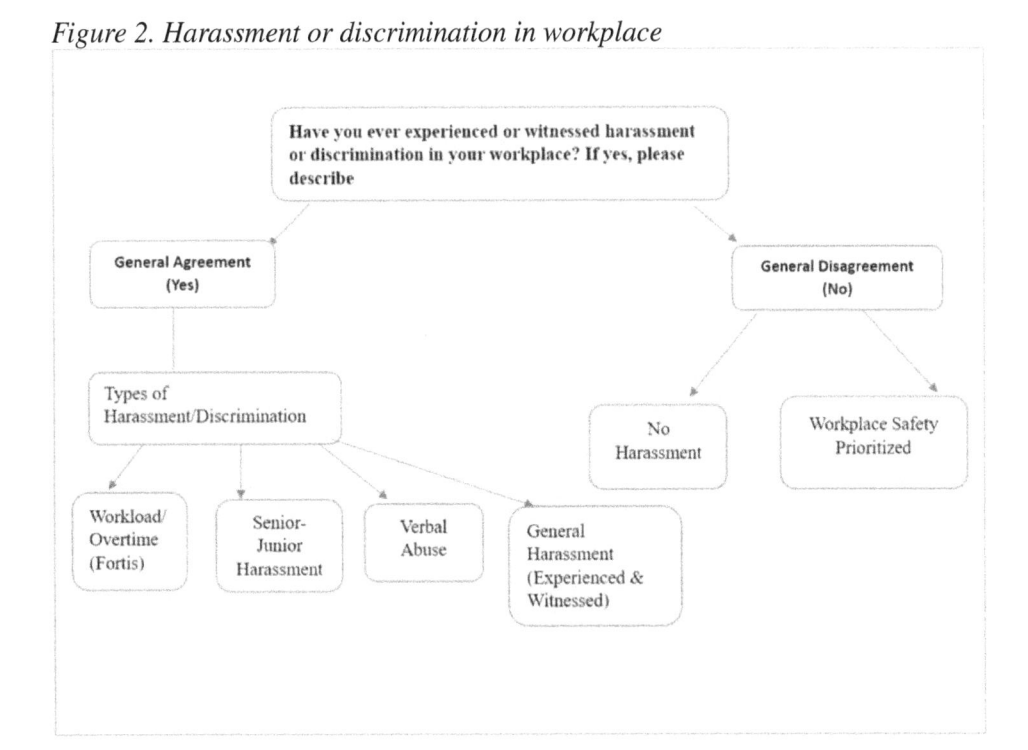

Figure 2. Harassment or discrimination in workplace

- *In your opinion, what are the main challenges women face regarding safety in the healthcare environment?*

Figure 3 presents Security concerns rank among the top issues faced by employees, particularly during night shifts, where the absence of adequate security personnel and transportation options exacerbates safety risks. Additionally, the demands of heavy workloads and the challenges associated with night shifts contribute to these safety concerns, with respondents mentioning the lack of menstrual leave and the negative impacts on mental health. Harassment and violence remain critical issues, encompassing physical violence, verbal abuse, and mental harassment. While some respondents noted the existence of supportive committees within their workplaces, the effectiveness of these support systems appears to vary, suggesting that more robust and consistent measures may be needed to enhance employee safety and well-being.

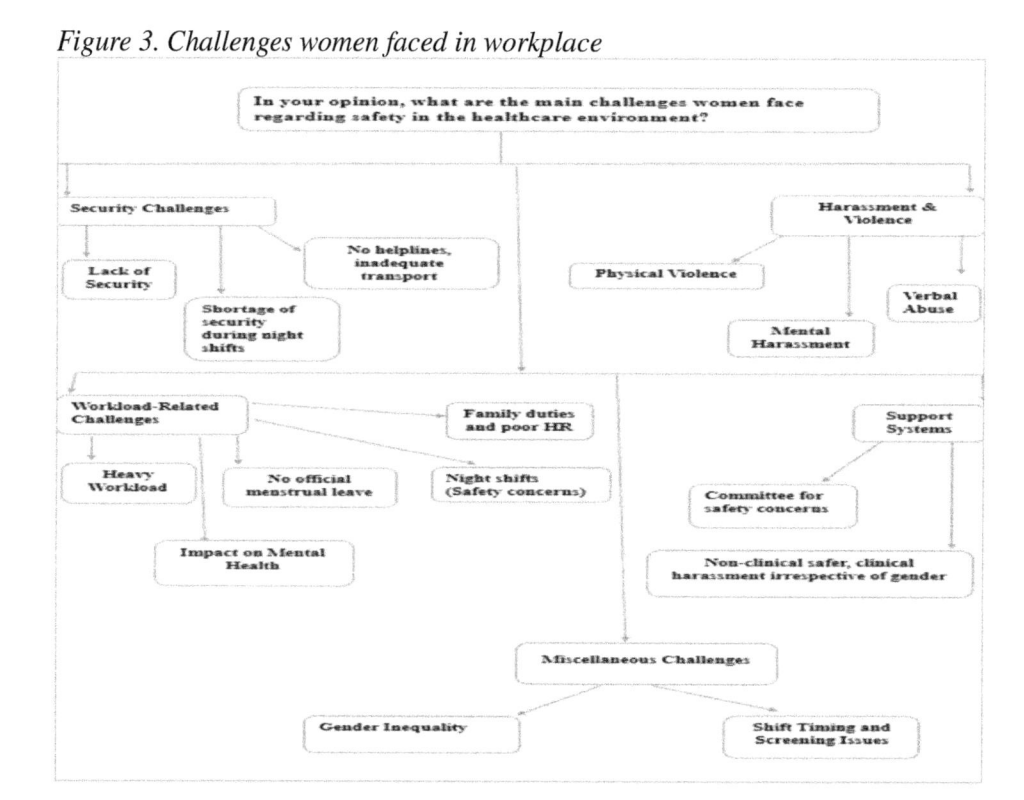

Figure 3. Challenges women faced in workplace

- **What improvements would you suggestion to enhance safety for women in your workplace?**

The most commonly suggested improvements focus on enhancing security, with recommendations for increasing the number of female guards, installing CCTV cameras, implementing emergency codes, and providing properly secured rooms with locks. There is a strong emphasis on ensuring safety during night shifts, with suggestions for conducting group duties and providing transportation options to enhance safety during off-hours. Respondents also advocated for clear and strict sexual harassment policies, emphasizing the need for equal security rights for both men and women. A safe working environment is viewed as a fundamental goal, with the necessity for punitive measures against those who violate safety protocols being highlighted. However, some respondents felt that their workplaces already have adequate safety measures in place and did not propose any additional improvements (see Figure 4).

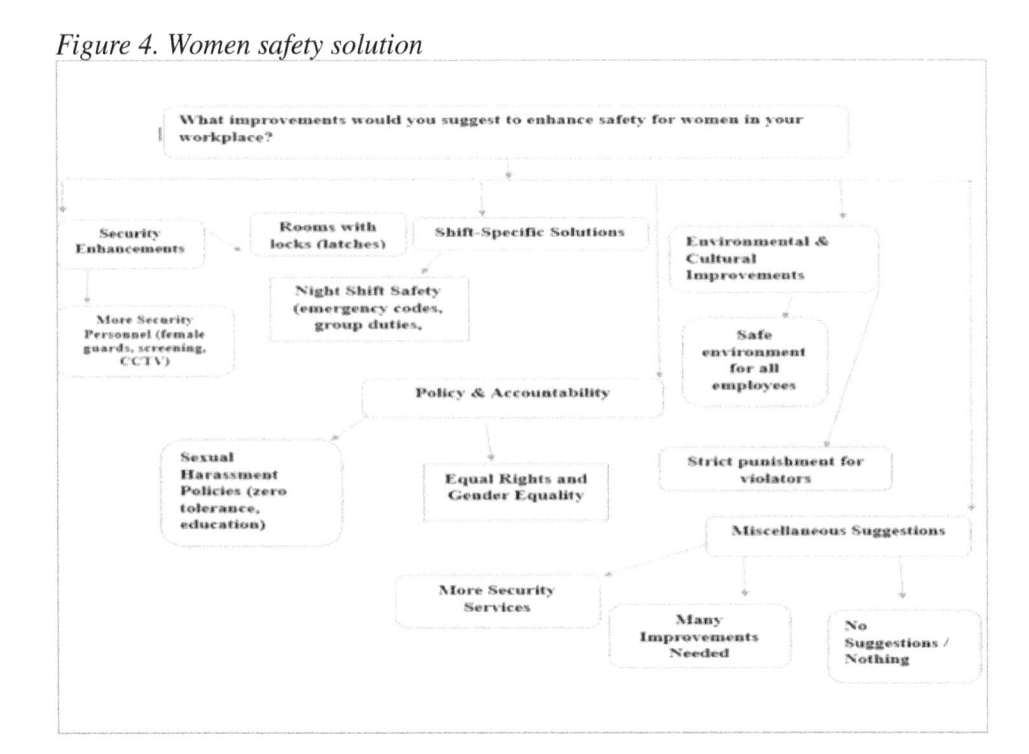

Figure 4. Women safety solution

- *Do you believe that women's safety issues are prioritized in your workplace? Why or why not?*

The Figure 5 presents those respondents who answered "yes" generally highlighted the effectiveness of measures such as counseling, legal support, and grievance policies like POSH as positive initiatives aimed at protecting women in the workplace. In contrast, those who answered "no" emphasized the inadequate security during night shifts, raising specific concerns about the lack of security personnel, surveillance cameras, and proper lighting in certain areas. There were mixed feelings regarding support systems; while some individuals felt that day shift support is sufficient, they identified significant gaps in night shift security. Practical safety concerns, such as the presence of street dogs and poorly lit areas, were noted as urgent issues that require immediate attention. Additionally, some respondents advocated for broader improvements, including stricter security measures, comprehensive training programs, and robust anti-harassment policies to enhance overall workplace safety.

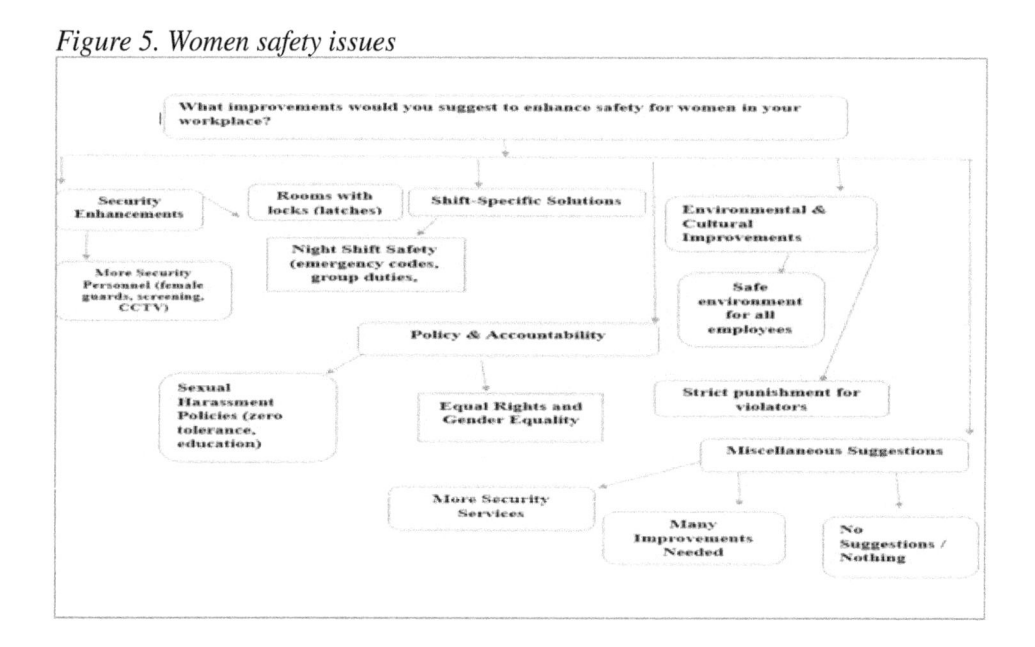

Figure 5. Women safety issues

Topic Analysis

Topic analysis is a text mining technique used to identify and categorize key themes or subjects within large sets of unstructured data, such as documents, articles, or customer reviews (Alghamdi and Alfalqi, 2015). By grouping words with similar meanings or contexts into coherent topics, it helps to uncover patterns and trends that may not be immediately obvious. This process is commonly used in fields like marketing, content analysis, and research to better understand large amounts of textual information. Methods such as Latent Dirichlet Allocation (LDA) and Term Frequency-Inverse Document Frequency (TF-IDF) are often employed to detect the most relevant topics, enabling businesses and researchers to gain insights, organize data efficiently, and make more informed decisions based on the discovered themes.

Latent Dirichlet Allocation (LDA) is a machine learning technique used for topic modelling, which helps identify hidden topics within large sets of text data (Jelodar et al., 2019). It assumes that each document in a collection is made up of several topics, and each topic is defined by a distribution of words. LDA works by determining the probability distribution of topics in each document and the distribution of words within each topic. Through an iterative process, the model assigns topics to words based on how frequently they appear together, revealing the underlying themes or topics in the text. This technique is widely used for tasks such as document summarization, text classification, and exploring large datasets.

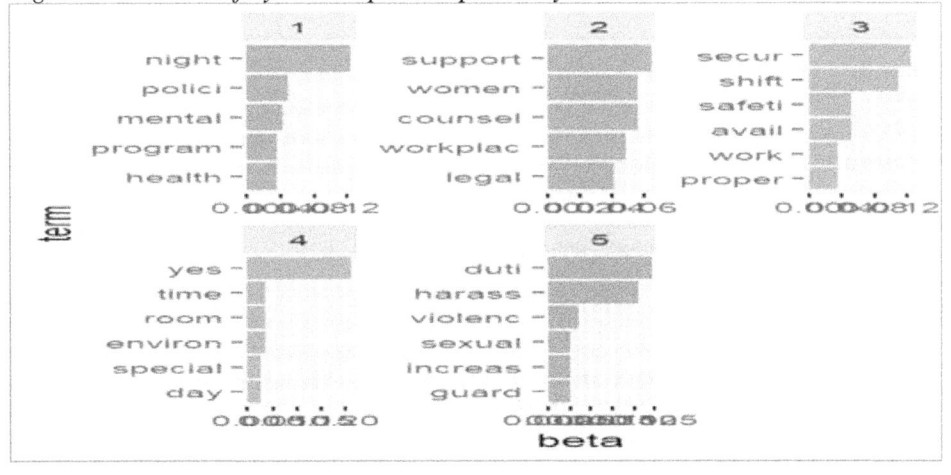

Figure 6. Women safety at workplace topic analysis

The LDA model identifies five key topics related to women's safety at work, each represented by a cluster of terms. Topic 1 focuses on policies and mental health programs for women working night shifts, indicated by terms like "night," "policy," and "health." Topic 2 highlights support systems, including counseling and legal help for women, with terms such as "support," "counsel," and "legal." Topic 3 revolves around security and safety measures during work shifts, as suggested by terms like "security" and "shift." Topic 4 reflects general workplace conditions, focusing on time and environment. Lastly, Topic 5 addresses workplace harassment and violence, with a focus on duties and security personnel in preventing such issues.

Topic 1: This topic could be focusing on policies and mental health programs, especially for women working night shifts. It might suggest that mental health and health programs are critical concerns for women's safety during night shifts.
Topic 2: This is clearly a support system topic, focusing on counseling, legal support, and workplace support available for women dealing with safety issues.
Topic 3: This topic is likely about security and safety measures available during work shifts, including how secure the workplace is and how safety measures are properly provided.
Topic 4: This topic might be capturing general responses about time and environment at the workplace, possibly reflecting on the timing of events or availability of safe spaces (like rooms or areas) during the workday.
Topic 5: This is a harassment and violence topic, focusing on duties related to handling harassment, addressing sexual violence, and the possible role of guards or other security personnel in preventing such issues.

Table 4. Topic 1 and Topic 2 relative importance

Questions	Policies and mental health programs	Support system
What support systems (e.g., counseling, legal support) are available to women facing safety issues at your workplace?	0.627	0.373
Have you ever experienced or witnessed harassment or discrimination in your workplace? If yes, please describe	0.529	0.471
In your opinion, what are the main challenges women face regarding safety in the healthcare environment?	0.552	0.448
What improvements would you suggest to enhance safety for women in your workplace?	0.588	0.413
Do you believe that women's safety issues are prioritized in your workplace? Why or why not	0.538	0.462

Source: Primary data

The Table 4 data shows that support systems for women facing safety issues at the workplace is strongly tied to Policies and mental health programs (62.7%), though Support systems (37.3%) also play a significant role, emphasizing both areas. The question of witnessing or experiencing harassment shows a more balanced association, with Policies and mental health programs (52.9%) and Support systems (47.1%) being nearly equally relevant, highlighting the need for both policy measures and support mechanisms. In addressing the challenges women face regarding safety in healthcare environments, the question is more linked to Policies and mental health programs (55.2%), but Support systems (44.8%) remain important. The question about suggested safety improvements similarly leans toward Policies and mental health programs (58.8%) but acknowledges the value of Support systems (41.3%). Finally, the question on whether women's safety issues are prioritized reflects a nearly even split, with Policies and mental health programs at 53.8% and Support systems at 46.2%, indicating that both are considered critical to addressing workplace safety concerns.

Table 5. Topic2 and Topic 3 relative importance

Questions	Support system	Security and safety measures
What support systems (e.g., counseling, legal support) are available to women facing safety issues at your workplace?	0.581	0.418
Have you ever experienced or witnessed harassment or discrimination in your workplace? If yes, please describe	0.600	0.400
In your opinion, what are the main challenges women face regarding safety in the healthcare environment?	0.508	0.491
What improvements would you suggest to enhance safety for women in your workplace?	0.507	0.492
Do you believe that women's safety issues are prioritized in your workplace? Why or why not	0.666	0.333

Source: Primary data

The Table 5 data shows that Support systems and Security and safety measures shows varying degrees of association between these two aspects. The question about available support systems for women is more strongly linked to Support systems (58.1%) but still significantly connected to Security and safety measures (41.8%), reflecting the dual importance of both aspects in ensuring workplace safety. Similarly, the question about harassment or discrimination is primarily associated with Support systems (60%) but also involves Security and safety measures (40%), indicating that addressing such issues requires both support and security.

For questions about the challenges women face in the healthcare environment, there is a near-equal split, with Support systems (50.8%) and Security and safety measures (49.1%) being almost equally relevant, showing that both themes are essential in tackling safety concerns. The same balanced association is evident in the question on safety improvements, where Support systems (50.7%) and Security and safety measures (49.2%) are nearly equal, suggesting that effective improvements require attention to both. Lastly, the question on whether women's safety issues are prioritized at work shows a stronger emphasis on Support systems (66.6%) over Security and safety measures (33.3%), indicating that prioritization is seen more in terms of available support than physical security measures.

DISCUSSION

The study highlights persistent safety issues for women in healthcare, pointing to gender inequality, harassment, and weak enforcement of legal protections like India's Equal Remuneration Act and the Sexual Harassment Act. Despite these laws, insufficient training, underreporting, and fear of retaliation prevent women from safely addressing grievances. The research underscores that effective enforcement, coupled with cultural and systemic shifts, is essential to foster a genuinely safe and supportive environment for women in healthcare.

The case study of a female medical resident in a private medical college reveals alarming gaps in infrastructure, institutional support, and workplace safety that significantly impact the well-being and security of medical professionals, especially women. The hospital's lack of functional CCTV cameras, unhygienic restrooms, insufficient drinking water, and lack of a designated rest area for doctors highlight serious infrastructural deficiencies. These poor working conditions not only affect physical health but also demoralize residents, suggesting an urgent need for institutions to provide essential facilities that support the safety and dignity of their staff.

Additionally, the financial strain on the resident due to exorbitant transportation costs during night shifts exacerbates the stress of her low salary, creating an environment where institutional support is insufficient and exploitation is normalized. This financial burden, combined with inadequate wages, impacts mental health and heightens burnout risks. Furthermore, the resident's experiences of harassment from patients and colleagues, coupled with threats to her career when reporting these issues, reflect a troubling culture that often protects perpetrators rather than supporting victims. This lack of accountability contributes to a hostile environment, leaving individuals vulnerable and hesitant to speak out.

These findings underscore the urgent need for systemic reform in medical institutions, focusing on safety measures, robust anti-harassment policies, and support structures like counseling and legal assistance. Institutions must prioritize safety by addressing both physical security—such as improved lighting, transportation, and secure areas—and comprehensive support mechanisms to protect against harassment and exploitation. Effective policies must bridge the gap between preventive measures and responsive support to foster a safe and supportive work environment, essential for the well-being of healthcare workers and the quality of patient care.

One of the primary threats to women's safety is sexual harassment, which manifests in various forms such as verbal, physical, and quid pro quo harassment. The hierarchical structure of healthcare settings, where male colleagues often occupy senior roles, increases the risk of abuse. As noted in the case study sexual harassment from both patients and male colleagues is alarmingly normalized. The absence of prompt action or any institutional backing further aggravates the issue, as illustrated by the hospital's inadequate response to complaints.

This case also highlights a critical issue in healthcare environments—gender-based discrimination and the broader culture of misogyny. Women doctors and nurses are frequently subjected to derogatory remarks and inappropriate behavior, often under the guise of "workplace banter" or "professional hierarchy." Furthermore, physical safety concerns, such as poor lighting during night shifts, lack of transportation, and the absence of secure rest areas, compound the threat, especially for women working late hours.

Beyond physical safety, women in healthcare are also subjected to psychological abuse and bullying. This type of harassment, although less overt than sexual or physical violence, can have devastating consequences on mental health. As the research points out, bullying, intimidation, and social ostracism are common in male-dominated healthcare sectors, contributing to burnout, anxiety, and depression.

Intersectionality plays a key role in understanding these challenges. Women who belong to marginalized groups, such as those from lower socioeconomic backgrounds or minority ethnic communities, face compounded challenges. In such cases, gender-based violence is often intertwined with racial or caste-based discrimination, further complicating the process of seeking justice or protection.

Despite the overwhelming challenges, the research identifies several support systems that could help alleviate these issues. One of the most effective solutions is the implementation of robust anti-harassment policies and regular training initiatives that promote a culture of respect. Moreover, mentorship programs and leadership training for women can help break the glass ceiling in healthcare, where women occupy only 18% of leadership positions. These programs can encourage women to ascend to decision-making roles, thereby fostering an environment where gender-based issues are more effectively addressed.

The research also emphasizes the importance of collaborative efforts between all healthcare staff members to create a safe and supportive work environment. This requires a cultural shift, which cannot happen overnight but should be initiated by hospital administration and leadership. Leaders must show a commitment to addressing harassment by holding perpetrators accountable and creating an environment where women feel safe to report misconduct.

The research compares workplace safety laws and practices in five countries—India, the United States, Canada, Australia, and the United Kingdom—offering valuable insights into how different systems handle women's safety in healthcare. For instance, in the United States, Title VII of the Civil Rights Act and Occupational Safety and Health Administration (OSHA) regulations provide a strong legal framework for gender-based violence prevention. These laws are reinforced by the

Equal Employment Opportunity Commission (EEOC), which actively monitors workplaces to ensure compliance.

On the other hand, countries like Australia have more comprehensive approaches, combining legal protections with employee assistance programs (EAPs) and psychological counseling services. Such systems ensure that women not only have legal recourse but also access to mental health support, which is critical in high-stress healthcare environments. These global comparisons underscore the need for India to strengthen its enforcement mechanisms and create more comprehensive support systems, such as trauma-informed counseling and anonymous reporting channels, to better protect women in healthcare.

CONCLUSION

In conclusion, the study sheds light on the pressing issues surrounding women's safety in healthcare settings, where systemic challenges, cultural norms, and inadequate enforcement of existing legal frameworks create an environment fraught with risk and inequality. Despite the presence of laws aimed at protecting women's rights, such as the Equal Remuneration Act and the Sexual Harassment of Women at Workplace Act, the lack of effective implementation and support systems continues to undermine these protections. The experiences of female medical residents illustrate a troubling reality marked by harassment, discrimination, and a hostile work environment, highlighting the urgent need for comprehensive reforms.

To create a safer and more equitable workplace for women in healthcare, it is crucial to not only strengthen enforcement mechanisms but also cultivate a culture that empowers women to report incidents without fear of retaliation. This includes providing adequate infrastructure, support systems, and mental health resources to address both the physical and psychological impacts of harassment. Ultimately, fostering a supportive and respectful environment requires a collective commitment to change from all stakeholders within the healthcare system, ensuring that women's safety and well-being are prioritized and upheld.

REFERENCES

Ajuwa, M. E. P. E., Veyrier, C. A., Cabrolier, L. C., Chassany, O., Marcellin, F., Yaya, I., & Duracinsky, M. (2024). Workplace violence against female healthcare workers: A systematic review and meta-analysis. *BMJ Open*, 14(8), e079396. DOI: 10.1136/bmjopen-2023-079396 PMID: 39209501

Alghamdi, R., & Alfalqi, K. (2015). A survey of topic modeling in text mining. [IJACSA]. *International Journal of Advanced Computer Science and Applications*, 6(1). Advance online publication. DOI: 10.14569/IJACSA.2015.060121

Basharat, L., & Alam, M. J. (2024). Workplace Environment for Gender Equality and Sustainable Career Planning: The Case of Bangladesh. In *People, Spaces and Places in Gendered Environments* (Vol. 34, pp. 77-97). Emerald Publishing Limited.

Biasatti, A. (2024). No Girls Allowed: How Sexual Harassment and Gender Discrimination Keep Women out of Oil Fields. *ONE J*, 10, 95.

Bright, A. M., Higgins, A., & Grealish, A. (2023). Women's experiences of prison-based mental healthcare: A systematic review of qualitative literature. *International Journal of Prisoner Health*, 19(2), 181–198. DOI: 10.1108/IJPH-09-2021-0091 PMID: 35192246

Crenshaw, K. W. (2013). Mapping the margins: Intersectionality, identity politics, and violence against women of color. In *The public nature of private violence* (pp. 93–118). Routledge.

Elizabeth, H. (2022). Risks and Safety of Women Healthcare Workers in Aizawl District, Mizoram, India. *International Journal of Occupational Safety and Health*, 12(2), 111–116. DOI: 10.3126/ijosh.v12i2.39794

Forbes India. (2023, December 13). *Women occupy only 18 percent of healthcare leadership positions, earn 34 percent less than men: Dasra report*. Retrieved October 22, 2024, from https://www.forbesindia.com/article/news/women-occupy-only-18-percent-of-healthcare-leadership-positions-earn-34-percent-less-than-men-dasra-report/90313/1

Galsanjigmed, E., & Sekiguchi, T. (2023). Challenges women experience in leadership careers: An integrative review. *Merits*, 3(2), 366–389. DOI: 10.3390/merits3020021

García-Moreno, C., Hegarty, K., d'Oliveira, A. F. L., Koziol-McLain, J., Colombini, M., & Feder, G. (2015). The health-systems response to violence against women. *Lancet*, 385(9977), 1567–1579. DOI: 10.1016/S0140-6736(14)61837-7 PMID: 25467583

Geiger-Brown, J., & Lipscomb, J. (2010). The health care work environment and adverse health and safety consequences for nurses. *Annual Review of Nursing Research*, 28(1), 191–231. DOI: 10.1891/0739-6686.28.191 PMID: 21639028

Gershon, R. R., Karkashian, C. D., Grosch, J. W., Murphy, L. R., Escamilla-Cejudo, A., Flanagan, P. A., Bernacki, E., Kasting, C., & Martin, L. (2000). Hospital safety climate and its relationship with safe work practices and workplace exposure incidents. *American Journal of Infection Control*, 28(3), 211–221. DOI: 10.1067/mic.2000.105288 PMID: 10840340

Grzelec, A. (2024). Doing gender equality and undoing gender inequality—A practice theory perspective. *Gender, Work and Organization*, 31(3), 749–767. DOI: 10.1111/gwao.12935

Hackney, K. J., Daniels, S. R., Paustian-Underdahl, S. C., Perrewé, P. L., Mandeville, A., & Eaton, A. A. (2021). Examining the effects of perceived pregnancy discrimination on mother and baby health. *The Journal of Applied Psychology*, 106(5), 774–783. DOI: 10.1037/apl0000788 PMID: 32614204

Halder, A. (2024). Women Safety Matters: Addressing the Complexities and Violence Against Women. *International Journal of English Literature and Social Sciences*, 9(4), 297–302. DOI: 10.22161/ijels.94.42

Hobson, A. J., & Townsend, A. (2014). Interviewing as educational research. *Educational Research and Inquiry. Qualitative and Quantitative Approaches*, 223-238.

Hom, M. A., Stanley, I. H., Spencer-Thomas, S., & Joiner, T. E. (2017). Women firefighters and workplace harassment: Associated suicidality and mental health sequelae. *The Journal of Nervous and Mental Disease*, 205(12), 910–917. DOI: 10.1097/NMD.0000000000000759 PMID: 29088006

Jelodar, H., Wang, Y., Yuan, C., Feng, X., Jiang, X., Li, Y., & Zhao, L. (2019). Latent Dirichlet allocation (LDA) and topic modeling: Models, applications, a survey. *Multimedia Tools and Applications*, 78(11), 15169–15211. DOI: 10.1007/s11042-018-6894-4

Kutaula, S., Gillani, A., & Budhwar, P. S. (2020). An analysis of employment relationships in Asia using psychological contract theory: A review and research agenda. *Human Resource Management Review*, 30(4), 100707. DOI: 10.1016/j.hrmr.2019.100707

Leape, L. L., Berwick, D. M., & Bates, D. W. (2002). What practices will most improve safety?: Evidence-based medicine meets patient safety. *Journal of the American Medical Association*, 288(4), 501–507. DOI: 10.1001/jama.288.4.501 PMID: 12132984

Malik, M. A., Inam, H., Martins, R. S., Janjua, M. B. N., Zahid, N., Khan, S., Sattar, A. K., Khan, S., Haider, A. H., & Enam, S. A. (2021). Workplace mistreatment and mental health in female surgeons in Pakistan. *BJS Open*, 5(3), zrab041. DOI: 10.1093/bjsopen/zrab041 PMID: 34037208

Mayhew, C., & Chappell, D. (2007). Workplace violence: An overview of patterns of risk and the emotional/stress consequences on targets. *International Journal of Law and Psychiatry*, 30(4-5), 327–339. DOI: 10.1016/j.ijlp.2007.06.006 PMID: 17628681

Nayanar, B. S., Fareed, N., Battur, H., & Praveena, J. (2024). A Study on Nature of Violence Against Doctors in Tertiary Care Centers in Karnataka, India: A Cross-Sectional Study. *Indian Journal of Community Medicine*, 49(3), 472–474. DOI: 10.4103/ijcm.ijcm_1139_21 PMID: 38933800

Pai, D. D., Sturbelle, I. C. S., Santos, C. D., Tavares, J. P., & Lautert, L. (2018). Physical and psychological violence in the workplace of healthcare professionals. *Texto & Contexto Enfermagem*, 27, e2420016.

Paniello-Castillo, B., González-Rojo, E., González-Capella, T., Civit, N. R., Bernal-Triviño, A., Legido-Quigley, H., & Gea-Sánchez, M. (2023). "Enough is Enough": Tackling sexism, sexual harassment, and power abuse in Spain's academia and healthcare sector. *The Lancet Regional Health. Europe*, 34, 34. DOI: 10.1016/j.lanepe.2023.100754 PMID: 37927426

Pondomatti, S. C., Tyagi, I., Shrivastava, K. K., Mahajan, S., Patel, J., Shinde, M. A., & Shrivastava, K. K.Sr. (2024). A Literature Review of the Integration of Ancient Indian Mythology in Clinical Medicine: A Holistic Approach to Health and Healing. *Cureus*, 16(7). Advance online publication. DOI: 10.7759/cureus.63779 PMID: 39099985

Robu, M. (2023). The Gender Pay Gap: A Roadblock to Gender Equality and Sustainable Development. *Analele Universității Ovidius, Seria: Științe Economice*, 23(1), 496–504. DOI: 10.61801/OUAESS.2023.1.64

Rospenda, K. M., Fujishiro, K., Shannon, C. A., & Richman, J. A. (2008). Workplace harassment, stress, and drinking behavior over time: Gender differences in a national sample. *Addictive Behaviors*, 33(7), 964–967. DOI: 10.1016/j.addbeh.2008.02.009 PMID: 18384975

Sain, S., Chatterjee, A., & Nundy, S. (2024). When trust is betrayed: The horrific rape-murder of a young resident doctor on duty in Kolkata: A call for justice and change. *Current Medicine Research and Practice*, 14(5), 10–4103. DOI: 10.4103/cmrp.cmrp_142_24

Shaikh, N., Bamne, F., Ali, A., Momin, M., & Khan, T. (2024). Herbal Medicine: Exploring Its Scope Across Belief Systems of the Indian Medicine. In *Herbal Medicine Phytochemistry: Applications and Trends* (pp. 1279–1304). Springer International Publishing. DOI: 10.1007/978-3-031-43199-9_46

Singh, B., Malviya, R., & Kaunert, C. (2024). Elevating Workplace Sustainability for Employees Lensing Mental Health Advancements: Runway for Future Ready Healthcare Services Projecting SDG 3 (Good Health and Well-Being). In *Impact of Corporate Social Responsibility on Employee Wellbeing* (pp. 285-310). IGI Global.

Sojo, V. E., Wood, R. E., & Genat, A. E. (2016). Harmful workplace experiences and women's occupational well-being: A meta-analysis. *Psychology of Women Quarterly*, 40(1), 10–40. DOI: 10.1177/0361684315599346

Stier, H., Lewin-Epstein, N., & Braun, M. (2013). Work–family conflict in comparative perspective: The role of social policies. *Research in Social Stratification and Mobility*, 31, 1–16. DOI: 10.1016/j.rssm.2012.10.001

Sindhu, J., Sathish, K., KK, M. J., & Rajula, I. 2024. Violence Against Health Care Professionals:Synopsis, A. (●●●)... *The European Journal of Cardiovascular Medicine*, 14(1), 429–436.

Taykhman, N. (2016). Defying Silence: Immigrant Women Workers, Wage Theft, and Anti-Retaliation Policy in the States. *Colum. J. Gender & L.*, 32, 96.

Thomson Reuters. (Thomson Reuters Foundation). (June 26, 2018). Factors which make India the most dangerous country for women in 2018 (by ranking out of 10 where 1 is worst) [Graph]. In *Statista*. Retrieved October 25, 2024, from https://www.statista.com/statistics/909596/india-most-dangerous-country-for-women/

Tiwari, G., Sinha, A., & Mahapatra, M. (2018). Gender-based violence in the workplace: Health sector perspectives. *Indian Journal of Gender Studies*, 25(3), 357–376. DOI: 10.1177/0971521518786347

Verma, R. K., & Gupta, A. K. (2023). Role of Information and Communication Technology in the Digitalization of Violence and Sexual Politics in the Indian Scenario. In *Cyberfeminism and Gender Violence in Social Media* (pp. 35–48). IGI Global. DOI: 10.4018/978-1-6684-8893-5.ch003

Vimalaksha, A., Vinay, S., & Kumar, N. S. (2019, December). Hierarchical mind map generation from video lectures. In *2019 IEEE Tenth International Conference on Technology for Education (T4E)* (pp. 110-113). IEEE. DOI: 10.1109/T4E.2019.00-40

Weller, S. C. (1998). Structured interviewing and questionnaire construction. *Handbook of methods in cultural anthropology*, 365-409.

Wheebox. (January 12, 2024). Share of participation at work across India from 2014 to 2024, by gender [Graph]. In *Statista*. Retrieved October 25, 2024, from https://www.statista.com/statistics/1043300/india-work-participation-by-gender/

Compilation of References

Abdalla, M., & Abdalla, M. (2021). The grey hoodie project: Big tobacco, big tech, and the threat on academic integrity. *FACT '21: Proceedings of the 2021 ACM Conference on Fairness, Accountability, and Transparency*, 854-865. DOI: 10.1145/3461702.3462563

Abdullah, Y. I., Schuman, J. S., Shabsigh, R., Caplan, A., & Al-Aswad, L. A. (2021). Ethics of artificial intelligence in medicine and ophthalmology. *Asia-Pacific Journal of Ophthalmology*, 10(3), 289–298. DOI: 10.1097/APO.0000000000000397 PMID: 34383720

Abinsay, M. (2020). Porter's Five Forces Analysis of the Organic Farming in Laguna Province. *Agricultural Economics eJournal*. https://doi.org/DOI: 10.53378/34

Abuali, K. M., Nissirat, L., & Al-Samawi, A. (2023). Advancing network security with AI: SVM-b sed deep learning for intrusion detection. *Sensors (Basel)*, 23(21), 8959. DOI: 10.3390/s23218959 PMID: 37960661

Aburbeian, A. M., & Fernández-Veiga, M. (2024). Secure Internet Financial Transactions: A Framework Integrating Multi-Factor Authentication and Machine Learning. *AI*, 5(1), 177–194. https://doi-org.captechu.idm.oclc.org/10.3390/ai5010010

Adahman, Z., Malik, A. W., & Anwar, Z. (2022). An analysis of zero-trust architecture and its cost-effectiveness for organizational security. *Computers & Security*, 122, 102911. DOI: 10.1016/j.cose.2022.102911

Adam, N. A., & Alarifi, G. (2020). Innovation practices for enhancing small and medium-sized enterprises' (smes) performance and survival during coronavirus (covid-19) epidemic crisis: the moderating role of external support. DOI: 10.21203/rs.3.rs-125153/v1

Adams, J. S. (1965). Inequity in social exchange. *Advances in Experimental Social Psychology*, 2, 267–299. DOI: 10.1016/S0065-2601(08)60108-2

Adams-Prassl, A., Boneva, T., Golin, M., & Rauh, C. (2020). Furloughing. *Fiscal Studies*, 41(3), 591–622. DOI: 10.1111/1475-5890.12242 PMID: 33362312

Adelekan, O. A., Ilugbusi, B. S., Adisa, O., Obi, O. C., Awonuga, K. F., Asuzu, O. F., & Ndubuisi, N. L. (2024). Energy transition policies: A global review of shifts towards renewable sources. *Engineering Science & Technology Journal*, 5(2), 272–287. DOI: 10.51594/estj.v5i2.752

Adeniyi, I. S., Al Hamad, N. M., Adewusi, O. E., Unachukwu, C. C., Osawaru, B., Onyebuchi, C. N., Omolawal, S. A., Aliu, A. O., & David, I. O. (2024). E-learning platforms in higher education: A comparative review of the USA and Africa. *International Journal of Science and Research Archive*, 11(1), 1686–1697. DOI: 10.30574/ijsra.2024.11.1.0283

Advanced Manufacturing Growth Centre. (2020). Circular Economy in the Automotive Industry. *Retrieved from*https://www.amgc.org.au/project/circular-economy-in-the-automotive-industry/

Agbo, F. J. (2024). Broadening participation in adult education: A literature review of computer science education. *InProceedings of the 55thACM Technical Symposium on Computer Science Education*, 1, pp. 11-17. DOI: 10.1145/3626252.3630797

Agenda, D. (2023). Why we need global rules to crack down on cybercrime? *World Economic Forum*. https://www.weforum.org/agenda/2023/01/global-rules-crack-down-cybercrime

Agnihotri, A. (2015). Extending boundaries of blue ocean strategy. *Journal of Strategic Marketing*, 24(6), 519–528. DOI: 10.1080/0965254X.2015.1069882

Agoncillo, K. M. U. (2023). An integrative action research on improving the marketing strategies of Kumintang Republik Restaurant in Club Balai Isabel Resort and Hotel in Talisay, Batangas towards consistent growth in monthly sales.

Agor, S., Kanesie, D., Boateng, P., & Yamoah, P. (2023). Formulating Strategies that Align Corporate Goals with Organizational Capabilities. *International Journal of Research and Scientific Innovation*. .DOI: 10.51244/IJRSI.2023.1011053

Aguirre, R.R., Suarez, O., Fuentes, M., & Sanchez-Gonzalez, M. A. (2019). Electronic Health Record Implementation: A Review of Resources and Tools. *Cureus,*13,11(9), e5649. doi: .DOI: 10.7759/cureus

Ahmad, F., Bask, A., Laari, S., & Robinson, C. V. (2023). Business management perspectives on the circular economy: Present state and future directions. *Technological Forecasting and Social Change*, 187, 122182. DOI: 10.1016/j.techfore.2022.122182

Ahumada-Canale, A., Jeet, V., Bilgrami, A., Seil, E., Gu, Y., & Cutler, H. (2023). Barriers and facilitators to implementing priority setting and resource allocation tools in hospital decisions: A systematic review. *Social Science & Medicine*, 322, 115790. DOI: 10.1016/j.socscimed.2023.115790 PMID: 36913838

AI Now Institute. (2018). *AI Now 2018 report*. AI Now Institute. Retrieved from https://ainowinstitute.org/reports.html

AI Now Institute. (2020). *AI Now 2020 report*. AI Now Institute. Retrieved from https://ainowinstitute.org/reports.html

Aiwerioghene, E. M., Lewis, J., & Rea, D. (2024). Maturity models for hospital management: A literature review. *International Journal of Healthcare Management*, •••, 1–14. DOI: 10.1080/20479700.2024.2367858

Ajayi, F. A., & Udeh, C. A. (2024). Review of crew resilience and mental health practices in the marine industry: Pathways to improvement. *Magna Scientia Advanced Biology and Pharmacy*, 11(2), 033-049. DOI:DOI: 10.30574/msabp.2024.11.2.0021

Ajlouni, A., & Abdulrahman, M. (2023). Detection Methods of Counterfeit Drugs: A Systemic Review. *Journal of Pharmaceutical Research & Reports*. .DOI: 10.47363/JPRSR/2023(4)144

Ajuwa, M. E. P. E., Veyrier, C. A., Cabrolier, L. C., Chassany, O., Marcellin, F., Yaya, I., & Duracinsky, M. (2024). Workplace violence against female healthcare workers: A systematic review and meta-analysis. *BMJ Open*, 14(8), e079396. DOI: 10.1136/bmjopen-2023-079396 PMID: 39209501

Akbar, M. A., Khan, A. A., & Hyrynsalmi, S. (2024). Role of quantum computing in shaping the future of 6G technology. *Information and Software Technology*, 170, 107454. DOI: 10.1016/j.infsof.2024.107454

Åkerman, M. (2005). What does "natural capital" do? The role of metaphor in economic understanding of the environment. *Environmental Education Research*, 11(1), 37–52. DOI: 10.1080/1350462042000328730

Akhmetshin, E., Makushkin, S., Abdullayev, I., Yumashev, A., Kozachek, A., Shichiyakh, R., & Shakhov, D. (2024). Opportunities to Increase the Efficiency of Universities' Research and Innovation Activities: Scientometric Evaluation of Researchers' Work under External Information Constraints. *Qubahan Academic Journal*, 4(1), 240–249. DOI: 10.48161/qaj.v4n1a258

Akinsanya, M. O., Ekechi, C. C., & Okeke, C. D. Michael Oladipo Akinsanya Cynthia Chizoba Ekechi Chukwuekem David Okeke. (2024). Data sovereignty and security in network engineering: A conceptual framework for compliance. *International Journal of Science and Research Archive*, 11(2), 1832–1847. DOI: 10.30574/ijsra.2024.11.2.0682

Akinsanya, O. O., Papadaki, M., & Sun, L. (2019). Towards a maturity model for health-care cloud security (M^2 HCS). *Information and Computer Security*, 28(3), 321–345. DOI: 10.1108/ICS-05-2019-0060

Akpa, V. O., Asikhia, O. U., & Nneji, N. E. (2021). Organizational culture and organizational performance: A review of literature. *International Journal of Advances in Engineering and Management*, 3(1), 361–372. DOI: 10.35629/5252-030136137

Al-Abdallah, G. M., Abdallah, A. B., & Hamdan, K. (2014). The impact of supplier relationship management on competitive performance of manufacturing firms. *International Journal of Business and Management*, 9(2). Advance online publication. DOI: 10.5539/ijbm.v9n2p192

Alabi, R. O., Vartiainen, T., & Elmusrati, M. (2020). Machine learning for prognosis of oral cancer: What are the ethical challenges? *CEUR Workshop Proceedings*.

Alam, S., & Islam, M. (2017). Impact of Blue Ocean Strategy on Organizational Performance: A Literature Review Toward Implementation Logic. *Agricultural & Natural Resource Economics eJournal*. .DOI: 10.9790/487X-1901030119

Alderman, B. L., & Blair, R. D. (2024). *Monopsony in Labor Markets: Theory, Evidence, and Public Policy*. Cambridge University Press. DOI: 10.1017/9781009465212

Alderman, B. L., Blair, R. D., & Saygin, P. Ö. (2023). Monopsony, wage discrimination, and public policy. *Economic Inquiry*, 61(3), 572–583. DOI: 10.1111/ecin.13131

Alexander, L., & Moore, M. (2020). Deontological ethics. In Zalta, E. N. (Ed.), *The Stanford Encyclopedia of Philosophy*.

Alexander, M. (2010). *The new Jim crow: Mass incarceration in the age of colorblindness*. The New Press.

Alfaro Solano, M. J., & Preuß, M. (2019). *An alternative approach to resistance to change and leadership and its resulting development of Kotter's change models*. (Independent thesis Advanced level, Linnaeus University, School of Business and Economics, Department of Organisation and Entrepreneurship).

Alghamdi, R., & Alfalqi, K. (2015). A survey of topic modeling in text mining. [IJACSA]. *International Journal of Advanced Computer Science and Applications*, 6(1). Advance online publication. DOI: 10.14569/IJACSA.2015.060121

Ali, G & Hassan, M. (2022). A Review of Organization Change Management and Employee Performance. *Xi'an Dianzi Keji Daxue Xuebao/Journal of Xidian University*. 16. 494-506. .DOI: 10.37896/jxu16.1/043

Ali, M. A., Zafar, U., Mahmood, A., & Nazim, M. (2021). The power of ADKAR change model in innovative technology acceptance under the moderating effect of culture and open innovation. LogForum, 17(4).

Ali, S., & Shabir, G. (2024). *Advanced persistent threats (APTs): Analysis, detection, and mitigation*. https://easychair.org/publications/preprint/sNLP

Ali, M., Aini, M. A., & Alam, S. N. (2024). Integrating technology in learning in madrasah: Towards the digital age. [INJOE]. *Indonesian Journal of Education*, 4(1), 290–304.

Alkhars, M., Evangelopoulos, N., Pavur, R., & Kulkarni, S. (2019). Cognitive biases resulting from the representativeness heuristic in operations management: An experimental investigation. *Psychology Research and Behavior Management*, 12, 263–276. DOI: 10.2147/PRBM.S193092 PMID: 31040729

Allred, A. (2019). What if your university tuition was based on your future salary? *Harvard Business Review*. https://hbr.org/2019/10/what-if-your-university-tuition-was-based-on-your-future-salary. Digital article, H056AR. US Anderson, B. (2013). *Us and them?: The dangerous politics of immigration control*. (OUP Oxford).

Al-Maliki, S., Qayyum, A., Ali, H., Abdallah, M., Qadir, J., Hoang, D. T., & Niyato, D. (2023). Adversarial machine learning for social good: Reframing the adversary as an ally. *ArXiv. /abs/2310.03614*. https://doi.org/DOI: 10.48550/arXiv.2310.036144

Alnabhan, O. (2019). Strategic Marketing Recommendations for Lipitor Introduced by Pfizer.

Alnsour, M. S. (2013). How to retain a bank customer: A qualitative study of Jordanian banks relational strategies. *International journal of marketing studies*, 5(4), 123.

Alsajjan, B., & Dennis, C. (2006). The Impact of Trust on Acceptance of Online Banking *European Association of Education and Research in Commercial Distribution*. https://bura.brunel.ac.uk/bitstream/2438/738/1/trust%20impact%20on%20online%20banking%20acceptance%20conceptual%20framework%20-full%20paper.pdf

Amar, A. D., & Walsh, C. (2016). Learning in Organizations: Some Observations from the Practice. *International Journal of Human Capital and Information Technology Professionals*, 7(4), 50–60. DOI: 10.4018/IJHCITP.2016100104

Amazon (2020). *Amazon's approach to responsible AI*. Retrieved from https://aws.amazon.com/machine-learning/responsible-ai

Ambasht, A. (2023). Real-time data integration and analytics: Empowering data-driven decision making. *International Journal of Computer Trends and Technology*, 71(7), 8–14. DOI: 10.14445/22312803/IJCTT-V71I7P102

Amberger, C., & Schreyer, D. (2024). What do we know about no-show behavior? A systematic, interdisciplinary literature review. *Journal of Economic Surveys*, 38(1), 57–96. DOI: 10.1111/joes.12534

Amft, S., Höltervennhoff, S., Huaman, N., Krause, A., Simko, L., Acar, Y., & Fahl, S. (2023, November). We've disabled MFA for you: An evaluation of the security and usability of multi-factor authentication recovery deployments. In *Proceedings of the 2023 ACM SIGSAC Conference on Computer and Communications Security* (pp. 3138-3152). DOI:DOI: 10.1145/3576915.3623180

Analytics, H. I. M. S. S. (2006). EMRAM: An International Standard for EMR Adoption. Retrieved from https://www.himssanalytics.org/emram

Analytics, H. I. M. S. S. (2024). EMRAM: Electronic Medical Record Adoption Model. Healthcare Information and Management Systems Society. Retrieved from https://www.himss.org/resources/emram

Anderson, J., & Rainie, L. (2023). As AI spreads, experts predict the best and worst changes. Pew Research Center. https://www.pewresearch.org/internet/2023/06/21/themes-the-most-harmful-or-menacing-changes-in-digital-life-that-are-likely-by-2035/

Anderson, D. (2020). *Organization development: the process of leading organizational change* (5th ed.). Sage Publishers.

Anderson, M. H. (2007). "Why are there so many theories?" A classroom exercise to help students appreciate the need for multiple theories of a management domain. *Journal of Management Education*, 31(6), 757–776. DOI: 10.1177/1052562906297705

Angioni, D., Demetrio, L., Pintor, M., Onet, L., Anguita, D., Biggio, B., & Roli, F. (2024). Robustness-congruent adversarial training for secure machine learning model updates. *arXiv:2402.17390v1 [cs.LG]* https://doi.org//arXiv.2402.17390DOI: 10.48550

Anschütz, C., Ebner, K., & Smolnik, S. (2024). Size does matter: A maturity model for the special needs of small and medium-sized smart cities. *Cities (London, England)*, 150, 104998. DOI: 10.1016/j.cities.2024.104998

Anser, M. K., Yousaf, Z., Usman, M., & Yousaf, S. (2022). Towards strategic business performance of the hospitality sector: Nexus of ICT, E-marketing and organizational readiness. *Sustainability (Basel)*, 12(4), 1346. DOI: 10.3390/su12041346

Antony, J., Sony, M., McDermott, O., Jayaraman, R., & Flynn, D. (2023). An exploration of organizational readiness factors for Quality 4.0: An intercontinental study and future research directions. *International Journal of Quality & Reliability Management*, 40(2), 582–606. DOI: 10.1108/IJQRM-10-2021-0357

Apraiz, A., Lasa, G., Montagna, F., Blandino, G., Triviño-Tonato, E., & Dacal-Nieto, A. (2023). An experimental protocol for human stress investigation in manufacturing contexts: Its application in the no-stress project. *Systems*, 11(9), 448. DOI: 10.3390/systems11090448

Aral, S., Brynjolfsson, E., & Van Alstyne, M. (2006). Information, Technology and Information Worker Productivity Task Level Evidence. *Information Systems Research*, 23(3, part 2), 849–867. DOI: 10.1287/isre.1110.0408

Arar, K. (2020). *School leadership for refugees' education: Social justice leadership for immigrant, migrants and refugees*. Routledge. DOI: 10.4324/9780429021770

Ari, E. (2020). Human Resource Risks in the Hospitality Industry.

Arora, P. (2023). *Building Resilience in the future workforce: The role of continuous learning and transferable skills*. BSSS Journal of Education., DOI: 10.51767/je1207

Arrieta, A. B., Díaz-Rodríguez, N., Del Ser, J., Bennetot, A., Tabik, S., Barbado, A., Garcia, S., il-Lopez, S., Molina, D., Benjamins, R., Chatila, R., & Herrera, F. (2021). Explainable artificial intelligence (XAI): Concepts, taxonomies, opportunities and challenges toward responsible AI. *Information Fusion*, 58, 82–115. DOI: 10.1016/j.inffus.2019.12.012

Ashari, C., & Herachwati, N. (2023). Implementation of Organizational Agility Model in Improving Sustainable PHEIs Competitive Advantage: Narrative Literature Review. *RSF Conference Series: Business, Management and Social Sciences*. DOI: 10.31098/bmss.v3i3.725

Asunda, P., & Ware, S. (2015). Applying the congruence principle of Bloom's taxonomy to **develop an integrated stem experience through engineering design** https://www.researchgate.net/publication/323133638_applying_the_congruence _principle_of_bloom's_taxonomy_to_develop_an_integrated_stem_experience _through_engineering_design

Atadoga, A., Ike, C. U., Asuzu, O. F., Ayinla, B. S., Ndubuisi, N. L., & Adeleye, R. A. (2024). The intersection of AI and quantum computing in financial markets: A critical review. *Computer Science & IT Research Journal*, 5(2), 461–472. DOI: 10.51594/csitrj.v5i2.816

Atanasovska, I., Choudhary, S., Koh, L., Ketikidis, P. H., & Solomon, A. (2022). Research gaps and future directions on social value stemming from circular economy practices in agri-food industrial parks: Insights from a systematic literature review. *Journal of Cleaner Production*, 354, 131753. DOI: 10.1016/j.jclepro.2022.131753

Attaran, M., & Gunasekaran, A. (2019). Blockchain and Cybersecurity. In *Applications of Blockchain Technology in Business. SpringerBriefs in Operations Management.* Springer., DOI: 10.1007/978-3-030-27798-7_10

Attkan, A., & Ranga, V. (2022). Cyber-physical security for IoT networks: A comprehensive review on traditional, blockchain and artificial intelligence based key-security. *Complex & Intelligent Systems*, 8(35), 9–3591. DOI: 10.1007/s40747-022-00667-z

Australia, K. P. M. G. (2019). *Fighting food waste using the circular economy.* Retrieved from https://assets.kpmg.com/content/dam/kpmg/au/pdf/2019/fighting -food-waste-using-the-circular-economy-report.pdf

Australian Circular Economy Hub. (2024). *Our current economic model is unsustainable, explore the circular alternative.* Retrieved from https://acehub.org.au/

Australian Logistics Council. (2020). Sustainable Logistics: Leveraging Technology for Efficiency. Retrieved from https://www.austlogistics.com.au/sustainable-logistics -leveraging-technology-for-efficiency/

Awad, A.I., Babu, A., Barka, E.S., & Shuaib, K. (2024). AI-powered biometrics for Internet of Things security: A review and future vision. *Journal of Information Security and Applications*. DOI:DOI: 10.1016/j.jisa.2024.103748

Axelsson, K., Melin, U., & Granath, M. (2024). Exploring services in a smart city through socio-technical design principles: Revealing five tensions in a smart living context. *Government Information Quarterly*, 41(1), 101915. DOI: 10.1016/j. giq.2024.101915

Ayat, M. (2024). E-Health Implementation Challenges and HIS Evaluation in Accordance with EMRAM in Iran. *Health Technology Assessment in Action*, 8(2). Advance online publication. DOI: 10.18502/htaa.v8i2.15628

Azad, M. A., Abdullah, S., Arshad, J., Lallie, H., & Ahmed, Y. H. (2024). Verify and trust: A multidimensional survey of zero-trust security in the age of IoT. *Internet of Things : Engineering Cyber Physical Human Systems*, 27, 101227. DOI: 10.1016/j.iot.2024.101227

Azar, J., Huet-Vaughn, E., Marinescu, I., Taska, B., & Von Wachter, T. (2023). Minimum wage employment effects and labour market concentration. *The Review of Economic Studies*, •••, rdad091. Advance online publication. DOI: 10.3386/w26101

Badari, T. P., Machado, G., Moniz, F., Fontes, A., & Teoldo, I. (2021). Comparison of soccer players' tactical behaviour in small-sided games according to match status. *Journal of Physical Education and Sport*, 21(1), 12–20.

Bag, S., Telukdarie, A., & Pretorius, J. H. C. (2021). Industry 4.0 Technologies and Circular Economy Practices: A Comprehensive Review. *Sustainability*, 13(19), 10678.

Bagyendera, M., Nabende, P., & Nabukenya, J. (2023). Critical factors influencing data use and utilization in health systems: A focus on data and interoperability standards for health information exchange (HIE) in Uganda's health care system. *Oxford Open Digital Health*, 1, oqad015. Advance online publication. DOI: 10.1093/oodh/oqad015

Bailer, S. (2014). Interviews and surveys in legislative research. *The Oxford handbook of legislative studies*, 167-193.

Baily, M. N., Boswoth, B., & Kennedy, K. (2021). The contribution of human capital to economic growth: A cross-country comparison of Germany, Japan, and the United States. *The Brookings Economic Studies*.https://www.brookings.edu/wp-content/uploads/2021/09/20210928_BailyBosworthKennedy_Returns_to_education_final.pdf

Ballister, C. M. (2022). Protecting financial data under the Zero Trust buzz. Armed Forces Comptroller, 67(2).

Bandhu, D., Mohan, M. M., Nittala, N. A. P., Jadhav, P., Bhadauria, A., & Saxena, K. K. (2024). Theories of motivation: A comprehensive analysis of human behavior drivers. *Acta Psychologica*, 244, 104177. DOI: 10.1016/j.actpsy.2024.104177 PMID: 38354564

Bank of America. (2021, February 1). *70% of Bank of America Clients engaging digitally for more of their financial needs*. Author. https://newsroom.bankofamerica.com/content/newsroom/press-releases/2021/02/70--of-bank-of-america-clients-engaging-digitally-for-more-of-th.html

Bans-Akutey, A. (2021). The Path-Goal Theory of Leadership. *Academia Letters. Article*, 748. Advance online publication. DOI: 10.20935/AL748

Baporikar, N. (2022). Innovation Management Case Study. *International Journal of Innovation in the Digital Economy*, 13(1), 1–11. DOI: 10.4018/IJIDE.311515

Baranik, L. E., Cheung, J. H., Sinclair, R. R., & Lance, C. E. (2019). What happens when employees are furloughed? A resource loss perspective. *Journal of Career Development*, 46(4), 381–394. DOI: 10.1177/0894845318763880

Barber, P., & Wallace, L. (2009). The power of word-of-mouth marketing. *American Libraries*, 40(11), 36–39.

Barker, T. H., Stone, J. C., Sears, K., Klugar, M., Leonardi-Bee, J., Tufanaru, C., & Munn, Z. (2023). Revising the JBI quantitative critical appraisal tools to improve their applicability: An overview of methods and the development process. *JBI Evidence Synthesis*, 21(3), 478–493. DOI: 10.11124/JBIES-22-00125 PMID: 36121230

Barocas, S., Hardt, M., & Narayanan, A. (2019). *Fairness and Machine Learning*. MIT Press.

Barocas, S., Hardt, M., & Narayanan, A. (2023). *Fairness and machine learning: Limitations and opportunities*. MIT Press.

Barrett, M. (2018). *Framework for improving critical infrastructure cybersecurity version 1.1*. NIST Cybersecurity Framework., DOI: 10.6028/NIST.CSWP.04162018

Barros, L., & Fischmann, A. (2020). Strategy code: indicators of organisational alignment for obtaining strategy implementation effectiveness. *International Journal of Business Excellence*. .DOI: 10.1504/IJBEX.2019.10024140

Bartik, A. W., Bertrand, M., Lin, F., Rothstein, J., & Unrath, M. (2020. July). Measuring the labor market at the onset of the COVID-19 crisis. *Natural Bureau of Economic Research*. https://www.nber.org/papers/w27613

Basharat, L., & Alam, M. J. (2024). Workplace Environment for Gender Equality and Sustainable Career Planning: The Case of Bangladesh. In *People, Spaces and Places in Gendered Environments* (Vol. 34, pp. 77-97). Emerald Publishing Limited.

Bass, B., & Avolio, B. (1993). Transformational leadership and organizational culture. *Public Administration Quarterly*, 17(1), 112–121. https://www.jstor.org/stable/40862298

Baum, S., & Lee, V. (2018). Understanding endowments. *Urban Institute. April.*

Baxter, R. S., & Martinez, C. S., Jr. (2020). *Enhancing Identity And Access Management In The Us Navy Via Migration To More Modern Standards Of Authentication* (Doctoral dissertation, Monterey, CA; Naval Postgraduate School).

Baxter, G., & Sommerville, I. (2021). Socio-technical systems: From design methods to systems engineering. *Interacting with Computers*, 23(1), 4–17. DOI: 10.1016/j.intcom.2010.07.003

Beauchamp, T. L., & Childress, J. F. (2019). *Principles of biomedical ethics* (8th ed.). Oxford University Press., DOI: 10.1080/15265161.2019.1665402

Becker, J., Knackstedt, R., & Pöppelbuß, J. (2009). Developing Maturity Models for IT Management. *Business & Information Systems Engineering*, 1(3), 213–222. DOI: 10.1007/s12599-009-0044-5

Bécue, A., Praça, I., & Gama, J. (2021). Artificial intelligence, cyber-threats and industry 4.0: Challenges and opportunities. *Artificial Intelligence Review*, 54(5), 3849–3886. DOI: 10.1007/s10462-020-09942-2

Bedard, A. (2023, August 22). The 8-step process for leading change: Dr. John Kotter. K*otter International Inc.*https://www.kotterinc.com/methodology/8-steps/

Beine, M., Peri, G., & Raux, M. (2023). International college students' impact on the skilled labor supply. *Journal of Public Economics*, 223, 104917. DOI: 10.1016/j.jpubeco.2023.104917

Bella, G., Giustolisi, R., & Schürmann, C. (2022). Modelling human threats in security ceremonies. *Journal of Computer Security*, 30(3), 411–433. DOI: 10.3233/JCS-210059

Bellantuono, N., Nuzzi, A., Pontrandolfo, P., & Scozzi, B. (2021). Digital Transformation Models for the I4.0 Transition: Lessons from the Change Management Literature. *Sustainability (Basel)*, 13(23), 12941. Advance online publication. DOI: 10.3390/su132312941

Belliard, J. C. (2009). Applying Kotter's model of change to sustaining community engaged scholarship within a school of public health and its parent university. *Metropolitan Universities*, 20(2), 119–138.

Belmabrouk, K. (2023). Cyber Criminals and Data Privacy Measures. In *Contemporary Challenges for Cyber Security and Data Privacy* (pp. 198–226). IGI Global., DOI: 10.4018/979-8-3693-1528-6.ch011

Belton, I. K., & Dhami, M. K. (2020). Cognitive biases and debiasing in intelligence analysis. In *Routledge Handbook of Bounded Rationality* (pp. 548–560). Routledge. DOI: 10.4324/9781315658353-42

Benjamin, R. (2019). Race after technology: Abolitionist tools for the new Jim code. *Polity.*

Berg, C., Philipp, R., & Taff, S. D. (2023, January). Scoping Review of Critical Thinking Literature in Healthcare Education. *Occupational Therapy in Health Care*, 37(1), 18–39. DOI: 10.1080/07380577.2021.1879411 PMID: 33571065

Berkhout, F., Smith, A., & Stirling, A. (2021). Managing e-waste in Australia: Circular economy strategies and outcomes. *Waste Management (New York, N.Y.)*, 119, 230–240. DOI: 10.1016/j.wasman.2020.10.028

Berlilana, N., Noparumpa, T., Ruangkanjanases, A., Hariguna, T., & Sarmini, . (2021). Organization Benefit as an Outcome of Organizational Security Adoption: The Role of Cyber Security Readiness and Technology Readiness. *Sustainability (Basel)*, 13(24), 13761. DOI: 10.3390/su132413761

Bertsch, C., & Rosenvinge, C. J. (2019). FinTech credit: Online lending platforms in Sweden and beyond. *Sveriges Riksbank Economic Review*, 2, 42–70.

Bevan, R. (2015). *The Changemaking Checklists: A Toolkit for Planning, Leading, and Sustaining Change.* ChangeStart Press (Richard Bevan), Independently Published.

Bhattacharyya, S. C. (2019). *Energy economics: concepts, issues, markets and governance.* Springer Nature. DOI: 10.1007/978-1-4471-7468-4

Biancini, S., & Bombarda, P. (2021). Intellectual property rights, multinational firms and technology transfers. Journal of Economic Behavior &Amp. *Journal of Economic Behavior & Organization*, 185, 191–210. DOI: 10.1016/j.jebo.2021.02.005

Bianco-Mathis, V. (2023). *Culture Change: The Nexus Of Leadership.* Organizational Development Models, And Coaching Cultures.

Biasatti, A. (2024). No Girls Allowed: How Sexual Harassment and Gender Discrimination Keep Women out of Oil Fields. *ONE J*, 10, 95.

Bickmore, E., MacKinlay, A., & Tellez, Y. (2023). Old Program, New Banks: Online Banks in Small Business Lending. *Social Science Research Network*. DOI: 10.2139/ssrn.4537337

Bier, D. J. (2020). The facts about optional practical training (OPT) for foreign students. *Policy Commons, 20.500.12592/18qwk8.*

Bikard, M., Vakili, K., & Teodoridis, F. (2019). When collaboration bridges institutions: The impact of university–industry collaboration on academic productivity. *Organization Science*, 30(2), 426–445. DOI: 10.1287/orsc.2018.1235

Binns, R. (2018). Fairness in machine learning: Lessons from political philosophy. *In Conference on fairness, accountability and transparency 149-159.* PMLR. https://proceedings.mlr.press/v81/binns18a.html

Birhane, A., & Prabhu, V. U. (2021). Large image datasets: A pyrrhic win for computer vision? /arXiv.2006.16923DOI: 10.1109/WACV48630.2021.00158

Blackmon, R., & Ammanath, B. (2022). Building transparency into AI projects. *Harvard Business Review.* https://hbr.org/2022/06/building-transparency-into-ai-projects

Blanco, M., & Aguilar, A. (2021). Digitalization in agriculture: An overview of challenges and opportunities. *Agricultural Systems*, 191, 103137.

Bligh, M., Kohles, J., & Yan, Q. (2018). Leading and learning to change: The role of leadership style and mindset in error learning and organizational change. *Journal of Change Management*, 2(18), 116–141. DOI: 10.1080/14697017.2018.1446693

Blunden, C. (2022). Between market failures and justice failures: Trade-offs between efficiency and equality in business ethics. *Journal of Business Ethics*, 178(3), 647–660. DOI: 10.1007/s10551-021-04767-7

BMA. (2019). Technology, infrastructure and data supporting NHS staff. British Medical Association. https://www.bma.org.uk/media/2080/bma-vision-for-nhs-it-report-april-2019.pdf

Bobbert, Y., & Scheerder, J. (.2020). Zero Trust validation: From practical approaches to theory. *Sci J Research & Rev. 2*(5). SJRR.MS.ID.000546. DOI: .DOI: 10.33552/SJRR.2020.02.000546

Bobbert, Y., & Timmermans, T. (2024). Zero Trust and compliance with industry frameworks and regulations: A Structured Zero Trust Approach to Improve Cybersecurity and Reduce the Compliance Burden. *In Future of Information and Communication Conference (pp. 650-667).* Springer Nature Switzerland.

Böckel, A., Nuzum, A. K., & Weissbrod, I. (2021). Blockchain for the circular economy: Analysis of the research-practice gap. *Sustainable Production and Consumption*, 25, 525–539. DOI: 10.1016/j.spc.2020.12.006

Bocken, N. M. P., de Pauw, I., Bakker, C., & van der Grinten, B. (2016). Product design and business model strategies for a circular economy. *Journal of Industrial and Production Engineering*, 33(5), 308–320. DOI: 10.1080/21681015.2016.1172124

Bocken, N. M. P., de Pauw, I., Bakker, C., & van der Grinten, B. (2021). Circular business strategies for sustainable growth. *Journal of Cleaner Production*, 292, 125–136. DOI: 10.1016/j.jclepro.2021.125136

Bodimani, M. (2024). Assessing the impact of transparent AI systems in enhancing user trust and privacy. *Journal of Science and Technology*, 5(1), 50–67. https://www.thesciencebrigade.com/jst/article/view/68

Bohr, A, & Memarzadeh, K. (2020). The rise of artificial intelligence in healthcare applications. *Artificial Intelligence in Healthcare*, 25–60. .DOI: 10.1016/B978-0-12-818438-7.00002-2

Bond, B. (2019). International students: Language, culture and the 'performance of identity'. *Teaching in Higher Education*, 24(5), 649–665. DOI: 10.1080/13562517.2019.1593129

Bonderud, D. (2022, March 16). Federal agencies can strengthen identify verification methods with MFA. *FedTech Magazine*. https://fedtechmagazine.com/article/2022/03/federal-agencies-can-strengthen-identify-verification-methods-mfa

Bongitte, I. (2024). Impact of minimum wage increases on employment levels in the United States. *American Journal of Economics*, 8(1), 39–50. DOI: 10.47672/aje.1790

Bongomin, O., Gilibrays Ocen, G., Oyondi Nganyi, E., Musinguzi, A., & Omara, T. (2020). Exponential Disruptive Technologies and the Required Skills of Industry 4.0. *Journal of Engineering*, 2020, 1–17. DOI: 10.1155/2020/4280156

Boston University. (2023). Belonging & culture survey. *Boston University*. https://www.bu.edu/belonging-culture-survey/committee/

Boston University. (2024). Lobbying guidelines. Lobbying Guidelines | Federal Relations. *Boston University*. https://www.bu.edu/federal/bu-community/working-with-dc/lobbying-guidelines/

Bostrom, N., & Yudkowsky, E. (2014). The Ethics of Artificial Intelligence. In *Cambridge Handbook of Artificial Intelligence* (pp. 316–334). Cambridge University Press., DOI: 10.1017/CBO9781139046855.020

Bottomley, D., & Thaldar, D. (2023). Liability for harm caused by AI in healthcare: An overview of the core legal concepts. *Frontiers in Pharmacology*, 14, 1297353. DOI: 10.3389/fphar.2023.1297353 PMID: 38161692

Bouke, M. A., & Abdullah, A. (2024). *An empirical assessment of ML Models for 5G network intrusion detection: A data leakage-free approach. e-Prime-Advances in Electrical Engineering.* Electronics and Energy., DOI: 10.1016/j.prime.2024.100590

Boutin, C. (2022, March 16). *There's more to AI bias than biased data, NIST report highlights.* NIST https://www.nist.gov/news-events/news/2022/03/theres-more-ai-bias-biased-data-nist-report-highlights

Bowers, C. (2001). How language limits our understanding of environmental education. *Environmental Education Research*, 7(2), 141–151. DOI: 10.1080/13504620120043144

Boyd, J. (2003). A quest for cinergy: The war metaphor and the construction of identity. *Communication Studies*, 54(3), 249–264. DOI: 10.1080/10510970309363285

Bracken, M. (2023, October 6). Stumbling blocks abound in federal push to stronger identity and access management, CISA and NSA panel finds. *Fedscoop.* https://fedscoop.com/cisa-nsa-report-mfa-sso-identity-access-management/

Bracker, J. (1980). The historical development of the strategic management concept. *Academy of Management Review*, 5(2), 219–224. DOI: 10.2307/257431

Bragato, L., & Jacobs, K. (2003). Care pathways: The road to better health services? *Journal of Health Organization and Management*, 17(3), 164–180. DOI: 10.1108/14777260310480721 PMID: 14763100

Braithwaite, J., Matsuyama, Y., Mannion, R., & Johnson, J. (Eds.). (2015). *Healthcare reform, quality and safety: perspectives, participants, partnerships and prospects in 30 countries.* Ashgate.

Brayne, S. (2020). *Predict and surveil: Data, discretion, and the future of policing.* Oxford University Press. DOI: 10.1093/oso/9780190684099.001.0001

Brenya, B. (2024). Higher education in emergency situation: Blended learning prospects and challenges for educators in the developing countries. *Journal of Applied Research in Higher Education*, 16(4), 1015–1028. DOI: 10.1108/JARHE-01-2023-0044

Brereton, T. A., Malik, M. M., Lifson, M., Greenwood, J. D., Peterson, K. J., & Overgaard, S. M. (2023). The role of artificial intelligence model documentation in translational science: Scoping review. *Interactive Journal of Medical Research*, 12(1), e45903. DOI: 10.2196/45903 PMID: 37450330

Bright, A. M., Higgins, A., & Grealish, A. (2023). Women's experiences of prison-based mental healthcare: A systematic review of qualitative literature. *International Journal of Prisoner Health*, 19(2), 181–198. DOI: 10.1108/IJPH-09-2021-0091 PMID: 35192246

Bristol, E. J. (2023). *Developing specialized master's programs in business schools: The convergence of mission and markets* (Doctoral dissertation, University of Massachusetts Boston).

Broeders, H., & Khanna, S. 2015. Strategic choices for banks in the digital age. McKinsey & Company: Our Insights. www.mckinsey.com/industries/ financial-services/our-insights/strategic-choices-for-banks-in-the-digital-age

Browne, S. (2015). *Dark matters: On the surveillance of blackness*. Duke University Press., DOI: 10.2307/j.ctv11cw89p

Brown-Jackson, K. L. (2017). Disrupting and retooling: A model for an effective community-based telehealth program (Doctoral dissertation, The National Graduate School of Quality Management). https://www.proquest.com/openview/d0a3ddae9045391382a3e936ac33a126/1?pq-origsite=gscholar&cbl=44156

Brown, M., Treviño, L., & Harrison, D. (2005). Ethical leadership: A social learning perspective for construct development and testing. *Organizational Behavior and Human Decision Processes*, 2(97), 117–134. DOI: 10.1016/j.obhdp.2005.03.002

Brownstein, N. C., Louis, T. A., O'Hagan, A., & Pendergast, J. (2019). The role of expert judgment in statistical inference and evidence-based decision-making. The American Statistician, 73(sup1), 56-68. DOI: 10.1080/00031305.2018.1529623

Bruce, G. (2024). Healthcare data breaches set record in 2023. *Becker Hospital Review, 2024*(February 7). https://www.beckershospitalreview.com/cybersecurity/healthcare-data-breaches-set-record-in-2023.html

Brush, M. A. (2022). *Understanding declining international graduate student yield at a private university* (Doctoral dissertation, Northeastern University).

Bryson, J. M., Edwards, L. H., & Van Slyke, D. M. (2018). Getting strategic about strategic planning research. *Public Management Review*, 20(3), 317–339. DOI: 10.1080/14719037.2017.1285111

Buchanan, L. (2005). Let the analogies end. *Journal of Business. Harvard*, 83(3), 19.

Buchanan, T. W. (2007). Retrieval of emotional memories. *Psychological Bulletin*, 133(5), 761–779. DOI: 10.1037/0033-2909.133.5.761 PMID: 17723029

Budur, T., Abdullah, H., Rashid, C. A., & Demirer, H. (2024). The Connection Between Knowledge Management Processes and Sustainability at Higher Education Institutions. *Journal of the Knowledge Economy*, •••, 1–34. DOI: 10.1007/s13132-023-01664-4

Bumiller, A., Challita, S., Combemale, B., Barais, O., Aillery, N., & Le Lan, G. (2023). On Understanding Context Modelling for Adaptive Authentication Systems. *ACM Transactions on Autonomous and Adaptive Systems*, 18(1), 1–35. DOI: 10.1145/3582696

Buntin, M. B., Burke, M. F., Hoaglin, M. C., & Blumenthal, D. (2011). The Benefits of Health Information Technology: A Review of The Recent Literature Shows Predominantly Positive Results. *Health Affairs*, 30(3), 464–471. DOI: 10.1377/hlthaff.2011.0178 PMID: 21383365

Bunzel, D. L. (2007). Universities sell their brands. *Journal of Product and Brand Management*, 16(2), 152–153. DOI: 10.1108/10610420710740034

Buolamwini, J., & Gebru, T. (2018). Gender shades: Intersectional accuracy disparities in commercial gender classification. [Conference on Fairness, Accountability, and Transparency] [FAT]. *Proceedings of Machine Learning Research*, 81, 1–15.

Burgess, J., & Nye, M. (2022). Incentive structures for promoting pro-environmental behaviors: Insights from Australian case studies. *Environmental Science & Policy*, 128, 14–22. DOI: 10.1016/j.envsci.2021.12.009

Burns, T., & Stalker, G. M. (1961). *The management of innovation*. Tavistock Publications.

Burrell, D. (2024). Final case study assignment – 16-page double spaced paper- you are to only pick one. *Canvas*. https://marymount.instructure.com/courses/30592/assignments/336448

Burrell, D. N., Nobles, C., & Wright, J. B. (2021). Cybersecurity and the intersection of AI and healthcare: A critical analysis. *Journal of Healthcare Information Management*, 35(4), 23–31. DOI: 10.1002/jhim.2021.35.4.23

Burrell, G., & Morgan, G. (1979). *Sociological paradigms and organizational analysis: Elements of the sociology of corporate life*. Heinemann Educational Books., DOI: 10.4324/9781315609751

Burton, S. L. (2022). Cybersecurity leadership from a Telemedicine/Telehealth knowledge and organizational development examination(Order No. 29066056). Available from ProQuest Central; ProQuest Dissertations & Theses Global. (2662752457). https://www.proquest.com/dissertations-theses/cybersecurity-leadership-telemedicine-telehealth/docview/2662752457/se-2

Burton, S. L. (2022). *Cybersecurity leadership from a telemedicine/telehealth knowledge and organizational development examination*. ProQuest https://www.proquest.com/dissertations-theses/cybersecurity-leadership-telemedicine-telehealth/docview/2662752457/se-2?accountid=44888

Burton, S. L. (2024). Business Resilience in a Cyber World: Protect Against Attacks Part 2. In Innovations, Securities, and Case Studies Across Healthcare, Business, and Technology (pp. 1-25). IGI Global. DOI: DOI: 10.4018/979-8-3693-1906-2.ch001

Burton, S. L. (2023). Cybersecurity risk: The business significance of ongoing tracking. In Burrell, D. N. (Ed.), *Transformational Interventions for Business* (1st ed., pp. 245–268). Technology, and Healthcare., DOI: 10.4018/979-8-3693-1634-4.ch015

Burt, R. S. (1992). *Structural holes: The social structure of competition*. Harvard University Press. DOI: 10.4159/9780674029095

Burt, R. S. (2000). The network structure of social capital. *Research in Organizational Behavior*, 22, 345–423. DOI: 10.1016/S0191-3085(00)22009-1

Buscha, F., & Dickson, M. (2023). Returns to education: Individuals. In Zimmermann, K. F. (Ed.), *Handbook of Labor, Human Resources and Population Economics*. Springer., DOI: 10.1007/978-3-319-57365-6_377-1

Butarbutar, I. P., Purnamasari, N., & Safitri, K. (2023). An analysis on five forces dan bcg matrix for apple inc. company. Maker. *Jurnal Manajemen*, 9(2), 229–240. DOI: 10.37403/mjm.v9i2.615

Butcher, K., & Shiro, A. G. (2024, January). Policy brief: The high and lasting costs of job displacement. *Federal Reserve Bank of Chicago*. https://www.chicagofed.org/publications/chicago-fed-insights/2024/policy-brief-costs-of-job-displacement

Cabrera, Á. A., Perer, A., & Hong, J. I. (2023). Improving human-AI collaboration with descriptions of AI behavior. *Proceedings of the ACM on Human-Computer Interaction*, 7(CSCW1), 1-21. DOI: 10.1145/3579612

Cacciolatti, L., Rosli, A., Ruiz-Alba, J., & Chang, J. (2020). Strategic alliances and firm performance in startups with a social mission. *Journal of Business Research*, 106, 106–117. DOI: 10.1016/j.jbusres.2019.08.047

Camacho, N. G. (2024). The role of AI in Cybersecurity: Addressing threats in the digital age. *Journal of Artificial Intelligence General science (JAIGS) ISSN: 3006-4023, 3*(1), 143-154. DOI: 10.60087/jaigs.v3i1.75

Cameron, K. (2009). An introduction to the competing values framework. https://www.semanticscholar.org/paper/An-Introduction-to-the-Competing-Values-Framework-Cameron/45b05b0eebf2f4bc6e204f4559e91ab7e7e0272d

Camilleri, M. A. (2018). Closing the loop for resource efficiency, sustainable consumption and production: A critical review of the circular economy. *International Journal of Sustainable Development*, 21(1-4), 1–17. DOI: 10.1504/IJSD.2018.10012310

Camilleri, M. A. (2018). The circular economy: Scope and opportunities for higher education. *Journal of Cleaner Production*, 183, 517–525.

Campbell, F., Tricco, A. C., Munn, Z., Pollock, D., Saran, A., Sutton, A., White, H., & Khalil, H. (2023, March 15). White H, Khalil H. Mapping reviews, scoping reviews, and evidence and gap maps (EGMs): The same but different- the "Big Picture" review family. *Systematic Reviews*, 12(1), 45. DOI: 10.1186/s13643-023-02178-5 PMID: 36918977

Cannavò, A., & Lamberti, F. (2021). Immersive Design Environments with Virtual and Augmented Reality. *Journal of Computer-Aided Design*, 128, 102837.

Cantor, D. E., Yan, T., Pagell, M., & Tate, W. L. (2022). From the editors: introduction to the emerging discourse incubator on the topic of leveraging multiple types of resources within the supply network for competitive advantage. Journal of Supply Chain Management, 58(2), 3-7. DOI: 10.1111/jscm.12282

Cantwell, B. (2019). Are international students cash cows? Examining the relationship between new international undergraduate enrollments and institutional revenue at public colleges and universities in the U.S. *Journal of International Students*, 5(4), 512–525. DOI: 10.32674/jis.v5i4.412

Carroll, J. (2024, June). The US National Cybersecurity Strategy: A Vehicle with an International Journey. *InEuropean Conference on Cyber Warfare and Security, 23*(1), pp. 107-115). DOI: DOI: 10.34190/eccws.23.1.2300

Čartolovni, A., Tomičić, A., & Mosler, E. L. (2022). Ethical, legal, and social considerations of AI-based medical decision-support tools: A scoping review. *International Journal of Medical Informatics*, 161, 104738. DOI: 10.1016/j.ijmedinf.2022.104738 PMID: 35299098

Carvalho, J. V., Rocha, A., & Abreu, A. (2016). Maturity Models of Healthcare Information Systems and Technologies: A Literature Review. *Journal of Medical Systems*, 40(6), 131. DOI: 10.1007/s10916-016-0486-5 PMID: 27083575

Carvalho, J. V., Rocha, A., Vasconcelos, J., & Abreu, A. (2019). A health data analytics maturity model for hospitals information systems. *International Journal of Information Management*, 46, 278–285. DOI: 10.1016/j.ijinfomgt.2018.07.001

Cath, C., Wachter, S., Mittelstadt, B., & Floridi, L. (2017) Artificial Intelligence and the 'Good Society': the US, EU, and UK approach. *Sci Eng Ethics 24*, 505–528 (2018). DOI: 10.1007/s11948-017-9901-7

Cath, C. (2018). Governing artificial intelligence: Ethical, legal, and technical opportunities and challenges. *Philosophy & Technology*, 31(4), 685–692. DOI: 10.1098/rsta.2018.0080 PMID: 30322996

Caulfield, J., & Brenner, E. (2019). Resolving complex community problems: Applying collective leadership and Kotter's change model to wicked problems within social systems networks. *Nonprofit Management & Leadership*, 2020(30), 509–524.

Cautitanu, C.. (2018). Circular economy indicators for performance analysis. *Journal of Cleaner Production*, 200, 112–124.

Cavada, M., Tight, M. R., & Rogers, C. D. (2019). A smart city case study of Singapore—Is Singapore truly smart? *Smart City Emergence*, 295-314. DOI: 10.1016/B978-0-12-816169-2.00014-6

CCMM. (2017). Continuity of Care Maturity Model (CCMM): A Strategic Framework for Optimizing Healthcare Outcomes. HIMSS. Retrieved from https://www.himss.org/resources/continuity-care-maturity-model

Centers for Medicare & Medicaid Services. (2021). Risk management handbook, Chapter 8. *CMS Information Security and Privacy Group*. https://security.cms.gov/policy-guidance/risk-management-handbook-chapter-8-incident-response-ir

Chakravorti, B. (2021, July 20). How to close the digital divide in the U.S. *Harvard Business Review*. https://hbr.org/2021/07/how-to-close-the-digital-divide-in-the-u-s#:~:text=Policymakers%20should%3A%201%29%20pay%20for%20improvements%20using%20a,in%20future-proofing%2C%20and%207%29%20invest%20in%20digital%20literacy

Chandrika, H. N., & Jadhav, P. P. (2023). Strengthening authentication best practices for multi factor authentication deployment. *Journal of Data Acquisition and Processing*, 38(3), 6065. DOI: 10.5281/zenodo.7778218

Chane, M., & Atwal, H. (2023). The entrepreneurial ecosystem and the performance of micro and small enterprises (MSEs) in Amhara region, Ethiopia: The political-legal perspective. *Journal of Developmental Entrepreneurship*, 28(03), 2350020. DOI: 10.1142/S1084946723500206

Chan, G. S. H., Tang, I. L. F., & Sou, A. H. K. (2017). An exploration of consumer complaint behavior towards the hotel industry: Case study in Macao. *International Journal of Marketing Studies*, 9(5), 56–76. DOI: 10.5539/ijms.v9n5p56

Chao, C., Hu, H., Zhang, L., & Wu, J. (2016). Managing the challenges of pharmaceutical patent expiry: a case study of Lipitor., 7, 258-272. .DOI: 10.1108/JSTPM-12-2015-0040

Chappell, G., Harreis, H., Havas, A., Nuzzo, A., Pepanides, T., & Rowshankish, K. (2018, *August31*). The lending revolution: How digital credit is changing banks from the inside. *McKinsey & Company*. https://www.mckinsey.com/capabilities/risk-and-resilience/our-insights/the-lending-revolution-how-digital-credit-is-changing-banks-from-the-inside

Chatterjee, P., Da, D., & Rawat, D. B. (2024). Digital twin for credit card fraud detection: Opportunities, challenges, and fraud detection advancements. *Future Generation Computer Systems*, 158, 410–426. Advance online publication. DOI: 10.1016/j.future.2024.04.057

Chauhan, A. C., & Kularatne, I. (2021). REGAINING REPUTATION: AUCKLAND LUXURY HO S A STAKEHOLDERS' PERSPECTIVES. Rere Āwhio, 105.

Chen, A., Wang, C., & Zhang, X. (2023). Reflection on the equitable attribution of responsibility for artificial intelligence-assisted diagnosis and treatment decisions. *Intelligent Medicine*, 3(2), 139–143. Advance online publication. DOI: 10.1016/j.imed.2022.04.002

Chen, C. C., & Liao, C. C. (2021). Research on the development of Fintech combined with AIoT. *IEEE International Conference on Consumer Electronics-Taiwan (ICCE-TW)*1-2, DOI: 10.1109/ICCE-TW52618.2021.9602952

Cheng, R., Aggarwal, A., Chakraborty, A., Harish, V., McGowan, M., Roy, A., Szulewski, A., & Nolan, B. (2024). Implementation considerations for the adoption of artificial intelligence in the emergency department. *The American Journal of Emergency Medicine*, 82, 75–81. DOI: 10.1016/j.ajem.2024.05.020 PMID: 38820809

Chen, L. Y., & Nguyen, K. E. (2024). Challenges in measuring the returns to education: Human capital theory revisited. *The Journal of Human Resources*. Advance online publication. DOI: 10.3386/jhr.2024.0002

Chen, M. (2021). The impact of international students on U.S. colleges: Higher education as a service export. *SSRN*, 3859798, •••. https://papers.ssrn.com/sol3/papers.cfm?abstract_id=3859798

Chen, M., Howell, J., & Smith, J. (2023). Best and brightest? The impact of student visa restrictiveness on who attends college in the U.S. *Labour Economics*, 84, 102385. DOI: 10.1016/j.labeco.2023.102385

Chen, Y., So, W. W., Zhu, J., & Chiu, S. W. (2024). STEM learning opportunities and career aspirations: The interactive effect of students' self-concept and perceptions of STEM professionals. *International Journal of STEM Education*, 11(1), 1–21. DOI: 10.1186/s40594-024-00466-7

Chertoff, M. (2023, April 13). *Cyber risk is growing. here's how companies can keep up.* Harvard Business Review. https://hbr.org/2023/04/cyber-risk-is-growing-heres-how-companies-can-keep-up

Chi, Y.-L., & Bump, J. B. (2018). Resource allocation processes at multilateral organizations working in global health. *Health Policy and Planning*, 33(suppl_1), i4–i13. DOI: 10.1093/heapol/czx140 PMID: 29415239

Choi, S., Johnson, M., & Lehmann, C. (2019). Data breach remediation efforts and their implications for hospital quality. *Health Services Research*, 54(5), 971–980. DOI: 10.1111/1475-6773.13203 PMID: 31506956

Choi, T. M., Lo, C. K. Y., & Chan, H. K. (2018). Industry 4.0: A Bibliometric Analysis and Research Agenda. *International Journal of Production Research*, 56(1-2), 442–472. DOI: 10.1080/00207543.2017.1380226

Choi, T.-M., Liu, S., & Hsu, C.-H. C. (2021). Retail supply chain management with IoT and blockchain technology. *Journal of Retailing and Consumer Services*, 62, 102654. DOI: 10.1016/j.jretconser.2021.102654

Cho, M. K. (2021). Rising to the challenge of bias in health care AI. *Nature Medicine*, 27(12), 2079–2081. DOI: 10.1038/s41591-021-01577-2 PMID: 34893774

Chong, J., Jason, T., Jones, M., & Larsen, D. (2020). A model to measure self-assessed proficiency in electronic medical records: Validation using maturity survey data from Canadian community-based physicians. *International Journal of Medical Informatics*, 141, 104218. DOI: 10.1016/j.ijmedinf.2020.104218 PMID: 32574925

Choudhury, A. (2020). Four Barriers to Entry in the Pharmaceutical Manufacturing Industry | Infiniti's Experts Provide Unparalleled Market Entry Insights for Pharma Companies. In *Business Wire*. Business Wire.

Christensen, C. M. (2016). *The innovator's dilemma : when new technologies cause significant firms to fail* [Third edition?]. Harvard Business Review Press.

Christensen, C. M., Horn, M. B., & Johnson, C. W. (2008). *Disrupting class : how disruptive innovation will change the way the world learns*. McGraw-Hill.

Christodoulou, I., & Langley, P. A. (2020). A gaming simulation approach to understanding blue ocean strategy development as a transition from traditional competitive strategy. *Journal of Strategic Marketing*, 28(8), 727–752. DOI: 10.1080/0965254X.2019.1597916

Chua, J. (2020). Cybersecurity in the healthcare industry. *American Association for Physician Leadership, October 7, 2020*. https://www.physicianleaders.org/articles/cybersecurity-in-the-healthcare-industry

Chua, J. (2021). Cybersecurity in the healthcare industry: A collaborative approach. *American Association for Physician Leadership, January 8, 2021*.https://www.physicianleaders.org/articles/cybersecurity-healthcare-industry-collaborative-approach

Chung, Y. Y., Annaswamy, T. M., & Prabhakaran, B. (2023, June). Performance and user experience studies of HILLES: Home-based immersive lower limb exergame system. In *Proceedings of the 14th Conference on ACM Multimedia Systems* (pp. 62-73). DOI: DOI: 10.1145/3587819.3590985

Ciancio, N. (2007). The seven pillars of an effective ethics and compliance program. *Compliance Today, Health Care Compliance Association, 2007*(July). https://assets.hcca-info.org/Portals/0/PDFs/Resources/Compliance%20Today/0707/ct0707_42_Ciancio.pdf

Cimini, C., Lagorio, A., & Cavalieri, S. (2024). Development and application of a maturity model for industrial agile working. *Computers & Industrial Engineering*, 188, 109877. DOI: 10.1016/j.cie.2023.109877

Cirillo, D., Catuara-Solarz, S., Morey, C., Guney, E., Subirats, L., Mellino, S., Gigante, A., Valencia, A., Rementeria, M. J., Chadha, A. S., & Mavridis, N. (2020). Sex and gender differences and biases in artificial intelligence for biomedicine and healthcare. *NPJ Digital Medicine*, 3(1), 81. Advance online publication. DOI: 10.1038/s41746-020-0288-5 PMID: 32529043

Clancy, J. J. (1999). *The invisible powers: The language of business*. Lexington Books.

Clark, J. (2024, April 3). DOD cyber officials detail progress on Zero Trust framework roadmap. *U. S. Department of Defense.* https://www.defense.gov/News/News-Stories/Article/Article/3729448/dod-cyber-officials-detail-progress-on-zero-trust-framework-roadmap/

Clark, A., Stenholm, S., Pentti, J., Salo, P., Lange, T., Török, E., Xu, T., Fabricius, J., Oksanen, T., Kivimäki, M., Vahtera, J., & Hulvej Rod, N. (2021). Workplace discrimination as risk factor for long-term sickness absence: Longitudinal analyses of onset and changes in workplace adversity. *PLoS One*, 16(8), e0255697. DOI: 10.1371/journal.pone.0255697 PMID: 34351965

Clark, G., Marsden, R., Whyatt, J. D., Thompson, L., & Walker, M. (2015). 'It's everything else you do...': Alumni views on extracurricular activities and employability. *Active Learning in Higher Education*, 16(2), 133–147. DOI: 10.1177/1469787415574050

Cleavenger, D. J., & Munyon, T. P. (2013). It's how you frame it: Transformational leadership and the meaning of work. *Business Horizons*, 56(3), 351–360. DOI: 10.1016/j.bushor.2013.01.002

Clemens, J., & Wither, M. (2019). The minimum wage and the Great Recession: Evidence of effects on the employment and income trajectories of low-skilled workers. *Journal of Public Economics*, 170, 53–67. DOI: 10.1016/j.jpubeco.2019.01.004

Cleven, A., Mettler, T., Rohner, P., & Winter, R. (2016). Healthcare quality innovation and performance through process orientation: Evidence from general hospitals in Switzerland. *Technological Forecasting and Social Change,* 113(Part B), 386-395. .DOI: 10.1016/j.techfore.2016.07.007

Cleven, A., Winter, R., Wortmann, F., & Mettler, T. (2014). Process management in hospitals: An empirically grounded maturity model. *Business Research*, 7(2), 191–216. DOI: 10.1007/s40685-014-0012-x

CMMI Product Team. (2010). CMMI for Development, Version 1.3. Software Engineering Institute, Carnegie Mellon University. Retrieved from https://resources.sei.cmu.edu/library/asset-view.cfm?AssetID=9661

Cob-Parro, A. C., Lalangui, Y., & Lazcano, R. (2024). fostering agricultural transformation through AI: An open-source AI architecture exploiting the MLOps paradigm. *Agronomy (Basel)*, 14(2), 259. DOI: 10.3390/agronomy14020259

Collier, Z. A., & Sarkis, J. (2021). The zero trust supply chain: Managing supply chain risk in the absence of trust. *International Journal of Production Research*, 59(11), 3430–3445. DOI: 10.1080/00207543.2021.1884311

Coopwood, K.Sr, & Augustine, S. S. (2018). Engaging faculty in campus transformation: The diversity fellows program. In *Campus Diversity Triumphs: Valleys of Hope* (pp. 27–43). Emerald Publishing Limited. DOI: 10.1108/S1479-364420180000020002

Cornelissen, J. P., Lock, A. R., and Kafouros, M. (2005). Organizational metaphors: The process by which organizational scholars create and choose organizational metaphors. 1545–1578 in *Human Relation*, 58(12).

Cornelissen, J. P. (2004). What are we playing at? Theatre, organization, and the use of metaphor. *Organization Studies*, 25(5), 705–726. DOI: 10.1177/0170840604042411

Cornelissen, J. P., & Kafouros, M. (2008). Metaphors and theory building in organization theory: What determines the impact of a metaphor on theory? *British Journal of Management*, 19(4), 365–379. DOI: 10.1111/j.1467-8551.2007.00550.x

Cornelissen, J. P., Kafouros, M., & Lock, A. R. (2005). Metaphorical images of organization: How organizational researchers develop and select organizational metaphors. *Human Relations*, 58(12), 1545–1578. DOI: 10.1177/0018726705061317

Cornelissen, J. P., Oswick, C., Thøger Christensen, L., & Phillips, N. (2008). Metaphor in organizational research: Context, modalities and implications for research—Introduction. *Organization Studies*, 29(1), 7–22. DOI: 10.1177/0170840607086634

Correani, A., De Massis, A., Frattini, F., Petruzzelli, A. M., & Natalicchio, A. (2020). Implementing a Digital Strategy: Learning from the Experience of Three Digital Transformation Projects. *California Management Review*, 62(4), 37–56. DOI: 10.1177/0008125620934864

Correia e Silva, L. (2019). *O impacto da aplicação de modelos de maturidade nas áreas clínicas do Sistema Nacional de Saúde. Integrated master's in biomedical engineering*. Minho University.

Crawford, A., & Serhal, E. (2020). Digital health equity and COVID-19: The innovation curve cannot reinforce the social gradient of health. *Journal of Medical Internet Research*, 22(6), e19361. DOI: 10.2196/19361 PMID: 32452816

Crawford, K. (2021). *Atlas of AI: Power, politics, and the planetary costs of artificial intelligence*. Yale University Press.

Crawford, K., & Schultz, J. (2014). Big data and due process: Toward a framework to redress predictive privacy harms. *Boston College Law Review. Boston College. Law School*, 55(1), 93–128.

Crawford, K., & Schultz, J. (2019). AI systems as state actors. *Columbia Law Review*, 119(7), 1941–1972.

Crenshaw, K. W. (2013). Mapping the margins: Intersectionality, identity politics, and violence against women of color. In *The public nature of private violence* (pp. 93–118). Routledge.

Creswell, J. W., & Poth, C. N. (2018). *Qualitative inquiry and research design: Choosing among five approaches*. Sage Publications.

Crucial Steps in Addressing the Impact of Natural Disasters. IGI Global. DOI: 10.4018/979-8-3693-4288-6

Cuadros-Solas, P. J., Cubillas, E., & Salvador, C. (2023). Does alternative digital lending affect bank performance? Cross-country and bank-level evidence. *International Review of Financial Analysis*, 90, 102873. DOI: 10.1016/j.irfa.2023.102873

Cui, Y., He, Y., Xu, X., Zhou, L., Nutakor, J. A., & Zhao, L. (2024). Cultural capital, the digital divide, and the health of older adults: A moderated mediation effect test. *BMC Public Health*, 24(1), 302. DOI: 10.1186/s12889-024-17831-4 PMID: 38273305

Cummings, S. (1993). Brief case: The first strategists. *Long Range Planning*, 26(3), 133–135. DOI: 10.1016/0024-6301(93)90015-8

Curtis, B., & Alden, J. (2007). The Business Process Maturity Model (BPMM): What, Why and How. BPTRends, www.bptrends.com/publicationfiles/02-07-COLBPMMWhatWhyHow-CurtisAlden-Final.pdf

Curuksu, J. D., & Curuksu, J. D. (2018). Principles of Strategy: Primer. *Data Driven: An Introduction to Management Consulting in the 21st Century*, 129-152.

Daah, C., Qureshi, A., Awan, I., & Konur, S. (2024). Enhancing Zero Trust models in the financial industry through blockchain integration: A proposed framework. *Electronics (Basel)*, 13(5), 865. DOI: 10.3390/electronics13050865

Dai, X., & Qiu, Y. (2019, September 11). Minimum wage hikes and technology adoption: evidence from U.S. establishments. *Journal of Financial and Quantitative Analysis (JFQA)*. Available at *SSRN*: https://ssrn.com/abstract=3451663 or DOI: 10.2139/ssrn.3451663

Danks, D. (2022). Digital Ethics as Translational Ethics. In Vasiliu-Feltes, I., & Thomason, J. (Eds.), *Applied Ethics in a Digital World* (pp. 1–15). IGI Global., DOI: 10.4018/978-1-7998-8467-5.ch001

Daraghmeh, R., & Brown, R. (2021). A Big Data Maturity Model for Electronic Health Records in Hospitals. In proceedings of *2021 International Conference on Information Technology* (ICIT) July 14-15, 2021, Amman, Jordan. DOI: 10.1109/ICIT52682.2021.9491781

Das, S., Wang, B., Kim, A., & Camp, L. J. (2020, January). MFA is a necessary chore!: Exploring user mental models of multi-factor authentication technologies. *In Proceedings of the 53rd Hawaii International Conference on System Sciences (HICSS),* (pp. 1-10).: https://hdl.handle.net/10125/64411

Das, K., & Mitra, A. (2018). Integrating sustainability in the Design and Planning of Supply Chains. Operations and Supply Chain Management. *International Journal (Toronto, Ont.)*, 11(4), 161–185.

Dastin, J. (2018). *Amazon scrapped secret AI recruiting tool that showed bias against women.* Reuters. Retrieved from https://www.reuters.com/article/us-amazon-com-jobs-automation-insight-idUSKCN1MK08G

Davids, N., & Waghid, Y. (2019). *Universities, pedagogical encounters, openness, and free speech: Reconfiguring democratic education.* Rowman & Littlefield.

Davis, J. (2016). Millions of patient records reportedly for sale on the dark web after ransom demand. *HealthCare IT News.* https://www.healthcareitnews.com/news/millions-patient-records-reportedly-sale-dark-web-after-ransom-demand

Davis, A. J. (2017). *Policing the black man: Arrest, prosecution, and imprisonment* (1st ed.). Pantheon.

Davis, F. D., & Granić, A. (2024). Epilogue: What will the future of TAM be like? In *The Technology Acceptance Model: 30 Years of TAM* (pp. 103–108). Cham Springer International Publishing., DOI: 10.1007/978-3-030-45274-2_4

Davis, F. D., Granić, A., & Marangunić, N. (2024b). *The technology acceptance model: 30 years of TAM.* Springer International Publishing AG., DOI: 10.1007/978-3-030-45274-2

de Almeida, P. G. R., dos Santos, C. D., & Farias, J. S. (2021). Artificial Intelligence Regulation: A framework for governance. *Ethics and Information Technology*, 23(3), 505–525. DOI: 10.1007/s10676-021-09593-z

De Angelis, R., Howard, M., & Miemczyk, J. (2018). Supply chain management and the circular economy: Towards the circular supply chain. *Production Planning and Control*, 29(6), 425–437. DOI: 10.1080/09537287.2018.1449244 de Jager, P. (2002). Ethics: good, evil, and moral duty. *The Information Management Journal, September/October 2002*, 82-85.

De Vass, T., Shee, H., & Miah, S. J. (2021). The effect of "Internet of Things" on supply chain integration and performance: An organisational capability perspective. *AJIS. Australasian Journal of Information Systems*, •••, 25.

de Vries, T. A., van der Vegt, G. S., Scholten, K., & van Donk, D. P. (2022). Heeding supply chain disruption warnings: When and how do cross-functional teams ensure firm robustness? *The Journal of Supply Chain Management*, 58(1), 31–50. DOI: 10.1111/jscm.12262

De Weerdt, D., De Schepper, A., Kyndt, E., & Gijbel, D. (2024). Entering the Labor Market: Networks and Networking Behavior in the School-to-Work Transition. *Vocations and Learning*, 17(2), 311–332. DOI: 10.1007/s12186-024-09343-4

Decker, A., & Galer, D. (2013). *Enterprise Risk Management - Straight to the Point: An Implementation Guide Function by Function*. ERMSTTP, LLC.

Del Sol, P., & Ghemawat, P. (1999). Strategic valuation of investment under competition. *Interfaces*, 29(6), 42–56. DOI: 10.1287/inte.29.6.42

Den Hollander, M. C., Bakker, C. A., & Hultink, E. J. (2017). Product design in a circular economy: Development of a typology of key concepts and terms. *Journal of Industrial Ecology*, 21(3), 517–525. DOI: 10.1111/jiec.12610

Denneen, J., & Dretler, T. (2012). The financially sustainable university. *Bain & Company, 12*.

Derave, T., Sales, T. P., Gailly, F., & Poels, G. (2022). Sharing platform ontology development: Proof-of-concept. *Sustainability (Basel)*, 14(4), 2076. DOI: 10.3390/su14042076

Derecho, K.C., Cafino, R., Aquino-Cafino, S.L., Isla, A. Jr., Esencia, J.A., Lactuan, N.J., Maranda, J.A.G., Velasco, L.C.P. (2024). Technology adoption of electronic medical records in developing economies: A systematic review on physicians' perspective. *Digital Health*, 12, 10, 20552076231224605. .DOI: 10.1177/20552076231224605

Devisakti, A., Muftahu, M., & Xiaoling, H. (2024). Digital divide among B40 students in Malaysian higher education institutions. *Education and Information Technologies*, 29(2), 1857–1883. DOI: 10.1007/s10639-023-11847-w PMID: 37361786

Dewar, C. (2023). Leading with authenticity: A conversation with Bill George. *McKinsey & Company*. https://www.mckinsey.com/capabilities/strategy-and-corporate-finance/our-insights/leading-with-authenticity-a-conversation-with-bill-george

Dhar, S., & Agarwal, S. (2023). Disputes at Work and the Perceived Effects of Social Assistance on Worker Health. *Journal for ReAttach Therapy and Developmental Diversities*, 6(9s), 455–463.

Dhiman, P., Saini, N., Gulzar, Y., Turaev, S., Kaur, A., Nisa, K. U., & Hamid, Y. (2024). A review and comparative analysis of relevant approaches of zero trust network model. *Sensors (Basel)*, 24(4), 1328. DOI: 10.3390/s24041328 PMID: 38400486

Di Iorio, V., Testa, F., Korschun, D., Iraldo, F., & Iovino, R. (2023). Curious about the circular economy? Internal and external influences on information search about the product lifecycle. *Business Strategy and the Environment*, 32(4), 2193–2208. DOI: 10.1002/bse.3243

Di Maio, F., Rem, P. C., Baldé, K., & Polder, M. (2017). Measuring resource efficiency and circular economy: A market value approach. *Resources, Conservation and Recycling*, 122, 163–171. https://doi.org/https://doi.org/10.1016/j.resconrec.2017.02.009. DOI: 10.1016/j.resconrec.2017.02.009

Di Nocera, F., Tempestini, G., & Orsini, M. (2023). Usable Security: A Systematic Literature Review. *Information (Basel)*, 14(12), 641. DOI: 10.3390/info14120641

Dickson, E. B., & Whitehurst, R. (2016). Integrated project planning in a construction management environment: The College of DuPage's Naperville, Illinois, satellite campus. *Planning for Higher Education*, 45(1), 160.

Diener, F., & Špaček, M. (2021). Digital Transformation in Banking: A Managerial Perspective on Barriers to Change. *Sustainability (Basel)*, 13(4), 2032. DOI: 10.3390/su13042032

DiMaggio, P. J., & Powell, W. W. (1983). The iron cage revisited: Institutional isomorphism and collective rationality in organizational fields. *American Sociological Review*, 48(2), 147–160. DOI: 10.2307/2095101

Din, I. U., & Khan, K. K. H., Almogren, A., Zareei, M., & Pérez Díaz, J. A. (2024). Securing the metaverse: A Blockchain-enabled zero-trust architecture for virtual environments. *In IEEE Access*, 12, pp. 92337-92347. DOI: 10.1109/ACCESS.2024.3423400

Dnistran, I. (2023). Tesla Now Has An Almost 60-Percent Share Of The EV Market In The US. https://insideevs.com/news/686440/tesla-60-percent-ev-market-share-new-registrations-2024/. Accessed on May 22, 2024

Doan, T. (2022). Value Creation and Value Capture: Analysis of Apple Company. *International Journal of Current Science Research and Review*. .DOI: 10.47191/ijcsrr/V5-i4-30

Dobbs, M. E. (2014). Guidelines for applying porter's five forces framework: A set of industry analysis templates. *Competitiveness Review*, 24(1), 32–45. DOI: 10.1108/CR-06-2013-0059

Doherty, T., & Carroll, A. (2020). Believing in Overcoming Cognitive Biases.. *AMA journal of ethics*, 22 9, E773-778 . . Rajasekar, J. (N.D.). Porter's 5 Forces-A strategic planning model.DOI: 10.1001/amajethics.2020.773

Domenech, T., & Stegemann, J. A. (2021). *The Circular Economy: Concept, Tools and Implementation*. Royal Society of Chemistry., DOI: 10.1039/9781788016209-00027

Domlyn, A. M., Scaccia, J., Lewis, N., Coleman, S., Parry, G., Saha, S., Wandersmanm, A., & Ramaswamy, R. (2021). The community transformation map: A maturity tool for planning change in community health improvement for equity and well-being. *The American Journal of Orthopsychiatry*, 91(3), 322–331. DOI: 10.1037/ort0000526 PMID: 34138626

Donaldson, L. (2001). *The Contingency Theory of Organizations*. Sage Publications. DOI: 10.4135/9781452229249

Dongrey, R., & Rokade, V. (2021). Assessing the effect of perceived diversity practices and psychological safety on contextual performance for sustainable workplace. *Sustainability (Basel)*, 13(21), 11653. DOI: 10.3390/su132111653

Douglas, S., & Haley, G. (2023). Connecting organizational learning strategies to organizational resilience. *Development and Learning in Organizations*, 38(1), 12–15. DOI: 10.1108/DLO-01-2023-0018

Drabiak, K. (2022). Leveraging law and ethics to promote safe and reliable AI/ML in healthcare. *Frontiers in Nuclear Medicine*, 2, 983340. Advance online publication. DOI: 10.3389/fnume.2022.983340 PMID: 39354991

Dryzek, J. S. (2005). *The Politics of Earth*. Oxford University Press.

Dunbrack, L., & Hand, L. (2013). A maturity model for Mobile in healthcare. IDC health insights: Business strategy, doc # HI241777.

Duncan, R., Eden, R., Woods, L., Wong, I., & Sullivan, C. (2022). Synthesizing Dimensions of Digital Maturity in Hospitals: Systematic Review. *Journal of Medical Internet Research*, 24(3), e32994. DOI: 10.2196/32994 PMID: 35353050

Dunn, C. P., and Burton. B. K. 2005. Social concerns and the compassionate approach in management education. 29(3), 453–474, Journal of Management Education.

Du, X., & Li, B. (2021). Analysis of Tesla's Marketing Strategy in China. *Proceedings of the 2021 3rd International Conference on Economic Management and Cultural Industry (ICEMCI 2021)*. DOI: 10.2991/assehr.k.211209.270

Dvorak, J., & Razova, I. (2018). Empirical Validation of Blue Ocean Strategy Sustainability in an International Environment. *Foundations of Management*, 10(1), 143–162. DOI: 10.2478/fman-2018-0012

Dyer, J. H., & Singh, H. (1998). The Relational View: Cooperative Strategy and Sources of Interorganizational Competitive Advantage. *Academy of Management Review*, 23(4), 660–679. DOI: 10.2307/259056

Dyke, G. (2022, October 2). What is the background in a research paper? *AJE Scholar Articles*. https://www.aje.com/arc/what-is-the-background-in-a-research-paper/

Ecer, F. (2021). A consolidated MCDM framework for performance assessment of battery electric vehicles based on ranking strategies. *Renewable & Sustainable Energy Reviews*, 143, 110916. Advance online publication. DOI: 10.1016/j.rser.2021.110916

Ed-Dafali, S., Al-Azad, M. S., Mohiuddin, M., & Reza, M. N. H. (2023). Strategic orientations, organizational ambidexterity, and sustainable competitive advantage: Mediating role of industry 4.0 readiness in emerging markets. *Journal of Cleaner Production*, 401, 136765. DOI: 10.1016/j.jclepro.2023.136765

Eden, C.A., Chisom, O.N., & Adeniyi, I.S. (2024). Promoting digital literacy and social equity in education: Lessons from successful initiatives. *International Journal of Management & Entrepreneurship Research*. DOI:DOI: 10.51594/ijmer.v6i3.880

Einarsen, S. V., Hoel, H., Zapf, D., & Cooper, C. L. (2020). *Bullying and harassment in the workplace: Theory, research and practice*. CRC press. DOI: 10.1201/9780429462528

Eisler, M. (2016). A Tesla in every garage? *IEEE Spectrum*, 53(2), 34–55. DOI: 10.1109/MSPEC.2016.7419798

EL YAZIDI, R. (2023). Strategies for promoting critical thinking in the classroom. *International Journal of English Literature and Social Sciences (IJELS)*, 26.

Elizabeth, H. (2022). Risks and Safety of Women Healthcare Workers in Aizawl District, Mizoram, India. *International Journal of Occupational Safety and Health*, 12(2), 111–116. DOI: 10.3126/ijosh.v12i2.39794

Elkington, J. (1998). *Cannibals with forks: The triple bottom line of 21st century business*. Capstone.

Ellen MacArthur Foundation. (2013). Towards the Circular Economy Vol. 1: an economic and business rationale for an accelerated transition.

Ellen MacArthur Foundation. (2013). Towards the Circular Economy: Economic and Business Rationale for an Accelerated Transition. Retrieved from https://www.ellenmacarthurfoundation.org/assets/downloads/TCE_Ellen-MacArthur-Foundation_9-Dec-2015.pdf

Ellen MacArthur Foundation. (2021). *Financing the Circular economy.* Retrieved from https://www.ellenmacarthurfoundation.org/topics/finance/overview

Employment & Training Administration [ETA]. (n.d.). WIOA adult and dislocated worker program. *U. S. Department of Labor.* https://www.dol.gov/agencies/eta/workforce-investment/adult

Epizitone, A., Moyane, S. P., & Agbehadji, I. E. (2023). A Systematic Literature Review of Health Information Systems for Healthcare. *Health Care*, 11(7), 959. DOI: 10.3390/healthcare11070959 PMID: 37046884

Epstein, M. J., & McFarlan, F. W. (2011). Measuring the efficiency and effectiveness of a nonprofit's performance. *Strategic Finance*, 93(4), 27.

Eriksen, H. K., Dickinson, C., Lawrence, C. R., Baccigalupi, C., Banday, A. J., Górski, K. M., Hansen, F. K., Lilje, P. B., Pierpaoli, E., Seiffert, M. D., Smith, K. M., & Vanderlinde, K. (2006). Cosmic microwave background component separation by parameter estimation. *The Astrophysical Journal*, 641(2), 665–682. DOI: 10.1086/500499

Etin, D. (2014). Quality of care with IDC & HIMSS models - Where are eHealth projects going in EMEA? Retrieved Sep 2015, fromEMC Sparkhttp://sparkblog.emc.com/2014/05/quality-care-idc-himss-models-ehealth-projects-going-emea/

Eubanks, V. (2018). *Automating inequality: How high-tech tools profile, police, and punish the poor.* St. Martin's Press.

Evenseth, L. L., Sydnes, M., & Gausdal, A. H. (2022). Building organizational resilience through organizational learning: A systematic review. *Frontiers in Communication*, 7, 837386. Advance online publication. DOI: 10.3389/fcomm.2022.837386

Executive Order 1368- Improving the Security of Consumer Financial Transactions1 (2014, October 14). *Author.*

F.A, B. (. (2022). Blue Ocean strategy: Economic importance of applying in tourism. *International Journal of Multicultural and Multireligious Understanding*, 9(12), 1. DOI: 10.18415/ijmmu.v9i12.4294

Faliagka, E., Christopoulou, E., Ringas, D., Politi, T., Kostis, N., Leonardos, D., Tranoris, C., Antonopoulos, C. P., Denazis, S., & Voros, N. (2024). Trends in digital twin framework architectures for smart cities: A case study in smart mobility. *Sensors (Basel)*, 24(5), 1665. DOI: 10.3390/s24051665 PMID: 38475201

Familoni, B.Babajide Tolulope Familoni. (2024). Cybersecurity challenges in the age of AI: Theoretical approaches and practical solutions. *Computer Science & IT Research Journal*, 5(3), 703–724. DOI: 10.51594/csitrj.v5i3.930

Fang, X., Che, S., Mao, M., Zhang, H., Zhao, M., & Zhao, X. (2024). Bias of AI-generated content: An examination of news produced by large language models. *Scientific Reports*, 14(1), 5224. DOI: 10.1038/s41598-024-55686-2 PMID: 38433238

Farjoun, M. (2017). Contradictions, dialectics, and paradoxes. The Sage handbook of process organization studies, 87-109.

Fatmala, I., & Setiawan, H. (2022). *Analysis of Willingness to Pay Premium Apple Product Users in Indonesia. Jurnal Riset Ekonomi Manajemen*. REKOMEN., DOI: 10.31002/rn.v5i2.4193

Faunce, T. (2015). AUSTRALIAN COMPETITION AND CONSUMER COMMISSION v PFIZER: EVERGREENING AND MARKET POWER AS A BLOCKBUSTER DRUG GOES OFF PATENT. *Journal of Law and Medicine*, 22(4), 771–787. PMID: 26349378

Fawaz, M., & Le Quellec, E. (2024). Indirect rivalries and civil wars: Empirical evidence. *Defence and Peace Economics*, 35(1), 44–71. DOI: 10.1080/10242694.2022.2129350

Federal Communications Commission. (2020, October 29 – November 25). Auction 904: Rural digital opportunity fund. https://www.fcc.gov/auction/904

Federal Communications Commission. (2024, May). lifeline program for low-income consumers. https://www.fcc.gov/general/lifeline-program-low-income-consumers

Federal Deposit Insurance Corporation. (2020). The importance of community banks in paycheck protection program lending. *FDIC.gov*https://www.fdic.gov/analysis/quarterly-

Federal Register. (2014, October 23). Improving the security of consumer financial transactions. *National Archives and Records Administration.*https://www.federalregister.gov/documents/2014/10/23/2014-25439/improving-the-security-of-consumer-financial-transactions

Federal Trade Commission [FTC] (2021). FTC strengthens security safeguards for consumer financial information following widespread data breaches. *Author*. https://www.ftc.gov/news-events/news/press-releases/2021/10/ftc-strengthens-security-safeguards-consumer-financial-information-following-widespread-data

Fedotov, P. (2022). Critical analysis of the electric vehicle industry. Exchanges. *The Interdisciplinary Research Journal*, 10(1), 43–56. DOI: 10.31273/eirj.v10i1.362

Felch, V., & Asdecker, B. (2020). How to make business process maturity models better drawing on design science research. PACIS 2020 Proceedings, 50. https://aisel.aisnet.org/pacis2020/50

Feldstein, S. (2021). *The rise of digital repression: How technology is reshaping power, politics, and resistance*. Oxford University Press. DOI: 10.1093/oso/9780190057497.001.0001

Feng, S., Li, Y., & Zhang, S. (2022). Skills for the circular economy: Challenges and opportunities. *Journal of Cleaner Production*, 332, 129877. DOI: 10.1016/j.jclepro.2021.129877

Ferdinansyah, A., & Purwandari, B. (2021). Challenges in Combining Agile Development and CMMI: A Systematic Literature Review. In Proceedings of ICSCA '21-10th International Conference on Software and Computer Applications Pages, 63 – 69. https://doi.org/DOI: 10.1145/3457784.3457803

Ferede, W. L., Endawoke, Y., & Tessema, G. (2024). Change management through strategic leadership: The mediating effect of knowledge management in public organizations, Ethiopia. *Future Business Journal*, 10(1), 93. DOI: 10.1186/s43093-024-00363-z

Ferguson, A. G. (2020). *The rise of big data policing: Surveillance, race, and the future of law enforcement*. NYU Press. DOI: 10.18574/nyu/9781479854608.001.0001

Ferguson, A. G. (2021). *Surveillance and the tyrant test*. Heinonline.

Ferguson, S. N. (2021). Effects of faculty and staff connectedness on student self-efficacy. *The Journal of Scholarship of Teaching and Learning*, 21(2). Advance online publication. DOI: 10.14434/josotl.v21i2.28597

Fernández, M. E., Ruiter, R. A. C., Markham, C., & Kok, G. (2019). Intervention mapping: theory- and evidence-based health promotion program planning: perspective and examples. *Frontiers in Public Health*, 7, 209. Advance online publication. DOI: 10.3389/fpubh.2019.00209 PMID: 31475126

Fernando, K., Menon, S., Jansen, K. U., Naik, P. S., Nucci, G., Roberts, J., Wu, S. S., & Dolsten, M. (2022). Achieving end-to-end success in the clinic: Pfizer's learnings on R&D productivity. *Drug Discovery Today*, 27(3), 697–704. DOI: 10.1016/j.drudis.2021.12.010 PMID: 34922020

Fernando, Y., Jabbour, C. J. C., & Wah, W. X. (2022). Exploring the role of digitalization on circular economy practices: A systematic literature review. *Sustainable Production and Consumption*, 32, 207–222.

Fernando, Y., Tseng, M. L., Aziz, N., Ikhsan, R. B., & Wahyuni-TD, I. S. (2022). Waste-to-energy supply chain management on circular economy capability: An empirical study. *Sustainable Production and Consumption*, 31, 26–38. DOI: 10.1016/j.spc.2022.01.032

Ferreira, J., Coelho, A., & Moutinho, L. (2020). Strategic alliances, exploration and exploitation and their impact on innovation and new product development: The effect of knowledge sharing. *Management Decision*, 59(3), 524–567. DOI: 10.1108/MD-09-2019-1239

Filho, W., Trevisan, L., Eustachio, J., Rampasso, I., Anholon, R., Platje, J., Will, M., Doni, F., Mazhar, M., Borsatto, J., & Marcolin, C. (2023). Assessing ethics and sustainability standards in corporate practices. *Social Responsibility Journal*. Advance online publication. DOI: 10.1108/SRJ-03-2023-0116

Fischer, C. S., & Hout, M. (2006). *Century of difference: How America changed in the last one hundred years*. Russell Sage Foundation.

Floridi, L. (2013). *The ethics of information*. Oxford University Press. DOI: 10.1093/acprof:oso/9780199641321.001.0001

Floridi, L., Cowls, J., Beltrametti, M., Chatila, R., Chazerand, P., Dignum, V., & Schafer, B. (2018). AI4People—An ethical framework for a good AI society: Opportunities, risks, principles, and recommendations. *Minds and Machines*, 28(4), 689–707. DOI: 10.1007/s11023-018-9482-5 PMID: 30930541

Flott, K., Callahan, R., Darzi, A., & Mayer, E. (2016). A Patient-Centered Framework for Evaluating Digital Maturity of Health Services: A Systematic Review. *Journal of Medical Internet Research*, 18(4), e75. DOI: 10.2196/jmir.5047 PMID: 27080852

Foldy, E. (2004). Learning from Diversity: A Theoretical Exploration. *Public Administration Review*, 64(5), 529–538. DOI: 10.1111/j.1540-6210.2004.00401.x

Food and Drug Administration. (2022, November 9). *Medical Product Safety Information*. https://www.fda.gov/safety/medwatch-fda-safety-information-and-adverse-event-reporting-program/medical-product-safety-information

Food and Drug Administration. (2024, July 25). *MedWatch: The FDA Safety Information and Adverse Event Reporting Program.* https://www.fda.gov/safety/medwatch-fda-safety-information-and-adverse-event-reporting-program

Forbes India. (2023, December 13). *Women occupy only 18 percent of healthcare leadership positions, earn 34 percent less than men: Dasra report.* Retrieved October 22, 2024, from https://www.forbesindia.com/article/news/women-occupy-only-18-percent-of-healthcare-leadership-positions-earn-34-percent-less-than-men-dasra-report/90313/1

Franky, F., & Syah, T. (2023). *The Effect of Customer Experience, Customer Satisfaction, and Customer Loyalty on Brand Power and Willingness to Pay a Price Premium.* Quantitative Economics and Management Studies., DOI: 10.35877/454RI.qems1639

Fraser, P., Moultrie, J., & Gregory, M. (2002). The use of maturity models/grids as a tool in assessing product development capability, in: *IEEE International Engineering Management Conference. IEEE,* 244–249. DOI: 10.1109/IEMC.2002.1038431

Freeman, R. E. (1984). *Strategic management: A stakeholder approach.* Pitman.

Frei, F., & Morriss, A. (2020). Begin with trust. *Harvard Business Review,* 98(3), 112–121.

Friedrich, K., Patel, M., & Stewart, K. (2022). Engaging consumers in the circular economy: Strategies and outcomes. *Journal of Cleaner Production,* 350, 131650. DOI: 10.1016/j.jclepro.2022.131650

Fu, W., & Chen, Y. (2022). The Impact of Pfizer-BioNTech COVID-19 Vaccine Development on the Companies Involved. In *2022 7th International Conference on Financial Innovation and Economic Development (ICFIED 2022)* (pp. 1271-1276). Atlantis Press. DOI: 10.2991/aebmr.k.220307.210

Fuchs, M. & others. (2022). Crisis communication and corporate social responsibility: A case study on IHG Hotels & Resorts and what organizations can learn from Covid-19 [PhD Thesis].

Fu, L., Zeng, Y., & Kang, X. (2024). Bridging the urban–rural gap: A qualitative examination of perceived access, barriers, risks and opportunities of children's digital learning during the COVID-19 pandemic. *Child & Family Social Work,* 29(1), 1–11. DOI: 10.1111/cfs.13045

Fuller, M. B. (2014). A history of financial aid to students. *Journal of Student Financial Aid,* 44(1), 4. DOI: 10.55504/0884-9153.1078

Fung, C., Tsui, B., & Hon, A. H. (2020). Crisis management: A case study of disease outbreak in the Metropark Hotel group. *Asia Pacific Journal of Tourism Research*, 25(10), 1062–1070. DOI: 10.1080/10941665.2020.1784245

Fuster, A., Goldsmith-Pinkham, P., Ramadorai, T., & Walther, A. (2018). 'Predictably Unequal? The Effects of Machine Learning on Credit Markets', https://haas.berkeley.edu/wp-content/uploads/Predictably-Unequal-The-Effects-of-Machine-Learning-on-Credit-Markets.pdf

Gallo, M. L. (2018). How are graduates and alumni featured in university strategic plans? Lessons from Ireland. *Perspectives: Policy and Practice in Higher Education*, 22(3), 92–97.

Galsanjigmed, E., & Sekiguchi, T. (2023). Challenges women experience in leadership careers: An integrative review. *Merits*, 3(2), 366–389. DOI: 10.3390/merits3020021

Gándara, P., & Ee, J. (2018). U.S. immigration enforcement policy and its impact on teaching and learning in the nation's schools. *Escholarship.org*, p. 1.

Gao, J., & Zhang, Y. (2023). *Assessing the Financial Stability & Investment Potential of Pfizer Inc*. Highlights in Business, Economics and Management., DOI: 10.54097/hbem.v15i.9223

Gao, L., Zhang, L., & Zhang, Y. (2022). Digital twin technology for circular economy: A review. *Journal of Cleaner Production*, 331, 129865. DOI: 10.1016/j.jclepro.2021.129865

García-Moreno, C., Hegarty, K., d'Oliveira, A. F. L., Koziol-McLain, J., Colombini, M., & Feder, G. (2015). The health-systems response to violence against women. *Lancet*, 385(9977), 1567–1579. DOI: 10.1016/S0140-6736(14)61837-7 PMID: 25467583

Garcia, R., Rathi, S., & Keirstead, J. (2015). Application of industrial ecology principles and tools to design a sustainable urban district in Curitiba, Brazil. *Journal of Cleaner Production*, 96, 387–393.

Gardner, T. A., Barlow, J., Chazdon, R., Ewers, R. M., Harvey, C. A., Peres, C. A., & Sodhi, N. S. (2019). A framework for integrating biodiversity concerns into national and global climate change mitigation strategies. *Nature Climate Change*, 2(1), 72–79.

Gardner, T. A., Benzie, M., Börner, J., Dawkins, E., Fick, S., Garrett, R., Godar, J., Grimard, A., Lake, S., Larsen, R. K., Mardas, N., McDermott, C. L., Meyfroidt, P., Osbeck, M., Persson, M., Sembres, T., Suavet, C., Strassburg, B., Trevisan, A., & Wolvekamp, P. (2019). Transparency and sustainability in global commodity supply chains. *World Development*, 121, 163–177. DOI: 10.1016/j.worlddev.2018.05.025 PMID: 31481824

Garets, D., & Davis, M. (2006). Electronic Medical Records vs. Electronic Health Records: Yes, There Is a Difference. White paper. HIMSS Analytics. Retrieved from https://www.aao.org/asset.axd?id=8e9b1f20-0ed6-4d2b-92f8-e28fbaf378ec

Garousi, V., Pfahl, D., Fernandes, J. M., Felderer, M., Mäntylä, M., Shepherd, D., Arcuri, A., Coşkunçay, A., & Tekinerdoğan, B. (2019). Characterizing industry-academia collaborations in software engineering: Evidence from 101 projects. *Empirical Software Engineering*, 24(4), 2540–2602. DOI: 10.1007/s10664-019-09711-y

Garvie, C., Bedoya, A. M., & Frankle, J. (2016). *The perpetual lineup: Unregulated police face recognition in America.* Georgetown Law, Center on Privacy & Technology. https://www.perpetuallineup.org/

Gasser, U., & Almeida, V. (2017). A layered model for AI governance. *IEEE Internet Computing*, 21(6), 58–62. DOI: 10.1109/MIC.2017.4180835

Gasser, U., & Schulz, W. (2015). *Governance of online intermediaries: Observations from a series of national case studies*. Berkman Klein Center Research Publication.

Geelan, D. R. (2015). Open forums for teaching in an open online world. *International Journal of Continuing Engineering Education and Lifelong Learning*, 25(1), 28–38. DOI: 10.1504/IJCEELL.2015.066545

Geiger-Brown, J., & Lipscomb, J. (2010). The health care work environment and adverse health and safety consequences for nurses. *Annual Review of Nursing Research*, 28(1), 191–231. DOI: 10.1891/0739-6686.28.191 PMID: 21639028

Geissdoerfer, M., Savaget, P., Bocken, N. M. P., & Hultink, E. J. (2017). The Circular Economy—A new sustainability paradigm? *Journal of Cleaner Production*, 143, 757–768. DOI: 10.1016/j.jclepro.2016.12.048

Gemmel, P., Vandaele, D., & Tambeur, W. (2008). Hospital Process Orientation (HPO): The development of a measurement tool. *Total Quality Management & Business Excellence*, 19(12), 1207–1217. DOI: 10.1080/14783360802351488

Gener, C. E. (2023). The Development of Academic Course Package for Digitalized Instruction in Educational Technology Management. *European Journal Of Innovation In Nonformal Education, 3*(7), 317–340. https://inovatus.es/index.php/ejine/article/view/1911

Genovese, A., Acquaye, A. A., Figueroa, A., & Koh, S. C. L. (2017). Sustainable supply chain management and the transition towards a circular economy: Evidence and some applications. *Omega*, 66, 344–357. DOI: 10.1016/j.omega.2015.05.015

George, B. (2010). *True north: Discover your authentic leadership* (Vol. 143). John Wiley & Sons.

Gershon, R. R., Karkashian, C. D., Grosch, J. W., Murphy, L. R., Escamilla-Cejudo, A., Flanagan, P. A., Bernacki, E., Kasting, C., & Martin, L. (2000). Hospital safety climate and its relationship with safe work practices and workplace exposure incidents. *American Journal of Infection Control*, 28(3), 211–221. DOI: 10.1067/mic.2000.105288 PMID: 10840340

Ghasabeh, M. S., Soosay, C., & Reaiche, C. (2015). The emerging role of transformational leadership. *Journal of Developing Areas*, 49(6), 459–467. DOI: 10.1353/jda.2015.0090

Ghemawat, P. (1991). *Commitment : the dynamic of strategy*. Free Press.

Ghodsi, M., Stehrer, R., & Barišić, A. (2024). Assessing the impact of new technologies on wages and labour income shares (No. 240). wiiw Working Paper.

Ghoshal, S. (2005). Bad management theories are destroying good management practices. *Academy of Management Learning & Education*, 4(1), 75–91. DOI: 10.5465/amle.2005.16132558

Giachetti, C. (2018). Explaining Apple's iPhone Success in the Mobile Phone Industry: The Creation of a New Market Space., 9-48. .DOI: 10.1007/978-3-319-67973-0_2

Gibbs, C., Achebe, N., Johnson, B., Nwaiche, C., & Ortiz, D. V. (2023). Constructing college-level diversity, equity, and inclusion (DEI) minors—Moving from performative to transformative DEI. *The Radical Teacher*, 127, 41–50. DOI: 10.5195/rt.2023.977

Gidney, C., & Ekerå, M. (2019). How to factor 2048-bit RSA integers in 8 hours using 20 million noisy qubits. *Quantum : the Open Journal for Quantum Science*, 5, 433. DOI: 10.22331/q-2021-04-15-433

Gikuhi, E. H. (2020). Crisis Management Strategies and Business Continuity for Star Rated Hotels in Kenya [PhD Thesis]. University of Nairobi.

Gilligan, C. (1982). *In a different voice: Psychological theory and women's development*. Harvard University Press.

Gillmore, S., & Tenhundfeld, N. (2020). The Good, The Bad, and The Ugly: Evaluating Tesla's Human Factors in the Wild West of Self-Driving Cars. *Proceedings of the Human Factors and Ergonomics Society Annual Meeting*, 64(1), 67–71. DOI: 10.1177/1071181320641020

Giotis, G. (2024). Labor Market Institutions and Employment. *Encyclopedia*, 4(1), 273–294. DOI: 10.3390/encyclopedia4010021

Gladwin, T. N., Kennelly, J. J., & Krause, T. S. (1995). Shifting paradigms for sustainable development: Implications for management theory and research. *Academy of Management Review*, 20(4), 874–907. DOI: 10.2307/258959

Global Partnership for Sustainable Development Data. (2022). Better data. Better decisions. Better lives. *Author*. https://www.data4sdgs.org/

Godfray, H. C. J., Beddington, J. R., Crute, I. R., Haddad, L., Lawrence, D., Muir, J. F., Pretty, J., Robinson, S., Thomas, S. M., & Toulmin, C. (2010). Food security: The challenge of feeding 9 billion people. *Science*, 327(5967), 812–818. DOI: 10.1126/science.1185383 PMID: 20110467

Goksen, Y., Cevik, E., & Avunduk, H. (2015). A Case Analysis on the Focus on the Maturity Models and Information Technologies. *Procedia Economics and Finance*, 19, 208–216. DOI: 10.1016/S2212-5671(15)00022-2

Goldman, I. (2023, July 20). Applying for a personal loan online vs. in person. *Discover Personal Loans*.https://www.discover.com/personal-loans/resources/learn-about-personal-loans/applying-for-a-personal-loan-online-versus-a-physical-branch/

Goldstein, I., Burnett, A., Rosen, R., Park, P., & Stecher, V. (2019). The Serendipitous Story of Sildenafil: An Unexpected Oral Therapy for Erectile Dysfunction. *Sexual Medicine Reviews*, 7(1), 115–128. DOI: 10.1016/j.sxmr.2018.06.005 PMID: 30301707

Gomes, J., & Romão, M. (2015). Maturity, Benefits and Project Management shaping Project Success. In *the series Advances in Intelligent Systems and Computing* (Vol. 353, pp. 435–448). New Contributions in Information Systems and Technologies. DOI: 10.1007/978-3-319-16486-1_43

Gomes, J., & Romão, M. (2018). Information system maturity models in healthcare. *Journal of Medical Systems*, 42(12), 1–14. DOI: 10.1007/s10916-018-1097-0 PMID: 30327955

Gong, L., Jiang, S., & Liang, X. (2022). Competing value framework-based culture transformation. *Journal of Business Research*, 145, 853–863. DOI: 10.1016/j.jbusres.2022.03.019

González-Gonzalo, C., Thee, E. F., Klaver, C. C., Lee, A. Y., Schlingemann, R. O., Tufail, A., Verbraak, F., & Sánchez, C. I. (2022). Trustworthy AI: Closing the gap between development and integration of AI systems in ophthalmic practice. *Progress in Retinal and Eye Research*, 90, 101034. Advance online publication. DOI: 10.1016/j.preteyeres.2021.101034 PMID: 34902546

Gonzalez, M., & Reider, P. (2021). Behavioral incentives for environmental sustainability: Evidence from Australian markets. *Ecological Economics*, 182, 106931. DOI: 10.1016/j.ecolecon.2021.106931

Gonzalez, S. (2022). AI in Waste Management: Transforming Recycling Processes. *Journal of Environmental Management*, 254, 109899.

Goodfellow, I., Bengio, Y., & Courvill, A. (2023). *Deep Learning* (2nd ed.). MIT Press., https://www.deeplearningbook.org/

Google. (2020). *Google AI principles*. Google AI. Retrieved from https://ai.google/principles

Göral, R. (2015). Competitive Analysis of the Hotel Industry in Konya by Using Porter's Five Forces Model. *European Journal of Economics and Business Studies*, 3(1), 106–115. DOI: 10.26417/ejes.v3i1.p106-115

Gordon, C. (2021, Summer). Protecting the security of digital health records: A brief overview of HIPAA and the breach notification rule. *Journal of Government Financial Management*, 41–45.

Gorman, L. (2022). *How the U.S.-China trade war affected the rest of the world*. National Bureau of Economic Research.

Goumaa, R., & Anderson, L. (2024). Developing critical reflection in asynchronous discussions; the role of the instructor. *Journal of Management Education*, 48(3), 427–458. DOI: 10.1177/10525629231215245

Gowen, G. H., & Hengesteg, P. S. (2021). Gaming the rankings: Richard Freeland and the dramatic rise of Northeastern University. In *The Marketisation of Higher Education: Concepts, Cases, and Criticisms* (pp. 235–265). Springer International Publishing. DOI: 10.1007/978-3-030-67441-0_11

Grandy, G., & Mills, A. J. (2004). Strategy as simulacra? A radical reflexive look at the discipline and practice of strategy. *Journal of Management Studies*, 41(7), 1153–1170. DOI: 10.1111/j.1467-6486.2004.00470.x

Granovetter, M. S. (1973). The strength of weak ties. *American Journal of Sociology*, 78(6), 1360–1380. https://www.jstor.org/stable/2776392. DOI: 10.1086/225469

Grassi, P. A., Garcia, M. E., & Fenton, J. L. (2017). *Draft NIST special publication 800-63-3 digital identity guidelines*. National Institute of Standards and Technology.

Green, B., & Viljoen, S. (2020). Algorithmic realism: Expanding the boundaries of algorithmic thought. *FAT '20: Proceedings of the 2020 Conference on Fairness, Accountability, and Transparency*, 19-31. DOI: 10.1145/3351095.3372840

Greene, C., & Stavins, J. (2017). Did the Target data breach change consumer assessments of payment card security? *Journal of Payments Strategy & Systems*, 11(2), 121–133. DOI: 10.69554/DISO6037

Green, K. W.Jr, Zelbst, P. J., Meacham, J., & Bhadauria, V. S. (2012). Green supply chain management practices: Impact on performance. *Supply Chain Management*, 17(3), 290–305. DOI: 10.1108/13598541211227126

Green, S. L. (2009). Why 5 percent? An analysis of optimal endowment spending rates. *Studies in Economics and Finance*, 26(4), 216–231. DOI: 10.1108/10867370910995681

Greiner, L. E., Bhambri, A., & Cummings, T. G. (2003). Searching for a strategy to teach strategy. *Academy of Management Learning & Education*, 2(4), 402–420. DOI: 10.5465/amle.2003.11902092

Grimaldi, M., Greco, M., & Cricelli, L. (2021). A framework of intellectual property protection strategies and open innovation. *Journal of Business Research*, 123, 156–164. DOI: 10.1016/j.jbusres.2020.09.043

Grimes, N. D., & Porter, W. (2023). Closing the digital divide through digital equity: The role of libraries and librarians. *Public Library Quarterly*, 43(3), 307–338. DOI: 10.1080/01616846.2023.2251348

Grin, J., Hassink, J., Karadzic, V., & Moors, E. H. (2018). Transformative leadership and contextual change. *Sustainability (Basel)*, 10(7), 2159. DOI: 10.3390/su10072159

Groene, O., Skau, J. K., & Frolich, A. (2008). An international review of projects on hospital performance assessment. *International Journal for Quality in Health Care : Journal of the International Society for Quality in Health Care*, 20(3), 162–171. DOI: 10.1093/intqhc/mzn008 PMID: 18339665

Grosen, S. L., & Edwards, K. (2023). Learning from experiments: Exploring how short time-boxed experiments can contribute to organizational learning. *Journal of Workplace Learning*, 36(1), 96–112. DOI: 10.1108/JWL-08-2023-0138

Gross, A. E., & MacDougall, C. (2020). Roles of the clinical pharmacist during the covid-19 pandemic. Jaccp. *Journal of the American College of Clinical Pharmacy: JAACP*, 3(3), 564–566. DOI: 10.1002/jac5.1231

Grundy, T. (2006). Rethinking and reinventing Michael Porter's five forces model. *Strategic Change*, 15(5), 213–229. DOI: 10.1002/jsc.764

Grzelec, A. (2024). Doing gender equality and undoing gender inequality—A practice theory perspective. *Gender, Work and Organization*, 31(3), 749–767. DOI: 10.1111/gwao.12935

Gubernskaya, Z., & Dreby, J. (2017). U.S. immigration policy and the case for family unity. *Journal on Migration and Human Security*, 5(2), 417–430. DOI: 10.1177/233150241700500210

Gupta, D., & Garg, J. (2020). Sexual harassment at workplace. International Journal of Legal Science and Innovation.

Gupta, K., Sleezer, C. M., & Russ-Eft, D. (2014). *A practical guide to needs assessment* (3rd ed.). John Wiley.

Habbal, A., Ali, M. K., & Abuzaraida, M. A. (2024). Artificial intelligence trust, risk and security management (AI TRiSM): Frameworks, applications, challenges and future research directions. *Expert Systems with Applications*, 240, 122442. DOI: 10.1016/j.eswa.2023.122442

Haber, M. J., Chappell, B., & Hills, C. (2022). Attack vectors. In *Cloud Attack Vectors: Building Effective Cyber-Defense Strategies to Protect Cloud Resources* (pp. 117–219). Apress., DOI: 10.1007/978-1-4842-8236-6_6

Hackney, K. J., Daniels, S. R., Paustian-Underdahl, S. C., Perrewé, P. L., Mandeville, A., & Eaton, A. A. (2021). Examining the effects of perceived pregnancy discrimination on mother and baby health. *The Journal of Applied Psychology*, 106(5), 774–783. DOI: 10.1037/apl0000788 PMID: 32614204

Halder, A. (2024). Women Safety Matters: Addressing the Complexities and Violence Against Women. *International Journal of English Literature and Social Sciences*, 9(4), 297–302. DOI: 10.22161/ijels.94.42

Haleem, A., Javaid, M., Qadri, M. A., & Suman, R. (2022). Understanding the role of digital technologies in education: A review. *Sustainable Operations and Computers*, 3, 275–285. DOI: 10.1016/j.susoc.2022.05.004

Hamington, M. (2009). *The social philosophy of Jane Addams*. University of Illinois Press.

Hamizan, M., Abu, N., Mansor, M., & Zaidi, M. (2023). An Analysis of the Effect of Price and Quality on Customer Buying Patterns: An Empirical Study of iPhone Buyers. *International Journal of Interactive Mobile Technologies (iJIM)*. .DOI: 10.3991/ijim.v17i18.42917

Hammad, M., Yahaya, J., & Mohamed, I. (2024). A model for enterprise resource planning implementation in the Saudi public sector organizations. *Heliyon*, 10(2), e24531. DOI: 10.1016/j.heliyon.2024.e24531 PMID: 38312684

Hamon, R., Junklewitz, H., Garrido, J. S., & Sanchez, I. (2024). *Three challenges to secure AI systems in the context of AI regulations*. IEEE., DOI: 10.1109/ACCESS.2024.3391021

Hanifah, H., Halim, H. A., Ahmad, N. H., & Vafaei-Zadeh, A. (2019). Emanating the key factors of innovation performance: Leveraging on the innovation culture among smes in malaysia. *Journal of Asia Business Studies*, 13(4), 559–587. DOI: 10.1108/JABS-04-2018-0130

Hanif, S. (2023). Developing Organizational Change Capabilities using ADKAR model of Change: The Efficacy of Context Sensitive Training: Organizational Change using ADKAR Model. *Journal of Workplace Behavior*, 4(1), 81–93. DOI: 10.70580/jwb.04.01.0176

Han, J. (2021). How does Tesla Motors achieve a competitive advantage in the global automobile industry? *Journal of Next-generation Convergence Information Services Technology*, 10(5), 573–582. DOI: 10.29056/jncist.2021.10.09

Han, K., Chang, Y. B., & Hahn, J. (2011). Information Technology Spillover and Productivity: The Role of Information Technology Intensity and Competition. *Journal of Management Information Systems*, 28(1), 115–145. DOI: 10.2753/MIS0742-1222280105

Hanna, A., Denton, E., Smart, A., & Smith-Loud, J. (2020). Towards a critical race methodology in algorithmic fairness. In *Proceedings of the 2020 Conference on Fairness, Accountability, and Transparency* (pp. 501-512). DOI: 10.1145/3351095.3372826

Hanson, M., & Checked, F. (2023). Average cost of college [2023]: yearly tuition + expenses. *Education Data Initiative.* https://educationdata.org/average-cost-of-college

Hardt, M., Price, E., & Srebro, N. (2016). Equality of opportunity in supervised learning. *Advances in Neural Information Processing Systems*, 29, 3315–3323. DOI: 10.48550/arXiv.1610.02413

Harker Roa, A., Córdoba Flechas, N., Moya, A., & Pineros-Leano, M. (2023). Implementing psychosocial support models in contexts of extreme adversity: Lessons from a process evaluation in colombia. *Frontiers in Psychology*, 14, 1134094. Advance online publication. DOI: 10.3389/fpsyg.2023.1134094 PMID: 37284476

Harmon, P. (2004). Evaluating an organization's business process maturity. *Business Process Trends*, 2, 1–11.

Harris, J., Taylor, K., & Green, T. (2022). Consumer incentives and sustainable behavior in the Australian context. *Sustainability*, 14(5), 2823. DOI: 10.3390/su14052823

Hashjin, A. A., Kringos, D. S., Manoochehri, J., Aryankhesal, A., & Klazinga, N. (2014). Development and impact of the Iranian hospital performance measurement program. *BMC Health Services Research*, 14(1), 448. DOI: 10.1186/1472-6963-14-448 PMID: 25269656

Hashmi, M. A., Jalees, T., Qabool, S., & Aziz, A. (2020). Consequences of Organizational Culture and the Mediating Role of Job Satisfaction and Turnover Intentions. Abasyn University Journal of Social Sciences, 13(1).

Hassija, V., Chamola, V., Mahapatra, A., Singal, A., Goel, D., Huang, K., Scardapane, S., Spinelli, I., Mahmud, M., & Hussain, A. (2023). Interpreting black-box models: A review on explainable artificial intelligence. *Cognitive Computation*, 16(1), 45–74. DOI: 10.1007/s12559-023-10179-8

Hawk, T. F., & Lyons, P. R. (2008). Please don't give up on me: When faculty fail to care. *Journal of Management Education*, 32(3), 316–338. DOI: 10.1177/1052562908314194

Hazari, A. (2024). Manuscript Preparation and Writing. In Research Methodology for Allied Health Professionals: A comprehensive guide to Thesis & Dissertation (pp. 99-103). Singapore: Springer Nature Singapore. DOI: 10.1007/978-981-99-8925-6_11

Hazen, B. T., Russo, I., Confente, I., & Pellathy, D. (2021). Supply chain management for circular economy: Conceptual framework and research agenda. *International Journal of Logistics Management*, 32(2), 510–537. DOI: 10.1108/IJLM-12-2019-0332

He, M. (2021). Analysis of iPhone's Marketing Strategy., 669-672. .DOI: 10.2991/aebmr.k.210319.124

Health and Human Services. (2021). *HIPAA for Professionals*. https://www.hhs.gov/hipaa/for-professionals/index.html

He, B., Wang, W., Sharifi, A., & Liu, X. (2023). Progress, knowledge gap and future directions of urban heat mitigation and adaptation research through a bibliometric review of history and evolution. *Energy and Building*, 287, 112976. DOI: 10.1016/j.enbuild.2023.112976

Heever, H. V. D., & Oosthuizen, R. (2024). Application of cognitive work analysis in support of systems engineering of a socio-technical system. *International Journal of Industrial and Systems Engineering*, 46(1), 90–106. DOI: 10.1504/IJISE.2024.135830

Heischmidt, K. A., & Gordon, P. (2020). Different strategic planning models: Considerations for international study programs. *Journal of Higher Education Theory and Practice*, 20(15), 27–35.

Held, V. (2006). *The ethics of care: Personal, political, and global*. Oxford University Press.

Heller, A., & Varney, J. (2013). *Using Process Management Maturity Models: A path to attaining process management excellence*. APQC.

Hendrick, K., & Engelbrecht, A. (2019). The principled leadership scale: An integration of value-based leadership. *SA Journal of Industrial Psychology*, 45(0), 1–10.

Henriques, V., & Tanner, M. (2017). A systematic literature review of agile and maturity model research. *Interdisciplinary Journal of Information, Knowledge, and Management*, 12, 53–73. DOI: 10.28945/3666

Heracleous, L., & Jacobs, C. D. (2008). Crafting strategy: The role of embodied metaphors. *Long Range Planning*, 41(3), 309–325. DOI: 10.1016/j.lrp.2008.02.011

Hermawan, I., & Suharnomo, S. (2020). Information technology as a strategic resource in encouraging organizational change readiness through the role of the human capital effectiveness. [Jurnal Dinamika Manajemen]. *Journal of Database Management*, 11(2), 242–254.

He, W., Hung, J., & Liu, L. (2022). Impact of big data analytics on banking: A case study. *Journal of Enterprise Information Management*. Advance online publication. DOI: 10.1108/JEIM-05-2020-0176

He, Y., Kiehbadroudinezhad, M., Hosseinzadeh-Bandbafha, H., Gupta, V. K., Peng, W., Lam, S. S., Tabatabaei, M., & Aghbashlo, M. (2023). Driving sustainable circular economy in electronics: A comprehensive review on environmental life cycle assessment of e-waste recycling. *Environmental Pollution*, •••, 123081. PMID: 38072018

He, Y., Wang, L., & Liu, H. (2023). A novel sustainable supply chain performance evaluation framework based on circular economy principles. *Journal of Cleaner Production*, 318, 128577.

Heydarov, K. (2020). "The Blue Ocean Strategy" is against "Porter's Five Competitive Powers". *Science Bulletin*, 1(1), 115–120. Advance online publication. DOI: 10.54414/zomg4450

Hickman, E., & Petrin, M. (2021). Trustworthy AI and corporate governance: The EU's ethics guidelines for trustworthy artificial intelligence from a company law perspective. *European Business Organization Law Review*, 22(4), 593–625. DOI: 10.1007/s40804-021-00224-0

Hidayat, S., Affandi, N., Eryanto, H., & Hidayat, D. R. (2023). Higher Education Governance and Lecturer Performance: The Role of Leadership, Commitment, and Culture. *Journal of Higher Education Theory and Practice*, 23(6).

Higgins, J. P. T., Thomas, J., Chandle, J., Cumpston, M., Li, T., Page, M. J., & Welch, V. A. (Eds.). (2023). *Cochrane Handbook for Systematic Reviews of Interventions* version 6.4 (updated August 2023). Available from www.training.cochrane.org/handbook

Hijfte, S. (2020). Continuous Learning. *Make Your Organization a Center of Innovation*, 113 - 122. .DOI: 10.1021/bk-2010-1055.ch007

Hill, R. (2017). Failure of ethical leadership: Implications for stakeholder theory and "anti-stakeholders". *Business and Society Review, Journal of the Center for Business Ethics. Bentley University*, 122(2), 165–190.

Hine, E., & Floridi, L. (2024). Artificial intelligence with American values and Chinese characteristics: A comparative analysis of American and Chinese governmental AI policies. *AI & Society*, 9, 257–278. DOI: 10.1007/s00146-022-01499-8

Hinlicky v. Dreyfuss, 848 N.E.2d 1285, 6 N.Y.3d 636, 815 N.Y.S.2d 908 (2006).

Hinrichs-Krapels, S., Hinrichs-Krapels, B., Ditewig, H., Boulding, A., Chalkidou, J., & Erskine, F. (2022). Purchasing high-cost medical devices and equipment in hospitals: A systematic review. *BMJ Open*, 12(9), e057516. Advance online publication. DOI: 10.1136/bmjopen-2021-057516 PMID: 36581959

Hiscox. (2023). *Hiscox research finds increased prevalence of cyber attacks on businesses for fourth consecutive year.* https://www.hiscoxgroup.com/sites/group/files/documents/2023-10/Hiscox-Cyber-Readiness-Report-2023.pdf

Hitka, M., Kucharčíková, A., Štarchoň, P., Balážová, Ž., Lukáč, M., & Stacho, Z. (2019). Knowledge and human capital as sustainable competitive advantage in human resource management. *Sustainability (Basel)*, 11(18), 4985. DOI: 10.3390/su11184985

Hitt, M., Keats, B., & DeMarie, S. (1998). Navigating in the new competitive landscape: Building strategic flexibility and competitive advantage in the 21st century. *The Academy of Management Perspectives*, 12(4), 22–42. DOI: 10.5465/ame.1998.1333922

Hobson, A. J., & Townsend, A. (2014). Interviewing as educational research. *Educational Research and Inquiry. Qualitative and Quantitative Approaches*, 223-238.

Hoffmann, M., & Mehler, M. (2023). An industry-specific investigation on artificial intelligence adoption: The cases of financial services and manufacturing. *PACIS 2023 Proceedings. 1*. https://aisel.aisnet.org/pacis2023/1

Hofmann, E., & Busch, T. (2013). How to integrate sustainability into logistics. *Logistics Research*, 6(2), 83–94. DOI: 10.1007/s12159-013-0098-8

Hogler, R., & Gross, M. A. (2009). Journal rankings and academic research: Two discourses about the quality of faculty work. *Management Communication Quarterly*, 23(1), 107–126. DOI: 10.1177/0893318909335419

Holland, M., Dunbrack, L., & Piai, S. (2008). Healthcare IT maturity model: Western European hospitals - The leading countries. European IT opportunity: healthcare provider IT strategies. Health Industry Insights, an IDC Company.

Hollebeek, L., Sprott, D., Andreassen, T., Costley, C., Klaus, P., Kuppelwieser, V., Karahasanovic, A., Taguchi, T., Islam, J., & Rather, R. (2019). Customer engagement in evolving technological environments: Synopsis and guiding propositions. *European Journal of Marketing*, 53(9), 2018–2023. Advance online publication. DOI: 10.1108/EJM-09-2019-970

Holstein, K., Wortman Vaughan, J., Daumé, H.III, Dudik, M., & Wallach, H. (2019). Improving fairness in machine learning systems: What do industry practitioners need? *Proceedings of the 2019 CHI Conference on Human Factors in Computing Systems*, 1-16. DOI: 10.1145/3290605.3300830

Holt, A. (2024, January). Unions, industrial concentration, and economic rents: How the Wagner Act increased wages during the 1930s. *Industrial Concentration, and Economic Rents: How the Wagner Act increased wages during the 1930s.SSRN.* DOI: 10.2139/ssrn.4698381

Homauni, A., Markazi-Moghaddam, N., Mosadeghkhah, A., Noori, M., Abbasiyan, K., & Balaye Jame, S. Z. (2023). Budgeting in Healthcare Systems and Organizations: A Systematic Review. *Iranian Journal of Public Health*, 52(9), 1889–1901. DOI: 10.18502/ijph.v52i9.13571 PMID: 38033850

Hom, M. A., Stanley, I. H., Spencer-Thomas, S., & Joiner, T. E. (2017). Women firefighters and workplace harassment: Associated suicidality and mental health sequelae. *The Journal of Nervous and Mental Disease*, 205(12), 910–917. DOI: 10.1097/NMD.0000000000000759 PMID: 29088006

Hopkins, C. D., Raymond, M. A., & Carlson, L. (2011). Educating students to give them a sustainable competitive advantage. *Journal of Marketing Education*, 33(3), 337–347. DOI: 10.1177/0273475311420241

Hossain, M. B., Rahman, M. U., Čater, T., & Vasa, L. (2024). Determinants of SMEs' strategic entrepreneurial innovative digitalization: Examining the mediation role of human capital. *European Journal of Innovation Management*. Advance online publication. DOI: 10.1108/EJIM-02-2024-0176

Houchil, K. (2023, May 3). Governor Hochul announces historic agreement to increase New York's Minimum Wage and index to inflation as part of FY 2024 budget. *New York State*. https://www.governor.ny.gov/news/governor-hochul-announces-historic-agreement-increase-new-yorks-minimum-wage-and-index

Houde, N. (2007). The six faces of traditional ecological knowledge: Challenges and opportunities for Canadian co-management arrangements. *Ecology and Society*, 12(2), art34. DOI: 10.5751/ES-02270-120234

House, R. J., & Howell, J. M. (1992). Personality and charismatic leadership. *The Leadership Quarterly*, 3(2), 81–108. DOI: 10.1016/1048-9843(92)90028-E

Hou, Y., Chen, S., & Lin, X. (2024). Parental digital involvement in online learning: Addressing the digital divide, not redressing digital reproduction. *European Journal of Education*, 59(2), e12635. DOI: 10.1111/ejed.12635

Hsu, C. H., & Lee, A. H. I. (2017). Information logistics: A bibliometric review. *Journal of Organizational Computing and Electronic Commerce*, 27(3), 253–275. DOI: 10.1080/10919392.2017.1348302

Hu, B., Malik, i., Noman, S. M., & Irshad, M. (2023). A sustainable retrospective analysis of cultural innovative approaches in technology management. Second International Conference on Sustainable Technology and Management (ICSTM 2023). DOI: 10.1117/12.3005508

Huang, Y., Li, X., & Yang, X. (2022). Lifecycle assessment and resource efficiency in Australian agriculture: A case study. *Resources, Conservation and Recycling*, 179, 106023. DOI: 10.1016/j.resconrec.2021.106023

Hubbart, J. (2023). Organizational Change: The Challenge of Change Aversion. *Administrative Sciences*, 13(7), 162. Advance online publication. DOI: 10.3390/admsci13070162

Huebner, C., & Flessa, S. (2022). Strategic Management in Healthcare: A Call for Long-Term and Systems- Thinking in an Uncertain System. *International Journal of Environmental Research and Public Health*, 19(14), 8617. DOI: 10.3390/ijerph19148617 PMID: 35886468

Huff, A. J., Burrell, D. N., Nobles, C., Richardson, K., Wright, J. B., Burton, S. L., Jones, A., Springs, D., Omar, M., & Brown-Jackson, K. L. (2023). Management practices for mitigating cybersecurity threats to biotechnology companies, laboratories, and healthcare research organizations. In *Applied Research Approaches to Technology* (pp. 1–12). Healthcare, and Business., DOI: 10.4018/979-8-3693-1630-6.ch001

Hu, J., & Dutta, T. (2022). What's charisma got to do with it? Three faces of charismatic leadership and corporate social responsibility engagement. *Frontiers in Psychology*, 13, 829584. DOI: 10.3389/fpsyg.2022.829584 PMID: 35941945

Hung, S., Hung, S., & Lin, M. (2015). Are alliances a panacea for SMEs? The achievement of competitive priorities and firm performance. *Total Quality Management & Business Excellence*, 26(1-2), 190–202. DOI: 10.1080/14783363.2014.927133

Hurst, E., Kehoe, P., Pastorino, E., & Winberry, T. (2022, July). The distributional impact of the minimum wage in the short and long run. NBER Working Paper No. w30294. *SSRN*: https://ssrn.com/abstract=4177541 DOI: 10.2139/ssrn.4177541

Hursthouse, R. (2001). *On virtue ethics*. Oxford University Press., DOI: 10.1093/0199247994.001.0001

Hurst, J. (2017). Robotic swarms in offensive maneuver. *Joint Force Quarterly*, 87(4), 105–111.

Hussain, S.T., Lei, S., Akram, T., Haider, M., Hussain, S.H., and Ali, M. (2016). Kurt Lewin's change model: A critical review of the role of leadership and employee involvement in organizational change. *Journal of Innovation & Knowledge, 3*(2018), 123-127. DOI: 10.1016/j.jik.2016.07.002

Huỳnh, Q. H., & Phan, T. T. V. (2022). The impacts of eco-friendly activities from resorts on guests' satisfaction. A case study of 5-star beach resorts in Da Nang, Vietnam [PhD Thesis]. FPTU \DJà N ng.

Hwang, Y. I. J., Hagos, A., Withall, A., Hampton, S., Snoyman, P., & Butler, T. (2024). Population ageing, incarceration and the growing digital divide: Understanding the effects of digital literacy inequity experienced by older people leaving prison. *PLoS One*, 9(4), e0297482. DOI: 10.1371/journal.pone.0297482 PMID: 38630834

IEEE. (2019). Ethically aligned design: A vision for prioritizing human well-being with autonomous and intelligent systems *(First Edition)*. The IEEE Global Initiative on Ethics of Autonomous and Intelligent Systems. Retrieved from Autonomous and Intelligent Systems (AIS)

Iftikhar, N., & Nordbjerg, F. (2021). Adopting Artificial Intelligence in Danish SMEs: Barrier to Become a Data Driven Company, Its Solutions and Benefits. *In Proceedings of the 2nd International Conference on Innovative Intelligent Industrial Production and Logistics - IN4PL*. SciTePress, 131-136. DOI: 10.5220/0010691800003062

Igbinenikaro, E., & Adewusi, A. O. (2024). Navigating the legal complexities of artificial intelligence in global trade agreements. *International Journal of Applied Research in Social Sciences*, 6(4), 488–505. DOI: 10.51594/ijarss.v6i4.987

Imprivata (2021, June 30). *Hackers, breaches, and the value of healthcare data.* https://www.imprivata.com/blog/healthcare-data-new-prize-hackers

İnce, F. F., Öztürk, B., Kumkale, İ., Tüt, K., Karaca, O., & Sağlam, Ş. B. (2022). Evaluation of Contemporary Management Approaches in Hotel Businesses: A Qualitative Application in Four and Five Star Hotels. *Journal of Management and Economic Studies*, 4(1), 59–81. DOI: 10.26677/TR1010.2022.959

Indrarathne, P., Ranadewa, K., & Shanika, V. (2020). Impact of competitive forces to the contractors in Sri Lanka: an industry analysis using Porter's five forces. DOI: 10.31705/FARU.2020.21

Infrastructure Sustainability Council of Australia. (2019). Building a Circular Economy: Sustainable Practices in Construction. Retrieved from https://www.isca.org.au/b

Iqbal, G. M. D., Ha, L., Anoruo, E., Gregory, S., & Rosenberger, J. M. (2022). Assigning faculty to university committees by considering priorities: an optimization approach. In *IIE Annual Conference. Proceedings* (pp. 1–6). Institute of Industrial and Systems Engineers (IISE).

Irani, Z., Abril, R., Weerakkody, V., Omar, A., & Sivarajah, U. (2023). The impact of legacy systems on digital transformation in European public administration: Lesson learned from a multi case analysis. *Government Information Quarterly*, 40(1), 101784. DOI: 10.1016/j.giq.2022.101784

Isabella, L. A., Yemen, G., & Hepler, K. (2015). So long to SingleStop? (A). Charlottesville: *Darden Graduate School of Business Administration*. UV7051-PDF-ENG.

ISACA (2023). Updates CMMI Model with Three New Domains That Help Organizations Improve Quality. Retrieved from ISACA website.

ISC2. (2023). H*ow the economy, skills gap and artificial intelligence are challenging the global cybersecurity workforce. Author.*https://www.isc2.org/-/media/Project/ISC2/Main/Media/documents/research/ISC2_Cybersecurity_Workforce_Study_2023.pdf

Ivanov, D. (2018). Revealing interfaces of supply chain resilience and sustainability: A simulation study. *International Journal of Production Research*, 56(10), 3507–3523. DOI: 10.1080/00207543.2017.1343507

Ives, Y. (2008). What is 'coaching'? An exploration of conflicting paradigms. *International Journal of Evidence Based Coaching and Mentoring*, 6(2), 100–113.

Iyanna, S., Kaur, P., Ractham, P., Talwar, S., & Najmul Islam, A. (2022). Digital transformation of healthcare sector. What is impeding adoption and continued usage of technology-driven innovations by end-users? *Journal of Business Research*, 153, 150–161. DOI: 10.1016/j.jbusres.2022.08.007

Iyer, S., Goss, E., Browder, C., Paccione, G. A., & Arnsten, J. H. (2019). Development and evaluation of a clinical reasoning curriculum as part of an internal medicine residency program. *Diagnosis (Berlin, Germany)*, 6(2), 115–119. DOI: 10.1515/dx-2018-0093 PMID: 30901312

Jacobsen, J. T., & Liebetrau, T. (2023). Artificial intelligence and military superiority: How the 'cyber-AI offensive-defensive arms race' affects the US vision of the fully integrated battlefield. In *Artificial Intelligence and International Conflict in Cyberspace* (pp. 135–156). Routledge., DOI: 10.4324/9781003284093-8

Jaffe-Walter, R. (2018). Leading in the context of immigration: Cultivating collective responsibility for recently arrived immigrant students. *Theory into Practice*, 57(2), 147–153. DOI: 10.1080/00405841.2018.1426934

Jäger-Roschko, J., & Petersen, M. (2022). Interorganizational communication and incentives for data exchange in circular economy. *Sustainable Development*, 30(2), 303–315.

Jagtap, S., & Rahimifard, S. (2019). Improving efficiency and productivity in agri-food supply chains through information logistics. *The Journal of Supply Chain Management*, 55(2), 89–105.

Jahya, A., Azlin, S. N. I., Othman, R., & Romaiha, N. R. (2020). Turnover intention among Gen-Y: The role of training and development, compensation and organizational culture. *International Journal of Academic Research in Business & Social Sciences*, 10(10), 765–782. DOI: 10.6007/IJARBSS/v10-i10/7975

Jain, A., Brooks, J. R., Alford, C. C., Chang, C. S., Mueller, N. M., Umscheid, C. A., & Bierman, A. S. (2023). Awareness of Racial and Ethnic Bias and Potential Solutions to Address Bias With Use of Health Care Algorithms. *JAMA Health Forum*, 4(6), e231197. Advance online publication. DOI: 10.1001/jamahealthforum.2023.1197 PMID: 37266959

Jain, A., Hisam, M. W., Azad, I., Dar, A. A., Malhotra, M., & Khan, M. S. (2024). Digitalization's revolutionary effect on education and career development. *Information Sciences Letters*, 13(1), 149–157. DOI: 10.18576/isl/130112

Jalali, M., & Kaiser, J. (2018). Cybersecurity in hospitals: A systemic, organizational perspective. *Journal of Medical Internet Research*, 20(5), e10059. Advance online publication. DOI: 10.2196/10059 PMID: 29807882

James, M., Newe, T., O'Shea, D., & O'Mahony, G. D. (2024, June). Authentication and authorization in zero trust IoT: A survey. *In 2024 35th Irish Signals and Systems Conference (ISSC)* (pp. 1-7). IEEE.

Järvenpää, M.. (2022). Data-driven logistics optimization in circular economy business models for SMEs. *Journal of Industrial Information Integration*, 25, 100234.

Jarvis, L. (2007). PHARMA'S TOUGH BALANCING ACT: Weaker third-quarter earning at the major drug companies reflect DRUG WITHDRAWALS and generic competition. *Chemical and Engineering News*, 85, 32–33. DOI: 10.1021/cen-v085n047.p032

Jarvis, L. (2013). Pfizer's Academic Experiment. *Chemical and Engineering News*. Advance online publication. DOI: 10.1021/cen-09040-bus1

Jarvis, L. (2018). Pfizer capitulates on prices. *Chemical and Engineering News*, 96(29), 12. Advance online publication. DOI: 10.1021/cen-09629-buscon3

Jarvis, L.LISA M. JARVIS. (2012). GENERIC ONSLAUGHT HITS PHARMA PROFITS. *Chemical and Engineering News*, 90(20), 30–31. DOI: 10.1021/cen-09020-bus3

Javaid, M., Haleem, A., Singh, R., & Suman, R. (2023, December). Towards insighting cybersecurity for healthcare domains: A comprehensive review of recent practices and trends. *Cyber Security and Applications*, 1, 1–13. DOI: 10.1016/j.csa.2023.100016

Jelodar, H., Wang, Y., Yuan, C., Feng, X., Jiang, X., Li, Y., & Zhao, L. (2019). Latent Dirichlet allocation (LDA) and topic modeling: Models, applications, a survey. *Multimedia Tools and Applications*, 78(11), 15169–15211. DOI: 10.1007/s11042-018-6894-4

Jerotich, C., & Chen, J. (2023). CEO tenure rates. The Harvard law school forum on corporate governance. *Harvard Law School*. https://corpgov.law.harvard.edu/2023/08/04/ceo-tenure-rates-2/#:~:text=The%20data%20reveals%2039%25%20of,for%2010%20years%20or%20less

Jesse, D. (2023). College presidents are less experienced than ever — and eyeing the exit. *Chronicle.com*. https://www.chronicle.com/article/college-presidents-are-less-experienced-than-ever-and-eyeing-the-exit

Jiang, H., & Shen, H. (2023). Toward a relational theory of employee engagement: Understanding authenticity, transparency, and employee behaviors. *International Journal of Business Communication*, 60(3), 948–975. DOI: 10.1177/2329488420954236

Jiang, X., Xu, J., & Xu, X. (2024). An overview of domestic and international applications of digital technology in teaching in vocational education: Systematic literature mapping. *Education and Information Technologies*, 29(13), 1–33. DOI: 10.1007/s10639-024-12528-y

Jiang, Y., Chen, X., & Xu, L. (2022). Circular business models and platform economy: Innovations in Australia. *Sustainability*, 14(8), 4911. DOI: 10.3390/su14084911

Jobin, A., Ienca, M., & Vayena, E. (2019). The global landscape of AI ethics guidelines. *Nature Machine Intelligence*, 1(9), 389–399. DOI: 10.1038/s42256-019-0088-2

Johnson, C., Bash, H. L., Song, J., Dunlap, K., Lagdamen, J., Suvak, M. K., & Stirman, S. W. (2022). The role of the consultant in consultation for an evidence-based treatment for ptsd. *Psychological Services*, 19(4), 760–769. DOI: 10.1037/ser0000592 PMID: 34735197

Johnson, M. W., Christensen, C. M., & Kagermann, H. (2008). Reinventing your business model. *Harvard Business Review*, 86(12), 50–59.

Johnstone, B. (2002). Challenges of financial austerity: Imperatives and limitations of revenue diversification in higher education. *Wales Journal of Education*, 11(1), 18–36. DOI: 10.16922/wje.11.1.3

Jones, D. and Moses, R. (2012). Insuring health care compliance: Reducing RAC audit and HIPAA breach risk exposure. *Journal of Health Care Compliance, January-February 2012*, 33-36.

Jones, P., & Comfort, D. (2020). Circular economy and competitive advantage: Innovations in sustainable business practices. *Sustainability*, 12(4), 1289–1305.

Joshi, A. M. (2022). A Study on work life balance of middle management employees with special reference to five star hotels in pune city [PhD Thesis]. Tilak Maharashtra Vidyapeeth, Pune.

JP Morgan & Chase, Co. (2021, December 16). Chase's 2021 digital banking attitudes study finds consumers continue to adopt digital banking tools to manage their finances. *Author*. https://media.chase.com/news/chases-2021-digital-banking-attitudes-study

Jun, W., Nasir, M. H., Yousaf, Z., Khattak, A., Yasir, M., Javed, A., & Shirazi, S. H. (2022). Innovation performance in digital economy: Does digital platform capability, improvisation capability and organizational readiness really matter? *European Journal of Innovation Management*, 25(5), 1309–1327. DOI: 10.1108/EJIM-10-2020-0422

Junyu, S. (2022). Analysing the External Environment and Industrial Competition of High-Tech Companies—Using Tesla as an Example. *Journal of Psychology Research*. .DOI: 10.17265/2159-5542/2022.09.009

Jurkiewicz, C., & Massey, T.Jr. (1998, December). The influence of ethical reasoning on leader effectiveness: An empirical study of nonprofit executives. *Nonprofit Management & Leadership*, 9(2), 173–186. DOI: 10.1002/nml.9204

Jyoti, R. (2022). IDC MaturityScape: Artificial Intelligence 2.0. IDC. https://www.idc.com/getdoc.jsp?containerId=US49037422&pageType=PRINTFRIENDLY

Kache, F., & Seuring, S. (2017). Challenges and opportunities of digital information at the intersection of Big Data Analytics and supply chain management. *International Journal of Operations & Production Management*, 37(1), 10–36. DOI: 10.1108/IJOPM-02-2015-0078

Kafoe, A. S. (2024). Supply Chain Resilience Strategy for Healthcare Organizations: Crucial Steps in Addressing the Impact of Natural Disasters. In Burrell, D. (Ed.), *Leadership Action and Intervention in Health, Business, Education, and Technology* (pp. 1–54). IGI Global., DOI: 10.4018/979-8-3693-4288-6.ch001

Kahneman, D., & Tversky, A. (1979). Prospect Theory: An Analysis of Decision under Risk. *Econometrica*, 47(2), 263–291. DOI: 10.2307/1914185

Kaiser, C., Miedzinski, M., McDowall, W., & McCarney, G. R. (2024). reflective appraisal of transformative innovation policy: Development of the sustainability transition and innovation review (STIR) approach and application to Canada. *Sustainability (Basel)*, 16(12), 5106. DOI: 10.3390/su16125106

Kaleli, Z., Konteos, G., Avlogiaris, G., & Kilintzis, P. (2024). Total Quality Management as Competitive Advantage for the Internal Strategy and Policy of Greek Special Education School Units. *Journal of the Knowledge Economy*, •••, 1–20. DOI: 10.1007/s13132-024-01987-w

Kalghatgi, G. (2019). Development of Fuel/Engine Systems—The Way Forward to Sustainable Transport. *Engineering (Beijing)*, 5(3), 510–518. Advance online publication. DOI: 10.1016/j.eng.2019.01.009

Kalinke, U., Barouch, D. H., Rizzi, R., Lagkadinou, E., Türeci, Ö., Pather, S., & Neels, P. (2022). Clinical development and approval of COVID-19 vaccines. *Expert Review of Vaccines*, 21(5), 609–619. DOI: 10.1080/14760584.2022.2042257 PMID: 35157542

Kalmykova, Y., Sadagopan, M., & Rosado, L. (2018). Circular economy – From review of theories and practices to development of implementation tools. *Resources, Conservation and Recycling*, 135, 190–201. DOI: 10.1016/j.resconrec.2017.10.034

Kamel, F. O., Magadmi, R., Magadmi, M. M., Alfawaz, F. A., & Alfawaz, M. (2022). Patients' perceptions and satisfaction regarding teleconsultations during the covid-19 pandemic in Jeddah, Saudi Arabia. *Journal of Pharmaceutical Research International*, •••, 15–27. DOI: 10.9734/jpri/2022/v34i31B36093

Kamilaris, A., Kartakoullis, A., & Prenafeta-Boldú, F. X. (2019). The role of information logistics in food traceability and safety. *Journal of Agricultural and Food Chemistry*, 67(15), 4251–4261.

Kane, E. (2016). A theory of how and why central-bank culture supports predatory risk-taking at megabanks. *Atlantic Economic Journal*, 2016(44), 51–71. DOI: 10.1007/s11293-016-9482-x

Kang, S. P., Chen, Y., Svihla, V., Gallup, A., Ferris, K., & Datye, A. K. (2022). Guiding change in higher education: An emergent, iterative application of Kotter's change model. *Studies in Higher Education*, 47(2), 270–289. DOI: 10.1080/03075079.2020.1741540

Kanungo, S. (2024). AI-driven resource management strategies for cloud computing systems, services, and applications. *World Journal of Advanced* Engineering Technology and Sciences, 11(2), 559-5 6. DOI: 10.30574/wjaets.2024.11.2.0137

Kanvaria, V. K., & Yadav, A. (2024). Integrating and Innovating: The Role of ICT in Education's Evolution-An In-depth Analysis of Emerging Technologies, Current Trends, Challenges, and Future Directions in the Digital Age. *International Journal for Multidimensional Research Perspectives*, 2(2), 33–48.

Kanwal, H., & Van Hoye, G. (2020). Inconsistent organizational images of luxury hotels: Exploring employees' perceptions and dealing strategies. *Tourism Management Perspectives*, 36, 100738. DOI: 10.1016/j.tmp.2020.100738

Karalis, V. D. (2024). The Integration of Artificial Intelligence into Clinical Practice. *Applied Biosciences*, 3(1), 14–44. DOI: 10.3390/applbiosci3010002

Karangutkar, A.Amogh Amol Karangutkar. (2023). The Impact of Artificial Intelligence on Job Displacement and the Future of Work. *International Journal of Advanced Research in Science. Tongxin Jishu*, 635–638. Advance online publication. DOI: 10.48175/IJARSCT-12096

Karapancheva, M. (2020). The future of organizational culture. *Journal of Sustainable Development*, 10(25), 42–52.

Kara, S., Hauschild, M., Sutherland, J., & McAloone, T. (2022). Closed-loop systems to circular economy: A pathway to environmental sustainability? *CIRP Annals*, 71(2), 505–528. DOI: 10.1016/j.cirp.2022.05.008

Kara, S., Sasan, E., & Lu, J. (2022). Circular economy and business model innovation. *Sustainability*, 14(4), 2277.

Karlén, N., & Rauta, V. (2023). Dealers and brokers in civil wars: Why states delegate rebel support to conduit countries. *International Security*, 47(4), 107–146. DOI: 10.1162/isec_a_00461

Katebi, A., Mohammadhosseini, A., Najmeddin, M., & Homami, P. (2024). The moderating impact of organizational readiness, competitive pressure and compatibility on the cost of using precast concrete components. *Journal of Financial Management of Property and Construction*, 29(2), 274–294. DOI: 10.1108/JFMPC-01-2023-0003

Kaur, R., Gabrijelčič, D., & Klobučar, T. (2023). Artificial intelligence for cybersecurity: Literature review and future research directions. *Information Fusion*, 97, 101804. DOI: 10.1016/j.inffus.2023.101804

KC. S. F. F. (2022). Discrimination law. Oxford University Press.

Kebede, S., & Wang, A. (2022). Organizational justice and employee readiness for change: The mediating role of perceived organizational support. *Frontiers in Psychology*, 13, 806109. DOI: 10.3389/fpsyg.2022.806109 PMID: 35369209

Kelly, R., Rogers, A., Wynne, B., & Peaden, M. (N.D). Competitive Analysis Tesla Inc.

Kerrigan, T. (2021). *An exploratory study of management perceptions of the role of Kotter's urgency in creating a future change agenda* (Doctoral dissertation, Dublin, National College of Ireland).

Kerstetter, J. (2019). $10m grant supports Harvard's work within rural schools. *Harvard Gazette*. https://news.harvard.edu/gazette/story/2019/02/10m-grant-supports-harvards-work-within-rural-schools/

Khalid, A. (2011). Effect of organizational change on employee job involvement: Mediating role of communication, emotions, and psychological contract. *Information Management and Business Review*, 3(3), 178–184. DOI: 10.22610/imbr.v3i3.931

Khan, A., Han, Y., & Zhang, C. (2023). The role of digital twins in supporting circular economy practices. *Computers & Industrial Engineering*, 169, 108110. DOI: 10.1016/j.cie.2022.108110

Khanchel, H. (2019). The Impact of Digital Transformation on Banking. *Journal of Business Administration Research*, 8(2), 20. DOI: 10.5430/jbar.v8n2p20

Khanday, S. (2024). Horizon of Healthcare: AI's Evolutionary Journey and Future Implications. *World Journal of Advanced Engineering Technology and Sciences*, 11(2), 308–324. DOI: 10.30574/wjaets.2024.11.2.0118

Khan, I. (2024). Strategic Planning in Business Management: Key Principles and Practices. *Management Science Research Archives*, 2(01), 31–39.

Khan, M. F. I., & Masum, A. K. M. (2024). Predictive *analytics and* machine learning for real-time detection of software defects and agile test management. *Educational Administration: Theory and Practice*, 30(4), 1051–1057. DOI: 10.1080/01616412.2019.1609159

Khan, M. J. Muhammad Jamshid Khan. (2023). Zero Trust architecture: Redefining network security paradigms in the digital age. *World Journal of Advanced Research and Reviews*, 19(3), 105–116. DOI: 10.30574/wjarr.2023.19.3.1785

Khan, M., & Ghafoor, L. (2024). Adversarial machine learning in the context of network security: Challenges and solutions. *Journal of Computational Intelligence and Robotics*, 4(1), 51–63. https://thesciencebrigade.com/jcir/article/view/118

Khan, M., Hussain, M., & Saber, H. M. (2016). Information sharing in a sustainable supply chain. *International Journal of Production Economics*, 181, 208–214. DOI: 10.1016/j.ijpe.2016.04.010

Khan, M., Parvaiz, G. S., Dedahanov, A. T., Abdurazzakov, O. S., & Rakhmonov, D. A. (2022). The impact of technologies of traceability and transparency in supply chains. *Sustainability (Basel)*, 14(24), 16336. DOI: 10.3390/su142416336

Khanna, T., Palepu, K., & Sinha, J. (2005). Strategies that fit emerging markets. *Harvard Business Review*, 83(6), 63–74, 76, 148. PMID: 15938439

Khan, S. A., Dong, Q. L., Zhang, Y., & Anwar, S. (2022). Big data-driven supply chain visibility and decision-making: A case of the circular economy within the agri-food sector. *Technological Forecasting and Social Change*, 170, 120894.

Khan, S. A., Dong, Q. L., Zhang, Y., & Yu, Z. (2016). The circular economy in China: Sectoral effects on industrial circularity and efficiency. *Journal of Environmental Management*, 197, 49–61.

Kharrazi, H., Gonzalez, C. P., Lowe, K. B., Huerta, T. R., & Ford, E. W. (2018). Forecasting the Maturation of Electronic Health Record Functions Among US Hospitals: Retrospective Analysis and Predictive Model. *Journal of Medical Internet Research*, 20(8), e10458. DOI: 10.2196/10458 PMID: 30087090

Khurram, A. (2020). Revisiting porter five forces model: Influence of non-governmental organizations on competitive rivalry in various economic sectors. *Pakistan Social Sciences Review*, 4(1), 1–15. DOI: 10.35484/pssr.2020(4-I)01

Kim, C., Yang, K., & Kim, J. (2008). A strategy for third-party logistics systems: A case analysis using the blue ocean strategy. *Omega*, 36(4), 522–534. DOI: 10.1016/j.omega.2006.11.011

Kim, J., & Park, M. J. (2022). Influence of entrepreneurship manifestation factor on organisational innovation: The role of corporate entrepreneurship and imperative innovation culture. *The Journal of Entrepreneurship*, 31(3), 514–545. DOI: 10.1177/09713557221135558

Kim, S. S., Watkins, E. A., Russakovsky, O., Fong, R., & Monroy-Hernández, A. (2023, April). "Help Me Help the AI": Understanding How Explainability Can Support Human-AI Interaction. *InProceedings of the 2023 CHI Conference on Human Factors in Computing Systems* (pp. 1-17). DOI: 10.1145/3544548.3581001

Kim, T., Peck, D., & Gee, B. (2020). *Race, gender and the double glass ceiling: An analysis of EEOC national workforce data*. Ascend Foundation. Ascendleadershipfoundation. Org/Research/Race-Gender-Doubleglass-Ceiling.

Kim, W. C., & Mauborgne, R. (2005). *Blue ocean strategy: how to create uncontested market space and make the competition irrelevant*. Harvard Business School Press.

King, H. D. (2022). *A case study exploring how culturally intelligent transformational higher education leaders foster organizational innovations in a multicultural student environment* (Doctoral dissertation, Indiana Institute of Technology).

Kingsbury, K. (2017). Secret lives of admissions officers. *The Daily Beast*. https://www.thedailybeast.com/secret-lives-of-admissions-officers

Kingsbury, P., Abajian, H., Abajian, M., Angyan, P., Espinoza, J., MacDonald, B., Meeker, D., Wilson, J., & Bahroos, N. (2023). SEnDAE: A resource for expanding research into social and environmental determinants of health. *Computer Methods and Programs in Biomedicine*, 238, 107542. DOI: 10.1016/j.cmpb.2023.107542 PMID: 37224727

Kirchherr, J., Reike, D., & Hekkert, M. (2017). Conceptualizing the circular economy: An analysis of 114 definitions. *Resources, Conservation and Recycling*, 127, 221–232. DOI: 10.1016/j.resconrec.2017.09.005

Kırmızı, M., & Kocaoglu, B. (2022). Digital transformation maturity model development framework based on design science: Case studies in manufacturing industry. *Journal of Manufacturing Technology Management*, 33(7), 1319–1346. DOI: 10.1108/JMTM-11-2021-0476

Kizza, J. M. (2024). Authentication. In *Guide to Computer Network Security 6thEd* (pp. 215–238). Springer International Publishing. DOI: 10.1007/978-3-031-47549-8_10

Klein, N., Stockwell, M., Demarco, M., Gaglani, M., Kharbanda, A., Irving, S., Rao, S., Grannis, S., Dascomb, K., Murthy, K., Rowley, E., Dalton, A., DeSilva, M., Dixon, B., Natarajan, K., Stenehjem, E., Naleway, A., Lewis, N., Ong, T., & Verani, J. (2022). Effectiveness of COVID-19 Pfizer-BioNTech BNT162b2 mRNA Vaccination in Preventing COVID-19–Associated Emergency Department and Urgent Care Encounters and Hospitalizations Among Nonimmunocompromised Children and Adolescents Aged 5–17 Years — VISION Network, 10 States, April 2021–January 2022. *MMWR. Morbidity and Mortality Weekly Report*, 71(9), 352–358. DOI: 10.15585/mmwr.mm7109e3 PMID: 35239634

Klein, R., & Rai, A. (2009). Interfirm strategic information flows in logistics supply chain relationships. *Management Information Systems Quarterly*, 33(4), 735–762. DOI: 10.2307/20650325

Kleizen, B., Wynen, J., Boon, J., & De Roover, J. (2023). Bullying and harassment as a consequence of workplace change in the Australian civil service: Investigating the mediating role of satisfaction with change management. *Review of Public Personnel Administration*, 43(1), 56–79. DOI: 10.1177/0734371X211036732

Kline, M. (2018). Survey results: Short tenure for higher ed's top leaders. *CUPA*. https://www.cupahr.org/blog/survey-results-administrators/#:~:text=Data%20from %20CUPA%2DHR%27s%202017,three%20years%20in%20their%20position

Knight, M., Kolin, J., Widergren, S., Narang, D., Khandekar, A., & Nordman, B. (2020). The Interoperability Maturity Model (IMM): A Qualitative and Quantitative Approach for Measuring Interoperability. PNNL-29683, GRID – Modernization Laboratory Consortium, US Department of Energy. https://www.osti.gov/servlets/purl/1804457

Knights, D., & Morgan, G. (1990). The concept of strategy in sociology: A note of dissent. *Sociology*, 24(3), 475–483. DOI: 10.1177/0038038590024003008

Kochura, O. (2024). The art of letting go: Corporate divestitures in the biopharmaceutical industries. In *Mergers and Acquisitions* (pp. 13–28). Routledge. DOI: 10.4324/9781003245438-3

Koenig, S., Bee, C., Borovika, A., Briddell, C., Colberg, J., Humphrey, G., Kopach, M., Martínez, I., Nambiar, S., Plummer, S., Ribe, S., Roschangar, F., Scott, J., & Sneddon, H. (2019). A Green Chemistry Continuum for a Robust and Sustainable Active Pharmaceutical Ingredient Supply Chain. *ACS Sustainable Chemistry & Engineering*, 7(20), 16937–16951. Advance online publication. DOI: 10.1021/acssuschemeng.9b02842

Kokila, M., & Reddy, K. S. (2025). Authentication, access control and scalability models in Internet of Things Security–A review. *Cyber Security and Applications*, 3, 100057. DOI: 10.1016/j.csa.2024.100057

Kong, A., Kwan, M., & Qiao, G. (2022). How to lead and deliver true hospitality to restore guest's confidence during COVID-19 pandemic? Case of InterContinental Zhuhai Hotel. MAIN CONFERENCE PROCEEDINGS, 141.

Korbi, K. (2015). Leadership and Strategic Change. *The Journal of Organizational Management Studies*, 2015, 638847. Advance online publication. DOI: 10.5171/2015.638847

Korejan, M. M., & Shahbazi, H. (2016). An analysis of the transformational leadership theory. *Revue des Sciences Fondamentales et Appliquées*, 8(3), 452–461. DOI: 10.4314/jfas.v8i3s.192

Korhonen, V. (2023, August 29). U.S. college enrollment and forecast 1965-2031. *Statista*. https://www.statista.com/statistics/183995/us-college-enrollment-and-projections-in-public-and-private-institutions/

Kotapati, B. A. P. U., Mutungi, S., Newham, M., Schroeder, J., Shao, S., & Wang, M. (2020). The antitrust case against Apple. *Available atSSRN* 3606073.

Kotter, J. P. (2007). *Leading change: Why transformation efforts fail. Harvard Business Review*. March-April Magazine.

Kotze, F. P., & Ferreira, E. J. (2020). Financial sustainability and profitability of high performance training centres. *S.A. Journal for Research in Sport Physical Education and Recreation*, 42(2), 77–94.

Kou, H., Zhang, Y., & Lee, H. P. (2024). Dynamic optimization based on Quantum computation-A comprehensive review. *Computers & Structures*, 292, 107255. DOI: 10.1016/j.compstruc.2023.107255

Kouhizadeh, M., Zhu, Q., & Sarkis, J. (2020). Blockchain and the circular economy: Potential tensions and critical reflections from practice. *Production Planning and Control*, 31(11-12), 950–966. DOI: 10.1080/09537287.2019.1695925

Kouroubali, A., Papastilianou, A., & Katehakis, D. G. (2019). Preliminary Assessment of the Interoperability Maturity of Healthcare Digital Services vs Public Services of Other Sectors. *Studies in Health Technology and Informatics*, 264, 654–658. DOI: 10.3233/SHTI190304 PMID: 31438005

Kraft, T., Alagesan, S., & Shah, J. (2021). The New War of the Currents: The Race to Win the Electric Vehicle Market. *Darden Case: Business Communications (Topic)*. DOI: 10.2139/ssrn.3771785

Krasuska, M., Williams, R., Sheikhm, A., Franklin, B.D., Heeney, C., Lane, W., Mozaffar, H., Mason, K., Eason, S., Hinder, S., Dunscombe, R., Potts, H.W.W., & Cresswell, K. (2020). Technological Capabilities to Assess Digital Excellence in Hospitals in High Performing Health Care Systems: International eDelphi Exercise. Journal of Medical Internet Research,18, 22, 8, e17022. .DOI: 10.2196/17022

Krogstad, J. M. (2022, January 11). Key facts about U.S. immigration policies and Biden's proposed changes. *Pew Research Center*. https://www.pewresearch.org/short-reads/2022/01/11/key-facts-about-u-s-immigration-policies-and-bidens-proposed-changes/

Kronk, H. (2019). How do colleges and universities earn revenue? 2019 update. *eLearningInside News*. https://news.elearninginside.com/how-do-colleges-and-universities-earn-revenue-2019-update/

Krstić, M. (2021). Higher education as determinant of competitiveness and sustainable economic development. In *The Sustainability Debate* (Vol. 14, pp. 15–34). Emerald Publishing Limited. DOI: 10.1108/S2043-905920210000015002

Kshetri, N. (2021). *Artificial Intelligence and Cybersecurity*. Springer.

Kuhn, T. S. (1962). *The Structure of scientific revolutions* (2nd ed.). University of Chicago Press.

Kumar, A. (2020). Disruptive Technologies and Impact on Industry- An Exploration. *Journal of Business Management and Information Systems*. .DOI: 10.48001/jbmis.2020.0701001

Kumar, B. (2018). *Acquisitions by Pfizer*. Wealth Creation in the World's Largest Mergers and Acquisitions., DOI: 10.1007/978-3-030-02363-8_8

Kumar, R., Chambers, E.IV, Chambers, D. H., & Lee, J. (2021). Generating new snack food texture ideas using sensory and consumer research tools: A case study of the japanese and south korean snack food markets. *Foods*, 10(2), 474. DOI: 10.3390/foods10020474 PMID: 33671546

Kumar, R., & Srivastava, P. (2022). Enhancing data quality for AI in network security. *International Journal of Information Security and Privacy*, 16(3), 134–150. DOI: 10.4018/IJISP.202203011

Kunduru, A. R. (2023). Industry best practices on implementing oracle cloud ERP security. *International Journal of Computer Trends and Technology*, 71(6), 1–8. DOI: 10.14445/22312803/IJCTT-V71I6P101

Kunttu, L. (2017). Educational Involvement in Innovative University–Industry Collaboration. *Technology Innovation Management Review*, 7(12), 14–22. DOI: 10.22215/timreview/1124

Kutaula, S., Gillani, A., & Budhwar, P. S. (2020). An analysis of employment relationships in Asia using psychological contract theory: A review and research agenda. *Human Resource Management Review*, 30(4), 100707. DOI: 10.1016/j.hrmr.2019.100707

L'Écuyer, F., Raymond, L., Fabi, B., & Uwizeyemungu, S. (2019). Strategic alignment of IT and human resources management in manufacturing SMEs: Empirical test of a mediation model. *Employee Relations*, 41(5), 830–850. DOI: 10.1108/ER-09-2018-0258

Lacatus, M. L. (2013). Organizational culture in contemporary university. *Procedia: Social and Behavioral Sciences*, 76, 421–425. DOI: 10.1016/j.sbspro.2013.04.139

Ladd, T. D., Jelezko, F., Laflamme, R., Nakamura, Y., Monroe, C., & O'Brien, J. L. (2010). Quantum Computing. *Nature*, 464(7285), 45–53. DOI: 10.1038/nature08812 PMID: 20203602

Ladha, S. (2024, February 24). Identity report. *Okta*. https://www.okta.com/blog/2024/02/key-findings-from-our-2023-state-of-secure-identity-report/#:~:text=Attackers%20target%20MFA&text=We%20found%20that%2012.7%25%20of,engineering%20and%20SIM%20swap%20attacks

Laig, R. B. D., & Abocejo, F. T. (2021). Change management process in a mining company: Kotter's 8-step change model. *Journal of Management, Economics, and Industrial Organization*, 5(3), 31–50. DOI: 10.31039/jomeino.2021.5.3.3

LastPass Sesurity Report. (2019). The 3rd annual global password security report. *Author*. https://www.lastpass.com/-/media/10aa2f653c774e428aa4cc6732734828.pdf

Latta, G. (2009). A Process Model of Organizational Change in Cultural Context (OC3 Model). *Journal of Leadership & Organizational Studies*, 16(1), 19–37. DOI: 10.1177/1548051809334197

Lauer, T. (2019). Generic Strategies, Outpacing and Blue Ocean - Discussing the Validity of Three Strategic Management Theories Using Case Studies from Airlines and Grocery Retail. *Theory, Methodology. Practice*, 15(1), 57–66. Advance online publication. DOI: 10.18096/TMP.2019.01.06

Lawrence, P. R., & Lorsch, J. W. (1967). Differentiation and Integration in Complex Organizations. *Administrative Science Quarterly*, 12(1), 1–47. DOI: 10.2307/2391211

Leape, L. L., Berwick, D. M., & Bates, D. W. (2002). What practices will most improve safety?: Evidence-based medicine meets patient safety. *Journal of the American Medical Association*, 288(4), 501–507. DOI: 10.1001/jama.288.4.501 PMID: 12132984

LeCun, Y., Bengio, Y., & Hinton, G. (2015). Deep learning. *Nature*, 521(7553), 436–444. DOI: 10.1038/nature14539 PMID: 26017442

Lee, J., Kim, H., & Choi, S. (2024). Do hospital data breaches affect health information technology investment? *Digital Health*, 10, 1–11. DOI: 10.1177/20552076231224164 PMID: 39286785

Lee, M. C., Scheepers, H., Lui, A. K., & Ngai, E. W. (2023). The implementation of artificial intelligence in organizations: A systematic literature review. *Information & Management*, 60(5), 103816. DOI: 10.1016/j.im.2023.103816

Lee, S. J. (2023). An Exploratory Study on Human Factor Analysis of Medical Accidents Using the SHELL (Software, Hardware, Environment, Liveware) Model. *Korean Journal of Aerospace and Environmental Medicine*, 33(3), 94–99. DOI: 10.46246/KJAsEM.230019

Lee, S. M., Lee, D., & Kim, Y. (2022). Policy frameworks and industry standards for circular economy implementation. *Resources, Conservation and Recycling*, 177, 106069. DOI: 10.1016/j.resconrec.2021.106069

Lefebvre, V. (2024). Layoffs in SMEs: The role of social proximity. *Journal of Business Ethics*, 190(4), 801–820. DOI: 10.1007/s10551-023-05414-z PMID: 37359804

Leibold, J. (2020). *Surveillance in China's Xinjiang region: ethnic sorting, coercion, and inducement*. La Trobe. Journal contribution. DOI: 10.26181/17102798.v1

Leone, J. &Lo Casio, e. J. (2020). Income gaps: Education and inequality. *Economics and Business Review*, 6(4).

Leong, S., & Lee, T. (2021). The Internet in Singapore: From 'Intelligent Island' to 'Smart Nation'. In: Global internet governance. *Palgrave Pivot*, Singapore. DOI: 10.1007/978-981-15-9924-8_3

Leoni, S. (2023). A historical review of the role of education: From human capital to human capabilities. *Review of Political Economy*, •••, 1–18. DOI: 10.1080/09538259.2023.2245233

Le, T. T., Nhu, Q. P. V., & Behl, A. (2024). Role of digital supply chain in promoting sustainable supply chain performance: The mediating of supply chain integration and information sharing. *International Journal of Logistics Management*. Advance online publication. DOI: 10.1108/IJLM-01-2024-0031

Le, T., Chang, H. C., & Chan, H. K. (2024). Blockchain technology and circular economy: A literature review and future research agenda. *International Journal of Production Research*, •••, 1–24.

Levasseur, R. (2001). People skills: Change Management Tools–Lewin's change model. *Interfaces*, 31(4), 71–73.

Lezoche, M., Hernandez, J. E. R., Alemany Díaz, M. M. E., Panetto, H., & Kacprzyk, J. (2020). Agri-food 4.0: A survey of the supply chains and technologies for the future agriculture. *Computers in Industry*, 117, 103187. DOI: 10.1016/j.compind.2020.103187

Liaw, S. T. & Godinho, M.A (2023). Digital health and capability maturity models-a critical thematic review and conceptual synthesis of the literature. *Journal of the American Medical Informatics Association*, 18, 30(2), 393-406. .DOI: 10.1093/jamia/ocac228

Li, B., Qi, P., Liu, B., Di, S., Liu, J., Pei, J., Yi, J., & Zhou, B. (2023). Trustworthy AI: From principles to practices. *ACM Computing Surveys*, 55(9), 1–46. https://dl.acm.org/doi/10.1145/3555803. DOI: 10.1145/3555803

Li, J., Wang, S., Zheng, H., Pan, D., Wang, Y., & Yang, Y. (2020). Overseas study experience and global processing style. *Current Psychology (New Brunswick, N.J.)*, 39(3), 913–918. DOI: 10.1007/s12144-018-9805-y

Li, M. (2023). *Five-Force Analysis, SWOT Analysis, Value Chain Analysis of Apple in Technology Industry*. Advances in Economics, Management and Political Sciences., DOI: 10.54254/2754-1169/4/2022946

Lin, C.-Y., & Huang, C.-K. (2021). Employee turnover intentions and job performance from a planned change: The effects of an organizational learning culture and job satisfaction. *International Journal of Manpower*, 42(3), 409–423. DOI: 10.1108/IJM-08-2018-0281

Liou, D. D., & Hermanns, C. (2017). Preparing transformative leaders for diversity, immigration, and equitable expectations for school-wide excellence. *International Journal of Educational Management*, 31(5), 661–678. DOI: 10.1108/IJEM-10-2016-0227

Li, T., Mayo-Wilson, E., Shaughnessy, D., & Qureshi, R. (2024). Studying harms of interventions with an equity lens in randomized trials. *Trials*, 25(1), 403. DOI: 10.1186/s13063-024-08239-x PMID: 38902776

Litchfield, I., Shukla, D., & Greenfield, S. (2021). Impact of COVID-19 on the digital divide: A rapid review. *BMJ Open*, 11(10), e053440. Advance online publication. DOI: 10.1136/bmjopen-2021-053440 PMID: 34642200

Liu, L., Song, W., & Liu, Y. (2023). Leveraging digital capabilities toward a circular economy: Reinforcing sustainable supply chain management with Industry 4.0 technologies. *Computers & Industrial Engineering*, 178, 109113. DOI: 10.1016/j.cie.2023.109113

Liu, X., Wang, J., & Ma, H. (2022). Educational programs and certifications for circular economy in Australia. *Resources, Conservation and Recycling*, 180, 106158. DOI: 10.1016/j.resconrec.2022.106158

Liu, Y., Evans, L., Kwan, T., Callister, J., Poon, S., Byth, K., & Harnett, P. (2021). Developing a maturity model for cancer multidisciplinary teams. *International Journal of Medical Informatics*, 156, 104610. DOI: 10.1016/j.ijmedinf.2021.104610 PMID: 34649110

Liu, Y., Li, X., & Wu, Y. (2023). Green supply chain management and circular economy integration. *Journal of Cleaner Production*, 359, 133722. DOI: 10.1016/j.jclepro.2022.133722

Liu, Y., Yang, Y., & Liu, X. (2023). Information logistics: A study of the impact of supply chain information on performance. *Journal of Business Research*, 156, 113396.

Li, Y., Dai, S., Zhou, X., He, K., & Sun, X. (2024). Chinese students' attitudes towards U.S. universities in the U.S.–China conflict. *Journal of Consumer Behaviour*, 23(2), 929–938. DOI: 10.1002/cb.2241

Llewelyn, S. (2003). What counts as "theory" in qualitative management and accounting research? Introducing five levels of theorizing. *Accounting, Auditing & Accountability Journal*, 16(4), 662–708. DOI: 10.1108/09513570310492344

Lombardi, R., Leach, D., & Thong, N. (2022). Public awareness and engagement with circular economy practices: Lessons from Australia. *Journal of Environmental Management*, 317, 115323. DOI: 10.1016/j.jenvman.2022.115323

Long, Z., Axsen, J., Miller, I., & Kormos, C. (2019). What does Tesla mean to car buyers? Exploring the role of automotive brand in perceptions of battery electric vehicles. *Transportation Research Part A, Policy and Practice*, 129, 185–204. Advance online publication. DOI: 10.1016/j.tra.2019.08.006

Lukyanenko, R., Maass, W., & Storey, V. C. (2022). Trust in artificial intelligence: From a foundational trust framework to emerging research opportunities. *Electronic Markets*, 32(4), 1993–2020. DOI: 10.1007/s12525-022-00605-4

Lyon, D. (2003). *Surveillance after September 11*. Blackwell Publishing Ltd.

Lyon, G. (2024). Informational inequality: The role of resources and attributes in information security awareness. *Information and Computer Security*, 32(3), 197–217. DOI: 10.1108/ICS-04-2023-0063

Machado, C. G., Winroth, M., Almström, P., Ericson Öberg, A., Kurdve, M., & AlMashalah, S. (2021). Digital organisational readiness: Experiences from manufacturing companies. *Journal of Manufacturing Technology Management*, 32(9), 167–182. DOI: 10.1108/JMTM-05-2019-0188

MacIntyre, A. (1981). *After virtue: A study in moral theory*. University of Notre Dame Press.

Madnick, S. (2024). Why data breaches spiked in 2023. *Harvard Business Review, 2024*(February 19). https://hbr.org/2024/02/why-data-breaches-spiked-in-2023

Madrid, A. P., & Wright, C. (2023). Trustworthy AI alone is not enough. *Dykinson*. https://www.dykinson.com/libros/trustworthy-ai-alone-is-not-enough/9788411706001/

Madsen, D. Ø., & Slåtten, K. (2019). Examining the emergence and evolution of blue ocean strategy through the lens of management fashion theory. *Social Sciences (Basel, Switzerland)*, 8(1), 28. DOI: 10.3390/socsci8010028

Mak, S., & Thomas, A. (2022). Steps for conducting a scoping review. *Journal of Graduate Medical Education*, 14(5), 565–567. DOI: 10.4300/JGME-D-22-00621.1 PMID: 36274762

Malatji, W. R., Eck, R. V., & Zuva, T. (2020). Understanding the usage, modifications, limitations and criticisms of technology acceptance model (TAM). *Advances in Science, Technology and Engineering Systems Journal, 5(6)*, 113-117. https://api.semanticscholar.org/CorpusID:229219113

Malekpour, M., Caboni, F., Nikzadask, M., & Basile, V. (2024). Taste of success: A strategic framework for product innovation in the food and beverage industry. *British Food Journal*, 126(13), 94–118. DOI: 10.1108/BFJ-02-2023-0138

Malik, H., Chaudhary, G., & Srivastava, S. (2021). Digital transformation through advances in artificial intelligence and machine learning. *Journal of Intelligent & Fuzzy Systems*, 42(2), 615–622. DOI: 10.3233/JIFS-189787

Malik, M. A., Inam, H., Martins, R. S., Janjua, M. B. N., Zahid, N., Khan, S., Sattar, A. K., Khan, S., Haider, A. H., & Enam, S. A. (2021). Workplace mistreatment and mental health in female surgeons in Pakistan. *BJS Open*, 5(3), zrab041. DOI: 10.1093/bjsopen/zrab041 PMID: 34037208

Mallick, M. A. I., & Nath, R. (2024). Navigating the cyber security landscape: A comprehensive review of cyber-attacks, emerging trends, and recent developments. *World Scientific News*, 190(1), 1–69. https://worldscientificnews.com/wp-content/uploads/2024/01/WSN-1901-2024-1-69-1.pdf

Mamman-Daura, F. N., de Weever-Lista, E., & Bertrand, W. (2023). Best Practices for Sexual Harassment Training in the Workplace. In Real-World Solutions for Diversity, Strategic Change, and Organizational Development: Perspectives in Healthcare, Education, Business, and Technology (pp. 91–100). IGI Global. DOI: 10.4018/978-1-6684-8691-7.ch006

Mangan, D. (2024). *Meta agrees to $1.4 billion settlement in Texas biometric data lawsuit over Facebook images.* Retrieved from https://www.cnbc.com/2024/07/30/meta-agrees-to-1point4-billion-settlement-in-texas-biometric-data-lawsuit.html

Manjunath, P., Prakruthi, M. K., & Shah, P. G. (2018, August). IoT driven with big data analytics and block chain application scenarios. In *2018 Second International Conference on Green Computing and Internet of Things (ICGCIoT)* (pp. 569-572). IEEE. DOI: 10.1109/ICGCIoT.2018.8752973

Mankins, M. C., & Steele, R. (2005). Turning great strategy into great performance. *Harvard Business Review*, 83(7/8), 64–72. PMID: 16028817

Manning, L., Soon, J. M., & Smith, R. (2022). The role of digital technology in enabling food security. *Trends in Food Science & Technology*, 124, 170–182.

Mann, M., & Lichtenstein, S. (2021). Effective communication strategies for promoting circular economy principles. *Journal of Business Research*, 132, 145–157. DOI: 10.1016/j.jbusres.2021.01.007

Mann, S. (2024). Evaluating Longevity as a Farm Animal Welfare Indicator. *Food Ethics*, 9(1), 4. DOI: 10.1007/s41055-023-00137-3 PMID: 34805483

Mansoor, T., & Hussain, S. (2024). Impact of knowledge oriented leadership on sustainable service quality of higher education institutes. *VINE Journal of Information and Knowledge Management Systems*, 54(4), 705–724. DOI: 10.1108/VJIKMS-09-2021-0176

Mansour, S., & Nogues, S. (2022). Advantages of and Barriers to Crafting New Technology in Healthcare Organizations: A Qualitative Study in the COVID-19 Context. *International Journal of Environmental Research and Public Health*, 12, 19(16), 9951. .DOI: 10.3390/ijerph19169951

Mantere, S., Sillince, J. A., & Hämäläinen, V. (2007). Music as a metaphor for organizational change. *Journal of Organizational Change Management*, 20(3), 447–459. DOI: 10.1108/09534810710740236

Maradin, D., Malnar, A., & Kaštelan, A. (2022). *Sustainable and Clean Energy: The Case of Tesla Company. JOURNAL OF ECONOMICS*. FINANCE AND MANAGEMENT STUDIES., DOI: 10.47191/jefms/v5-i12-10

Markevych, M., & Dawson, M. (2023, July). A review of enhancing intrusion detection systems for cybersecurity using artificial intelligence (AI). *In International conference Knowledge-based Organization* (pp. 30-37). https://intapi.sciendo.com/pdf/10.2478/kbo-2023-0072

Marr, B. (2023, August 23). 9 vital steps to create a digital transformation strategy. *Forbes*. https://www.forbes.com/sites/bernardmarr/2023/08/22/9-vital-steps-to-create-a-digital-transformation-strategy/

Marshall, A. (2023). A new rural digital divide? Taking stock of geographical digital inclusion in Australia. *Media International Australia*. Advance online publication. DOI: 10.1177/1329878X231202274

Martinez, J., Sagarra, M., & Sancho, M. (2021). Barriers to maturity model implementation in hospitals: A case study analysis. *Journal of Health Organization and Management*, 35(4), 375–392. DOI: 10.1108/JHOM-11-2019-0336

Martin, R. E. (2000). Enrollment management as a portfolio investment problem. *College and University*, 76(1), 25.

Martins, J. M. (2024). Strategic management in an uncertain environment: A review. *Sustainable Economies*, 2(2), 64. DOI: 10.62617/se.v2i2.64

Masi, D., Frey, M., & Finkbeiner, M. (2021). Circular economy and the role of information logistics in waste management. *Waste Management (New York, N.Y.)*, 118, 138–149. DOI: 10.1016/j.wasman.2020.10.033

Masi, D., Montagnini, F., & Finkbeiner, M. (2021). Advancing circular economy practices through technological innovations. *Journal of Environmental Management*, 291, 112847. DOI: 10.1016/j.jenvman.2021.112847

Masoumian Hosseini, M., Masoumian Hosseini, S. T., Qayumi, K., Ahmady, S., & Koohestani, H. R. (2023). The Aspects of Running Artificial Intelligence in Emergency Care; a Scoping Review. *Archives of Academic Emergency Medicine*, 11(1), e38. DOI: 10.22037/aaem.v11i1.1974 PMID: 37215232

Masrom, M. (2007). Technology acceptance model and e-learning. *Technology (Elmsford, N.Y.)*, 21(24), 81.

Mastroprieto, F., & Blini, L. (n.d.). Why digital lending is the future for banks and smes. *EY*. https://www.ey.com/en_gl/insights/financial-services/emeia/why-digital-lending-is-the-future-for-banks-and-smes

Mathrani, S., & Lai, X. (2021). Big data analytic framework for organizational leverage. *Applied Sciences (Basel, Switzerland)*, 11(5), 2340. DOI: 10.3390/app11052340

Mathur, P. (2024). Cloud computing infrastructure, platforms, and software for scientific research. *High Performance Computing in Biomimetics: Modeling, Architecture and Applications*, 89-127. DOI:DOI: 10.1007/978-981-97-1017-1_4

Matt, C., Hess, T., & Benlian, A. (2015, September). (PDF) Digital Transformation Strategies. *ResearchGate*.https://www.researchgate.net/publication/281965523 _Digital_Transformation_Strategies

Ma, Y. (2023). *A Comparative Analysis of Amazon, Microsoft, and Apple's Stock Investment Value*. Highlights in Business, Economics and Management., DOI: 10.54097/hbem.v13i.8825

Mayhew, C., & Chappell, D. (2007). Workplace violence: An overview of patterns of risk and the emotional/stress consequences on targets. *International Journal of Law and Psychiatry*, 30(4-5), 327–339. DOI: 10.1016/j.ijlp.2007.06.006 PMID: 17628681

McCabe, D. L., Butterfield, K. D., & Trevino, L. K. (2006). Academic dishonesty in graduate business programs: Prevalence, causes, and proposed action. *Academy of Management Learning & Education*, 5(3), 294–305. DOI: 10.5465/amle.2006.22697018

McCormack, K. P., & Johnson, W. C. (2001). *Business process orientation: Gaining the e-business competitive advantage*. CRC Press.

McDermott, O., Antony, J., Sony, M., & Daly, J. S. (2021). Barriers and enablers for continuous improvement methodologies within the irish pharmaceutical industry. *Processes (Basel, Switzerland)*, 10(1), 73. DOI: 10.3390/pr10010073

McGee, E. O. (2021). *Black, Brown, Bruised: How Racialized STEM Education Stifles Innovation*. Harvard Education Press.

McKenna, S. M. (1998). *The application of a corporate cultural change model to an institution of higher education*. (Doctoral dissertation, University of Connecticut).

McLuhan, M. (1964). *Understanding Media: The Extensions of Man*. McGraw-Hill.

McNamara, J., Sweetman, S., Connors, P., Lofgren, I., & Greene, G. (2020). Using interactive nutrition modules to increase critical thinking skills in college courses. *Journal of Nutrition Education and Behavior*, 52(4), 343–350. DOI: 10.1016/j.jneb.2019.06.007 PMID: 31353275

Mehrabi, N., Morstatter, F., Saxena, N., Lerman, K., & Galstyan, A. (2021). A survey on bias and fairness in machine learning. *ACM Computing Surveys*, 54(6), 1–35. DOI: 10.1145/3457607

Meiser, J. W., Cramer, T., & Turner-Brady, R. (2021). What good is military strategy? An analysis of strategy and effectiveness in the first Arab-Israeli War. *An Analysis of Strategy and Effectiveness in the First Arab-Israeli War (January 28, 2021). Meiser, J., Cramer, T., & Turner-Brady*, 37-49.

Melesse, H. S., & Knatko, D. M. (2024). The contingent effects of strategic orientations and strategic capabilities on competitive performance: Evidence from Ethiopian manufacturing enterprises. *Heliyon*, 10(15), e35497. DOI: 10.1016/j.heliyon.2024.e35497 PMID: 39170336

Melville, N., Kraemer, K. L., & Gurbaxani, V. (2004). Information Technology and Organizational Performance: An Integrative Model of IT Business Value. *Management Information Systems Quarterly*, 28(2), 283–321. DOI: 10.2307/25148636

Mennella, C., Maniscalco, U., De Pietro, G., & Esposito, M. (2024). Ethical and regulatory challenges of AI technologies in healthcare: A narrative review. *Heliyon*, 10(4), e26297. Advance online publication. DOI: 10.1016/j.heliyon.2024.e26297 PMID: 38384518

Mensah, J. (2019). Sustainable development: Meaning, history, principles, pillars, and implications for human action: Literature review. *Cogent Social Sciences*, 5(1), 1653531. DOI: 10.1080/23311886.2019.1653531

Menukin, O., Mandungu, C., Shahgholian, A., & Mehandjiev, N. (2023). Guiding the integration of analytics in business operations through a maturity framework. *Annals of Operations Research*. Advance online publication. DOI: 10.1007/s10479-023-05614-w

Mettler, T., & Rohner, P. (2009). An analysis of the factors influencing networkability in the healthcare sector. *Health Services Management Research*, 22(4), 163–169. DOI: 10.1258/hsmr.2009.009004 PMID: 19875837

Meyer, I. H. (2003). Prejudice, social stress, and mental health in lesbian, gay, and bisexual populations: Conceptual issues and research agenda. *Psychological Bulletin*, 129(5), 674–697. DOI: 10.1037/0033-2909.129.5.674 PMID: 12956539

Mhlanga, D. (2024). Digital transformation of education, the limitations and prospects of introducing the fourth industrial revolution asynchronous online learning in emerging markets. *Discover Education*, 3(32), 32. Advance online publication. DOI: 10.1007/s44217-024-00115-9

Microsoft Build. (2024, May 21-23). Security at your organization - Multifactor authentication (MFA) statistics. *Author*. https://learn.microsoft.com/en-us/partner-center/security/security-at-your-organization

Microsoft Security. (2019, August 20). One simple action you can take to prevent 99.9 percent of attacks on your accounts. *Author*. https://www.microsoft.com/en-us/security/blog/2019/08/20/one-simple-action-you-can-take-to-prevent-99-9-percent-of-account-attacks/#:~:text=However%2C%20one%20of%20the%20best,percent%20of%20account%20compromise%20attacks

Microsoft. (2021). *Microsoft AI principles: Responsible AI in practice.* Retrieved from https://www.microsoft.com/ai/responsible-ai

Mikalef, P., & Gupta, M. (2021). Artificial intelligence capability: Conceptualization, measurement calibration, and empirical study on its impact on organizational creativity and firm performance. *Information & Management*, 58(3), 103434. DOI: 10.1016/j.im.2021.103434

Miller, C. J., Barnett, M. L., Baumann, A. A., Gutner, C. A., & Stirman, S. W. (2021). The frame-is: A framework for documenting modifications to implementation strategies in healthcare. *Implementation Science : IS*, 16(1), 36. Advance online publication. DOI: 10.1186/s13012-021-01105-3 PMID: 33827716

Mill, J. S. (1863). *Utilitarianism.* Parker, Son, and Bourn.

Milne, M. J., Kearins, K., & Walton, S. (2006). Creating adventures in wonderland: The journey metaphor and environmental sustainability. *Organization*, 13(6), 801–839. DOI: 10.1177/1350508406068506

Miloslavskaya, N., & Tolstaya, S. (2022). Information security management maturity models. *Procedia Computer Science*, 213, 49–57. DOI: 10.1016/j.procs.2022.11.037

MindTools. (n.d.). PDCA (Plan Do Check Act), also known as PDSA, The "Deming Wheel," and "Shewhart Cycle". *MindTools.com*. https://www.mindtools.com/as2l5i1/pdca-plan-do-check-act

Minh-Ha, L. (2024). *Beyond recognition: Privacy protections in a surveilled world.* Linkoping University. DOI: 10.3384/9789180756761

Miotto, G., Del-Castillo-Feito, C., & Blanco-González, A. (2020). Reputation and legitimacy: Key factors for Higher Education Institutions' sustained competitive advantage. *Journal of Business Research*, 112, 342–353. DOI: 10.1016/j.jbusres.2019.11.076

Mishra, B., & Mishra, J. (2015). Discrimination in the workplace. *Journal of Higher Education Theory and Practice*, 15(4).

Mishra, S. (2023). Exploring the impact of AI-based cyber security financial sector management. *Applied Sciences (Basel, Switzerland)*, 13(10), 5875. DOI: 10.3390/app13105875

Mishra, V. T., & Sharma, M. G. (2022). Digital transformation evaluation of telehealth using convergence, maturity, and adoption. *Health Policy and Technology*, 11(4), 100684. DOI: 10.1016/j.hlpt.2022.100684

Mitchell, I. K., & Saren, M. (2008). The living product–Using the creative nature of metaphors in the search for sustainable marketing. *Business Strategy and the Environment*, 17(6), 398–410. DOI: 10.1002/bse.526

Moerschell, L., & Novak, S. S. (2020). Managing crisis in a university setting: The challenge of alignment. *Journal of Contingencies and Crisis Management*, 28(1), 30–40. DOI: 10.1111/1468-5973.12266

Moges Dereje, H., & Assefa Habete, G. (2023). The Adoption of Electronic Procurement and Readiness Assessment in Central Ethiopia Regional State. *International Journal of Engineering and Advanced Technology (IJEAT) ISSN*, 2249-8958.

Moghaddam, Y., Russell, M., Yuen, J., & Demirkan, H. (2023). *Roadmap to close the gap between undergraduate education and STEM Employment across industry sectors, further studied*. The Human Side of Service Engineering., DOI: 10.54941/ahfe1003109

Mohamed, N. (2023). Current trends in AI and ML for cybersecurity: A state-of-the-art survey. *Cogent Engineering*, 10(2), 2272358. Advance online publication. DOI: 10.1080/23311916.2023.2272358

Mohammadpoor, M., & Torabi, F. (2020). Big data analytics in oil and gas industry: An emerging trend. *Petroleum*, 6(4), 321–328. DOI: 10.1016/j.petlm.2018.11.001

Mohammed, A. H. Y., Dziyauddin, R. A., & Latiff, L. A. (2023). Current multi-factor of authentication: Approaches, requirements, attacks and challenges. *International Journal of Advanced Computer Science and Applications*, 14(1). Advance online publication. DOI: 10.14569/IJACSA.2023.0140119

Mok, K. H., Shen, W., & Gu, F. (2024). The impact of geopolitics on international student mobility: The Chinese students' perspective. *Higher Education Quarterly*, 78(4), 12509. DOI: 10.1111/hequ.12509

Möller, D. P. (2023). Cybersecurity in digital transformation. In *Guide to Cybersecurity in Digital Transformation: Trends* (pp. 1–70). Methods, Technologies, Applications and Best Practices., DOI: 10.1007/978-3-031-26845-8_1

Monaco, R., Bergaentzlé, C., Leiva Vilaplana, J. A., Ackom, E., & Nielsen, P. S. (2024). Digitalization of power distribution grids: Barrier analysis, ranking and policy recommendations. *Energy Policy*, 188, 114083. DOI: 10.1016/j.enpol.2024.114083

Monzani, L., Seijts, G. H., & Crossan, M. M. (2021). Character matters: The network structure of leader character and its relation to follower positive outcomes. *PLoS One*, 16(9), e0255940. DOI: 10.1371/journal.pone.0255940 PMID: 34469454

Moody, B. K. (2023). *Bearing witness to terror and triumph: A narrative inquiry into black men's healing after police brutality*. Retrieved from https://marymountuniv.idm.oclc.org/login?url=https://www.proquest.com/dissertations-theses/bearing-witness-terror-triumph-narrative-inquiry/docview/2838439933/se-2

Moon, S., Guan, S. A., Vargas, J. H., Lin, J. C., Kwan, P., Saetermoe, C. L., Flores, G., & Chavira, G. (2024). Critical mentorship in undergraduate research experience BUILDs science identity and self-efficacy. *International Journal of Science and Mathematics Education*. Advance online publication. DOI: 10.1007/s10763-024-10476-0

Moore, J., & Pratt, M. K. (2023). *What is digital transformation?: Definition and guide from TechTarget CIO*. TechTarget https://www.techtarget.com/searchcio/definition/digital-transformation#:~:text=Digital%20transformatio %20is%20the%20incorporation,improve%20their%20ability%20to%20compete.

Moreno-Ortiz, A. (2024). Keywords. In *Making Sense of Large Social Media Corpora: Keywords, Topics, Sentiment, and Hashtags in the Coronavirus Twitter Corpus* (pp. 59-102). Springer Nature Switzerland.

Morgan, M., Mallett, R., Hutchinson, G., & Bagalkote, H. (2000). Morgan, K. Mungham, G. Redesigning democracy: The making of the Welsh Assembly. Bridgend: Seren.

Morley, J., Floridi, L., Kinsey, L., & Elhalal, A. (2020). From what to how: An initial review of publicly available AI ethics tools, methods and research to translate principles into practices. *Science and Engineering Ethics*, 26(4), 2141–2168. DOI: 10.1007/s11948-019-00165-5 PMID: 31828533

Morrell, C., Hu, H., & Bai, Y. (2022). Innovative models for circular economy integration. *Journal of Cleaner Production*, 330, 129852. DOI: 10.1016/j.jclepro.2021.129852

Morris, C. (2024). The number of data breach victims is up 490% in the first half of 2024. *Fast Company, July 18, 2024.* https://www.fastcompany.com/91158122/data-breach-victims-up-490-percent-first-half-2024

Morrison, M., Davidson, M., & Fletcher, R. (2023). Workforce development for sustainable practices in circular economy. *Journal of Environmental Management*, 306, 114333. DOI: 10.1016/j.jenvman.2022.114333

Mosqueira-Rey, E., Hernández-Pereira, E., Alonso-Ríos, D., Bobes-Bascarán, J., & Fernández-Leal, Á. (2023). Human-in-the-loop machine learning: A state of the art. *Artificial Intelligence Review*, 56(4), 3005–3054. DOI: 10.1007/s10462-022-10246-w

Mostafa, A. M., Rushdy, E., Medhat, R., & Hanafy, A. (2023). An identity management scheme for cloud computing: Review, challenges, and future directions. *Journal of Intelligent & Fuzzy Systems*, 45(12), 1–23. DOI: 10.3233/JIFS-231911

Moutousi, O., & May, D. (2018). How change-related unethical leadership triggers follower resistance to change: A theoretical account and conceptual model. *Journal of Change Management*, 18(2), 142–161. DOI: 10.1080/14697017.2018.1446695

Movsesyan, E., & Anokhina, M. (2020). TESLA VERTICAL INTEGRATION STRATEGIES: THEORY, PRACTICE, RESULTS. *Business Strategies*. .DOI: 10.17747/2311-7184-2020-7-184-188

Mowreader, A. (2023). How a WashU success center will serve first-gen, limited-income students. *Inside Higher Ed | Higher Education News, Events and Jobs*. https://www.insidehighered.com/news/student-success/college-experience/2023/04/12/program-launch-success-center-first-gen-limited

Mubarak, M. F. (2022). The Role of Artificial Intelligence in Circular Economy: Opportunities, Challenges, and the Path Forward. *Journal of Cleaner Production*, 362, 131949.

Mubeen, M. (2024). Biometric authentication: Past, present, and future perspectives. *International Journal of Innovative Research in Technology and Science*, 12(2), 351–362.

Mullard, A. (2017). FDA approves Novartis's CDK4/6 inhibitor. *Nature Reviews. Drug Discovery*, 16(4), 229–229. DOI: 10.1038/nrd.2017.62 PMID: 28356596

Müllner, J. (2016). From uncertainty to risk—A risk management framework for market entry. *Journal of World Business*, 51(5), 800–814. DOI: 10.1016/j.jwb.2016.07.011

Munee, S., Farooq, U., Athar, A., Raza, M. A., Ghazal, T., & Sakib, S. (2024). A critical review of artificial intelligence based approaches in intrusion detection: A comprehensive analysis. *Journal of Engineering*, 2024(1), 3909173. DOI: 10.1155/2024/3909173

Muraleedhara, P. (2024). The Need For AI-Powered Cybersecurity to Tackle AI-Driven Cyberattacks. ISACA. https://www.isaca.org/resources/news-and-trends/isaca-now-blog/2024/the-need-for-ai-powered-cybersecurity-to-tackle-ai-driven-cyberattacks

Murillo-Oviedo, A. B., Pimenta, M. L., Hilletofth, P., & Reitsma, E. (2019). Achieving market orientation through cross-functional integration. Operations and Supply Chain Management: An International Journal, 175-185. DOI: 10.31387/oscm0380241

Murugalakshmi, S., & Robin, C. R. (2023). Advancements in mobile security: A comprehensive study of sim card swapping and cloning-trends, challenges and innovative solutions. *I-Manager's Journal on Mobile Applications & Technologies*, 10(1). Advance online publication. DOI: 10.26634/jmt.10.1.20103

Musonera, E., & Cagle, C. (2019). Electric Car Brand Positioning in the Automotive Industry: Recommendations for Sustainable and Innovative Marketing Strategies. *Journal of Strategic Innovation and Sustainability*. .DOI: 10.33423/jsis.v14i1.991

Myers, K. (2023, February). Digital insanity: Exploring the flexibility of NIST digital identity assurance levels. *In International Conference on Cyber Warfare and Security 18*(1), pp. 273-278. DOI: 10.34190/iccws.18.1.1032

Nadler, D. A., & Tushman, M. L. (1990). Beyond the charismatic leader: Leadership and organizational change. *California Management Review*, 32(2), 77–97. DOI: 10.2307/41166606

Nae, T. M., Florescu, M. S., & Bălă oiu, G. I. (2024). Towards social justice: Investigating the role of labor, globalization, and governance in reducing socio-economic inequality within post-communist countries. *Sustainability (Basel)*, 16(6), 2234. DOI: 10.3390/su16062234

Naik, N., Hameed, B. M. Z., Shetty, D. K., Swain, D., Shah, M., Paul, R., Aggarwal, K., Ibrahim, S., Patil, V., Smriti, K., Shetty, S., Rai, B. P., Chlosta, P., & Somani, B. K. (2022). Legal and Ethical Consideration in Artificial Intelligence in Healthcare: Who Takes Responsibility? *Frontiers in Surgery*, 9, 862322. Advance online publication. DOI: 10.3389/fsurg.2022.862322 PMID: 35360424

Najjar, A., Amro, B., & Macedo, M. (2021). The adoption level of electronic medical records in hebron hospitals based on the electronic medical record adoption model (EMRAM). *Health Policy and Technology*, 10(4), 100578. DOI: 10.1016/j.hlpt.2021.100578

Najjar, R. (2023). Redefining Radiology: A Review of Artificial Intelligence Integration in Medical Imaging. *Diagnostics (Basel)*, 13(17), 2760. Advance online publication. DOI: 10.3390/diagnostics13172760 PMID: 37685300

Nakagawa, K., Takata, M., Kato, K., Matsuyuki, T., & Matsuhashi, T. (2017). A University–Industry Collaborative Entrepreneurship Education Program as a Trading Zone: The Case of Osaka University. *Technology Innovation Management Review*, 7(6), 38–49. DOI: 10.22215/timreview/1083

Nalebuff, B. J., & Brandenburger, A. M. (1997). Co-opetition: Competitive and cooperative business strategies for the digital economy. *Strategy and Leadership*, 25(6), 28–33. DOI: 10.1108/eb054655

Nam, K., Dutt, C. S., Chathoth, P., Daghfous, A., & Khan, M. S. (2021). The adoption of artificial intelligence and robotics in the hotel industry: Prospects and challenges. *Electronic Markets*, 31(3), 553–574. DOI: 10.1007/s12525-020-00442-3

Namugenyi, C., Nimmagadda, S. L., & Reiners, T. (2019). Design of a SWOT Analysis Model and Its Evaluation in Diverse Digital Business Ecosystem Contexts. *Procedia Computer Science*, 159(159), 1145–1154. https://demo.dspacedirect.org/server/api/core/bitstreams/c5fcc52d-13fe-4a94-ae78-24f2a820a312/content. DOI: 10.1016/j.procs.2019.09.283

Naor, M., Coman, A., & Wiznizer, A. (2021). Vertically Integrated Supply Chain of Batteries, Electric Vehicles, and Charging Infrastructure: A Review of Three Milestone Projects from Theory of Constraints Perspective. *Sustainability (Basel)*, 13(7), 3632. DOI: 10.3390/su13073632

Naranjo, F. V.. (2023). Blockchain in Collaborative Processes: Transparency, Security, and Traceability. *Journal of Blockchain Technology*, 9(2), 112–128.

National Conference of State Legislatures. (2024). *Artificial intelligence 2023 legislation*. National Conference of State Legislatures https://www.ncsl.org/technology-and-communication/artificial-intelligence-2023-legislation

Navarro, J. G. (2024). Marketing in the United States – statistics & facts. https://www.statista.com/topics/8972/marketing-in-the-united-states/#topicOverview

Nayanar, B. S., Fareed, N., Battur, H., & Praveena, J. (2024). A Study on Nature of Violence Against Doctors in Tertiary Care Centers in Karnataka, India: A Cross-Sectional Study. *Indian Journal of Community Medicine*, 49(3), 472–474. DOI: 10.4103/ijcm.ijcm_1139_21 PMID: 38933800

Nazer, L. H., Zatarah, R., Waldrip, S., Ke, J. X. C., Moukheiber, M., Khanna, A. K., Hicklen, R. S., Moukheiber, L., Moukheiber, D., Ma, H., & Mathur, P. (2023). Bias in artificial intelligence algorithms and recommendations for mitigation. *PLOS Digital Health*, 2(6), e0000278. DOI: 10.1371/journal.pdig.0000278 PMID: 37347721

NEJM Catalyst. (2018). What is risk management in healthcare? *New England Journal of Medicine, April 25, 2018*. https://catalyst.nejm.org/doi/full/10.1056/CAT.18.0197

Neumann, W. P., & Purdy, N. (2023). The better work, better care framework: 7 strategies for sustainable healthcare system process improvement. *Health Systems (Basingstoke, England)*, 12(4), 429–445. DOI: 10.1080/20476965.2023.2198580 PMID: 38235296

Neuwirth, L. S., Jović, S., & Mukherji, B. R. (2021). Reimagining higher education during and post-COVID-19: Challenges and opportunities. *Journal of Adult and Continuing Education*, 27(2), 141–156. DOI: 10.1177/1477971420947738

Newton, B. (2024). Economic impact of international students: The power of international education. *IIE*. https://www.iie.org/research-initiatives/open-doors/economic-impact-of-international-students/

Nguyen, C., & Kebede, M. (2017). Immigrant students in the Trump era: What we know and do not know. *Educational Policy*, 31(6), 716–742. DOI: 10.1177/0895904817723740

Nieto, C., & Zoller Booth, M. (2010). Cultural competence: Its influence on the teaching and learning of international students. *Journal of Studies in International Education*, 14(4), 406–425. DOI: 10.1177/1028315309337929

Nigam, I. (2023). *Marketing Strategies of Apple Inc.* International Journal For Multidisciplinary Research., DOI: 10.36948/ijfmr.2023.v05i02.2059

Nili, A., Tate, M., & Barros, A. (2020). A disciplined approach for enhancing the technology acceptance model. *In European Conference on Information Systems (ECIS) 2020 Proceedings*. https://eprints.qut.edu.au/202630/

Nivarthi, K. S. P., & Gatla, G. (2022). Fighting cybercrime with Zero Trust. [ASR-JETS]. *American Academic Scientific Research Journal for Engineering, Technology, and Sciences*, 90(1), 371–381.

Noble, S. U. (2018). *Algorithms of oppression: How search engines reinforce racism*. NYU Press. DOI: 10.18574/nyu/9781479833641.001.0001

Noennig, J. R., Mello Rose, F., Stadelhofer, P., Jannack, A., & Kulashri, S. (2024). Agile development for urban digitalisation: Insights from the creation of dresden's smart city strategy. *Measuring Business Excellence*, 28(2), 193–208. DOI: 10.1108/MBE-09-2023-0142

Nohria, N. (2021). What the case study method really teaches. *Harvard Business Review, December 21, 2021*. https://hbr.org/2021/12/what-the-case-study-method-really-teaches

Northouse, P. (2016). *Leadership theory and practice* (7th ed.). Sage Publications.

Notarnicola, B., Tassielli, G., Renzulli, P. A., Castellani, V., & Sala, S. (2017). Environmental impacts of food consumption in Europe. *Journal of Cleaner Production*, 140, 753–765. DOI: 10.1016/j.jclepro.2016.06.080

Ntizikira, E., Lei, W., Alblehai, F., Saleem, K., & Lodhi, M. A. (2023). Secure and privacy-preserving intrusion detection and prevention in the internet of unmanned aerial vehicles. *Sensors (Basel)*, 23(19), 8077. DOI: 10.3390/s23198077 PMID: 37836907

O'Connor, P. (2021). Loyalty programs and direct website performance: An empirical analysis of global hotel brands. *Information and Communication Technologies in Tourism*, 2021, 150–161. DOI: 10.1007/978-3-030-65785-7_13

O'Neil, C. (2016). *Weapons of Math Destruction: How Big Data Increases Inequality and Threatens Democracy*. Crown Publishing Group.

Ochuba, N. A., Amoo, O. O., Okafor, E. S., Akinrinola, O., & Usman, F. O. (2024). Strategies for leveraging big data and analytics for business development: A comprehensive review across sectors. *Computer Science & IT Research Journal*, 5(3), 562–575. DOI: 10.51594/csitrj.v5i3.861

Odiaga, J., Guglielmo, M. J., Catrambone, C., Gierlowski, T., Bruti, C., Richter, L., & Miller, J. (2021). Kotter's change model in higher education: Transforming siloed education to a culture of interprofessionalism. *Journal of Organizational Culture. Communications and Conflict*, 25(2), 1–7.

Odumeru, J. A., & Ogbonna, I. G. (2013). Transformational vs. transactional leadership theories: Evidence in literature. *International review of management and business research, 2*(2), 355.

Office of the Governor Tim Waltz & Lt. Governor Peggy Flanagan. (2024, June 5). Governor Walz, Lieutenant Governor Flanagan announce opening of applications for Minnesota student teacher grants and loan repayment programs. *Author*. https://mn.gov/governor/newsroom/press-releases/

Ofori-Parku, S. (2021). When public and business interests collide: An integrated approach to the altruism-instrumentalism tension and corporate social responsibility theory. *Journal of Medical Ethics*, 36(1), 2–19. DOI: 10.1080/23736992.2020.1857254

Oke, A., Prajogo, D. I., Idiagbon-Oke, M., & Edwin, T. (2022). Linking environmental forces, absorptive capacity, information sharing, and innovation performance. Industrial Management &Amp. *Industrial Management & Data Systems*, 122(7), 1738–1755. DOI: 10.1108/IMDS-12-2021-0732

Okorie, O., Salonitis, K., Charnley, F., Moreno, M., Turner, C., & Tiwari, A. (2018). Digitisation and the circular economy: A review of current research and future trends. *Energies*, 11(11), 3009. DOI: 10.3390/en11113009

Okta. (2023). The secure sign-in trends report. *Author.* https://www.okta.com/sites/default/files/2023-06/Okta_MFA_Report_06_21.pdf

Olabanji, S.O., Olaniyi, O.O., Adigwe, C.S., Okunleye, O.J., & Oladoyinbo, T.O. (2024). AI for Identity and Access Management (IAM) in the Cloud: Exploring the Potential of Artificial Intelligence to Improve User Authentication, Authorization, and Access Control within Cloud-Based Systems. *Asian Journal of Research in Computer Science*. DOI:DOI: 10.9734/ajrcos/2024/v17i3423

Oladoyinbo, T. O., Olabanji, S. O., Olaniyi, O. O., Adebiyi, O. O., Okunleye, O. J., & Ismaila Alao, A. (2024). Exploring the challenges of artificial intelligence in data integrity and its influence on social dynamics. *Asian Journal of Advanced Research and Reports*, 18(2), 1–23. https://ssrn.com/abstract=4693987. DOI: 10.9734/ajarr/2024/v18i2601

Oliveira, V. A. R. D.. (2023). Green logistics and resource-saving technologies in circular economy. *Transportation Research Part D, Transport and Environment*, 95, 102849.

Olorunsogo, T., Jacks, B. S., & Ajala, O. A. (2024). Leveraging quantum computing for inclusive and responsible AI development: A conceptual and review framework. *Computer Science & IT Research Journal*, 5(3), 671–680. DOI: 10.51594/csitrj.v5i3.927

Omodan, B. I. (2024). Redefining university infrastructure for the 21st century: An interplay between physical assets and digital evolution. *Journal of Infrastructure. Policy and Development*, 8(4), 3468. DOI: 10.24294/jipd.v8i4.3468

Opoku, E. K., Wimalasena, L., & Sitko, R. (2024). Sexism and workplace interpersonal mistreatment in hospitality and tourism industry: A critical systematic literature review. *Tourism Management Perspectives*, 53, 101285. DOI: 10.1016/j.tmp.2024.101285

Opportunities and challenges in online marketplace lending. *U.S. department of the treasury*. (2016). https://home.treasury.gov/system/files/231/Opportunities_and_Challenges_in_Online_Marketplace_Lending_white_paper.pdf

Orem, S., Binkert, J., & Clancy, A. L. (2007). *Appreciative coaching: A positive process for change*. Jossey-Bass/Wiley.

Osmëi, T., & Ali, M. (2023, August). Hands-on cyber risk management scepticism. *In 2023 International Conference on Computing, Electronics & Communications Engineering (iCCECE)* (pp. 89-94). IEEE. DOI: 10.1109/iCCECE59400.2023.10238544

Oswick, C., Keenoy, T., & Grant, D. (2002). Note: Metaphor and analogical reasoning in organization theory: Beyond orthodoxy. *Academy of Management Review*, 27(2), 294–303. DOI: 10.2307/4134356

Owoseni, A. (2023). What is digital transformation? Investigating the metaphorical meaning of digital transformation and why it matters. *Digital Transformation and Society*, 2(1), 78–96. DOI: 10.1108/DTS-10-2022-0049

Oxford Analytica. (2023). Cyber trends underline need for mature MFA. *Emerald Expert Briefings*, (oxan-db).

Ozkan-Ozay, M., Akin, E., Aslan, Ö., Kosunalp, S., Iliev, T., Stoyanov, I., & Beloev, I. (2024). *A comprehensive survey: Evaluating the efficiency of artificial intelligence and machine learning techniques on cyber security solutions*. IEEE., DOI: 10.1109/ACCESS.2024.3355547

Özlen, M. K., & Djedovic, I. (2017). Online banking acceptance: The influence of perceived system security on perceived system quality. *Accounting and Management Information Systems*, 16(1), 164–178. DOI: 10.24818/jamis.2017.01008

Özşahan, H. (2023, November 23). 40+ Multi-factor authentication (MFA) statistics to know in 2024. *Resmo Inc*.https://www.resmo.com/blog/multifactor-authentication-statistics#:~:text=In%20companies%20with%20over%2010%2C000%20employees%2C%2087%25%20use,the%20adoption%20rate%20is%20even%20lower%20at%2027%25

Oztemel, E., & Gursev, S. (2020). Literature review of industry 4.0 and related technologies. *Journal of Intelligent Manufacturing*, 31(1), 127–182. DOI: 10.1007/s10845-018-1433-8

Page, M. J., Page, J. E., McKenzie, P. M., Bossuyt, I., Boutron, T. C., Hoffmann, C. D., Mulrow, L., Shamseer, J. M., Tetzlaff, E. A., Akl, S. E., Brennan, R., Chou, J., Glanville, J. M., Grimshaw, A., Hróbjartsson, M. M., Lalu, T., Li, E. W., Loder, E., Mayo-Wilson, S., & McGuinness, L. A. (2021). The PRISMA 2020 statement: An updated guideline for reporting systematic reviews. *BMJ (Clinical Research Ed.)*, 372, n71. Advance online publication. DOI: 10.1136/bmj.n71 PMID: 33782057

Pagoropoulos, A., Pigosso, D. C. A., & McAloone, T. C. (2017). Integration of circular economy into existing systems and infrastructure. *Resources, Conservation and Recycling*, 126, 52–60.

Pahlevi, A. and Laksana, R. D. (2022). The influence of organizational politics on organizational commitment and job satisfaction and its influence on organizational citizenship behavior. Eduvest - Journal of Universal Studies, 2(7). DOI: 10.36418/eduvest.v2i7.497

Pai, D. D., Sturbelle, I. C. S., Santos, C. D., Tavares, J. P., & Lautert, L. (2018). Physical and psychological violence in the workplace of healthcare professionals. *Texto & Contexto Enfermagem*, 27, e2420016.

Pai, D. R. (2023). Complexities of Simultaneously Improving Quality and Lowering Costs in Hospitals Comment on Hospitals Bending the Cost Curve with Increased Quality: A Scoping Review into Integrated Hospital Strategies. *International Journal of Health Policy and Management*, 12, 7442. DOI: 10.34172/ijhpm.2022.7442 PMID: 36404505

Pamungkas, Y., Santoso, A., Ashari, B., Sensuse, D., Mishbaha, M., & Meiyanti, R. (2019). Evaluation of Interoperability Maturity Level: Case Study Indonesian Directorate General of Tax. *Procedia Computer Science*, 157, 543–551. DOI: 10.1016/j.procs.2019.09.012

Pangarkar, N., & Prabhudesai, R. (2024). Using porter's five forces analysis to drive strategy. *Global Business and Organizational Excellence*, 43(5), 24–34. DOI: 10.1002/joe.22250

Paniello-Castillo, B., González-Rojo, E., González-Capella, T., Civit, N. R., Bernal-Triviño, A., Legido-Quigley, H., & Gea-Sánchez, M. (2023). "Enough is Enough": Tackling sexism, sexual harassment, and power abuse in Spain's academia and healthcare sector. *The Lancet Regional Health. Europe*, 34, 34. DOI: 10.1016/j.lanepe.2023.100754 PMID: 37927426

Papageorgiou, L. G., & Tzanetakis, M. (2021). Technological advancements supporting circular economy in logistics. *Computers & Chemical Engineering*, 147, 107244. DOI: 10.1016/j.compchemeng.2021.107244

Papaspirou, V., Papathanasaki, M., Maglaras, L., Kantzavelou, I., Douligeris, C., Ferrag, M. A., & Janicke, H. (2023). A novel authentication method that combines honeytokens and Google authenticator. *Information (Basel)*, 14(7), 386. DOI: 10.3390/info14070386

Papernot, N. (2021). Adversarial Machine Learning. In *Encyclopedia of Cryptography, Security and Privacy* (pp. 1–4). Springer Berlin Heidelberg., DOI: 10.1007/978-3-642-27739-9_1635-1

Pargaonkar, Y. (2016). Leveraging patent landscape analysis and IP competitive intelligence for competitive advantage. *World Patent Information*, 45, 10–20. DOI: 10.1016/j.wpi.2016.03.004

Paris, R. A. (2024). Intersectionalities of systematic barriers set upon underrepresented students in STEM: Capturing the potential benefits of online modality. *University Honors Theses. Paper 1441.* DOI: 10.15760/honors.1473

Pascoe, E. A., & Richman, L. S. (2009). Perceived discrimination and health: A meta-analytic review. *Psychological Bulletin*, 135(4), 531–554. DOI: 10.1037/a0016059 PMID: 19586161

Pasini, M. L., Yin, J., & Li, Y. W. (2021). A scalable algorithm for the optimization of neural network architectures. *Parallel Computing*, 104-105, 102788. DOI: 10.1016/j.parco.2021.102788

Patel, P. C. (2024). Out of the frying pan into the fire: Displaced workers' vocational skill specificity, self-employment, and income. *Small Business Economics*, 63(3), 1–27. DOI: 10.1007/s11187-023-00856-1

Patel, P., & Rietveld, C. (2020). The impact of financial insecurity on the self-employed's short-term psychological distress: Evidence from the COVID-19 pandemic. *P*, 14, e00206. Advance online publication. DOI: 10.1016/j.jbvi.2020.e00206

Patel, S., Kumar, R., & Smith, T. (2023). Correlating EMRAM stages with clinical outcomes and operational efficiency. *Health Informatics Journal*, 29(1), 15–29. DOI: 10.1177/14604582221103612

Patty, R. (2015). Credit card issuers' claims arising from large-scale data breaches. *Journal of Taxation and Regulation of Financial Institutions*, 28(3), 5–18.

Paul, J., Khatri, P., & Kaur Duggal, H. (2023). Frameworks for developing impactful systematic literature reviews and theory building: What, Why and How? *Journal of Decision Systems*, •••, 1–14. DOI: 10.1080/12460125.2023.2197700

Paulk, M. C. (2009). A history of the Capability Maturity Model for software. Software Quality Professional, 12, 9, 12-19.

Pei, H., Yu, S., & Tian, B. (2014). Analysis of Apple's Design Management Policy. *Applied Mechanics and Materials*, 496-500, 2626–2629. . DOI: 10.4028/www.scientific.net/AMM.496-500.2626

Pekrun, R. (2024). Overcoming fragmentation in motivation science: Why, When, and How should we integrate theories? *Educational Psychology Review*, 36(1), 27. DOI: 10.1007/s10648-024-09846-5

Peng, J., Li, M., Wang, Z., & Lin, Y. (2021). Transformational leadership and employees' reactions to organizational change: Evidence from a meta-analysis. *The Journal of Applied Behavioral Science*, 57(3), 369–397. DOI: 10.1177/0021886320920366

Peter, M. K., Kraft, C., & Lindeque, J. (2020). Strategic action fields of digital transformation: An exploration of the strategic action fields of Swiss SMEs and large enterprise. *Journal of Strategy and Management*, 13(1), 160–180. DOI: 10.1108/JSMA-05-2019-0070

Pew. (2021, May 2). what policymakers can learn from the 'Minnesota Model' of broadband expansion. *Author*. https://www.pewtrusts.org/en/research-and-analysis/articles/2021/03/02/what-policymakers-can-learn-from-the-minnesota-model-of-broadband-expansion

Pfeffer, J., & Sutton, R. I. (2006). Profiting from evidence-based management. *Strategy and Leadership*, 34(2), 35–42. DOI: 10.1108/10878570610652617

Pfizer (2023). Annual Report. https://annualreport.stocklight.com/nyse/pfe/23658781.pdf

Pierce, S., Bolter, J., & Selee, A. (2018). U.S. immigration policy under Trump: Deep changes and lasting impacts. *Migration Policy Institute*, 9, 1–24.

Pietrzak, M., & Paliszkiewicz, J. (2015). Framework of strategic learning: The PDCA cycle. *Management*, 10(2), 149–161.

Pinder, C. C., & Bourgeois, V. W. (1982). Controlling tropes in administrative science. *Administrative Science Quarterly*, 27(4), 641–652. DOI: 10.2307/2392535

Pirandola, S., Andersen, U. L., Banchi, L., Berta, M., Bunandar, D., Colbeck, R., Englund, D., Gehring, T., Lupo, C., Ottaviani, C., Pereira, J. L., Razavi, M., Shamsul Shaari, J., Tomamichel, M., Usenko, V. C., Vallone, G., Villoresi, P., & Wallden, P. (2020). Advances in quantum cryptography. *Advances in Optics and Photonics*, 12(4), 1012. DOI: 10.1364/AOP.361502

Plotinsky, D., & Cinelli, G. M. (2024). *Existing and proposed federal AI regulation in the United States*. https://www.morganlewis.com/pubs/2024/04/existing-and-proposed-federal-ai-regulation-in-the-united-states

Polacko, M. (2021). Causes and consequences of income inequality: An overview. *Statistics, Politics, and Policy*, 12(2), 341–357. DOI: 10.1515/spp-2021-0017

Pondomatti, S. C., Tyagi, I., Shrivastava, K. K., Mahajan, S., Patel, J., Shinde, M. A., & Shrivastava, K. K.Sr. (2024). A Literature Review of the Integration of Ancient Indian Mythology in Clinical Medicine: A Holistic Approach to Health and Healing. *Cureus*, 16(7). Advance online publication. DOI: 10.7759/cureus.63779 PMID: 39099985

Ponnahennedige, U. (2021). Service recovery in luxury hotels and resorts in Sri Lanka.

Pooranam, N., Surendran, D., Karthikeyan, N., & Rajathi, G. I. (2023). *Quantum computing: Future of artificial intelligence and its applications. Quantum Computing and Artificial Intelligence: Training Machine and Deep Learning Algorithms on Quantum Computers*. Walter de Gruyter GmbH & Co KG.

Pope County Minnesota. (2019). Total broadband coverage in county now in sight; Pope county Starbuck telephone project receives $4.2mm deed grant. *Author*. https://www.popecountymn.gov/total-broadband-coverage-in-county-now-in-sight-pope-county-starbuck-telephone-project-receives-4-2mm-deed-grant-2/

Porter, M. E. (2008). Competitive advantage: Creating and sustaining superior performance. simon and schuster.

Porter, M. E. (1979). HBR. *Harvard Business Review*.

Porter, M. E. (2008). The five competitive forces that shape strategy. *Harvard Business Review*, 86(1), 78–93. PMID: 18271320

Portier, C., Vervaet, C., & Vanhoorne, V. (2021). Continuous twin screw granulation: A review of recent progress and opportunities in formulation and equipment design. *Pharmaceutics*, 13(5), 668. DOI: 10.3390/pharmaceutics13050668 PMID: 34066921

Powell, D., Reich, M., Allegretto, S., & Jacobs, K. (2021). Minimum wage effects across state borders: Estimates using contiguous counties. *Journal of Labor Economics*, 39(S1), S139–S186.

Prahalad, C. K., & Hamel, G. (1990). The core competence of the corporation. (also includes a related article on the corporate structure at Vickers Co.). [-). Harvard Business School Press.]. *Harvard Business Review*, 68(3), 79.

Prakash, S., Balaji, J. N., Joshi, A., & Surapaneni, K. M. (2022). Ethical Conundrums in the Application of Artificial Intelligence (AI) in Healthcare—A Scoping Review of Reviews. *Journal of Personalized Medicine*, 12(11), 1914. Advance online publication. DOI: 10.3390/jpm12111914 PMID: 36422090

Prem, E. (2023). From ethical AI frameworks to tools: A review of approaches. *AI and Ethics*, 3(3), 699–716. DOI: 10.1007/s43681-023-00258-9

Preskill, J. (2021). Quantum computing: Current status and future prospects. *Bulletin of the American Physical Society*, 65, •••. https://meetings.aps.org/Meeting/MAR20/Session/P00.5

Proehl, R. (1996). Enhancing the effectiveness of cross-functional teams. *Leadership and Organization Development Journal*, 17(5), 3–10. DOI: 10.1108/01437739610127450

Proença, D., & Borbinha, J. (2017). Enterprise Architecture: A Maturity Model Based on TOGAF ADM, In proceedings of the *2017 IEEE 19th Conference on Business Informatics*, 24-27 July 2017, Thessaloniki, Greece.

Puck, J. F., Rogers, H., & Mohr, A. T. (2013). Flying under the radar: Foreign firm visibility and the efficacy of political strategies in emerging economies. *International Business Review*, 22(6), 1021–1033. DOI: 10.1016/j.ibusrev.2013.02.005

Pumplun, L., Tauchert, C., & Heidt, M. (2019). A new organizational chassis for artificial intelligence-exploring organizational readiness factors.

Quaglini, S. (2010). Information and communication technology for process management in healthcare: A contribution to change the culture of blame. *Journal of Software Maintenance and Evolution: Research and Practice*, 22(6-7), 435–448. DOI: 10.1002/smr.461

Queensland Government. (2021). *Sustainable Agricultural Practices - Improve Farm Operations*. Retrieved from https://www.qrida.qld.gov.au/program/sustainability-loan?gad_source=1&gclid=CjwKCAjwnqK1BhBvEiwAi7o0XzNwiNGmORPRQW4UQo1YFrZKX16G3FC5tSIF1BOX-0L1WZmjZ9MQJRoC-FIQAvD_BwE

Quinn, R., Hopkins, M., & García Bedolla, L. (2017). The politics of immigration and education. *Educational Policy*, 31(6), 707–715. DOI: 10.1177/0895904817725729

Quispe Mamani, J. C., Flores Turpo, G. A., Calcina Álvarez, D. A., Yapuchura Saico, C. R., Velásquez Velásquez, W. L., Aguilar Pinto, S. L., Quispe, B., & Quispe Maquera, N. B. (2022). Gap and inequality in the economic income of independent workers in the region of Puno-Peru and the effect of the pandemic, 2019–2020. *Frontiers in Sociology*, 7, 7. DOI: 10.3389/fsoc.2022.858331 PMID: 35495574

Qureshi, R., Mayo-Wilson, E., & Li, T. (2022). Harm in Systematic Reviews Paper 1: An introduction to research on harm. *Journal of Clinical Epidemiology*, 143, 186–196. DOI: 10.1016/j.jclinepi.2021.10.023 PMID: 34742788

Rachels, J., & Rachels, S. (2015). *The elements of moral philosophy* (8th ed.). McGraw-Hill Education.

Rahimi, K. (2019). Digital health and the elusive quest for cost savings. *The Lancet. Digital Health*, 1(3), e108–e109. DOI: 10.1016/S2589-7500(19)30056-1 PMID: 33323258

Rahman, H. A. (2021). Key technologies driving the car of the future. *Journal of the Society of Automotive Engineers Malaysia*, 3(1), 2–4. DOI: 10.56381/jsaem.v3i1.101

Raji, I. D., Gebru, T., Mitchell, M., Buolamwini, J., Lee, J., & Denton, E. (2020). Saving Face: Investigating the Ethical Concerns of Facial Recognition Auditing. *In Proceedings of the 2020 AAAI/ACM Conference on AI, Ethics, and Society* (AIES '20). DOI: 10.1145/3375627.3375820

Raji, I. D., & Buolamwini, J. (2020). Actionable Auditing: Investigating the Impact of Publicly Naming Biased Performance Results of Commercial AI Products. *Proceedings of the 2019 AAAI/ACM Conference on AI, Ethics, and Society*, 429-435.

Rajpurkar, P., Chen, E., Banerjee, O., & Topol, E. J. (2022). AI in health and medicine. *Nature Medicine*, 28(1), 31–38. DOI: 10.1038/s41591-021-01614-0 PMID: 35058619

Rake, B. (2019). Do publication activities of academic institutions benefit from formal collaborations with firms? *Innovation (North Sydney, N.S.W.)*, 23(2), 241–265. DOI: 10.1080/14479338.2019.1679024

Rakesh, C., Harika, A., Chahuan, N., Sharma, N., Zabibah, R. S., & Nagpal, A. (2023). Towards a circular economy: challenges and opportunities for recycling and re-manufacturing of materials and components. In *E3S Web of Conferences* (Vol. 430, p. 01129). EDP Sciences. DOI: 10.1051/e3sconf/202343001129

Rakha, N. A. (2023). Ensuring Cyber-security in Remote Workforce: Legal Implications and International Best Practices. *International Journal of Law and Policy*, 1(3). Advance online publication. DOI: 10.59022/ijlp.43

Ramezan, C. A. (2023). Examining the cyber skills gap: An analysis of cybersecurity positions by sub-field. *Journal of Information Systems Education*, 34(1), 94–105.

Ramezankhani, M. J., Torabi, S. A., & Vahidi, F. (2018). Supply chain performance measurement and evaluation: A mixed sustainability and resilience approach. *Computers & Industrial Engineering*, 126, 531–548. DOI: 10.1016/j.cie.2018.09.054

Ramirez, R., Melville, N., & Lawler, E. (2010). Information technology infrastructure, organizational process redesign, and business value: An empirical analysis. *Decision Support Systems*, 49(4), 417–429. DOI: 10.1016/j.dss.2010.05.003

Rane, N.. (2023). The Role of AI in Enhancing Decision-Making, Trend Prediction, and Prototyping. *Artificial Intelligence Review*, 56(4), 677–692.

Rao, V. (2024). *Massed Muddler Intelligence.* https://studio.ribbonfarm.com/p/massed-muddler-intelligence?utm_source=tldrnewsletter

Raquib, M. A., Anantharaman, R. N., Eze, U. C., & Murad, M. W. (2010). Empowerment practices and performance in Malaysia-an empirical study. *International Journal of Business and Management*, 5(1), 123.

Raschke, D., & Peace, C. (2021). Remapping Career Counseling for Future Work. *TMS Proceedings 2021.* DOI: 10.1037/tms0000104

Rath, K., Altintas, S., & Ulrich, S. (2022). Advances in closed-loop packaging systems: Case studies from the Australian industry. *Packaging Technology & Science*, 35(1), 23–35. DOI: 10.1002/pts.2819

Ratiu, R. (2024). *Securing the future: Enhancing cybersecurity in 2024 and beyond.* https://www.isaca.org/resources/news-and trends/isaca-now-blog/2024/securing-the-future-enhancing-cybersecurity-in-2024-and-beyond

Ravi, G., Nur, M., & Kiswara, A. (2023). *Analyzing Changes in Traditional Industries: Challenges and Opportunities in the E-commerce Era. IAIC Transactions on Sustainable Digital Innovation.* ITSDI., DOI: 10.34306/itsdi.v5i1.608

Rawls, J. (1971). *A Theory of justice.* Harvard University Press. DOI: 10.4159/9780674042605

Rea, L. M., & Parker, R. A. (2014). *Designing and conducting survey research: A comprehensive guide.* John Wiley & Sons.

Reddy, M. V. R. (2012). Status of supply chain management in India. *International Journal of Emerging Technology and Advanced Engineering*, 2(7), 429–432.

Reddy, S., Allan, S., Coghlan, S., & Cooper, P. (2020). A governance model for the application of AI in health care. *Journal of the American Medical Informatics Association : JAMIA*, 27(3), 491–497. DOI: 10.1093/jamia/ocz192 PMID: 31682262

Redmond, P., & McGuinness, S. (2021). The impact of the 2016 minimum wage increase on average labour costs, hours worked and employment in Irish firms. *Fiscal Studies*. Advance online publication. DOI: 10.26504/rs118

Rehof, L. A. (2021). Guide to the Travaux Préparatoires of the United Nations Convention on the Elimination of all Forms of Discrimination against [). Brill.]. *Women*, 29, •••.

Reissner, S., Pagan, V., & Smith, C. (2011). 'Our iceberg is melting': Story, metaphor and the management of organisational change. *Culture and Organization*, 17(5), 417–433. DOI: 10.1080/14759551.2011.622908

Reyna, A., Martín, C., Chen, J., Soler, E., & Díaz, M. (2018). On blockchain and its integration with IoT. Challenges and opportunities. *Future Generation Computer Systems*, 88, 173–190. DOI: 10.1016/j.future.2018.05.046

Richardson, R., Schultz, J., & Crawford, K. (2019). Dirty data, bad predictions: How civil rights violations impact police data, predictive policing systems, and justice. New York

Riggi, J. (n.d.). The importance of cybersecurity in protecting patient safety: A high-level guide for hospital and health system senior leaders. *American Hospital Association Center for Health Innovation*. https://www.aha.org/center/cybersecurity-and-risk-advisory-services/importance-cybersecurity-protecting-patient-safety

Rivera, J. J. D., Muhammad, A., & Song, W. C. (2024). Securing digital identity in the Zero Trust architecture: A Blockchain approach to privacy-focused multi-factor authentication. *IEEE Open Journal of the Communications Society*, 5, 2792–2814. Advance online publication. DOI: 10.1109/OJCOMS.2024.3391728

Rizos, V., Behrens, A., Kafyeke, T., Hirschnitz-Garbers, M., & Ioannou, A. (2016). The Circular Economy: Barriers and Opportunities for SMEs. Retrieved from https://ec.europa.eu/environment/eussd/pdf/Circular_Economy_Barriers_and_Opportunities_for_SMEs.pdf

Robaki, G., Papaioannou, A., Yfantidou, G., Kourtesopoulou, A., & Dalakis, A. (2020). Organizational culture and business performance in tourism and hospitality industry: The case of A luxury tourist resort. Cultural and Tourism Innovation in the Digital Era: Sixth International IACuDiT Conference, Athens 2019, 533–542.

Robert, M., Giuliani, P., & Gurau, C. (2022). Implementing industry 4.0 real-time performance management systems: The case of Schneider Electric. *Production Planning and Control*, 33(2–3), 244–260. DOI: 10.1080/09537287.2020.1810761

Roberts, H., Cowls, J., Hine, E., Mazzi, F., Tsamados, A., Taddeo, M., & Floridi, L. (2024). Achieving a 'Good AI Society': Comparing the Aims and Progress of the EU and the US. *Science and Engineering Ethics*, 27(6), 68. DOI: 10.1007/s11948-021-00340-7 PMID: 34767085

Robu, M. (2023). The Gender Pay Gap: A Roadblock to Gender Equality and Sustainable Development. *Analele Universităţii Ovidius, Seria: Ştiinţe Economice*, 23(1), 496–504. DOI: 10.61801/OUAESS.2023.1.64

Rohner, P. (2012). Achieving impact with clinical process management in hospitals: An inspiring case. *Business Process Management Journal*, 18(4), 600–624. DOI: 10.1108/14637151211253756

Rollo, J. M., & Zdziarski, E. L. (2020). Developing a crisis management plan. In *Campus Crisis Management* (pp. 67–85). Routledge. DOI: 10.4324/9780429321658-4

Roscigno, V. J. (2019). Discrimination, sexual harassment, and the impact of workplace power. *Socius: Sociological Research for a Dynamic World*, 5, 2378023119853894. DOI: 10.1177/2378023119853894

Rospenda, K. M., Fujishiro, K., Shannon, C. A., & Richman, J. A. (2008). Workplace harassment, stress, and drinking behavior over time: Gender differences in a national sample. *Addictive Behaviors*, 33(7), 964–967. DOI: 10.1016/j.addbeh.2008.02.009 PMID: 18384975

Rossi, F., & Goglio, V. (2020). Satellite university campuses and economic development in peripheral regions. *Studies in Higher Education*, 45(1), 34–54. DOI: 10.1080/03075079.2018.1506917

Rothblatt, S. (2008). Global branding and the celebrity university. *Liberal Education*, 94(4), 26–33.

Rothwell, W., Bakhshandeh, B., & Imroz, S. M. (2021). *Organization development interventions: Executing effective organizational change*. Productivity Press. DOI: 10.4324/9781003019800

Ruggless, M. A. (2023). *Exploring the development and decision-making process of cost of attendance at American colleges and universities* (Doctoral dissertation, Saint Louis University).

Russo, S., Besmer, M. D., Blumensaat, F., Bouffard, D., Disch, A., Hammes, F., Hess, A., Lürig, M., Matthews, B., Minaudo, C., Morgenroth, E., Tran-Khac, V., & Villez, K. (2021). The value of human data annotation for machine learning based anomaly detection in environmental systems. *Water Research*, 206, 117695. DOI: 10.1016/j.watres.2021.117695 PMID: 34626884

Saadi, I. A., & Razak, R. C. (2019). Organizational Change and Organizational Sustainability: The mediating effect of Innovative Human Capital. Opción. *Revista de Ciencias Humanas y Sociales*, (89), 180.

Sablone, S., Bellino, M., Cardinale, A. N., Esposito, M., Sessa, F., & Salerno, M. (2024). Artificial intelligence in healthcare: An Italian perspective on ethical and medico-legal implications. *Frontiers in Medicine*, 11, 1343456. DOI: 10.3389/fmed.2024.1343456 PMID: 38887675

Sadat, S. E., Lodin, H., & Ahmadzai, N. (2023). Highly secure and easy to remember password-based authentication approach. *Journal for Research in Applied Sciences and Biotechnology*, 2(1), 134–141. DOI: 10.55544/jrasb.2.1.18

Sain, S., Chatterjee, A., & Nundy, S. (2024). When trust is betrayed: The horrific rape-murder of a young resident doctor on duty in Kolkata: A call for justice and change. *Current Medicine Research and Practice*, 14(5), 10–4103. DOI: 10.4103/cmrp.cmrp_142_24

Saldaña, J. (2021). *The Coding Manual for Qualitative Researchers*. Sage Publishers.

Saleem, S., Moosa, K., Imam, A., & Ahmed Khan, R. (2017). Service quality and student satisfaction: The moderating role of university culture, reputation and price in education sector of pakistan. *Iranian Journal of Management Studies*, 10(1), 237–258.

Saleminezhadl, A., Remmele, M., Chaudhari, R., & Kashef, R. (2021). *IoT Analytics and Blockchain*. arXiv preprint arXiv:2112.13430.

Samimi, M., Cortes, A. F., Anderson, M. H., & Herrmann, P. (2022). What is strategic leadership? Developing a framework for future research. *The Leadership Quarterly*, 33(3), 101353. DOI: 10.1016/j.leaqua.2019.101353

Şanlıöz-Özgen, H. K., & Kozak, M. (2023). Customer experience in five-star hotel businesses: Is it an "experience" for customers? *Consumer Behavior in Tourism and Hospitality*, 18(3), 306–320. DOI: 10.1108/CBTH-11-2022-0197

Saravanan, K., Anitha, R., Kamarajapandian, P., Arockiadoss, T. P. R., Kumar, K. S., & Hariharan, R. (2024). Design and Elevating Cloud Security Through a Comprehensive Integration of Zero Trust Framework. *International Journal of Intelligent Systems and Applications in Engineering*, 12(11s), 214–219.

Saritha, K.. (2021). Convergence of AI, IoT, and Blockchain: Opportunities and Challenges. *Journal of Emerging Technologies*, 24(3), 215–234.

Sarker, I. H. (2021). Deep Learning: A Comprehensive Overview on Techniques, Taxonomy, Applications and Research Directions. *SN Computer Science*, 2(6), 420. DOI: 10.1007/s42979-021-00815-1 PMID: 34426802

Sarker, I. H., Furhad, M. H., & Nowrozy, R. (2021). AI-Driven cybersecurity: An overview, security intelligence modeling and research directions. *SN Computer Science*, 2(173), 173. Advance online publication. DOI: 10.1007/s42979-021-00557-0

Sarkis, J. (2022). *Handbook on the Circular Economy*. Edward Elgar Publishing.

Sarkis, J., & A. Z. (. (2021). Circular economy and the future of sustainable supply chains. *International Journal of Production Economics*, 236, 108089. DOI: 10.1016/j.ijpe.2021.108089

Sarkis, J., Kouhizadeh, M., & Zhu, Q. S. (2021). Digitalization and the greening of supply chains. *Industrial Management & Data Systems*, 121(1), 65–85. DOI: 10.1108/IMDS-08-2020-0450

Sarkodie-Mensah, K. (1998). International students in the US: Trends, cultural adjustments, and solutions for a better experience. *Journal of Education for Library and Information Science*, 39(3), 214–222. DOI: 10.2307/40324159

Saros, D. E. (2019). *Principles of Political Economy* (3rd ed.). Valparaiso University.

Sauntson, H., & Morrish, L. (2010). Vision, values and international excellence: The 'products' that university mission statements sell to students. In *The marketisation of higher education and the student as consumer* (pp. 87–99). Routledge.

Scaringella, L., Górska, A., Calderon, D., & Benitez, J. (2022). Should we teach in hybrid mode or fully online? A theory and empirical investigation on the service–profit chain in MBAs. *Information & Management*, 59(1), 103573. DOI: 10.1016/j.im.2021.103573

Schein, E. (2010). *Organizational Culture and Leadership* (3rd ed.). Jossey-Bass.

Schein, E. H. (1984). Coming to a new awareness of organizational culture. *Sloan Management Review*, 25(2), 3–16.

Schiff, D., Borenstein, J., Biddle, J., & Laas, K. (2021). *AI ethics in the public, private, and NGO sectors: A review of a global document collection*. DOI:DOI: 10.36227/techrxiv.14109482

Schneider, D. and Henriques, J. (2020). Compliance program implementation when you are not in the same family. *Journal of Health Care Compliance, January-February 2020*, 53-56.

Schneider, K. T., Swan, S., & Fitzgerald, L. F. (1997). Job-related and psychological effects of sexual harassment in the workplace: Empirical evidence from two organizations. *The Journal of Applied Psychology*, 82(3), 401–415. DOI: 10.1037/0021-9010.82.3.401 PMID: 9190147

Schwartz, N. (2023). *4 charts explaining international enrollment trends*. Education Dive.

Schwartz, R., Vassilev, A., Greene, K., Perine, L., Burt, A., & Hall, A. (2022). *Towards a standard for identifying and managing bias in artificial intelligence*. NIST., DOI: 10.6028/NIST.SP.1270

Scott, J. E. (2007). Mobility, Business Process Management, Software Sourcing, and Maturity Model Trends: Propositions for the IS Organization of the Future. *Information Systems Management*, 24(2), 139–145. DOI: 10.1080/10580530701221031

Scott, P. (2018). *The crisis of the university*. Routledge. DOI: 10.4324/9780429446870

Scott, W. R. (2014). *Institutions and Organizations: Rational, natural, and open systems* (7th ed.). Pearson.

Scown, C. D., Cordeiro, S., & Kueh, J. (2021). Sustainable water management in the Australian wine industry: Challenges and innovations. *Journal of Cleaner Production*, 307, 127362. DOI: 10.1016/j.jclepro.2021.127362

Sefil-Tansever, S., & Yılmaz, E. (2024). Minimum wage and spillover effects in a minimum wage society. *Labour*, 38(1), labr.12259. Advance online publication. DOI: 10.1111/labr.12259

Selvarajan, S., Srivastava, G., Khadidos, A. O., Baza, M., Alshehri, A., & Lin, J. C. (2023). An artificial intelligence lightweight blockchain security model for security and privacy in IIoT systems. *Journal of Cloud Computing (Heidelberg, Germany)*, 12(1), 1–17. DOI: 10.1186/s13677-023-00412-y PMID: 36937654

Selye, H. (1956). *The stress of Life*. McGraw-Hill.

Sen, A. (2009). *The Idea of Justice*. Harvard University Press.

Shah, V. (2021). Machine Learning Algorithms for Cybersecurity: Detecting and preventing threats. *Revista Española de Documentación Cientifica*, 15(4), 42–66. https://redc.revistas-csic.com/index.php/Jorunal/article/view/156

Shaikh, N., Bamne, F., Ali, A., Momin, M., & Khan, T. (2024). Herbal Medicine: Exploring Its Scope Across Belief Systems of the Indian Medicine. In *Herbal Medicine Phytochemistry: Applications and Trends* (pp. 1279–1304). Springer International Publishing. DOI: 10.1007/978-3-031-43199-9_46

Shamim, M. M. I. (2024). Artificial Intelligence in Project Management: Enhancing Efficiency and Decision-Making. *International Journal of Management Information Systems and Data Science*, 1(1), 1–6. DOI: 10.62304/ijmisds.v1i1.107

Shandilya, S. K., Datta, A., Kartik, Y., & Nagar, A. (2024). Achieving digital resilience with cybersecurity. In *Digital Resilience: Navigating Disruption and Safeguarding Data Privacy* (pp. 43–123). Springer Nature Switzerland. DOI: 10.1007/978-3-031-53290-0_2

Sharif, M. H. U., & Mohammed, M. A. (2022). A literature review of financial losses statistics for cyber security and future trend. *World Journal of Advanced Research and Reviews,* 15(1, 138-156. DOI: 10.30574/wjarr.2022.15.1.0573

Sharma, B. (2008). Electronic Healthcare Maturity Model (eHMM). White Paper. Quintegra Solutions Limited.

Sharma, K. (2023). Enhancing cybersecurity through AI: A look into the future. *ISC2*.https://www.isc2.org/Insights/2023/09/Enhancing-Cybersecurity-through-AI-A-Look-into-the-Future

Sharma, S., Yadav, P., & Singh, R. (2020). Data-driven decision-making in agricultural and environmental management. *Environmental Management*, 66(1), 78–91.

Sharton, B. R. (2021). Ransomware attacks are spiking. Is your company prepared? *Harvard Business Review.*https://hbr.org/2021/05/ransomware-attacks-are-spiking-is-your-company-prepared

Shaygan, A., & Daim, T. (2023). Technology management maturity assessment model in healthcare research centers. *Technovation*, 120, 102444. DOI: 10.1016/j.technovation.2021.102444

Shebeshe, E. N., & Sharma, D. (2024). Sustainable supply chain management and organizational performance: The mediating role of competitive advantage in Ethiopian manufacturing industry. *Future Business Journal*, 10(1), 47. DOI: 10.1186/s43093-024-00332-6

Shipsy, (2024). What is Logistics Information System: Your Guide to Smart Logistics. https://shipsy.io/blogs/what-is-logistics-information-system/. Accessed date: 31 July 2024.

Shivashankar, S., Mitra, I., Prakash, A., & Panwar, N. (2020). The effect of gender and work experience on psychological attributes at workplace. *Ushus Journal of Business Management*, 19(2), 1–19.

Shukla, A. K., & Dubey, A. K. (2024). Deployment issues in industrial resolution. In *Computational Intelligence in the Industry 4.0* (1st ed., pp. 161–188). CRC Press. DOI: 10.1201/9781003479031-10

Siddiqui, F. (2011). *Impact of employee's willingness on organizational ... - core*. Journal of Economics and Sustainable Development. https://core.ac.uk/download/pdf/234645454.pdf

Siemon, D. (2022). Elaborating team roles for artificial intelligence-based teammates in human-ai collaboration. *Group Decision and Negotiation*, 31(5), 871–912. DOI: 10.1007/s10726-022-09792-z

Silva, F. S., Soares, F. S. F., Peres, A. L., Azevedo, I. M., Vasconcelos, A. P. L., Kamei, F. K., & Meira, S. R. L. (2015). Using CMMI together with agile software development: A systematic review. *Information and Software Technology*, 58, 20–43. DOI: 10.1016/j.infsof.2014.09.012

 Sindhu, J., Sathish, K., KK, M. J., & Rajula, I. 2024. Violence Against Health Care Professionals:Synopsis, A. (●●●)... *The European Journal of Cardiovascular Medicine*, 14(1), 429–436.

Singareddy, S., Sn, V. P., Jaramillo, A. P., Yasir, M., Iyer, N., Hussein, S., & Nath, T. S. (2023). Artificial intelligence and its role in the management of chronic medical conditions: A systematic review. *Cureus*, 15(9). Advance online publication. DOI: 10.7759/cureus.46066 PMID: 37900468

Singer, P. (2002). *One world: The ethics of globalization*. Yale University Press.

Singh, B., Malviya, R., & Kaunert, C. (2024). Elevating Workplace Sustainability for Employees Lensing Mental Health Advancements: Runway for Future Ready Healthcare Services Projecting SDG 3 (Good Health and Well-Being). In *Impact of Corporate Social Responsibility on Employee Wellbeing* (pp. 285-310). IGI Global.

Sintani, L., Fransisca, Y., Anjarini, A. D., & Mulyapradana, A. (2021). Identification of the effectiveness of higher education marketing strategies using social media. *International Research Journal of Management. IT and Social Sciences*, 9(1), 1–9.

Siqi, J. (2023). China unveils new childbirth support as population on verge of shrinking. South *China Morning Post*. https://www.scmp.com/economy/china-economy/article/3206420/china-unveils-new-childbirth-incentives-population-growth-set-turn-negative# Spence, E. D. (2023). *Transformational leadership among chairs of academic departments in U.S. colleges and universities* (Doctoral dissertation, Trident University International).

Siwach, A., & Pathak, P. (2020). Evaluating the growing importance of IT in the management of logistics and supply chain. *Evaluating the growing importance of IT in the management of logistics and supply chain.*, 45(1), 18-18.

Slobogin, C., & Brayne, S. (2023). Surveillance Technologies and Constitutional Law. *Annual Review of Criminology*, 6(1), 219–240. DOI: 10.1146/annurev-criminol-030421-035102 PMID: 38074421

Smajli, E., Feldman, G., & Cox, S. (2024). Exploring the Limitations of Business Process Maturity Models: A Systematic Literature Review. *Information Systems Management*, 1–20. Advance online publication. DOI: 10.1080/10580530.2024.2332210

Smith, H., Patel, V., & Anderson, J. (2023). Advancing IT process improvement with IDC MaturityScape: A roadmap for success. *International Journal of Information Systems*, 58(1), 75–90. DOI: 10.1016/j.ijinfomgmt.2023.02.004

Smith, J., Brown, A., & Liu, H. (2020). Enhancing supply chain resilience through information logistics. *International Journal of Production Economics*, 220, 233–247.

Smith, J., Brown, A., & Liu, H. (2022). Advanced recycling technologies and their impact on circular economy. *Waste Management (New York, N.Y.)*, 139, 125–137. DOI: 10.1016/j.wasman.2022.01.008

Smith, R., King, D., Sidhu, R., & Skelsey, D. (2014). *The effective change manager's handbook: essential guidance to the change management body of knowledge.* Kogan Page Publishers.

Sojo, V. E., Wood, R. E., & Genat, A. E. (2016). Harmful workplace experiences and women's occupational well-being: A meta-analysis. *Psychology of Women Quarterly*, 40(1), 10–40. DOI: 10.1177/0361684315599346

Solomon, N. O., Simpa, P., Adenekan, O. A., & Obasi, S. C. (2024). Circular economy principles and their integration into global supply chain strategies. *Finance & Accounting Research Journal*, 6(5), 747–762. DOI: 10.51594/farj.v6i5.1133

Soroka, L., Danylenko, A., Sokiran, M., Levchenko, D., & Zubko, O. (2023). Public-private collaboration for national security: Challenges and opportunities. *Amazonia Investiga*, 12(70), 43–45. DOI: 10.34069/AI/2023.70.10.4

Sousa, M. J., Cruz, R., Dias, I., & Caracol, C. (2017). Information management systems in the supply chain. In *Handbook of Research on Information Management for Effective Logistics and Supply Chains* (pp. 469–485). IGI Global. DOI: 10.4018/978-1-5225-0973-8.ch025

Srivastava, P., & Bhatnagar, J. (2010). Vision: The Journal of Business Perspective.

Srivastava, S. K. (2006). Logistics and supply chain management practices in India. *Indian Journal of Marketing*, 36(10).

Srivastava, S. K. (2006). Logistics and supply chain practices in India. *Vision (Basel)*, 10(3), 69–79. DOI: 10.1177/097226290601000307

Stacy, M., Gross, G., & Adams, L. (2022). Applying organizational change theory to address the long-standing problem of harassment in medical education. *Teaching and Learning in Medicine*, 34(3), 313–321. DOI: 10.1080/10401334.2021.1954523 PMID: 34493134

Stahel, W. R. (2016). The circular economy. *NATNews*, 531(7595), 435. PMID: 27008952

Stahl, B. C., Antoniou, J., Bhalla, N., Brooks, L., Jansen, P., Lindqvist, B., Kirichenko, A., Marchal, S., Rodrigues, R., Santiago, N., Warso, Z., & Wright, D. (2023). A systematic review of Artificial intelligence impact assessment. *Artificial Intelligence Review*, 56(11), 12799–12831. DOI: 10.1007/s10462-023-10420-8 PMID: 37362899

Starman, A. B. (2013). The case study as a type of qualitative research. *Journal of Contemporary Educational Studies/Sodobna Pedagogika*, 64(1).

Stęchły, A., & Szpunar, A. (2023). Analysis of potential risks of SMS-based authentication. *Advances in Web Development Journal*, 1(1). Advance online publication. DOI: 10.5281/zenodo.10049987

Stewart, J., Lu, J., Goudie, A., Bennamoun, M., Sprivulis, P., Sanfillipo, F., & Dwivedi, G. (2021). Applications of machine learning to undifferentiated chest pain in the emergency department: A systematic review. *PLoS One*, 16(8), e0252612. DOI: 10.1371/journal.pone.0252612 PMID: 34428208

Stier, H., Lewin-Epstein, N., & Braun, M. (2013). Work–family conflict in comparative perspective: The role of social policies. *Research in Social Stratification and Mobility*, 31, 1–16. DOI: 10.1016/j.rssm.2012.10.001

Stoller, G. (2024). Questrom learning community with Greg Stoller. *YouTube*. Retrieved January 20, 2024, from https://www.youtube.com/watch?v=B_f8m3U0OJ4

Stoppel, C. A. (2023). *What is influencing net tuition revenue?: A panel data study of public doctoral universities* (Doctoral dissertation, University of Kansas).

Stosic, K., Dahlstrom, N., & Boonchai, C. (2023). Applying lessons from aviation safety culture in the hospitality industry: A review and road map. *International Journal of Occupational Safety and Ergonomics*, 29(3), 1025–1036. DOI: 10.1080/10803548.2022.2108638 PMID: 35915910

Stoumpos, A.I., Kitsios, F., & Talias, M. A. (2023). Digital Transformation in Healthcare: Technology Acceptance and Its Applications. *International Journal of Environmental Research and Public Health*, 15;20(4):3407. .DOI: 10.3390/ijerph20043407

Stowe, K., & Komasara, D. (2016). An analysis of closed colleges and universities. *Planning for Higher Education*, 44(4), 79.

Strahilevitz, L. (2020). Data security's unjust enrichment theory. *Chicago Unbound. University of Chicago Law School*, 87, 2477–2491.

Strohm, M., & Horton, C. (2023, November 24). 5 benefits of Digital Banking. *Forbes*. https://www.forbes.com/advisor/banking/benefits-of-digital-banking/

Strubell, E., Ganesh, A., & McCallum, A. (2019). Energy and Policy Considerations for Deep Learning in NLP. *Proceedings of the 57th Annual Meeting of the Association for Computational Linguistics*. DOI: 10.18653/v1/P19-1355

Suárez-Orozco, C., & López Hernández, G. (2020). "Waking up every day with the worry": A mixed-methods study of anxiety in undocumented Latinx college students. *Frontiers in Psychiatry*, 11, 568167. DOI: 10.3389/fpsyt.2020.568167 PMID: 33281641

Subramanian, N., & Suresh, M. (2022). Integrated circular economy framework for resilient supply chains: A digital transformation perspective. *Business Strategy and the Environment*, 31(5), 2035–2049.

Subramanian, N., & Suresh, M. (2022). The contribution of organizational learning and green human resource management practices to the circular economy: A relational analysis–evidence from manufacturing SMEs (part II). *The Learning Organization*, 29(5), 443–462. DOI: 10.1108/TLO-06-2022-0068

Suhrab, M., Chen, P., & Ullah, A. (2024). Digital financial inclusion and income inequality nexus: Can technology innovation and infrastructure development help in achieving sustainable development goals? *Technology in Society*, 76, 102411. DOI: 10.1016/j.techsoc.2023.102411

Suleski, T., Ahmed, M., Yang, W., & Wang, E. (2023). A review of multi-factor authentication in the Internet of Healthcare Things. *Digital Health*, 9, 20552076231177144. Advance online publication. DOI: 10.1177/20552076231177144 PMID: 37252257

Sumagaysay, L., & Agrawal, S. (2023, December 21). New California laws raise the minimum wage for 2 industries. Others could see pay hikes, too. *CAL Matters*. https://calmatters.org/economy/2023/12/minimum-wage-2024/

Sun, J., Lenz, D., Yu, H., & Peterka, T. (2024). MFA-DVR: Direct volume rendering of MFA models. *Journal of Visualization / the Visualization Society of Japan*, 27(1), 109–126. DOI: 10.1007/s12650-023-00946-y

Suresan, V., Jnaneswar, A., Swati, S. P., Jha, K., Goutham, B. S., & Kumar, G. (2019). The impact of outreach programs on academics development, personal development and civic responsibilities of dental students in Bhubaneswar city. *Journal of Education and Health Promotion*, 8(1), 188. DOI: 10.4103/jehp.jehp_56_19 PMID: 31867373

Sustainable Development Goals Academy. (2019). Circular economy and e-waste management in Australia. *International Journal of Environmental Research and Public Health*, 16(4), 607. DOI: 10.3390/ijerph16040607 PMID: 30791457

Swan, M., & dos Santos, R. P. (2023). Quantum intelligence: responsible human-ai entities. In *AAAI Spring Symposium* (pp. 21–31). SRAI., https://ceur-ws.org/Vol-3527/Paper_2896.pdf

Sweeney, L. (2013). Discrimination in online ad delivery. *Communications of the ACM*, 56(5), 44–54. DOI: 10.1145/2447976.2447990

Taddeo, M., & Floridi, L. (2018). How AI can be a force for good. *Science*, 361(6404), 751–752. DOI: 10.1126/science.aat5991 PMID: 30139858

Tambunan, P. N. P., Legowo, N., & Tambunan, D. R. (2024). Strengthening payment card data security: A study on compliance enhancement and risk mitigation through MFA implementation under PCI DSS 4.0. *Journal of Theoretical and Applied Information Technology*, 102(9).

Tanjung, I. U., & Annisa, S. (2024). Comparative Analysis of Efforts to Prevent Sexual Violence and Legal Protection for Women in the Criminal Code and Sexual Violence Crime Law (UU NO. 12 of 2022). International Journal of Synergy in Law. *Criminal Justice*, 1(1), 37–50.

Tarhan, A., Turetken, O., & Reijers, H. A. (2015). Do mature business processes lead to improved performance? a review of literature for empirical evidence. In: Proceedings of the *23rd European Conference on Information Systems* (ECIS), 26-29 May 2015, Munster, Germany, Association for Information Systems, 1-6.

Tarhan, A., Garousi, V., Turetken, O., Soylemez, M., & Garossi, S. (2020). Maturity assessment and maturity models in health care: A multivocal literature review. *Digital Health*, 6, 1–20. DOI: 10.1177/2055207620914772 PMID: 32426151

Tarhan, A., Turetken, O., & Reijers, H. A. (2016). Business process maturity models: A systematic literature review. *Information and Software Technology*, 75, 122–134. DOI: 10.1016/j.infsof.2016.01.010

Tasseron-Dries, P. E., Smaling, H. J., Nakanishi, M., Achterberg, W. P., & van der Steen, J. T. (2023). What are best practices for involving family caregivers in interventions aimed at responsive behaviour stemming from unmet needs of people with dementia in nursing homes: A scoping review. *BMJ Open*, 13(12), e071804. DOI: 10.1136/bmjopen-2023-071804 PMID: 38149428

Taykhman, N. (2016). Defying Silence: Immigrant Women Workers, Wage Theft, and Anti-Retaliation Policy in the States. *Colum. J. Gender & L.*, 32, 96.

Taylor, Z. W., & Bicak, I. (2020). First-generation college student financial aid: Results from a national financial aid jargon survey. *The College Student Affairs Journal*, 38(1), 91–109. DOI: 10.1353/csj.2020.0006

Teh, Y. F., & Ramli, S. N. (2023). Implementation of multi-factor authentication on A vaccination record system. *Applied Information Technology and Computer Science*, 4(1), 019-039. https://publisher.uthm.edu.my/periodicals/index.php/aitcs/article/view/7327

Teh, Y., Tan, Y., & Wong, S. (2021). 5G cybersecurity: risk assessment and incident response in the healthcare industry. *International Conference on Digital Transformation and Applications (ICDXA)*, 25-26 October 2021, 145-152. DOI: 10.56453/icdxa.2021.1015

Temoshok, D. (2022, February, 15). NIST Update: Multi-factor authentication and SP 800-63 digital identity guidelines. *NIST; United stated Department of Commerce*. https://csrc.nist.gov/csrc/media/Presentations/2022/multi-factor-authentication-and-sp-800-63-digital/images-media/Federal_Cybersecurity_and_Privacy_Forum_15Feb2022_NIST_Update_Multi-Factor_Authentication_and_SP800-63_Digital_Identity_%20Guidelines.pdf

Thanh, U. P. T. (2022). The application of Kotter's model of change in higher education: A case study in Vietnam private universities. *International Journal of Social Science And Human Research*, 05(1), 1. DOI: 10.47191/ijsshr/v5-i1-01

The Federal Science, Technology, Engineering, And Mathematics (Stem) Education Strategic Plan. *Author*. https://www.whitehouse.gov/wp-content/uploads/2024/04/2023-CoSTEM-Progress-Report.pdf

The Johns Hopkins Health System/Johns Hopkins School of Nursing (2022). Johns Hopkins evidence-based practice for nurses and healthcare professionals: Model and guidelines.

The White House. (2024, April 16). Progress Report on the Implementation of the Federal Science, Technology, Engineering, and Mathematics (STEM) Education Strategic Plan. *Author*. https://www.whitehouse.gov/ostp/news-updates/2024/04/16/2023-progress-report-on-the-implementation-of-the-federal-science-technology-engineering-and-mathematics-stem-education-strategic-plan/

The World Bank. (2020). Tackling the impact of job displacement through public policies. *Author*. https://www.worldbank.org/en/news/feature/2020/10/20/tackling-the-impact-of-job-displacement-through-public-policies

Thekkekara, J. V. & others. (2023). Change Management: A Survey of Literature in View of Analysing the Advantages of ADKAR Model. RGUHS Journal of Allied Health Sciences, 3(2).

Thibaut, J. W., & Walker, L. (1975). *Procedural justice: A psychological analysis*. Lawrence Erlbaum Associates.

Thomson Reuters. (Thomson Reuters Foundation). (June 26, 2018). Factors which make India the most dangerous country for women in 2018 (by ranking out of 10 where 1 is worst) [Graph]. In *Statista*. Retrieved October 25, 2024, from https://www.statista.com/statistics/909596/india-most-dangerous-country-for-women/

Thorbecke, C., & Ziady, H. (2024). *Microsoft is laying off 10,000 employees*. https://www.cnn.com/2023/01/18/tech/microsoft-layoffs/index.html

Tierney, W. G. (1988). Organizational culture in higher education: Defining the essentials. *The Journal of Higher Education*, 59(1), 2–21. DOI: 10.1080/00221546.1988.11778301

Tierney, W. G. (2008). *The impact of culture on organizational decision-making: Theory and practice in higher education* (1st ed.). Routledge., DOI: 10.4324/9781003447887

Timmons, A. C., Duong, J. B., Simo Fiallo, N., Lee, T., Vo, H. P. Q., Ahle, M. W., Comer, J. S., Brewer, L. P. C., Frazier, S. L., & Chaspari, T. (2023). A call to action on assessing and mitigating bias in artificial intelligence applications for mental health. *Perspectives on Psychological Science*, 18(5), 1062–1096. DOI: 10.1177/17456916221134490 PMID: 36490369

Tiwari, G., Sinha, A., & Mahapatra, M. (2018). Gender-based violence in the workplace: Health sector perspectives. *Indian Journal of Gender Studies*, 25(3), 357–376. DOI: 10.1177/0971521518786347

Tjahjadi, B., Soewarno, N., Nadyaningrum, V., & Aminy, A. (2022). Human capital readiness and global market orientation in Indonesian Micro-, Small-and-Medium-sized Enterprises business performance. *International Journal of Productivity and Performance Management*, 71(1), 79–99. DOI: 10.1108/IJPPM-04-2020-0181

Torab-Miandoab, A., Samad-Soltani, T., Jodati, A., & Rezaei-Hachesu P. (2023). Interoperability of heterogeneous health information systems: a systematic literature review. *BMC Medical Informatics and Decision Making*, 24, 23(1),18. .DOI: 10.1186/s12911-023-02115-5

Treece, K., & Tarver, J. (2023, September 28). Should you apply for a loan online or in person? *Forbes*. https://www.forbes.com/advisor/personal-loans/online-or-in-person-loans/

Trezzini, A. (2024, February). Hazel Kyrk, The Economics of the Social Relevance of Consumption and John Maynard Keynes' Consumption Function. *In Research in the History of Economic Thought and Methodology: Including a Symposium on Hazel Kyrk's: A Theory of Consumption 100 Years after Publication*, 41, pp. 69-93. Emerald Publishing Limited.

Trist, E. L. (1981). *The Evolution of Socio-Technical Systems. A conceptual framework and an action research program*. Internet Archive. https://archive.org/details/39120320010110

Trivedi, N. K., Tiwari, R. G., Jain, A. K., Sharma, V., & Gautam, V. (2023, August). Impact analysis of integrating AI, IoT, Big Data, and Blockchain Technologies: A comprehensive study. In *2023 3rd Asian Conference on Innovation in Technology (ASIANCON)* (pp. 1-6). IEEE.

Tsai, C.H., Eghdam, A., Davoody, N., Wright, G., Flowerday, S., & Koch, S. (2020). Effects of Electronic Health Record Implementation and Barriers to Adoption and Use: A Scoping Review and Qualitative Analysis of the Content. *Life*, 4, 10(12), 327. .DOI: 10.3390/life10120327

Tsoukas, H. (1991). The missing link: A transformational view of metaphors in organizational science. *Academy of Management Review*, 16(3), 566–585. DOI: 10.2307/258918

Tukker, A. (2015). Product services for a resource-efficient and circular economy – a review. *Journal of Cleaner Production*, 97, 76–91. DOI: 10.1016/j.jclepro.2013.11.049

Tura, N., Hanski, J., Ahola, T., Ståhle, M., Piiparinen, S., & Valkokari, K. (2019). Unlocking circular business: A framework of barriers and drivers. *Journal of Cleaner Production*, 212, 90–98. DOI: 10.1016/j.jclepro.2018.11.202

Turk, M., & Pentland, A. (1991). Face recognition using eigenfaces. *InProceedings of the IEEE Computer Society Conference on Computer Vision and Pattern Recognition* (pp. 586-591). IEEE.

Turner, M. J. (2023). IDC MaturityScape: Digital Infrastructure Operating Model 2.0. IDC. https://www.idc.com/getdoc.jsp?containerId=US50401123

Turner, A., & Fok, L. (2020). The role of circular economy in transforming advanced manufacturing. *Resources, Conservation and Recycling*, 163, 105–116. DOI: 10.1016/j.resconrec.2020.105116

Tyagi, A. K., Mishra, A. K., Aswathy, S. U., & Kumari, S. (2024). *Quantum computing, qubits with artificial intelligence, and blockchain technologies: A roadmap for the future*. Automated Secure Computing for Next-Generation Systems, 367-384. DOI: 10.1002/9781394213948.ch18

Tyler, T. R. (1990). *Why people obey the law*. Yale University Press.

Tyler, T. R. (2006). Psychological perspectives on legitimacy and legitimation. *Annual Review of Psychology*, 57(1), 375–400. DOI: 10.1146/annurev.psych.57.102904.190038 PMID: 16318600

Tyler, T. R., & Lind, E. A. (1992). *A relational model of authority in groups* (Vol. 25). Advances in Experimental Social Psychology. Academic Press., DOI: 10.1016/S0065-2601(08)60283-X

Tytler, R. (2020). STEM Education for the Twenty-First Century. In Anderson, J., & Li, Y. (Eds.), *Integrated approaches to STEM Education. Advances in STEM education*. Springer., DOI: 10.1007/978-3-030-52229-2_3

U. S. Bureau of Labor Statistics [U. S. BLS]. (2024, May). Characteristics of minimum wage workers, 2023. *Author*. https://www.bls.gov/opub/reports/minimum-wage/2023/home.htm

U. S. Department of Labor. (2024, January 1). Consolidated minimum wage table. *Author.*https://www.dol.gov/agencies/whd/mw-consolidated

U.S. Congressional Office. (2024, January 24). How Increasing the federal minimum wage could affect employment and family income. *Author*. https://www.cbo.gov/publication/55681

U.S. Department of the Treasury. (2023, June 15). Paycheck protection program. *Treasury.Gov*https://home.treasury.gov/policy-issues/coronavirus/assistance-for-small-businesses/paycheck-protection-program#:~:text=This%20program%20provides%20small%20businesses,mortgages%2C%20rent%2C%20and%20utilities

Ueda, D., Kakinuma, T., Fujita, S., Kamagata, K., Fushimi, Y., Ito, R., Matsui, Y., Nozaki, T., Nakaura, T., Fujima, N., Tatsugami, F., Yanagawa, M., Hirata, K., Yamada, A., Tsuboyama, T., Kawamura, M., Fujioka, T., & Naganawa, S. (2024). Fairness of artificial intelligence in healthcare: Review and recommendations. *Japanese Journal of Radiology*, 42(1), 3–15. DOI: 10.1007/s11604-023-01474-3 PMID: 37540463

Umbaugh, S. E. (2010). *Digital image processing and analysis: Human and computer vision*. Taylor & Francis Group. DOI: 10.1201/9781439802069

Uzialko, A. (2023, November 20). How small businesses are affected by minimum wage. *Business News Daily*. https://www.businessnewsdaily.com/8984-increased-minimum-wage.html

Vada, S., Dupre, K., & Zhang, Y. (2023). Route tourism: A narrative literature review. *Current Issues in Tourism*, 26(6), 879–889. DOI: 10.1080/13683500.2022.2151420

Valdez, V. B., & Javier, S. P. (2020). Digital divide: From a peripheral to a core issue for all SDGs. In Leal Filho, W., Azul, A. M., Brandli, L., Lange Salvia, A., Özuyar, P. G., & Wall, T. (Eds.), *Reduced Inequalities. Encyclopedia of the UN Sustainable Development Goals*. Springer., DOI: 10.1007/978-3-319-71060-0_107-1

Van der Zande, J. (2018). Banks and digitalization. In *The rise and development of fintech* (pp. 327–349). Routledge. DOI: 10.4324/9781351183628-18

Van Dyk, L., Schutte, C., & Fortuin, J. (2012). A maturity model for telemedicine implementation. In *eTelemed 2012, The Fourth International Conference on eHealth, Telemedicine, and Social Medicine*. 10, 56116.

Van Looy, A., De Backer, M., & Poels, G. (2011). Defining business process maturity. A journey towards excellence. *Total Quality Management & Business Excellence*, 22(11), 1119–1137. DOI: 10.1080/14783363.2011.624779

van Wijngaarden, H., Braam, A., Buljac-Samardžić, M., & Hilders, M. (2023). Towards Process-Oriented Hospital Structures; Drivers behind the Development of Hospital Designs. *International Journal of Environmental Research Public Health*, 21, 20(3),1993. .DOI: 10.3390/ijerph20031993

Vashishth, T. K., Sharma, V., Sharma, K. K., Kumar, B., Chaudhary, S., & Panwar, R. (2024). Security and privacy considerations in cloud-based data processing solutions for sensitive data. In *Developments Towards Next Generation Intelligent Systems for Sustainable Development* (pp. 35–61). IGI Global., DOI: 10.4018/979-8-3693-5643-2.ch002

Vassolo, R. S., Vassolo, A. F., Mac Cawley, G. L., Tortorella, F. S., Fogliatto, D., & Tlapa, G. (2021). Hospital Investment Decisions in Healthcare 4.0 Technologies: Scoping Review and Framework for Exploring Challenges, Trends, and Research Directions. *Journal of Medical Internet Research*, 23(8), e27571. Advance online publication. DOI: 10.2196/27571 PMID: 34435967

Velsen, L., Hermens, H., & d'Hollosy, W. O. (2016). A maturity model for interoperability in eHealth. *IEEE 18th International Conference on e-Health Networking, Applications and Services* (Healthcom). Munich, Germany, 1-6. DOI: 10.1109/HealthCom.2016.7749533

Vera, D., Tabesh, P., Velez-Castrillon, S., Kachra, A., & Werner, S. (2024). Improvisational decision making: Context, antecedents, and outcomes. In *The Routledge companion to improvisation in organizations* (pp. 144–163). Routledge.

Verhoef, P. C., Broekhuizen, T., Bart, Y., Bhattacharya, A., & Dong, Q. J., Fabian, N., & Haenlein, M. (2021). Digital transformation: a Multidisciplinary Reflection and Research Agenda. *Journal of Business Research, 122*(122), 889–901. ScienceDirect. https://www.sciencedirect.com/science/article/pii/S0148296319305478

Veritti, D., Rubinato, L., Sarao, V., De Nardin, A., Foresti, G. L., & Lanzetta, P. (2024). Behind the mask: A critical perspective on the ethical, moral, and legal implications of AI in ophthalmology. *Graefe's Archive for Clinical and Experimental Ophthalmology*, 262(3), 975–982. DOI: 10.1007/s00417-023-06245-4 PMID: 37747539

Verma, R. K., & Gupta, A. K. (2023). Role of Information and Communication Technology in the Digitalization of Violence and Sexual Politics in the Indian Scenario. In *Cyberfeminism and Gender Violence in Social Media* (pp. 35–48). IGI Global. DOI: 10.4018/978-1-6684-8893-5.ch003

Vespa, J. E., Armstrong, D. M., & Medina, L. (2018). Demographic turning points for the United States: Population projections for 2020 to 2060 (pp. 25–1144). Washington, DC: U.S. Department of Commerce, Economics and Statistics Administration, *U.S. Census Bureau.*

Viceira, Luis M., Emily R. McComb, & Dean Xu. (2021). Modern endowment management: Paula Volent and the Bowdoin endowment. *Harvard Business School Case 221–101.*

Vimalaksha, A., Vinay, S., & Kumar, N. S. (2019, December). Hierarchical mind map generation from video lectures. In *2019 IEEE Tenth International Conference on Technology for Education (T4E)* (pp. 110-113). IEEE. DOI: 10.1109/T4E.2019.00-40

Vo, T., Ballinger, C., Shain, K., Schweikert, N., O'Hara, A., Ali, A., Young, C., Dudash, A., O'Hara, J., & Wunderlich, K. (2023). Operational concepts for distributed ledger in ITS use cases: Blockchain research and deployment technical services support (No. FHWA-JPO-23-119). *United States. Department of Transportation. Intelligent Transportation Systems Joint Program Office.*

Von Ghyczy, T. (2003). The fruitful flaws of strategy metaphors. *Harvard Business Review*, 81(9), 86–94. PMID: 12964396

Vo, V., Chen, G., Aquino, Y. S. J., Carter, S. M., Do, Q. N., & Woode, M. E. (2023). Multi-stakeholder preferences for the use of artificial intelligence in healthcare: A systematic review and thematic analysis. *Social Science & Medicine*, 338, 116357. Advance online publication. DOI: 10.1016/j.socscimed.2023.116357 PMID: 37949020

Wachter, S., Mittelstadt, B., & Floridi, L. (2016). Why a right to explanation of automated decision-making does not exist in the general data protection regulation. SSRN *Electronic Journal*. DOI:DOI: 10.2139/ssrn.2903469

Wada, M. (2014). *Studying Overseas: Friends, School and Life*(Doctoral dissertation,).

Wagner, B. (2019). *Ethics as an escape from regulation: From ethics-washing to ethics-shopping?* Being Profiled., DOI: 10.1515/9789048550180-016

Wakiru, J. M., Pintelon, L., Muchiri, P. N., & Chemweno, P. (2020). A simulation approach for investigating the impact of food loss and waste reduction on circular economy: The case of fresh fruits and vegetables supply chain. *Sustainability*, 12(5), 2073.

Walker, B., & Soule, S. (2017, November 16). Changing company culture requires a movement, not a mandate. *Harvard Business Review.*https://hbr.org/2017/06/changing-company-culture-requires-a-movement-not-a-mandate

Walker, D.M., Tarver, W.L., Jonnalagadda, P., Ranbom, L., Ford, E.W, & Rahurkar, S. (2023). Perspectives on Challenges and Opportunities for Interoperability: Findings From Key Informant Interviews With Stakeholders in Ohio. *JMIR Medical Informatics*, 24,11,e43848. .DOI: 10.2196/43848

Walker, G., Stanton, N., Salmon, P., & Jenkins, D. (2021). A review of sociotechnical systems theory: A classic concept for new command and control paradigms. *Theoretical Issues in Ergonomics Science*, 9(6), 479–499. DOI: 10.1080/14639220701635470

Wang, C., Xu, X., & Zhang, L. (2022). IoT applications and their role in circular economy practices. *Journal of Cleaner Production*, 341, 130852. DOI: 10.1016/j.jclepro.2022.130852

Wang, C., Xu, X., & Zhang, L. (2023). Public-private partnerships and their role in circular economy implementation. *Journal of Cleaner Production*, 373, 131771. DOI: 10.1016/j.jclepro.2022.131771

Wang, Y., Bao, Q., Wang, J., Su, G., & Xu, X. (2024). Cloud computing for large-scale resource computation and storage in machine learning. *Journal of Theory and Practice of Engineering Science*, 4(03), 163–171. DOI: 10.53469/jtpes.2024.04(03).14

WANJIKU. A. M. (2022). STRATEGIC CHANGE MANAGEMENT PRACTICES AND PERFORMANCE OF FIVE STAR HO S IN NAIROBI COUNTY, KENYA [PhD Thesis]. KENYATTA UNIVERSITY.

Waqas, M., Tu, S., Halim, Z., Rehman, S. U., Abbas, G., & Abbas, Z. H. (2022). The role of Artificial Intelligence and machine learning in wireless networks security: Principle, practice and challenges. *Artificial Intelligence Review*, 55(7), 5215–5261. DOI: 10.1007/s10462-022-10143-2

Ward, J., & Daniels, E. (2012). The Effectiveness of IT Investments: A Review of Empirical Studies. *European Journal of Information Systems*, 21(3), 245–260. DOI: 10.1057/ejis.2011.36

Waring, T. S. (2015). Information management and technology strategy development in the UK's acute hospital sector: A maturity model perspective. *Public Money & Management*, 35(4), 281–288. DOI: 10.1080/09540962.2015.1047271

Warschauer, M. (2001). Singapore's dilemma: Control versus autonomy in IT-led development. *The Information Society*, 17(4), 305–311. DOI: 10.1080/019722401753330922

Wasserman, L., & Wasserman, Y. (2022). Hospital cybersecurity risks and gaps: Review (for the non-cyber professional). *Frontiers in Digital Health*, 4, 862221. Advance online publication. DOI: 10.3389/fdgth.2022.862221 PMID: 36033634

Watt, H., & Gardiner, R. (2016). Satellite programmes: Barriers and enablers for student success. Wellington, New Zealand: *Ako Aotearoa* (National Centre for Tertiary Teaching Excellence).

Watts, L., & Buckley, M. (2015). A dual-processing model of moral whistleblowing in organizations. *Journal of Business Ethics*, 2017(146), 669–683.

Waugh, E. (2023). What is personally identifiable information? https://www.experian.com/blogs/ask-experian/what-is-personally-identifiable-information/

Webb, S. (1912). The Economic Theory of a Legal Minimum Wage. *Journal of Political Economy*, 20(10), 973–998. Advance online publication. DOI: 10.1086/252125

Weber, M. (1978). *Economy and society: An outline of interpretive sociology.* University of California Press.

Weisbord, M. R. (1976). Organizational Diagnosis: Six Places To Look for Trouble with or Without a Theory. *Group & Organization Studies*, 1(4), 430–447. https://doi-org.proxymu.wrlc.org/10.1177/105960117600100405. DOI: 10.1177/105960117600100405

Weller, S. C. (1998). Structured interviewing and questionnaire construction. *Handbook of methods in cultural anthropology*, 365-409.

Wels, J., Booth, C., Wielgoszewska, B., Green, M., Gessa, G., Huggins, C., Griffith, G., Kwong, A., Bowyer, R., Maddock, J., Patalay, P., Silverwood, R., Fitzsimons, E., Shaw, R., Steptoe, A., Hughes, A., Chaturvedi, N., Steves, C., Katikireddi, S., & Ploubidis, G. (2021). Association of COVID-19 employment disruption with mental and social wellbeing: evidence from nine UK longitudinal studies. DOI: 10.1101/2021.11.15.21266264

Wendler, R. (2012). The maturity of maturity model research: A systematic mapping study. *Information and Software Technology*, 54(12), 1317–1339. DOI: 10.1016/j.infsof.2012.07.007

Wen, T., Puett, R. C., Liao, D., Kanter, J., Mittleman, M. A., Lanzkron, S. M., & Yanosky, J. D. (2024). Short-term air pollution levels and sickle cell disease hospital encounters in South Carolina: A case-crossover analysis. *Environmental Research*, 252, 118766. DOI: 10.1016/j.envres.2024.118766 PMID: 38583660

Wheebox. (January 12, 2024). Share of participation at work across India from 2014 to 2024, by gender [Graph]. In *Statista*. Retrieved October 25, 2024, from https://www.statista.com/statistics/1043300/india-work-participation-by-gender/

Whelehan, D. F. (2020). Students as partners: A model to promote student engagement in post-COVID-19 teaching and learning. *All Ireland Journal of Higher Education, 12*(3).

White House. (2024). FACT SHEET: President Biden takes action to protect American workers and businesses from China's unfair trade practices. The White House. https://www.whitehouse.gov/briefing-room/statements-releases/2024/05/14/fact-sheet-president-biden-takes-action-to-protect-american-workers-and-businesses-from-chinas-unfair-trade-practices/

Whittaker, M., Crawford, K., Dobbe, R., Fried, G., Kaziunas, E., Mathur, V., West, S. M., Richardson, R., Schultz, J., & Schwartz, O. (2018). *AI Now 2018 report.* AI Now Institute.

Wight, C. (2013). Philosophy of social science and international relations. Handbook of international relations, 29-56. DOI: 10.4135/9781446247587.n2

Williams, C. K., Guthery, F. S., Applegate, R. D., & Peterson, M. J. (2004). The northern bobwhite decline: Scaling our management for the twenty-first century. *Wildlife Society Bulletin*, 32(3), 861–869. DOI: 10.2193/0091-7648(2004)032<0861:TNBDSO>2.0.CO;2

Williams, D. R., & Mohammed, S. A. (2009). Discrimination and racial disparities in health: Evidence and needed research. *Journal of Behavioral Medicine*, 32(1), 20–47. DOI: 10.1007/s10865-008-9185-0 PMID: 19030981

Williamson, S. M., & Prybutok, V. (2024). Balancing privacy and progress: A review of privacy challenges, systemic oversight, and patient perceptions in ai-driven healthcare. *Applied Sciences (Basel, Switzerland)*, 14(2), 675. DOI: 10.3390/app14020675

Williams, R. (2011, May-June). Cause for HIPAAnoia? *Journal of Health Care Compliance*, 5-8, 75–76.

Wilson, L. (2022). Americans Deserve to Get a Better Value From CMMI. *INQUIRY: The Journal of Health Care Organization, Provision, and Financing*, 59, 1–4. DOI: 10.1177/00469580221141806 PMID: 36541229

Winner, L. (1980). Do artifacts have politics? *Daedalus*, 109(1), 121–136. https://www.jstor.org/stable/20024652

Woldemariam, M. T., & Jimma, W. (2023). Adoption of electronic health record systems to enhance the quality of healthcare in low-income countries: A systematic review. *BMJ Health & Care Informatics*, 30(1), e100704. DOI: 10.1136/bmjhci-2022-100704 PMID: 37308185

Woods, L., Dendere, R., Eden, R., Grantham, B., Krivit, J., Pearcem, A., McNeil, K., Green, D., & Sullivan, C. (2023). Perceived impact of digital health maturity on patient experience, population health, health care costs, and provider experience: Mixed methods case study. *Journal of Medical Internet Research*, 25, e45868. DOI: 10.2196/45868 PMID: 37463008

Worke, M. D., Koricha, Z. B., & Debelew, G. T. (2021). Coping strategies and perceived barriers of women hospitality workplace employees to sexual harassment in Bahir Dar city, Ethiopia: A grounded theory approach. *BMC Psychology*, 9(1), 1–14. DOI: 10.1186/s40359-021-00648-w PMID: 34530938

World Health Organization. Social determinants of health. Retrieved from https://www.who.int/health-topics/social-determinants-of-health#tab=tab_1

WRAP. (2020). *WRAP and the circular economy*. Retrieved from https://www.wrap.ngo/taking-action/climate-change/circular-economy

Yaghoubi, N. M., & Bahmani, E. (2010). Factors affecting the adoption of online banking: An integration of technology acceptance model and theory of planned behavior. *International Journal of Business and Management*, 5(9), 159–165. DOI: 10.5539/ijbm.v5n9p159

Yaseen, A. (2024). Enhancing Cybersecurity through Automated Infrastructure Management: A Comprehensive Study on Optimizing Security Measures. *Quarterly Journal of Emerging Technologies and Innovations*, 9(1), 38–60.

Young, S. D. (2022, January 26). Memorandum for the heads of executive departments and agencies. *Executive Office of the President Office Of Management And Bud Get*.https://www.whitehouse.gov/wp-content/uploads/2022/01/M-22-09.pdf

Yousefnezhad, N., & Costin, A. (2024, June). Understanding SBOMs in real-world systems–A Practical DevOps/SecOps Perspective. *InInternational Symposium on Business Modeling and Software Design(pp.293-304)*. Springer Nature Switzerland. DOI: 10.1007/978-3-031-64073-5_20

Yu, T., & Wu, N. (2009). A review of study on the competing values framework. *International Journal of Business and Management*, 4(7), 37–42. DOI: 10.5539/ijbm.v4n7p37

Zaakiyyah, H. K. A. (2024). Innovative Strategies to Enhance the Quality of Higher Education Management: Human Resource Development and the Critical Role of Communication. [ADMAN]. *Journal of Contemporary Administration and Management*, 2(1), 331–336.

Zak, P. (2017, January). The Neuroscience of Trust. *Harvard Business Review*. https://hbr.org/2017/01/the-neuroscience-of-trust

Zarbakhshnia, N., Kannan, D., Kiani Mavi, R., & Soleimani, H. (2020). A novel sustainable multi-objective optimization model for forward and reverse logistics system under demand uncertainty. *Annals of Operations Research*, 295(2), 1–38. DOI: 10.1007/s10479-020-03744-z

Zhang, F. (2023). Why is everyone quitting their jobs? *Berkeley Economic Review*. https://econreview.berkeley.edu/why-is-everyone-quitting-their-jobs/

Zhang, J., & Tenney, D. (2023). The evolution of integrated advance persistent threat and its defense solutions: A literature review. *Open Journal of Business and Management*, 12(1), 293–338. DOI: 10.4236/ojbm.2024.121021

Zhang, L., Carter, R. A.Jr, Greene, J. A., & Bernacki, M. L. (2024). Unraveling challenges with the implementation of universal design for learning: A systematic literature review. *Educational Psychology Review*, 36(1), 35. DOI: 10.1007/s10648-024-09860-7

Zhang, M., Lu, S., Zhang, S., & Bai, Y. (2023). The unintended consequence of minimum wage hikes: Evidence based on firms' pollution emission. *Energy Economics*, 125, 106857. DOI: 10.1016/j.eneco.2023.106857

Zhang, W., Zeng, X., Liang, H., Xue, Y., & Cao, X. (2023). Understanding How Organizational Culture Affects Innovation Performance: A Management Context Perspective. *Sustainability (Basel)*, 15(8), 6644. DOI: 10.3390/su15086644

Zhang, X. Y., & Zhang, P. (2016). Recent perspectives of electronic medical record systems. *Experimental and Therapeutic Medicine*, 11(6), 2083–2085. DOI: 10.3892/etm.2016.3233 PMID: 27284289

Zhang, X., Wu, D. D., Wang, X., & Lu, Y. (2019). The influence mechanism of information logistics on supply chain integration and competitive advantage. *Industrial Management & Data Systems*, 119(7), 1437–1457. DOI: 10.1108/IMDS-02-2019-0067

Zhang, Y., Liu, X., & Chen, C. (2021). Developing educational pathways for circular economy competencies. *Journal of Cleaner Production*, 280, 124173. DOI: 10.1016/j.jclepro.2020.124173

Zhang, Y., Liu, X., & Li, H. (2023). AI-Powered Predictive Analytics for Supply Chain Optimization. *International Journal of Production Economics*, 239, 108298.

Zhang, Y., Li, X., & Wang, X. (2022). Sustainable packaging innovations for circular economy. *Packaging Technology & Science*, 35(2), 85–97. DOI: 10.1002/pts.2847

Zhang, Y., Yang, S., & Xu, H. (2020). Data privacy and security concerns in large-scale information logistics. *Journal of Information Privacy and Security*, 16(2), 115–130.

Zhang, Z., Ning, H., Shi, F., Farha, F., Xu, Y., Xu, J., Zhang, F., & Choo, K.-K. R. (2021). Artificial Intelligence in cyber security: Research advances, challenges, and opportunities. *Artificial Intelligence Review*, 55(2), 1029–1053. DOI: 10.1007/s10462-021-09976-0

Zhao, J., & Gómez Fariñas, B. (2023). Artificial intelligence and sustainable decisions. *European Business Organization Law Review*, 24(1), 1–39. DOI: 10.1007/s40804-022-00262-2

Zhou, J. (2015). International students' motivation to pursue and complete a Ph. D. in the US. *Higher Education*, 69(5), 719–733. DOI: 10.1007/s10734-014-9802-5

Zhou, W., Yu, H., & Xu, Z. (2021). Blockchain-based supply chain management: A case study in the Australian retail industry. *Computers & Industrial Engineering*, 154, 107140. DOI: 10.1016/j.cie.2021.107140

Zhuo, Y., Solak, S., Zou, Y., & Hu, B. (2024). Sharing is caring: Designing incentive rebate strategies for information-sharing alliances. *Decision Sciences*, deci.12640. Advance online publication. DOI: 10.1111/deci.12640

Ziaei Nafchi, M., & Mohelská, H. (2020). Organizational culture as an indication of readiness to implement industry 4.0. *Information (Basel)*, 11(3), 174. DOI: 10.3390/info11030174

Zlatolas, L., Welzer, T., & Lhotska, L. (2024). Data breaches in healthcare: Security mechanisms for attack mitigation. *Cluster Computing*, 2024(7), 8639–8654. Advance online publication. DOI: 10.1007/s10586-024-04507-2

Zuboff, S. (2019). *The age of surveillance capitalism: The fight for a human future at the new frontier of power*. Public Affairs.

About the Contributors

Sharon L. Burton leads in product management and development, Organizational Development Change Management, Cyber-Security/Technology, Process Improvement, Telemedicine/Telehealth and Learning & Development. Education includes: Ph.D. in Cybersecurity Leadership, and a DBA in Business Process Improvement; and two MBA degrees - Human Resources Management, and Management. Certifications in the following: AI Prompting Essentials; Project Management Essentials; Master Lean Six Sigma Black Belt; Kaizen Leader; Change Management Professional; Strategic Workforce Planning; Human Capital Strategist; Kirkpatrick Four Levels Evaluation; and Advanced Communicator Gold Toastmaster. As a facilitator and educator of audiences, she has more than 100 academic publications and has presented at over 30 professional conferences. Dr. Burton is available to present at conferences, participate in forums, and other initiatives. She may be reached at sharonlburton2@comcast.net and 302-547-8010.

S. L. Burton is a highly accomplished senior leader with over 25+ years of expertise spanning various domains. Her professional focal points and proficiencies encompass multiple skills and competencies: change management, human performance technology- organizational; development technology/cybersecurity, management, training/development, practical teaching/ facilitation, management, technical writing, engaging presentation skills, adept interviewer capabilities, and expert project and program/project management expertise. Dr. Burton's leadership journey encompasses the following significant roles, including Chief Learning and compliance Officer-Administrator Representative for the Board of Trustees, Chief Cognitive Officer, Chief Learning Officer, Compliance and Information Assurance Officer, Senior Change Management Officer, Senior Business Process Engineer, and Senior Program/Project Manager. She is widely recognized for her exceptional ability to lead transformative organizational change initiatives. She is also at the forefront of leading the development of business impact analysis and business continuity plans. Her skills extend to developing and executing process improvement strategies, authoring insightful content, and fostering a culture of continuous improvement. Beyond her remarkable achievements, Dr. Burton excels in various roles, serving as a dissertation chair, faculty member, facilitator, author, speaker, consultant, and TV co-host. This leader has a portfolio boasting 100+ scholarly publications and active participation in 30+ professional conferences. She uniquely translates technical intricacies for non-technical audiences and senior leadership while offering valuable business process insights to technical teams. Her academic accomplishments include a Ph.D. in Cybersecurity Leadership, a DBA in Quality Systems Management focusing on Business Process Improvement, and two MBA degrees in Human Resources Management and Management. Her impressive credentials also feature certifications, including Project Management Professional), Artificial Intelligence Professional Education and Certification, Master Lean Six Sigma Black Belt, Advanced Telemedicine/Telehealth Professional, Certified Change Management Professional, and Strategic Workforce Planning. Dr. Burton is a highly sought-after speaker who welcomes speaking engagements. She can be contacted at 302-547-8010 or via email at sharonlburton2@comcast.net.

Saumendra Das presently working as an Associate Professor at the School of Management Studies, GIET University, Gunupur, Odisha. He has over 21 years of teaching, research, and industry experience. He has published more than 102 articles in national and international journals, conference proceedings, and book chapters. He also authored and edited 15 books. Dr Das has participated and presented many papers in seminars, conferences, and workshops in India and abroad. He has organized many FDPs and workshops in his career. He is an academician, author, and editor. He has also published two patents. He is an active member of various professional bodies such as ICA, ISTE and RFI. In the year 2023, he was awarded as the best teacher by Research Foundation India.

Jorge Gomes is Professor of Strategy and Management at Universidade Lusófona and researcher at ADVANCE/CSG/ISEG - University of Lisbon. He holds a PhD in Management from ISEG and a Master's in Management Sciences from ISCTE-IUL, a postgraduate degree in Project Management from INDEG / ISCTE and a degree in Geographic Engineering from the Faculty of Sciences of the University of Lisbon. For the last 35 years he has worked as an engineer, project manager, quality auditor and consultant. His research interests include Strategy and Operations, Benefits Management, Project Management, Project Success, Maturity Models, IS/IT Investment Management.

Avery Greene brings a strong and diverse skill set in Incident Response, backed by over 26 years of IT experience across multiple platforms in both private and public organizations. With over 12 years in cybersecurity, Avery is a seasoned security analyst skilled in vulnerability scanning and assessments, policy creation and documentation, and event/incident handling. As a People Leader, Avery has led engineering teams in intrusion detection and network security, demonstrating strong communication skills to promote organizational goals, facilitate presentations, and collaborate with diverse audiences. Known for building successful relationships, Avery excels in consensus building, collaborative working groups, and team development at all organizational levels. Avery holds a Bachelor's degree in Interdisciplinary Studies and a Master's in Cybersecurity from UMBC. He is currently a PhD candidate in Cyber Leadership at Capitol Technology University where Avery focuses on the integration of AI and Network Security.

Cakesha Hardin is now in her first year of doctoral studies in the field of business intelligence within the College of Business, Innovation, Leadership, and Technology at Marymount University. Her main area of interest is in the enhancement of the federal government workforce's agility, with a specific emphasis on the development of digital literacy skills to facilitate more informed decision-making via data analysis. In conjunction with conventional written research, she has conducted thorough research pertaining to the heightened use of artificial intelligence, namely machine learning algorithms, within the realm of clinical decision-making. Mrs. Hardin has a Master of Business Administration degree from the Darden School of Business at the University of Virginia.

Alieu Stephen Kafoe is a doctoral student in Business Intelligence at Marymount University, USA, bringing over two decades of extensive experience in the Food, Beverage, and Process Automation industries. Parallel to his academic pursuits, Alieu is an entrepreneur and a business consultant, helping clients solve complex challenges surrounding implementing business strategy, process control in production, and supply chain operations and management. Alieu's multidimensional professional journey has encompassed diverse leadership positions, including Chief Operating Officer, Director of Brewing Operations, and Sales Director, wherein he has consistently spearheaded initiatives to drive operational excellence, optimize processes, and catalyze revenue growth. His career has been marked by a global presence, living and working in numerous countries across Africa, Europe, and North America, giving him a broad cross-cultural perspective. Alieu's professional accomplishments showcase a proven track record of delivering tangible results. He has successfully implemented the Entrepreneurial Operating System (EOS) across entire organizations, increased production capacity by more than

Sunil Kumar, currently an Associate Professor at Faculty of Management Sciences, Shoolini University, possesses extensive academic and research experience. With a background in Business Administration, Sunil's research endeavors span multiple domains, including human resource management, e-training, and the application of artificial intelligence in business. His prolific contributions are evidenced by numerous research papers, book chapters, copyrights, and patents. Dr. Kumar has a knack for teaching with expertise in subjects like HR Analytics, Talent Management, Industrial Psychology, and more. He has also successfully guided PhD students and actively contributes to various academic administrative roles. Dr. Kumar's vast research landscape includes topics like AI-based chatbots in recruitment, e-training impact, and more. His papers have been published in esteemed journals like Journal of Workplace Learning and International Journal of Law and Management. Moreover, he has authored books and edited volumes touching upon themes related to the contemporary business environment. Dr. Sunil has been a dynamic participant in numerous workshops, ranging from data analysis to stress

Karteek Madapana is a Assistant professor of Financial Management at the GIET UNIVERSITY, Gunupur, Odisha. where he has been teaching since 2013. He has more than 11 years of wide-ranging experience in teaching, research, consulting, and academic administration and qualified in UGC-NET in Management and AP-SLET in Management and Commerce.

Maria Montano is a community professional with a demonstrated history working in the U.S. Senate and the City of Orlando. She is skilled in social media, government relations, constituent outreach, and marketing. She specializes in working with government, private businesses, and non-profit sectors, specifically in government affairs, advocacy, and public relations. She graduated from St. John's University with a master's degree in international relations. She is pursuing her doctorate in business administration at Marymount University.

Tapaswini Panda is presently working as Internal Full Time Research Scholar at VIT VELLORE, TAMILNADU. She has completed Master of Business Administration from GIET University, Gunupur, India. Her research interest is on Talent Management, Work Life Balance, Quality of Work Life and Human Resource Information System. She has published three patents in India and abroad. She is a passionate researcher and a true academician teaches the subject such as Principles of Management, Human Resource Management, Organizational Development and Change. She has published Two Scopus,2 paper in National Journal, 1 UK Patent and two book chapters.

Udaya Sankar Patro is a renowned and successful research scholar who has made significant and innovative contributions to the field of Digital Branding at the National Institute of Technology, Tiruchirappalli. Driven by a fervent desire to expand knowledge and tackle intricate problems, he has committed his professional life to pushing the limits of comprehension in the field of Marketing. He obtained a Bachelor's degree in Chemistry Honors from Berhampur University and thereafter pursued a Master's degree in MBA (Marketing & Human Resource Management) at GIET University, Gunupur. Motivated by an unquenchable thirst for knowledge and a determination to create a significant influence, he is currently pursuing his doctoral studies in Digital Branding at the National Institute of Technology, Tiruchirappalli. He has obtained three patents in India and Internationally. He has authored fifteen book chapters, papers, books and journals across several levels of publication.

Mário José Batista Romão is an Associate Professor of Information Systems at ISEG – University of Lisbon. He is Director of the Masters program in Computer Science and Management. He holds a PhD in Management Sciences by ISCTE-IUL and by Computer Integrated Manufacturing at Cranfiel University (UK). He also holds a MsC in Telecommunications and Computer Science, at IST - Instituto Superior Técnico, University of Lisbon. He is Pos-Graduated in Project Management and holds the international certification Project Management Professional (PMP), by PMI – Project Management International. He has a degree in Electrotecnic Engineer by IST.

Mallika Roy is working as an associate professor (study leave) at the Department of Economics, University of Chittagong, Bangladesh. Mallika completed her Honours (Economics) and Masters' (Economics) at the University of Chittagong. She achieved the Prestigious Prime Minister Gold Medal Award Bangladesh for her scholastic academic results. Being a recipient of a UGC-funded scholarship throughout her studies, she earned her M. Phil (Economics) from the City University of Hong Kong. Her research interests include Macroeconomics, Environmental Economics, Agricultural Economics, Supply Chain, and Economic Development. She has teaching experience of above 12 years. She worked as a research fellow and teaching assistant at the Department of Economics and Finance of the City University of Hong Kong. She worked in Islamia University College and BGC Trust University Bangladesh as a lecturer for several years. After joining the University of Chittagong, she worked at the University of Professional (BUP) Bangladesh, Premier University, and BGC Trust University Bangladesh as an adjunct faculty. She published a good number of her research papers in national and international journals. She also published several newspaper articles.

Fauziatu Salifu-Sidii is currently pursuing a Doctor of Business Administration at Marymount University. With a robust academic background that includes a Master's in Public Administration from Sungkyunkwan University, Ms. Salifu-Sidii has focused their research on exploring the digital transformation of Ghana: analyzing the adoption, legitimacy, and diffusion of digital technologies through the lens of the technology acceptance model and digital era theory from an institutional theory perspective. Their work has been shaped by a passion for digital transformation in emerging economies. She aims to contribute valuable insights to the field of technology adoption. She is committed to advancing knowledge in business Intelligence and bridging the gap between theory and practice.

Jaba Rani Sarker completed her Bachelor's and Master's degrees from Bangladesh Agricultural University. She is currently an associate professor (on leave) at Bangabandhu Sheikh Mujibur Rahman Agricultural University, Bangladesh. She was awarded PhD from Central Queensland University, Australia. Currently, she is a Postdoctoral Research Fellow at CQ University, Australia.

Gregory Stoller is a master lecturer in strategy and innovation at Boston University's Questrom School of Business. He is actively involved in building entrepreneurship, experiential learning and international business programs at Boston University. He also actively mentors student teams which participate in business plan and venture capital competitions. He is the owner of a commercial real estate holding company and speaks, reads and writes 7 different languages.

Eleanor J. Thompson is a doctoral student in Business Intelligence at Marymount University's School of Business, Innovation, Leadership and Technology, where her research focuses on neurodiversity in the workplace. She earned master's degrees from Southern Methodist University (Liberal Arts) and Regis University (Organizational Leadership) and an undergraduate degree in Law from Carleton University in Ottawa, Canada. Her varied professional experience includes time as a stockbroker and options trader, followed by management in the fields of corporate governance, securities compliance, shareholder relations, healthcare mergers and acquisitions, vendor relationships, PPO networks, contract negotiation, medical bill review processes, and operational efficiency maximization.

Index

A

AI Ethics 222, 245, 330, 344, 345, 346
Algorithmic Bias 232, 312, 318, 319, 374
Analogy 2, 3, 4, 5, 7, 8, 9, 11, 13, 14, 16, 217
Authentication Factors 256, 258, 260, 266, 267, 268, 269, 270, 282

B

Biometric Verification 255, 266, 267, 268, 282
Blue Ocean Strategy 53, 54, 55, 56, 57, 58, 59, 61, 62, 63, 64, 65, 67, 68, 69, 70, 73, 74, 75, 77, 78, 80, 82, 83, 85, 87, 88, 89, 91, 92, 94, 95

C

Change Management Theory 112, 137
Circular Economy 449, 450, 451, 452, 453, 454, 455, 456, 457, 458, 459, 460, 461, 462, 463, 464, 465, 466, 467, 468, 469, 470, 471, 472, 473, 474, 475, 476, 477, 478, 479, 480, 481, 482, 483, 484, 485, 486, 487, 488, 489
College Tuition 131
Competitive Advantage 16, 20, 21, 22, 25, 26, 27, 28, 29, 30, 31, 32, 33, 34, 35, 36, 37, 38, 40, 41, 43, 44, 45, 46, 47, 48, 49, 51, 53, 57, 58, 59, 62, 64, 65, 66, 68, 70, 74, 79, 80, 82, 86, 87, 88, 91, 92, 98, 120, 207, 208, 220, 327, 388, 407, 424, 449, 452, 453, 469, 482, 488
Competitive Strategy 73, 74, 82, 87
Compliance 28, 116, 117, 119, 221, 224, 226, 227, 229, 247, 249, 251, 252, 253, 254, 257, 258, 259, 263, 264, 267, 268, 270, 271, 273, 274, 280, 282, 295, 324, 327, 328, 329, 333, 337, 349, 350, 351, 354, 356, 357, 359, 361, 362, 363, 365, 367, 368, 370, 371, 382, 390, 470, 516
Compliance Program 349, 351, 357, 361, 362, 363, 365, 368, 371
Corporate Culture 34, 113, 115, 121, 122, 124, 350, 367
Culture 28, 29, 30, 31, 32, 33, 34, 43, 46, 47, 51, 78, 79, 80, 82, 91, 94, 101, 102, 103, 104, 105, 106, 108, 109, 110, 111, 112, 113, 114, 115, 116, 117, 118, 119, 120, 121, 122, 123, 124, 125, 126, 127, 128, 129, 130, 132, 133, 134, 135, 136, 137, 141, 144, 147, 148, 149, 150, 151, 152, 170, 205, 206, 213, 214, 215, 217, 218, 219, 220, 221, 222, 325, 327, 334, 350, 355, 356, 357, 358, 359, 360, 362, 365, 366, 367, 370, 371, 381, 384, 393, 394, 403, 407, 410, 415, 416, 426, 428, 432, 433, 434, 435, 436, 437, 441, 443, 447, 473, 476, 494, 497, 499, 505, 514, 515, 516
Cyber Incident 245
Cybersecurity 202, 205, 207, 208, 213, 215, 218, 219, 223, 227, 231, 235, 236, 237, 238, 240, 242, 243, 247, 248, 249, 250, 251, 252, 253, 254, 255, 257, 259, 260, 261, 263, 264, 269, 270, 271, 272, 274, 275, 280, 282, 349, 350, 352, 354, 356, 357, 361, 368, 369, 371, 404, 483
Cyber Threats 206, 207, 208, 209, 210, 211, 212, 213, 222, 223, 228, 229, 232, 245, 249, 250, 251, 252, 254, 255, 256, 257, 260, 263, 264, 267, 269, 271

D

Decision-Making Process 151, 293, 312, 376, 390
Digital Divide 155, 156, 158, 160, 161, 165, 167, 168, 169, 172, 173, 176, 177, 180, 181, 182, 183, 184, 185, 186, 187, 188, 189, 191, 195, 196, 197, 198, 199, 202, 203
Digital Transformation 48, 77, 87, 96, 184, 199, 206, 208, 215, 219, 240, 241, 242, 245, 371, 393, 400, 401, 403,

404, 407, 408, 423, 425, 426, 431, 432, 436, 438, 440, 441, 442, 444, 445, 447, 453, 487
Discrimination 101, 102, 103, 104, 105, 106, 107, 109, 110, 111, 113, 116, 118, 119, 121, 122, 124, 125, 127, 128, 129, 172, 193, 284, 285, 301, 302, 303, 304, 305, 306, 307, 308, 309, 311, 312, 315, 316, 323, 326, 329, 331, 332, 346, 347, 348, 373, 375, 376, 377, 382, 384, 491, 492, 493, 494, 495, 496, 497, 498, 501, 502, 507, 512, 513, 515, 516, 517, 518

E

Economic Stability 155, 157, 158, 161, 165, 166, 173, 174, 175, 177, 203
Employee Resistance 430, 436, 440, 441
Enterprises 5, 8, 30, 32, 34, 35, 49, 50, 51, 85, 213, 214, 223, 228, 231, 245, 386, 438, 459
ERM 349, 350, 351, 354, 356, 365
Ethics 9, 21, 88, 89, 198, 208, 222, 232, 236, 237, 242, 245, 274, 283, 285, 287, 323, 325, 327, 330, 333, 334, 336, 341, 343, 344, 345, 346, 347, 351, 355, 357, 358, 360, 361, 366, 368, 369, 370, 371, 393, 394
Ethiopia 25, 26, 27, 28, 29, 30, 32, 33, 34, 35, 37, 49, 50, 130

F

Facial Recognition Technology 283, 284, 285, 286, 287, 288, 289, 291, 292, 295, 296, 301, 303, 307, 309, 310, 311, 312, 315, 318, 321, 322, 328, 330, 331, 332, 334, 335, 337, 338, 340
Financial Institutions 219, 221, 222, 265, 370
Free Choice Idea 433

G

Gender Bias 315, 505

H

Healthcare 72, 73, 93, 96, 129, 134, 177, 181, 183, 184, 194, 235, 238, 244, 257, 274, 275, 280, 349, 350, 351, 352, 353, 354, 356, 360, 361, 362, 365, 368, 369, 370, 371, 372, 373, 374, 375, 376, 377, 381, 383, 384, 385, 386, 387, 388, 389, 390, 391, 392, 393, 394, 395, 396, 397, 399, 400, 401, 402, 403, 404, 406, 407, 408, 409, 412, 413, 414, 415, 416, 417, 418, 419, 420, 421, 422, 423, 424, 425, 426, 428, 458, 491, 492, 494, 495, 496, 497, 498, 499, 500, 501, 502, 504, 505, 507, 512, 513, 514, 515, 516, 517, 519, 520
Historical Mistrust 286, 332, 335
Human Capital 25, 26, 27, 28, 29, 30, 31, 32, 33, 34, 35, 36, 37, 38, 40, 41, 43, 44, 45, 46, 47, 48, 49, 50, 51, 85, 169, 170, 171, 172, 194, 195, 198

I

Incident Response 349, 353, 356, 364, 365, 367, 371
Industry Analysis 56, 63, 88, 92
Information Logistics 449, 450, 451, 452, 453, 454, 455, 456, 458, 459, 460, 461, 462, 463, 464, 465, 466, 467, 468, 469, 470, 471, 472, 473, 474, 475, 476, 481, 482, 484, 487, 488, 489
Innovation 26, 28, 32, 34, 36, 45, 46, 50, 51, 53, 54, 55, 56, 57, 58, 59, 60, 61, 62, 63, 64, 65, 67, 69, 70, 73, 74, 77, 79, 80, 82, 85, 86, 87, 89, 90, 91, 94, 95, 96, 97, 98, 99, 127, 128, 129, 166, 184, 186, 187, 193, 195, 196, 198, 201, 208, 215, 218, 220, 221, 225, 226, 323, 328, 330, 339, 342, 345, 369, 371, 407, 413, 420, 428, 430, 431, 436, 441, 454, 458, 467, 469, 471, 475, 476, 482, 488, 494
International Students 131, 132, 133, 137, 141, 142, 143, 144, 145, 150, 151, 153
IS 2, 3, 5, 7, 8, 9, 10, 11, 12, 13, 14, 15,

16, 17, 18, 26, 27, 28, 29, 30, 31, 32, 33, 34, 35, 38, 39, 40, 41, 42, 43, 44, 45, 46, 47, 48, 51, 53, 54, 55, 58, 59, 61, 62, 66, 69, 70, 71, 72, 73, 74, 75, 77, 81, 82, 91, 96, 102, 103, 104, 105, 106, 107, 108, 109, 110, 111, 112, 113, 114, 115, 116, 117, 119, 120, 121, 122, 125, 126, 129, 131, 132, 133, 134, 135, 136, 137, 138, 140, 141, 142, 152, 153, 155, 156, 157, 158, 159, 160, 161, 162, 164, 165, 166, 167, 168, 169, 170, 171, 172, 173, 174, 175, 176, 177, 179, 180, 181, 183, 184, 185, 186, 187, 188, 189, 190, 191, 192, 195, 196, 203, 205, 206, 207, 208, 209, 211, 212, 213, 214, 215, 216, 217, 218, 219, 220, 221, 222, 223, 224, 225, 226, 227, 228, 229, 230, 231, 232, 236, 239, 240, 241, 243, 244, 245, 247, 248, 249, 250, 251, 252, 253, 254, 255, 256, 257, 258, 259, 260, 261, 262, 263, 264, 265, 266, 267, 268, 269, 270, 271, 276, 281, 282, 284, 286, 287, 290, 291, 292, 294, 296, 298, 299, 300, 301, 302, 303, 304, 305, 306, 307, 308, 309, 310, 311, 312, 313, 314, 315, 316, 317, 318, 319, 320, 321, 323, 324, 325, 326, 327, 328, 330, 332, 333, 334, 335, 336, 339, 343, 349, 350, 351, 352, 353, 354, 355, 356, 357, 358, 359, 360, 361, 362, 363, 364, 365, 366, 370, 371, 373, 374, 375, 376, 381, 382, 383, 384, 385, 386, 387, 389, 390, 391, 392, 399, 400, 401, 402, 403, 404, 405, 406, 407, 408, 409, 410, 411, 412, 413, 414, 415, 421, 423, 426, 429, 430, 431, 432, 433, 434, 435, 436, 437, 438, 439, 440, 441, 442, 444, 445, 446, 450, 451, 453, 455, 456, 457, 458, 459, 460, 462, 463, 466, 467, 468, 469, 470, 471, 472, 474, 475, 476, 477, 486, 492, 493, 494, 497, 498, 499, 500, 501, 502, 503, 504, 505, 506, 509, 510, 511, 512, 513, 514, 515, 516, 519, 520

L

Law Enforcement 284, 285, 286, 287, 288, 289, 296, 297, 299, 303, 304, 305, 306, 307, 310, 312, 315, 321, 322, 331, 332, 333, 334, 335, 339, 343, 356, 361

Leadership 2, 3, 4, 7, 10, 11, 12, 13, 14, 15, 16, 21, 22, 31, 32, 33, 46, 49, 51, 64, 70, 80, 93, 97, 99, 102, 106, 109, 111, 112, 114, 115, 119, 121, 122, 123, 124, 125, 131, 132, 134, 135, 136, 137, 141, 144, 145, 146, 147, 149, 152, 218, 220, 236, 275, 317, 318, 321, 327, 334, 336, 339, 340, 349, 355, 356, 357, 358, 359, 360, 362, 363, 365, 366, 367, 368, 369, 370, 371, 382, 383, 384, 387, 407, 410, 429, 432, 433, 434, 435, 436, 440, 441, 443, 444, 445, 446, 495, 499, 515, 517

Leadership Theory 16, 134, 136, 149, 359, 435, 446

M

Machine Learning 77, 81, 96, 207, 209, 229, 234, 235, 238, 239, 240, 241, 243, 244, 245, 270, 271, 273, 326, 341, 342, 344, 345, 373, 376, 377, 386, 387, 393, 396, 444, 477, 511

Mass Muddler Intelligence 215, 217, 245

Maturity Models 399, 400, 401, 402, 403, 404, 406, 410, 413, 414, 416, 418, 419, 421, 422, 424, 425, 426, 427

Metaphors 2, 3, 5, 6, 8, 10, 11, 12, 13, 14, 15, 16, 17, 19, 20, 22

Minimum Wage Policy 168, 190, 203

Minority Communities 285, 286, 298, 299, 331, 335

O

Online Lending Platforms 429, 430, 431, 435, 442, 443

Organizational Culture Theory 108, 136

Organizational Readiness 25, 26, 27, 28, 29, 31, 32, 33, 34, 35, 36, 37, 38, 40,

41, 43, 44, 45, 49, 50, 51, 205, 206, 207, 208, 212, 213, 214, 218, 219, 232

P

Policing 285, 286, 297, 298, 299, 306, 307, 311, 312, 315, 331, 335, 341, 342, 343, 346
Porter's Five Forces 53, 54, 55, 56, 57, 58, 59, 60, 62, 63, 65, 67, 68, 70, 71, 74, 75, 77, 78, 80, 82, 83, 85, 88, 90, 91, 92, 98
Principle of Congruence 433
Psychological Impact 179, 203, 302, 303, 305, 306, 504

Q

Quantum Computing 215, 222, 223, 224, 234, 239, 241, 242, 244, 245

R

Racial Bias 283, 284, 285, 286, 287, 289, 293, 294, 307, 315, 316, 318, 320, 321, 322, 325, 327, 328, 330, 331, 336, 337, 338, 339, 340
Racial Profiling 285, 286, 306, 307, 311, 316, 331, 335
Recovery Mechanisms 260, 269, 270, 282
Regional Bank 429, 430, 431, 432, 433, 434, 435, 436, 437, 438, 439, 440, 441, 442
Regulatory Frameworks 250, 251, 252, 258, 282, 287, 289, 311, 321, 324, 327, 328, 330, 337, 338, 340
Reputation 21, 32, 71, 101, 102, 106, 107, 108, 109, 117, 118, 119, 120, 123, 124, 125, 126, 127, 151, 225, 258, 349, 363, 367, 374, 388
Resource Efficiency 449, 450, 451, 453, 454, 457, 459, 461, 462, 463, 464, 465, 466, 467, 472, 474, 478, 479, 481
Risk Management 64, 72, 80, 82, 97, 101, 115, 116, 120, 188, 215, 252, 279, 349, 350, 351, 353, 354, 361, 362, 364, 365, 367, 368, 369, 370, 381

S

Stem Education 155, 156, 161, 166, 168, 175, 177, 185, 187, 189, 195, 201, 203, 345
Strategic Management 3, 7, 9, 11, 14, 16, 18, 27, 55, 56, 57, 58, 59, 70, 95, 96, 343, 400, 422
Strategic Positioning 34
Strategy 3, 7, 9, 10, 11, 12, 14, 15, 16, 20, 21, 22, 30, 46, 48, 53, 54, 55, 56, 57, 58, 59, 60, 61, 62, 63, 64, 65, 67, 68, 69, 70, 72, 73, 74, 75, 77, 78, 80, 81, 82, 83, 85, 86, 87, 88, 89, 90, 91, 92, 93, 94, 95, 96, 97, 98, 108, 109, 110, 117, 118, 120, 121, 125, 131, 132, 135, 136, 146, 158, 187, 207, 215, 219, 224, 225, 228, 231, 232, 242, 248, 252, 258, 270, 275, 292, 318, 358, 369, 377, 384, 389, 406, 407, 410, 412, 415, 420, 428, 429, 430, 433, 434, 435, 438, 439, 441, 445, 474, 479, 487
Supply Chain Management 51, 87, 97, 450, 451, 452, 453, 454, 458, 459, 461, 467, 472, 474, 478, 479, 480, 481, 482, 483, 484, 486, 487, 489
Support Systems 105, 155, 178, 179, 186, 190, 191, 426, 455, 491, 496, 501, 502, 504, 506, 508, 510, 511, 512, 513, 515, 516
Sustainable 1, 2, 3, 4, 5, 11, 12, 13, 17, 20, 21, 22, 49, 51, 53, 54, 55, 58, 64, 65, 68, 69, 70, 74, 77, 80, 81, 82, 86, 88, 92, 93, 94, 96, 97, 99, 109, 116, 117, 122, 123, 126, 127, 146, 157, 180, 181, 182, 188, 196, 197, 201, 202, 218, 219, 225, 245, 281, 370, 400, 409, 425, 447, 449, 450, 451, 452, 453, 454, 455, 456, 457, 458, 459, 461, 462, 464, 465, 466, 467, 468, 469, 471, 472, 473, 474, 475, 477, 478, 479, 480, 481, 482, 483, 484, 485, 486, 487, 488, 500, 517, 519
Sustainable Growth 4, 11, 53, 54, 55, 58, 81, 454, 478
Sustainable Practices 450, 451, 453, 454,

457, 465, 466, 467, 472, 474, 481, 484

T

Technological Advancements 77, 157, 161, 166, 167, 169, 170, 175, 177, 178, 179, 186, 187, 188, 190, 203, 210, 216, 218, 250, 254, 259, 287, 299, 310, 319, 325, 328, 330, 438, 459, 471, 485

Technological Displacement 179, 203

Technology Acceptance Model 215, 216, 236, 239, 241, 437, 445, 447

U

Uncontested Market Spaces 53, 56, 58, 59, 61, 64, 74, 77, 79, 80, 83

W

Women's Safety 492, 493, 495, 496, 497, 502, 509, 511, 512, 513, 514, 515, 516

Workforce Adaptability 155, 203

Workforce Retraining 189, 203

Workplace 33, 91, 101, 102, 103, 104, 105, 109, 110, 111, 113, 114, 116, 117, 118, 119, 120, 121, 122, 123, 124, 125, 126, 127, 128, 129, 130, 160, 170, 247, 365, 385, 434, 441, 491, 492, 493, 494, 496, 497, 498, 499, 500, 501, 502, 506, 507, 509, 510, 511, 512, 513, 514, 515, 516, 517, 518, 519, 520

Workplace Culture 101, 102, 103, 113, 114, 116, 117, 118, 120, 122, 170, 365